QuickAccess Bar 2—Graphics

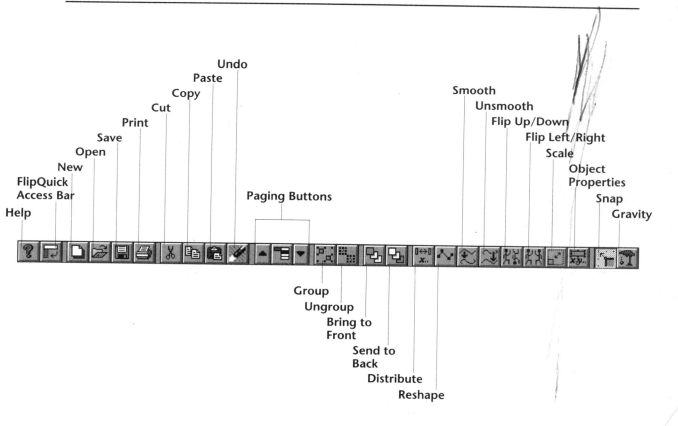

Mastering
FrameMaker® 5

Tom Neuburger

SYBEX

San Francisco • Paris • Düsseldorf • Soest

Acquisitions Manager: Kristine Plachy
Developmental Editors: Jim Sumser, Brenda Kienan
Editor: Peter Weverka
Project Editors: Lee Ann Pickrell, Stephanie La Croix, Emily Smith
Technical Editor: Denise Martineau
Book Designer: London Road
Technical Artists: Dan Schiff, Lynell Decker
Desktop Publisher: Lynell Decker
Proofreader/Production Assistant: Alexa Riggs
Indexer: Nancy Guenther
Cover Designer: Design Site
Cover Photographer: Mark Johann

Screen reproductions produced with Collage Complete.

Collage Complete is a trademark of Inner Media Inc.

SYBEX is a registered trademark of SYBEX Inc.

TRADEMARKS: SYBEX has attempted throughout this book to distinguish proprietary trademarks from descriptive terms by following the capitalization style used by the manufacturer.

Every effort has been made to supply complete and accurate information. However, SYBEX assumes no responsibility for its use, nor for any infringement of the intellectual property rights of third parties which would result from such use.

Library of Congress Card Number: 95-70848
ISBN: 0-7821-1712-0

Manufactured in the United States of America
10 9 8 7 6 5 4 3 2 1

For Alida, my river of gold

Acknowledgments

Thanks are due to many for the success of this project. First, to Brenda Kienan and Jim Sumser, those wise folks at SYBEX who thought the book might be a good idea and guided its development.

Thanks to all the good people in editorial and production—Lee Ann Pickrell and the crew behind her—who struggle hard with impossible deadlines and authors who always want to make things just a little bit better.

A big debt is owed to Peter Weverka for his excellent and timely text editing, and Denise Martineau, the technical guru who allowed herself to be swamped with more details about this program than most people will ever have to deal with.

And finally to Kenn Halliwell, a terrific writer in his own right, who contributed volumes of much needed source material for a project not his own. Thanks to you all.

Contents at a Glance

		Introduction	xix
Part One		**The Least You Need to Know**	**1**
	1	Getting Started	2
	2	Windows and Commands	22
	3	Controlling What You See Onscreen	46
	4	Editing Documents	74
	5	Getting Help	96
Part Two		**Basic Work with Documents**	**105**
	6	Starting a Document	106
	7	Saving and Printing Documents	138
Part Three		**Formatting and Editing Text**	**153**
	8	What Is a FrameMaker Document	154
	9	Characters and Character Formats	206
	10	Paragraphs and Paragraph Formats	236
	11	Editing Text	266
	12	Controlling the Look of the Page	306
Part Four		**Doing More with FrameMaker**	**325**
	13	Adding Graphics to Documents	326
	14	Working with Tables	386

Part Five   Advanced Freatures   411

15	Working with Color	412
16	Creating and Working with Book Files	442
17	Tables of Contents, Indexes, and Other Book Features	466
18	Using Hypertext in View-Only Files	522
19	Other FrameMaker Features	544

Appendices   597

A	Installing FrameMaker	598
B	FrameMaker Templates	608
	Index	665

Contents

Introduction   xix

Part One   ***The Least You Need to Know***   **1**

Chapter 1   **Getting Started**   2
Starting FrameMaker   3
   Starting the Windows Version of FrameMaker   3
   Starting the Mac Version of FrameMaker   5
   Starting the UNIX Version of FrameMaker   7
Creating a Document from a Template   8
   Choosing a Template   8
   Turning a Template into a Document   10
Saving a New Document   12
Editing a Document   15
Printing a Document   18
Quitting FrameMaker   18

Chapter 2   **Windows and Commands**   22
Exploring FrameMaker Windows   23
   The Application Window   23
   The Document Window   31
   Dialog Boxes   35
   Palettes—Windows That Stay Open   37
Issuing Commands with the Mouse and the Keyboard   41
   Using the Mouse   41
   Using the Keyboard   42

Chapter 3   **Controlling What You See Onscreen**   46
Arranging Windows in the Working Area   49
Document Guidelines and Display Options   54
   Different Ways of Viewing a Document   54
   The View Options Dialog Box: More Ways to View Documents   56
   Working with the Ruler   60
Zooming In and Out of Documents   66
   How Zooming Works   66
   Making Windows and Pages Fit Onscreen   68
   Changing Zoom Settings   71
Moving Quickly from Page to Page   71

Chapter 4   **Editing Documents**   74
Editing Basics   75
   FrameMaker Cursors   75
   Selecting Text and Objects   77

Deleting Text 84
Cutting, Copying, and Pasting Text and Objects 85
Undoing Mistakes 87
Searching for and Replacing Text 88
Changing the Look of Text 90
Changing the Look of Paragraphs 91
Checking the Spelling of Words in a Document 93

Chapter 5 Getting Help 96
Help: The Basics 97
Getting Context-Sensitive Help 98
The Help Main Menu 100
Viewing FrameMaker Online Manuals 101
The Help Index 102
Returning to the Pages You Just Left 103

Part Two   Basic Work with Documents   105

Chapter 6 Starting a Document 106
Creating a New Document 107
Opening an Existing FrameMaker Document 110
Importing Documents into FrameMaker 111
Importing a Non-FrameMaker Document 112
Importing Text into a FrameMaker Document 116
Using Document Templates 120
Creating Documents from Templates 121
Modifying a Document to Look Like a Template 124
Some Sample Document Templates 126
Creating Your Own Templates 128

Chapter 7 Saving and Printing Documents 138
Saving Documents 139
Saving Documents in FrameMaker Document Format 140
Changing the Name or Location of a Document 141
Saving a Document as a Text File 142
Saving Documents in Specialized Formats 143
Using Save to Undo Changes 145
Preferences for Saving Files Automatically 146
Printing Documents 147
Print Options 149
Creating Acrobat Files 150

Part Three   Formatting and Editing Text   153

Chapter 8 What Is a FrameMaker Document? 154
Pages, Text Flows, and Text Frames 155
When Text "Overflows" 156

Connected and Unconnected Text Frames   159
How Autoconnected Text Frames Work   160
Connecting Text Frames with the Autoconnect Feature   162
Turning Autoconnect On and Off   164
What to Do about Empty Pages   165
Connecting and Disconnecting Text Frames   166
What Are Body, Master, and Reference Pages?   166
Working with Body Pages   167
How Body Pages Use Background Text and Graphics   167
Adding New Body Pages   168
Deleting Body Pages   169
Changing the Master Page Used by a Body Page   169
Changing the Layout of a Body Page   170
Working with Master Pages   174
A Quick Tour of Master Pages   174
Basic Operations with Master Pages   180
Working with Reference Pages   183
Adding Graphics Frames to Reference Pages   184
Adding, Deleting, and Renaming Reference Pages   185
Creating Special Page Layouts   186
Creating Multicolumn Pages   186
Using "Sideheads" in Documents   192
Getting Text to "Straddle" Columns   195
Anchored Frames That Move with the Text Flow   195
Using Anchored Frames in a Text Flow   197
Anchored Frames That "Straddle" Columns   203
Importing Graphics into Anchored Frames   203
Importing Text into Anchored Frames   204

Chapter 9   Characters and Character Formats   206
All about Fonts   207
Symbol, or Character, Sets   208
Font Families   209
Type Size   210
Font Angle   211
Weight   211
Variation   211
Style   211
Color   214
The Character Designer Window   214
Defining the Properties of Characters   215
Changing the Look of Superscript, Subscript, and Small
Cap Characters   217
Character Designer Controls   220
Applying a Character Tag to Text   221
Applying Character Tags with the Character Catalog   224
Copying Character Formats from One Document to Another   225
Working with Character Formats and Character Tags   226
Applying and Copying Character Formats and Tags   226
Creating, Changing, and Copying Character Tags   227

Working with Groups of Tags and Characters   230
Practice with Character Formats   231

Chapter 10   Paragraphs and Paragraph Formats   236
What Is a FrameMaker Paragraph?   237
Paragraph Tags and the Paragraph Catalog   238
Changing the Look of Paragraphs with the Paragraph Designer Window   239
The Basic Paragraph Properties for Generic Paragraphs   240
Default Font Paragraph Properties for Text   244
Pagination Paragraph Properties for How Paragraphs Fit on the Page   245
Numbering Paragraph Properties for Numbered and Bulleted Lists   246
Advanced Paragraph Properties   249
Table Cell Paragraph Properties for Defining the Look of Tables   250
Paragraph Designer Controls   251
Applying Tags to Text with the Paragraph Catalog   256
Copying Paragraph Formats from One Document to Another   257
Sample Paragraph Formats   258
Paragraphs for Manuscripts and Personal Letters   258
Paragraphs for Business Memos and Business Letters   258
Indented Paragraphs   259
Paragraphs with Hanging Indents   259
Complex Numbered Paragraphs   263
Run-In Paragraphs   265

Chapter 11   Editing Text   266
Selecting, Copying, Pasting, and Deleting Text and Formats   267
Selecting Text   267
Copying Text, Formats, and Other Elements   269
Pasting from the Clipboard   269
Quick-Copying and Pasting Text   271
Deleting—Cutting and Clearing Text   271
Undoing Mistakes   273
Changing the Capitalization of Text   274
Customizing Smart Quotes, Smart Spaces, and Line Breaks   275
Finding and Replacing Text and Formats   276
Finding Text and Formats with the Find/Change Palette   276
Replacing Text and Formats   283
Conducting the Search   284
Finding and Changing Text and Formats from the Keyboard   285
Formatting Imported Text   286
Formatting an Imported Text File   287
Formatting an Imported Flow   290
Editing the Properties of Text Insets   292
Correcting Spelling Mistakes in Documents   293
Exploring the Spelling Checker Window   293
Correcting a Misspelled Word   295
Customizing Spell Checking Options   296
Customizing the FrameMaker Dictionaries   298
Editing FrameMaker's Dictionary Files   301

Keyboard Shortcuts for Spell-Checking | 302
Using the Thesaurus to Find the Right Word | 303
The Thesaurus Window | 305
The Thesaurus Look Up Window | 305

Chapter 12 Controlling the Look of the Page | 306
Elements of a Page Layout | 307
Laying Out the Page | 308
Laying Out a New Document | 308
Changing the Layout of Existing Documents | 309
Handling Headers and Footers | 313
Adding Headers and Footers to Master Pages | 314
Including Page Numbers and Other Variables in Headers and Footers | 317
Changing the Page Number Style | 318
Creating Running Headers and Footers | 319

Part Four   Doing More with FrameMaker   325

Chapter 13 Adding Graphics to Documents | 326
Exploring the Tools Window | 327
The Selection Tools | 330
The Drawing Tools | 330
Drawing Commands for Manipulating Graphics | 338
Three More Drawing Commands: Join, Runaround, and Overprint | 347
Connecting Objects with the Gravity Feature | 350
Aligning Objects with the Snap Grid | 350
Choosing Patterns and Colors for Objects | 351
Telling FrameMaker How to Draw Lines | 353
Creating a Drawing | 356
Techniques for Selecting Objects | 358
Practice in Working with Graphic Objects | 359
Copying, Pasting, and Moving Objects | 359
Moving Objects by Increments | 362
Working with Bezier Curves | 363
Aligning, Distributing, Rotating, and Scaling Objects | 363
Importing Graphic Images | 367
Importing Bitmap Images | 368
Importing Vector Graphics | 371
Importing Desktop Color Separation Files | 374
Importing QuickTime Movies (Mac Only) | 375
Importing PostScript Code | 377
Making Text Run Around Graphics | 378
Changing the Size, Color, and Position of Objects | 380

Chapter 14 Working with Tables | 386
How Tables Work in FrameMaker | 387
Creating and Editing New Tables | 388
Creating an Empty Table in a Document | 388

Default A and B Table Formats in New Documents 389
Entering Text and Other Objects into Table Cells 389
Cutting, Copying, and Pasting Table Cells 390
Adding New Rows and Columns to Tables 392
Changing the Shape and Look of a Table 392
Changing the Size of Columns and Rows 392
Making Cells Straddle Columns and Rows 394
Rotating Cells 394
Controlling How Tables Look 395
Table Designer Controls 402
Customized Ruling Lines and Shading 405
From Text to Tables and Back Again 407
Converting Text into Tables 407
Converting Tables into Text 409
Copying Table Formats from One Document to Another 409

Part Five   Advanced Features   411

Chapter 15   Working with Color 412
Adding Color to Text and Graphics 413
Adding Color to Text 413
Adding Color to Graphics 417
Creating, Modifying, and Importing Colors 418
What Is a Color Model? 418
Creating New Colors 421
Changing the Definition of a Color 428
Importing Color Definitions from Other Documents 428
Changing How Colors Are Shown on the Screen 429
Dealing with Color Separations 431
Spot Color Separations 431
Four-Color Process Separations 432
Printing Spot Color Separations 433
Printing Four-Color Separations 437

Chapter 16   Creating and Working with Book Files 442
Creating a Book 443
Gathering and Preparing Files for a Book 444
Generating a Book File 445
Renaming and Saving a Newly Created Book File 446
Adding Document Files to a Book 447
Setting Up Document Files 449
Working with Book Files 451
Opening, Saving, and Closing Book Files 453
Operating on Document Files 454
Changing and Updating the Format of Document Files 455
Deleting and Rearranging Document Files 457
When Document Files Are Renamed... 458
Printing a Book 459
Comparing Books 460

Chapter 17   Tables of Contents,Indexes, and Other Book Features   466

Generated Files   467
Creating a Table of Contents   467
    Making Sure Source Documents Are Tagged Correctly   468
    Generating a Table of Contents   468
    Regenerating a Table of Contents   471
    Formatting a Table of Contents   472
    Troubleshooting a Table of Contents   482
Creating an Index   484
    Marking Documents for an Index   486
    Generating and Regenerating an Index   494
    Formatting an Index   497
    Troubleshooting an Index   515
Creating Master Indexes and TOC That Cover Several Books   517
Table, Figure, Paragraph, and Other Generated Lists   518
Using Hypertext in Generated Files   519
    Hypertext in Editable Documents   519
    Hypertext in View-Only Documents   520

Chapter 18   Using Hypertext in View-Only Files   522

View-Only Documents   523
Setting Up Hypertext Areas   524
    Making Text Active   525
    Making Graphics Active   526
Preventing Hypertext Graphics from Being Printed   529
Working with Hypertext Markers   530
    Inserting Hypertext Markers and Commands   530
    Editing Hypertext Commands   531
    Deleting Hypertext Markers   532
Hypertext Commands: A Quick Reference   533
    Matrix   536
Testing a Hypertext Document for Incorrect Links   541

Chapter 19   Other FrameMaker Features   544

Placing Cross References in Documents   545
    Inserting Cross-References   546
    Updating Cross-References   550
    Creating Your Own Cross-Reference Formats   553
    Importing Cross-Reference Formats   557
Including Footnotes and Endnotes in Documents   558
    How FrameMaker Handles Footnotes   558
    Inserting Footnotes   559
    Deleting a Footnote   559
    Referencing a Footnote from Several Places   559
    Separators for Dividing the Text from Footnotes   560
    Formatting Footnotes   561
    Creating Endnotes   564
Variables   564

System Variables and User Variables   565
Creating User Variables   567
Changing a Variable's Definition   569
Inserting Variables in a Document   570
Conditional Text   571
Condition Tags for Setting the Document Version   571
How Conditional Text Interacts with Other FrameMaker Features   576
Change Bars for Marking Changes to Documents   578
Adding Change Bars Automatically   579
Adding Change Bars Manually   580
Removing Change Bars   580
Formatting Change Bars   581
Document Comparison   582
Comparing Documents   583
Ways to Compare Documents   585
Creating and Formatting Equations   587
Creating Equations   587
Math Elements   588
Editing Equations   593
Formatting Equations   594
Evaluating Equations   594
HyperText Markup Language with FrameMaker   595

Appendices   597

Appendix A   Installing FrameMaker   598
Installing FrameMaker for Windows   600
Installing FrameMaker for the Macintosh   601
Installing FrameMaker for UNIX   604
Using the FrameMaker Introduction and Tutorial   606

Appendix B   FrameMaker Templates   608
Business Templates   609
Business Letter Template   609
Business Memo Template   613
Fax Cover Page Template   616
Viewgraph Templates   619
Business Envelope Template   622
Business Cards Template   624
Reports Templates   625
Plain Report Template   626
Numbered Report Template   629
Sidehead Report Template   633
Outlines Templates   637
Harvard Outline Template   637
Numeric Outline Template   640
Small Outline Template   643

Special Templates   646
    Pagination Sheet Template   646
    Newsletter Template   649
Book Templates   653
    Book Chapter Template   653
    Book Frontmatter Template   657
    Book Table of Contents Template   660
    Book Index Template   663

Index   665

Introduction

Mastering FrameMaker 5 shows you in detail how to use FrameMaker's many word-processing and desktop publishing features, from the most simple to the very advanced. And it covers all three versions of Frame-Maker 5—Windows, Mac, and UNIX. Where these versions are in "sync" (as most of the time they are), instructions for using the Windows version are presented, but the information in this book applies to all three platforms. Where the versions differ from each other, special Windows Notes, Mac Notes, and UNIX Notes appear in the text to show you just what those differences are and how to make use of the version on *your* computer.

What's in This Book

Mastering FrameMaker 5 is divided, unlike Gaul, into five parts.

Part One, "The Least You Need to Know," is a quick tutorial that introduces the program to you. If you are a new user or you want to brush up on the basic skills, start here. In a couple of fast sessions, you'll learn everything you need to know to start doing real work with the program.

Part Two, "Basic Work with Documents," examines all of the ways you can start a document, FrameMaker's templates and file importing and filtering capabilities, how to save a document in various formats, and the many valuable print options.

Part Three, "Formatting and Editing Text," covers FrameMaker's text and document-control features in detail. It begins with a chapter that shows you how a FrameMaker document is put together and how to control the page layout with a minimum of fuss and bother. Then it moves through chapters on character and paragraph formatting, shows you how to edit text quickly and easily, and closes with information on page layout options.

Part Four, "Doing More with FrameMaker," explains valuable proce-dures for adding graphics to documents and working with tables.

Part Five, "Advanced Features," tackles the advanced stuff. It shows you how to use color, create and maintain books and book files, generate automatic tables of contents and indexes, and work with hypertext. It concludes with a chapter on a host of useful features, including text cross-references, variables, conditional text, document comparison, footnotes, change bars, equations, and HTML document conversion.

Appendix A explains how to install FrameMaker 5. Appendix B shows what is in the many templates offered by the program.

A Quick Tour of FrameMaker

FrameMaker is different from other desktop publishing and word-processing programs because it is both a top-notch word processor *and* a first-rate desktop publisher. Since it originated in the UNIX environment, where program size is not an issue, FrameMaker could, from the start, incorporate sophisticated word-processing features into a fully functional desktop publishing program, and still do a great job of both.

Because of this background, FrameMaker was designed well right from the beginning. It didn't have to be twisted out of (or into) shape to accommodate new capabilities, like many of its competitors. As it grew in features, the original design allowed new features to be incorporated smoothly.

In addition, FrameMaker excels at both short and long documents. It began as a long document handler, but it also has all the layout features it takes to handle short, complex documents.

As a desktop publishing program, FrameMaker can compete with the best of them. As a word processor, it has as many advanced features as the most popular word processors on the market, if not more. FrameMaker has become, for many writers, the program of choice for both desktop publishing and word-processing chores. Its popularity continues to grow.

A Full-Featured Word Processor

As a word-processing program, FrameMaker can do all of the following:

- Select text by the character, word, line, sentence, or paragraph
- Format individual characters or whole paragraphs either on the fly or by reference to paragraph and character tags—remembered character and paragraph formats

▶ Cut, copy, and paste both text and formatting

▶ Perform simple and complex search-and-replace operations

▶ Check spelling and suggest alternate word choices from its built-in dictionary and thesaurus

▶ Automatically create, format, and maintain tables

▶ Create and update cross-references (statements like "See page 29 for more information") from one place in the text to another

▶ Insert variables (such as the current page number or the current date) into text

▶ Insert and maintain footnotes at the bottom of a page and endnotes at the end of a document

▶ Format and update change bars

▶ Automatically generate lists (tables of contents, indexes, lists of figures, lists of authorities, and the like)

▶ Build entire books from multiple documents

With all of these capabilities (each of which is fully covered in this book), FrameMaker is probably the only word processor you will ever need.

A Powerful Desktop Publisher

FrameMaker also excels at desktop publishing. Almost any page format you can visualize can be created in FrameMaker. For example, Frame-Maker allows you to:

▶ Create complex multicolumn pages containing a variety of articles that flow newspaper-style from one page to the next

▶ Import, resize, and reshape graphics in a variety of file formats

▶ Create drawings with the full-featured graphics toolbox

▶ Anchor graphics to text or paste them directly to specific pages

▶ Rotate text and graphics to a precision of one-fourth of a degree

▶ Wrap text around graphics

▶ Create color documents using one of four color-definition schemes

▶ Create color separations, printed pages that can be used directly for CMYK printing in print shops

▶ Create master pages, pages that contain background material for all body pages that use them

Working with FrameMaker Files

One of the advantages of using FrameMaker is something called *cross-platform compatibility*. This phrase, which may sound complex, simply means that all versions of FrameMaker work in the same way on different types of computers. You can work on the Windows version, the Mac version, or the UNIX version, and never see an appreciable difference in the program.

FrameMaker files are also compatible across platforms—you can take a Frame-Maker 5 file from your PC, load it into a Mac, and the Mac version of FrameMaker will read that file perfectly. (Of course, the Mac has to be able to read a PC-created disk, or vice versa, but with today's computers that's much less of a problem than it used to be.)

All of this means you can take FrameMaker files from home to the office and back again, or from your computer to a friend's—even if one is a PC, one a Mac, and one is a UNIX-based machine. All you need is the same version of FrameMaker running on all the machines.

FrameMaker can also create the print files that service bureaus use to turn desktop publishing output into four-color slides or typeset-quality pages for printing.

What's New in FrameMaker 5

FrameMaker Release 5, the latest version of FrameMaker, offers a number of new and exciting features and enhancements.

Text Frames That Support Columns

Text frames now support multiple columns, eliminating the complexity of management in most multicolumn layouts. See Chapters 8 and 12 for more on these new page layout possibilities.

Headings and Tables That Straddle Columns

With FrameMaker 5 you can make paragraphs, footnotes, tables, and graphics straddle text columns and even the area set aside for sideheads, if your document has them. FrameMaker "straddles" flow with the text—they move when the text moves—so they can be used easily and effectively without a lot of the "tweaking" that makes creating this effect a chore on other programs. Chapters 8 and 12 have information on paragraph straddles. Chapter 14 deals with tables and table options.

Text That Runs around Graphics

FrameMaker 5 can now make text run around graphics automatically. The lines of text can either follow the contours of the picture or form a rectangular boundary around the picture area. All of FrameMaker's graphics features are covered in Chapter 15.

New Anchored Frame Positions

There are a number of new positions for anchored frames, including *run into text*, which allows special effects like drop caps and run-in graphics that flow with the text. Anchored frames can also be made to straddle columns, allowing you to create "straddle graphics" easily. For more on anchored frames, look ahead to Chapter 8.

Text Imported by Reference

You could always import graphics by reference into FrameMaker. Now you can import text by reference as well. You can import from Frame-Maker files, text files, and a number of popular word-processing file formats. Chapter 6 shows how to import text by reference. Chapter 11 talks about how to format imported text.

Enhanced Drawing Tools

FrameMaker's drawing tools have been enhanced for Release 5 to allow graphic lines and curves to be joined into a single object. This allows you to build complex line drawings and then reduce the number of objects in those drawings for easy manipulation. Check out Chapter 15 for information on these new features.

HTML Output for Internet Publishing

FrameMaker 5 comes with a unique add-on, a conversion tool that turns FrameMaker documents into HTML documents that are ready for publishing on the World Wide Web. See Chapter 19 for more on HTML conversion.

Support for Adobe Acrobat

FrameMaker 5 supports Adobe Acrobat 2.0. It can create enhanced PostScript files that can be used by Adobe Distiller to create Acrobat PDF files. In Chapter 7, all of FrameMaker's print options are covered in detail.

QuickAccess Bar on All Platforms

The QuickAccess Bar, which gives you one-touch access to dozens of commonly used commands, has been added to all platforms for FrameMaker 5. See Chapter 2 for more on the QuickAccess Bar.

Online Tutorial

A modular, interactive tutorial is available online. It offers step-by-step instructions for using the program.

Conventions Used in This Book

This book serves as both a tutorial and a reference. It is designed so you can find the information you need quickly. To help you learn FrameMaker and get the most out of the program, you'll find the following special features in this book.

Hands-On Instructions

Step-by-step exercises take you easily through the procedures for completing all important tasks. By doing these exercises, you'll get the experience you need to gain a solid understanding of how FrameMaker works and the many program options available to you.

Notes, Tips, Warnings

Where applicable, this book provides special notes, tips, and warnings.

 NOTE   Notes define terminology, or refer you to other parts of the book for further information, or remind you how to complete an action or where something is located on the screen. Notes provide all-purpose information to help you become a better FrameMaker user.

In addition, *Mastering FrameMaker 5* contains three special kinds of notes.

 MAC NOTE   Mac notes offer information specific to the Macintosh version of the program.

 UNIX NOTE   Unix notes help FrameMaker's many UNIX users work with parts of the program found only in this powerful version.

 WINDOWS NOTE   Windows notes provide the same information for users of the Windows version of FrameMaker 5.

Other special aids include tips and warnings.

 TIP   Tips provide shortcuts or insights for using the program better.

 WARNING   Warnings, for example, let you know when completing an action is essential or when you are in danger of losing data. Pay close attention to warnings.

Sidebars

You will find sidebars—short essays about using the program—throughout this book. Sidebars provide helpful advice and tell you how to make important decisions. Each has a title. Sidebars appear in boxes with a dark background.

Endpapers

Inside the front and back cover of this book are charts that show what all the buttons on the QuickAccess Bars do.

Pull-Down Menus

FrameMaker, like most programs, has a pull-down menu structure. In other words, to complete a task with the menus, you start at the main menu, select an option, and from the next menu that appears you select another option.

As a shorthand method of showing you how to use the pull-down menus, this book uses the ➤ symbol to show menu selections. For example, "Choose File ➤ Open" means "From the main menu, choose the File option, and then select Open from the File menu." You will find this shorthand method easy to follow.

Numbered Lists

For your convenience, step-by-step instructions are numbered. Simply follow the numbered steps to learn a new procedure or to remind yourself how to do something you haven't done in a while.

Bulleted Lists

Sometimes, in step-by-step instructions, you will be given options for completing a task. These options are shown in bulleted lists, like so:

1. Now begin to create the index file:

   - If your index is for a single document, select File ➤ Generate/Update from the document menu.

   - If your index is for a book, select File ➤ Generate/Book from the book file menu.

Boldface

When you see boldface text in a step-by-step instruction list, it means to type something at your keyboard. For example, an instruction that says "Type the file name **trudy.doc** in the dialog box" means type those characters.

The Least You Need to Know

1

Chapter 1
Getting Started

In this chapter, you will learn the least you need to know to work on simple documents. This chapter and the four that follow work like a tutorial. If you can, work hands-on with FrameMaker running on your computer as you read these chapters. You'll learn a lot in a very short time.

This chapter includes information on

Starting and quitting FrameMaker

Using a template to create a memo

Editing a document

Saving a document

Printing a document

The following chapters in Part One contain information on what Frame-Maker windows do and how to work with them, mouse and keyboard commands, basic editing techniques, and so on.

If you work only on basic documents, you may not need to go much further than these few chapters, at least not for now, to use FrameMaker successfully.

 NOTE The early chapters in this book cover the basics. To learn more about a technique, see the chapter devoted to that technique in Part Two.

Starting FrameMaker

How you start FrameMaker varies with the operating system you are using. In this section you'll find instructions for starting the Windows, Mac, and UNIX versions of FrameMaker.

 NOTE The following procedure assumes FrameMaker is correctly installed. If you have not installed FrameMaker or you installed the program incorrectly, see Appendix A.

Starting the Windows Version of FrameMaker

Starting FrameMaker is easy. After installation, FrameMaker places itself in a Windows group called Frame Products.

To start the Windows version of FrameMaker:

1. Start Windows by typing **win** at the DOS command line and pressing ↵.

2. Open the group called Frame Products, if it isn't open already, by double-clicking on the Frame Products icon. The Frame Products group window appears, as in Figure 1.1.

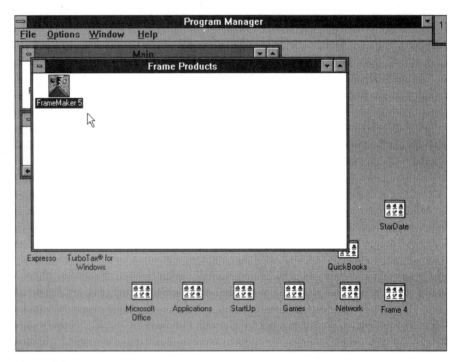

Figure 1.1   *Frame Products program group. Double-click the FrameMaker icon to start the program.*

3. Double-click on the Frame Products icon that says "FrameMaker."

That's all there is to it. In a moment the main FrameMaker application window appears, as in Figure 1.2.

NOTE Sometimes messages appear during startup. FrameMaker places these messages in a window called the Console window. If you see a Console window icon, click it from time to time to see messages from the program.

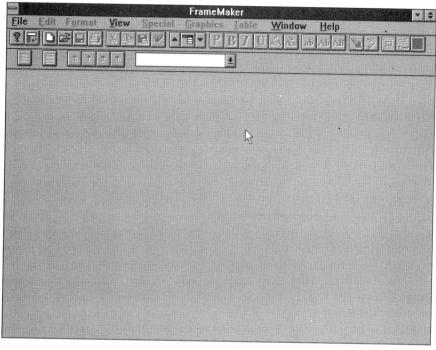

Figure 1.2 **FrameMaker 5 application window (Windows)**

Starting the Mac Version of FrameMaker

There are several ways to start the Mac version of FrameMaker. During installation, you are asked in which folder FrameMaker should be installed. The simplest way to start the Mac version of FrameMaker is as follows:

1. Navigate through the various disk and folder icons until you open the FrameMaker installation folder. It is shown in Figure 1.3.

2. Double-click on the icon that says FrameMaker.

   This launches the FrameMaker executable file. In a moment FrameMaker appears, as shown in Figure 1.4.

   Other ways to start the Mac version of FrameMaker include configuring and using the Launcher program (if it is available), and adding FrameMaker to the Apple menu. See your operating system documentation for more information on these procedures.

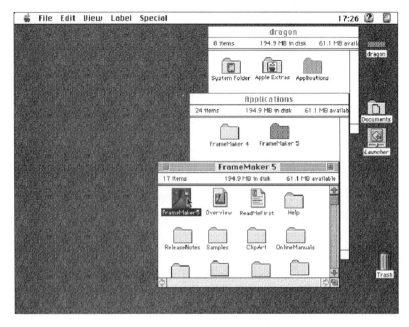

Figure 1.3   The FrameMaker installation folder. Double-click on the FrameMaker icon to launch FrameMaker.

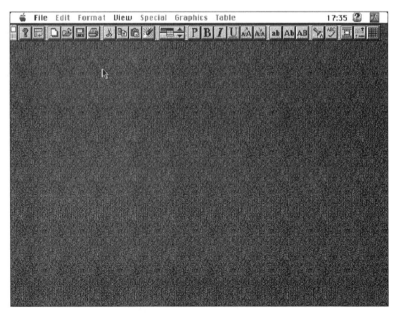

Figure 1.4   FrameMaker 5 main screen (Mac)

Starting the UNIX Version of FrameMaker

Since your UNIX version of FrameMaker was probably installed by a system administrator, the way you start FrameMaker may vary considerably from the method described here. This method, explained below, should work no matter how your copy of FrameMaker was installed, but it may not be the most efficient way to start FrameMaker, since it doesn't take advantage of special setups at your site. See your system administrator for information on the best way to start FrameMaker.

The UNIX version of FrameMaker can be started as follows:

1. Open a shell tool or command tool window.

2. Enter the command **cd $FMHOME** at the UNIX prompt. (If the FMHOME variable has not been defined for your account, see your system administrator.)

3. Enter the command **maker** at the UNIX prompt. After a moment, the UNIX FrameMaker window appears:

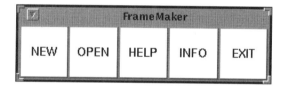

The UNIX Version Main Menu

In the Windows and Mac versions of FrameMaker, the FrameMaker main menu (the menu that contains the commands File, Edit, Format, and the like) appears either at the top of the screen (Mac) or at the top of the program Application window (Windows).

In the UNIX version, however, the main menu appears at the top of each document window. The buttons in the UNIX FrameMaker window shown above are simply ways of opening documents, getting help and licensing information, and exiting the program when no document windows are open. In almost every other respect, the three versions of the program are identical.

Creating a Document from a Template

In this section, we're going to open a document template, create a memo from that template, edit the memo, and save it. Later we'll explore some of the basic FrameMaker windows and dialog boxes.

Though templates are not the only way to start a document, they are one of the easiest. A *template* is simply a preformatted model document (like a letter or a memo) that you can modify for your own use. In FrameMaker, each template comes in two flavors, an empty version that has no writing in it, and a sample version with example headings and paragraphs.

Here we will work with an empty version of the memo template. Later, when templates are more fully discussed, we'll show you how to use both versions. (See Chapter 6 for more on templates and how to use them.)

NOTE   There are lots of ways to start a FrameMaker document. Chapter 6 has a full explanation of all of them.

Choosing a Template

Creating a document using a FrameMaker template is easy:

1. Select File ➤ New. The New file dialog box appears, as in Figure 1.5.

NOTE   Throughout this book, I will abbreviate multiple menu selections by using the ➤ symbol, as in "Select File ➤ New." This is a shorthand way of saying, "Select File from the main menu, and then select New."

UNIX NOTE   Open a new document by clicking on New in the UNIX Frame-Maker window.

2. Select the Explore Standard Templates button at the bottom of the box. The Standard Templates dialog box appears, as in Figure 1.6.

This dialog box contains a list of useful templates in the left column. If the template you want isn't in the list, select the More button at the bottom of the column to see more templates.

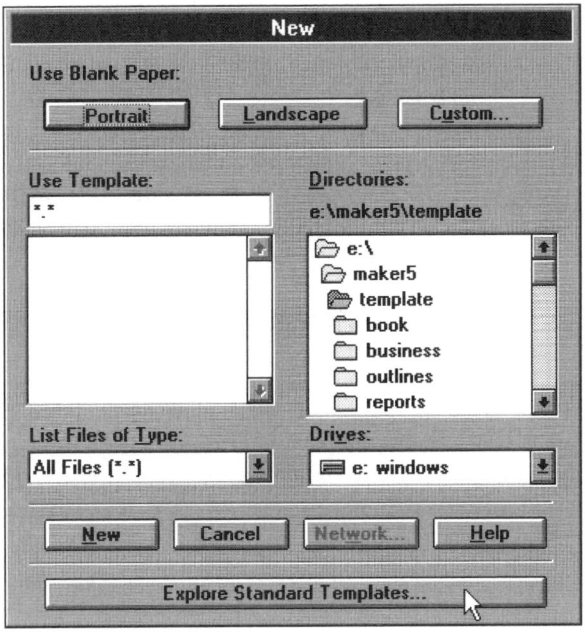

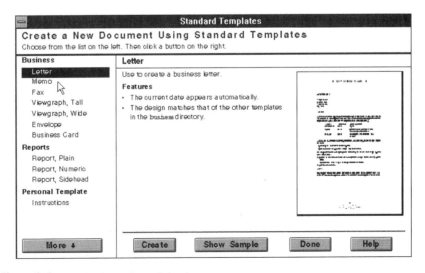

Figure 1.5   The New File dialog box

Figure 1.6   Standard Templates dialog box

You can click on the name of a template to see a description of that template along with a thumbnail view, which appears in the right-hand portion of the dialog box. Notice that the Letter template is shown in Figure 1.6.

3. Click on Memo in the template list on the left side of the dialog box.

4. Select the Create button on the bottom of the dialog box. An empty memo made from the template you selected appears in the working area, as shown in Figure 1.7.

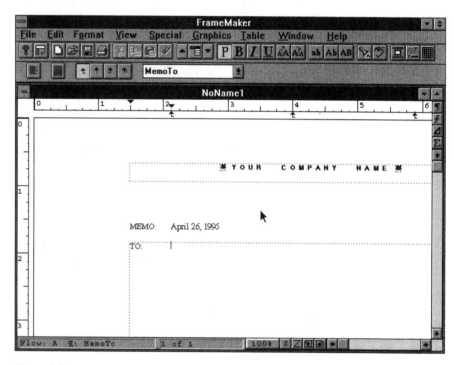

Figure 1.7 **An empty sample memo template**

You are ready to begin creating your first memo with FrameMaker.

Turning a Template into a Document

Let's start by changing the *view* of the document (the way the document appears on the screen) and filling in some information. Note that today's date is already filled in for you, and that the *typing cursor* (a flashing vertical line) appears after the word *TO:*.

1. Type a name—**Sam Spade,** for example—after the TO: heading and press ↵.

   When you pressed ↵, you created a new paragraph that already has the heading FROM:. This bit of template magic will be explained later.

   Let's turn text symbols on so we can see paragraph marks, tab symbols, and other nonprinting text symbols.

2. Select View ➤ Text Symbols. Notice that paragraph marks (¶) and tab symbols (>) appear in the text. Viewing these symbols is useful when you want to see precisely how a document is laid out on the screen.

   Let's fill in the rest of the information needed for a memo:

3. On the FROM: line, type **Trudy Dutweiler** and press ↵.

4. On the RE: line, type **Rental Fees Past Due** and press ↵. More magic—a horizontal line appears after the new CC: paragraph.

5. On the CC: line, we're going to type two names in a single paragraph. First type **Sidney Greenstreet** and press Shift-↵. ("Shift-↵" means to hold down the Shift key, press and release ↵, and then release the Shift key.)

   Pressing Shift-↵ creates a new line without making a new paragraph. With text symbols turned on, you can see that the symbol for "new line" (<) is different from the symbol for a paragraph (¶).

6. Type **Peter Lorre** and press ↵. The typing cursor is now in the memo's main text area.

7. Type the following, starting at the current cursor position. This will be the message portion of the memo.

   ```
   Sam, I hate to ask again, but last month's rent on your of-
   fice is past due. I know you've had a run of bad luck, what
   with the Falcon disappearing, but if you don't pay, you're
   going to have to vacate the premises.

   Sorry,

   Trudy
   ```

WARNING   As you type the memo, do *not* press ↵ (or Shift-↵) after each line, only after each paragraph. Within a paragraph, just type the words and let FrameMaker take care of the line breaks for you. If you press ↵ after each line in a paragraph, FrameMaker will not be able to format the paragraphs properly.

8. Turn text symbols off by selecting File ➤ Text Symbols. Now you can see what the document will look like when it is printed.

That's all there is to it. You've just created your first memo. The completed document should look like Figure 1.8. Now all you have to do is save your new document. How to do that is explained in the next section.

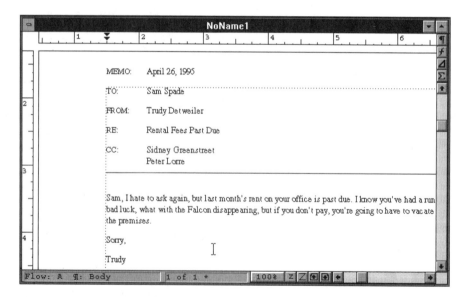

Figure 1.8 *A sample FrameMaker memo*

Saving a New Document

Before going on, the new document should be saved. Notice that the document has a strange name (NoName1) in the title bar. We are going to give it a new name.

NOTE   All of the FrameMaker "save" options are discussed in Chapter 7.

 MAC AND UNIX NOTE   The Save dialog boxes in the Mac and UNIX operating environments use conventions that are typical of those environments. As a result, the Mac and UNIX Save boxes are different from the Windows box illustrated here. The principles of selecting a directory (folder) and a file name are the same, however.

To save a document with a new name:

1. Select File ➤ Save or File ➤ Save As. (If you are saving a document for the first time, it doesn't matter which command you choose.) The Save dialog box appears, as shown in Figure 1.9.

Figure 1.9   *The Save dialog box*

2. The generic file name (*.*) is highlighted in the Save in File box. Start typing your new name for the memo—for example, **TRUDY.DOC**.

Notice that the old text disappears as soon as you start typing. If it doesn't, just click in the typing box with the mouse cursor and press Backspace to get rid of the text that appears there. Then start typing.

Saving a Document under a New Name

The first time you save a new document, it doesn't matter whether you select File ►Save or File ► Save As, because both commands take you to the Save dialog box (see Figure 1.9).

But what if you want to change the name of a document you've already saved and named? With an existing (named) document, selecting File ► Save simply saves the document under its own name. To save an existing document under a new name, you must select File ► Save As. This command saves the document to the disk under the new name. (Note that the old file, with the old name, still exists, so you can still go back to it if you want to.)

TIP Whenever you select (highlight) text in FrameMaker and then start typing, the old text automatically disappears and what you type replaces it.

3. Go to the right side of the dialog box and select a drive and directory to store your file. (The following instructions assume you are saving to the root directory of drive C.)

   • Using the Drives pull-down menu, select drive C:.

   • Using the Directories selection list, open C:\ (the root directory of drive C) by double-clicking on the top entry in the list.

   • If you wanted to save your file to a different directory than the root directory of drive C, you would double-click on that folder name. You could keep opening new folders if you liked until you found the one you wanted to store the file in. Most likely, though, the root directory of drive C will do for now. This is a document you will probably delete sometime soon, and the root directory is easy to get to, so let's save the memo file on the root directory, C.

WINDOWS NOTE Double-clicking on a folder icon "opens" the folder. (A *folder* is the same as a directory or subdirectory.)

After double-clicking, your screen will look something like Figure 1.10. Notice that only the top folder (labeled C:\) is "open." All of the other folders are closed. Notice also that the name of the currently open folder appears above the folder selection box and below the "Directories" label.

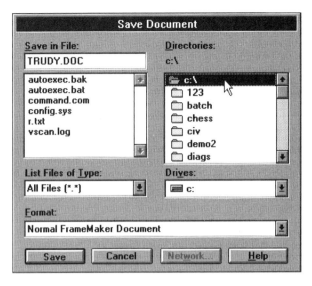

Figure 1.10 *An open C:\ folder showing the subfolders in the C drive*

To make sure you save your file in the right directory, always check the directory name below the "Directories" label before you save your file.

4. Leave the rest of the settings in the Save dialog box alone for now. When the directory name is right and the file name is right, use the mouse to click on the Save button or press ↵.

> **TIP** Pressing ↵ in a dialog box selects the *default* button and closes the box. You can identify the default button easily—it's the one with the dark black line around it. In the Save dialog box, the default button is Save.

A copy of the memo is now saved in a file on disk. You can retrieve that memo anytime you want, even if someone accidentally turns off your machine while you are working. (Of course, if your machine does accidentally get turned off, all of your unsaved changes will be lost!)

Editing a Document

Now let's make some simple edits to the memo. Suppose Trudy decides that stronger language is needed, so instead of writing "vacate the premises," she wants to substitute the phrase "get out."

You can make this change in two ways. The first is to delete one letter at a time with the Del (Delete) or Backspace key. The second is to highlight entire words and delete them.

Deleting a Letter at a Time

To edit letter by letter:

1. Move the mouse cursor in front of the *v* in "vacate." Notice that the cursor changes into a vertical bar when it's over editable text:

   ```
   ast due. I know you've had a run of
   , you're going to have to|vac ate
   ```

2. Click the mouse once. There is now a flashing text cursor in front of the letter *v*:

   ```
   ast due. I know you've had a run of
   , you're going to have to|vac ate
   ```

   Now you can move the mouse cursor anywhere you want, and the text cursor remains where it is.

3. Press Del or Backspace as many times as it takes to delete the words "vacate the premises." Be sure *not* to delete the period at the end of the sentence, since the new sentence will need it.

4. Now type the words **get out**:

   ```
   ast due. I know you've had a run of
   , you're going to have to get out|
   ```

   You're done. By using the mouse to move the text cursor, the Backspace key or the Del key to remove text, and the typing keys to insert text, you can change any text in any document.

Highlighting and Deleting Text

The second way of making these changes, by highlighting and deleting text, is much faster. In this case, you replace whole words with whole words.

To edit by changing whole words:

1. Double-click on the word *vacate*, and without releasing the mouse button, drag the mouse cursor over the words "the premises." (Be careful not to get the period at the end of the sentence.) When you are done, the whole phrase "vacate the premises" should be selected, or highlighted:

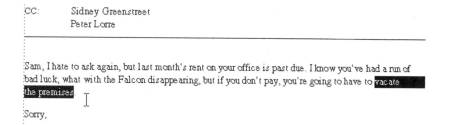

Highlighting words this way takes some practice, but it's worth it. You can double-click to highlight an entire word—in this case, *vacate*. Then, by dragging the mouse, you can continue selecting word by word, not just letter by letter.

2. Now start typing the new phrase—in this case, **get out. The new phrase replaces the old one.**

Either of these methods of editing works equally well. Use whichever one you prefer.

NOTE   There are many fast and easy ways to select and edit text in FrameMaker. See Chapter 11 for an explanation of all of them.

You can make any changes you like to the document. Feel free to play. When you are finished making changes, select File ➤ Save to save the file to disk (in the directory you specified last time). You won't see the Save document dialog box.

Keyboard Shortcuts

Did you notice the Ctrl+S next to the Save command? Ctrl+S is an example of a *keyboard shortcut*. Pressing a keyboard shortcut—Ctrl+S in this case—does the same action as a menu command does. If you prefer using the keyboard instead of the mouse, you can save your documents by typing Ctrl+S instead of going through the File menu. There are lots of keyboard shortcuts in FrameMaker. Many of them are listed in the menus next to the commands they activate. You can also get a list of shortcuts for your environment through the Help menu.

Printing a Document

Now that we have completed, edited, and saved the memo document, let's take a look at how printing works. This section gives the basics of printing just to get you started.

NOTE   Printing is covered in detail in Chapter 7.

This procedure assumes that your printer has already been set up to print with your operating environment. To print your memo:

1. Turn on your printer.

2. Select File ➤ Print. The Print Document dialog box appears, as in Figure 1.11.

3. For now, leave all the settings in this box as they are. The Print Page Range parameters should already specify All, and Copies should already be set to 1.

4. Select the Print button at the bottom of the dialog box.

    That's all there is to it. Trudy's memo is on its way to the printer.

Quitting FrameMaker

Quitting FrameMaker is as easy as starting it. To quit FrameMaker:

1. Click once on the File command to pull down the File menu.

2. Click on Exit, the last command on the menu, as in Figure 1.12. That's it. You'll be returned to the Program Manager.

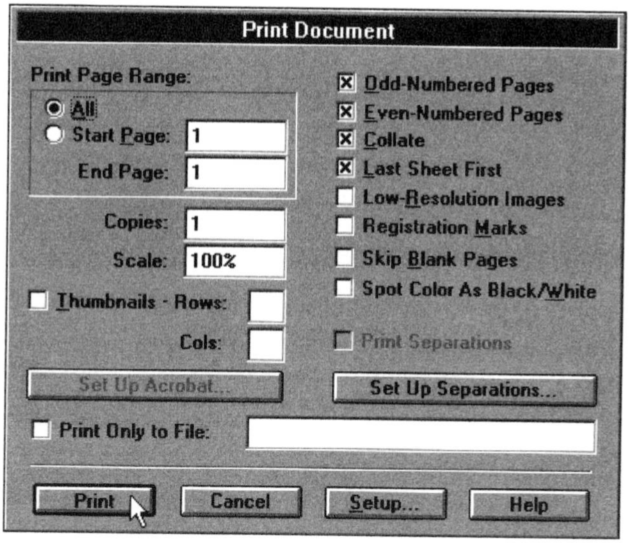

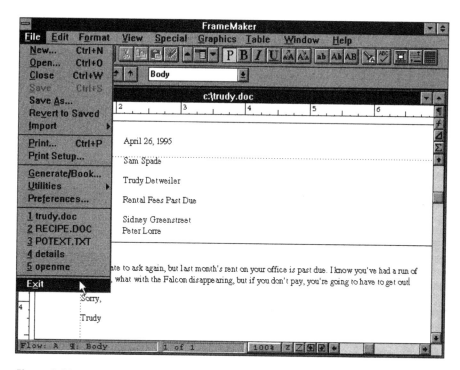

Figure 1.11   **The Print Document dialog box**

Figure 1.12   **Choose File ➤ Exit to quit FrameMaker.**

UNIX NOTE   To quit FrameMaker, click on the Exit button in the UNIX FrameMaker window.

 MAC NOTE   To quit FrameMaker, select File ➤ Quit.

The next chapter continues showing you the "least you need to know" to run FrameMaker. It introduces FrameMaker windows and basic FrameMaker techniques. After that, you can strike out on your own if you like, or continue working through more of this book. In either case, you will be ready to make FrameMaker start working for you.

Chapter 2

Windows and Commands

T his chapter continues the idea of Part One—it explains "the least you need to know about FrameMaker." Here you will learn basic information about FrameMaker windows and screens, and how to use the mouse and the keyboard to issue commands.

NOTE This chapter uses the sample document you created in Chapter 1, the memo from Trudy Dutweiler to Sam Spade. If you haven't created that document yet, you may want to go back and do so now.

Exploring FrameMaker Windows

FrameMaker uses many kinds of windows. Two of them, the main application window and the document window, you have already seen. Others, like most of the dialog boxes, you have not seen. This section takes you on a tour of all the windows you see in FrameMaker and shows you how to use them.

We'll start with the main window, the FrameMaker application window. Then we'll look at the document window, dialog boxes, and special windows, called *palettes*, that stay open even when you are working in another FrameMaker window.

MAC AND UNIX NOTE Except for the application window (as noted below), differences between FrameMaker windows on the three platforms are minor. The differences among document windows, dialog boxes, and palettes all have to do with characteristics that are typical of the various operating environments. Since the windows are familiar to users of Frame-Maker in the different environments, most differences between windows are not noted here.

The Application Window

When FrameMaker is first installed, and before any modifications are made to it, the main FrameMaker application window looks like the one shown in Figure 2.1.

MAC NOTE In the Mac environment, the FrameMaker application window always takes up the full screen. The main menu always appears across the top of the screen.

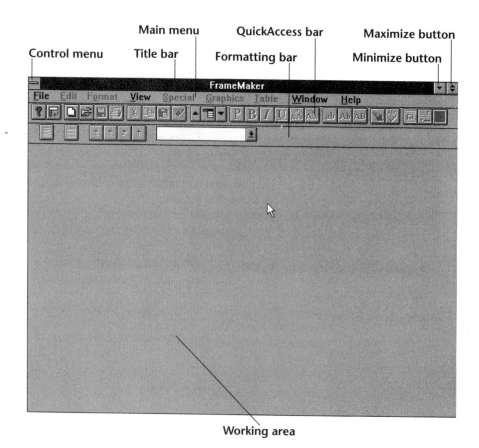

Figure 2.1   The FrameMaker application window. This application window is from the Windows environment.

 UNIX NOTE   In the UNIX environment, there is no FrameMaker application window as such. There is a UNIX FrameMaker menu that contains the five buttons illustrated in Chapter 1, and there are document windows that lie on the workspace. Each document window contains a FrameMaker main menu.

The application window contains a number of features. The following pages explain what these features are. As you read this section, refer to Figure 2.1, where the different features are labeled.

Title Bar

The *title bar* is the Windows "title stripe." It contains these items:

▶ The Windows Control menu button, a square button on the upper-left side of the title bar. If you click the Control menu button, you see the Windows control menu:

Double-clicking on this button selects the Close menu item, and shuts down FrameMaker.

▶ The name of the program (FrameMaker 5) and, if there is a document in "full-screen" view, the name of that document.

▶ The Minimize button (the one on the left) reduces the window to an icon.

▶ The Maximize button (the one on the right) makes the window take up the full screen (called "maximizing the window"), or, if the window is already maximized, reduces it back to a smaller working size.

WINDOWS NOTE   If you're playing around, try double-clicking on the title bar a couple of times. There are lots of shortcuts in Windows.

FrameMaker Menu

Directly below the title bar is the FrameMaker main menu. The items on this menu are discussed in the course of this book. If you want information on a specific menu item or command, check the index.

UNIX NOTE   In the UNIX version, the FrameMaker main menu is part of each document window.

QuickAccess Bar

The *QuickAccess Bar* sits just below the main menu. It contains a number of buttons that execute common commands, including Open, Save, and Spelling Checker. The buttons are shown in Figure 2.2.

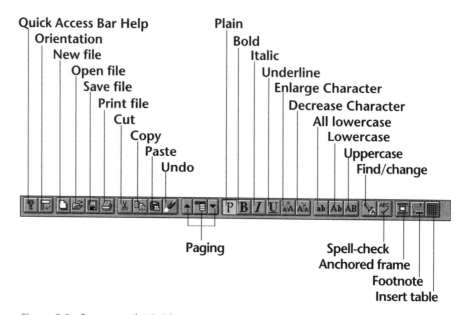

Figure 2.2   **Buttons on the QuickAccess Bar**

The QuickAccess Bar is actually four button bars, only one of which is visible at a time. You can select which QuickAccess Bar to display by using the QuickAccess Paging buttons. These buttons are located in the middle of the QuickAccess Bar. They are shown here:

Click these buttons to "page through" the four QuickAccess bars. Try using the paging buttons shown above and you'll see what I mean. There are a lot of QuickAccess buttons to make your work with FrameMaker easier.

The orientation of the QuickAccess Bar—whether it is displayed vertically or horizontally—can also be changed by using the QuickAccess Orientation button, the second-from-left button on the bar.

Viewing the QuickAccess Bar   To make the QuickAccess Bar appear or disappear in the Windows version of FrameMaker, select View ➤ QuickAccess Bar from the main menu. The QuickAccess Bar command is a toggle command. Notice that a check mark appears when the QuickAccess Bar is displayed, and does not appear when the QuickAccess Bar is not displayed. A command that alternately turns something on or off is called a *toggle* command. A number of FrameMaker commands are toggles.

 MAC AND UNIX NOTE   In the Mac and UNIX versions of the program, the View ➤ QuickAccess Bar command is *not* a toggle. To make the QuickAccess Bar disappear, click on the Close box at the left end of the QuickAccess Bar.

Help with the QuickAccess Bar   As you saw, the QuickAccess Bar has a great many buttons. To get online help on the QuickAccess Bar, click on the Question button on the QuickAccess Bar itself. You can also select Help ➤ Context Sensitive, then click on the QuickAccess Bar after the mouse cursor changes. In either case, a Help window on the Quick-Access Bar appears.

 MAC NOTE   Context-sensitive help is available from the Apple menu.

 WINDOWS NOTE   To make the Help window go away, double-click on the Control menu box in the upper-left corner of the Help window title stripe.

Formatting Bar

The *Formatting Bar* is another button bar with command shortcuts. As shown in Figure 2.3, it contains the following items:

▶ Two buttons that bring up paragraph pop-up menus—the Alignment menu and the Spacing menu.

▶ Four buttons that select tab styles. These are called *tab wells* because they stay down when "pushed" (that is, they stay down when they are selected with the mouse).

▶ A Paragraph Format pull-down menu that lists all the paragraph formats, or *paragraph tags*, that have been created for the current document.

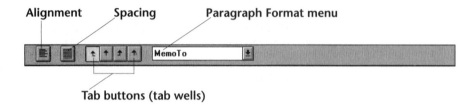

Alignment   **Spacing**   **Paragraph Format menu**

Tab buttons (tab wells)

Figure 2.3   The Formatting Bar

Aligning Paragraphs   The Alignment pop-up menu, which you access by clicking the Alignment button on the Formatting Bar, contains items for making paragraphs left-aligned, center-aligned, right-aligned, or left-and-right justified. When you click this button, you see the following pop-up menu:

Controlling Paragraph Spacing   The Spacing pop-up menu, which you access by clicking the Spacing button on the Formatting Bar contains items for controlling line spacing in paragraphs and the space between paragraphs. Click the Spacing button and you see the following pop-up menu:

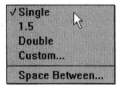

Choosing a Paragraph Format   To access the Paragraph Format pull-down menu, either click on the down arrow next to the white text box or click on the white text box itself. The menu lists all of the paragraph formats available in the current document, as shown in Figure 2.4. (To learn about paragraph formats, turn to Chapter 10.)

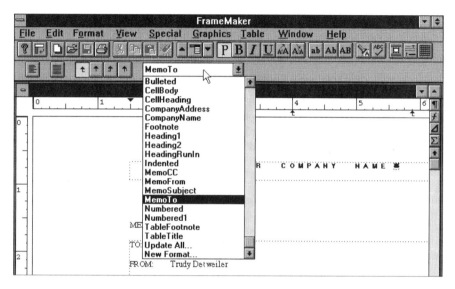

Figure 2.4   *The Paragraph Format pull-down menu*

Viewing the Formatting Bar   In the Windows version of FrameMaker, make the Formatting Bar appear or disappear by selecting View ➤ Formatting Bar. Formatting Bar is another toggle command. A check mark appears when the Formatting Bar is displayed, but does not appear when it is not displayed.

MAC AND UNIX NOTE   In the Mac and UNIX versions of the program, the Formatting Bar is part of each document window and not the main application window. You can toggle its appearance on or off for each document window by clicking on the arrow in the upper-left corner of that window. In these versions, there is no View ➤ Formatting Bar command.

Working Area

The *working area* is the large white area where documents and document windows reside. Document windows can be displayed to take up part or all of the working area, or they can be reduced to icons that lie on the working area and are ready to be opened up and worked on. Figure 2.5 shows a document and some document icons in the working area.

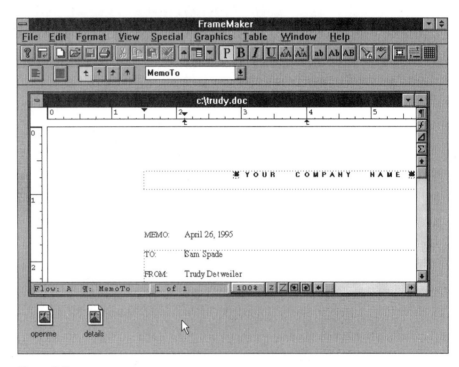

Figure 2.5   A document and some document icons in the working area

NOTE   The working area is larger than what you see on screen. FrameMaker windows, including document windows, can be moved partially off the screen. Don't worry about losing things, however. Nothing can be moved entirely off the screen, and when documents are moved partially off the screen, scroll bars appear below and/or at the side of the working area so you can scroll and see the entire document.

The Document Window

Each FrameMaker document is displayed in a document window. Figure 2.6 shows a FrameMaker document window in the FrameMaker working area.

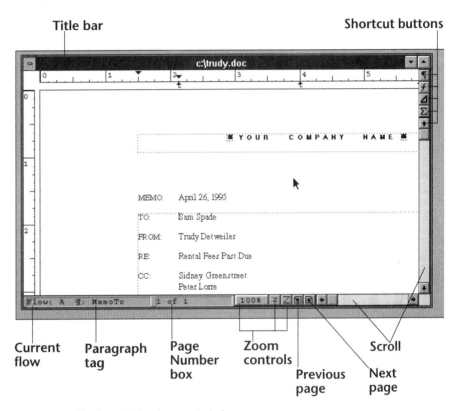

Figure 2.6   The FrameMaker document window

 UNIX NOTE   In the UNIX environment, each FrameMaker document appears in a separate window on the workspace and can be manipulated like any other Motif/OpenLook window.

The top of the document window contains a title bar—just like the application window. The document window title bar tells you the name of the document in the document window.

Document Window Shortcut Buttons

On the right side of the document window are four shortcut buttons and a scroll bar. The shortcut buttons let you bring up commonly used dialog boxes and windows quickly:

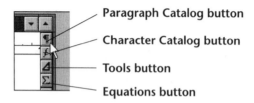

Paragraph Catalog button

Character Catalog button

Tools button

Equations button

Paragraph Catalog Button   The *Paragraph Catalog button* brings up the Paragraph Catalog window, a window that lists all of the paragraph formats defined for the current document. If you have two documents open and you switch from one to the other, you may notice the contents of this window change. (You'll learn about paragraph formats in Chapter 10.)

Character Catalog Button   The *Character Catalog button* calls the Character Catalog window, a window like the Paragraph Catalog window, except that it lists character formats instead of paragraph formats. (Chapter 9 tells you more about character formats.)

Tools Button   The *Tools button* calls the Tools window, a special window that contains a full spread of drawing tools and pop-up menus. (Drawing with FrameMaker drawing tools is discussed in detail in Chapter 9. Look ahead if you like.)

Equations Button   The *Equations button* brings up the Equations window, which allows you to build equations that look professionally typeset, just like in math books. You may never use this feature, but it's there if you need it, and it works very well!

NOTE   Each of the windows mentioned above is a *palette*—a window that stays open while you work. If you want to play with these palette windows, open up your practice document, TRUDY.DOC, then open up these special windows and start experimenting. Just remember *not* to save TRUDY.DOC after you've changed it.

Scroll Bar

The *scroll bar,* located below the shortcut buttons and shown back in Figure 2.6, allows you to see more of your document by scrolling through it vertically.

To use the scroll bar, click the up or down arrow to move the document up or down in the document window a line at a time. The *scroll box*—the white box that moves up or down in the scroll bar area—will show you roughly what part of the document you are viewing.

To move the document up or down one screen at a time, click in the gray area above or below the scroll box.

Finally, to move quickly through a document—to go from near the beginning to near the end, for example—you can drag the scroll box itself up or down in the scroll bar area.

The bottom of the document window also contains a horizontal scroll bar that works just like the vertical scroll bar, only it allows you to move your document left and right in the document window.

Status Information

The bottom of the document window displays status information, such as the current flow and paragraph tag names, if any, and the current page number. (Don't worry about what "flow" means for now. We'll cover that in Chapter 8.)

The current page number box tells you which page you're on and how many pages are in the document. Sometimes you see an asterisk (*) next to the last number. When the asterisk appears, it means that the document contains unsaved edits, as shown here:

You can see the asterisk in the page number box of the TRUDY.DOC if you like. Just go to the end of the document and add a space character. Voilà, the asterisk appears. Save the document and the asterisk goes away.

TIP   If you click on the box that shows the current page number, the Go to Page dialog box appears. From there, you can just type in the number of the page to go to, and click Go.

Controlling the Size of Your Document

Next to the status boxes are buttons that allow you to control the magnification of your document and buttons that let you go to the next or the previous page (see Figure 2.6).

Zooming In and Out   If you click the box that shows the zoom percentage, you'll see the Zoom pop-up menu:

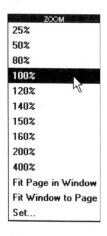

Pressing the Zoom buttons (the buttons with the big and little Z's on them) moves the document up and down through the percentages in the Zoom menu list.

TIP   Use the Set command at the bottom of the Zoom pop-up menu to change the percentage settings in the Zoom menu. Look ahead to Chapter 3 for more on the zoom feature.

Resizing the Document Window   You can resize the document window in the same way you resize other windows. In the Windows version, either use the Maximize or Minimize button at the top, or grab the sides or corners of the window with the mouse cursor and move them. When you grab the side of a window, the cursor changes to a two-headed arrow, as shown here:

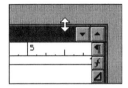

The resizing conventions of the other versions of FrameMaker are similar, and follow the standards of their environments.

There are also four View menu toggle commands (Borders, Text Symbols, Rulers, and Grid Lines) that change the display in the Document window, and a fifth (Options) that brings up a View Options dialog box. These commands and settings are discussed in Chapter 3.

Dialog Boxes

Like most applications, FrameMaker provides a number of dialog boxes. Dialog boxes demand attention. Once a dialog box is open, it must be dealt with and closed before any other FrameMaker work can be done.

 NOTE   You can always select Cancel to close a dialog box without doing anything. Every dialog box has a Cancel button.

A good example of a dialog box is the View Options box shown in Figure 2.7. To see the View Options dialog box, first make sure there is a document in the working area—TRUDY.DOC, for example. Then select View ➤ Options from the main menu.

 NOTE   Some menu items are not selectable under certain conditions. You'll recognize them because they appear in gray instead of black. The Options item on the View menu is not selectable unless a document is being viewed.

Every dialog box has at least one of the features described here.

Pull-Down Menus   You've seen *pull-down menus* before, on the Formatting Bar. When you click on the box or on the arrow pointing down, a menu list appears. Try it with any of the four pull-down menus in the View Options dialog box—for example, the one labeled Display Units.

Check boxes   Pull-down menus   Text boxes

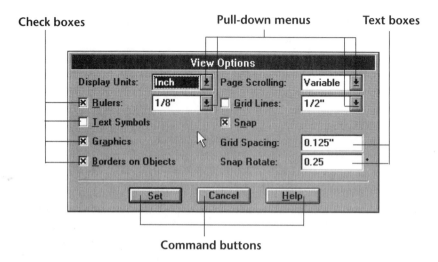

Command buttons

Figure 2.7   View Options dialog box. This is a typical dialog box.

Check Boxes   *Check boxes* can be toggled to turn features on or off. From the View Options dialog box, you can toggle the following features—Rulers, Text Symbols, Graphics, Borders on Objects, Grid Lines, and the Snap feature. If an item is checked, it means it has been activated.

Text Boxes   *Text boxes* are boxes you can type in. The View Options dialog box contains two text boxes, Grid Spacing and Snap Rotate.

Command Buttons   Though *command buttons* can appear anywhere, they're usually found at the bottom of dialog boxes. They are always gray, and one of them will have a dark line around it. This one is the *default* command button—if you press ↵ on the keyboard while the dialog box is up, the default command is selected.

The View Options dialog box has three command buttons—Set, Cancel, and Help. Set is the default button.

Radio, or Option, Buttons   *Radio buttons*, also known as *option buttons*, are like check boxes, except that like the station buttons on a radio, only one can be pressed at a time. FrameMaker radio buttons are round.

The View Options dialog box doesn't have any radio buttons, but there are two in the Print Document dialog box. To see the Print Document dialog box, click Cancel to close the View Options dialog box and select File ➤ Print. The Print Page Range area of the Print Document dialog box has two radio buttons, All and Start/End Page:

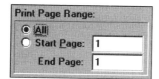

These are radio buttons. You can either select the All radio button or enter a Start/End Page range, but you can't do both—which makes sense if you think about it. In the above example, the All button is selected, and any text in the Start Page and End Page boxes is ignored.

Palettes—Windows That Stay Open

Palettes are special windows. They are like dialog boxes in many ways, and have all of the features of dialog boxes listed above.

But palettes can stay open while you are working elsewhere. They don't demand that you deal with them. You can click on something else—a document, for example—and the palette will just sit there waiting for you to get back to it.

Determining Which Window Is the Active One

You can always tell which window is the active one in FrameMaker—it's the one with the marked or specially colored title bar. (The marking or color varies with your operating environment and its configuration.) All other visible windows have unmarked (often white) title bars, which indicate they are "sleeping." To wake up a sleeping window, click on the title bar. Be careful, though, because if you click elsewhere in the box—for example, on a command button—you will wake up the window *and* start working in the box at the same time.

A good example of a palette, and one you will probably use frequently, is the Paragraph Catalog box. To see it, bring up TRUDY.DOC, then click on the Paragraph Catalog button on the right side of the document window (it has a ¶ symbol on it). A window that says "¶ Catalog" in the title bar will appear:

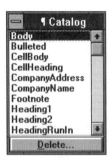

Notice that the title bar is specially colored or marked, meaning that the window is active.

WINDOWS NOTE　In the Windows version of FrameMaker, the title bar of most palettes has a square Control menu button in the upper-left corner. This button brings down a modified Control menu with three items—Move, Size, and Close. (Some palettes don't offer the Size option because they can't be resized.)

Working with Palettes

Following are instructions for working with palettes:

Action	Instructions
Opening	Select its command or button— just as you do with a dialog box.
Closing	Double-click on the Control menu button or select Close on the Control menu (Windows). (Closing a palette in the Mac and UNIX versions follows similar conventions.)

Action	Instructions
Moving	Grab the title bar and drag it. Palettes can be moved nearly off the screen, since they float on top of the FrameMaker application window and can therefore be moved anywhere in the Windows workspace. In fact, if the FrameMaker application window is small, a palette can be moved completely away from it.
Activating	Click on the title bar. To make a palette active *and* start working in it, click on a command button or other active area of the palette.

More Palette Features

To see a few more features of palettes, let's bring up another commonly used palette, the Paragraph Designer. To bring up the Paragraph Designer palette, which is shown in Figure 2.8, go to the main menu and select Format ➤ Paragraphs ➤ Designer. The Paragraph Designer is the box that allows you to control the "look" of a paragraph. You can use it to create paragraph formats and add them to the Paragraph Catalog list.

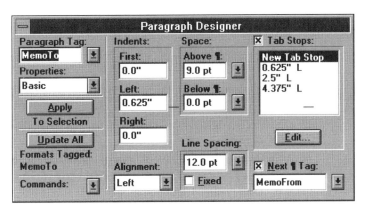

Figure 2.8   The Paragraph Designer palette

MAC AND WINDOWS NOTE   You can also bring up the Paragraph Designer
by typing the keyboard shortcut Ctrl+M (Windows) or ⌘+M (Mac).

Many palettes are responsive, even when they are "sleeping." To see this,
click to place the text cursor in the first paragraph of the TRUDY.DOC
document, and then press the ↑ and ↓ keys to move the text cursor from
paragraph to paragraph. Even though the Paragraph Designer is "sleeping," it still responds to the position of the cursor—that is, it shows the
setting of the current paragraph and changes when the cursor encounters
a paragraph with different settings.

A second feature of palettes is that some of them have multiple "pages"
of information. The Properties box of the Paragraph Designer, for
example, probably says "Basic:"

This means that the basic group of paragraph properties is displayed—
Indents, Alignment, Tab Stops, and so on. The basic paragraph properties appear in the Paragraph Designer palette shown in Figure 2.8.

But if you pull down the Properties menu, you will see a list of property
pages:

Select Default Font, for example, and the Paragraph Designer shows a
whole new group of properties to work with—in this case, properties
related to the default font of the paragraph.

 TIP   Another way to select a new page in a palette is to press the PgDn or
PgUp key.

Again, paragraph formatting and everything associated with that subject will be discussed later, in Chapter 10. But feel free to experiment with these settings as long as you have the Paragraph Catalog and Paragraph Designer up. Just be careful not to save TRUDY.DOC after you've made changes to it. We'll be using that document later.

Issuing Commands with the Mouse and the Keyboard

FrameMaker, like many programs, lets you give commands in a number of ways. You can use the mouse to select commands, buttons, and other active areas of the screen. You can use the keyboard to access the menu and issue keyboard shortcuts.

Some people are mouse users, while others prefer the keyboard. Whichever you prefer, it's a good idea to know what options are available. Let's look at how to use the mouse and keyboard with FrameMaker.

MAC AND UNIX NOTE While many of the conventions in this section are the same or similar across platforms, some are different. This book assumes that you are familiar with your operating environment (Windows, Mac, or Motif/OpenLook), so most of the differences between platforms are not noted. The following information documents the Windows version of the program.

Using the Mouse

We've done a lot of mousework already, so much of this section will be familiar to you.

Giving Commands with the Mouse

To select a single menu command with the mouse, click with the mouse button on the command. You can also select a series of menu commands with the mouse. There are two ways to do this:

▶ Click on the menu commands in order, starting with the main menu command and working your way down, until you select the last command in the chain.

▶ Click the first command, and without releasing the mouse button, *drag* the mouse cursor through the list of menus and commands until you land on the one you want. At that point, release the mouse button.

 NOTE   *Drag* means to hold down the mouse button while moving the mouse cursor.

For example, you can bring up the Document Reports dialog box with either the click method or the click-and-drag method:

▶ Click on File on the main menu, then click on Utilities in the File menu, then click on Document Reports.

▶ Move the mouse cursor to File in the main menu, click and hold the left mouse button, and then drag the cursor first down to Utilities, then across to Document Reports in one smooth (or not so smooth) motion.

In either case, when you release the left button on the Designer menu item, the Document Reports dialog box appears.

Your choice of method will probably depend on how good you are at dragging mouse cursors (I'm personally terrible at it). Both methods work just fine, however.

Using the Mouse with Buttons and Active Screen Areas

Using the mouse with buttons and active screen areas is pretty simple— just click on the button or active area. The only trick is knowing what the buttons do and which areas of the screen are active.

For online help about any button or window item, select Help ➤ Context Sensitive, then click on the item. A FrameMaker Help screen will appear. (For Mac users, context-sensitive help is available from the Apple menu.)

Using the Keyboard

Any command that can be issued with the mouse can also be issued with the keyboard, often in more than one way. The keyboard can be used to:

▶ Access the menu directly (in Windows)

▶ Issue keyboard shortcuts for commands

Accessing the Menu in Windows

In Windows, the keyboard as well as the mouse can be used to select and pull down menu items. In fact, anything that can be done with a mouse in Windows can also be done with the keyboard.

If you look at the main menu, you will see that each command has an underlined letter—for example, the *F* in File and the *o* in Format. Take a look at the main menu to see which letters are underlined:

| <u>F</u>ile | <u>E</u>dit | F<u>o</u>rmat | <u>V</u>iew | <u>S</u>pecial | <u>G</u>raphics | <u>T</u>able | <u>W</u>indow | <u>H</u>elp |

By pressing the Alt key and an underlined letter, you can pull down a menu. By typing Alt+O, for example, you can bring down the Format menu:

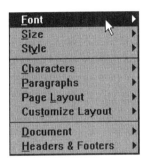

Notice that the items in the Format menu also have underlined letters. By typing the underlined letter, you select the item. If, after bringing down the Format menu, you pressed P (for the Paragraph item) and then D (for the Designer item), you would open the Paragraph Designer.

Every FrameMaker menu item can be selected in this way. Windows has keyboard ways of doing other mouse actions as well (see the Windows manual for details). So if your mouse breaks (or goes on strike), you can still get work done!

Using Keyboard Shortcuts

A *keyboard shortcut* is a way of bypassing the menus to issue a command or cause an action. When you use a keyboard shortcut, the menus never appear. In fact, some actions that can be done with keyboard shortcuts don't have menu commands associated with them at all.

There are actually two kinds of keyboard shortcuts in FrameMaker. Some require the Ctrl, Shift, or Alt key; others require the Esc key.

Shortcuts with Ctrl, Shift, and Alt Shortcuts that use the Ctrl, Shift, and Alt (or the Meta key, for UNIX users) include the key combinations printed next to commands in the various menus. Usually the menu shortcut keys involve the Ctrl key. For example, pressing Ctrl+S is the Windows shortcut for giving the Save command. Occasionally, menu shortcut keys use Shift or one of the other special keys, like the Alt key (or for UNIX users, the Meta key).

If you want to see some of these shortcuts, select File and look at the menu. You'll see several shortcuts listed. If you find yourself using a menu command often, see if a shortcut key is listed next to the menu command. Next time you want to give the command, try using the shortcut key instead of clicking on the menu. You might save time this way.

Shortcuts Using the Esc Key A second kind of keyboard shortcut uses the Esc key. These combinations are available in all three versions of FrameMaker.

To execute an Esc key combination, press the Esc key as you would any other key—that is, tap and then release it. *Do not* hold down the Esc key while you press the other keys. Then, after you've pressed the Esc key, press the other two keys in turn. For example, *Esc f s* is yet another shortcut for the Save command. To execute this Esc key combination, press and release the Esc key, then the f key, then the s key.

Esc key combinations were created when FrameMaker was first developed for UNIX systems, and there are quite a few of them. In early versions of FrameMaker, almost every program task was assigned an Esc key combination, and the program code still contains these features.

While the Esc key shortcuts are documented, they are little known to Windows and Mac users. Some of them, however, are extremely handy. They can be used, for example, when building scripts and macros (many Mac and Windows macro programs are available). The only menu items that lack these combinations are generally those that do not exist in the UNIX code, such as Print ➤ Setup, which is a Windows innovation.

WARNING Esc key shortcuts are case-sensitive—it matters if you type a capital letter or a lowercase letter. For example, pressing *Esc f p* (lowercase *p*) executes the File ➤ Print command, while pressing *Esc f P* (capital *P*) executes the File ➤ Preference command.

Let's start with some simple Esc key shortcuts first, so you can see the pattern. Here are the Esc key combinations for most of the items in the File menu. The *f* stands for "File," the name of the menu. The second letter, as nearly as possible, corresponds to the command name.

File Menu Item	Esc Key Shortcut
New	*Esc f n*
Open	*Esc f o*
Close	*Esc f c*
Save	*Esc f s*
Save As	*Esc f a*
Revert to Saved	*Esc f r*
Print	*Esc f p*
Generate	*Esc f g*
Preferences	*Esc f p*

Quite a few non-menu actions (actions that don't have menu items associated with them) can be performed with Esc shortcuts. For example, here are some of the more useful Esc key shortcuts for selecting text:

To Select	Press
Next character	*Esc h c*
Current word	*Esc h w*
Current line	*Esc h l*
Current sentence	*Esc h s*
Current paragraph	*Esc h p*

The *h* in these key combinations stands for "highlight," which is what happens onscreen when text is selected. This group of shortcuts can be quite useful, as you might imagine. Try working with them and see.

Chapter 3

Controlling What You See Onscreen

n this chapter you will learn how to control FrameMaker windows to get the view you want of your documents. This chapter covers many areas, all related to how windows and documents appear on the screen.

Here you will learn about:

Arranging windows in the working area

Controlling document guidelines, such as rulers and grid lines

Controlling the magnification of documents (often called "zooming")

Moving from page to page in a document

NOTE   This chapter offers hands-on procedures to get you familiar with the techniques being demonstrated. These procedures assume that you created the document TRUDY.DOC in Chapter 1. However, you can substitute another document if you wish.

MAC AND UNIX NOTE   While most of the commands described in this chapter have counterparts in Mac and UNIX, not all of the responses will be the same as those shown here. This is due to the way the three operating environments (Windows, Mac, and OpenLook/Motif) organize the visual workspace. Even though your system may not respond exactly as shown, the exercises in this chapter are still useful for understanding what actions have what effect in your environment. In this chapter, the responses shown are Windows program responses.

Let's start with a clean working area in this chapter. If the program is not running, bring it up, but don't open any documents yet. If the program is running, close all documents that are open, so that only a blank working area remains. When you are finished, your screen should look like Figure 3.1.

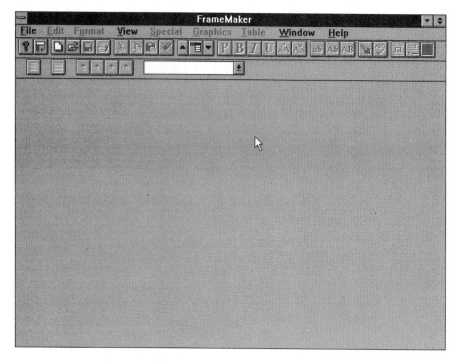

Figure 3.1   FrameMaker application window with no document

Now let's bring up TRUDY.DOC, the sample document you created in Chapter 1, and save it under a new name.

1. Select File ➤ Open, then select TRUDY.DOC from the list. If you saved the document in the root directory, it will be found in C:\TRUDY.DOC.

2. With the document open, select File ➤ Save As and enter a new name for the document—for example, enter **TRUDY1.DOC** to keep things simple.

3. Finally, open the original TRUDY.DOC by selecting File ➤ Open, then TRUDY.DOC. Now both documents are open at once.

TIP FrameMaker displays the names of the five most recently opened documents just above the Exit command in the File menu. Since you opened TRUDY.DOC recently, it's probably listed there. If so, you can select TRUDY.DOC from that list without going through the Open dialog box.

Arranging Windows in the Working Area

Now that you have two open documents, you can play around a little. The following exercises will give you good hands-on practice with window-arranging options.

> **MAC AND UNIX NOTE**   There is no Window menu in the Mac and UNIX environments, so much of the following has no Mac or UNIX counterpart.

First, let's *cascade* the two document windows. Cascaded windows are laid out one over the other, with title bars visible for easy selection.

1. Select Window ➤ Cascade. Your screen should now look like Figure 3.2. (If your screen doesn't look like Figure 3.2, it will shortly.)

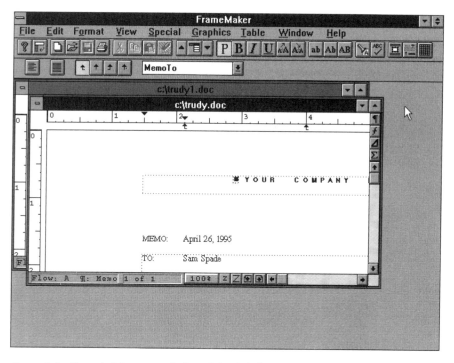

Figure 3.2   Cascaded document windows. Select Window ➤ Cascade to get cascaded windows.

Now let's *tile* the windows. Tiled windows are laid out next to each other like tiles on a floor. They allow you to work on documents side by side.

2. Select Window ➤ Tile. Your screen will now look like Figure 3.3.

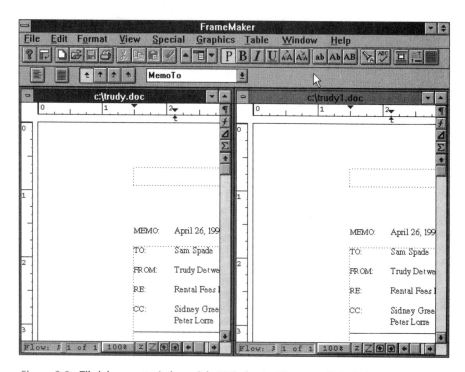

Figure 3.3   *Tiled document windows. Select Window ➤ Tile to get tiled windows.*

Let's say you now want TRUDY.DOC to take up the whole working area. To do this:

3. Find TRUDY.DOC and *maximize* it, either by clicking on the Maximize button (the up arrow on the far right of the title bar) or by double-clicking on the title bar itself. The screen will look like Figure 3.4.

Now let's make both windows into icons. To do this, you first have to make both documents visible onscreen.

4. Select Window ➤ Cascade or click on the Maximize button again. (This time the Maximize button has both an up and a down arrow in it.) Your screen will look like Figure 3.2. You should see cascaded windows.

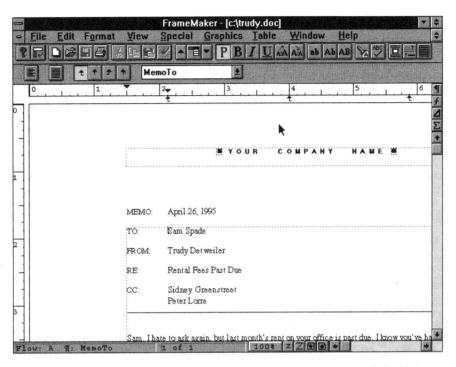

Figure 3.4 **A maximized document. Click the Maximize button or double-ckick the title bar to maximize a document.**

5. Now click the Minimize button in both windows. (The Minimize button is the down-arrow button next to the Maximize button.) Both windows are now reduced to icons:

6. Move the icons around by dragging them with the mouse cursor. Feel free to leave them in random places on the working area.

> **NOTE**   Click only once on an icon to move it. If you double-click an icon, it will open and you will have to make it an icon again by clicking the Minimize button.

Now let's rearrange the icons at the bottom of the working area:

7.   Select Window ➤ Arrange Icons. The icons are instantly back in a neat row.

Let's say you want to work on TRUDY.DOC. How do you make a document icon into a full-fledged document again?

8.   Double-click on the TRUDY.DOC icon. It opens into a document window that partially fills the working area. Notice that the TRUDY1.DOC icon is still visible as an icon, as Figure 3.5 shows.

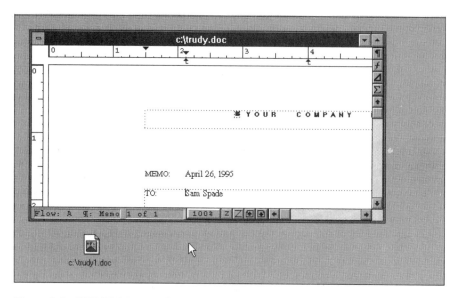

Figure 3.5   TRUDY.DOC restored to its original size. TRUDY1.DOC is still an icon.

Now let's say you decide to work on TRUDY1.DOC. You could double-click on its icon, but let's open it up in a different way:

9.   Select Window to bring up the Window menu. Notice the list of open documents at the bottom. Notice also that TRUDY.DOC is checked off to show that it is the current document.

10. Select the other open document, TRUDY1.DOC, from the list.

    Now both document windows are open again, and TRUDY1.DOC is the current document. Let's say you want to keep them both open, but you want TRUDY.DOC out of the way while you work on TRUDY1.DOC.

11. Click on the TRUDY.DOC title bar to make TRUDY.DOC the current document.

12. Place the mouse cursor on the far left side of the title bar (but still in the colored area of the bar) and drag the window to the right edge of the working area as far as it will go. You should be able to get most of it off the screen, as shown in Figure 3.6.

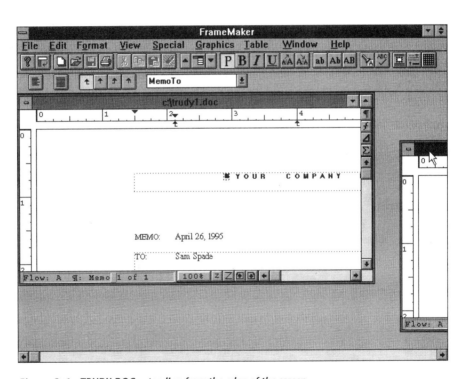

Figure 3.6   **TRUDY.DOC extending from the edge of the screen**

Finally, let's close both documents:

13. Double-click on each document's Control menu button. If you inadvertently changed the contents of these files, you will be asked if you want to save unsaved changes. Say No.

That's it. I hope you did that exercise onscreen. It gave you practice in using most of the window-arranging options.

Document Guidelines and Display Options

A number of display options and features allow you to work more easily with documents and document layouts. These include:

▶ Borders on text frames and objects

▶ Text symbols

▶ Rulers along the top and side of document windows

▶ Background grid lines in the document (grid lines do not appear on print documents)

▶ The "snap" feature

The first four of these items—borders, text symbols, rulers, and grid lines—can be turned on and off from the View menu. Additional display options not presented in the View menu are available from the View Options dialog box. All the display options are explained here.

Different Ways of Viewing a Document

Four document window toggle commands appear in the View menu. (Notice once again the check marks next to the menu items. A check mark shows whether a feature is turned on or off.) The functions of the four document window toggle commands are described in the following list.

The Least You Need...

Command	What It Does
Borders	Makes a light, dotted line appear around page objects, such as graphics and text frames. (*Text frames* are frames that can hold paragraphs. There are other kinds of frames in FrameMaker, as you will see in later chapters.)
Text Symbols	Makes non-printing text symbols, such as paragraph marks (¶), new-line characters (<), and tab characters (>), appear and disappear. Turn this feature on to see these symbols. Turn it off to see what the page will look like when printed. The text symbols are explained in Table 3.1.
Rulers	Makes the rulers at the top and right side of the document window appear and disappear. Most people like to leave rulers turned on, since the ruler bar allows them to change paragraph margins and tabs easily.
Grid Lines	Places a visible grid behind the objects on the page. This feature allows you to position objects on the page more exactly.

You will probably want to turn grid lines on for some jobs, especially jobs like brochures and newsletters that require a lot of hand-placement of objects. But for most work, like memos and letters, the grid can be distracting.

These features can also be controlled from the View Options dialog box.

NOTE   View settings are saved as part of the document when a document is saved. Each document has its own view settings.

Symbol	What It Means
¶	End of paragraph
<	New line (a forced new line within a paragraph)
>	Tab
§	End of flow
⊥	Anchor for anchored frame or table
⊤	Marker (for index entries, cross-references, and so on)
␣	Nonbreaking space
⊤	Discretionary hyphen
—	Suppressed hyphenation
[ ]	Macintosh publisher boundaries (Mac created, but viewable on all platforms)

Table 3.1   Text Symbols

The View Options Dialog Box: More Ways to View Documents

The View Options dialog box allows you to control many document window view features. Besides the ones available from the View menu, it allows you to control those available from the Document menu.

To bring up the View Options dialog box, select View ➤ Options. You'll see the dialog box shown in Figure 3.7. After you've made your changes in this dialog box, select Set, which confirms your changes and returns you to the document. If you want to cancel your changes and return to the document, select Cancel. Now let's look at what the View Options dialog box can do.

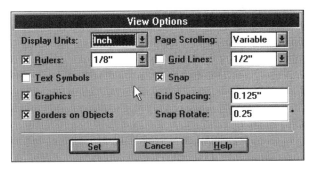

Figure 3.7 **The View Options dialog box**

Display Units

The Display Units pull-down menu allows you to specify which unit of measurement will be used when distances and lengths are specified in documents. For example, the distance of an object from the top of the page, or the length of a rectangle are measured in the display unit you choose here.

The choices are:

Centimeter

Millimeter

Inch

Pica

Point

Didot

Cicero

You probably know about centimeters, millimeters, and inches. Most people leave the unit as inches.

Didots and ciceros are used mostly in Europe. A *didot* is about $^1/_8$ millimeter, and a *cicero* is about 4.55 millimeters.

Picas and *points* are common typesetting units. There are six picas per inch, roughly 72 points per inch, and therefore about 12 points per pica. (Why there are "roughly" and not exactly 72 points per inch is a long story....) There are a couple of reasons for using either picas or points as the display unit as an alternative to inches.

Picas In the United States, the pica is the most common unit of measurement for page layouts. For example, the space between columns in your favorite newspaper is probably measured in picas or parts of picas. Consider setting Display Units to Pica if you do a lot of page layout work—with newsletters or brochures, for example. The results can be very pleasing. (You can get a pica ruler by selecting either Pica or $^1/_{12}''$ from the Rulers pull-down menu.)

Points The *point* is a useful setting for several reasons. Points are small units that can be mentally converted into inches without much trouble. (Seventy-two points = 1 inch, 36 points = $^1/_2$ inch, and 18 points = $^1/_4$ inch. Therefore, a standard $^1/_4''$ indent for paragraphs is 18 points, $1^1/_2$ picas, or three notches on a ruler set to $^1/_{12}''$.)

If you want to specify small changes in an object's size or position, changing the number of points gives you a lot of control. With just a little practice, for example, you'll learn to imagine what a 2-point change in a line's thickness looks like.

On the other hand, if your display unit is inches, sizes and distances will be shown in decimal inches (for example, 1.954″ or 3.45″). Many people find decimal inches hard to work with, since it's hard to picture the results of your changes.

If the same is true for you, consider setting the display unit to points and learning to measure that way. There are many benefits. (The best ruler to use with points is probably $^1/_{12}''$, since it gives you the ability to work in picas, points, and inches at the same time.)

Rulers, Text Symbols, Borders, and Grid Lines

The Rulers, Text Symbols, Borders, and Grid Lines options have the same meaning here as they do in the View menu (see "Different Ways of Viewing a Document" earlier in this chapter to learn about these options). In the View Options dialog box, these options appear as check boxes. If the box is checked, the feature is turned on.

However, the View Options dialog box also offers pull-down menus for choosing ruler subdivisions of your own. To choose ruler subdivisions, pull down the Rulers menu. To choose where grid lines fall, pull down the Grid Lines menu.

NOTE For more information on rulers and ruler subdivisions, see "Working with the Ruler" later in this chapter.

Graphics

The Graphics check box allows you to make graphic objects either appear on the screen or be hidden. (Of course, graphic objects will still print when the document is printed.) Turning Graphics off allows documents with lots of drawings and imported graphics to appear onscreen faster.

Page Scrolling

The Page Scrolling pull-down menu allows you to determine how pages are displayed in the document window. There are four choices:

▶ **Vertical**—Displays document pages one above the other.

▶ **Horizontal**—Displays pages next to each other in a row.

▶ **Facing Pages**—Displays pages two at a time next to each other in a *spread*, the way magazine and book pages are displayed when a book or magazine is laid open.

▶ **Variable**—Fills the document window with as many pages as will fit in it, laying pages out in rows, one below the other.

The default selection for most documents is Variable. At large magnifications (large enough for most people to read comfortably), Variable lays out the document pages vertically.

Snap

Snap refers to the tendency of an object, when moved near a *snap line*, to gravitate or "snap" next to it. Snap lines are invisible lines in documents that act like magnets—objects are pulled into place next to snap lines. Snap lines make it easier to line up objects on a page. They allow you to put objects into preset positions easily and precisely.

Snap also affects the behavior of objects on the ruler. When snap is turned on, objects on the ruler snap to the marked ruler divisions you have chosen.

You will get a chance to see the snap feature in action in the next section, "Working with the Ruler."

 TIP   If you like using the ruler to place tabs and change margins, you will probably want to keep snap turned on.

The snap feature is controlled by these three items in the View Options dialog box:

Snap check box	Turns snap on or off for all three snap items at once—the snap grid, snap rotation, and the top ruler.
Grid Spacing text box	Specifies the distance between invisible snap lines. (Note that the snap grid is not the same as the visible grid controlled by the Grid Lines pull-down menu.)
Snap Rotate text box	Controls the angles that objects snap to when they are rotated.

Snap Grid vs. Visible Grid

The snap grid is *not* visible, and it is *not* the same as the visible grid. But you can make them the same by making them lie on top of one another. To do this, make the Grid Lines setting (for the visible grid) the same as the Grid Spacing setting (for the snap grid). For example, you could make both settings $^1/_2$".

You can also make the snap grid smaller or larger than the visible grid and still have them lie on top of each other. Do this by making one grid spacing a multiple of the other one. For example, you could set the visible grid to $^1/_4$" and the snap grid to $^1/_8$". Objects would then snap to the visible grid (when snap was turned on), and also snap to an invisible line halfway between the lines of the visible grid.

Note that the snap grid spacing also works on the ruler.

Working with the Ruler

The FrameMaker rulers allow you to see roughly where things are on a page by giving you a measurement guide across the top and down the left side of the page.

Each document has its own ruler, and the settings for one document may be different from the settings for another. As you saw, rulers can be turned on or off, and the display units on rulers may be changed.

The ruler across the top has another important feature. With it you can manually control the margins, first-line indentation, and tabs of a paragraph. Let's see how the ruler works. Open the document TRUDY.DOC, if it isn't open already, and do the following:

1. Expand the document so it takes up the entire screen. (Do this by double-clicking on the title bar.)

2. Reduce the document to 80 percent by clicking on the Zoom Out button (the button with the small "z" on it). The Zoom buttons are located at the bottom of the document window. Your screen will look like Figure 3.8.

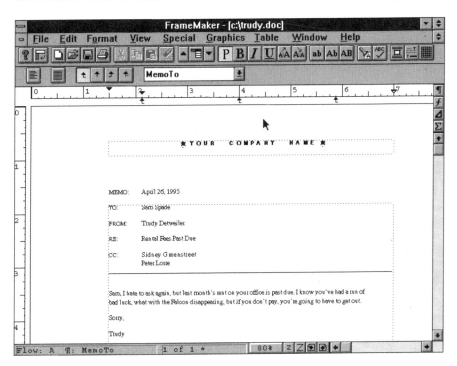

Figure 3.8 **TRUDY.DOC expanded full-screen**

3. Make sure snap is turned on. Go to the View Options dialog box (select View ➤ Options), and turn Snap on by clicking in the Snap check box.

4. Click the Set button to close the View Options box and apply the changes to the document.

5. Click anywhere in the paragraph that says "TO: Sam Spade" and look at the top ruler.

   You should see three small triangles above the ruler line (where the numbers are), and three small arrows below the ruler line:

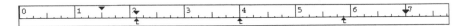

   The two triangles on the left side of the line and above it show the two left margins for the paragraph—one for the first line and one for all of the other lines. The single triangle on the right shows the right margin for the paragraph. The three small arrows below the ruler line show where the tab stops are located.

6. Press the ↓ key to slowly move the cursor down through the document. Notice that the ruler display changes to reflect the settings of each paragraph.

7. When you get to the paragraph that starts "Sam, I hate to ask again," stop. We're going to practice changing settings on this paragraph.

8. Bring up the Paragraph Designer by pressing Crtl+M (2 +M on the Mac), and move it away from the paragraph we're working with. Your screen will look something like Figure 3.9.

   Notice that the three settings labeled Indents (First, Left, and Right) are all 0.0″, and that no tab stops are listed. The settings in these boxes reflect the settings on the ruler.

NOTE   The Paragraph Designer says that the paragraph is indented 0″, while the ruler shows $1^{1}/_{2}$″. This is because they are measuring from different places. The ruler always measures from the edge of the page. The Paragraph Designer, on the other hand, measures from the edge of the text frame—the box with the dotted-line border that contains the paragraph.

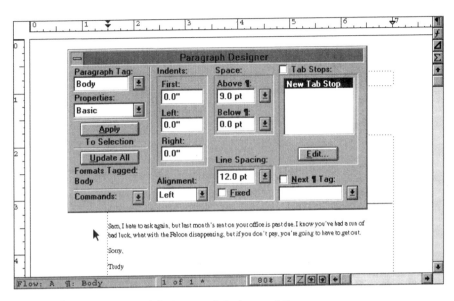

Figure 3.9   TRUDY.DOC and the Paragraph Designer palette

Let's start by changing the first-line margin:

9.   With the mouse cursor, grab the *upper* dark triangle and move it across from the $1^1/_2''$ mark to the $1^3/_4''$ mark on the ruler. (If this movement seems difficult at first, just stay with it. It will come easily in a moment.)

You should have noticed three things:

- That the triangle seemed to "hop" from one ruler division to the next. This is the snap feature in action.

- That the first line of the paragraph moved $^1/_4''$ to the right from its previous position.

- That the Indents setting labeled First in the Paragraph Designer changed to 0.25".

Now let's change the left and right margins and create a different paragraph style—one with a *hanging indent.*

10.   On the ruler, move the upper-left arrow (first-line indent mark) back to the $1^1/_2''$ mark, and move the lower-left arrow (rest-of-the-paragraph indent mark) over to $1^3/_4''$.

Notice what the paragraph looks like now. You can probably see why this is called a "hanging indent."

Notice also the new settings that have appeared in the Paragraph Designer:

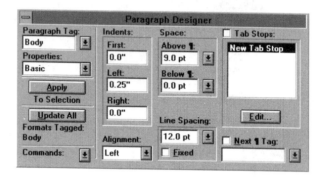

Let's place tabs in the new paragraph:

11. Look at the four tab buttons on the Formatting Bar and make sure the one on the left is "pushed in" (selected). If it isn't, select it now by clicking on it with the mouse cursor:

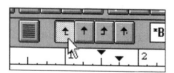

12. Now create a tab stop at the $1^3/4''$ mark on the ruler by clicking once at $1^3/4''$ below the line that contains the numbers and ruler divisions. A left tab symbol appears on the ruler:

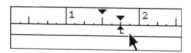

Notice that the left tab symbol is the same as the one on the tab button you just pressed. Had you pressed any of the other tab buttons (center, right, or decimal) you would have gotten one of those tabs instead, and the symbol would have reflected that. If you look at the Paragraph Designer, you'll see a left tab has appeared at 0.25".

Part
1

The Least You Need...

Let's do something with our new tab stop. We're going to create a *numbered paragraph.*

13. Move the text cursor into the first line of the paragraph, and then press the Home key. The cursor should move to the beginning of the paragraph.

14. Type **1.** (the number one followed by a period) and press the Tab key once. If text symbols were turned on, you would see the tab character. Now the entire paragraph has a hanging indent:

    1. Sam, I hate to ask again, but I
       run of bad luck, what with th
       to get out.

Paragraphs with hanging indents are often used to make numbered paragraphs, as you just saw, and also *bulleted paragraphs.* Bulleted paragraphs start with a bullet character, such as • or ■.

TIP   FrameMaker actually has some pretty sophisticated ways to make both numbered paragraphs and bulleted paragraphs. It can even automatically number the paragraphs for you. See Chapter 10 for more on this interesting subject.

If you want to continue playing with the ruler, feel free. Get as comfortable with its capabilities as you like. Try different types of tabs, or try turning snap off and moving things around to see what happens. Just make sure you don't save the document when you are finished!

15. When you are done, close the document by selecting File ➤ Close.

16. You are asked if you want to save unsaved changes. Select No.

17. Put away the Paragraph Designer by double-clicking on the Control menu button in the upper-left corner.

You should now have a pretty good idea of how to use the ruler. You should also know what its capabilities are.

Zooming In and Out of Documents

Unless you have one of those wonderfully expensive large-screen monitors, you will probably change the magnification of documents with some frequency. Do this with the zoom feature.

Zoom is controlled by three buttons at the bottom of the document window. These are called, in order from left to right, Zoom, Zoom Out, and Zoom In:

Every document window has these buttons, and you can have different zoom settings for each document.

NOTE Zoom settings are saved with the document when the document is saved.

How Zooming Works

The magnification of a document can be set in two ways. You can use either the Zoom menu, which is available by clicking the Zoom button, the button with the current zoom percent on it, or you can use the Zoom In and Zoom Out buttons, the buttons with the large and small letter "Z" on them.

To see how zooming works, let's bring up a clean copy of TRUDY.DOC:

1. Open TRUDY.DOC if it is not already open.

2. If the document is maximized, click on the Maximize button so that it has it's own title stripe.

3. Click once on the Zoom button, the button that shows the zoom percent. You will see the Zoom menu.

4. Click once on 25%. Your screen will look something like Figure 3.10.

Notice that the text has been reduced to gray lines. This is called *greeking* the text (as in Shakespeare's "It's Greek to me"), and it allows the screen display to be updated faster. Imagine how long it would take the computer to resize and print all those small fonts if it had to show them accurately—and how much good it would do if they *were* displayed. You'd wait a long time for something that couldn't be read anyway!

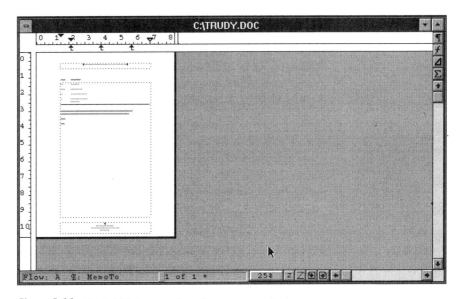

Figure 3.10 **TRUDY.DOC zoomed to 25 percent magnitude**

TIP At small font sizes, FrameMaker always greeks text. You can control the point size at which greeking starts by selecting File ➤ Preferences and changing the Greek Screen Text setting in the Preferences dialog box.

5. Start clicking on the Zoom In button, the button with the large "Z" on it. The document gets larger and larger. Zoom in as far as you like.

Notice that the zoom percentage display changes, and that the numbers are moving through the numbers listed in the Zoom menu.

TIP The part of the document that is currently selected or contains the text cursor is the part that's visible when a document is zoomed. This is a handy feature. When you are zooming in close on drawings, select the part of the drawing you want to look at before you zoom, then zoom away. The part you selected will always be in view.

6. Zoom back down, using the button with the smaller "z" on it. Stop when you get to 80%.

7. Save the document.

Using some combination of the zoom and window sizing features, you should be able to view the document in a way that's convenient for you.

> TIP When you do find the settings you like—window size and zoom setting—save the document. The settings will be saved along with it. When the document is reopened, it will have the settings you chose.

Making Windows and Pages Fit Onscreen

There are two more ways to zoom a document. From the bottom of the Zoom menu, you can select Fit Window to Page or Fit Page in Window. These choices may sound a bit confusing, so let's look at them more closely.

▶ **Fit Window to Page**—Keeps the zoom setting the same and makes the document window larger or smaller so that the window fits around the page.

▶ **Fit Page in Window**—Keeps the document window the same size and adjusts the zoom percentage of the page so that the whole document fits into the window.

In other words, "Fit Window" means change the window size, and "Fit Page" means change the zoom (in other words, the page size).

To see these commands in action, do the following:

1. Open TRUDY.DOC or a document of your own.

2. Select Window ➤ Cascade and set zoom to 80%. Your screen will look like Figure 3.11.

3. Click on the Zoom button (the one with the zoom percent) to bring up the Zoom menu.

4. Select Fit Window to Page. Notice that the document window gets a lot larger, as in Figure 3.12.

5. Now bring up the Zoom menu and select Fit Page in Window. The page gets a lot smaller but the window doesn't change, as in Figure 3.13.

6. Select Fit Window to Page again. The document window frame is now shrink-wrapped ("fit") to the document itself, as in Figure 3.14.

7. Close TRUDY.DOC without saving it.

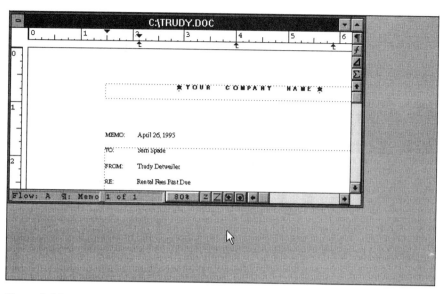

Figure 3.11   ***TRUDY.DOC at 80-percent zom***

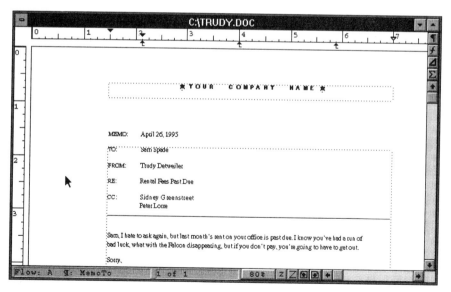

Figure 3.12   ***TRUDY.DOC after the Fit Window to Page command has been issued***

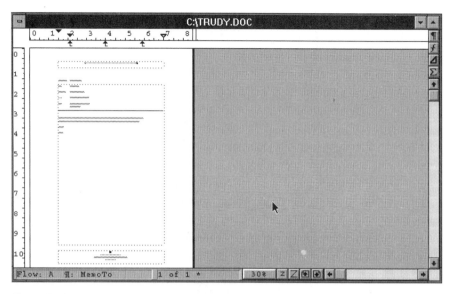

Figure 3.13   TRUDY.DOC after the Fit Page in Window command has been issued

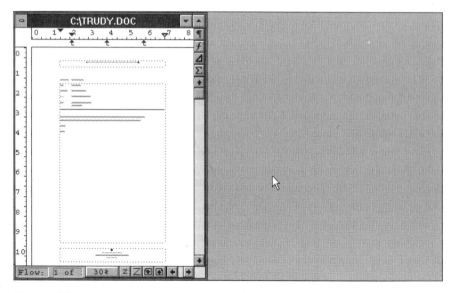

Figure 3.14   TRUDY.DOC after the second Fit Window to Page command

Changing Zoom Settings

The zoom percentages on the Zoom menu can be customized to your liking. To change the zoom percent settings:

1. Open TRUDY.DOC.

2. Bring up the Zoom menu by clicking on the Zoom button.

3. Select Set, the bottom-most menu item, to bring up the Zoom Menu Options dialog box:

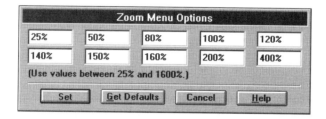

From this box, you can change any of the settings in the Zoom menu. In other words, the percents shown in the boxes will appear on the Zoom menu.

4. When you are finished, you can select either:

   • Set to confirm the current settings.

   • Get Defaults to return to the program's default list of settings.

   • Cancel to exit the dialog box without making any changes at this time.

Changes to the Zoom menu are saved whenever the document is saved. (We are leaving TRUDY.DOC onscreen through the rest of this chapter, so that you can work with the features and buttons discussed below. When you are done, close the document without saving it.)

Moving Quickly from Page to Page

Moving through pages of a document can be done in any of four ways:

▶ With the PgUp and PgDn keys

▶ With the Page Up and Page Down buttons on the bottom of the Document window

▶ With the scroll bar along the right side of the document window

▶ With the Go to Page dialog box

PgUp and PgDn Keys The PgUp and PgDn keys are the easiest to use, but they have one disadvantage. They always move to the top of the next or previous page. The bottoms of pages aren't displayed unless the zoom magnitude is very small (or your monitor is large enough to show a full page). Pressing PgUp and PgDn is useful if you want to turn pages quickly, but not if you want to see the next "screenful" of a document.

Page Up and Page Down Buttons The Page Up and Page Down buttons on the document window work just like the PgUp and PgDn keys, and have the same advantages and disadvantages.

Scroll Bar The scroll bar along the right side of the screen allows you to fine-tune what you see. To use the scroll bar, do any of the following:

▶ Drag the scroll box (the white box that appears in the scroll bar) up or down to move quickly to an approximate place in the document. (The page number status box will be updated as the button moves to show your new location.)

▶ Click on the up and down arrow buttons at the top and bottom of the scroll bar to move up or down in small increments.

▶ Click on the gray areas above or below the scroll box to move up or down one "screenful" at a time.

Go to Page Dialog Box You can bring up the Go to Page dialog box in any of three ways. You can

▶ select View ➤ Go to Page from the main menu.

▶ press Ctrl+G on the keyboard (⌘+G for Mac users).

▶ click on the page number status box at the bottom of the document window.

The Go to Page dialog box is shown in Figure 3.15. Its options are self-explanatory. Notice that the cursor always appears in the Page Number text area when the dialog box first comes up. To go to a specific page, just bring up the box, type a page number, and press ↵ (or select Go, the default button at the bottom of the box).

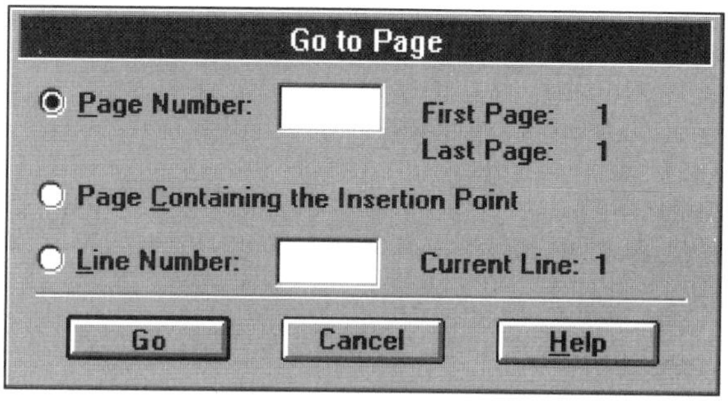

Figure 3.15 **The Go to Page dialog box**

The Go to Page dialog box is not a palette. It goes away as soon as you use it. To abandon the box without using it, select Cancel at the bottom of the box or press Esc.

Chapter 4
Editing Documents

This chapter explains "the least you need to know about" text editing and gives you a quick introduction to using color with FrameMaker.

NOTE This chapter uses the sample document you created in Chapter 1, the memo from Trudy Dutweiler to Sam Spade. If you haven't created that document yet, you may want to go back and do so now.

Editing Basics

This section covers some of the basics of text editing. It explains:

▶ Using FrameMaker cursors

▶ Selecting text and objects

▶ Deleting text

▶ Cutting, copying, and pasting text

▶ Undoing changes

▶ Searching for and replacing text

▶ Changing the look of text to bold, italic, and so forth

▶ Changing the look of paragraphs

▶ Checking spelling

Let's look at these one at a time, starting with the FrameMaker cursors.

FrameMaker Cursors

FrameMaker has three main cursors:

▶ The *text cursor*—what the mouse cursor looks like when it's over a text area. The text cursor looks like a skinny I-beam.

▶ The *object cursor*—what the mouse cursor looks like when it's *not* over a text area. The object cursor looks like a wide arrow.

▶ The *character cursor*—a marker in the text itself that shows where characters will be entered when you start typing. The character cursor is a flashing vertical line that sits in text next to text characters. It appears when the mouse is clicked once in a text frame, and disappears when the mouse cursor is clicked outside of a text frame:

TrudylDetweiler

Notice that two cursors (the text cursor and object cursor) are different flavors of the mouse cursor, while the character cursor is not.

The mouse cursor changes automatically from text to object, depending on what it is "over." That is, when the mouse cursor is within the borders of a text frame—the dotted-line box that can hold text paragraphs—it becomes a text cursor. When the mouse cursor is not within the borders of a text frame, it becomes an object cursor.

It's important to notice what kind of cursor you have, since different kinds of cursors can select different kinds of things.

 TIP You can force the text cursor to become an object cursor even when it's over a text frame. Just hold down the Ctrl key (or ⌘ key for Mac users) and "wiggle" the mouse a bit. The mouse cursor will become an object cursor and stay that way until the Ctrl key is released. To change the cursor back to text, release the Ctrl key and wiggle the mouse again.

 MAC NOTE Most Ctrl key combinations are available on the Mac as ⌘ key combinations.

Fast Ways to Move the Character Cursor

One of the fastest ways to move the character cursor is with the keys on the cursor keypad:

Key(s)	Moves the Character Cursor
↑, ↓, ←, or →	Up, down, left, or right
Home or End	To the beginning or end of a line
Ctrl+← or Ctrl+→	To the beginning or end of a word
Ctrl+Home or Ctrl+End	To the beginning or end of a sentence
Ctrl+↑ or Ctrl+↓	To the beginning or end of a paragraph

Key(s)	Moves the Character Cursor
Ctrl+PgUp *or* Ctrl+PgDn	To the beginning or end of a text frame
Alt+Shift+PgUp *or* Alt+Shift+PgDn	To the beginning or end of a flow

MAC AND UNIX NOTE   Some of these key combinations are not available on Mac and UNIX installations of the program.

The character cursor can also be moved around in a text frame by clicking the mouse cursor in various locations.

MAC AND UNIX NOTE   The keyboard and mouse button actions shown in this chapter are true for the Windows version of the program, and depend on conventions established for the Windows operating environment. Some of these conventions are different for the Mac and UNIX versions of Frame-Maker. Mac key and mouse actions will be consistent with the Mac interface. UNIX key and mouse actions will be consistent with the Motif interface (though the latter may be considerably modified by your system administrator).

Selecting Text and Objects

The text and object cursors are used to make selections in FrameMaker. Once text or objects are selected, they can be operated on. Selected text can be cut, copied, and reformatted, for example. Selected objects can be cut, copied, moved, resized, and reshaped.

This section explains how to select text with the text and object cursors.

Selecting Text with the Text Cursor

The text cursor is a mouse cursor that is used to place the character cursor (as you just saw) and to select text—for deleting, cutting, or copying, for example. Normally, the mouse cursor becomes a text cursor when it is within a text frame. In Figure 4.1, the mouse cursor, located in a text frame, has become a text cursor.

"Selecting" text means highlighting a group of characters. Highlighted text changes the text to "reverse video," so that the characters turn white

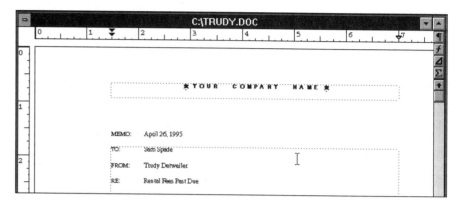

Figure 4.1   *A text cursor over a text frame*

and appear within a black highlight bar. Selected text can now be operated on—it can be cut, copied, changed to boldface, and so on.

There are lots of ways to select text with the text cursor:

To Select	Do This
Text letters	Click once at one end of the text you want to select, then hold the left mouse button and drag the cursor over the text. The character cursor widens into a black highlight bar, and the text over which you dragged is selected.
A word	Double-click on the word.
Several words	Double-click on the word, then hold the left mouse button and drag the cursor over text. The text will be selected word by word.
A paragraph	Click three times, or "triple-click," over the paragraph.
Several paragraphs	Click three times, or "triple-click," over a paragraph, then hold the left mouse button and drag the cursor over text. The text will be selected paragraph by paragraph.

If you practice highlighting text, and you get inspired to start deleting or making other changes, go ahead. Just don't save your work (my usual warning in these practice chapters).

Extending a Selection

Another way to highlight (select) a group of text characters is by *extending a selection*. To do this, click once at the beginning of the text you want to select, move the mouse cursor to the end of the intended selection, and *Shift-click* (press the Shift key and click once with the mouse button). Shift-clicking is a useful way to select text, especially large chunks of text—more than one page, for example. Shift-clicking is also a good way to extend an existing selection.

Why You Can't Select the Date in TRUDY.DOC

When you select text, you might notice that the date cannot be selected. Can you guess the reason? Look carefully and see if the date text is within the dotted line borders of a text frame.

The reason you can't select the date in this document is because it's not on the same page as the other text—it's on a *master page*, a page that shows through from "underneath" the page. Anything on a *master page* appears on a body page as part of the background. In this document, the date is on the master page. Master pages are discussed later (in Chapter 8). For now, just be aware that text that isn't within a visible text frame may not be selected with a text cursor.

Selecting Objects with the Object Cursor

The object cursor is a mouse cursor that can select *objects*—things on a page other than text characters, such as circles and rectangles. Once you've selected an object with the mouse cursor, you can delete, copy, move, or resize it, and do other operations as well.

Normally, as Figure 4.2 shows, the text cursor becomes an object cursor when the midpoint of the I-beam is moved outside the borders of a text frame. Notice in the figure that the object cursor is normally a *filled arrow*—it is entirely black inside.

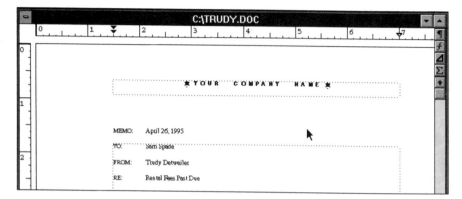

Figure 4.2 **An object cursor** *outside* **of a text frame. Outside a text frame, the cursor is a black arrow.**

When the object cursor is over something that can be selected, it becomes an *unfilled arrow*—an outline with a hollow center. Figure 4.3 shows an object cursor over something that can be selected.

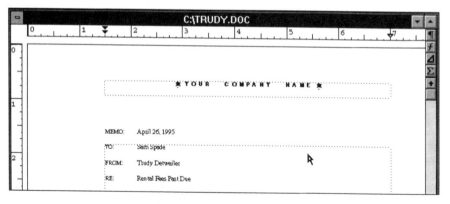

Figure 4.3 **An object cursor over a selectable object. Compare this cursor to the one in Figure 4.2.**

The Least You Need...

Here are some techniques for working with the object cursor:

To Do This	Action
Select an object	Click the left mouse button once and release it while the cursor is over the object. The object will be selected and black "handles" will appear around the object. (To select a text frame, the procedure is a little different. See below.)
Move an object	Click and hold the left mouse button over an object, then drag the cursor. The object will be selected and dragged along.
Select several objects	Click and hold the left mouse button outside the group of objects, then drag the mouse. A "rubber band" selector box appears. Keep dragging until the objects you want to select are all inside the box. Every object that is entirely within that box will be selected. (See "Selecting a Text Frame with the 'Rubber Band' Technique" later in this chapter for the details.)

Selecting a Text Frame   The procedure for selecting a text frame is different from the procedure for selecting other kinds of objects. The reason is simple—when you move the mouse cursor over a text frame, the object cursor disappears and the text cursor takes its place! You have to force the object cursor to stay an object cursor, even over a text frame, or you can't select the text frame as an object.

The following shows how this works:

1. Open a fresh copy of TRUDY.DOC.

2. Move the mouse cursor over the top text frame on the page—the one that contains the text YOUR COMPANY NAME. You should see the I-beam text cursor, as in Figure 4.4.

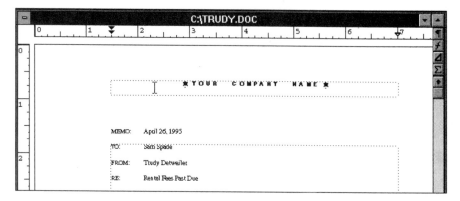

Figure 4.4   **The text cursor over a text frame**

3. Hold down the Ctrl key and click the mouse button once. The text cursor becomes an object cursor, and object handles appear on the selected text frame, as in Figure 4.5.

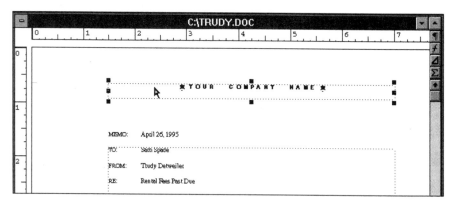

Figure 4.5   *Selecting a text frame with the object cursor*

The text frame can now be moved, resized, cut, or copied. You can perform other operations on it as well.

Selecting a Text Frame with the "Rubber Band" Technique   You can also use the "rubber band" technique to select a text frame, or any other object, for that matter.

To select an object with the rubber band selector box:

1. If necessary, open a fresh copy of TRUDY.DOC and double-click on the title bar to maximize the document window.

2. Make sure the document is zoomed to 80 percent. If it isn't, use the Zoom buttons to zoom it.

3. Move the mouse cursor above and to the left of the top text frame on the page—the one that contains the text YOUR COMPANY NAME. Figure 4.6 shows where to move the mouse cursor.

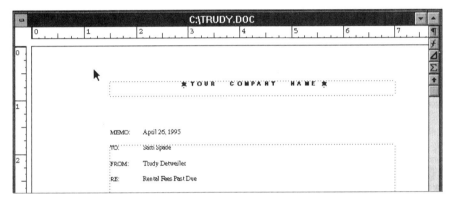

Figure 4.6 Positioning the mouse cursor for a "rubber band" selection

4. Hold the left mouse button down and drag the cursor to a position below and to the right of the same text frame, as shown in Figure 4.7. The rubber band selector box should entirely enclose the text frame.

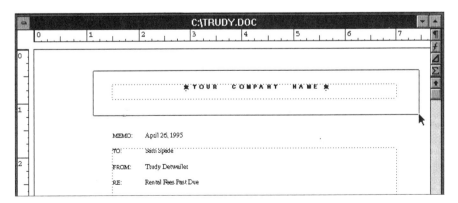

Figure 4.7 Drawing a rubber band selector box around a text frame

5. Release the left mouse button. The selector box disappears and the text frame is selected. Notice the black object handles, as in Figure 4.8.

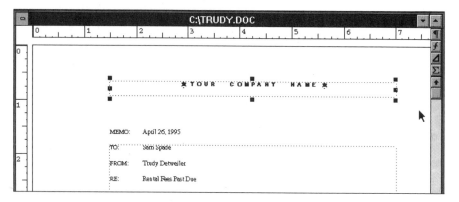

Figure 4.8   *A selected text frame. Notice the object handles.*

The text frame can now be moved, resized, cut, or copied. You can perform other operations on it as well.

TIP   Using a selector box is an easy way to select a group of objects. Just make sure every object you want to select is entirely within the selector box when you release the mouse button.

"Deselecting" an Object or Text Frame   To "deselect" an object or text frame, click somewhere else on the page with the object cursor. The object handles will disappear and the object will no longer be selected.

NOTE   The rest of this section deals only with operations that can be performed on text, since most documents don't contain objects, like circles and rectangles, and since text frames in most documents don't usually need to be moved. For more information on how to perform operations on objects with the object cursor, see Chapter 13.

Deleting Text

Text can be deleted, or cleared, by selecting Edit ➤ Clear from the main menu or by using the keyboard. "Delete" or "clear" means to completely remove something from a document. Deleted text isn't saved anywhere.

You can use a number of keys in FrameMaker to delete text. You are probably already using some of them. Others may be new to you. Table 4.1 lists the most useful keys and key combinations for deleting text.

To Delete	Press
Previous character	Backspace
Next character	Del (Delete)
To the end of the previous word	Ctrl+Backspace
To the end of the current word	Shift+Backspace
To the end of the current line	Ctrl+Shift+Del
To the end of the previous sentence	Esc k a
To the start of the next sentence	Esc k s

Table 4.1   **Deleting Text with the Keyboard**

MAC AND UNIX NOTE   Some of the key combinations in Table 4.1 are not available on Mac and UNIX installations of the program.

Cutting, Copying, and Pasting Text and Objects

Cutting, copying, and pasting are all operations that use the Clipboard. The *Clipboard* is a temporary storage location for text and objects that all applications, including FrameMaker, can use. (In the Windows version, you can see the contents of the Clipboard with the Clipboard Viewer, a program in the Program Manager Main program group.)

Here is what happens when you cut and copy things to the Clipboard, and what happens when you paste things from the Clipboard:

▶ **Cutting**—Deletes something from the document *and* saves it to the Clipboard. Cutting something changes the contents of the Clipboard, since what was there before the cut is removed.

▶ **Copying**—Copies something from the document to the Clipboard. The document remains intact, since nothing is taken from it. Copying something changes the contents of the Clipboard, since what was there before is removed.

▶ **Pasting**—Copies what is on the Clipboard to the document. Pasting something does *not* change the contents of the Clipboard. You can paste what is on the Clipboard into the document as many times as you like.

The Difference between Deleting and Cutting

Note that "deleting," or "clearing," is not quite the same as cutting, which you will read about shortly. Deleting text or objects does not change the contents of the Clipboard, a special storage area for text and objects. Cutting text or objects, on the other hand, does change the contents of the Clipboard, since it places what was cut on the Clipboard and removes what was there previously.

Cutting, copying, and pasting can be accomplished with the menus, keyboard shortcuts, or QuickAccess Bar buttons. Table 4.2 shows how. See the inside front and back covers of this book if you need to find where QuickAccess Bar buttons are located.

Action	Menu Selection	Keyboard Shortcut	QuickAccess Bar Button
Cut	Edit ➤ Cut	Ctrl+X, Shift+Del	Cut
Copy	Edit ➤ Copy	Ctrl+C, Ctrl+Ins	Copy
Paste	Edit ➤ Paste	Ctrl+V, Shift+Ins	Paste

Table 4.2   Techniques for Cutting, Copying, and Pasting

MAC AND UNIX NOTE   Some of the keyboard shortcuts shown here are not available on Mac and UNIX installations of the program.

Undoing Mistakes

Most changes you make in FrameMaker can be reversed. There are three ways to *undo,* or reverse, an action:

▶ By choosing Edit ➤ Undo.

▶ By pressing Ctrl+Z.

 ▶ By clicking the QuickAccess Bar Undo button.

After an action is undone, the Edit ➤ Undo menu item changes to Redo, so you can redo the undo, so to speak. Ctrl+Z and the QuickAccess Bar Undo button also change back and forth between undo and redo actions.

However, only the last change to a document can be undone. If you make several changes to a document and then notice that something you did six or seven changes ago needs correcting, you'll have to make that change manually. So if you've just done something that you're in doubt about—especially if it involves a big change, like cutting several paragraphs, or pages—stop and decide if you want to keep the change *before you do anything else to the document.* At this point, undo is still available.

 TIP   If you've just cut something large—like several pages—and you're concerned that you might want it back later, you can always paste it somewhere temporarily. One good place is the end of the current document, maybe separated with a row of *X*s; another is a second "scratch paper" document that you open with File ➤ New and one of the Blank Paper buttons.

Most actions can be undone, but not all. If an action cannot be undone, it will be marked "No Undo," and for many actions, you will be warned before the action is executed. All of the actions you have seen so far can be undone.

 TIP   There is a way to undo an action marked "No Undo." Simply save the document before performing the action. Then, if you don't like the result after the action is performed, select File ➤ Revert to Saved. The document will be returned to its last saved condition.

Searching for and Replacing Text

Like most word processors, FrameMaker allows you to search for and replace text and other items. This section presents a quick introduction to the search and replace capability. For more detailed information, see Chapter 11.

Searching for text is done with the Find/Change dialog box, shown in Figure 4.9. You can bring up this dialog box in three ways:

▶ With the Find/Change item on the Edit menu.

▶ With the keyboard shortcut Ctrl+F.

 ▶ With the QuickAccess Bar Find/Change button.

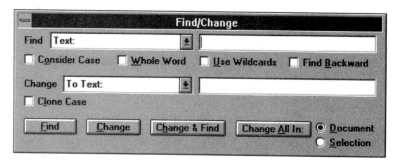

Figure 4.9   The Find/Change dialog box for searching for and replacing text

Finding Text

To find text, do the following:

1. Make sure the Find pull-down menu in the Find/Change dialog box says "Text." If it doesn't, use the menu to change it.

2. In the text box next to the Find pull-down menu, type the text you want to search for.

3. Check the Consider Case box if you want to find text that matches the upper- and lowercase letters you typed in the Find text box. If you leave Consider Case unchecked, both upper- and lowercase matches will be found. That is, if you were searching for "magic," both "magic" and "Magic" would be found.

4. Check Whole Word if you want to find only whole words. If you leave Whole Word unchecked and you search for the word "do," for example, FrameMaker will find all instances where the letters *do* appear together. It will find words like "done," "donut," and "doodle."

5. Check Find Backward if you want to search backward from the character cursor instead of forward. If you want to search forward, leave this box unchecked.

6. Click on the Document radio button to search the document (instead of the currently selected text).

7. Select the Find button at the bottom of the dialog box to start the search.

8. To continue to search after the first match is found, press Find again.

When you are done searching, you can return to the document without closing the Find/Change box (Find/Change is a palette—a box that stays open). Or you can close the box by double-clicking in the Control menu button at the top-left corner of the title bar.

 MAC AND UNIX NOTE   Close the Find/Change window (or any other palette) by clicking once in the upper-left corner of the title stripe.

You can search for many special items with the Find/Change window. To see what, open the Find pull-down menu. For now, though, searching for text is all we need to be concerned with.

Replacing Text

Replacing (changing) text is done with the Find/Change window as well. To replace text with new text, do the following:

1. Follow steps 1 through 6 in the procedure for finding text (above) to specify the text you want to find.

2. Make sure the Change pull-down menu says "To Text." If it doesn't, use the menu to change it.

3. Click once in the text box next to the Change pull-down menu box and type the text that will replace that in the Find text box.

4. Check Clone Case if you want the replacement to match exactly the case of the items that are found. In other words, if you were searching for "luck" and replacing it with "fortune," checking Clone Case would replace "luck" with "fortune" and "Luck" with "Fortune."

5. Select the Find button at the bottom of the dialog box to start the search.

6. When a match is found, select either Change to alter the text and stop searching, or Change & Find to change the text and continue searching.

As before, when you are done making changes, you can return to the document without closing the Find/Change box, or you can close the box by double-clicking on the Control menu button at the top-left corner of the title stripe. (Mac and UNIX users, click once in the upper-left corner of the box.)

Changing the Look of Text

Sometimes you may want to change the look of text characters. For example, you may change characters to **boldface**, or *italic*, or <u>underlined</u> for emphasis.

NOTE   Changing the look of text is called "changing its format." The word *format* turns up quite a lot in connection with FrameMaker and other desktop publishing programs.

These changes, and others like them, can be accomplished with an easy two-step process:

1. Select (highlight) the text you wish to change.

2. Apply the formatting you wish, using either the menus, keyboard shortcuts, or the QuickAccess Bar buttons.

Table 4.3 shows how to apply some of the common format changes. See the endpapers on the inside covers of this book if you need to find out where QuickAccess Bar buttons are located.

MAC AND UNIX NOTE   Some of the keyboard shortcuts in Table 4.3 are not available on Mac and UNIX installations of the program.

Format	With Menus	With the Keyboard	QuickAccess Bar Button
Boldface	Format ➤ Style ➤ Bold	Ctrl+B, Esc c b	Bold
Italic	Format ➤ Style ➤ Italic	Ctrl+I, Esc c I	Italic
Underlined	Format ➤ Style ➤ Underline	Ctrl+U, Esc c u	Underline
Plain	Format ➤ Style ➤ Plain	Esc c p	

Table 4.3   **Common Format Changes to Text**

You can make a number of other changes as well, as the Format ➤ Style menu and the other items on the QuickAccess Bar show. Feel free to experiment.

> **TIP** You can also format characters with the Character Designer and the Character Catalog boxes. A full discussion of character formatting appears in Chapter 9.

Changing the Look of Paragraphs

Just as you can alter the look of characters easily, you can also change the way paragraphs look (in other words, you can change their format). A paragraph's "format" generally refers to its margins, line spacing, whether it is left-aligned or not, and so on.

Many simple changes to paragraph formatting can be accomplished with this two-step process:

1. Click once with the mouse to place the character cursor anywhere in the paragraph whose format you wish to change. The paragraph does not have to be selected (highlighted), just identified.

2. Apply the formatting you wish, using either the ruler, keyboard short-cuts, or the Formatting Bar buttons.

With the Ruler With the ruler, you can change the left and right margins of a paragraph, the amount of first-line indentation, and the location of tab stops. Using the ruler was discussed in "Working with the Ruler" in Chapter 3.

With the Keyboard and Formatting Bar Table 4.4 below shows how to format paragraphs using keyboard shortcuts and the Formatting Bar. See the inside front and back covers of this book if you need to find out where Formatting Bar buttons are located.

Format	With the Keyboard	With the Formatting Bar
Centered	Esc j c	Alignment pull-down menu
Left-aligned	Esc j l	Alignment pull-down menu
Right-aligned	Esc j r	Alignment pull-down menu
Justified	Esc j f	Alignment pull-down menu
Single-spaced	Esc j 1	Spacing pull-down menu
Double-spaced	Esc j 2	Spacing pull-down menu
$1\text{-}1/2$ spaced	Esc j /	Spacing pull-down menu

Table 4.4 **Techniques for Formatting Paragraphs**

MAC AND UNIX NOTE   Some of the keyboard shortcuts in Table 4.4 are not available on Mac and UNIX installations of the program.

You can make a number of other changes as well. Feel free to experiment.

TIP   You can also format paragraphs with the Paragraph Designer and the Paragraph Catalog. A full discussion of paragraph formatting, the Paragraph Designer, and the Paragraph Catalog appears in Chapter 10.

Checking the Spelling of Words in a Document

FrameMaker allows you to check the spelling of the words in documents quickly and easily. There are a number of spell-checking options. You can check:

▶ All text in a document

▶ All text on the current page

▶ All text in a selection

▶ A specific word

In this section, we'll show you a simple procedure for checking an entire document. For more spell-checker options, see Chapter 11.

To check the spelling of an entire document:

1. Place the insertion point where you want the spell-checking to start.

2. Select Edit ➤ Spelling Checker, type *Esc e s* or use the QuickAccess Bar Spell Checker button.

   You will see the Spelling Checker window, which is shown in Figure 4.10. (The Spelling Checker window is a palette—it stays open after you are done with it.)

3. Make sure the Document check box is checked.

4. Click the Start Checking button. Spell-checking begins at the insertion point and continues through the entire document, goes back to the start of the document, and returns to the insertion point again.

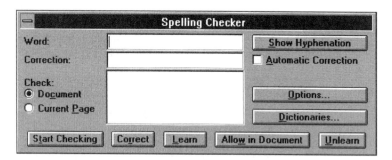

Figure 4.10   *The Spelling Checker window*

When a "misspelled" word is found (that is, a word the Spelling Checker *thinks* is misspelled), that word is selected (highlighted) in the document and displayed in the Spelling Checker in the text box labeled "Misspelling?". (Notice that the text box labeled "Word" changes its label to "Misspelling?" when a misspelled word is found.)

5. To correct the error (if it is an error—only you can judge that), you can either

    • Click on the correctly spelled word in the Correction scroll box and select the Correct button (spell-checking will continue when you do), or

    • Click anywhere in the document to make the document window the current window and then manually correct the misspelling. (If you choose this option, you must restart spell-checking by choosing Start Checking in the Spelling Checker dialog box.)

6. If the allegedly misspelled word is in fact just a correctly spelled word that is not in FrameMaker's dictionary, you can click on the Learn button. The highlighted word will be added to FrameMaker's list of words it knows are correctly spelled.

7. If the "misspelled" word is really a correctly spelled word and you do *not* want to add it to FrameMaker's dictionary, you can click on the Allow in Document button. FrameMaker will remember that the word is correct, but only for the current document.

NOTE Learned words are saved to dictionaries. FrameMaker has quite a number of dictionary options. For more on FrameMaker dictionaries, see Chapter 11.

When all words in the document have been checked for spelling, the words "Spelling OK" appear in the Spelling Checker window where the label "Misspelling?" previously appeared.

Don't Trust the Spell Checker with Important Documents

No spell checker can really check for all misspelled words. Some words (for example, words with numbers in them) are not questioned unless you specifically request it by resetting the spell checker options. Other misspelled words are mistaken for correctly spelled words if they are spelled like correctly spelled words. For example, if you misspell the word "on" by typing "no" instead, the spell checker will be none the wiser, since "no" is indeed a word. The bottom line is, always read over important documents (like job application letters!) before sending them out.

Chapter 5
Getting Help

T his chapter conludes the idea of Part One. It explains "the least you need to know about FrameMaker." Here you will learn how to use the online help facility to get help with the things you want to do in the program.

 NOTE The Help facilities in the Mac and UNIX environments work somewhat differently than they do in the Windows environment. The information in this chapter about Help functions and actions refers to the Windows Help facility. The text of the FrameMaker help screens, however, is nearly identical from platform to platform. It is different only in areas that are platform-dependent, such as keyboard shortcuts.

Help: The Basics

Online help is always available in FrameMaker. To get help, you can start by selecting Help from the main menu. You'll see the following menu of Help choices:

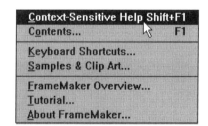

The choices on this menu are:

Help Command	How It Can Help You
Context-Sensitive Help	Lets you get help on a screen item or menu item by clicking on that item with a special context-sensitive Help cursor.
Contents	Shows you the Help main menu, a list of general topics for which FrameMaker Help is available.
Keyboard Shortcuts	Displays a menu that takes you to lists of keyboard shortcuts available on your platform.

Help Command	How It Can Help You
Samples & Clip Art	Takes you to the Samples page of the FrameMaker Overview document. From there you can see several document samples and view all of the clip art supplied with FrameMaker.
FrameMaker Overview	Opens the FrameMaker Overview document. This document was opened for you the first time you used the program.
Tutorial	Takes you to the FrameMaker online tutorial.
About Frame-Maker	Displays copyright, version, and serial number information about FrameMaker.

 UNIX NOTE   If no document windows are open, you can click on the Help button in the UNIX FrameMaker window to go to the Help main menu (discussed below). The Help menu item in the document window main menu works much the same on both UNIX and Windows versions of the program.

 MAC NOTE   The Help and Context-Sensitive Help menu items are available in the Apple menu. You can also access Context-Sensitive Help by typing 2-?.

Getting Context-Sensitive Help

 When you choose Context-Sensitive Help from the Help menu, the cursor changes to an arrow with a question mark. *Context-sensitive* means that the type of help offered is sensitive to what you happen to be doing in the program when you call for help. When you click on a window item with the question mark cursor, a Help window comes up that explains the item you clicked on. This allows you to get help on a specific subject without going through a lot of menus.

For example, if you click on the Equations button after choosing Context-Sensitive Help from the Help menu, you see a Help screen that looks like the one in Figure 5.1.

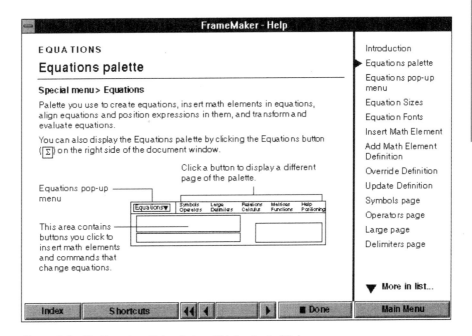

Figure 5.1   The Equations Help window. This is a typical Help screen.

A table of contents for the subject (in this case, Equations) is listed down the right side of the screen. These items can be selected with the mouse.

Across the bottom of the Help screen are buttons that allow you to go to the Help Index, bring up the Keyboard Shortcuts help pages, close the Help screen (Done), or go to the Help main menu. All FrameMaker Help screens have these buttons.

WINDOWS NOTE   Close the Help screen when you are done by clicking twice on the Control menu button in the upper-left corner of the title bar. The FrameMaker Help utility is a separate program that stays running until you shut it down.

The Help Main Menu

Select Contents from the Help menu, and a main menu of Help topics appears, as shown in Figure 5.2. To use the Help main menu, just click on an item. For example, Character Formats has been clicked on in Figure 5.2. A list of Help menu items for that subject appears in the right-hand column of the Help screen.

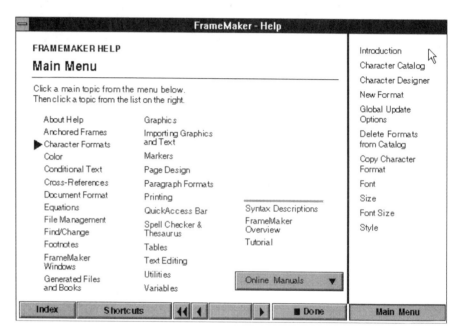

Figure 5.2   The main menu of Help topics. Click on a topic and menu items for the topic appear in the right-hand column.

TIP This main menu of Help topics is organized into a short list of very broad subjects. If you want to see an alphabetical index of much narrower subjects, select the Index button at the bottom of the Help main menu screen. Using the Help Index is discussed a little later in this section.

You can now click on an item in the right-hand column or choose another subject from the Help main menu. If you click on one of the items on the right side, the Help screen changes and the text for the item you clicked on appears in the middle of the window. In Figure 5.3,

Introduction was selected in the right-hand column, so an Introduction to character formats appears in the middle of the window.

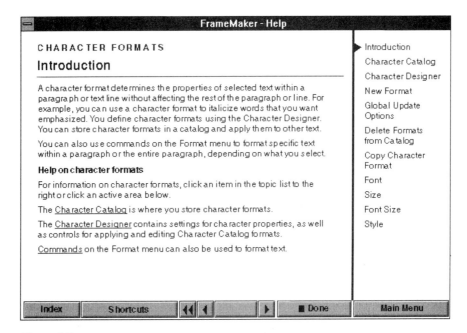

Figure 5.3 **Character formats introduction Help text**

To return to the main menu, select the Main Menu button in the lower-right corner of the screen.

Viewing FrameMaker Online Manuals

The Help main menu window (see Figure 5.2) has a special button for calling up FrameMaker's online manuals. This button is located above the Done button. Click the mouse cursor on the Online Manuals button to make the Online Manuals pull-down menu appear.

Click on the name of the manual you want to view. The manual will appear in a FrameMaker Document window in *view-only* mode (*view-only* mode simply means a document cannot be edited).

> **NOTE**   You can tell when a document is displayed in view-only mode because the FrameMaker main menu lists fewer items, including one new one, Navigation, which allows you to go from one page to the next. When you switch from a view-only document to an editable one, the FrameMaker main menu returns to its old, full-length self.

You cannot edit or save a FrameMaker online manual. Note, however, that you *can* print it.

Close the online manual just as you would any FrameMaker document—by selecting File ➤ Close, typing Ctrl+W, or double-clicking on the Control menu button.

The Help Index

Once the FrameMaker Help screen is up, you can see a comprehensive, alphabetical Index of help subjects by selecting the Index button in the lower-left corner of the screen. The first page of the Index is shown in Figure 5.4.

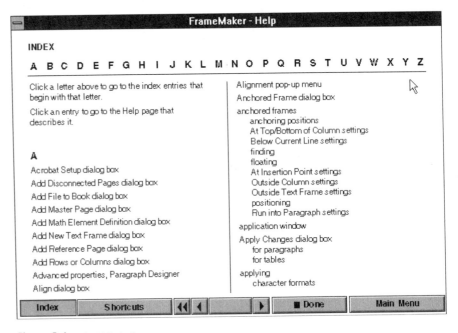

Figure 5.4   *The Help Index*

You can navigate through the Index in a number of ways:

▶ To see the entry for one of the Index items, select that item.

▶ To page through the Index, click the Previous Page and Next Page buttons (the buttons marked with left and right arrows) at the bottom of the screen.

▶ To jump through the index, select one of the letters listed at the top of the page.

▶ To return to the main menu, select the Main Menu button at the bottom the screen.

▶ To quit Help, select the Done button at the bottom the screen, or double-click on the Control menu button on the left side of the title bar.

Returning to the Pages You Just Left

FrameMaker Help provides one more capability—it remembers which pages you view, in the order you view them, no matter how much jumping around you do.

You can walk backwards through the path you took by pressing the Previously Viewed Page button at the bottom of the screen.

Being able to look at what you saw before can be handy if you moved through a lot of Help topics and want to go back to something you read earlier. Thanks to the Previously Viewed Page button, you don't have to walk through all of the menus it took to get to the topic you're interested in.

Just keep in mind that FrameMaker's Help memory lasts through only one Help session. When you close Help, the list of previously viewed pages is thrown away.

You do not have to close the Help utility before going back to a FrameMaker document. Help is a separate program, so you can keep it open while you do other FrameMaker work.

WINDOWS NOTE   If the Help screen gets hidden behind the FrameMaker application window, just call up the Windows task list (Ctrl+Esc) and reselect it. The Help screen will immediately appear on top of the other windows you have up.

That's it for Part One, the FrameMaker tutorial. If you stop here (or just pause to catch your breath), you will know enough to use the program easily and productively.

Part Two begins our in-depth coverage of FrameMaker's features and operations, starting with the many ways you can open and create documents. Feel free to go through the chapters in Part Two in any order you wish.

Basic Work
with Documents

Chapter 6
Starting a Document

This chapter begins the in-depth coverage of FrameMaker's many word processing and desktop publishing features, beginning with how to start a document.

You can start a FrameMaker document in many ways. You can

Create a new document using "blank paper"

Create a new document using a template

Open an existing document and continue work on it

Open an existing document, change it into a new document, and save it under a new name

Import a document from another program into Frame-Maker, then work on it as a FrameMaker document

Each of these ways will be covered in this chapter.

Creating a New Document

New documents can be created either from "blank paper" or from a template. In both cases, you use the File ➤ New command. When you issue this command, you see the New file dialog box shown in Figure 6.1.

 MAC AND UNIX NOTE The New file dialog box in the Mac and UNIX versions of the program uses the conventions of the Macintosh and Motif Window Manager interfaces, respectively. The Mac and UNIX dialog boxes contain slightly different features than the Windows version.

Across the top, under the heading Use Blank Paper, are three buttons: Portrait, Landscape, and Custom. These buttons are for choosing a page orientation for the document.

Click the Portrait button to create a new document the same size as a piece of typing paper ($8^1/_2$" x 11"). A portrait document is taller than it is wide, and has a number of useful features built into it:

➤ The page is laid out with a single text column and standard one-inch margins on all four sides of the page.

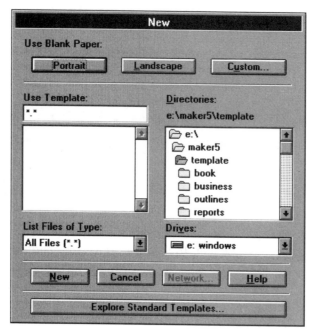

Figure 6.1   The New File dialog box

▶ There are prebuilt header and footer areas about $^1/_2$" from the top and bottom edges of the page.

▶ The built-in paragraph catalog contains good basic paragraph styles—12-point Times Roman body paragraphs, with appropriate heading, footnote, and other paragraph styles.

TIP   Selecting Portrait in the New file dialog box is an excellent way to start simple one-column documents, such as letters and reports. Another is to open an existing letter with the same formatting as the one you are creating, save it with a new name, and replace the old text with your new writing.

Click the Landscape button to create a new document just like the portrait document, except that the page is turned on its side—that is, it is wider than it is long. The built-in margins, text columns, and paragraph tags are otherwise identical to those of a portrait page.

By clicking the Custom button, you can design your own page. It brings up the Custom Blank Paper dialog box shown in Figure 6.2.

Custom Blank Paper

Page Size:	US Letter ±	Columns:	
Width:	8.5"	Number:	1
Height:	11.0"	Gap:	0.25"

Column Margins:

Top:	1.0"
Bottom:	1.0"
Left:	1.0"
Right:	1.0"

Pagination:
- ● Single-Sided
- ○ Double-Sided
- Right 1st Page ±

Units:
Inch ±

[Create] [Cancel] [Help]

Figure 6.2 *The Custom Blank Paper dialog box*

With this box you can create pages with many sizes and layouts. To do so:

1. Select the page size, using either the Page Size pull-down menu or the Width and Height text boxes.

2. Enter a number of columns for the page with the Columns text boxes. ("Gap" refers to the gap between columns, and affects only pages with more than one column.)

3. Enter top, bottom, left, and right margins in the Column Margins text boxes.

4. Choose whether the document will be single-sided or double-sided with the Pagination radio buttons. For a double-sided document, choose whether the first page falls on a right-hand page or a left-hand page by selecting either Right 1st Page or Left 1st Page from the pull-down list.

5. Select the default unit of measurement (inches, centimeters, picas, points, and so on) from the Units pull-down menu.

NOTE For more information on the units of measurement available in FrameMaker, see "The View Options Dialog Box: More Ways to View Documents" in Chapter 3.

6. When you are done, click Create. The document will be created for you. Now you can enter your text.

All newly created documents have funny default names—NoName1, NoName2, and so on. When you save documents for the first time, you are prompted to give them more meaningful names.

The New file dialog box also allows you to explore and open templates that can be turned into documents. This feature is discussed in "Creating Your Own Templates" at the end of this chapter.

Opening an Existing FrameMaker Document

Opening an existing document (a FrameMaker document that has been previously created and saved) is a simple matter. If you worked through the tutorial in Chapters 2 and 3, you've done it already.

To open an existing document:

1. Select File ➤ Open from the FrameMaker menu. The Open file dialog box appears, as in Figure 6.3.

2. Select a drive from the Drives pull-down menu (in the lower-right corner of the box).

3. Choose a directory by double-clicking on a directory name in the Directories list in the upper-right portion of the box.

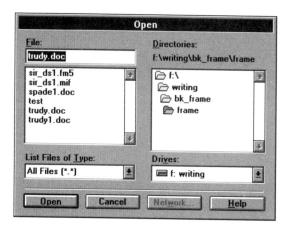

Figure 6.3   The Open file dialog box

Basic Work with
Documents

 WINDOWS NOTE   You must double-click on a directory name to open and select the directory. Single-clicking simply selects the directory. To make sure you've opened the directory, look at the directory icon next to the name—the folder will appear to be open and grayed (this means opened and selected). You can also look at the directory name listed just below the heading Directories. This is the name of the currently opened, selected directory.

When you open a directory, its files are listed in the File list (in the left-hand portion of the box).

If you don't see the file you are looking for, check the pull-down menu labeled "List Files of Type" in the lower-right portion of the box.

4.   Highlight the name of the file to be opened and click the Open button. The dialog box disappears and the file is opened in a document window.

 NOTE   Another way to open an existing document is to look at the list of files at the bottom of the File menu. If you opened the file recently, it may be listed there. If it is, just click on the file name to open the file.

Importing Documents into FrameMaker

You can import whole documents created by other programs into Frame-Maker, usually with excellent results. When you open a non-FrameMaker document, it is passed through a filter provided by Frame and turned into a FrameMaker document.

Besides importing whole documents, you can import both FrameMaker and non-FrameMaker text into the middle of a FrameMaker document.

 In FrameMaker 4, you could copy an imported document directly, and you still can. But in FrameMaker 5, you can also import a document by reference. In this case, the Frame file contains, instead of a copy of the second document, a pointer to the disk location where the second document resides. When the second document is changed, the Frame file can be updated to match the new contents, either automatically or with a single command. In other words, the changes don't have to be made twice. FrameMaker automatically picks up changes to the external document. The ability to create and maintain reference links between documents is a nice feature of this version of FrameMaker.

Importing a Non-FrameMaker Document

You can import a non-FrameMaker document and make it a Frame-Maker document by using the File ➤ Open command. You will see the Open file dialog box (see Figure 6.3). Simply select the file to be opened from the list of files and press the Open button.

FrameMaker will recognize that the file is not a normal FrameMaker document format and attempt to filter it. *Filter* means to translate all the formatting codes in the original document into formatting codes that FrameMaker uses. You will see the Unknown File Type dialog box, as in Figure 6.4.

Figure 6.4 *The Unknown File Type dialog box*

 MAC NOTE Mac versions of FrameMaker are able to recognize file types "on sight" and perform translations without showing the Unknown File Type dialog box.

When the dialog box is opened, FrameMaker attempts to analyze the type of file you are opening. In the dialog box, it highlights the file type it thinks it is dealing with. You can choose any file type you wish (by clicking elsewhere with the mouse), or accept FrameMaker's suggestion.

When you are ready to convert the file to a FrameMaker file, click on the Convert button.

FrameMaker will create a FrameMaker document that closely resembles the original, though some hand-editing may still be necessary to clean up formats.

Formats that FrameMaker Recognizes

FrameMaker can convert documents from many non-FrameMaker formats, including:

▶ Microsoft Word

▶ QuickDraw PICT

▶ Rich Text Format (RTF)

▶ Text (plain old ASCII text files)

▶ Ventura Publisher

▶ WordPerfect

MAC AND UNIX NOTE The Mac and UNIX formats that can be converted are slightly different, and may reflect the presence of installed optional filters.

FrameMaker also recognizes two other file formats, both created by Frame Technology:

▶ MIF (Maker Interchange Format)

▶ MML (Maker Markup Language)

MIF Files

The first format is used for MIF (Maker Interchange Format) files. A *MIF file* is a text file that completely describes a FrameMaker document. Every feature that can be found in a FrameMaker document is mentioned in the MIF version of that document, even if that feature is never used.

The MIF standard was created by Frame for the earliest versions of the program, and has been maintained through every iteration of the program.

MIF files can be created by FrameMaker using the Save As command. Some non-FrameMaker applications, especially some graphics programs, can save files in MIF format.

NOTE See the next chapter, "Saving and Printing Documents," for information on creating MIF files from FrameMaker documents.

Even though MIF files are text files, when FrameMaker encounters a MIF file, either through the File ➤ Open command or the File ➤ Import command, it interprets the file and creates the FrameMaker document described in the MIF file.

TIP You can force FrameMaker to open a MIF file as text. Simply hold down the correct modifier key while selecting File ➤ Open or File ➤ Import. The correct modifier key is platform-dependent—Ctrl for Windows, Option for Mac users, and Shift for UNIX. (When you're done, be sure to save the file as text!)

MIF files are just text files, so they are often used to pass FrameMaker documents from one user to another over e-mail networks that do not accept binary file transfers. Note, however, that because they are text file descriptions of complex documents and because they always describe every feature a FrameMaker document *could* contain, MIF files tend to be large. TRUDY.DOC, the one-page memo you created in Chapter 2, is about 14K in size. TRUDY.MIF, the same file saved as a MIF file, is about 68K!

MIF files are also handy if you want to do advanced work with Frame files, or groups of Frame files. As a simple example, suppose you were responsible for collecting documents from a workgroup of ten people and making sure that all references to imported graphics files in these documents pointed to the same network directory (say, F:\WORK-GROUP\ARTFILES, to use the PC file-naming convention).

You soon discovered, however, that some references in these documents were incorrect, since they pointed to copies of the graphics files that were kept temporarily in another place (say, F:\TEMPDIR\STUFF). You want to make the directory F:\TEMPDIR\STUFF go away (by deleting it!), but you can't because when FrameMaker opens some of those documents, it looks in the STUFF directory for imported graphics. So all references to the STUFF directory that are internal to those document files must be changed to point to the ARTFILES directory.

There are several ways to solve this problem. One is to open each document individually and reimport each graphics file from the right place. That sounds like a lot of work, and it is. But with a little advanced programming, you could write a batch file that does the following:

1. Opens each FrameMaker document file in a directory.

2. Saves each file as MIF.

3. Performs a search-and-replace on each MIF file, and changes all occurrences of the string F:\TEMPDIR\STUFF to the string F:\WORKGROUP\ARTFILES.

4. Saves each file as text.

5. Reopens each MIF file as a FrameMaker document.

6. Saves each file in normal FrameMaker format.

This batch file could operate sequentially on any number of files, and be working away while you were at lunch—or dinner!

Advanced uses of MIF files require a knowledge of programming tools, but this example shows the range of operations that can be performed on and with FrameMaker documents.

MML Files

Another file format devised by Frame is the MML (Maker Markup Language) format. MML is a kind of cousin to MIF, but easier to use. An MML file is a text-only file that contains document contents and MML statements that specify formatting for the document.

Unlike MIF files, MML files do not completely describe a FrameMaker document. There is no need for table statements in an MML file, for example, if there are no tables in the document. But MML files can be used to create fully formed, sophisticated FrameMaker documents.

The advantage of using MML files is that you can create them with a text editor and then import them into FrameMaker and get a nice FrameMaker document. And they are simple enough to be usable by mere mortals—you only need to learn the MML statements that describe the features you are actually using in your document. Often this includes only a few words about character and paragraph formatting.

Part
2

Basic Work with
Documents

FrameMaker opens or imports an MML file in the same way it opens or imports an MIF file, by interpreting it and creating the FrameMaker document it describes.

TIP   You can open an MML file as text in the same way you open a MIF file as text. Simply hold down the Ctrl (Windows), Option (Mac), or Shift (UNIX) key before you select File ➤ Open or File ➤ Import. (If you do open the MML file as text, be sure to save it as text when you are done!)

Finding out More about MIF and MML Files

MIF and MML files are fully documented in the FrameMaker online manuals *MIF Reference* and *MML Reference.* To read or print these manuals:

1. Select Help ➤ Contents from the FrameMaker main menu. The FrameMaker Help main menu appears.

2. Click on the Online Manuals button.

3. Select MIF Reference or MML Reference. A read-only version of the document's table of contents appears. The items on this page are hypertext links to headings in the manual itself.

4. To read about any topic, click on the item of interest.

5. To print the entire manual, click on the Print Manual button near the top of the page.

Importing Text into a FrameMaker Document

You can also import text from another document—either a FrameMaker document or a non-FrameMaker document—into the FrameMaker document you are working on.

MAC NOTE   In addition to imported text, the Mac version of FrameMaker supports the Mac Publish-and-Subscribe feature. See your Macintosh documentation for more information on using this unique platform capability.

To import text into a FrameMaker document:

1. Place the character cursor in the FrameMaker document where you want the imported text to appear.

2. Select File ➤ Import ➤ File. The Import File dialog box appears, as in Figure 6.5.

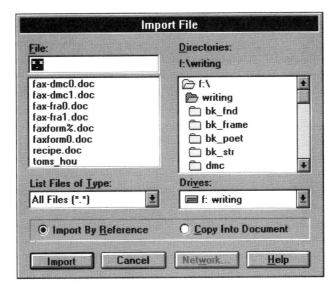

Figure 6.5 **The Import File dialog box**

This box is identical to the Open file dialog box, except for the radio buttons at the bottom. With these buttons, you can either import the file by reference or place a copy of the file into the document.

3. Select the file to be imported, using the Drives, Directories, and File areas of the dialog box.

4. Select either Import by Reference or Copy into Document.

5. Select Import to import (or copy) the document.

> **NOTE** The names of all open FrameMaker documents and Maker Inter-change Format (MIF) documents are shown at the bottom of the File ➤ Import submenu. This list is similar to the list of recently opened files that appears at the bottom of the File menu.

What happens next depends on whether you are importing text from a FrameMaker document or a non-FrameMaker document.

Importing Text from a Non-FrameMaker Document

If you are importing text from a non-FrameMaker document, you see the Unknown File Type dialog box (see Figure 6.4). Select Convert in this dialog box, and a dialog box appropriate to the type of file you are converting appears.

For example, if you are importing a simple text file by reference (as opposed to a file from a word processing program), you will see the Import Text File by Reference dialog box shown in Figure 6.6.

     MAC NOTE   File formats that can be converted are recognized automatically by the Mac version of FrameMaker.

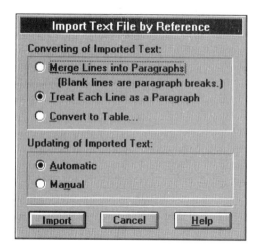

Figure 6.6   *The Import Text File by Reference dialog box*

In this dialog box, you can choose line break options and specify manual or automatic updating of the text. "Automatic" means that the imported text is updated every time the file is opened.

The Import Text File by Copy dialog box is similar to the Import Text File by Reference dialog box, except that it contains no update options.

Make your selections and click Import to complete the process.

NOTE   Formatting options for imported files are discussed in Chapter 11.

Importing Text from a FrameMaker Document

If you are importing text from a FrameMaker document, you see either the Import Text Flow by Copy dialog box or the Import Text Flow by Reference dialog box. Both dialog boxes look like Figure 6.7. Both of these dialog boxes allow you to select the flow to be imported, specify how the flow is to be formatted, and, if the import is by reference, specify how updating will occur. Make your selections and press Import to complete the process.

Unnamed flows and duplicate flow names do not appear in the Flow to Import pull-down lists. Therefore, if a flow is unnamed or named the

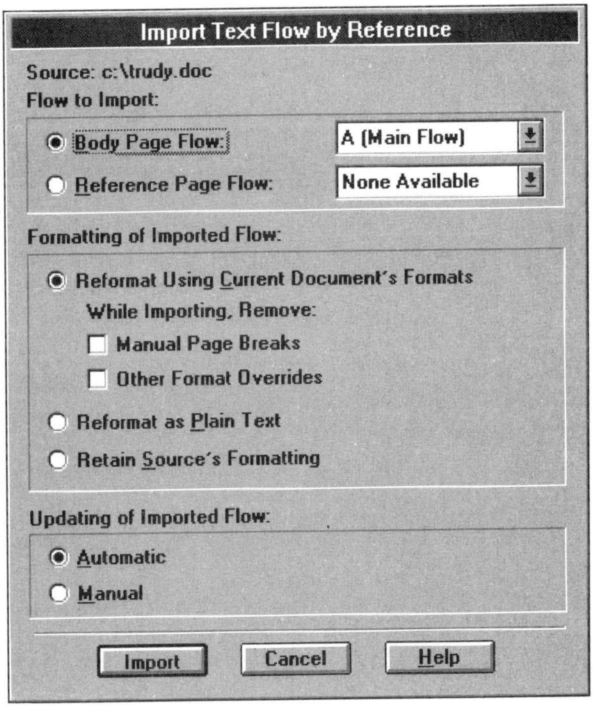

Figure 6.7 The Import Text Flow by Reference dialog box

same as another flow in the same document, it cannot be imported. Keep this in mind when creating documents with multiple flows.

NOTE　Text flows are an important concept in FrameMaker documents. For a complete explanation of text flows, see Chapter 8.

Note that when you import a file by reference, you cannot select individual characters with the mouse—only the entire block of text is selectable.

If you double-click on a text block, the Text Inset Properties dialog box appears, as in Figure 6.8. This handy dialog box allows you to revise or change any of the settings you specified when the text was first imported.

TIP　It's worth remembering that double-clicking on many "special" items in FrameMaker, like cross-references, imported text, and variables, brings up the dialog box that deals with those items—and saves a lot of mousing through menus.

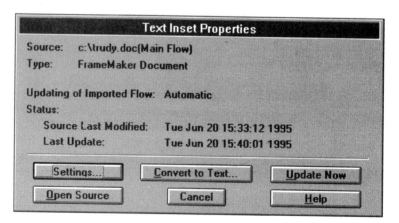

Figure 6.8　*The Text Inset Properties dialog box*

Using Document Templates

Document templates are a fast way to create new documents from old ones. Any FrameMaker document can become a template. In fact, every

FrameMaker document is already a template. Simply by opening it and changing the text, you change the document while keeping the formatting.

This section covers how to create a document from an existing Frame-Maker template and how to modify a document to look like a FrameMaker template. It describes some useful FrameMaker templates and tells you how to create your own templates and place them in the templates directory.

Creating Documents from Templates

When you select File ➤ New, you see the New file dialog box shown in Figure 6.9. We've used this box before to create documents from the special "blank paper" templates. Now let's use it to create a document from one of FrameMaker's templates.

To create a document from a FrameMaker template:

1. Select File ➤ New. The New file dialog box appears.

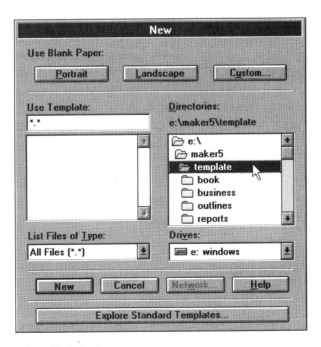

Figure 6.9 **The New file dialog box**

Note that you are taken to the MAKER5\TEMPLATES directory (or its Mac or UNIX equivalent). Under this directory, you will find a list of subdirectories in which FrameMaker templates reside. These subdirectories are simply ways to organize templates into logical groups:

▶ Book

▶ Business

▶ Outlines

▶ Reports

▶ Special

2. From here, there are two ways of working. You can either:

- Select a subdirectory, then a template name, and then click the New button. This opens a blank version of a template into which you can enter text.

- Select Explore Standard Templates at the bottom of the dialog box. This brings up the Standard Templates window, from which you can see what the various templates look like. From there you can click on either the Create button to open a blank version of the template (as above) or Show Sample to bring up an example of the template ready for modification.

It is generally easier to work with templates by clicking on Explore Standard Templates, selecting a template (for example, the Letter template listed under the Business group), and clicking on Show Sample.

If you click on Show Sample, you get a document containing text that shows how the paragraph tags should be used. If you did indeed select the Business/Letter template and then Show Sample, your screen will look something like Figure 6.10.

3. Begin working in the document by replacing text. Notice, in the Formatting Bar or the Paragraph Catalog, the paragraph tags for the various paragraphs and how they are used. As you create your own paragraphs, you will want to use the appropriate tags yourself.

NOTE   **Paragraph tags are discussed in Chapter 10.**

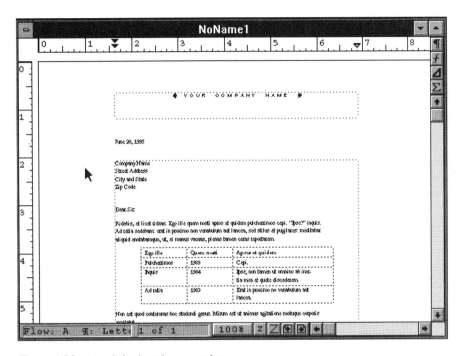

Figure 6.10 Sample business letter template

4. When you are done, select File ➤ Save. You will see the Save Document dialog box, as in Figure 6.11.

   Because the document was opened with File ➤ New instead of File ➤ Open, FrameMaker gave it one of those Clint Eastwood names (NoName1, NoName2, etc.) and knows it has to ask you for a better name before saving the document for the first time.

5. Select a drive and directory location for the file, give it a better file name, and select Save.

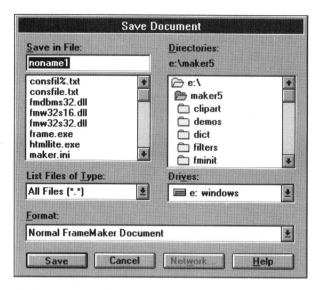

Figure 6.11   **The Save Document dialog box**

Modifying a Document to Look Like a Template

You can also use a template to modify the look of an existing document. Here's how:

1. Choose File ➤ Open and open the document you want to change.

2. Choose File ➤ New and open the template you wish the document to look like.

3. Save the template under a new name, but leave it open. (This can be a temporary save—FrameMaker just needs to see a saved version to work with the open document as we are about to do. The saved version can be deleted later.)

4. Click on the document you wish to change (to make it the current document), and select File ➤ Import ➤ Formats. The Import Formats dialog box appears, as in Figure 6.12.

5. From the Import from Document pull-down list, select the name of the open template document.

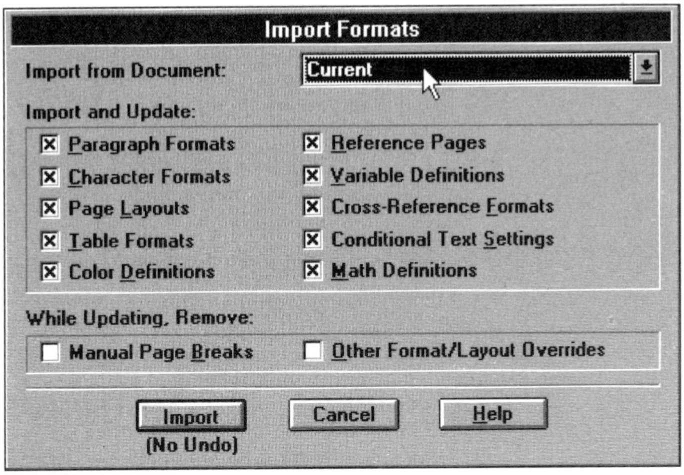

Figure 6.12 The Import Formats dialog box

6. Select the formats you wish to import. To make the existing document as similar to the template as possible, leave all of the options selected, though you may unselect any of the options you like.

7. If you wish to remove "overrides"—in-paragraph changes to the original format definitions such as manual page breaks, modifications to paragraphs that make them no longer identical to their paragraph tag definitions, and other formatting and layout changes—click the appropriate check box under the While Formatting, Remove heading.

8. Click the Import button to import the formats.

9. Save the document under a new name if you wish.

10. Delete the saved, renamed template document if you wish.

All formats, master pages, and definitions you specify for importation will be added from the template to the document you are changing. Formats, master pages, and definitions in the template replace equivalent elements in the changed document if the names are the same.

In addition, all text (paragraphs, characters, variables, and so on) in the changed document is updated to reflect the new definitions (subject to the conditions specified in the While Updating, Remove overrides boxes).

Paragraphs and other elements that are formatted with names that do not appear in the template will not be affected, so some retagging might be necessary.

 NOTE   This technique is especially useful for documents that have been created from templates and then modified in a way you dislike—in this case, you are simply returning the formatting of the document to its initial state as a template. And the process is fast and easy, since most or all of the paragraph tags and other elements will still have the same names as they do in the template.

Some Sample Document Templates

FrameMaker comes with some pretty useful templates. The business templates subdirectory, for example, offers templates for these kinds of documents:

▶ Letter

▶ Memo

▶ Fax cover page (with blank message page)

▶ Viewgraphs (tall and wide)

▶ Envelope

▶ Business cards (eight to a page)

To give you a clear idea of what these templates look like, samples are shown in Figures 6.13 through 6.19.

The reports templates subdirectory offers three report styles:

▶ Plain (simple formatting, numbered headings)

▶ Numeric (fancy formatting, numbered headings)

▶ Sidehead (fancy formatting, unnumbered side-headings)

The first pages of these templates look like the ones in Figures 6.20 through 6.22.

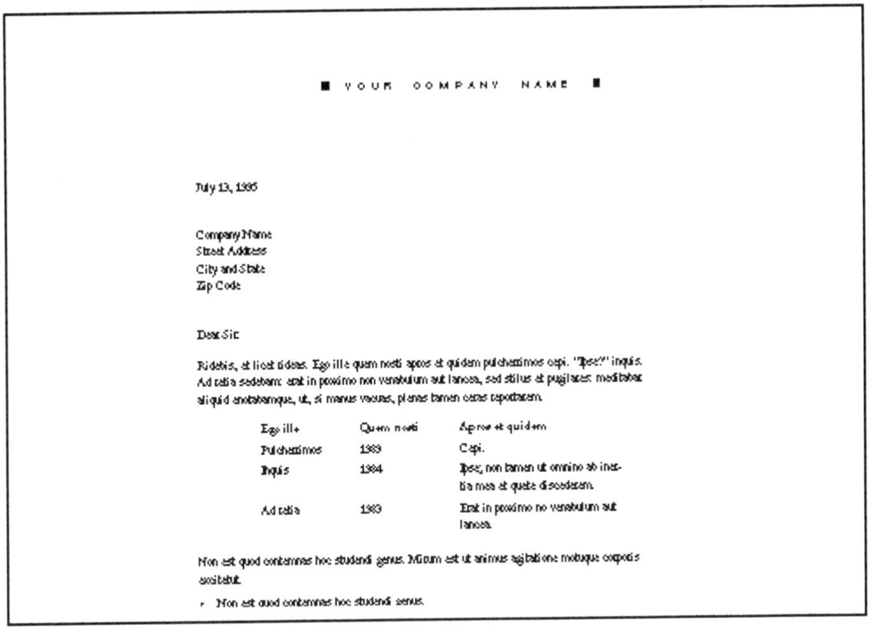

■ YOUR COMPANY NAME ■

July 13, 1995

Company Name
Street Address
City and State
Zip Code

Dear Sir:

Ridebis, et licet rideas. Ego ille quem nosti apros et quidem pulcherrimos cepi. "Ipse?" inquis. Ad retia sedebam: erat in proximo non venabulum aut lancea, sed stilus et pugillares: meditabar aliquid enotabamque, ut, si manus vacuas, plenas tamen ceras reportarem.

Ego ille	Quem nosti	Apros et quidem
Pulcherrimos	1989	Cepi.
Inquis	1984	Ipse, non tamen ut omnino ab inertia mea et quate discederem.
Ad retia	1983	Erat in proximo no venabulum aut lancea.

Non est quod contemnas hoc studendi genus. Mirum est ut animus agitatione motuque corporis excitatur.

- Non est quod contemnas hoc studendi genus.

Figure 6.13 **Business letter template sample**

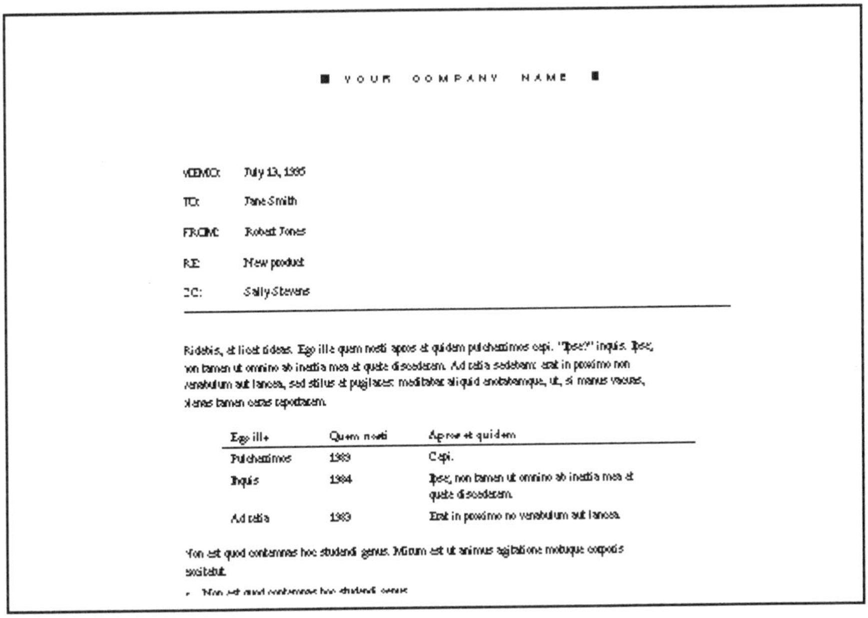

■ YOUR COMPANY NAME ■

MEMO: July 13, 1995

TO: Jane Smith

FROM: Robert Jones

RE: New product

CC: Sally Stevens

Ridebis, et licet rideas. Ego ille quem nosti apros et quidem pulcherrimos cepi. "Ipse?" inquis. Ipse, non tamen ut omnino ab inertia mea et quate discederem. Ad retia sedebam: erat in proximo non venabulum aut lancea, sed stilus et pugillares: meditabar aliquid enotabamque, ut, si manus vacuas, plenas tamen ceras reportarem.

Ego ille	Quem nosti	Apros et quidem
Pulcherrimos	1989	Cepi.
Inquis	1984	Ipse, non tamen ut omnino ab inertia mea et quate discederem.
Ad retia	1983	Erat in proximo no venabulum aut lancea.

Non est quod contemnas hoc studendi genus. Mirum est ut animus agitatione motuque corporis excitatur.

- Non est quod contemnas hoc studendi genus.

Figure 6.14 **Business memo template sample**

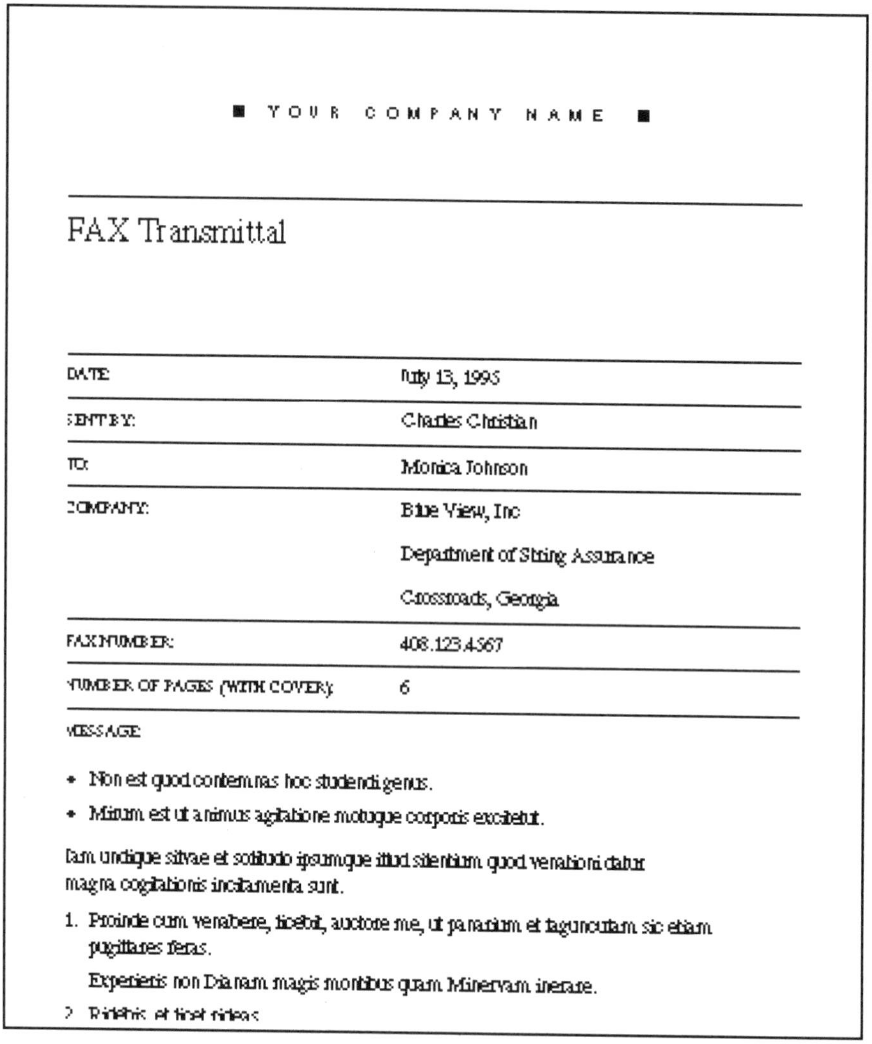

■ Y O U R   C O M P A N Y   N A M E ■

FAX Transmittal

DATE:	July 13, 1995
SENT BY:	Charles Christian
TO:	Monica Johnson
COMPANY:	Blue View, Inc
	Department of String Assurance
	Crossroads, Georgia
FAX NUMBER:	408.123.4567
NUMBER OF PAGES (WITH COVER):	6

MESSAGE

* Non est quod contemnas hoc studendi genus.
* Mirum est ut animus agitatione motuque corporis excitetur.

Iam undique silvae et solitudo ipsumque illud silentium quod venationi datur magna cogitationis incitamenta sunt.

1. Proinde cum venabere, licebit, auctore me, ut panarium et lagunculam sic etiam pugillares feras.

   Experieris non Dianam magis montibus quam Minervam inerrare.

2. Ridebis, et licet rideas.

Figure 6.15   **Fax cover page template sample**

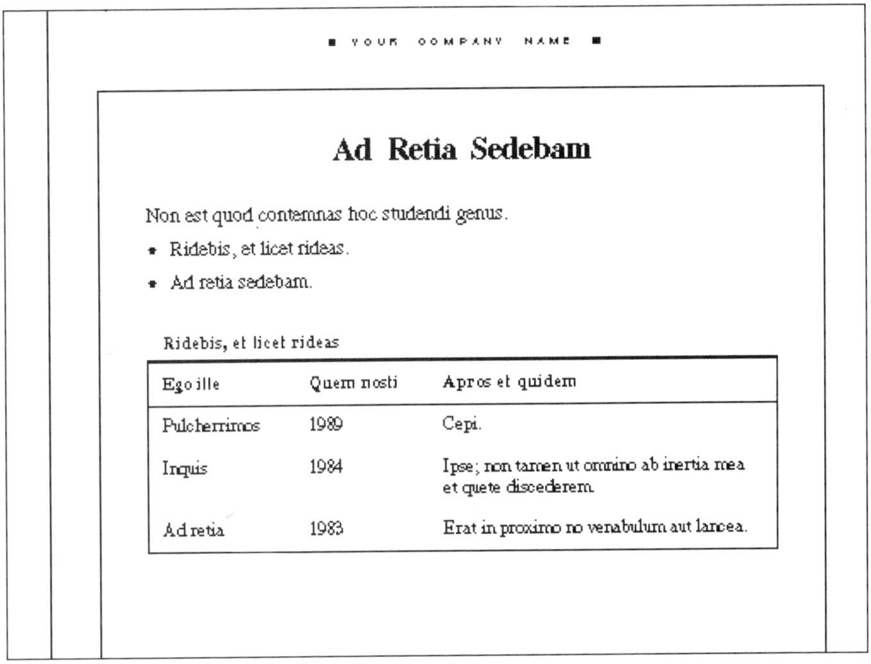

Figure 6.16 **Tall viewgraph template sample**

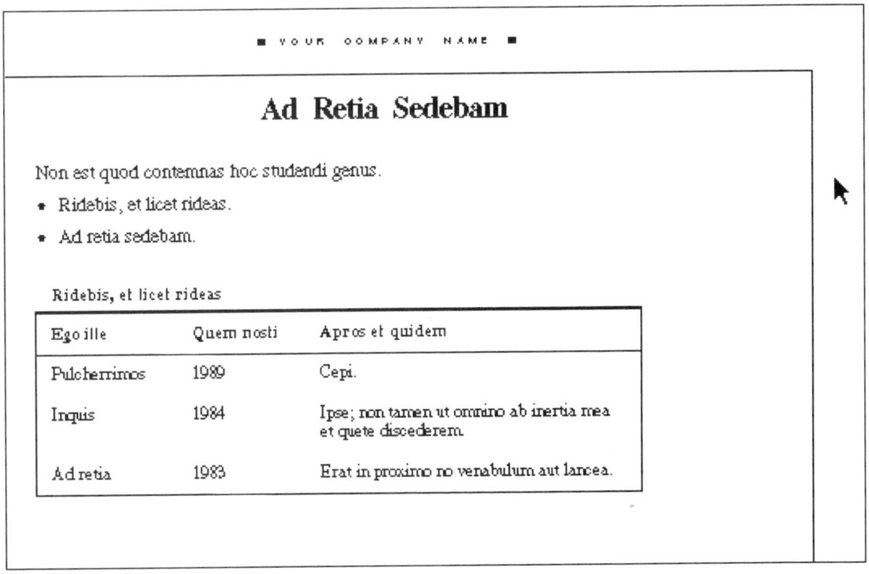

Figure 6.17 **Wide viewgraph template sample**

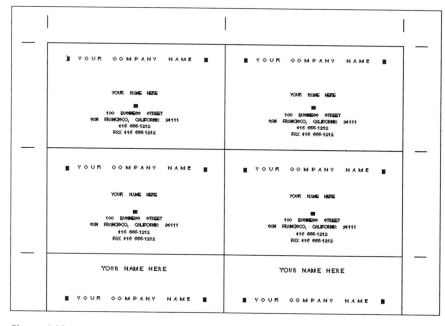

Figure 6.18   Business envelope template sample

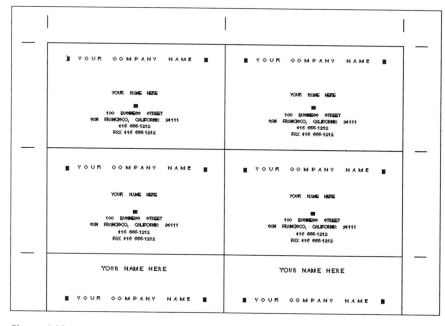

Figure 6.19   Business cards template sample

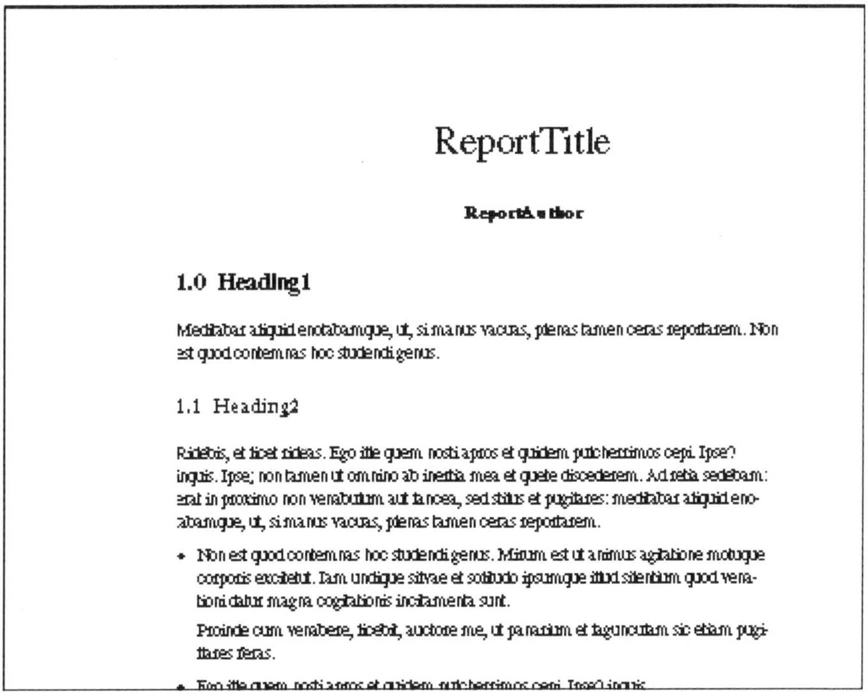

ReportTitle

ReportAuthor

1.0 Heading1

Meditabar aliquid enotabamque, ut, si manus vacuas, plenas tamen ceras reportarem. Non est quod contemnas hoc studendi genus.

1.1 Heading2

Ridebis, et licet rideas. Ego ille quem nosti apros et quidem pulcherrimos cepi. Ipse? inquis. Ipse; non tamen ut omnino ab inertia mea et quiete discederem. Ad retia sedebam: erat in proximo non venabulum aut lancea, sed stilus et pugillares: meditabar aliquid enotabamque, ut, si manus vacuas, plenas tamen ceras reportarem.

- Non est quod contemnas hoc studendi genus. Mirum est ut animus agitatione motuque corporis excitetur. Iam undique silvae et solitudo ipsumque illud silentium quod venationi datur magna cogitationis incitamenta sunt.

  Proinde cum venabere, licebit, auctore me, ut panarium et lagunculam sic etiam pugillares feras.

- Ego ille quem nosti apros et quidem pulcherrimos cepi. Ipse? inquis.

Figure 6.20 "Plain" report template

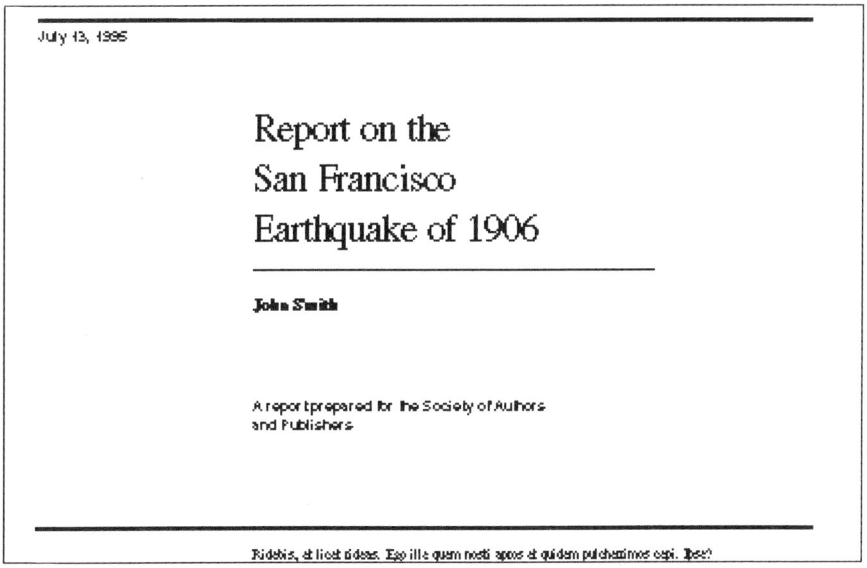

July 13, 1995

Report on the
San Francisco
Earthquake of 1906

John Smith

A report prepared for the Society of Authors and Publishers

Ridebis, et licet rideas. Ego ille quem nosti apros et quidem pulcherrimos cepi. Ipse?

Figure 6.21 "Numbered" report template

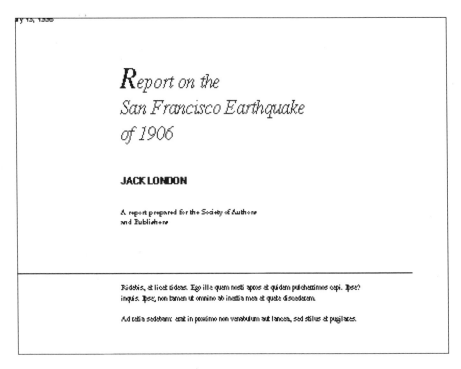

Figure 6.22   *"Sidehead" report template*

The outlines templates subdirectory contains three outline styles:

- Harvard (numbered I., A., 1., a), etc.)
- Numeric (numbered 1.0, 1.1, 1.1.1, etc.)
- Small ($5\frac{1}{2}''\times11''$ format, informal level indications)

The first pages of these templates are shown in Figures 6.23 through 6.25.

The newsletter template contains four pages that look similar to this first page shown in Figure 6.26.

By following the instructions in "Creating Documents from Templates," you can use these templates "as is" to create polished-looking documents.

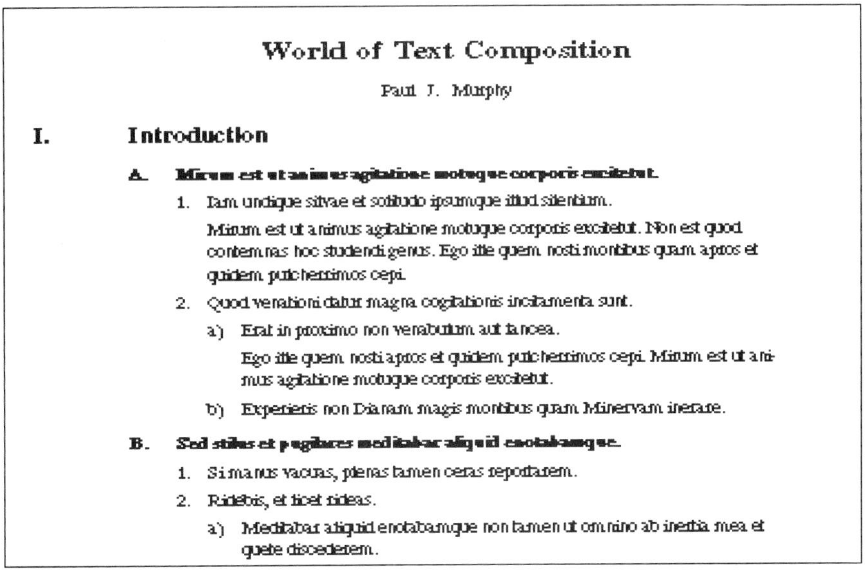

World of Text Composition

Paul J. Murphy

I. **Introduction**

A. **Mirum est ut animus agitatione motuque corporis excitetur.**

1. Iam undique silvae et solitudo ipsumque illud silentium.

   Mirum est ut animus agitatione motuque corporis excitetur. Non est quod contemnas hoc studendi genus. Ego ille quem nosti apros et quidem pulcherrimos cepi.

2. Quod venationi datur magna cogitationis incitamenta sunt.

   a) Erat in proximo non venabulum aut lancea.

      Ego ille quem nosti apros et quidem pulcherrimos cepi. Mirum est ut animus agitatione motuque corporis excitetur.

   b) Experieris non Dianam magis montibus quam Minervam inerrare.

B. **Sed stilus et pugillares meditabar aliquid enotabamque.**

1. Si manus vacuas, plenas tamen ceras reportarem.
2. Ridebis, et licet rideas.

   a) Meditabar aliquid enotabamque non tamen ut omnino ab inertia mea et quiete discederem.

Figure 6.23 ***Harvard-style report template***

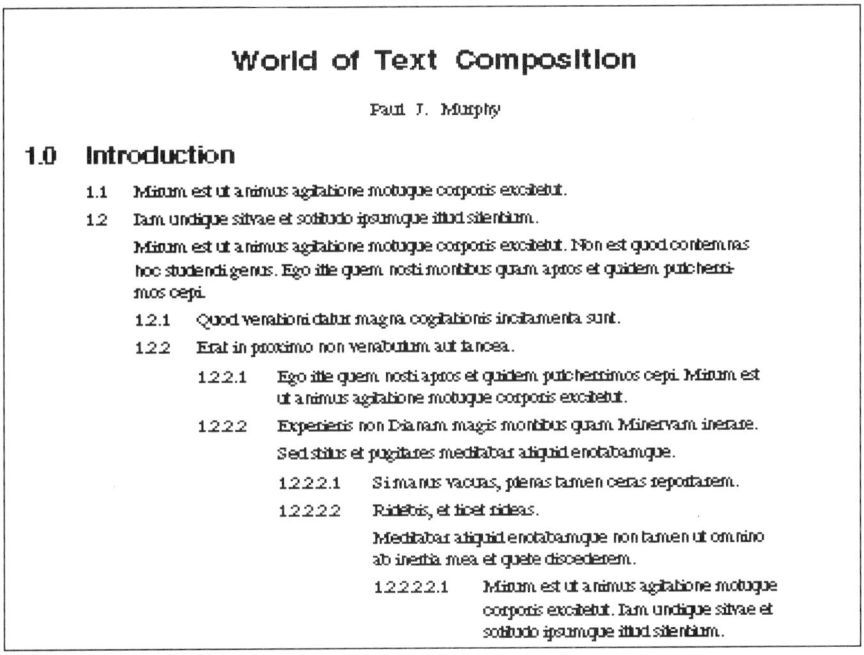

World of Text Composition

Paul J. Murphy

1.0 **Introduction**

1.1 Mirum est ut animus agitatione motuque corporis excitetur.

1.2 Iam undique silvae et solitudo ipsumque illud silentium.

Mirum est ut animus agitatione motuque corporis excitetur. Non est quod contemnas hoc studendi genus. Ego ille quem nosti montibus quam apros et quidem pulcherrimos cepi.

1.2.1 Quod venationi datur magna cogitationis incitamenta sunt.

1.2.2 Erat in proximo non venabulum aut lancea.

1.2.2.1 Ego ille quem nosti apros et quidem pulcherrimos cepi. Mirum est ut animus agitatione motuque corporis excitetur.

1.2.2.2 Experieris non Dianam magis montibus quam Minervam inerrare.

Sed stilus et pugillares meditabar aliquid enotabamque.

1.2.2.2.1 Si manus vacuas, plenas tamen ceras reportarem.

1.2.2.2.2 Ridebis, et licet rideas.

Meditabar aliquid enotabamque non tamen ut omnino ab inertia mea et quiete discederem.

1.2.2.2.2.1 Mirum est ut animus agitatione motuque corporis excitetur. Iam undique silvae et solitudo ipsumque illud silentium.

Figure 6.24 ***Numeric-style report template***

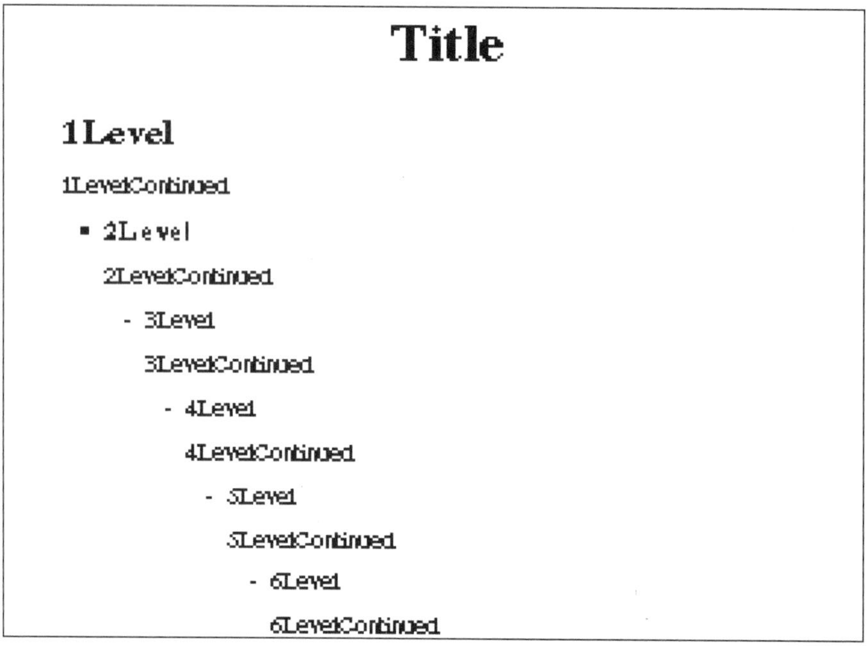

Figure 6.25   Small report template

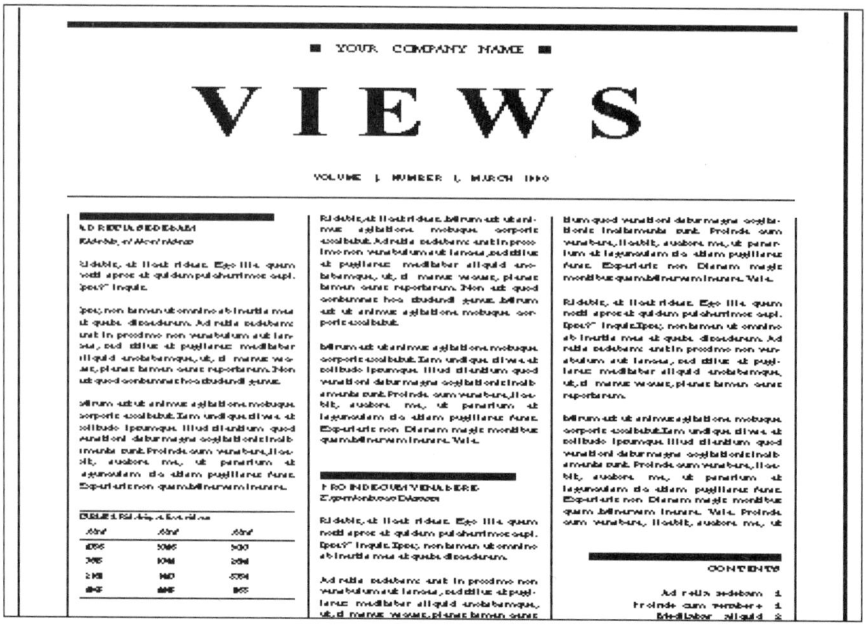

Figure 6.26   Newsletter template sample

Creating Your Own Templates

Not only do you have all of the FrameMaker-supplied templates available to you, but you can create new templates of your own. In fact, every FrameMaker document can be used as a template. There are a couple of ways to make your own templates:

▶ The first option is to simply open an existing document with File ➤ Open, save it under a new name, and change the old text. The modified old document becomes the basis for the new document.

▶ Option two is to move an existing document to a personal templates directory (any directory will do), open the document with File ➤ New, change the old text, and save it.

▶ Finally, you can copy one of the FrameMaker templates or template examples to a personal directory, modify it as you like, and save it. You can then open it with File ➤ New, as above, when you want to use it.

All three options work well. The first is the simplest, but if you use it you run the risk of automatically saving the new document with the same name as the old one, which overwrites the old document on the disk.

Opening new documents with File ➤ New avoids that problem. Documents opened with File ➤ New are always named "NoName," and you will always be prompted to change the name the first time you save the document.

You can navigate to any directory with File ➤ New, so you could, of course, open any document with that command. However, if you frequently use documents as "models" (another name for templates), you might as well put them all in one place. Just as File ➤ Open remembers the last place you looked to open a file, so does File ➤ New. So once you go to your personal templates place with File ➤ New, the command will default to that location (until you go fishing someplace else, of course). For that reason the second option is, for most people, the most practical.

Use the third option if you find a FrameMaker template you really like, but you want to change it some. In this case, start with a version of the template that you have modified to your liking, and choose a personal templates directory for storage.

NOTE   Modifying templates is no more difficult than modifying other documents. It involves making changes to the paragraph and character catalogs, column layouts, master and reference pages, and other elements like variables and cross-reference formats. You will learn how to do all of this in this book. Just see the appropriate chapter for the subject you are interested in.

Chapter 7

Saving and Printing Documents

This chapter contains information on the options available when saving or printing a document. Here you will learn how to save documents in a variety of formats, and to use the many print features available to FrameMaker users.

Saving Documents

Saving documents is as easy in FrameMaker as it is in most programs. Simply select File ➤ Save (or click the Save icon on the QuickAccess Bar, or press any of the keyboard shortcuts for saving, like Ctrl+S).

> **TIP**   If you want to save changes to all open files, hold down the Shift key before selecting File. The Save command becomes Save All Open Files. Try pressing the Shift key with other menu selections—you will see some interesting changes!

If the document already has a name, it will be saved to disk without further notice or intervention from you. However, if the document has just been created with the File ➤ New command, it will have a funky name (NoName1, or the like), and you will be prompted to give it a new name with the Save Document dialog box.

You can bring up the Save Document dialog box yourself by choosing the File ➤ Save As command. This dialog box, shown in Figure 7.1, lets you specify the location, name, and format of the file you're saving. All of the format options available through this box are discussed in this chapter.

> **UNIX NOTE**   The Save Document dialog box in the UNIX version of the program uses the conventions of the Motif Window Manager interface. While it contains the same options as the other versions, the way directory locations and file names are selected is slightly different. In addition, the UNIX version allows you to set Group and Public read and write permissions when saving a document.

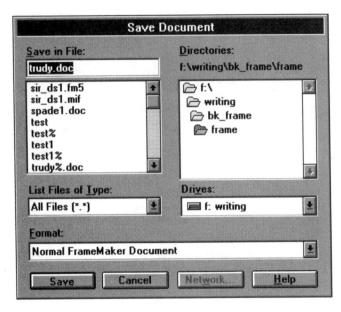

Figure 7.1   *Save Document dialog box*

Saving Documents in FrameMaker Document Format

The natural format for a FrameMaker document is called "Normal FrameMaker Document Format." Under this format, the file is saved as a *binary* file, which means that it contains formatting codes that the machine can read but you can't. A Normal FrameMaker Document Format file usually (but not necessarily) has the extension .DOC.

When FrameMaker imports a non-FrameMaker file, it attempts to create a FrameMaker format file, and it saves the file in Normal FrameMaker Format unless you specify otherwise. (See the previous chapter for more information on importing non-FrameMaker files.)

NOTE   Knowing that FrameMaker files are binary files can be important when you attempt to transfer them. FrameMaker files are easy to transfer, but the file transfer "mode" must be set to binary. If binary transfers are not possible but text files can be sent, save the FrameMaker file in MIF format and then send it. MIF files are FrameMaker files converted to ASCII in a special format designed by Frame Technology. Chapter 6 has more information on MIF files.

In the Save Document dialog box, the Normal FrameMaker Document format is the first one in the pull-down list under the heading Format. It is the default format—you have to actively select something else to save a file in another format. Even text files are saved in this format unless you specify otherwise.

Changing the Name
or Location of a Document

To save a document under a new name, select File ➤ Save As and make changes to the Drives, Directories, or Save in File specifications, as you wish.

In the Save Document dialog box, Drives is a pull-down list of the drives connected to your system, including network drives, if any. Select a drive to make it current.

> **WINDOWS NOTE**   The Network button at the bottom of Windows version of the Save Document dialog box is used with Windows for Workgroups and network file-sharing software for saving to network files.

The Directories box displays a directory tree of the current drive. Double-click on a directory to open it and make it current. If you are in doubt about which directory is current, look just above the Directories scroll list (and just below the label *Directories*). The current drive and directory is written out for you, like so:

The Save in File text box is where you can type in the new file name. If you highlight a file name in the list below this text box, that name appears in the text box. You can then save the file under the name or modify the name before actually saving the file.

TIP   You can manually control which files are listed below the Save in File text box by typing wildcards in the text box and pressing ↵. Only files that meet the wildcard specification will be shown. (For example, to see only files with the extension .BAK, type *.BAK in the text box and press ↵. Only .BAK files will be listed.)

The List Files of Type drop-down list at the bottom of the Save Document dialog box controls which files are listed *below* the Save in File text box. This box does not control the name of the file you are saving.

When you are ready to save the file under the new name or save it to a new location, click the Save button.

Saving a Document as a Text File

A *text* file (or ASCII file) is a file that contains primarily text characters (like *a*, *b*, *c*, and the like) and uses an agreed-upon standard (the ASCII standard) for describing those characters in computer language. This means that "text" files can usually be moved freely from one program to another, since all word processors (and many other programs as well) can read and save text files. But it also means that all formatting in the original file (like bolding and so on) is lost when a text file is moved between programs.

To save a FrameMaker file as a text file:

1.   Select File ➤ Save As.

2.   Specify a new file name or location if you like.

3.   In the Format drop-down menu, select Text Only.

4.   Select Save. The Save As Text dialog box appears, as in Figure 7.2.

5.   Use the radio buttons to specify where carriage returns should be placed.

A *carriage return* is a paragraph break. You enter a carriage return when you press the Enter key. The term is a holdover from the typewriter days, when to start a new line you actually had to hit the carriage—the thing that held the paper in place—to make it slide back.

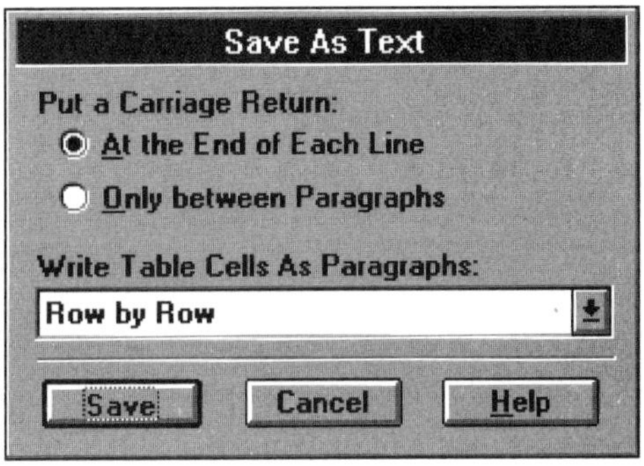

Save As Text

Put a Carriage Return:
- ⦿ **At the End of Each Line**
- ◯ **Only between Paragraphs**

Write Table Cells As Paragraphs:

Row by Row ⬦

[**Save**]   [Cancel]   [**Help**]

Figure 7.2   *The Save As Text dialog box*

Placing carriage returns at the end of each line of a text file makes sense, since that's the only reliable way to show a new line in a text file. But placing carriage returns after every line also breaks the document into lots of paragraphs and defeats the word-wrap feature the we love so much in word processors. In general, carriage returns should be placed at the end of each line only in specialized files like computer code.

6.   Use the drop-down menu to specify how tables should be written.

Table options are used with specialized files, and are discussed in Chapter 11. Unless you imported the file from a spreadsheet or a database program, you can accept the program's default table setting, since nothing you say here will have any effect anyway.

7.   Select Save.

An ASCII text file version of your FrameMaker file is written to disk.

WARNING   Even if you started with a text file (by opening it with File ➤ Open), you must specify Text Only to save the file as a text file. If you don't, the file will be saved as a FrameMaker file.

Saving Documents in Specialized Formats

The Format pull-down menu of the Save Document dialog box (see Figure 7.1) contains a number of options beyond those discussed. With this menu, you can save documents in many other formats, including:

▶   View-only (FrameMaker format)

▶ MIF (Maker Interchange Format)

▶ Text-only (ASCII format)

▶ RTF (Rich Text Format)

You can also save documents in file formats specific to other applications.

UNIX NOTE   The list of formats in which documents can be saved varies by platform. The UNIX version, for example, can also save documents in CCITT Group 4 (a TIFF format used for faxing), WordPerfect, and Interleaf formats.

FrameMaker View-Only File Mode   This format is useful for documents that are distributed online. Documents saved in this format can be opened and printed in FrameMaker (or FrameViewer, a companion product), but cannot be edited or saved. In view-only documents, all hypertext commands and all cross-references are converted to active, clickable links.

MIF (Maker Interchange Format) Files   Files saved in this format are ASCII text files that completely describe FrameMaker documents, including formatting. Because they are text files, they can be moved easily from one platform to another. Though the MIF format was designed by FrameMaker, many other applications, especially graphics applications, can read and write MIF files. MIF files can also be edited by any text editor, which means that they can be changed using batch files and scripts. (See "Importing a Non-FrameMaker Document" in the previous chapter for a short discussion of MIF files.)

Text-Only Files   Files saved in this format are ASCII text files. These were discussed in the previous section of this chapter.

RTF (Rich Text Format)   RTF is, like MIF, another ASCII description of a word processing file, including its formatting. RTF files are often used in building online help files.

To save a FrameMaker file in another format:

1. Select File ➤ Save As.

2. Specify a new file name or location if you like.

3. In the Format drop-down menu, select the format in which the file will be saved.

4. Select Save.

   Notice that if you don't change the name of the file, your new file will overwrite the old one.

Unlocking View-Only Files

If you are saving the file as a view-only file, the file on your screen will become a view-only (locked) version of the original file—it can no longer be saved or edited. To unlock a locked view-only file, use the keyboard shortcut *Esc F l k*. Be sure to use a capital *F*, and the letter *l*, not the number *1*. (*Esc F l k* is a toggle—it will both lock and unlock files.)

Using Save to Undo Changes

You may have noticed that some FrameMaker commands are marked "No Undo." This means, of course, that once the change is made, the Undo command can not reverse it.

There is a way around this limitation, however. The File menu provides a Revert to Saved command, which returns files to their last saved version. In essence, this command rereads the file from disk.

You can use Revert to Saved to undo a command that is marked "No Undo," but it takes a little forethought:

1. Immediately before making the change marked "No Undo," save the file.

2. Now make the change.

3. If you don't like the result, select File ➤ Revert to Saved. The only changes you will lose are those that resulted from step 2.

   It's important to save the file just before making the change in question. If you save it earlier, other changes or edits will also be lost when the file is reread from disk.

Preferences for Saving Files Automatically

With the Preferences dialog box, shown in Figure 7.3, you can customize how you save your files. The save options of interest are Automatic Backup on Save and the Automatic Save - Every time setting.

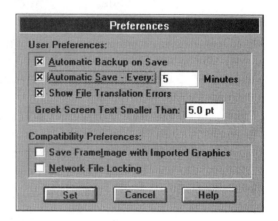

Figure 7.3   *The Preferences dialog box (Windows)*

 MAC AND UNIX NOTE   The Mac version of the Preferences dialog box contains additional options, though none are related to saving documents. The UNIX version contains fewer options than the Windows version, but retains the save options discussed below.

If you select Automatic Backup on Save, FrameMaker creates a *backup file* every time you manually save a file (with Save or Save As). A backup file is identical to the old saved version, but FrameMaker renames it. For example, if the original file is MYFILE.DOC (Windows), MyFile (Mac), or MyFile.doc (UNIX), saving the file also creates a backup file named MYFILE%.DOC (Windows), MyFileBackup (Mac), or Myfile.backup (UNIX).

If you select Automatic Save, FrameMaker automatically saves your files. Autosave files are identical to backup files, but are named differently. For example, if the original file is MYFILE.DOC (Windows), MyFile (Mac), or MyFile.doc (UNIX), the autosave file will be named MYFILE$.DOC (Windows), MyFileAutosave (Mac), or Myfile.auto (UNIX).

Autosave files are deleted when you manually save a file.

> **TIP** You can open a backup or autosave file in the same way you open any other file—by selecting it in the Open file dialog box. Backup and autosave files can be edited just like other FrameMaker files.

Turning Automatic Backup and Automatic Save on is generally a good thing to do, since most of us forget to save a document sometime in our lives when it really, really matters. The only negatives involve disk space and time. For very large files, the backup file can crowd an already crowded disk, and autosaving a very large file can cause regular, irritating interruptions in your work flow.

> **NOTE** FrameMaker sometimes creates a third kind of backup file, called a *recover file*. Recover files are created if FrameMaker detects that your system is starting to crash. Don't depend on recover files, however, as a substitute for saving regularly. Recover files are named like backup and autosave files— MYFILE#.DOC (Windows), MyFileRecover (Mac), and MyFile.recover (UNIX).

Printing Documents

All FrameMaker documents (even view-only documents) can be printed from FrameMaker with the File ➤ Print command. When you choose this command, the Print Document dialog box shown in Figure 7.4 or 7.5 appears.

> **UNIX NOTE** The UNIX version of the Print Document dialog box is nearly identical to the Windows version. The differences are slight and easy to figure out.

> **MAC NOTE** The Mac version of the Print Document dialog box varies, depending on the print driver your system is currently using.

Most of the time, you can simply select the number of copies to print, which pages to print (all pages or a page range), and click the Print button.

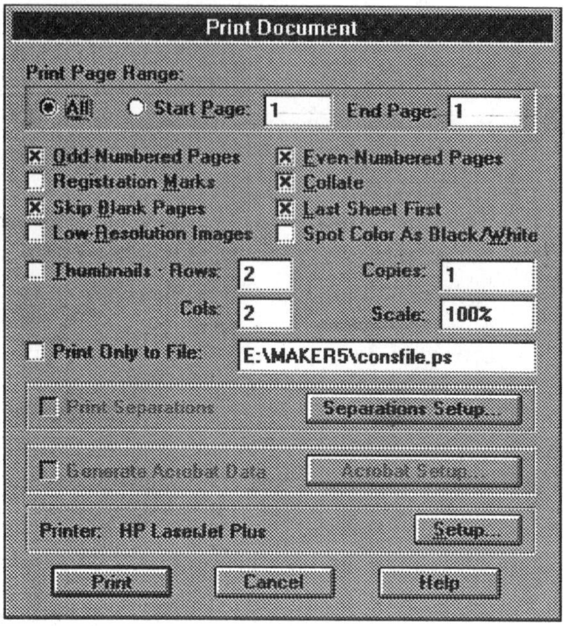

Figure 7.4 **The Print Document dialog box (Windows)**

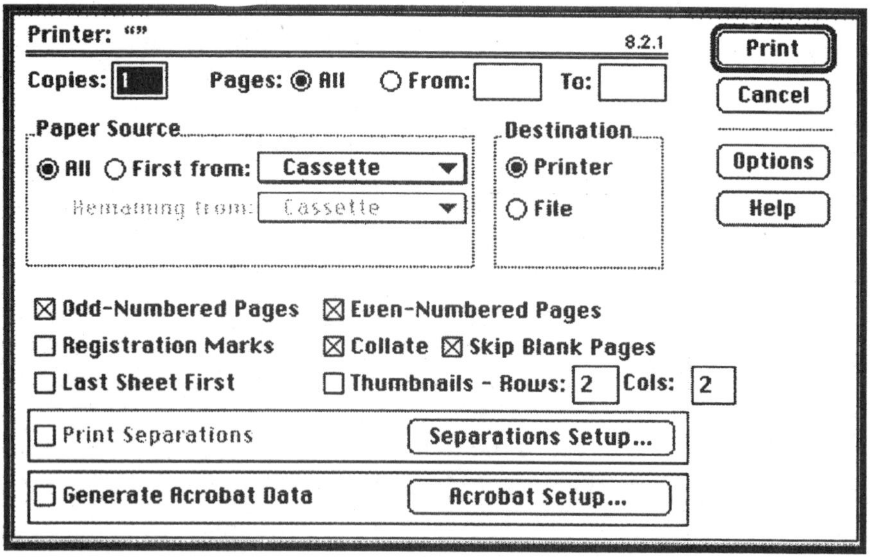

Figure 7.5 **The Printer dialog box (Mac)**

If you need to change the printer, you can click on the Setup button (Windows version), go to the Chooser (Mac), or enter another printer name in the Printer Name text box (UNIX).

The Print Document dialog box has other options, however, whose purposes may not be obvious. These options are discussed below.

Print Options

Some options in the Print Document dialog box may require explanation.

The Odd-Numbered Pages and Even-Numbered Pages settings are for printing duplex (double-sided copies) on a nonduplex printer. Just print all odd-numbered pages, then turn the pages over in the printer, re-feed them, and print all even-numbered pages.

The Registration Marks check box is for adding crop marks and lines that show where pages start and stop. Commercial print shops use these marks to make pages and text line up correctly.

Click the Low-Resolution Images check box if you want to print imported graphics as gray boxes. You might use this option when you print draft copies of documents, since graphics take less time to print this way. (The Mac version does not have this setting.)

Thumbnails are used to print greatly reduced images of document pages. Professionals often print thumbnail documents so they can review the layout of a whole document at a glance.

For documents that contain color, you can make sure that all colors print as either black or white (not shades of gray):

▶ In the Windows version, select Spot Color as Black/White.

▶ In the Mac version, select Options, then select Black and White from the Print pop-up menu.

▶ In the UNIX version, you must edit setup files for your system. See "Changing Setup Files" in the set of online manuals for more information.

Select Print Only to File to create a PostScript file on disk. (In the Mac version, select File in the Destination area. Note that, depending on the configuration of your Mac system, you can also choose Fax as a destination!)

Print Separations are special pages that printers use to make color plates for documents. Documents that contain several colors are printed in several passes through the printing press. With each pass, a new print separation, or color, is applied to the document. The Separations Setup button brings up a dialog box that allows you to say which color(s) will be printed (as black). This setting can be used in conjunction with Skip Blank Pages. (Printing color separations is covered much more thoroughly in Chapter 15.)

 The Generate Acrobat Data (Mac) and the Acrobat Setup buttons (Windows) are available for converting FrameMaker files to PDF (Portable Document Format) for use with Adobe Acrobat. (*Adobe Acrobat* is a set of programs and utilities for managing and reading special view-only files containing hypertext links. These view-only files are not the same ones that FrameMaker produces.)

Creating Acrobat Files

 Adobe Acrobat Exchange and Acrobat Reader are programs used to distribute view-only documents that contain hypertext links and other useful online-document-oriented features. FrameMaker Release 5 can convert its own files into a format that can then be converted by Acrobat Distiller to produce Acrobat-compatible files. (In effect, FrameMaker creates a modified PostScript file that Acrobat Distiller interprets and converts.)

During the conversion, cross-references and hypertext commands are converted into Acrobat links, hypertext alert messages become Acrobat notes, and FrameMaker paragraph tags can be turned into hierarchical Acrobat bookmarks. In addition, named FrameMaker flows become Acrobat article threads. Most features of Adobe Acrobat are supported.

To create a file for conversion by Acrobat Distiller, open the file you want to convert and select File ➤ Print. Then do the following:

1. Select All as the page range.

2. Turn on Odd-Numbered Pages and Even-Numbered Pages.

3. Make sure that Last Sheet First and Skip Blank Pages are turned off.

4. Make sure that the selected printer is a PostScript printer, and then turn on Print Only to File.

5. Type ★ in the file name box to preserve the default file name for the PostScript file. (An appropriate extension will be automatically added to the file name.)

6. Turn on Generate Acrobat Data and click the Set Up Acrobat button. (The UNIX version does not have a separate Generate Acrobat Data check box.) The Acrobat Setup dialog box appears, as in Figure 7.6.

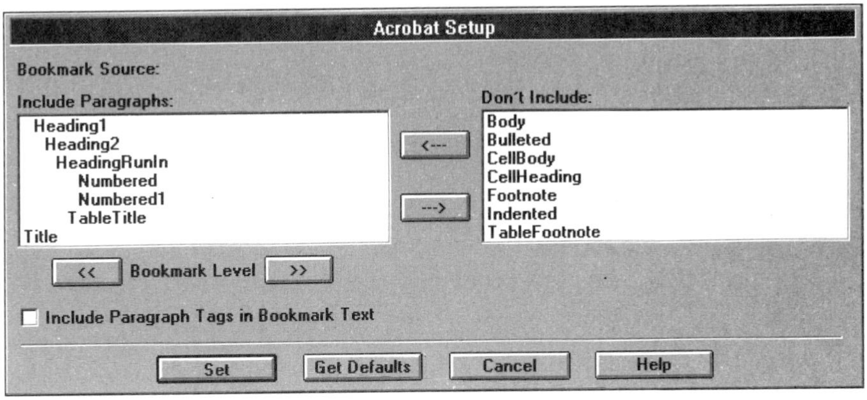

Figure 7.6   The Acrobat Setup dialog box

7. Select paragraph tags for use as bookmarks and specify their hierarchy.

8. Select Set to confirm the settings and close the dialog box.

9. Select Print (or Save on the Mac version) to create the PostScript file.

   The PostScript file can now be used by Acrobat Distiller to create a PDF file.

Formatting and Editing Text

3

Chapter 8

What Is a FrameMaker Document?

This chapter defines a FrameMaker document and explains three of the most basic concepts in the program: pages, text frames, and text flows. "Text flow" is just the term for how text behaves on the page—how it fills columns, how it relates to figures, and so on. This chapter also shows you how to work with body pages, master pages, and reference pages, and how to use anchored frames as places to put imported text and graphics.

 NOTE   This is perhaps one of the most important chapters in the book, in that understanding these concepts is an excellent foundation for working easily and successfully with FrameMaker.

Pages, Text Flows, and Text Frames

A FrameMaker *page* is a representation of a sheet of paper on which objects may be pasted. That's it—the whole definition. By contrast, a document is the contents of a FrameMaker file. A document contains (among other things) pages displayed in a certain order. (Documents also contain other things—like Character and Paragraph Catalogs, which you will see in later chapters.) A document's pages may or may not contain text or other objects, but the order of pages is fixed. You cannot, for example, zoom out to a 25-percent view of document pages and then drag pages from one place to another in a document.

Objects are placed on pages. FrameMaker objects include anything that can be drawn with the Tools palette—rectangles, circles, frames of various types, straight and curved lines, and so on. Figure 8.1 shows two document pages with objects drawn on them.

What about text? We could paste words on the page, in the same way that we could paste rectangles on them, but text is different from objects in a very important way: We don't want words to be pasted in place on pages, because we want words to *flow* onto pages in the right order. Then, when we insert a word near the beginning of a "flow," we want all of the other words to move over automatically to make room for the new word. You could say we don't just put the *words* onto a page, we want to put the *flow of words* onto a page.

But suppose you wanted words to stay in one place on the page? For example, suppose you had a notice of some kind that you wanted words to flow around? FrameMaker has a clever way of doing this. To keep text

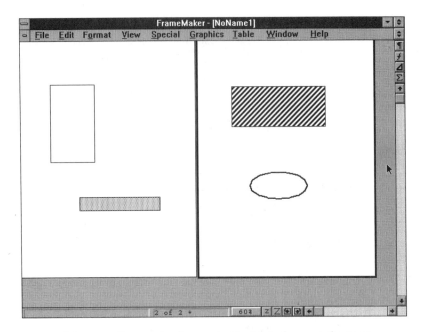

Figure 8.1　**A two-page Framemaker document with objects drawn on the pages**

in one place, you paste an object called a *text frame* onto the page. And since a text frame is an object that can hold a "flow of words," or *flow*, the problem is solved. The text frame can be pasted down, but within the text frame, the words in the flow shift and shimmy as much as they like.

In fact, a text frame gives the flow some shape. And within the text frame, the flow can be formatted—it can be divided into paragraphs, left and right margins can be applied to it, the words can be split into columns, and so on.

Figure 8.2 shows our two-page document with a symbolic text frame pasted onto each page, and a text flow in each text frame. Note the end-of-flow character that marks the end of each of the flows. In a real FrameMaker document, this arrangement looks like Figure 8.3.

When Text "Overflows"

If you add a word to a text flow, the other words move over automatically. That's what a flow is designed to do. You can make flows longer or shorter just by adding or removing words. But what happens if you add too many

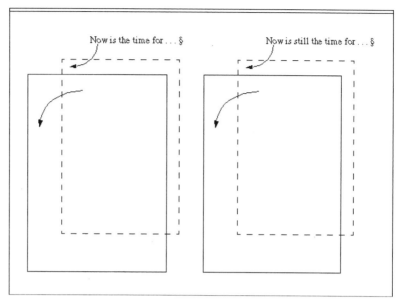

Figure 8.2   *A symbolic representation of a two-page document with two text frames and two text flows*

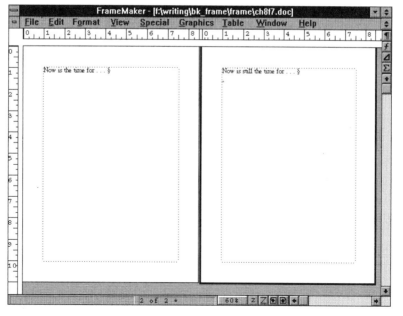

Figure 8.3   *A "real" Framemaker document with two text frames and two text flows*

Part
3

Formatting and
Editing Text

words, so that the text frame fills up and "overflows?" One of two things can happen, either

▶ the flow of words fills up the frame until the end, and then disappears through the bottom of the text frame, or

▶ the flow spills over into another text frame that has been connected to the first.

Either of these two results is desirable, depending on the situation. Let's look at them one at a time.

"Overflows" in an Unconnected Text Frame

When the flow of words reaches the end of a text frame and no other text frame is connected to it, words disappear through the bottom of the frame. They don't go away, but you can't see them. To show where text has spilled over, a dark line appears at the bottom of the text frame. It reminds you that the text flow continues below the frame. Figure 8.4 shows a two-page document. This time, the first flow is too full (note the dark line), and the second flow is empty (note the end-of-flow character).

"Overflows" in Connected Text Frames

To avoid the problem of text frames that become too full, you can connect text frames to each other. This allows the overflow to move from the bottom of one text frame to the top of another one, usually the one on the next page. Figure 8.5 and 8.6 show this. In Figure 8.5, the first text frame is *not* overflowing into the second text frame, which is connected to the first. Notice that the second frame does not have its own flow, but shares a flow with the first frame, and therefore it has its own end-of-flow character. Figure 8.6 shows what happens if text is added to the first frame, so that it fills up. The words spill out of the bottom of the first frame and in through the top of the second. This can only happen if the two text frames are connected.

NOTE   Text frames can be connected manually, or they can be automatically created whenever they are needed. You will see both methods later in this chapter.

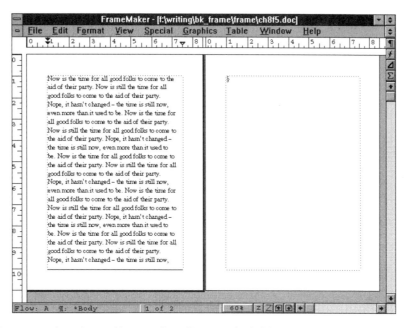

Figure 8.4   A text frame with too much text flow. Note the dark line at the bottom of the flow on the first page.

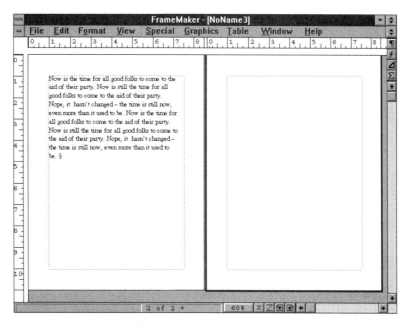

Figure 8.5   A text frame on the first page and a connected text frame on the second

Part
3

Formatting and
Editing Text

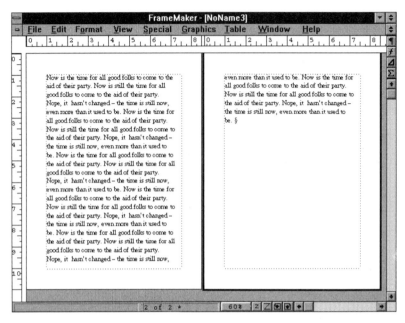

Figure 8.6 The same as Figure 8.5, but here the flow from the first text frame is long and flows into the second.

Connected and Unconnected Text Frames

Each of these situations—unconnected and connected text frames—has its uses. Sometimes you don't want text frames to be connected. In a business "slide" presentation, for example, where each slide has a title and its own message, you might want each text frame to have its own flow. Spillovers from one text frame to another might move things around too much. Better to shorten the text in the frame with the spillover or create a new slide to hold the rest of the message.

Figure 8.7 shows a short slide presentation in which each text frame has its own flow. In a longer document, however, you almost always want the text frames to be connected, often because there is only one long flow in the whole document. A letter, for example, should have only one flow in it, and it should have connected text frames, as in Figure 8.8.

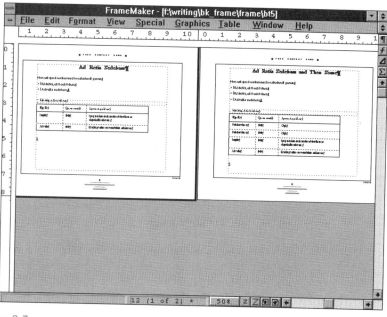

Figure 8.7 *A two-page viewgraph, or slide presentation, in which each text frame has its own flow*

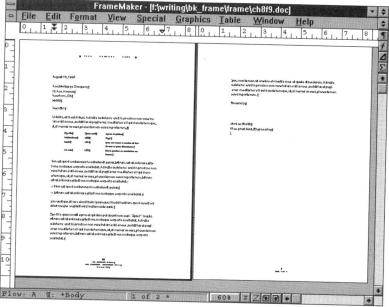

Figure 8.8 *A two-page letter with one flow*

How Autoconnected Text Frames Work

To make it easier to work with documents with multiple pages and only one flow, FrameMaker allows text frames to be "autoconnected." When the autoconnect setting is "on" and a text flow gets to the end of the last text frame in a connected series, FrameMaker does the following:

▶ Adds a new page to the document at that point (usually at the end of the document)

▶ Creates a new text frame (or frames) on the new page it creates

▶ Automatically connects the new text frame to the end of the old one

▶ Lets the excess text flow from the previous text frame into the new text frame on the new page

When autoconnect is turned on, page after page is automatically added to the document without any further action from you. You never have to add pages yourself. For example, if the flow in Figure 8.8 gets too long for the two text frames, the two-page letter automatically becomes a three-page letter with a single flow and a connected text flow on each page:

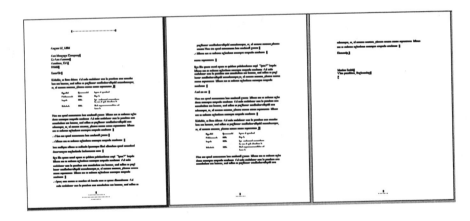

TIP   In fact, for most documents it's important that you *not* add pages manually, but that you let FrameMaker take care of creating new pages for you with the autoconnect feature.

Connecting Text Frames with the Autoconnect Feature

Most of the time, the documents you work with have autoconnect turned on. For example, most FrameMaker templates, including the ones you create with File ➤ New and the Blank Paper buttons, have one page to start with, a single text frame on that page, and a flow in that text frame with autoconnect on. In addition, thanks to the Delete Empty Pages setting, whenever you print or save one of these documents, the empty pages at the end are automatically deleted.

In combination, the autoconnect feature and the Delete Empty Pages setting allow you to use blank paper and template documents in an easy and natural way. Just bring them up, put the character cursor where you want to type, and start typing. Don't worry about adding or deleting pages—just type. Pages will be added and deleted for you. They will be added when they are needed and deleted when you save or print your document.

Test this now if you like:

1. Select File ➤ New and the Portrait button. You see a single blank sheet of paper.

    Notice, at the bottom in the Page Status area, that it says, "Page 1 of 1." Notice also the single text frame on the page and the end-of-flow character in that frame.

2. Start typing characters and pressing Enter to create words and paragraphs. When you get to the bottom of page 1, you will find yourself automatically at the top of page 2. This is autoconnect in action!

3. Go to page 1 again. In the Page Status area it says, "Page 1 of 2."

Part
3

Formatting and
Editing Text

Empty Pages

FrameMaker has its own definition of what an empty page is. An empty page is either a page with nothing at all on it—no text, no paragraph symbols (¶), no end-of-flow symbol, nothing.

By this definition, a page with a text frame and empty paragraphs (paragraph marks but no text) is *not* empty. In the same way, a page with a text frame that contains only an end-of-flow symbol is *not* empty. These pages would not be deleted when the document is saved, and they would be printed.

4. Delete enough paragraphs to make page 2 empty. Check this by pressing PgDn and looking at page 2. There should be nothing at all on it—just a completely empty text frame.

5. Save the document.

When you are done, the Page Status area reads "Page 1 of 1" again. The empty page was automatically deleted. If you press PgDn now, nothing happens.

The following sections show you how to control the autoconnect feature and how to change the Delete Empty Pages setting. Then you learn about the types of pages in FrameMaker and how to use them to design documents of your own that take advantage of these features.

Turning Autoconnect On and Off

The autoconnect feature is a property of a flow, and since text flows only exist inside of text frames, the autoconnect setting is grouped with text frame properties and controlled through the Customize Text Frame dialog box.

TIP If autoconnect is not working, check the master pages of the document to make sure autoconnect is turned on there as well. (You'll learn about master pages shortly.)

If you are editing a document and you find that autoconnect is not working, use the following procedure to turn the autoconnect setting on. To turn autoconnect on or off:

1. Put the character cursor anywhere in a flow and bring up the Customize Text Frame dialog box by selecting Format ➤ Customize Layout ➤ Customize Text Frame. The dialog box shown in Figure 8.9 appears. You can also bring up this box by selecting the text frame as an *object*—by Ctrl+clicking on the text frame (Option+clicking, for Mac users)—and then selecting Graphics ➤ Object Properties.

UNIX AND MAC NOTE UNIX and Mac users can also display the Customize Text Frame dialog box by selecting the text frame as an object and clicking on Properties in the large Tools window.

Customize Text Frame

Type: Text Frame

Unrotated Size: Color: Black

Width: 6.5"   Angle: 0.0

Height: 9.0"   Border Width: 1.0 pt

Offset From: Flow Tag: A

Top: 1.0"   ☒ Autoconnect

Left: 1.0"   ☐ PostScript Code

                         ☐ Room for Side Heads:

Columns:

Number: 1   Width: 1.5"

Gap: 0.25"   Gap: 0.25"

☐ Balance Columns   Side: Left

Set   Cancel   Help

Figure 8.9   *The Customize Text Frame dialog box*

2. In the first row under the Flow settings (Tag, Autoconnect, and Post-Script Code), click the Autoconnect check box.

    When this box is checked, autoconnect is on, and a new page with a new, connected text frame is created to hold excess characters in the flow. When this box is unchecked, however, autoconnect is off, and excess characters in the flow disappear through the bottom of the text frame. (They aren't deleted; you just can't see them.)

3. Click on the Set button to apply your changes.

What to Do about Empty Pages

What about empty pages? FrameMaker creates them in order to handle text flows, but you can do what you will with empty pages by changing the Delete Empty Pages setting in the Numbering Properties dialog box:

1. Bring up the Numbering Properties dialog box by selecting Format ➤ Document ➤ Numbering:

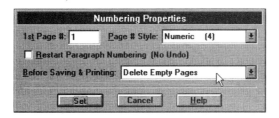

Numbering Properties

1st Page #:   1   Page # Style: Numeric   (4)

☐ Restart Paragraph Numbering (No Undo)

Before Saving & Printing: Delete Empty Pages

Set   Cancel   Help

2. Bring down the Before Saving & Printing menu. You will see four items:

    - **Delete Empty Pages**—Deletes pages with no contents or with text frames with no contents *from the end of the document.*

    - **Make Page Count Even**—Makes sure that the last page of the document is an even number by adding one disconnected page, if necessary. (A "disconnected page" is a page with its own text flow.) This setting is especially useful for two-sided documents, since it makes sure that for every front page there is a back page.)

    - **Make Page Count Odd**—Makes sure that the last page of the document is an odd number by adding one disconnected page, if necessary.

    - **Don't Change Page Count**—Neither adds nor deletes pages.

3. If Delete Empty Pages is not selected, select it now.

4. Confirm your setting by clicking the Set button. Pages will be added or deleted as though you just saved the document.

Connecting and Disconnecting Text Frames

Text frames may be connected and disconnected from each other. To connect text frames, select the text frames to be connected *in the order in which you wish them connected*, and then select Format ➤ Customize Layout ➤ Connect Text Frames.

To disconnect a text frame from the previous text frame in the flow, place the cursor in the frame and select Format ➤ Customize Layout ➤ Disconnect Previous. To disconnect a text frame from the next text frame in the flow, place the cursor in the frame and select Format ➤ Customize Layout ➤ Disconnect Next. To disconnect a text frame from both the previous and the next text frame in the flow, place the cursor in the frame and select Format ➤ Customize Layout ➤ Disconnect Both.

To split a text frame into two text frames, place the character cursor in the line below which you wish to make the split, and then select Format ➤ Customize Layout ➤ Split Text Frames. The old text frame will be split into two just below the line containing the cursor, and the new text frames will be connected in the same flow.

What Are Body, Master, and Reference Pages?

There are three kinds of pages in a FrameMaker document: body pages, master pages, and reference pages. We have been working with the first kind—body pages. Body pages are the ones on which you place the main text of your document.

Master pages look like body pages. They have text frames on them that look like the text frames on body pages. However, master pages have a different use, as you will see shortly. Master pages are used as models when new body pages are created. A document can have many master pages, each used for a different purpose.

Reference pages are not like either body pages or master pages. Reference pages are used to hold objects that are referred to. For example, they hold frames that contain lines used above and below paragraphs, frames used by the hypertext feature, and frames used to generate tables of contents and indexes

Seeing and Moving Around in Body, Master, and Reference Pages

To see and edit body, master, and reference pages, use one of the three options on the View menu—Body Pages, Master Pages, or Reference Pages. Move from page to page in master and reference pages just as you would in the body pages—with PgUp and PgDn, the scroll bar, the Go to Page dialog box, and so on. Only body pages can be printed, though.

Working with Body Pages

Let's look at body pages first. Even though we have been dealing with body pages all along, there are a few features we haven't touched on yet. Body pages are printable pages that contain the main text of a document. In most documents, each body page is linked to a particular master page. From the master page, the body page gets two types of information:

▶ Background text and graphics, such as headers and footers, which are displayed automatically at the tops and bottoms of body pages

▶ Models for the editable text frame (or frames) on the body page

Part
3

Formatting and
Editing Text

How Body Pages Use Background Text and Graphics

The text and graphics on master pages can be made to appear in the background of a body page or a group of body pages. For example, if you draw a rectangle on a master page, all body pages that use that master page also have the rectangle. In addition, if you add a text frame to a master page and mark it as background, anything written in the text frame appears in the background of each body page that uses that master page.

Background text and graphics cannot be edited on body pages, only on master pages. To edit a header or footer, for example, you have to view master pages (with View ➤ Master Pages) and perform your edits there.

Adding New Body Pages

New body pages are created when the autoconnect feature adds a "connected page," a page with a connected text frame, or when you manually add a "disconnected page," a page with a text frame that has its own, separate flow.

When Autoconnect Adds a Page...

When autoconnect adds a page, it uses the default master page as a model. Any objects on the master page that are marked as background are placed in the background of the new body page. New text frames are created on the body page and modeled after text frames on the master page, if there are any, that have named flows (flow tags that are not blank). You'll see what all this means in a moment.

The default master page in a one-sided document (a document printed on only one side of a page) is the master page named Right. The default master page in a two-sided document is either the master page named Right or the one named Left, depending on whether the new body page is a left-hand or right-hand page.

When You Add Body Pages...

When you add disconnected body pages manually, you can assign any master pages you wish, or no master page, to the new pages. Add disconnected pages by selecting Special ➤ Add Disconnected Pages. The Add Disconnected Pages dialog box appears:

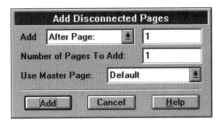

Here you can specify where and how many pages to add, and also which master pages to use as a model, if any. Selections on the Use Master Page pull-down list include Default (which has the same meaning discussed above), None, and each named master page, including Right and Left (if they exist).

Deleting Body Pages

As you saw, empty body pages can be automatically deleted from the end of a document with the Delete Empty Pages setting. But you can also delete body pages manually. To do so, select Special ➤ Delete Pages, and in the Delete Pages dialog box, specify which pages to delete and click Delete. Then click OK when the "cannot be undone" warning message appears.

If the pages you deleted contained *disconnected* text frames, both the pages and the frames are deleted. If the pages contain *connected* text frames, the pages, the frames, and the part of the text flow that appears in those frames are deleted.

Changing the Master Page Used by a Body Page

You can change which master page is used by any body page. For example, you would do this to get a different background on a page. To do so:

1. Select Format ➤ Page Layout ➤ Master Page Usage to see the Master Page Usage dialog box shown in Figure 8.10.

Part 3

Formatting and Editing Text

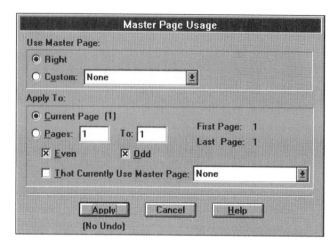

Figure 8.10   *The Master Page Usage dialog box. Use it to change which master page is assigned to a body page.*

2. Under the heading Use Master Page, click the first radio button to select the default master page (either Right or Left/Right) or use the Custom pull-down list to select a specific master page, including one that you created yourself.

3. Under the heading Apply To, apply the specified usage to either the current page, or all pages in a range that

   • Are even-numbered

   • Are odd-numbered

   • Use a specified master page

   • Are any combination of the above

4. Click the Apply button to apply the changes.

Changing the Layout of a Body Page

You can change the column layout and the line layout of the flow where the character cursor is located. You can also change the page size of the entire document (but not individual pages), and you can make the first page a left- or right-hand page (a quality called "Pagination" in Frame-Maker). Finally, you can rotate pages, so that they lie on their sides or appear upside-down. How to do this is discussed in the following pages.

Changing the Column Layout

To change the column layout:

1. Select Format ➤ Page Layout ➤ Column Layout. The Column Layout dialog box appears, as in Figure 8.11.

2. Modify Columns, Margins, and Side Heads settings as you wish.

3. Click the Update Entire Flow button to apply the changes.

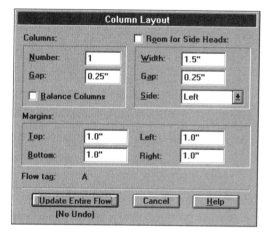

Figure 8.11   *The Column Layout dialog box*

TIP   You can also make column layout modifications from the Customize Text Frame dialog box. Open this box by selecting either Format ➤ Customize Layout ➤ Customize Text Frame or Graphics ➤ Object Properties, then update the column layout to the entire flow and the underlying master page by selecting Format ➤ Page Layout ➤ Update Column Layout. (Unlike the Column Layout dialog box, the Customize Text Frame dialog box changes only the current text frame.)

Changing the Line Layout

Line layout refers to two qualities, baseline synchronization and feathering.

Baseline synchronization aligns the "baselines" (the invisible lines that the letters sit on) of some paragraphs with horizontal lines in an invisible synchronization grid. (This is *not* the same grid as the one set in the View Options dialog box.) Only paragraphs with the same line spacing as the line spacing of the synchronization grid are affected. If the grid has a line spacing of 14 points, all paragraphs with line spacings of 14 points are aligned with the grid.

TIP   Baseline synchronization is especially effective when used with body text paragraphs, so the synchronization grid is often set to match the line spacing of those paragraphs. The effect is terrific in multicolumn pages—all of the body text paragraphs sit on the same baselines from one column to the next.

Feathering simply means adding extra space between lines and paragraphs so that the last line on the page reaches the bottom of the text frame. Feathering does vertically what right-justification does horizontally—it adds padding.

To change the line layout of a flow:

1. Select Format ➤ Page Layout ➤ Line Layout. The Line Layout dialog box appears, as in Figure 8.12.

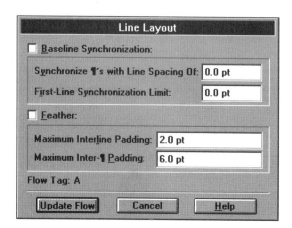

Figure 8.12   *The Line Layout dialog box*

2. If you wish, turn Baseline Synchronization on by clicking the check box, and then enter values in the two text boxes:

   • Enter the line spacing of the invisible synchronization grid in the box labeled Synchronize ¶'s with Line Spacing Of. All paragraphs in the flow with this line spacing will have baselines synchronized with the grid.

   • Enter a value in the box labeled First-Line Synchronization Limit. This allows run-in headings to extend above the top of the text frame if they appear in the first line on the page. Headings taller than this value will not be allowed to extend above the text frame.

3. If you wish, turn Feathering on by clicking the check box and entering values in the Maximum Interline Padding and Maximum Inter-¶ Padding text boxes. Feathering overrides baseline synchronization when both are turned on.

4. Click the Update Flow button to apply the changes.

Changing the Page Size and Pagination

To change the page size or pagination for all the pages in a document:

1. Select Format ➤ Page Layout ➤ Page Size. The Page Size dialog box appears:

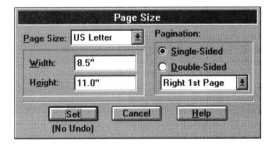

2. Select a page size—either by selecting a size from the Page Size pull-down list (it includes most common sizes and a few uncommon ones) or by entering values in the Width and Height text boxes.

3. Use the Pagination controls to select whether the document is single-sided or double-sided and whether the first page is a left- or right-hand page.

Rotating Body Pages

Body pages can be rotated in 90° increments so that they lie on their sides or appear upside down. Rotated pages change their orientation, from portrait to landscape, for example. The text frame rotates with the page, so that its text appears to be printed on its side.

To rotate a body page, go to the page to be rotated and select Format ➤ Customize Layout. Then select either Rotate Page Clockwise, Rotate Page Counterclockwise, or Unrotate Page.

Working with Master Pages

Master pages are not printed, exactly. Body pages use them for background text and graphics. Master pages also contain models of the editable text frames that appear on body pages when body pages are created.

Using master pages, you can create complex page layouts. Using multiple master pages, you can create complex-looking documents that are nevertheless easy to manage.

A Quick Tour of Master Pages

To see how master pages work, let's look again at the master page of a simple document, in this case, the one-page piece of blank paper you get when you use the Blank Portrait Page template. We're going to examine the master page, make some changes, and see how those changes affect the body page.

1. Select File ➤ New and click the Portrait button. The first (and only) body page appears.

2. Select View ➤ Master Pages. The document is a one-sided document, so it has only one master page, named "Right." Right is shown in Figure 8.13.

   Notice that even though there is only one text frame on the body page, there are three text frames on the master page, two small ones at the top

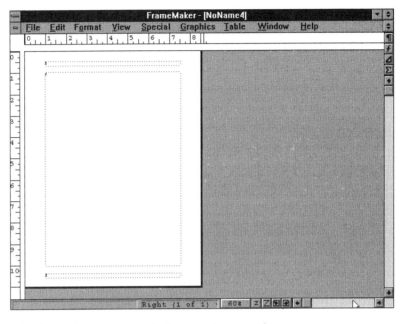

Figure 8.13 *"Right" master page of the Blank Portrait Page template*

and bottom, and one big one in the middle. The top and bottom text frames (the two flat ones) hold the header and footer, respectively. Both of these text frames are marked as background—that's why they don't appear on the body page. If you typed text into them, however, the text would appear in the background on the body page.

3. Click the mouse anywhere in the top text frame and type **This is a header.**

4. Select View ➤ Body Pages. As Figure 8.14 shows, even though the text frame for the header does not appear on the body page, any text you type into it does.

NOTE FrameMaker always updates body pages from master pages whenever the view changes from master pages to body pages.

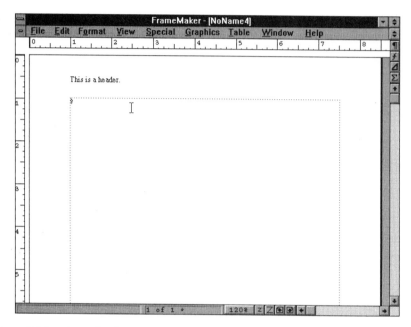

Figure 8.14   *The new header appears on the body page.*

5. Try to select and edit the header text on the body page. You'll discover that you can't.

   To see why that is, let's go back to the master page and look more closely at that text frame:

6. Select View ➤ Master Pages.

7. Click the mouse in the top text frame, the one with the header text you just typed.

8. Select Format ➤ Customize Layout ➤ Customize Text Frame. The Customize Text Frame dialog box appears, as in Figure 8.15.

   In the Flow group of settings, there is no flow tag name in the text box and autoconnect is turned off. That's because any master page text frame *without* a flow tag is used as background by the body page.

   You can also place graphics in the background. To see how:

9. Click Cancel in the Customize Text Frame dialog box to close it.

10. Bring up the Tools window by clicking on the Tools button (the one with the triangle) on the side of the document window.

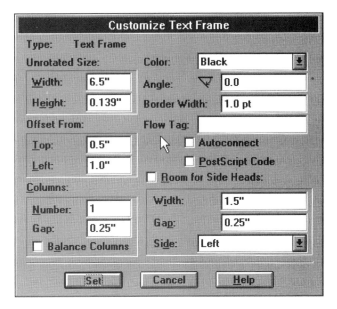

Figure 8.15   The Customize Text Frame dialog box for the header text frame

11. Select the Rectangle tool.

12. Draw a rectangle anywhere near the top of the page by holding down the mouse button, dragging, and releasing.

Now let's look at the body page again:

13. Select View ➤ Body Pages. The rectangle appears on the body page, but can't be selected.

Let's look at the main text frame on the master page to see what's happening there:

14. Select View ➤ Master Pages.

15. Click the mouse cursor in the main text frame and select Format ➤ Customize Layout ➤ Customize Text Frame once again. The Customize Text Frame dialog box appears, but this time it looks a little different.

In the Flow group of settings, notice that the flow is named (Flow Tag = A) and that autoconnect is on. Any master page text frame *with* a flow tag is used as a template for a body page text frame when the body page is created. In addition, if you change the size or position of a master page text frame with a flow tag, or if you change any of its layout settings in the Customize Text Frame dialog box, you change every text frame with the same flow tag name on every body page that uses that master page.

There are lots of variations on these possibilities. Let's look at just a few of them:

16. Click Cancel in the Customize Text Frame dialog box to close it. You will see that the text frame has been selected as an object (it has little black handles on its border.)

17. Move the mouse cursor near one of the corner handles and move it somewhere else. (Note that the mouse cursor changes to an arrowhead when it touches an object handle.)

18. Look at the body page one more time. Select View ➤ Body Pages. You'll see that the text frame has been similarly resized, as Figure 8.16 shows.

One more test. Let's see what happens when you add text to the main (named) flow on the master page:

19. Select View ➤ Master Pages and click anywhere in the main text frame.

20. Type anything.

21. Select View ➤ Body Pages. The text you typed does not appear.

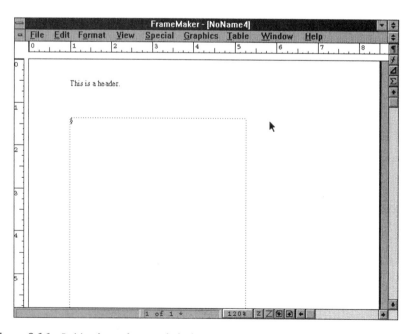

Figure 8.16   Resizing the text frame on the body page

That's it for this exercise. You could do other experiments as well, though, to see how master pages and body pages interact. What happens, for instance, if you rename the body page text flow so that it no longer matches the flow tag of the master page text flow? Let's see.

View body pages, change the flow tag name of the body page text frame (from A to AA, for example), and when you see a message asking whether to rename just the current flow or all similarly named flows on body pages *and* master pages, choose to rename only the current flow (the one on the body page). The master page and body page are now "out of sync" with each other—the body page no longer contains a text frame with the same named flow as the master page. In FrameMaker terminology, the body page now contains "overrides" to the master page. An override is a text flow named A on the master page that is missing from the body page.

Now go to the master page and change the shape of the text frame with the flow labeled A (so, for the purposes of this experiment, it *looks* different from the body page flow named AA), and try to view body pages. FrameMaker attempts to update body pages from the master page, discovers that the body page does *not* contain a text flow named A (as it should), and warns you about these overrides. You then have two options—to keep the overrides or to remove them:

▶ If you *keep* overrides, the named text frame on the master page will not appear on the body page (since the body page has its own, differently named text frame). Overrides are retained.

▶ If you *remove* overrides, the named text frame on the master page (A) will appear on the body page *in addition* to the text frame named AA, which was already there. Overrides are removed in the sense that the body page is updated from the master page, and the master page text flow is added to the body page.

As another experiment, change the size of the text frame on the body page but leave the flow tag alone. The body page is again out of sync with the master page (that is, it contains overrides), but this time the names of the flows are still the same. The override is not a missing text flow, but a differently sized text frame with the same named flow.

This creates a different situation than the one we just looked at. If you viewed master pages, then viewed body pages again, FrameMaker would try to apply the master page to the body pages, discover the overrides, and display the overrides message again. This time, though, because the flows are named the same, the results of your two choices would be a little different.

▶ If you *keep* overrides, the text frame on the body page remains the same size as it was before. (Overrides are retained.)

▶ If you *remove* overrides, the text frame on the body page adopts the size and shape of the text frame on the master page. (Since their flow tags are the same, FrameMaker makes them match each other, using the master page flow as a model.)

TIP The overrides message can be useful. With complex documents, you may need a warning about overrides when you make changes to master pages—you may not remember whether you changed body pages independently or not.

There are lots of ways master pages can affect body pages. As you might expect, if you put two text frames with named flows on a master page (one called A, for example, and one called B), you would get two similar text frames on any body page that uses that master page.

The following section shows just a few basic operations with master pages. The possibilities for their use are too numerous to describe here. An hour or two of experimentation, however, will teach you a lot about the interaction between master pages and body pages.

Basic Operations with Master Pages

This section includes some of the basic master page operations, in fairly abbreviated form. By now, though, you should be familiar with operations like viewing master pages, so this section can serve as a reference.

Adding Master Pages

To add a master page to a document:

1. Select View ➤ Master Pages.

2. Go to the master page *before* which you want to add the new page. (Master pages can be used no matter what their order in the set of master pages, but, like body pages, they cannot be moved. So if the order of master pages matters to you, select its position now.)

3. Select Special ➤ Add Master Page. The Add Master Page dialog box appears:

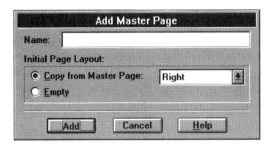

4. In the Name field, type a name for the new master page. Choose a name that describes the use of this page.

    There are already default Right and/or Left master pages. A master page called First is common when the first page of a document has a different layout (no headers, for example, or a special graphic in the background).

5. Under Initial Page Layout, select a master page to copy from or choose to create an empty master page. Whichever you select, you can make any modifications you wish later.

6. Click the Add button to create the page and add it after the current master page.

    The new master page is now the current master page. It can be modified in any way you like.

> **TIP**   You can also bring up the Add Master Page dialog box without viewing master pages first by selecting Format ➤ Page Layout ➤ New Master Page.

Adding Background Text and Graphics to Master Pages

Adding background text and graphics to a master page is easy:

▶   **To add a drawing,** such as a rectangle, use the Tools palette to put the drawing directly on the master page. (See Chapter 13 for more on the Tools palette.)

▶   **To add text,** for example, a header or footer, use the Tools palette to draw a text frame directly onto the page (again, see Chapter 13). In the Add New Text Frame dialog box, specify Background Text as the Text

Part 3

Formatting and Editing Text

Type, adjust the Columns settings as you wish, and click Add. Then enter your text. (See Chapter 12 for more on adding headers and footers.)

➤ **To add an imported graphic,** such as clip art, use the File ➤ Import command to import the art directly onto the page.

Whatever you add as background will appear on every body page that uses that master page.

Adding Template Text Frames to Master Pages

The same method that adds background text frames can also be used to add text frames that will be used as templates for body text frames. In general, any master page text frame *with* a flow tag is used as a template for a body page text frame when the body page is created. If a master page contains two or more text frames with differently named flow tags, each text frame appears on the associated body pages.

To add a text frame template to a master page, use the Tools palette to draw a text frame directly onto the page. (See Chapter 13 for information on the Tools palette.) Then, in the Add New Text Frame dialog box, specify Template for Body Page Text Frame as the Text Type, name the flow in the Flow Tag text box, and adjust Columns settings as you wish. When you are done, press Add. The text frame is added and selected.

Deleting and Renaming Master Pages

Master pages can be deleted and renamed. To delete a master page, select View ➤ Master Pages, go to the master page you wish to delete, and select Special ➤ Delete Page *XXX*, where *XXX* is the name of the master page to be deleted. When the "cannot be undone" message appears, press OK.

To rename a master page, select View ➤ Master Pages, go to the master page you wish to rename, and click once on the page status box at the bottom of the document window. A dialog box appears so you can enter a new name for the current master page.

Applying a Master Page to a Body Page

To apply a master page to a body page (that is, to specify that a body page use a certain master page), select Format ➤ Page Layout ➤ Master Page Usage and use the Master Page Usage dialog box to select which master pages to apply and which body page(s) will use that master page.

For more information, see "Changing the Master Page Used by a Body Page" earlier in this chapter.

Updating the Column Layout of a Master Page

If you change the size, position, or column layout of a body page text frame with a named flow, you can update the master page used by that body page to match the new body page. To do so, simply move to the body page you wish to change, make changes as you wish to text frames with named flows, and then select Format ➤ Page Layout ➤ Update Column Layout. When the confirming message appears, press Update. The master page used by that body page *and* all body pages that use that master page will be updated to match the current body page.

Rotating Master Pages

Like body pages, master pages can be rotated in 90° increments so that they lie on their sides or appear upside-down. Rotated master pages can be used as background for rotated body pages. Text frames on rotated pages may be rotated back to their original orientation with the Graphics ➤ Rotate command, or to any other 90° orientation you like. (See Chapter 13 for more on the Rotate command.)

To rotate a body page, go to the page to be rotated and select Format ➤ Customize Layout, and then select Rotate Page Clockwise, Rotate Page Counterclockwise, or Unrotate Page.

Working with Reference Pages

Reference pages are the last kind of pages contained in a document. Reference pages are not printed. They contain information (graphics frames and text flows) used by various aspects of the program.

For example, the first reference page of every new document contains a group of frames with lines in them, and looks something like Figure 8.17. This reference page contains four named reference frames—Footnote, TableFootnote, Single Line, and Double Line. These frames contain lines that are used by the Frame Above and Frame Below features of the Paragraph Designer to add ruling lines to paragraphs.

NOTE   See Chapter 10 for more on Frame Above and Frame Below.

Part
3

Formatting and
Editing Text

Other reference pages are used by generated files (like tables of contents and indexes), by hypertext elements in view-only files, and by equations. These subjects are covered in later chapters.

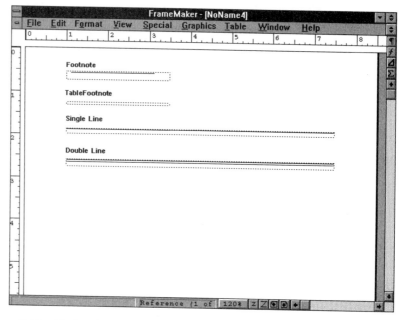

Figure 8.17　*The first reference page of a new document*

Adding Graphics Frames to Reference Pages

Adding a graphics frame to a reference page for use by the Paragraph Designer is a simple process:

1.　Select View ➤ Reference Pages. The first reference page of the document is displayed.

2.　Bring up the Tools palette by clicking on the Tools button. (See Chapter 13 for information on the Tools palette.)

3.　Select the Frame tool and draw the frame on the reference page. When you are finished, the Frame Name dialog box appears.

4.　Type the name of the frame in the dialog box and click on Set. The dialog box disappears, the frame is selected, and the name of the frame appears in the status area at the bottom of the document window.

TIP   When you size the frame, remember that the *entire frame* will be placed above or below the specified paragraphs, not just the graphic elements in the frame.

5. Again using the Tools palette, place any graphic element you wish into the frame. For example, to draw a ruling line to be used above or below certain paragraphs, use the Line tool to draw the line.

6. As a reminder to yourself of the name of the reference frame, use the Text Line tool to add the name of the frame *above* the frame itself. (Other frames on the page are similarly labeled.) This step is not necessary, but it's convenient to have these labels where you can see them.

7. Repeat this process for each frame you wish to add.

You will probably have to go back and forth between reference pages and body pages several times to adjust the interaction between the reference frame and the paragraph that uses it.

Adding, Deleting, and Renaming Reference Pages

You can add, delete, and rename reference pages in the same way you add, delete, and rename master pages. To add a reference page, go to the page after which the new page should be added, select View ➤ Reference Pages, select Special ➤ Add Reference Page, and fill in the Add Reference Page dialog box.

To delete a reference page, select View ➤ Reference Pages, go to the page to delete, and select Special ➤ Delete Page *XXX,* where *XXX* is the name of the master page to be deleted. When the "cannot be undone" message appears, press OK.

To rename a reference page, select View ➤ Reference Pages, go to the page to be renamed, and click once on the page status box at the bottom of the document window. A dialog box appears so you can enter a new name for the current reference page.

Creating Special Page Layouts

 FrameMaker can create a number of effects within text frames. For one thing, the text in a text frame can be divided into columns. This is a new feature of FrameMaker 5. In previous versions, having more than one column on a page required more than one text frame.

It's also possible to reserve an area on the side of single- or multicolumn text frame for "sideheads." A sidehead is a heading that appears alongside body text paragraphs instead of between them.

Finally, you can make paragraphs, tables, and anchored frames straddle columns and sidehead areas. Anchored frames are "boxes" that can be anchored into a certain place in the text flow so that they move along with the flow. Unanchored frames are pasted onto the page and don't move with the flow.

Both anchored and unanchored frames can hold anything, but they are used primarily as a place to put pictures and drawings, with anchored frames being far more common. Anchored frames are discussed in the next section.

Creating Multicolumn Pages

There are two ways to create multicolumn pages: you can divide a single text frame into columns or you can paste multiple text frames on a page and connect them in any order you wish. Dividing a text frame into columns is new with FrameMaker 5.

Dividing a Text Frame into Columns

 The first method mentioned above, dividing a single text frame into multiple columns, is the easiest way to create multicolumn documents. It can be used in most situations. This method creates pages in which there is only one text flow that moves in an orderly way from one column to the next and from one page to the next. (The opposite is newsletter- or newspaper-style columns, in which several flows or "articles" are started on one page and continued on some random future page.)

TIP   A template for a multicolumn newsletter using a single text flow is provided with FrameMaker. In this template, the articles in the newsletter appear continuously, one after the other, with no jumping to other pages. To see or use this template, select File ➤ New and click on Explore Standard Templates. Then find the Newsletter template in the list and click on Show Sample.

Figure 8.18 shows a one-column text frame. Figure 8.19 shows a three-column text frame. Notice the dotted line that marks the gutter, or gap between the columns.

To divide a text frame into multiple columns:

Part 3

1. Place the character cursor into the text frame.

2. To change column settings for *all text frames in a main flow*, including those on master pages, select Format ➤ Page Layout ➤ Column Layout. The Column Layout dialog box appears, as shown in Figure 8.20. (A "main flow" is a flow that appears on a master page as well as on the corresponding body page.)

3. To change column settings for the *current text frame only* or for a text frame that is not part of a main flow, select Format ➤ Customize Layout ➤ Customize Text Frame. The Customize Text Frame dialog box appears, as in Figure 8.21.

4. In either dialog box, select the number of columns and the gap between them by using the Columns and Gap text boxes.

5. To divide the text on unfilled pages (usually the last page in a text flow) evenly between all columns, turn on the Balance Columns check box. The effect of balanced columns is to use only the top part of the page for text, so that all columns on the page are partially filled, as shown in Figure 8.22.

6. Make any other changes you wish. Remember, though, that the Column Layout dialog box makes global changes (it changes all text frames in the flow, including those on master pages), while the Customize Text Frame dialog box changes only the current text frame. (The exceptions are the Room for Sideheads settings, which are discussed below.)

7. Click on Update Entire Flow (in the Column Layout dialog box) or Set (in the Customize Text Frame dialog box) to apply your changes.

Formatting and Editing Text

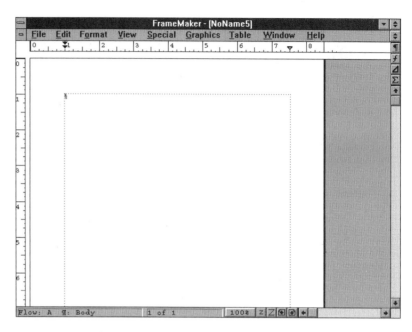

Figure 8.18   **A one-column text frame**

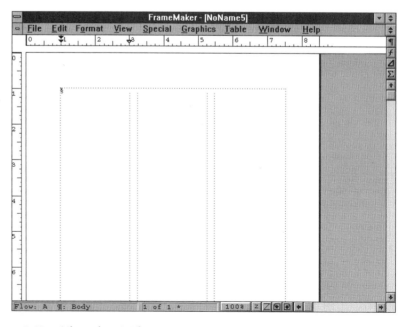

Figure 8.19   **A three-column text frame**

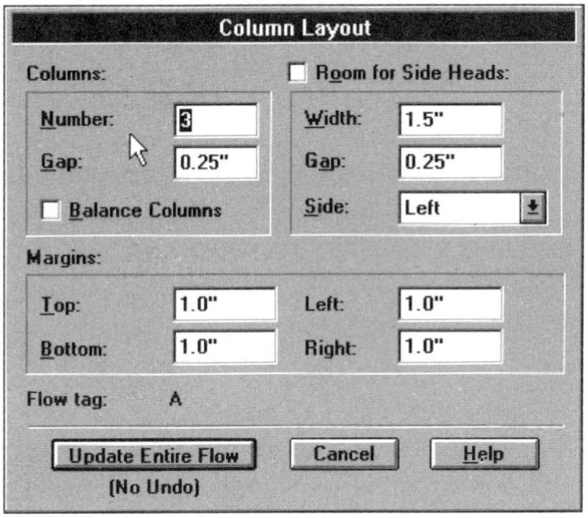

Figure 8.20   The Column Layout dialog box

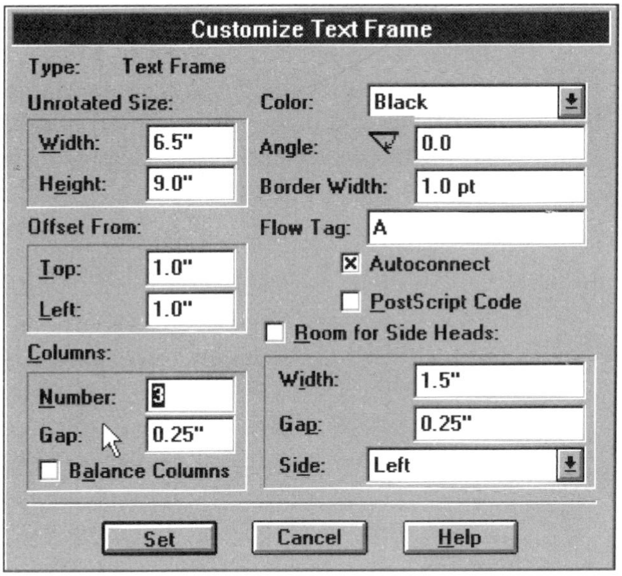

Figure 8.21   The Customize Text Frame dialog box

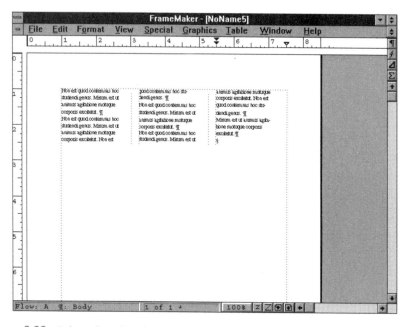

Figure 8.22   Balanced text in columns

Using Multiple Text Frames to Create Multiple Columns

The second method, using multiple text frames to create multiple columns, is used primarily in newsletters and newspapers in which several flows, or "articles," start on one page and are continued on future pages and columns. In this kind of newsletter, the articles "jump" from one page to another.

This kind of newsletter requires each article to be a separate flow and each flow to have its own text frame or text frames. The frames can be connected in whatever order you wish the text to appear. In other words, if an article starts on page one, column one, it might continue and end on page three, column two. To do this, there has to be a text frame on page one, column one, that is connected to a separate text frame on page three, column two. In this way, the "overflow" from page one can go to page three.

In addition, the text frame on page three has to be shortened by hand so it is exactly as long as the text, and the text frames below it have to resized to fill the available space. Either that, or a full-column text frame on page three has to be split into two text frames immediately below the end of the article.

While the effect of this kind of layout can be quite impressive, creating it involves a certain amount of cutting, pasting, and connecting and splitting of text frames, all done "by hand." If this is what you wish to do, here's one way to do it:

1. Start with a blank document with *no* text frames on it by selecting File ➤ New, clicking on the Portrait button, and deleting the text frame that appears on the first body page. Do that by Ctrl+clicking on the text frame (Option+clicking on the Mac) and pressing the Backspace or Delete key.

2. Specify a background grid by selecting View ➤ Options and using the Grid Lines setting in the View Options dialog box. Be sure to select a grid size whose lines you can use as guidelines when you draw and place your document's text frames.

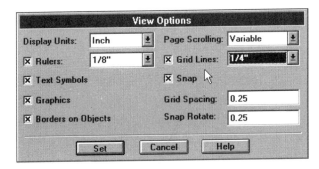

3. Turn on the Snap feature and specify a snap Grid Spacing that is identical to the Grid Lines setting. (It's not absolutely necessary for these settings to be the same, but it sure helps.)

4. Turn on Borders on Objects.

5. Click on the Set button to close the dialog box and apply your settings. The document should now have gridlines on its body pages.

6. Draw text frames on the first page to hold the beginnings of each article, as well as any other information, such as the title of the newsletter or document. Do this with the Tools window, as explained in Chapter 15. Make sure that for each text frame you add, autoconnect is turned off.

7. Type or import (by using File ➤ Import) the front-page articles into the text frames on that page. Type or import one article for each text frame.

8.   When an article needs to be continued, do the following:

- Add extra pages as necessary with the Special ➤ Add Disconnected Pages command. Be sure to specify None in the Use Master Page box so that you get a blank page with no text frames on it.

- Draw a text frame to hold the "continued article" on this page, just as you did on the first page. Make sure that, here again, autoconnect is turned off.

- Connect the two text frames by clicking on them in the order in which you want them connected, and then selecting Format ➤ Customize Layout ➤ Connect Text Frames. The flow will move from the first text frame you selected to the second.

9.   Continue this process until all articles are added and all pages appear as you want them to appear. Feel free to move text frames around and resize them to get the layout you want.

10.   When you are done, save the document.

You can also do this by starting with a master page that has several long, full-page text frames, one for each column in the newsletter. On the various body pages, lay your articles into the frames, and split, disconnect, and reconnect them as needed to accommodate the size and placement of each one. With either method, when you are done, each article will occupy its own text flow.

Using "Sideheads" in Documents

"Sideheads" are headings that appear alongside body text paragraphs instead of above or between them. A good example of a sidehead can be seen in the "sidehead report" template provided with FrameMaker. It is shown in Figure 8.23. This template is discussed in Chapter 6. You can take a look at it by selecting File ➤ New, clicking on Explore Standard Templates, selecting "Report, Sidehead" from the list, and clicking on Show Sample.

If you want to leave room for sideheads, you must do so for an entire flow, not just for a single text frame. To turn on the Room for Sideheads option, select Format ➤ Customize Layout ➤ Customize Text Frame, click on the Room for Sideheads setting in the Customize Text Frame dialog box shown in Figure 8.24. Specify the width of the sidehead area, the

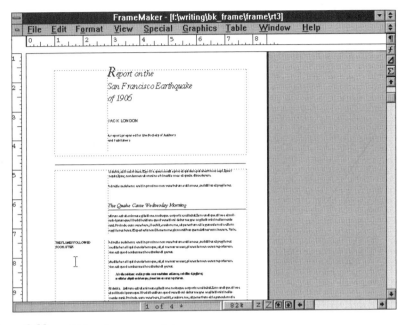

Figure 8.23 **A sidehead report template**

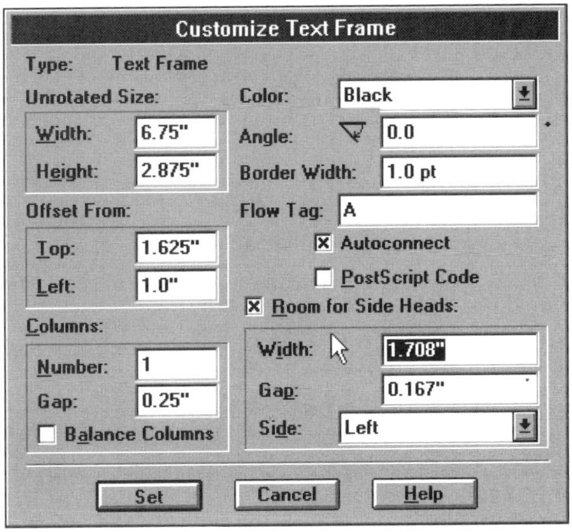

Figure 8.24 **The Customize Text Frame dialog box**

gap between the sidehead area and the text area, and which side the sidehead area should occupy by using the Width, Gap, and Side settings.

Next, turn on sidehead placement for any paragraph you wish to appear in the sidehead area. Do this with the Paragraph Designer, using the Pagination Properties page. "Sidehead" is a radio button under the Format heading:

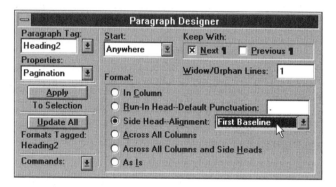

You have several choices of alignment when you make a paragraph into the sidehead area:

► **First Baseline**—Aligns the first baseline of the sidehead text with the first baseline of the paragraph next to it in the text area. In other words, the first lines in each paragraph appear to rest on the same horizontal line, no matter how tall the letters in each paragraph are. (Keep in mind that heading paragraphs are frequently in a larger font than body paragraphs, so they tend to look taller than body paragraphs.)

► **Top Edge**—Aligns the top of the tallest letter in the first line of the sidehead paragraph with the top of the tallest letter in the first line of the text paragraph next to it. The baselines don't necessarily line up, but the top edges of the paragraphs do.

► **Last Baseline**—Aligns the last baseline of the sidehead text with the first baseline of the paragraph next to it in the text area. In other words, the last line of the sidehead paragraph appears to rest on the same horizontal line as the first line of the paragraph in the text area.

Getting Text to "Straddle" Columns

 In documents with multiple columns or areas set aside for sideheads, you can make individual paragraphs, tables, or anchored frames straddle either all columns or all columns plus the sidehead area, if there is one. "Straddling" paragraphs can be headings, body text paragraphs, footnotes, or any other paragraph you choose. If you place a straddling paragraph, table, or anchored frame (we'll just call it a "straddle" for now) on a page, the text in the columns fills all columns above the straddle before moving below the straddle.

The straddle property for paragraphs, including footnote paragraphs, is specified with the Pagination Properties page of the Paragraph Designer. The straddle property for tables and anchored frames is specified as follows:

▶ A table or anchored frame that is anchored in a straddle paragraph has the same straddle properties as the paragraph.

▶ A table or anchored frame that is wider than one column but not wider than the text area automatically straddles columns but not the sidehead area.

▶ A table or anchored frame that is wider than all columns automatically straddles columns *and* the sidehead area.

Anchored Frames
That Move with the Text Flow

As you saw earlier in this chapter, objects can be pasted directly to FrameMaker pages, and when they are, they don't move when the words of a flow move. These objects can include imported graphics, FrameMaker drawings like rectangles and the like, and graphic frames that hold graphics, drawings, and the like.

More often, though, you want objects like drawings and imported graphics to move with the flow of words—in other words, you want them to be "anchored" to a certain position in the flow. A picture that illustrates something said in the text—like the figures in this book, for example—should stay with the text it illustrates, and move when that text moves.

To allow objects to move with the text flow, FrameMaker provides an object called an *anchored frame*. An anchored frame is a frame or box for holding things that is tied to a certain position in the text flow by an anchor symbol. The anchor symbol moves with the text, as does the anchored frame. There are lots of options for positioning an anchored frame relative to the position of the symbol—below the line containing the anchor symbol, between words in the line of text that contains the anchor symbol, and at the top or bottom of the column that holds the anchor symbol are just a few. We'll look at these placement options in a moment.

Here you can see an anchor symbol in a line of text, and immediately below it, an empty anchored frame with its dotted-line border:

tabamque, ut, si manus vacuas, plenas tamen ceras reportarem. Mirum est ut animus agitatione motuque corporis excitetut.↓¶

The border of the anchored frame is like the border of a text frame. When View Borders is turned on, the border appears, but it doesn't get printed when the page is printed. When View Borders is turned off, the border still exists, but it disappears.

NOTE You can treat an anchored frame just like any other object in FrameMaker. You can change its borders to lines of some thickness, fill it with colors and patterns, and so on—by using the Tools window. See Chapter 15 for more on how to do this.

Let's look at how to use anchored frames to hold imported text, imported graphics, and FrameMaker drawings so that they move when the text flow moves.

Using Anchored Frames in a Text Flow

There are several ways to import graphics or text into an anchored frame, but the simplest is to place the character cursor in the text where you want the anchor to appear and select the File ➤ Import command.

FrameMaker creates a default anchored frame to hold the imported material. The default anchored frame is sized appropriately, positioned below the current line, and centered. (Other ways to create anchored frames and to import graphics and text into them are covered later in this section.)

After an anchored frame is created, resizing handles appear on its border to show it is selected, and you can immediately change its properties. Do this by selecting Special ➤ Anchored Frame. The Anchored Frame dialog box appears, as illustrated in Figure 8.25. Notice that the first button at the bottom says Edit Frame. If it said Add Frame instead, you would know that the anchored frame was not selected, and you would have to go back and select it.

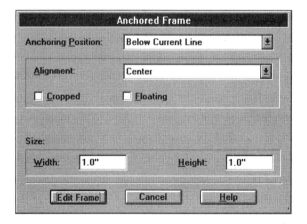

Figure 8.25   *The Anchored Frame dialog box*

The Anchored Frame dialog box is where all the action is regarding anchored frames. The first line allows you to select an Anchoring Position for the frame from a pull-down list. Here's where you select positions like below the current line, or at the top of the current column. The bottom of the box allows you to specify a width and height using type-in text boxes. In between is an area that changes depending on the anchoring position you selected.

A bunch of anchoring positions are available. Let's look at them one at a time.

Anchored Frames below the Current Line

Below the current line is one of the most common positions for anchored frames. This setting produces a frame that sits exactly below the current line, with no white space above it, and within the borders of the column or text frame.

The Alignment pull-down list controls how the frame is positioned horizontally—Left, Center, Right, Side Closer to Binding, and Side Farther from Binding. The last two alignments apply to two-sided documents only.

Changing the Size of an Anchored Frame

Anchored frames can also be resized by dragging on their resizing handles with the mouse. In addition, many can be repositioned by dragging on their borders.

Whether an anchored frame can be repositioned in this way depends on its original positioning setting. In general, the most flexible positioning settings are Outside Column and Outside Text Frame. If you want to move an anchored frame into an eccentric position on the page, select one of these settings. Note, however, that *no* anchored frame can be moved above or below the text frame that contains its anchor!

The Cropped check box decides whether a frame that is wider than the current column will be clipped (or cropped) at the column boundaries or whether it will be allowed to extend beyond them on either side.

The Floating check box determines whether the frame will be forced to appear together in the same text column all the time or whether the frame can move below the anchor into the next column (leaving the anchor behind) if the current column doesn't have enough room to hold the frame. If Floating is turned off and there isn't much room at the bottom of the column or text frame, both the anchored frame and the line containing the anchor symbol will be moved to the top of the next column or text frame. This situation always leaves white space at the bottom of the original column.

If Floating is turned on and there isn't much room at the bottom of the column or text frame, the line with the anchor can stay in the original column while the frame can move (or float) to the top of the next column or text frame that can hold it. The space below the line with the anchor is then padded with whatever text would normally appear there, and the columns or text frames have a nicely filled-out, even appearance.

Note that while this positioning (Below Current Line) gives the "look" that most people desire (a drawing that lies below the text that refers to it), the only way to control the space between the drawing and the text above is to leave extra space between the drawing and the top of the anchored frame. This is because you can't control how far below the current line the anchored frame is placed—that distance is fixed at a pretty small number. A better way to create this "look" and at the same time control the space above and below the drawing or picture automatically is presented below, where anchoring frames at the insertion point are discussed.

Anchored Frames at the Top or Bottom of the Column

Positioning anchored frames at the top or bottom of the column provides the same choices as positioning an anchored frame below the current line. The only difference is the vertical placement of the frame. Instead of being a fixed distance below the current line, the anchored frame is placed in a fixed position—at the top or bottom of the current column (aligned left, right, or centered, and so on).

Note, however, that if the current column contains a paragraph that straddles the columns, the Top of Column setting will move the frame up only as far as the straddle, not above it. Similarly, the Bottom of Column setting will move the frame down only as far as the straddle, not below it. This is because many—or most—straddle paragraphs are headings, and you wouldn't want the anchored frame to be above a heading that introduces the paragraph with the anchor.

Anchored Frames at the Insertion Point

Anchoring frames at the insertion point produces a paragraph in which the anchored frame (and whatever graphic it contains) is in line with the text of the paragraph containing the anchor.

With this setting, the only option is Distance above Baseline, which can be zero, a positive number, or a negative number. Zero distance above the baseline produces a frame that sits right on the baseline with the rest of the characters. A negative number produces a frame that sits on a line some distance below the baseline.

If you place a space character on either side of an anchored frame in this position, the frame is treated as a word in the paragraph—perhaps a tall word, but a word nonetheless. Otherwise, the frame is treated as a letter of the word the anchor is next to.

> **TIP**   To keep the frame from moving up into the lines above or below it, open the Paragraph Designer (with Format ➤ Paragraphs ➤ Designer) and, on the Basic Properties page, turn Fixed Line Spacing off. This allows the line spacing to vary to accommodate the height of the "letters" it contains—and in this instance, the anchored frame is nothing more than a big letter in the paragraph.

You can use the At Insertion Point setting to create figures that always have a fixed distance above or below them—in effect, to create a nicer "below the current line" anchored frame. Simply create a paragraph format especially for anchored frames (called "Figure Paragraph," for example) and let the anchored frame be the only thing in it, positioned At Insertion Point. Then you can use the Space Above and Space Below settings of the Paragraph Designer to control with precision the padding above and below the anchored frame. You'll end up with a perfectly positioned figure every time.

Anchored Frames outside the Column or the Text Frame

Use the Outside Column or Outside Text Frame settings for anchored frames that you want to move freely around on the page. While all the previous settings restrict an anchored frame from moving outside the borders of the column or text frame, these positions allow you to place the frame anywhere on the page you wish—anywhere, that is, except above or below the text frame that contains the anchor.

Anchored frames with these settings can be dragged freely with the mouse, so repositioning them is easy.

For both of these positions, you can select one of six places for the frame from the Side pull-down list—Left, Right, Side Closer to Binding, Side Farther from Binding, Side Closer to Page Edge, and Side Farther from Page Edge. The Side Closer to Binding and Side Farther from Binding settings apply to two-sided documents only. Figure 8.26 shows the dialog box that appears when the Outside Column position is selected. The selections for Outside Text Frame are almost identical to these.

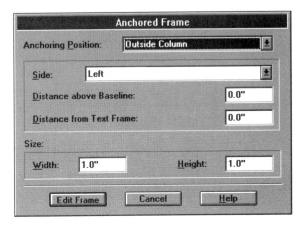

Figure 8.26 Anchored Frame dialog box for frames positioned outside the column

You can specify a vertical distance from the baseline (above with a positive number or below with a negative number). You can also specify a horizontal distance from the edge of the column (for anchored frames positioned with the Outside Column setting) or from the text frame (for anchored frames positioned with the Outside Text Frame setting). This type of anchored frame is often used to produce "margin graphics," the pictures and icons that appear in the margin next to the text to which they refer.

In a single-column layout, Outside Column and Outside Text Frame yield the same result. In a multicolumn layout, the Outside Column setting can produce an anchored frame that overlaps text in a neighboring column. If this is undesirable, you have two choices. You can manually reposition the anchored frame in the margins outside the text frame and leave the anchoring position setting as it is, or you can choose Outside Text Frame as an anchoring position.

The first choice is fast, but the second is better if you want to place margin graphics a standard distance away from the text frame, since the Distance from Text Frame setting can be set exactly and identically for each anchored frame.

Drop Caps: Anchored Frames That Run into the Paragraph

You can also use anchored frames to produce an effect known as "drop capitals," or simply *drop caps*. Drop caps are those large first letters at the start of paragraphs:

datur magna cogitationis incitar

E go ille quem nosti apros
inquis. Mirum est ut ani
excitetut. Ad retia sedeb
lancea, sed stilus et pugilares: m
manus vacuas, plenas tamen cer
tatione motuque corporis excite

Drop caps are created with the Run into Paragraph Anchoring Position setting. The anchored frame is always positioned so that the top of the frame is aligned with the top of the first line of the paragraph, no matter where in the paragraph the anchor is placed.

The general procedure for creating a drop capital is pretty simple. Just create a new anchored frame in the paragraph with the Run into Paragraph setting, select an alignment and gap setting, size the frame with the mouse or the size settings, and use the Text Line tool to place a single letter into the frame. Adjust the size of the frame and the position of the letter and you're done.

To create a new anchored frame for a drop cap, place the character cursor anywhere in the paragraph and select Special ➤ Anchored Frame. When you are finished with the Anchored Frame dialog box, click on New Frame.

To place a single letter in the frame, bring up the Tools window, select the anchored frame, select the Text Line tool, and type the letter into the frame. Then size the letter with the Character Designer, size the frame with the mouse, and use the Graphics ➤ Align command to center the letter in the frame.

Anchored Frames That "Straddle" Columns

Just as paragraphs can be made to straddle columns or columns and the sidehead area, so can anchored frames. With paragraphs, straddling is done with settings in the Paragraph Designer, which controls how paragraphs look, but with anchored frames, straddling is *not done with the Anchored Frame dialog box. Instead, an anchored frame becomes a straddle according to these principles:*

▶ A frame anchored to a straddle paragraph straddles whatever the paragraph straddles.

▶ An anchored frame that is wider than the column in which it appears straddles all columns, if the Cropped setting is turned off.

▶ An anchored frame that is wider than all columns in the text area straddles columns and the sidehead area, if it exists and if the Cropped setting is turned off.

In a single-column text frame, an overly wide anchored frame simply extends into the margins of the page if the Cropped setting is not selected, or else it is clipped at the borders of the text frame if Cropped is selected.

Importing Graphics into Anchored Frames

It is easy to import graphics and drawings into anchored frames. Simply place the character cursor where you want the imported art to be anchored, select File ➤ Import ➤ File, and select the file to be imported. The file appears in a ready-made anchored frame. Then use the mouse, the Tools window, and the Graphics menu commands to size and position the frame and the art within it. It's that simple.

If you want to create the anchored frame yourself first, place the character cursor where you want the anchor to appear, select Special ➤ Anchored Frame, use the Anchored Frame dialog box to position and size the frame, and click on the New Frame button. Then, with the frame selected, choose File ➤ Import ➤ File and select the file to be imported.

TIP You can also paste graphics or drawings from the Clipboard into selected anchored frames. You can even drag art from elsewhere on the page into an anchored frame.

Importing Text into Anchored Frames

Anchored frames can also be used to hold the single-character text lines used in drop caps and text imported by reference. The procedure for placing a text line into an anchored frame was given earlier in the chapter.

To import text by reference into an anchored frame, just place the character cursor where you want the frame's anchor to appear, choose File ➤ Import ➤ File, and select the file. You will see a series of dialog boxes that allow you to specify a filter for the file (if needed) and format the imported text. (These dialog boxes are discussed in detail in Chapters 6 and 11.) Then use the Anchored Frame dialog box and the mouse to size and position the frame as needed.

Chapter 9

Characters and Character Formats

Though the term "format properties" usually applies to paragraphs, in a FrameMaker document you can change the format properties of individual characters as well. You can make characters bold, for example, change the font to Palatino, or the type size to 24 point.

When you change a character's format properties, they are retained by the characters that have them, even when the paragraph formats are changed later. In other words, if you make text bold, italic, and 12 points in size, the text stays that way even if you change the paragraph format of the paragraph it is in.

In this chapter you will learn about character format properties and how to select a character format. You will learn how to apply formats to selected text characters in a document, and save the format for repeated use as a "character tag."

 NOTE This chapter uses the sample document you created in Chapter 1, TRUDY.DOC, the memo from Trudy Dutweiler to Sam Spade. If you'd like to follow along with the exercises here and you don't have TRUDY.DOC, you might go to Chapter 1 and create the document.

All about Fonts

Typeset characters are grouped by their characteristics into sets called fonts. A *font* is a group of characters (letters and symbols) that look the same and have the same size. Fonts have names like Helvetica, Courier, and Times. Font sizes are usually measured in points. One point is approximately equal to $\frac{1}{72}$ of an inch.

 NOTE Which fonts are available for use with FrameMaker depends on which fonts are installed on your system.

The following are all different fonts:

12-point Times

12-point Times Bold

12-point Times Italic

14-point Times

12-point Courier New

18-point Courier New

Font characteristics include:

- Symbol, or character, sets
- Family
- Size
- Angle
- Weight
- Variation
- Style

Each of these characteristics (except symbol set) can be selected to suit your needs and applied to one character or several. All are explained below.

Symbol, or Character, Sets

A *symbol,* or *character, set* is a set of all the characters (letters and symbols) that can be printed in a given font. Roman-8 is an example of a symbol set. Below is a sample of Roman-8 characters printed in 12-point Courier type (not all symbols available in the set are shown):

```
! " # $ ' ( ) * + , - . /
0 1 2 3 4 5 6 7 8 9 : ; < = >
A B C D E F G H I J K L M N O P Q R S T U V W X Y Z
a b c d e f g h i j k l m n o p q r s t u v w x y z
```

The same symbol set printed in 12-point Helvetica type looks like this:

```
! " # $ ' ( ) * + , - . /
0 1 2 3 4 5 6 7 8 9 : ; < = >
A B C D E F G H I J K L M N O P Q R S T U V W X Y Z
a b c d e f g h i j k l m n o p q r s t u v w x y z
```

Font Families

A *font family,* also called a *typeface,* refers to the actual design of the characters themselves. Even when they are the same size, style, and weight, Helvetica characters have a different design than Times characters. The first line below is 12-point Helvetica type; the second is 12-point Times:

a b c d e f g
a b c d e f g

Font families can be classed in two groups, serif and sans serif:

▶ *Serif* font families have little lines at the ends of the character strokes. The lines lead the eye from one character to another, like so:

m

▶ *Sans serifs* font families lack these lines:

m

Another characteristic of font families is *spacing.* Spacing refers to the horizontal space occupied by characters on a line. There are two kinds of character spacing: *fixed,* or *monospaced,* characters and *proportionally spaced* characters. Below, the first line is monospaced, and the second is in a proportionally spaced font:

```
In a monospaced font, all letters are the same length.
```
In a proportionally spaced font, letters have different lengths.

Part 3

Formatting and Editing Text

Fixed, or *monospaced, characters* are designed to occupy the same amount of space, no matter what the character is. In a monospaced font such as Courier, the character *i* takes up the same amount of space as the character *m*.

Monospaced character spacing is sometimes measured in *pitch,* or characters per inch. The 12-point Courier font is a 10-pitch font. Each character measures $\frac{1}{10}$ of an inch in width, and there are ten characters per inch, hence the term *10-pitch*. As the pitch becomes larger, the characters become smaller.

Proportionally spaced characters occupy different amounts of space on a line, depending on the width of each character. In a proportionally spaced font like Helvetica, the character *i* takes less space on a line than the character *m* does, because in a proportionally spaced font, an *m* is always wider than an *i*.

Notice that the characters of a monospaced font are designed differently than those of a proportionally spaced font. No font can be both monospaced and proportionally spaced.

Type Size

The *size* of the characters in a font is measured in points. One point is approximately $\frac{1}{72}$ of an inch. A 14-point font is taller than a 10-point font. Figure 9.1 shows examples of different type sizes. Notice that each character of a 12-point font is not 12 points high. For example, a *t* is taller than an *n*. But a 12-point *t* will be taller than a 10-point *t*, and so on.

This is 10-point type.

This is 12-point type.

This is 16-point type.

This is 24-point type.

Figure 9.1 Comparing type sizes

Font Angle

The *angle* of a font refers to its slant. *Italicized* characters are slanted to the right, whereas regular characters, sometimes called *roman* characters, are upright—straight up and down.

Other character angles are available for some fonts. Sometimes you see terms like "oblique" and "slanted" to describe a font's angle. Often these are just another way to say "italic."

Weight

The *weight* of a font is the thickness of the characters. The two most common weights are regular and **bold.** Regular characters are just that—regular in weight. This is the weight the font designer started with when designing the font. **Bold characters** are thicker, of course. They look the same as the regular characters, but the lines used to draw them are thicker by a definite amount.

Other character weights are available, depending on the font. Terms such as book, demi, demibold, light, extra light, heavy, medium, semibold, thin, ultra, ultrabold, and ultralight are sometimes used to describe the weight of type.

Variation

Several *variations* are available. Depending on the font, variations can include condensed, copy, engraved, extended, gray, headline, inline, narrow, ornaments, tall, titling, and ultra condensed, to name just a few. A look through any font book or catalog will show you what these fancy fonts look like.

Style

Several other character properties can be adjusted in FrameMaker, and they fit in the catchall category called "style." (All of these "style" properties are specified using the Character Designer, a window for specifying character properties. The Character Designer is discussed in the next section of this chapter.)

Spread and Kerning   *Spread* is extra space between characters. If two characters seem jammed together, you can remedy that by increasing the spread. Spread is expressed as a percentage of an em dash in the font you're working with. An *em dash* is a long dash and is defined as the length of an *m* in the font you're using. Specifying a spread of, say, 20 percent means adding space between each character equal to 20 percent of an em dash in whatever font you're using.

Pair kerning refers to adjusting the spacing between pairs of characters to improve the appearance of the text. For example, with pair kerning turned on, the space between the characters *A* and *W* is narrower so the letters look better together. Which character pairs are kerned and how much kerning is applied depends upon the font being used.

Underline, Double Underline, Numeric Underline, Overline   An underline is a line under a character. The offset (distance below the characters) and thickness of the underline depend on the weight and size of the character's font. The line under bold text, for example, is thicker than the line under regular text.

A *double underline* is two lines under a character.

A *numeric underline* places a line under a character with the same offset and thickness regardless of the weight and size of the character's font. A numeric underline under bold text is the same as a line under regular text. Numeric underlines are also placed further below characters than regular underlines, a quality that makes them more attractive for many people. Numeric underlines were used originally to draw lines under columns of added or subtracted numbers.

An *overline* is a line over a character.

Strikethrough and Change Bar   A Strikethrough is a line through the middle of a character. Lawyers often use strikethrough text to show where language has been removed from legal contracts.

A *change bar* is another way to show where changes have been made to text. A change bar is a vertical bar in the margin next to a line of characters that have been changed. With change bars, a reader can quickly see what's different in a new version of a manuscript.

Super- and Subscript   *Superscript* makes a character smaller and moves it above the text *baseline,* the line that characters rest on. The size of a superscripted character and the offset (distance) above the baseline are specified as a percentage of the font size. Superscripts are frequently used in math equations, like so:

$$E = mc^2$$

Subscript is the opposite of superscript. Subscripted characters are smaller and rest on a line below the baseline. The size of a subscript character and the offset below the baseline are specified as a percentage of the font. Subscripts look like this:

$$water = H_2O$$

NOTE   When FrameMaker spell-checks a document, it does not check super-scripted and subscripted characters.

Small Caps   Everybody knows what lowercase and uppercase letters are (they have these names because, back in the days of moveable type printing presses, lowercase characters were kept in the "lower case," or tray, and uppercase letters were kept in the "upper case"). However, there is also such a thing as *small caps*. A small cap has the form of a capital letter but is the size of a lowercase letter. Small caps are used in certain publishing conventions. For example, they are often used in dates and in times, like so:

8:00 A.M.
500 B.C.

MAC NOTE   The Mac version of FrameMaker allows two other character properties, *outline* and *shadow*. Outline produces a character with a white center and black border. Shadow produces a character with a white center and black border, with the appearance of a shadow falling away from the character.

Color

Though color is not a traditional character property, in FrameMaker you can change the color of a character or group of characters. The available predefined colors include black, white, red, green, blue, cyan, magenta, and yellow. You can also define your own colors, as Chapter 15 explains.

The Character Designer Window

You can change the format of characters by using the Character Designer window. To open the Character Designer window in a document, select Format ➤ Characters ➤ Designer. You can also use the keyboard shortcuts Ctrl+D (⌘+D on a Mac) and *Esc o c d*. The Character Designer window will appear, as shown in Figure 9.2.

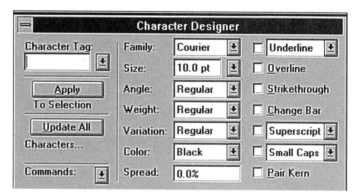

Figure 9.2   *The Character Designer window. On the right are the character properties. On the left are the character controls.*

On the right side of the vertical line dividing the window are the character properties. You should recognize them from reading the first part of this chapter. On the left side are the character controls. Let's take a close look at each of these sections, starting with the properties.

Defining the Properties of Characters

The following character properties can be specified using the Character Designer:

Property	Description
Family	This pull-down menu lists the font families available for use with FrameMaker. Which fonts are available for use depends upon which fonts are loaded on your system.
Size	Here you can enter a custom point size in the range of 2 to 400 points, or pull down a list and select a common point size.
Angle	This pull-down list shows the angles available for the selected font family. "Italic" is the most common angle. If you see "oblique" listed, it probably means "italic."
Weight	This pull-down list shows the weights available for the selected font family. Bold is the most common weight available.
Variation	This pull-down list shows the variations available for the selected font family.
Color	This pull-down list shows the available colors (black, white, red, green, blue, cyan, magenta, and yellow, plus any custom colors you have defined).

Part
3

Formatting and
Editing Text

Property	Description
Spread	This text field allows you to specify extra space between characters. Remember that spread is expressed as a percentage of an em dash in the selected font's size. Positive values increase the space. Negative values decrease the space. The default value is 0 percent.
Overline, Strikethrough, Outline (Shadow), Change Bar, Pair Kern	These are check boxes. An X in the box indicates that the property is turned on for the characters selected (highlighted) in the current document. An empty (white) box means that the property is turned off. A gray square means the property is left "as is." (See below for more information on the "As Is" setting.)
Underline, Super-script, Small Caps	These are check boxes and pull-down lists. You can choose Underline, Double Underline, or Numeric Underline from the Underline menu.
Superscript	The Superscript menu allows you to select Superscript or Subscript.
Small Caps	The Small Caps list allows to choose Small Caps, Uppercase, or Lowercase.

TIP Changing capitalization from the Uppercase/Lowercase/Small Caps list changes the appearance of the characters only as they are displayed here, on the current page. It does not change the characters as the program stores them. This can be a benefit. For example, if you want a heading to appear as uppercase, but you also want a cross-reference to the text of the heading to be in mixed upper- and lowercase, you can type the heading as you want it to appear in the cross-reference (mixed case), and then apply the Uppercase property to it using the Character Designer. This way, the text will be uppercase in the heading and mixed case in the cross-reference.

The look of superscripts, subscripts, small caps, and change bars can be modified for the current document. See "Changing the Look of Superscript, Subscript, and Small Cap Characters" below.

The As Is Property Setting

If you look through the various Character Designer pull-down lists, you sometimes see gray squares. Gray squares indicate the As Is setting. As Is means, in essence, "Leave the property settings for the characters highlighted in the document alone. Let them be whatever they are."

The As Is setting allows you to modify some properties with the Character Designer, but let others be what they are. You will see how the As Is setting is used in the sections below.

Changing the Look of Superscript, Subscript, and Small Cap Characters

The definitions of some character properties can be changed. You can change how superscript characters, subscript characters, small caps, and change bars appear in your documents.

To modify the look of superscripts, subscripts, and small caps:

1. Select Format ➤ Document ➤ Text Options. The Text Options dialog box appears, as in Figure 9.3.

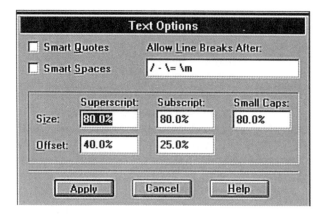

Figure 9.3   The Text Options dialog box

2. Specify the Size and Offset values you prefer.

Size is a percentage of the selected font's size, so choosing 50%, for example, would make the characters half the size they are now.

Offset specifies how far above or below the baseline superscripts or subscripts should be moved. Again, offset is expressed as a percentage of the font's size. A superscript offset of 40% moves superscript characters *up* 40 percent of the font's size, whatever that is. Likewise, a subscript offset of 25% moves subscript characters *down* 25 percent of the font's size.

3. When you are finished, click the Apply button.

NOTE   Besides the size and offset values for superscript, subscript, and small caps, the Text Options dialog box also controls smart quotes, smart spaces, and where line breaks fall after special characters. These features are discussed in Chapter 11.

To modify the look of change bars:

1. Select Format ➤ Document ➤ Change Bar Properties to open the Change Bar Properties dialog box shown in Figure 9.4.

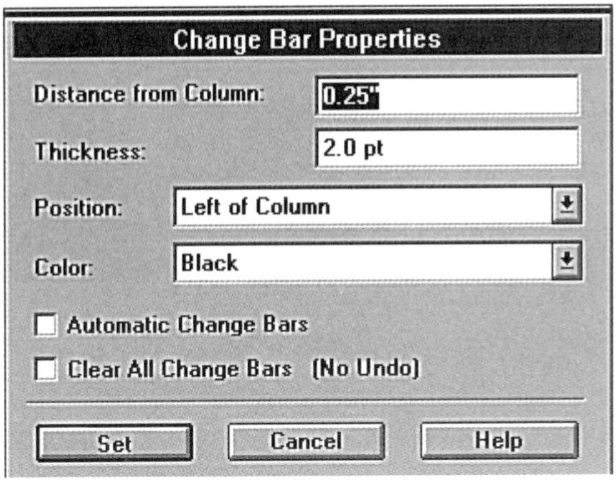

Change Bar Properties

Distance from Column: `0.25"`

Thickness: `2.0 pt`

Position: `Left of Column`

Color: `Black`

☐ Automatic Change Bars

☐ Clear All Change Bars [No Undo]

[Set] [Cancel] [Help]

Figure 9.4 *The Change Bar Properties dialog box*

2. In the Distance from Column text box, set the distance of the change bar from the text column.

3. Specify a thickness for the change bars.

4. Use the Position pull-down menu to select where the change bar will appear. The choices are Left of Column (the default), Right of Column, Side Closer To Page Edge, or Side Farther From Page Edge. The last two settings are used primarily with double-sided documents—documents with both left- and right-hand pages.

5. Specify a color for change bars with the Color pull-down menu.

6. Use the Automatic Change Bars check box to place a change bar automatically next to any line of text to which changes are made.

NOTE You can place change bars manually as well, with the Character Designer.   •

7. When you are finished, click the Set button. The changes will be applied and the dialog box will close.

Character Designer Controls

The control area on the left side of the Character Designer window (see Figure 9.2) has options for defining character tags.

A *character tag* is a predefined set of font characteristics that you can apply to text. Character tags are extremely handy. For example, one of the character tags that every FrameMaker document comes with is called Emphasis. With this character tag, you can italicize any group of characters. You can also create your own character tags, give them names, and apply them to text as you wish.

You create and apply character tags with the Character Tag field on the left side of the Character designer window. This field is both a text box (you can type in it) and a pull-down menu that lists all the character tags that have been defined for the current document.

The Character Tag field is used to:

- Show the definition of a character tag
- Change existing character tags
- Create new character tags
- Apply character tags to selected characters in a document
- Show what tags have been applied to selected characters in a document

NOTE   The list of character tags in a document is called the "Character Catalog." The Character Catalog is discussed later in this chapter.

To see the definition of a character tag, select the tag from the Character Tag pull-down list. The settings in the Character Designer window will show all the properties that have been defined for the character tag.

NOTE   Notice all the As Is settings in the definition of Emphasis, including the gray check boxes. When you are defining your own character tags, using As Is will be important.

Applying a Character Tag to Text

To apply a character tag to selected text, select the text and display the Character Designer window by choosing Format ➤ Characters ➤ Designer. Choose the tag you wish to apply from the Character Tag pull-down list. Then click the Apply or Update All button. Each of these options is discussed below.

NOTE If the Character Tag field is blank, it means that no character tag has been defined for the characters selected in the document, or multiple tags are present. Blank is the field's usual condition.

The Apply button applies all the properties in the Character Designer window, including the character tag if one has been selected, to the characters that are highlighted in the document. Clicking the Apply button does *not* change the definition of a character tag in the Character Catalog.

To apply a set of properties but not a tag to selected text:

1. Bring up the Character Designer.

2. Select the text you wish to modify.

   Note that the Character Designer displays the properties of the text you selected, including the setting As Is if some of the properties are different from one character to another.

3. Change the properties to the ones you want. To turn on underlining, for example, click the Underline check box.

4. Leave all of the other properties the same.

5. Click the Apply button. The selected characters now have the new properties you specified.

   The As Is setting keeps you from changing properties you don't want to change. For example, if some of the selected text is all caps, the All Caps check box will be gray. Applying As Is to All Caps allows each character you selected to retain whatever its All Caps setting was originally.

To apply a character tag to selected text:

1. Bring up the Character Designer.

2. Select the text you wish to modify.

3. Select the tag you wish to apply from the Character Tag pull-down list.

4. Click the Apply button. The selected characters are given the properties of the character tag you applied, including any As Is settings in the tag's definition.

The Update All Button: Other Ways to Modify Characters and Tags

The Update All button in the Character Designer window (see Figure 9.2) is actually several buttons in one.

Update All Characters   If the text below the button says "Characters," clicking the Update All button updates all characters, and when you click Update All, you see the Global Update Options dialog box shown in Figure 9.5.

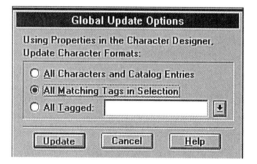

Figure 9.5   The Global Update Options dialog box

From here, you can choose one of three options:

▶ **All Character and Catalog Entries**—Allows you to change *all* characters in the document, *all* character tag definitions, and *all* default font definitions for *all* paragraph tags to match the properties in the Character Designer. That's a lot of changes!

▶ **All Matching Tags in Selection**—Allows you to make changes for only those tags in the text selected in the document, if characters of more than one tag were selected.

▶ **All Tagged**—Allows you to make changes for only one tag—the one selected from the pull-down menu.

The changes are applied both to characters in the document that are tagged with a particular tag and to the tag definitions themselves. (In the first option, changes are applied to *everything*.)

In all three cases, changes are applied both to specified tags (definitions) and to the characters that have those tags applied to them. They are different in this way: the first option changes everything, all characters and all tags; the second option changes tags (and characters with those tags) that are included in selected text; the third option changes a specific, named tag that you get to select from a list.

Update All Formats Tagged   On the other hand, if the text below the Update All button says "Formats Tagged *XXX*," (where *XXX* is some character tag), then Update All makes changes to only one tag (the one called *XXX*) and to the characters that have that tag.

Update All becomes Update All Characters when you select (highlight) text in the document that either has no tag or contains characters with more than one tag.

Update All becomes Update All Formats Tagged when you select text in the document that contains characters all having the same format tag, or when you select a character tag from the Character Tag pull-down list.

You can even use Update All to rename a tag:

1. Select the tag to rename in the Character Tag pull-down list. Update All now says "Update All Formats Tagged," followed by the tag you just selected.

2. Type a new name for the tag in the Character Tag field.

3. Select Update All. You will see a box asking you to confirm the renaming.

4. Press OK in the confirmation box.

Applying Character Tags with the Character Catalog

The Character Catalog window is a palette, which, you may remember, is a window that stays open. The Character Catalog shows a list of the defined character tags for the document. Your Character Catalog will look something like the one in Figure 9.6.

Figure 9.6   **The Character Catalog palette**

You can open the Character Catalog either by:

▶ Selecting Format ➤ Characters ➤ Catalog.

▶ Clicking on the Character Catalog button at the upper-right side of the document window.

▶ Entering the keyboard shortcut *Esc o c c*.

You can use the Character Catalog to apply character tags to text and to delete tags from the catalog.

To apply a character tag, select some text in the document and then select a tag with the mouse.

To delete a format from the catalog, select a tag name in the palette and click the Delete button at the bottom of the catalog. The Delete Format from Catalog dialog box appears. Click the Delete button, and then click Done.

Copying Character Formats from One Document to Another

When you have a particularly nice set of character formats, you might want to copy them from one document to another. To do so:

1. Open the document you want to copy the formats from.

2. Open the new document if it is not already open.

3. With the new document active, select File ➤ Import ➤ Formats. The Import Formats dialog box appears, as in Figure 9.7.

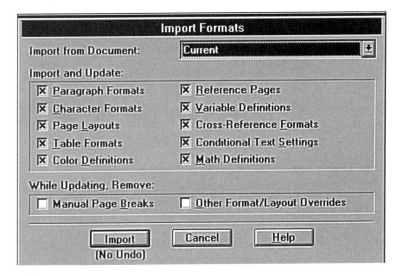

Figure 9.7   *The Import Formats dialog box*

4. Select the document you want to copy the formats from by using the Import from Document pull-down list. (With only two documents open, there are only two selections.)

5. In the Import and Update section of the window, click the Character Formats check box. You can also select other choices, if they are available.

6. Click the Import button. The Character Catalog in the new document will be updated with all the formats from the original document.

NOTE   You can also use a document with a good set of formats as a template. See Chapter 6 for more information on turning documents into templates.

Working with Character Formats and Character Tags

There are three groups of character operations—those done to characters, those done to tags, and those done to groups of tags and characters in combination. This section describes how to work with character formats and character tags.

Applying and Copying Character Formats and Tags

To see the character formatting of a group of characters, bring up the Character Designer by choosing Format ➤ Characters ➤ Designer, and then select the tag from the Character Tag pull-down list. The Character Designer property settings will appear in the tag's definition.

To apply a set of character properties (not a tag) to a group of characters:

1. Bring up the Character Designer.

2. Select the text you wish to modify.

3. Change the properties in the Character Designer to the ones you want.

4. Leave all of the other properties the same.

5. Click the Apply button.

To apply a character tag to a group of characters:

1. Bring up either the Character Designer or Character Catalog. To bring up the Character Designer, choose Format ➤ Characters ➤ Designer. To bring up the Character Catalog, select Format ➤ Characters ➤ Catalog or click on the Character Catalog button at the upper-right side of the document window.

2. Select the text you wish to modify.

3. If you're using the Character Designer, select a tag from the Character Tag pull-down list and click the Apply button. If you're using the Character Catalog, click on the name of the tag to be applied.

To copy a character's format directly from one character to another:

1. Select the characters that have the format you want to copy.

2. Select Edit ➤ Copy Special ➤ Character Format. The character format is saved in the Clipboard.

3. Select the characters you want to apply the format to.

4. Select Edit ➤ Paste. The characters now have the new character format.

Creating, Changing, and Copying Character Tags

Before you perform an operation on a character tag, you may want to see its definition to find out exactly what you're working with. To do this, select Format ➤ Characters ➤ Designer to see the Character Designer window, and then select the tag from the Character Tag pull-down list. The Character Designer property settings will show the tag's definition.

Creating a New Character Tag

To create a new character tag:

1. Bring up the Character Designer by selecting Format ➤ Characters ➤ Designer.

2. Select Set Window to As Is in the Commands list.

3. Set the property settings you want the new tag to have.

4. Select New Format from the Commands list. The New Format dialog box appears, as in Figure 9.8.

5. Type a name for the new tag into the Tag field.

6. Select Store In Catalog.

7. Select Apply to Selection if you want the new tag to also be applied to the currently selected text.

8. Click on the Create button.

Part 3

Formatting and Editing Text

Figure 9.8 **The New Format dialog box**

You can also bring up the New Format dialog box by setting the character properties of the new format, typing a new tag name into the Character Tag field of the Character Designer, and clicking the Apply button.

TIP If characters in a document already have format properties that you would like to save in the Character Catalog, you can select those characters, name the format in the Character Designer, and save that format in the Character Catalog. Be careful, though. You will be saving *all* of the character's properties in the tag, including such properties as type size.

Changing the Properties of a Character Tag

To modify an existing character tag:

1. Bring up the Character Designer by selecting Format ➤ Characters ➤ Designer.

2. Select a tag in the Character Tag pull-down list. The Update All button now says "Update All Formats Tagged" followed by the tag you just selected.

3. Make changes to the tag's properties as you wish.

4. Click the Update All button.

At this point you may see a message that says "Some characters use format overrides." Select either Retain Overrides or Remove Overrides. *Format overrides* are changes to the formatting of a tagged group of characters that override part of definition contained in the tag. If you tagged a word as Italic, and it was then made bold with the QuickAccess Bar, the bolding would be a format override.

Renaming a Character Tag

To rename a character tag:

1. Bring up the Character Designer by selecting Format ➤ Characters ➤ Designer.

2. Select a tag in the Character Tag pull-down list. The Update All button now says "Update All Formats Tagged" followed by the tag you just selected.

3. Type a new name for the tag in the Character Tag field.

4. Click the Update All button. You will see a box asking you to confirm the renaming.

5. Press OK in the confirmation box.

Deleting a Character Tag

To delete a character tag from the catalog:

1. Bring up the Character Catalog by selecting Format ➤ Characters ➤ Designer.

2. Select Delete. The Delete Formats from Catalog dialog box appears, as in Figure 9.9.

3. Click on one of the tags in the scroll list.

4. Click on the Delete button.

5. Repeat this procedure until you have deleted all the character formats that you want deleted.

6. When you are finished deleting, select Done. (If you decide not to delete any of the tags after all, select Cancel.)

Figure 9.9   *The Delete Formats from Catalog dialog box*

You can also bring up the Delete Format from Catalog dialog box by selecting Delete Format from the Commands list of the Character Designer.

NOTE When a character format has been deleted from the Character Catalog, the characters in the document retain the character tag and format properties.

Working with Groups of Tags and Characters

You can perform a number of operations on groups of tags in combination with selected text. Operations on groups of tags and characters are done with the Global Update Options dialog box. There are two ways to open this dialog box:

▶ Click the Update All button in the Character Designer when no tag appears in the Character Tag field.

▶ Select Global Update Options from the Commands pull-down menu at the bottom-left of the Character Designer.

The combinations are many, but let's take a look at two common examples of working with groups of tags.

Suppose you have a letter in which all of the text and character tags specify the Times font family. You want to change everything to Garamond but leave all of the other settings alone. To do this:

1. Bring up the Character Designer by selecting Format ➤ Characters ➤ Designer.

2. Select Set Window to As Is from the Commands list.

3. Select Garamond from the Family pull-down list.

4. Click the Update All button. The Global Update Options dialog box appears.

5. Turn on All Characters and Catalog Entries and click the Update button.

    For a final example, let's say you have a document in which there are many character tags and you want two of them now to include underlines. You could change each tag, one at a time, or you could do the following:

1. Bring up the document and then bring up the Character Designer by selecting Format ➤ Characters ➤ Designer.

2. Select a group of text characters that includes both the tags you want to change. The text character must include *only* the two tags and no others.

3. Select Underline and turn on the Underline check box.

4. Click the Update All button. The Global Update Options dialog box appears.

5. Turn on All Matching Tags in Selection and click Update.

> **TIP** If characters already have the properties of a format you want to save in the Character Catalog, you can select those characters, rename the format in the Character Designer, and save that format in the Character Catalog.

Practice with Character Formats

Now let's practice creating character formats with the sample document TRUDY.DOC that you created in Chapter 1. First, we'll create two new character formats called "bold" and "italic." We'll save them to the Character Catalog.

Part 3

Formatting and Editing Text

1. Open a fresh copy of TRUDY.DOC.

2. Place the insertion point in the document by clicking once somewhere in the middle of the text.

3. Open the Character Designer window by selecting Format ➤ Character ➤ Designer.

4. Create the new character format "bold," as follows:

   • Select the command Set Window to As Is.

   • Use the Weight pull-down menu to select bold.

   • In the Character Tag text box, type **bold**.

   • Click on the Apply button (or select New Format from the Commands list). The New Format window appears. The new Character Format Tag, bold, should appear in the Tag text box.

   • Make sure Store in Catalog is checked.

   • Make sure Apply to Selection is turned off and is not checked.

   • Click on Create. The New Format window closes and the new format, bold, is added to the Character Catalog.

5. Create the new character format "italic" as follows:

   • Select the command Set Window to As Is.

   • Use the Angle pull-down menu to select Italic.

   • In the Character Tag text box, type **italic**.

   • Click on Apply (or select New Format from the Commands list). The New Format window appears. The Character Format Tag, "italic," appears in the Tag text box.

   • Make sure Store in Catalog is turned checked.

   • Make sure Apply to Selection is turned off and is not checked.

   • Click on the Create button. The New Format window closes and the new format, "italic," is added to the Character Catalog.

6. Open the Character Catalog by clicking the Character Format Catalog button. The character formats you just created, "bold" and "italic," should appear in the scroll list, as in Figure 9.10, alongside FrameMaker default formats.

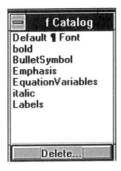

Figure 9.10 *New Formats, "bold" and "italic," in the Character Catalog*

Now let's put the new formats to use:

1. Select the text *past due* in the first sentence of the memo.

2. In the Character Catalog, click on the "bold" tag. The selected text takes on the new character format. That's all there is to it!

    Take a moment to look at the page, but don't read it. Notice how your eye is drawn to the emphasized text, *past due*.

    Now, let's emphasize the text even further:

1. Select the text *get out* in the second sentence of the memo.

2. In the Character Catalog, click on the "bold" tag. The selected text takes on the new character format.

    Again, look at the document. Your eye is drawn to the emphasized text. You can scan the document quickly and get the key points, *past due* and *get out*.

    Adding more emphasis to this short document would dilute the effect. For example, if you emphasized the text *last month's rent, past due, don't pay,* and *get out* with bold text, the key points of the memo would be lost. The reader's eye would jump around too much and not really know what to concentrate on. The impact of emphasis would be lost.

    Before trying the italic character format, we need to restore the text to a less drastic condition:

1. Select the *entire paragraph* that begins "Sam, I hate to ask again" by triple-clicking anywhere in the paragraph.

2. In the Character Catalog, click on the first tag in the list, Default ¶ Font. (Recall that Default Font means "whatever font is already defined for that paragraph.")

3. Select the text *past due*.

4. In the Character Catalog, click on "bold."

Now let's try another character format, "italic."

1. Select the complimentary close, *Sorry,* by double-clicking on the word.

2. Type the French phrase **Au revoir**. (Trudy has apparently decided to get fancy.)

3. Now select *Au revoir*.

4. In the Character Catalog, click on the "italic" tag **italic**. The text takes on the new character format.

Once you set up character formats and save them to the catalog, applying the format to text is a simple, fast operation.

Create some character formats on your own. Try combining different properties, such as italic and bold, in a format (bold-italic) and applying them to text to see the results. Play around with the character properties. You can define character tags for any purpose, from numeric underlines to font family changes (to Symbol or Dingbat font, for example).

When you are finished, close TRUDY.DOC without saving your changes.

Chapter 10

Paragraphs and Paragraph Formats

Just as you can change the properties of characters in FrameMaker, as you saw in the last chapter, you can change the properties of paragraphs. That is the subject of this chapter. You can change basic properties such as the margins, indentation, and line spacing. You can change font properties, such as type style and size, and more advanced properties as well, including hyphenation, autonumbering, and the way graphics frames are used. And when you've found a set of paragraph properties you like, you can save them, name them, and store them in a Paragraph Catalog that is also part of the document.

In this chapter you will learn:

How to use the paragraph properties in FrameMaker

How to use the Paragraph Designer and the Paragraph Catalog to manage and apply paragraph tags

How to create special paragraphs, such as hanging indents

How to use paragraph autonumbering

What Is a FrameMaker Paragraph?

In FrameMaker, a *paragraph* is a group of characters that ends in a carriage-return. You enter a carriage-return by pressing the Enter or Return key. When you do that, a paragraph symbol (¶) appears on the screen . (To see the ¶ symbol and other nonprinting text symbols, select View ➤ Text Symbols.) The paragraph symbol is part of the paragraph. If you type new characters into a paragraph, they adopt the default character formatting of the paragraph unless they have had character formatting specially applied to them.

Just as characters have qualities that, taken as a group, define character formatting, paragraphs have qualities that, taken as a group, define paragraph formatting. In FrameMaker, these paragraph qualities are divided into sets, called "properties." You'll learn about paragraph properties throughout this chapter. Each property is controlled using the Paragraph Designer.

Paragraph Tags and the Paragraph Catalog

A *paragraph tag* is a named set of paragraph format properties. Paragraph tags are stored with other named properties in a catalog, called the *Paragraph Catalog*. For example, suppose you want all of the body text in a document to look the same. To do this easily, you could create a tag (called "Body" or "Body Text"), store it in the catalog, and apply it to all body text paragraphs. If you wanted all headings to look the same, you could do the same with all headings, or have one tag for first-level headings, another for second-level headings, and so on.

Paragraph tags help give a consistent and polished look to a document. At the same time, they allow you to change that look easily, since all you have to do is modify a tag and apply the changes to all paragraphs that have that tag to make all the changes at once. If you wanted all of your body text paragraphs to be in 10-point Times instead of 12-point Helvetica, for example, you could simply change the Body Text tag.

You can also apply paragraph properties directly to paragraphs, without using tags. You can change the line spacing from single- to double-spacing, for example, using either the Paragraph Designer or the QuickAccess Bar. You can even apply properties to tagged paragraphs, overriding the properties of the tag. FrameMaker is quite flexible in this regard. Still, using tags is preferred if you manage many similar documents.

NOTE   If you apply properties to a paragraph and those properties override the properties of the tag that has already been applied, the paragraph no longer has the same properties. To indicate this, an asterisk appears before the name of the tag in both the Formatting Bar and the status area at the bottom of the document window.

The Paragraph Designer window, which you will see shortly, is the premier place for managing paragraphs. It is where you assign properties to individual paragraphs, as well as create tags and place them in the Paragraph Catalog.

NOTE   You can assign tags to paragraphs with both the Paragraph Catalog and the Paragraph Designer. The Paragraph Catalog is explained later in this chapter.

Changing the Look of Paragraphs with the Paragraph Designer Window

You can assign Paragraph format properties to a paragraph or a group of paragraphs with the Paragraph Designer window. You can also create paragraph tags of your own and assign them to paragraphs.

To open the Paragraph Designer window from a document, select Format ➤ Paragraphs ➤ Designer. The Paragraph Designer window appears, as in Figure 10.1. Notice that the Paragraph Designer is another palette. It stays open while you work, and you can move back and forth from it to other windows without closing it first.

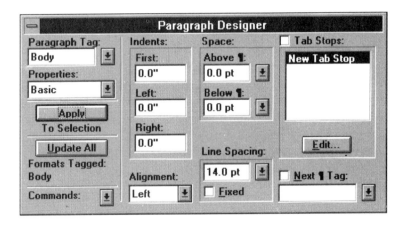

Figure 10.1   *The Paragraph Designer window*

On the right side of the Paragraph Designer are groups of paragraph properties. On the left are the controls—the group of buttons and pull-down menus that allow you to apply properties to paragraphs, create and modify paragraph tags, and so on. Notice that in the controls section is a pull-down list labeled Properties. This list controls which set (or "page") of properties is displayed in the right side of the window. When the Paragraph Designer window first opens, the Basic set of properties is displayed. To see another set of properties, make another selection from the pull-down list.

In this section, we'll examine the pages of properties one at a time, starting with the Basic properties. Then we'll look at the controls.

NOTE   All paragraph properties in the Paragraph Designer can be set to the As Is setting. Chapter 9 explains how important this setting is. See that chapter for more information on what As Is means and how it is used.

The Basic Paragraph Properties for Generic Paragraphs

When you select Basic from the Properties pull-down list, you see the Basic set of properties shown in Figure 10.2. These are the properties you will probably deal with most often.

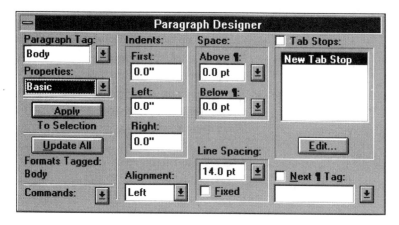

Figure 10.2   *Basic Properties page of the Paragraph Designer*

Indents   Under the heading Indents, there is a setting for First, Left, and Right. These settings determine the margins for the first line of the paragraph, the left edge of the paragraph, and the right edge of the paragraph, respectively. All are measured from the edge of the text frame, not the edge of the page.

A first indent of $\frac{1}{2}''$ (or 36 points) greater than the setting for the right indent produces a standard first-line paragraph indentation. The indentation of the current paragraph is also shown on the top ruler, if it is visible. Chapter 2 contains more information on the relationship between the ruler and the Paragraph Designer.

Alignment From the Alignment pull-down list, you can specify Left, Center, or Right alignment, and a paragraph style known as Justified:

▶ **Left**—The left edge of the paragraph is smooth ("justified"), but the right side is uneven ("ragged"). This kind of paragraph is sometimes called "left-justified," or "ragged-right."

▶ **Right**—The right edge of the paragraph is smooth, but the left side is uneven. This kind of paragraph is sometimes called "right-justified" or "ragged-left."

▶ **Center**—Each line is centered between the margins specified by the Indents setting, and as a result, both edges are uneven.

▶ **Justified**—Extra space is added to each line so that both edges are smooth, or justified. Note, however, that because of this extra space, justified paragraphs are frequently hard to read. As a result, justified paragraphs should probably be avoided unless the style of the document requires it.

Alignment settings for individual paragraphs can also be set by using the Formatting Bar.

Space Above and Below the Paragraph Under the Space heading are the following settings:

▶ **Above**—Determines how much white space is added above the first line of the paragraph. The measurement is presented in points. You can use the pull-down list or enter your own values.

▶ **Below**—Determines how much white space is added below the last line of the paragraph. This measurement is also presented in points. You can use the pull-down list or enter your own values.

The Space Above and Space Below settings are useful for controlling inter-paragraph spacing. Normally, you create inter-paragraph spacing in a document with one of these settings, but not both. Note that the distance between two adjacent paragraphs is not the sum of the Space Below the upper paragraph and the Space Above the lower one. Instead, the larger of the two numbers is used. In other words, if one paragraph has 12 points below it and the following paragraph has 10 points above it, FrameMaker places 12 points of white space between the paragraphs, not 22 points.

Part 3

Formatting and Editing Text

Negative numbers are allowed. You can make paragraphs appear next to each other by giving a negative Space Below to the first paragraph and a negative Space Above to the next one. Of course, you would also have to manipulate the margins to make them sit next to each other, instead of one on top of the other.

Line Spacing With the Line Spacing box, you can specify how much white space, also called leading, appears between paragraphs. The term comes from the typesetting days when thin strips of lead were used to create space between lines of type.

The pull-down menu allows you to specify Single, 1.5, or Double spacing, and you can also enter your own values in the Line Spacing box, including decimal fractions. FrameMaker calculates these values relative to the size of the default font (see the next set of properties for more on paragraph fonts). Single spacing for a 10-point font is 12 points between lines (10 points for the letters with 2 points of leading). Another way to say this is that the baselines of the lines in a paragraph are 12 points apart.

Fixed The Fixed check box determines whether line spacing is fixed, regardless of the size of the tallest character on a line, or whether extra space is allowed for lines that have large characters on them. (A gray square here, or in any check box, means the property is left As Is.) The Fixed setting should be turned off for paragraphs with anchored frames in them.

TIP **You can also set the line spacing for individual paragraphs with the Formatting Bar.**

Tab Stops In the Tab Stops box is a list of tabs settings for the paragraph. By clicking the Tab Stops check box, you can turn the list of tabs on or off as a group.

Edit Click the Edit button to change the tab stop settings in the list. When you click Edit, you see the Edit Tab Stop dialog box shown in Figure 10.3. Here you can enter a new tab position in the New Position text box, select an alignment from the Alignment radio buttons, and select a pattern of leader characters from the Leader radio buttons.

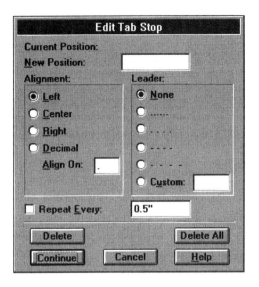

Figure 10.3   **The Edit Tab Stop dialog box**

The Alignment text box lets you specify the alignment character for decimal tabs. In the United States, text is usually aligned on the period, but in other countries it's frequently aligned on the comma.

The Custom radio button in the Leader area of the Edit Tab stop dialog box is for entering a character or group of characters to use as your own tab leader.

You can make the current tab repeat at regular intervals with the Repeat Every setting. This means that if you place a tab stop at 1″ and repeat it every .5″, you will get a tab stop at 1″, 1.5″, 2″, 2.5″, and so on until the right margin is reached. These tabs are added to the other tab stops in the paragraph.

Press Continue to confirm your changes to the current tab stop and return to the Paragraph Designer. Press the Delete button to delete the current tab or Delete All to delete all tabs from the paragraph.

TIP   **You can also bring up the Edit Tab Stops dialog box by double-clicking on a tab setting in the Tab Stops list. Tabs may also be added and deleted from a paragraph by using the ruler and the Formatting Bar.**

Next Paragraph Tag Meanwhile, back in the southeast corner of Paragraph Designer (see Figure 10.2), there is the Next ¶ Tag setting. It operates only in a narrowly defined situation. If the character cursor is at the end of the current paragraph and you press Enter, the new paragraph that is created will have the tag listed in this box. Otherwise, Next ¶ Tag has no effect.

Click the pull-down list to see all the paragraph tags in the Paragraph Catalog. The check box allows you to turn this feature on or off.

Usually the Next ¶ Tag box contains the tag name of the current paragraph, since body paragraphs usually follow body paragraphs, and so on. This setting is put there as a convenience in special situations. Use it with heading paragraphs, for example, when you may want a paragraph tagged Body Text to be created if you press Enter after typing a paragraph tagged Heading 1.

Default Font Paragraph Properties for Text

When you select Default Font from the Properties pull-down list, you see the Paragraph Designer window shown in Figure 10.4. These are the same properties that are presented in the Character Designer. The only difference is that, instead of applying the properties to selected characters, they are applied to selected paragraphs.

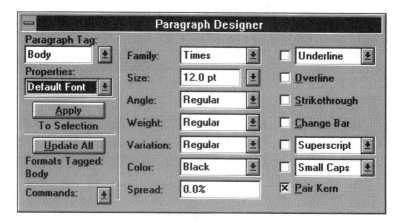

Figure 10.4   Default Font Properties page of the Paragraph Designer

When you use the Paragraph Designer to create a paragraph tag, the Default Font properties are applied to all characters in paragraphs with that tag. See "All about Fonts" in Chapter 9 to see how these properties work.

Pagination Paragraph Properties for How Paragraphs Fit on the Page

When you select Pagination from the Properties pull-down list, you see the Paragraph Designer window shown in Figure 10.5. Following is a rundown of the properties on this page of the Paragraph Designer.

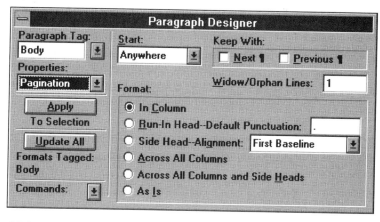

Figure 10.5   *The Pagination Properties page of the Paragraph Designer*

Part 3

Formatting and Editing Text

Start   Start is a pull-down list that allows you to say where the paragraph starts—Anywhere, Top of Column, Top of Page, Top of Left Page, or Top of Right Page. Use this setting to create paragraph tags for paragraphs that must start at the top of a page, or a certain type of page—for example, all first-level headings. You can also apply this setting directly to any paragraph to create a page break above that paragraph.

Keep With Next/Previous   The Keep With Next and Keep With Previous check boxes keep the end of the current paragraph on the same page as the start of the next, or keep the start of the current paragraph on the same page as the end of the previous one. Choose these settings when you don't want FrameMaker to place a page break between two paragraphs.

Widow/Orphan Lines *Widows* and *orphans* are lines at the start or end of a paragraph that appear on the previous or following page and are separated from the rest of the paragraph. This setting specifies the minimum number of lines that can be widowed or orphaned in this way.

Format The Format area offers a number of radio buttons that tell where the paragraph is placed. This is where run-in headings, side headings, and paragraph straddles are controlled:

▶ **In Column**—Makes the paragraph appear within the borders of the column. (This is the setting used for most paragraphs.)

▶ **Run-In Head**—Allows the current paragraph to occupy the same line as the start of the next paragraph, in effect running the paragraph into the next paragraph. It produces an effect called *run-in headings*. The heading "Format" at the beginning of this section is a run-in heading. Enter the kind of punctuation you want to use between the run-in heading and the paragraph into the Default Punctuation text box. The initial setting is a period and a space, but you can change this to anything you wish.

▶ **Side Head**—Places the paragraph in the sidehead area instead of the text column. To create a sidehead area, use the Room for Sideheads setting in the Column Layout dialog box or Customize Text Frame dialog box. (Select Format ▶ Page Layout ▶ Column Layout or Format ▶ Customize Layout ▶ Customize Text Frame, respectively.) From the Alignment pull-down list, you can choose to line the sidehead paragraph up with the First Baseline, Top Edge, or Last Baseline of the paragraph in the text column area that the sidehead will appear next to. Sideheads are discussed in Chapter 8.

▶ **Across All Columns**—Creates a paragraph that straddles all columns but not the sidehead area. "Straddles" are discussed in Chapter 8.

▶ **Across All Columns and Side Heads**—Creates a paragraph that straddles all columns and the sidehead area.

Numbering Paragraph Properties for Numbered and Bulleted Lists

When you select Numbering Properties from the Properties pull-down list, the Numbering Properties page of the Paragraph Designer appears, as in Figure 10.6. This is where you create "autonumbered" paragraphs.

"Autonumbering" is just a fancy word for automatically placing numbers and other characters at the start or the end of a paragraph.

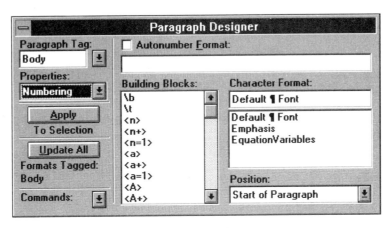

Figure 10.6 Numbering Properties Page of the Paragraph Designer

FrameMaker automatically increments and maintains numbers placed with the autonumber feature. If your document has figure captions numbered "Figure 1", "Figure 2," for example, FrameMaker can maintain those numbers for you. If you added a figure or deleted one, all the rest would be renumbered, or "autonumbered."

Autonumbers can be used for figures, tables, steps in a procedure, outline heading numbers (like I, A, i, a) and paragraph numbering (like 1.3.12). You can also use autonumbers to create bulleted paragraphs and paragraphs that start with words like "NOTE."

Autonumber Format The Autonumber Format text line allows you to define a format for the numbers that are generated automatically. A format is made up of several elements:

▶ An optional series label

▶ A group of counters

▶ Special symbols for the bullet and tab characters

▶ Text and punctuation of your own

A *series label* is a single character followed by a colon—for example, *A:*, *a:*, and so on. A series label allows you to have a separate numbering sequence for figures (perhaps labeled series F:), another for tables (labeled series T:, if you like), and still more for other elements. The series label is case-sensitive, so more than 52 (2 × 26) are available. Numbering series are maintained separately for each flow in the document.

Counters are listed in the Building Blocks scroll list. FrameMaker replaces the counters with the appropriate number or letter in the sequence. All counters are delimited by angle braces (< >) and indicate both the format of the number to be displayed and its value. For example, using the counter <*n*+> says to increment the value of the counter by 1 and display the result in Arabic format (1, 2, 3, and so on). Other formats include:

▶ Lower- and uppercase Roman numerals, which use the counters <*r*> and <*R*> and are displayed i, ii, iii, or I, II, III.

▶ Lower- and uppercase letters, which use counters like <*a*> and <*A*> and are displayed as a, b, c, and A, B, C.

A single format or series can have multiple counters, allowing for complex autonumbers like *1.3.12.*

Text can include any characters you wish. Tabs are inserted with \t. A common format for figure captions, for example, is "F:Figure <n+>.\t", which specifies the series label (F:), prints the word "Figure" followed by a space, increments the counter by one and displays that value in Arabic format, prints a period, and then inserts a tab character—all before the text of the caption itself. The result can look like "Figure 12. Market Share by Manufacturer," with everything before the word *Market* controlled by the autonumber setting.

You can use a special building block to insert a round bullet character. There are also ways to use other bullet characters. (For more on special paragraph formats, including bulleted paragraphs and examples of autonumbered paragraphs, see "Sample Paragraph Formats" later in this chapter.)

Character Format   The Character Format scroll list on the Numbering Properties page of the Paragraph Designer (see Figure 10.6) allows you to apply any format in the Character Catalog to the autonumber. If you have an Italics format, for example, the entire autonumber, including text, can be italicized.

Position   The Position drop-down list has two options, Start of Paragraph and End of Paragraph, for placing the autonumber. End-of-paragraph autonumbers might include paragraph numbers in square brackets.

Advanced Paragraph Properties

When you select Advanced Paragraph from the Properties pull-down list, the Advanced group of properties shown in Figure 10.7 appears. From here you can control:

▶ Automatic hyphenation and language selection

▶ Word spacing for justified paragraphs

▶ Reference frames used to place graphics above or below the paragraph

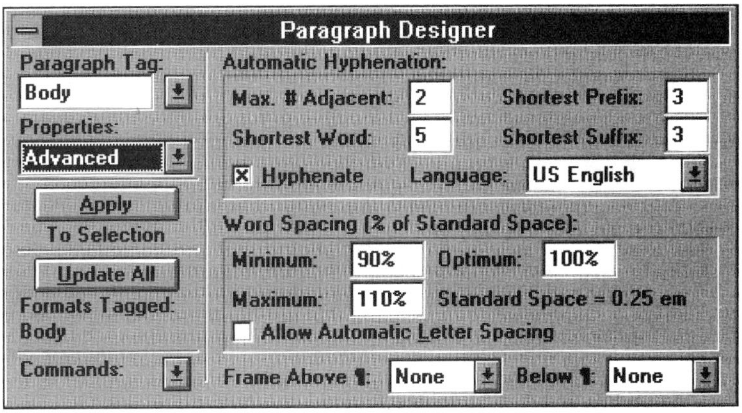

Figure 10.7   *The Advanced Properties page of the Paragraph Designer*

Automatic Hyphenation and Language Selection   With the Automatic Hyphenation properties, you can control how a paragraph is hyphenated. The choices are self-explanatory.

The Language pull-down list is for selecting the language to be used when the paragraph is spell-checked. Your choices include any language whose dictionary is installed, and None. None keeps a paragraph from being spell-checked and is a useful selection if the paragraph contains computer code, for example.

Word Spacing   The Word Spacing area allows you to control how much space (horizontal padding) can be added to lines when FrameMaker is trying to create justified paragraphs. The Minimum, Maximum, and Optimum determine how wide or narrow the spaces between characters can become. The Allow Automatic Letter Spacing check box tells FrameMaker whether to try to add space between the letters of a word.

A Standard Space is defined by FrameMaker as a fraction of an em space, a space that is as wide as the point size of the font. Thus, in a 12-point font, an em space would be 12 points wide, and a Standard Space of .25 em would be 3 points wide.

Frame Above/Below   Frame Above ¶ and Frame Below ¶ place a "reference frame" immediately above and/or below the paragraph. A *reference frame* is a named graphics frame on any reference page of a document. Reference frames can contain anything, though a graphic element, often a ruling line, is their usual content. Click the pull-down list to see what reference frames are available.

NOTE   To see reference frames, select View ➤ Reference Pages.

Keep in mind that the whole reference frame is placed above or below the paragraph, not just the graphic it contains. If the frame is large, the space above the paragraph occupied by the graphic will also be large.

Table Cell Paragraph Properties for Defining the Look of Tables

When you select Table Cell Properties from the Properties pull-down list, the Table Cell properties page of the Paragraph Designer appears. It is shown in Figure 10.8. This is where you determine how text paragraphs are placed vertically within table cells and where you decide what the minimum margins of the paragraph are relative to the four "walls" of the cell. Their use is self-explanatory.

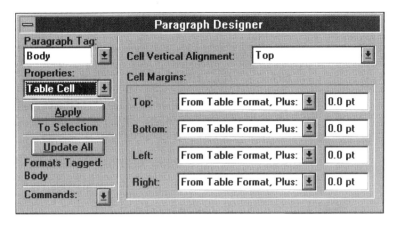

Figure 10.8   Table Cell Properties page of the Paragraph Designer

With these properties, you can get a number of different "looks" for the placement of text in table cells. If you use the Table Designer for these settings, you must specify margins for all cells in the table at once, not for individual cells. For more on tables, see Chapter 14.

Paragraph Designer Controls

The control area of the Paragraph Designer has the Paragraph Tag pull-down list, a Properties pull-down list, the Apply button, the Update All button, and a Commands pull-down menu. What do these controls do? Read on.

The Paragraph Tag field is both a text box (you can type in it) and a pull-down menu. It lists all the paragraph tags that have been defined for the current document. Use the Paragraph Tag field to:

▶ See the definition of a paragraph tag

▶ Modify existing paragraph tags

▶ Create new paragraph tags

▶ Apply paragraph tags to selected paragraphs in a document

▶ Show what tags have been applied to selected paragraphs in a document

Part
3

Formatting and
Editing Text

To see the definition of a paragraph tag, select the tag from the Paragraph Tag pull-down list. The Paragraph Designer property settings show the tag's definition. If the Paragraph Tag field is blank, it means that no tag has been defined for the paragraphs selected in the document, or multiple tags are present. Blank is the field's usual condition.

To create new paragraph tags or modify existing ones, see Chapter 9, "Characters and Character Formats." The procedures for working with paragraph formats and tags are nearly identical to those for working with character formats and tags.

NOTE As you have seen, the properties pull-down list allows you to "page" through groups of paragraph properties, from Basic to Table Cell. You can also page though these properties by pressing PgUp and PgDn.

The Apply button applies the properties on the current page of the Paragraph Designer, whatever they are, to a paragraph or paragraphs you've selected. If a paragraph tag is listed in the Paragraph Tag field, it is also applied. Clicking the Apply button does not update the definition of a tag in the Paragraph Catalog.

NOTE If you apply properties to a paragraph and the properties override the properties of the tag that has already been applied, the paragraph no longer matches the tag's definition. FrameMaker indicates this by placing an asterisk before the name of the tag in both the Formatting Bar and the status area at the bottom of the document window.

Changing the Properties of Paragraphs with the Update All Button

The Update All button is actually several buttons in one. You use it to update, or change, the properties of paragraphs and paragraph tags. If the text below the button says "Paragraphs" (meaning "Update All Paragraphs"), then clicking the Update All button brings up the Global Update Options dialog box shown in Figure 10.9.

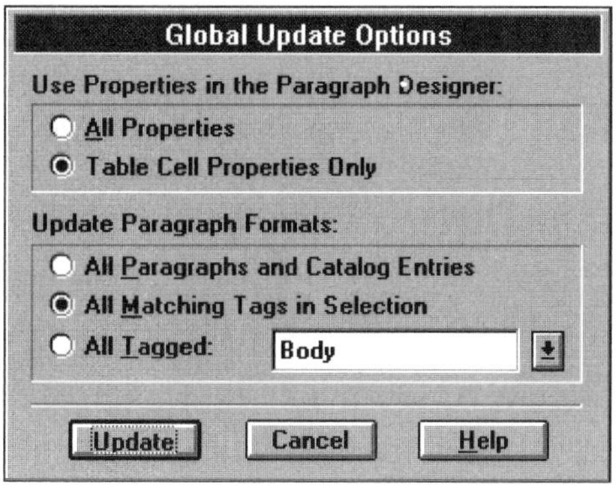

Figure 10.9   *Global Update Options dialog box*

From here, you can choose several options. First, decide which properties to update, all properties in the Paragraph Designer (i.e., all pages of properties) or the properties of the current page only.

Then decide where to apply those properties:

▶ **All Paragraphs and Catalog Entries**—Changes all paragraphs in the document and all paragraph tag definitions—a big change!

▶ **All Matching Tags in Selection**—Changes only those tags in the paragraphs selected in the document, if paragraphs of more than one tag were selected.

▶ **All Tagged**—Allows you to make changes for only one tag—the one selected from the pull-down list.

The changes are applied both to paragraphs of a particular tag and to the tags themselves. (In the first option, the changes are applied to *everything*.)

If the text below the Update All button says "Formats Tagged" (meaning "Update All Formats Tagged XXX", where XXX is a paragraph tag), then Update All makes changes to only one tag (the one called XXX) and to the paragraphs that have that tag.

You see "Update All Paragraphs" when the selected text either has no tag or contains paragraphs with more than one tag. You see "Update All Formats Tagged" when the selected text contains paragraphs that all have the same format tag, or when you select a paragraph tag from the Paragraph Tag pull-down list.

NOTE   You can also bring up the Global Update Options window with the Global Update Options command in the Commands pull-down menu. The only thing to remember about using this command is this: If a paragraph tag appears in the Paragraph Tag field, the update will retag selected paragraphs in the document. If no tag name appears in the Paragraph Tag field, then only properties of selected paragraphs will be updated.

Creating a New Paragraph Format

To create a new paragraph format using the current properties settings of the Paragraph Designer:

1. Click the New Format command on the Commands pull-down menu in the lower-left corner of the Paragraph Designer. The New Format dialog box appears:

2. Enter the name of the new tag.

3. Choose whether to store the tag in the catalog and/or apply it to the selected text.

4. Click Create.

 NOTE   The New Format dialog box also appears when you type a new tag name in the Paragraph Tag field and click the Apply button.

Deleting a Format

To delete a format from the Paragraph Catalog:

1. Click the Delete Formats command on the Commands pull-down menu. You'll see the Delete Formats from Catalog dialog box:

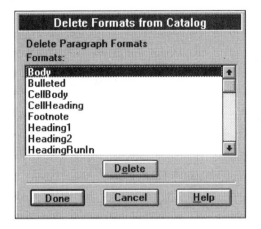

2. Select a format and click Delete.

3. When you are done deleting formats, select Done.

   Note that formats are not deleted for good until you press Done, so if you suddenly think you've deleted too much, press Cancel and your paragraph catalog will not be touched.

Two Final Commands

The Commands pull-down menu offers two final commands:

▶ **Set Window to As Is**—Sets all properties in the current page of the Paragraph Designer to As Is.

▶ **Reset Window from Selection**—Resets the current Paragraph Designer properties to the properties of the paragraph(s) selected in the document.

Applying Tags to Text with the Paragraph Catalog

The Paragraph Catalog window, shown in Figure 10.10 shows the list of defined paragraph tags for the document. You can use the Paragraph Catalog to apply paragraph tags to text and to delete tags from the catalog.

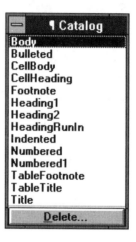

Figure 10.10 **Paragraph Catalog palette**

To open the Paragraph Catalog, do one of the following:

▶ Select Format ➤ Paragraphs ➤ Catalog

 ▶ Click on the Paragraph Catalog button at the upper-right side of the document window

▶ Enter the keyboard shortcut *Esc o p c*

To apply a paragraph tag, just select some text in the document and then select one of the tags by clicking it with the mouse.

To delete a format from the catalog, select Delete at the bottom of the catalog, highlight the format in the Delete Format from Catalog dialog box, click Delete, and click Done. (Again, no deletion is actually performed until you press the Done button.)

Copying Paragraph Formats from One Document to Another

Just as you can copy character formats from one document to another, you can copy paragraph formats also. To do so:

1. Open both the document you want to copy the formats from and the new document.

2. With the new document active, select File ➤ Import ➤ Formats. The Import Formats dialog box appears, as in Figure 10.11.

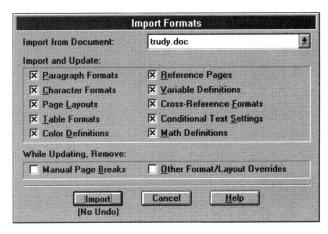

Figure 10.11   **The Import Formats dialog box**

3. Select the document you want to copy the formats from by using the Import from Document pull-down list. (With only two documents open, there are only two selections.)

4. In the Import and Update section of the window, click the Paragraph Formats check box. You can also select any or all of the other choices.

5. Click the Import button. The Paragraph Catalog in the new document is updated and is given all the formats from the original document.

TIP   You can also use a document with a good set of paragraph formats as a template. See Chapter 7 for more on turning documents into templates.

Sample Paragraph Formats

FrameMaker's Paragraph Designer is a powerful tool. You can use it to create almost any paragraph type you see in print. This section shows you how to set up some of the more common types of paragraphs.

Paragraphs for Manuscripts and Personal Letters

Basic body text paragraphs for manuscripts (for example, college papers) and personal letters should have one-inch margins (controlled by the placement of the text frame, not by the Indent settings of the Paragraph Designer), half-inch, first-line indents (controlled by the First Indent setting), and no extra space above or below the paragraph.

These paragraphs can be either single- or double-spaced, though double-spacing is more correct (for manuscripts) and generally easier to read. I recommend double-spacing even for personal letters and other informal writing.

The font should probably be one of the more basic fonts—Courier, Helvetica, Times, Palatino, and so on. Using fancy fonts in manuscripts makes the work seem somehow less professional.

Paragraphs for Business Memos and Business Letters

Business paragraphs are generally single-spaced and have no first-line indent. Paragraph separation is used instead of first-line indentation to show where new paragraphs begin. Use Space Above or Space Below to add this inter-paragraph space. A good choice is an amount equal to the default font size or an amount equal to the line spacing.

Be sure to use a plainer font for a more professional appearance. If you want to be more decorative than Times or Helvetica, try Palatino, Garamond, or something similar.

There are a number of good business templates in FrameMaker 5. View them by selecting File ➤ New, pressing the Explore Standard Templates button, and selecting Show Sample. Feel free to modify them as you wish and resave them in your own templates directory.

Indented Paragraphs

Indented paragraphs should always be created by changing the Left Indent value, not by entering a tab. Though you could create each indented paragraph as needed by manipulating the left indent arrow on the ruler, it's best to create a separate paragraph tag, perhaps called Indent or Body Text-Indent (depending on where in the Paragraph Catalog you want the indented paragraph format to be alphabetized).

Indented paragraphs are used for unnumbered lists under body text paragraphs, and also as continuation paragraphs following paragraphs with hanging indents, like bulleted paragraphs and numbered paragraphs.

Paragraphs with Hanging Indents

Paragraphs with hanging indents have a first line that is farther left than the rest of the lines in the paragraph. If they contain nothing but text, they look like this:

Ego ille quem nosti apros et quidem pulcherrimos cepi. "Ipse?" inquis. Mirum est ut animus agitatione motuque corporis excitetut. Ad retia sedebam: erat in proximo non venabulum aut lancea, sed stilus et pugilares: meditabar aliquid enotabamque, ut, si manus vacuas, plenas tamen ceras reportarem. Mirum est ut animus agitatione motuque corporis excitetut.

Hanging indents have two uses that you've seen fairly often. One is to create bulleted paragraphs:

- Ego ille quem nosti apros et quidem pulcherrimos cepi. "Ipse?" inquis. Mirum est ut animus agitatione motuque corporis excitetut. Ad retia sedebam: erat in proximo non venabulum aut lancea, sed stilus et pugilares: meditabar aliquid enotabamque, ut, si manus vacuas, plenas tamen ceras reportarem. Mirum est ut animus agitatione motuque corporis excitetut.

The other is to create numbered paragraphs:

1. Ego ille quem nosti apros et quidem pulcherrimos cepi. "Ipse?" inquis. Mirum est ut animus agitatione motuque corporis excitetut. Ad retia sedebam: erat in proximo non venabulum aut lancea, sed stilus et pugilares: meditabar aliquid enotabamque, ut, si manus vacuas, plenas tamen ceras reportarem. Mirum est ut animus agitatione motuque corporis excitetut.

In both cases, a tab is used to start the first word after the bullet or the number in the same place as the start of the other lines of the paragraph.

To create a hanging indent paragraph with a $\frac{1}{4}''$ indentation, set the First Indent to 0, the Left Indent to .25", and the Right Indent to 0 (or whatever you wish). Then set a tab stop at .25". Figure 10.12 shows the Paragraph Designer settings for such a paragraph.

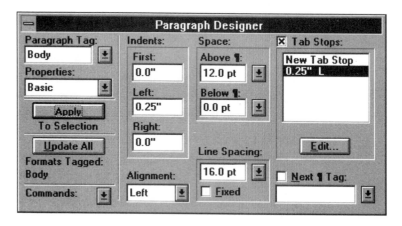

Figure 10.12 **Paragraph Designer settings for a hanging indent paragraph**

Simple Bulleted Paragraphs

To turn a hanging indent paragraph into a simple bulleted paragraph, go to the Numbering Properties page of the Paragraph Designer, click on the Autonumber Format check box, and use the building blocks \b\t in the Autonumber text area. This will add a standard round bullet character and a tab, which will line up the first line text with the rest of the text. Figure 10.13 shows these Paragraph Designer settings.

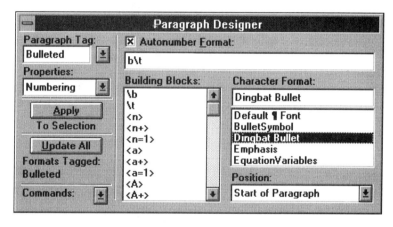

Figure 10.13 **Paragraph Designer settings for a bulleted paragraph**

Simple Numbered Paragraphs

To turn a hanging indent paragraph into a simple numbered paragraph, go to the Numbering Properties page of the Paragraph Designer, click on the Autonumber Format check box, and enter <n+>.\t in the Autonumber text area. This adds a number that increments from 0 (so the first number in the series is 1), followed by a period and a tab character. If your document has only one series of numbered paragraphs, this works just fine. Figure 10.14 shows these Paragraph Designer settings.

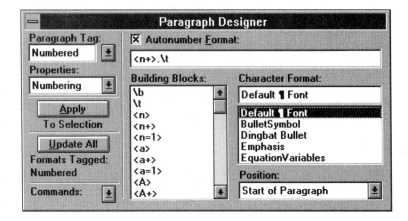

Figure 10.14   Paragraph Designer settings for a numbered paragraph

If you have more than one series of numbered paragraphs (such as a procedure that uses numbered steps), just use the building block $<n=1>$ instead of $<n+>$ to reset the counter to 1 at the start of each new group of steps.

An easy way to implement this numbering method with paragraph tags is to create two tags, one that uses the counter $<n=1>$ and another that uses the counter $<n+>$. Name the first one something like "Numbered Para 1" and the second "Numbered Para 2+." Use the first for each step 1 of any numbered list, and the other for steps 2 and beyond. (Frame-Maker templates contain paragraph tags named Numbered1 and Numbered for just these purposes.)

"Note" Paragraphs

You can also use autonumbering and hanging indent paragraphs to create paragraphs that start with words like "Note" and "Warning." To do this, type the text you wish to appear at the start of the paragraphs, followed by a tab (\t) in the Autonumber Format box. Then set the tab in the Basic Properties page of the Paragraph Designer to leave room for the "autonumber" text. Finally, save the format in the Paragraph Catalog under a descriptive name like "Note Para" (boring, but effective). The result looks like Figure 10.15.

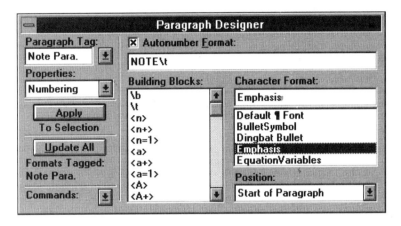

Figure 10.15   *Note Paragraph using autonumbering for the initial text*

Complex Numbered Paragraphs

The autonumbering feature is capable of many effects, the most complex of which involve the clever use of the autonumber building blocks—$<n>$, $<n+>$, and so forth. So let's look at these building blocks a little more closely.

All building blocks in FrameMaker must be delimited by angle braces ($<\ >$). The autonumber building blocks are called counters, because they act as placeholders, and are assigned a numerical value that can be incremented and reset. Example counters include $<n>$ and $<a=1>$.

The letters n, R, r, A, and a in the autonumber counters indicate the display style of the number, as shown in Table 10.1. The counters can take the forms shown in Table 10.2.

Part 3

Formatting and Editing Text

Style	Description	Example
n	Arabic	1, 2, 3
r	Lowercase Roman	i, ii, iii
R	Uppercase Roman	I, II, III
a	Lowercase letters	a, b, c
A	Uppercase letters	A, B, C

Table 10.1 **Autonumber Counters**

Counter Form	What It Means
<n>	Keeps the value of the counter the same
<n+>	Increments the value of the counter by 1
<n=0>	Assigns a value of 0 to the counter (other values may also be assigned)

Table 10.2 **Forms Counters Can Take**

There can be more than one counter in a single autonumber format specification. The specification <n>.<n>.<n+> would produce a number that looked like this: 2.3.13. In multi-counter numbers:

▶ Each counter has a value that is maintained separately.

▶ Each counter is incremented based on the corresponding counter (based on position) in the previous autonumbered paragraph of the same autonumber series of the same text flow.

NOTE For examples of using multiple autonumbering counters to create headings like 1.2.4 and outline-style paragraph numbering, see the outline templates supplied with FrameMaker.

Run-In Paragraphs

FrameMaker allows you to use the Paragraph Designer to create a paragraph style called a run-in heading. Run-in headings are printed on the same line as the start of the following paragraph, like this:

Ridebis. Ego ille quem nosti apros et quidem pulcherrimos cepi. "Ipse?" inquis. Mirum est ut animus agitatione motuque corporis excitetut. Ad retia sedebam: erat in proximo non venabulum aut lancea, sed stilus et pugilares: meditabar aliquid enotabamque, ut, si manus vacuas, plenas tamen ceras reportarem. Mirum est ut animus agitatione motuque corporis excitetut.

As you can see, run-in heads can be used to give a professional appearance to many kinds of documents.

Run-in headings are created with the Pagination page of the Paragraph Designer. Simply click on the Run-In Head radio button and type something in the Default Punctuation box. New FrameMaker documents have a period and a space in this box, but many people prefer the period with two or three spaces. Feel free to experiment. You could use em dashes, for example.

The text of run-in headings doesn't have to be the same size as the text of the following paragraph, but it generally is. Run-in heads are often boldface or italicized. Use the Space Above box to create extra separation between paragraphs that start with run-in heads and the paragraph above.

NOTE Many other kinds of heading styles are available in FrameMaker—for example, sideheads, headings that straddle columns, and so on. These heading styles are discussed in Chapter 12.

Part 3

Formatting and Editing Text

Chapter 11
Editing Text

This chapter covers FrameMaker's powerful text-editing capabilities. It includes information on:

Selecting, copying, and editing text and formats

Undoing changes

Changing the capitalization of words

Dealing with smart quotes, smart spaces, and line breaks

Finding and replacing text and formats

Formatting imported text

Making sure words are spelled correctly

Using FrameMaker's Thesaurus

Selecting, Copying, Pasting, and Deleting Text and Formats

This section summarizes the various ways to select, copy, paste, and delete text in FrameMaker. It also offers information on copying and pasting character and paragraph formats.

 NOTE Many of these actions are explained more fully in Chapter 4. This section simply provides a shorthand reference to most of the ways of selecting text in FrameMaker.

Selecting Text

Selecting *text* means highlighting a group of characters with the character cursor. Highlighted text changes to "reverse video"—in other words, it appears white against a black background. Selected text can be operated on—it can be cut, copied, changed to boldface, and so on.

There are three ways to select text: with the mouse cursor, with the keyboard (especially the cursor keys), and with Escape key combinations. You can also *extend* an existing selection with the mouse, cursor keys, or Escape key combinations. To extend a selection means to select yet more text after a selection has already been made.

You can select letters, words, lines, sentences, and paragraphs. You can even select an entire text flow. Table 11.1 summarizes techniques for selecting text.

MAC AND UNIX NOTE   In Table 11.1, Mac users should substitute the 2 key for the Ctrl key, and note that K1=End, K2=↓↓, etc. UNIX users should ignore the third column.

To Select	Mouse	Keyboard	Escape Key
Letters	Click and drag	Click, then press Shift+any cursor key	*Esc h c*, then *Esc h c*
Word	Double-click	Click, then press Ctrl+Shift+→	*Esc h w*
A group of words	Double-click and drag *or* Shift+Click	Click, then press Ctrl+Shift+→, then Ctrl+Shift+→	*Esc h w*, then *Esc h w*
Line		Shift+End	*Esc h l*
Group of lines		Shift+End, then Shift+End	*Esc h l*, then *Esc h l*
Sentence		Click, then press Ctrl+Shift+End	*Esc h s*
Group of sentences		Click, then Ctrl+Shift+End, then Ctrl+Shift+End	*Esc h s*, then *Esc h s*
Paragraph	Triple-click	Click, then press Ctrl+Shift+↓	*Esc h p*
Group of paragraphs	Triple-click and drag *or* Shift+Click	Click, then press Ctrl+Shift+↓, then Ctrl+Shift+↓	*Esc h p*, then *Esc h p*
Entire flow		Ctrl+A	*Esc e a*

Table 11.1   **Techniques for Selecting Text**

Selecting "Backward" Text

A number of the combinations in Table 11.1 can be modified to extend selections backward rather than forward:

▶ To select backward with the cursor keys, substitute ← for →, ↑ for ↓, and Home for End.

▶ To select backward with Escape key combinations, capitalize the letters of the combination (for example, *Esc H S* instead of *Esc h s*).

Copying Text, Formats, and Other Elements

Copying means copying something from the document to the Clipboard. Copying changes the contents of the Clipboard. When you copy something, the old contents of the Clipboard are lost and are replaced with the new contents.

You can copy selected text, character and paragraph formats, sets of conditional text settings, and even the width of a table column. To do so, simply select the element to be copied, and then do one of the actions described in Table 11.2.

Pasting from the Clipboard

Pasting means copying the contents of the Clipboard into the document. Pasting does *not* change the contents of the Clipboard.

Data can be copied to the Clipboard from FrameMaker documents and, on the Windows platform, from other applications:

▶ Text, character and paragraph formats, conditional text settings, and table column widths can be copied from FrameMaker documents.

▶ *(Windows only.)* Text and graphics can be copied from other Windows applications. This feature is generally not supported on other platforms, though Publish and Subscribe offers similar capabilities (for graphics only) on the Mac. UNIX systems, depending on their configuration, maintain several Clipboards, and copying from other applications to FrameMaker may or may not be supported.

To paste the contents of the Clipboard into a document, place the insertion point in the document where you want the text or format inserted. (If you're pasting a character format, select the text to be

To Copy	Menu	Keyboard	Escape Key	Quick-Access Bar
Text	Edit ➤ Copy	Ctrl+C (Windows), 2 +C (Mac), Meta+W (UNIX)	*Esc e c*	Copy
Character format	Edit ➤ Copy Special ➤ Character Format	2 +Opt+X (Mac)	*Esc e y c*	
Paragraph format	Edit ➤ Copy Special ➤ Paragraph Format	2 +Opt+C (Mac)	*Esc e y p*	
Conditional text setting	Edit ➤ Copy Special ➤ Conditional Text Settings	2 +Opt+Z (Mac)	*Esc e y d*	
Table column width	Edit ➤ Copy Special ➤ Table Column Width		*Esc e y w*	

Table 11.2   **Copying Text, Formats, and Other Elements**

reformatted. If you're pasting a paragraph format, just place the cursor somewhere in the paragraph.)

To paste the contents of the Clipboard into a document, place the insertion point in the document where you want the text or format inserted. (If you're pasting a character format, select the text to be reformatted. If you're pasting a paragraph format, just place the cursor somewhere in the paragraph.) Then, do one of the following, do one of the following:

➤ Choose Edit ➤ Paste

➤ Press Ctrl+V (Windows), ℅+V (Mac), Ctrl+Y, Meta+Y (UNIX)

➤ Press *Esc e p*

➤ Choose Paste on the QuickAccess Bar

 WINDOWS NOTE   Keep in mind that even when you use Copy Special to copy a format, you don't use Paste Special to paste it.

Quick-Copying and Pasting Text

Windows and Mac users of FrameMaker can also "quick-copy" and paste text. *Quick-copying* does not place text on the Clipboard; it just copies it from one part of the document to another.

To quick-copy and paste text, do one of the following:

▶ **In Windows—**Place the cursor at the insertion (destination) point, press Alt and drag through the text.

▶ **On the Mac—**Place the cursor at the insertion (destination) point, press Ctrl and drag through the text.

▶ **In UNIX—**Select the text, then middle-click at the insertion (destination) point.

When you release the mouse button, the selected text is copied and pasted at the insertion point.

Deleting—Cutting and Clearing Text

You can delete both selected (highlighted) or unselected text. Selected text can be deleted in either of two ways:

▶ By *cutting*. Cutting puts a copy of the text on the Clipboard.

▶ By *clearing*. Clearing does not put a copy on the Clipboard. Cleared text is gone forever.

You can delete unselected text by pressing certain keys or key combinations. Unselected text cannot be cut to the Clipboard. When you delete it, the text is cleared and cannot be recovered.

 WARNING   Be careful when you delete text by clearing, since you can only recover it by using Undo, and you can't use the Undo command in certain situations. See "Undoing Mistakes" later in this chapter.

Cutting and Clearing Selected Text

To delete (cut or clear) selected text, first highlight the text to be deleted, and then do one of the following to clear selected text:

▶ Choose Edit ➤ Clear

▶ Press Backspace *or* Del (Windows); Delete (Mac); Ctrl+D, Backspace, Delete (UNIX)

▶ Press *Esc e b*

To cut selected text:

▶ Choose Edit ➤ Cut

▶ Press Ctrl+X (Windows); ⌘+X, Shift+Delete (Mac); Ctrl+W, Shift+Backspace, Shift+Delete (UNIX)

▶ Press *Esc e x*

▶ Choose Cut from the QuickAccess bar

Cutting and Clearing Unselected Text

To clear unselected text, you can use the keys and key combinations in Table 11.3.

Item	Windows	Mac	UNIX	Escape Key
Next character	Del	Ctrl+D, Del	Ctrl+D	
Previous character	Backspace, Ctrl+H	Delete, Ctrl+H	Backspace, Delete, Ctrl+H	
Forward to end of current word	Ctrl+Del			*Esc k f*
Backward to start of current word				*Esc k b*
Forward to start of next word		⌘+Opt+G	Meta+D	
Backward to end of previous word	Ctrl+Backspace		Meta+Delete, Meta+H	
Forward to end of current line	Ctrl+Shift+Del	Ctrl+K	Ctrl+K	

Table 11.3 **Quick Ways to Clear Unselected Text**

Item	Windows	Mac	UNIX	Escape Key
Backward to start of current line	Shift+Backspace	Ctrl+Backspace, Ctrl+U	Ctrl+Backspace, Ctrl+Delete, Ctrl+U	
Forward to end of current sentence		Ctrl+Opt+K	Meta+K	
Forward to start of next sentence				*Esc k s*
Backward to end of previous sentence				*Esc k a*

Table 11.3   **Quick Ways to Clear Unselected Text (continued)**

Undoing Mistakes

Most mistakes you make in FrameMaker can be reversed. There are three ways to *undo,* or reverse, an action:

▶ Choose Edit ➤ Undo.

▶ Press Ctrl+Z in Windows, ⌘+Z on the Mac, or Meta+Backspace in UNIX.

▶ Press *Esc e u.*

▶ Click the Undo button on the QuickAccess Bar.

Only the last change made to the document command (such as a cut or paste) can be undone. If an action cannot be undone, you will be warned before the action is executed or you will see a "No Undo" comment next to the command in the dialog box.

After an action is undone, the Edit ➤ Undo menu item changes to Redo, so you can redo an undo, so to speak. All keyboard commands (such as Ctrl+Z and *Esc e u*) also toggle between Undo and Redo.

TIP   You can still undo an undoable action! Simply save the document before performing the action. Then, if you don't like the result after the action is performed, select File ➤ Revert to Saved. The document will be returned to its last saved condition.

Changing the Capitalization of Text

You can change the capitalization of text in a number of ways. To change the capitalization of a word, simply place the cursor anywhere in the word and then execute one of the following commands. Likewise, to change the capitalization of a group of words, select all of them and then execute one of the following commands. In the list below, "Initial caps" means that the first letter in the word or words is capitalized and the others are lowercased.

▶ To change text to lowercase, choose Lowercase from the QuickAcess Bar or press Ctrl+Alt+l (Windows), Ctrl+Option+l (Mac), Meta+l (UNIX).

▶ To change to uppercase, Choose uppercase on the QuickAccess Bar or press Ctrl+Alt+u (Windows), Ctrl+Option+u (Mac), Meta+u (UNIX).

▶ To change to initial caps, choose Initial caps on the QuickAccess Bar or press Ctrl+Alt+c (Windows), Ctrl+Option+c (Mac), Meta+c (UNIX).

▶ To change to small caps, choose Format ➤ Style ➤ Small Caps.

You can also change the capitalization of selected text with the Capitalization dialog box shown here:

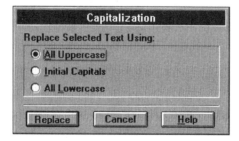

Bring up this box with the keyboard shortcut *Esc e C*. Click one of the radio buttons and your text will be changed to uppercase, lowercase, or initial capitals.

In addition, the Character Designer can be used to make capitalization uppercase and lowercase, or to define character tags that perform the same operations. (See Chapter 9 for more on the Character Designer and character tags.)

Customizing Smart Quotes, Smart Spaces, and Line Breaks

You can control how smart quotes, smart spaces, and line breaks appear or are used in your document. These options are set for each document and saved with the document.

▶ *Smart quotes* are quotation marks that curl instead of going straight up and down.

▶ *Smart spaces* simply means that only one empty space appears between words, never two or more empty spaces.

▶ *Line breaks,* of course, are the places where text is wrapped from one line to the next. You can control how words are broken and moved to the following lines in FrameMaker.

All these editing parameters are controlled from the Text Options window. To open the Text Options window, select Format ➤ Document ➤ Text Options. You'll see the dialog box in Figure 11.1.

Selecting Smart Quotes automatically makes the first quotation mark you type a curly open quote mark (") and the next quote a curly end quote mark (") in a paragraph. When Smart Quotes is not selected, you

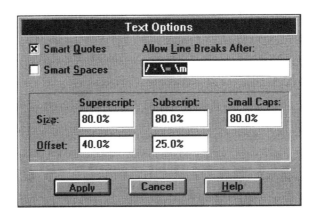

Figure 11.1   *The Text Options window*

get straight quotes (″) when you type quotation marks. Smart quotes operates on both single quotes (' ') and double quotes (" ").

Selecting Smart Spaces allows only one space character between words and sentences. If you type two spaces, you will still get only one.

The Allow Line Break After text box allows you to specify the characters after which FrameMaker will break a line and wrap it. The default characters shown in the box are: a slash (\), a hyphen (–), an en dash (represented as \=), and an em-dash (represented as \m). To add or delete characters, click in the dialog box and enter or delete characters. Note that you must use a backslash to represent characters that cannot be typed directly from the keyboard. For a list of those representations, see the next section of this chapter.

NOTE An explanation of the size and offset settings for the Superscript, Subscript, and Small Caps settings in the Text Options dialog box can be found in Chapter 9.

You can change these options at any time during an editing session. For example, if you want to insert two spaces between certain words, you could turn off Smart Spaces, type in the spaces, and then turn Smart Spaces back on for the rest of the editing session. When you save the document, the current text options settings will be saved along with it.

Finding and Replacing Text and Formats

You can find and replace text, formats, and other things in a Frame-Maker document. For example, you can search for special characters and use wildcards in searches. You can also conduct searches from the keyboard.

Finding Text and Formats with the Find/Change Palette

The Find/Change palette is where you go to search for and replace text and formatting. It provides a number of other options as well. To open the Find/Change palette, do one of the following:

▶ Choose Edit ➤ Find/Change

▶ Press Ctrl+F (Windows), ⌘+F (Mac), or Ctrl+S (UNIX)

▶ Press *Esc e f*

▶ Click the Find/Change button on the QuickAccess Bar

The Find/Change palette is a palette that will stay open while you work. It is shown in Figure 11.2.

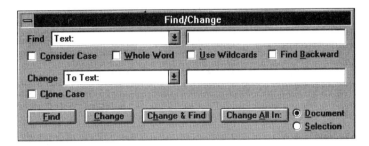

Figure 11.2   *The Find/Change palette*

 NOTE   The Find/Change palette searches only the page type that is currently displayed. For example, if a body page is displayed, only body pages are searched, not master pages or reference pages.

Telling FrameMaker What to Find

In the Find area of the Find/Change palette, you specify the type of item you want to find. It has a pull-down menu, a text box, and four check boxes. Using these items, you can specify any findable item. For example, to find text, select Text from the Find pull-down menu, and then type the text to be found in the box. To find a paragraph format, select Paragraph Tag from the pull-down menu, and then type the name of the tag in the text box.

What You Can Find   Using the Find pull-down menu, you can search for any of the following:

▶ **Text**—Any text matching that entered in the text box.

NOTE You can also search for characters not found on the keyboard (see below). To do this, you place a backslash character (\) before the special character you want to find. To find a single backslash, type two backslashes (\\) in the Find text box.

▶ **Character Format**—Any text whose formatting matches that specified in the Find Character Format dialog box shown in Figure 11.3. The Find Character Format dialog box appears when you make this selection. (Note that As Is settings are available.) Clicking Set returns you to the Find/Change palette, where you can start searching. (For an explanation of the character properties, see Chapter 9.)

TIP If your character cursor is sitting in text, the Find Character Format dialog box will pick up and display that text format.

▶ **Paragraph Tag**—Any paragraph whose tag matches that entered in the text box.

▶ **Character Tag**—Any character whose tag matches that entered in the text box.

▶ **Any Marker**—A marker of any type whatsoever. There are many types of markers in FrameMaker. To see the list, select Special ➤ Marker, and then look at the Marker Type pull-down list.

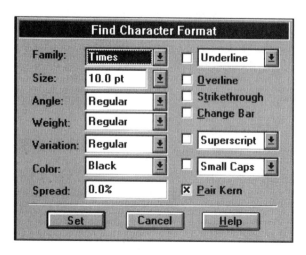

Figure 11.3 *The Find Character Format dialog box*

- **Marker of Type**—A marker of the type entered in the text box (for example, Index).

- **Marker Text**—A marker whose text contains the word or phrase entered in the text box (for example, an Index marker whose entry contains the word *allergy*). Note that Find/Change does not change marker text; it simply finds and selects markers. Use the Marker box to change marker text.

- **Any Cross-Reference**—Any cross-reference of any format.

- **Cross-Reference of Format**—A cross-reference with the same cross-reference format as that named in the text box.

- **Unresolved Cross-Reference**—Any cross-reference that could not be updated at the last cross-reference update. If Find/Change does find an unresolved cross-reference, it displays the marker text of the cross-reference in the Find text box.

- **Any Text Inset**—Any text imported by reference.

- **Unresolved Text Inset**—Any text imported by reference that could not be updated from its source file.

- **Any Publisher**—Any text (but not graphics) publisher (Macintosh version only).

- **Any Variable**—Any variable on the page type currently displayed (for example, any variable on a body page).

- **Variable of Name**—A variable whose name matches that entered in the text box.

- **Anchored Frame**—Any anchored frame.

- **Footnote**—Any footnote.

- **Any Table**—Any table.

- **Table Tag**—A table whose tag name matches that entered in the text box.

- **Conditional Text**—Any conditional text whose conditions match that specified in the Find Conditional Text dialog box shown in Figure 11.4. The Find Conditional Text dialog box appears when you make this selection.

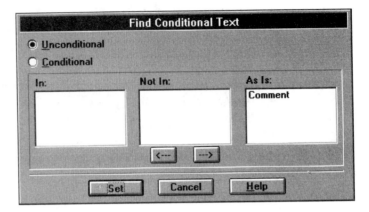

Figure 11.4   The Find Conditional Text dialog box

This dialog box is similar to the Conditional Text dialog box. Note that Find/Change does not find hidden conditional text, so you need to specify Show/Hide conditional text settings appropriate to your search.

▶ **Automatic Hyphen**—Any word that FrameMaker has automatically hyphenated.

▶ **Text & Character Formats on Clipboard**—Text (including capitalization and formatting) that matches the text on the Clipboard (up to the first 126 characters).

The Find Check Boxes   There are four Find check boxes:

▶ **Consider Case**—When checked, Find searches for an item with the same capitalization as the text in the Find text box. When unchecked, Find ignores capitalization.

▶ **Whole Word**—When checked, Find searches for complete words that match the text in the Find text box. When unchecked, Find searches for both whole words and partial words for matching text.

▶ **Use Wildcards**—Check this to turn on the use of wildcards in the Find text box. (See below for a list of Find wildcards.)

▶ **Find Backward**—Checking this box causes searches to proceed backward from the character cursor instead of forward. In either case, when Find/Change reaches the end of the document, it continues again at the other end until it has searched the complete document.

Using Wildcards in Searches

When the Use Wildcards check box in the Find/Change palette is turned on (see Figure 11.2), you can use wildcards in searches. Wildcard can find any string of characters, including none, but not spaces or punctuation marks. For example, *i*t* finds *it* and interpret. Table 11.4 explains how to use wildcards in searches.

Part 3

Formatting and Editing Text

What It Finds	Wildcard
|	One or more spaces and/or punctuation marks. For example, *like|* finds *like.*, *like;*, and *like .*, but not *likely*.
?	Any single character, but not spaces or punctuation marks. For example, *l??e* finds *like* and *lake*, but not *laminate*.
[xy]	Any one of the characters in the brackets. For example, *l[ia]ke* finds *like* and *lake*.
[^xy]	Any one of the characters *not* in the brackets. For example, *l[^ia]ke* finds *luke*, but does *not* find *like* and *lake*.
[a–f]	Any one of the characters in the range specified between the brackets. For example, *[g–l]ive* finds *give*, *hive*, *jive*, and *live*, but not *dive*.
^	The start of any line. For example, *^S* finds the letter *S* if it is the first word in a line of text.
$	The end of any line. For example, *t$* finds the letter *t if it is the last character in a line of text.*

Table 11.4 **Using Wildcards in Searches**

Searching for Special Characters

You can also search for special characters. These are characters that don't appear on the keyboard. For example, Tab characters (→) and end-of-paragraph symbols (¶) are special characters. To find special characters, you precede the character you want to search for with a backslash character (\). If you want to search for a backslash, enter two backslashes (\\) in the Find text box of the Find/Change palette (see Figure 11.2).

Table 11.5 explains how to search for special characters.

To Find	Enter
Tab	\t
New-line character (<)	\n or \r
End-of-paragraph character (¶)	\p
Start of paragraph	\P
Nonbreaking space	\ (following by space character)
Thin space	\st
En space	\sn
Em space	\sm
Numeric space	\s#
En dash (–)	\=
Em dash (—)	\m
Discretionary hyphen	\-
Nonbreaking hyphen	\+
Suppress hyphenation symbol	_
End-of-flow character (§)	\f
Start of word	\<
End of word	\>

Table 11.5   Searching for Special Characters

TIP Most of the special characters can be entered in the Change text box as well. (You cannot change the following—end of flow, start of word, end of word.)

Replacing Text and Formats

Using the Change area of the Find/Change palette (see Figure 11.2), you can change the item after you find it. The pull-down menu in the Change area is similar to the one in the Find area.

Using the Change pull-down menu, you can change items in the following ways:

▶ **To Text**—Replaces the found item with the text in the Change text box. The new text uses the same character format as the found text.

▶ **To Character Format**—Applies a specified character formatting to found text. When you select this item, the Change to Character Format dialog box opens, as in Figure 11.5. Here, you can select the character format to apply.

▶ **By Pasting**—Replaces the found item with the contents of the Clipboard, including capitalization and formatting. *Anything* that can be copied to the Clipboard can be pasted with Find/Change!

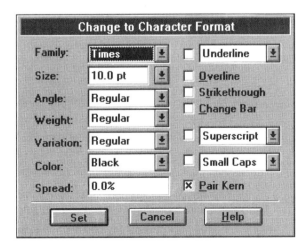

Figure 11.5 *The Change to Character Format dialog box*

Notice the Clone Case check box. Selecting Clone Case gives the replacement text the same capitalization as the found text.

For example, if you are searching for *luck* and you didn't check Consider Case, you would find *luck* as well as *Luck*. Checking Clone Case capitalizes the replacement word in the same way that the word it is replacing is capitalized. If the replacement word is *fortune* and you check Clone Case, *fortune* would replace *luck*, but *Fortune* would replace *Luck*.

Conducting the Search

Once you've told FrameMaker what to search for, how to search for it, and what to replace it with, click the Find button at the bottom of the Find/Change palette (see Figure 11.2). If it can do so, FrameMaker will find the item you are looking for. When that is done, click one of the buttons at the bottom of the Find/Change palette:

Button	What It Does
Find	Begins a search. If an item is found, it is selected. When one end of the document is reached, the search continues from the other end until the entire document has been searched.
Change	Pastes the item specified in the Change area at the character cursor. If you have previously executed a successful Find, the found item is selected, and the Change item replaces the found item.
Change & Find	Is like pressing Change and then pressing Find. You make the change and tell FrameMaker to start looking for the next instance of the item.
Change All In	Searches for every instance (within the range specified by the Document or Selection radio button) of the Find item and replaces it with the Change item.

Repeating a Search Straight from the Keyboard

With the Edit ➤ Find Next menu command, you can find the next occurrence of the item in the Find/Change palette, whether or not that window is open. If nothing is selected in the Find/Change palette, FrameMaker alerts you to select an item to find. The Find Next command always searches forward, regardless of the settings in the Find/Change palette, and it does not replace the items it finds.

TIP Change All cannot be undone, and you will be warned before continuing. If you aren't sure of the effect of your action (Change All is very powerful), save the document first. Then execute Change All. If you don't like the results, execute File ➤ Revert to Saved.

Finding and Changing Text and Formats from the Keyboard

You can issue many Find/Change commands from the keyboard as well as from the Find/Change palette. To do so:

1. Enter the keyboard shortcut *Esc f i s*. The Set Find/Change Parameters dialog box appears, as in Figure 11.6.

2. Specify Find/Change parameters.

The Set Find/Change Parameters window is almost identical to the Find/Change palette (see Figure 11.2), except that it doesn't have any buttons for finding or changing text. Use it as you would the regular Find/Change palette. You can use wildcards for any search that requires

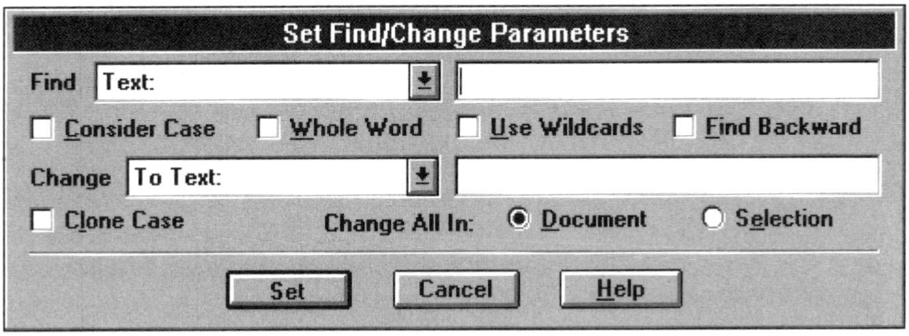

Set Find/Change Parameters

Find | Text: ⬧ | |

☐ <u>C</u>onsider Case   ☐ <u>W</u>hole Word   ☐ <u>U</u>se Wildcards   ☐ <u>F</u>ind Backward

Change | To Text: ⬧ | |

☐ C<u>l</u>one Case   Change All In: ⦿ <u>D</u>ocument   ○ S<u>e</u>lection

[<u>S</u>et]   [Cancel]   [<u>H</u>elp]

Figure 11.6   The Set Find/Change Parameters dialog box

text in the Find text box (see "Using Wildcards in Searches" earlier in this chapter), and search for or replace special characters as well (see "Finding Special Characters").

TIP You can change all settings in the Character Format box when it is displayed to As Is by typing Shift+F8 (Windows and UNIX) or ⌘+Shift+X (Mac). You can display the character settings of the current text by typing Shift+F9 (Windows and UNIX) or ⌘+Shift+V (Mac).

3. Press the Set button. The Find/Change Parameters dialog box closes.

4. Execute one of the following keyboard shortcuts:

   - Search forward: Press Ctrl+Shift+F or Ctrl+Alt+S (Windows), ⌘+G (Mac), Meta+S (UNIX), or *Esc e F.*

   - Search backward: Press Ctrl+Alt+F or Ctrl+Alt+R (Windows), ⌘+Shift+G (Mac), Meta+R (UNIX), or *Esc f i p.*

Formatting Imported Text

As you saw in Chapter 6, text can be imported into a FrameMaker document from another file. Imported files can be copied directly, or a reference to an imported file can be created and inserted. Imported text can come from a text flow in a FrameMaker document, an ASCII text file, or a file created by a different application (if FrameMaker has a filter for it).

Text that is imported by copying is stored directly in the document. It can be edited and formatted just like text you enter yourself.

On the other hand, text that is imported by reference is not stored word for word. Instead, a *text inset* is created. The text inset contains information on the formatting of the referenced text and also the path name of the source document. Referenced text (text insets) cannot be edited by FrameMaker, but when the source text changes, the inset can be updated, either automatically or manually.

Some formatting options are available, even with reference text. You can also change the formatting of text insets, even after they are created. This section contains information on both of these options.

Formatting an Imported Text File

You can control two elements of formatting when you import text files—how lines are treated and how paragraphs appear.

Specifying How Lines Are Treated in ASCII Files

When you import an ASCII text file, you see one of the Import Text File dialog boxes, either the Import Text File by Reference dialog box shown in Figure 11.7, or the Import Text File by Copy dialog box shown in Figure 11.8.

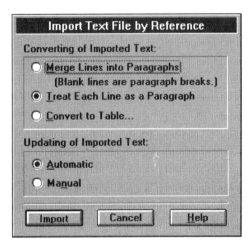

Figure 11.7   **Import Text File by Reference dialog box**

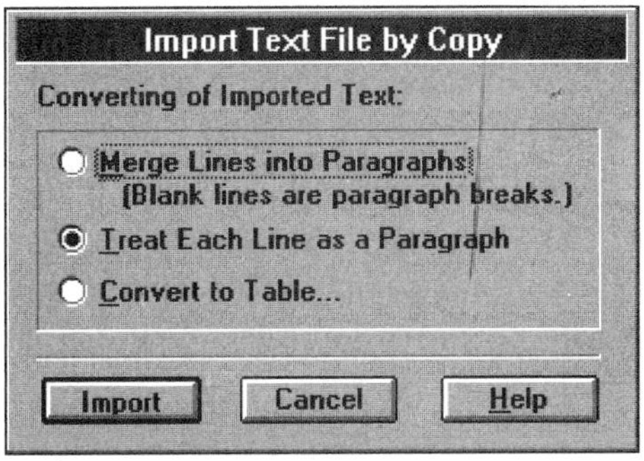

Figure 11.8   **Import Text File by Copy dialog box**

As you can see, both dialog boxes allow you to decide how lines are treated during importing. (Recall that in a text file, each line is a separate paragraph with a carriage return at the end.) Here are your options:

▶ **Merge Lines into Paragraphs**—Merges consecutive lines (that would normally be separate paragraphs) into a single paragraph. A blank line (i.e., two paragraph marks in a row) is turned into a paragraph break.

▶ **Treat Each Line as a Paragraph**—Keeps the file as is—it keeps each line of the text file as a separate paragraph, with its own paragraph mark.

▶ **Convert to Table**—Allows you to set up the imported text as a table.

Which option should you choose? It depends on the type of text file you are importing. For e-mail messages, for example, the first option is usually the best. In e-mail messages, paragraph marks come in the middle of paragraphs. You would have to delete them manually anyway, to allow the paragraphs to wrap between the margins of the new page.

For something like computer code (Pascal or C, for example) or poetry, you would *not* want the lines to merge together and wrap to fill the margins. You *do* want each line to stay separate. In this case, the second option is needed.

The third option assumes that the imported text was once a table and needs to become a table again. Data exported from spreadsheets (which are organized into cells arranged in rows and columns) and databases (which are organized into records and fields) often fall into this category. Both spreadsheets and databases are easy to present in table form.

Converting Imported Text from Spreadsheets and Databases

Choosing Convert to Table, the third option in the Import Text File dialog box (see Figure 11.7 or 11.8) opens the Convert to Table dialog box. This dialog box is shown in Figure 11.9.

Here you can treat each paragraph as either a row of cells, or as a cell itself. You can also specify the number of heading rows (if there are heading rows), and you can apply one of the table formats to the table.

The key decision is how to treat paragraphs. If you treat each paragraph as a row of cells, you have to say what character separates one cell from another. This character is often called the *delimiting character*, or the *delimiter*. The Tab character is the most commonly used delimiting character.

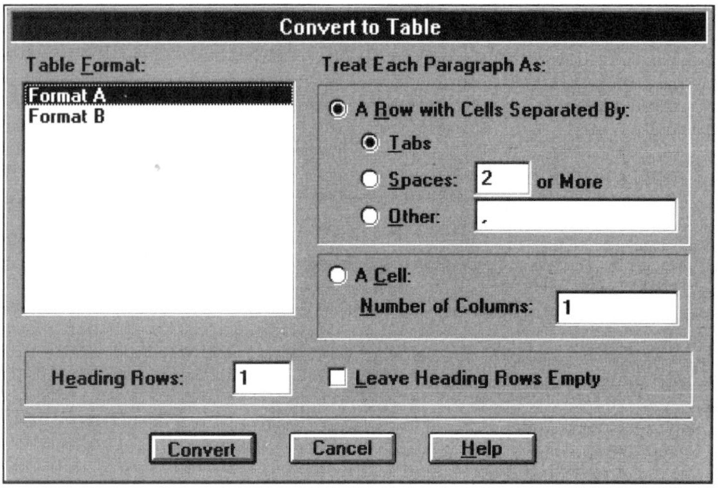

Figure 11.9 **Convert to Table dialog box**

Database programs often export their information this way. Tabs (or commas, or some other character) are used to separate fields from each other, and paragraph marks (carriage returns) are used to separate records. You may have heard ASCII database files being called "tab-delimited" or "comma-delimited," for example.

Spreadsheet data is often exported in the same way, so the first option (treat each paragraph as a row) is the most frequently used one.

Occasionally, though, a program (for example, a word processing program like FrameMaker) exports a table by making each cell a separate paragraph. In this case, choose the second option. Note, however, that you need to know how many cells make up one column, or the table won't look right after being imported.

In any case, you need to know something about the data you are importing as a table in order get it laid out correctly.

Controlling How Paragraphs and Tables Appear

How you control the appearance of paragraphs depends on whether or not you imported the text file by copy or by reference. If you imported it by copy, you can modify any of the paragraphs or words as you wish.

If you imported the text file by reference, you have fewer formatting options. You can, however, do the following, as long as you chose *not* to create a table:

▶ The character and paragraph formatting at the insertion point (the place where the character cursor was prior to importing the text) determines how each paragraph is formatted in the imported file. So if you want the imported text to look a certain way, make the paragraph with the insertion point look that way. (You can reformat that paragraph later, if you like, without altering the look of the imported text.)

▶ The paragraph tag of the paragraph that contained the insertion point becomes the paragraph tag of each paragraph of imported text. If you apply global changes to this paragraph tag, you will reformat the imported text.

TIP If you want to be able to format the imported text independently of the rest of the document, create a separate tag (named, say, Imported Text) for the paragraph that contains the insertion point, then import the text. Each paragraph of the imported text will have the tag Imported. Any changes to the Imported Text tag will affect only paragraphs with that tag.

You can do the following if you chose to create a table:

▶ The cells of the table will be formatted with the CellBody and CellHeading tags. Changes to these tags will cause the imported table text to be reformatted. In addition, you can make changes to the imported table with the Table Designer.

Formatting an Imported Flow

When you import a text flow from another document, whether by copying or by reference, you see either the Import Text Flow by Reference dialog box, shown in Figure 11.10, or the Import Text Flow by Copy dialog box, shown in Figure 11.11.

Both dialog boxes present the same formatting options. You can:

▶ Reformat the text using the paragraph tags in the current document. This assumes, of course, that the tags in the source document and in the current document are the same.

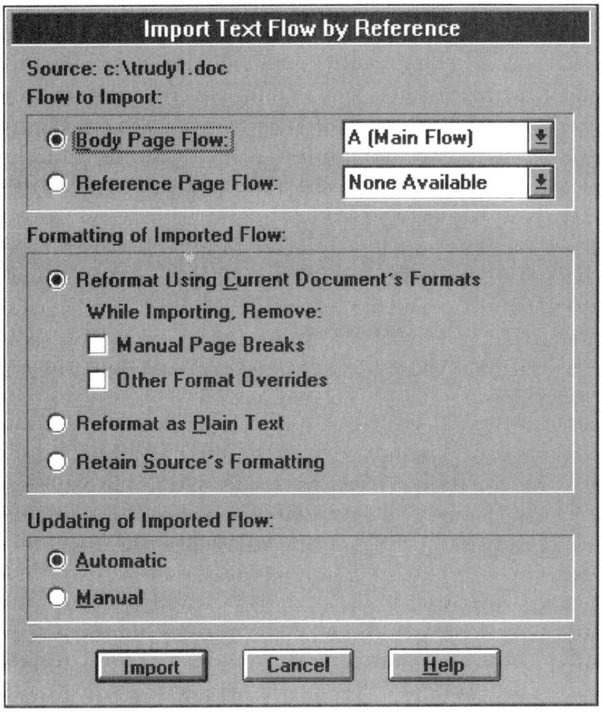

Figure 11.10   Import Text Flow by Reference dialog box

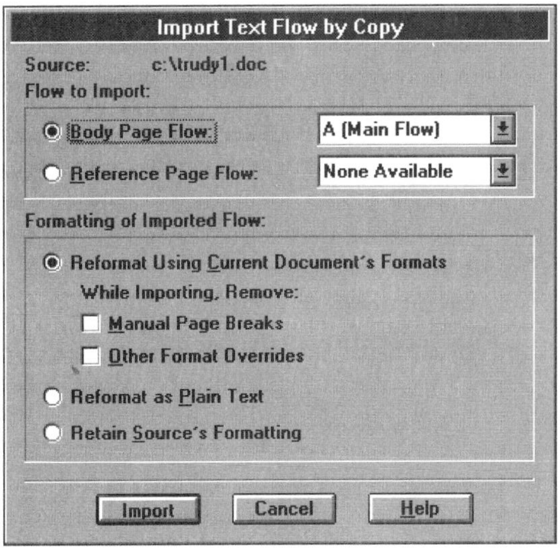

Figure 11.11   Import Text Flow by Copy dialog box

**Part
3**

Formatting and
Editing Text

▶ Reformat as "plain text." This works like formatting a text file (explained above). It removes all formatting from the source text and applies the character and paragraph formatting used at the insertion point (the place where the character cursor was when the text was imported).

▶ Retain the formatting of the source file regardless of the names of the paragraph tags.

Here again, if you import by copy, you can make any changes you like after importation, but if you import by reference, your options are more limited.

If you are importing by reference, the first choice (reformatting using paragraph tags in the current document) allows you the most reformatting options. Just make sure that the paragraph tags in the source document match the tag names in the current document. If they do, changes to the current document's tags will change the look of imported paragraphs with those tags.

If you are importing by reference, the second choice (reformatting as plain text) allows the same formatting changes as imported text files (discussed above under "Controlling How Paragraphs and Tables Appear").

The third choice (retaining the formatting of the source file) keeps the formatting of the source text just as it was in the original file. If you are importing by reference, you must change the formatting of the text in the source document to change its appearance in the current document.

Editing the Properties of Text Insets

Whatever decision you make when you import text by reference can easily by changed later. Just double-click on the text inset to make the Text Inset Properties dialog box appear. It is shown in Figure 11.12.

If you click on Settings, you will see the original Import dialog box—Import Text File by Reference (see Figure 11.7), Import Text Flow by Reference (see Figure 11.10), or Convert to Table (see Figure 11.9). Make whatever changes you like in those dialog boxes.

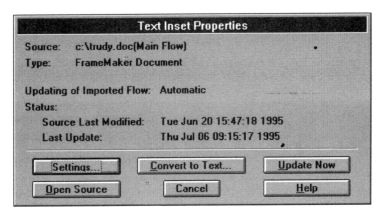

Figure 11.12   *The Text Inset Properties dialog box*

You can also convert the inset to editable text. Note, however, that once insets are converted, the procedure cannot be reversed, since all information about the source file will be lost. In addition, Convert to Text cannot be undone by the Undo command. (You will see a warning box before the conversion, just in case you wish to change your mind.)

Correcting Spelling Mistakes in Documents

The FrameMaker Spelling Checker can check a document for spelling errors, as well as many punctuation and formatting errors. The Spelling Checker also allows you to set up and maintain personal spelling and hyphenation dictionaries.

Exploring the Spelling Checker Window

Even though keyboard shortcuts are available for some types of spell-checking, most of your spell-checking will be done from the Spell Checker window.

To check the spelling of a document, select Edit ➤ Spelling Checker, or use the keyboard shortcut *Esc e s*, and click the Start Checking button. If FrameMaker finds a misspelled word or weird character pattern, the Spelling Checker window appears, as in Figure 11.13. Note that Spelling Checker is another FrameMaker palette, a window that stays open while you work.

Preventing FrameMaker from Spell-Checking a Paragraph or Text Line

You can keep FrameMaker from spell-checking any paragraph or text line you wish—for example, a paragraph containing computer code. To do this, set the Language setting of the paragraph or text line to None. (Set the language of a paragraph with the Advanced Properties page of the Paragraph Designer. Set the language of a text line with the command Graphics ➤ Object Properties.) Then, use the Object Properties dialog box. FrameMaker knows how to spell-check a paragraph or text line because each paragraph or text line is assigned a language. When spell-checking, FrameMaker uses a dictionary appropriate to that language (if that dictionary has been installed).

When the language of a paragraph or text line is set to None, FrameMaker ignores the paragraph or text line entirely when it checks spelling.

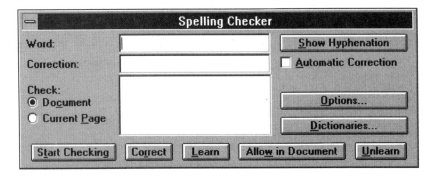

Figure 11.13   *The Spelling Checker window*

 NOTE   See Chapter 4 to learn the basic procedures for Spelling Checker. Spell-checking procedures are also summarized briefly later in this section. A table of keyboard shortcuts for spell-checking can also be found later in this section.

The Word text box displays the word or character pattern that Frame-Maker considers questionable. The label "Word" changes to "Misspelling?" and the questioned word appears in the text box.

The Correction area contains both a text box and a scroll list. When FrameMaker questions a word, it presents a list of possible corrections in the scroll list and displays the most likely suggestion in the Correction text box. If you don't like FrameMaker's suggestion, you can type in your own correction into the Correction text box.

The Check Document and Check Current Page radio buttons allow you to choose what you want spell-checked.

Click the Show Hyphenation button to see where hyphens appear in the word in the Word text box. FrameMaker uses dictionaries to determine where to place hyphens. If it can't find the word in the hyphenation dictionary, it calculates where the hyphens go (which means it guesses).

Click the Automatic Correction check box if you want FrameMaker to correct all future occurrences of each misspelled word or punctuation mistake without prompting you. Each time you press Correct, Frame-Maker adds the questioned word and its correction to an internal list of auto-corrections. It uses the corrections on the list to correct spelling errors until you exit FrameMaker. (You can clear this list without exiting FrameMaker by pressing the Dictionaries button and then selecting Clear Automatic Corrections.)

WARNING   Be careful with the Automatic Correction option. Sometimes a misspelled word can be corrected in more than one way. For example, if you auto-correct *fro* to *for, you will miss those times when fro* should be corrected to *from.*

NOTE   The Options button opens the Spelling Checker Options window. It is discussed below. The Dictionaries button opens the dictionary functions window. It is also discussed below.

Correcting a Misspelled Word

The five action buttons across the bottom of the window perform the most important spell-checking functions. These are the buttons you press to correct the misspelled word in the Word box:

▶ **Start Checking**—Besides starting the spell-checking, this button is also used to ignore a questioned word and continue checking. (You can also ignore a word by clicking Allow in Document, which also adds the word to the document dictionary.)

▶ **Correct**—Replaces the misspelled word with the text in the Correction text box. Note that you can use one of FrameMaker's suggested corrections, or type a correction of your own in the Correction text box.

▶ **Learn**—Adds the word shown in the Word text box to your personal dictionary. Once the word is in your personal dictionary, FrameMaker does not question it in any document you spell-check. Learn also adds hyphenation to your dictionary. You cannot add repeated words or unusual punctuation to your personal dictionary.

▶ **Allow in Document**—Adds the word shown in the Word text box to the *document dictionary*. FrameMaker does not question the word in the document, but it will question the word if it finds it in a different document. The document dictionary is stored with the document. Words in the document dictionary are considered correctly spelled words and are not flagged by the spell-checker.

▶ **Unlearn**—Removes the word shown in the Word text box from both your personal dictionary *and* from the document dictionary.

Customizing Spell Checking Options

You can decide for yourself what is checked in a document and what is ignored. To do so, select Options in the Spelling Checker window. You'll see the Spelling Checker Options window shown in Figure 11.14. The Find and Ignore options are described below. Click the Get Defaults button if you want to restore FrameMaker's default settings in this dialog box.

Find Options

The Spelling Checker can be told to find (or not to find) the following:

▶ **Repeated Words**—For example, if *the the* appears in a document, FrameMaker will flag it.

▶ **Unusual Hyphenation**—If the check box is off, a hyphenated word is checked as two (or more) separate words. If the check box is on, a hyphenated word is considered one word that requires one or more hyphens to be spelled correctly.

▶ **Unusual Capitalization**—Words with peculiar capitalization, such as *WordPerfect*.

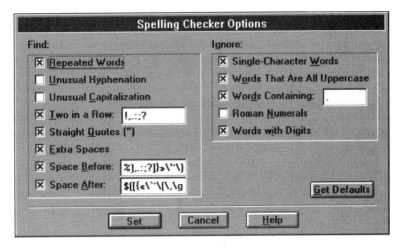

Figure 11.14   **The Spelling Checker Options window**

▶ **Two in a Row**—Two instances of the same punctuation in a row. The text box allows you to specify which characters should not be allowed two in a row. Thus, if you enter a comma and a semicolon, FrameMaker will question , and ;. However, FrameMaker it won't question ,; or any other instance of two unlike punctuation characters in a row.

▶ **Straight Quotes**—Quotation marks that look like " instead of this " or ". When Straight Quotes is turned on, FrameMaker finds both double-quote marks and single-quote marks.

▶ **Extra Spaces**—When checked, FrameMaker locates two spaces in a row and suggests replacing them with a single space. The Spelling Checker ignores more than two spaces in a row. Em and en spaces are not spell-checked.

▶ **Space Before *and* Space After**—Checks to see if a space appears before or after the characters in the Space Before and Space After text boxes. For example, you generally don't want a space after a dollar sign ($).

Ignore Options

The Spelling Checker can be told to ignore the following:

▶ **Single-Character Words**—Ignores words like *a* and *I*, as well as any other instances of single letters in a document.

Part
3

Formatting and
Editing Text

▶ **Words That Are All Uppercase**—Ignores words like DOS filenames (CONFIG.SYS), or the word *DOS* itself.

▶ **Words Containing**—Ignores words that contain any of the punctuation or other characters specified in the Words Containing text box. For example, if you place a period (.) here, FrameMaker will not spell-check file names that have a period in the middle and an extension.

▶ **Roman Numerals**—Ignores MCMLXXX (1980), iv (4), and the like.

▶ **Words with Digits**—Ignores words that contain numbers, like *test2*.

Spell-Checking Limitations

FrameMaker's Spelling Checker is quite versatile, but there are a few things it cannot do.

The Spelling Checker does *not* spell-check text inserts or text that was created in a dialog box (i.e., cross-references, variables, autonumbers, marker text) or in another window. It also does not check text in PostScript code columns.

The Spelling Checker only checks the page type (i.e., Body page) currently displayed. If a Body page is displayed, only the Body pages are checked. If a Master page is displayed, only Master pages are checked.

Customizing the FrameMaker Dictionaries

FrameMaker spell-checks documents against four dictionaries: the main dictionary, the site dictionary, your personal dictionary, and the document dictionary. You cannot change the contents of the main dictionaries. You can, however, change the site dictionary, your personal dictionary, and the document dictionaries.

 UNIX NOTE   Only the system manager can change the site dictionary.

The site dictionary is named SITE.DCT (Windows), site.dict (UNIX), or Site Dictionary (Macintosh). It is initially located in the DICT subdirectory (Windows), the fminit subdirectory (UNIX), or the Dictionaries folder (Mac) of the install directory.

When the program is first started, your personal dictionary is named USER.DCT (Windows), fmdictionary (UNIX), or Personal Dictionary

(Mac). It is located in the FrameMaker install directory ($HOME in UNIX installations). If this dictionary doesn't exist, FrameMaker creates it the first time you press Learn in the Spelling Checker.

Both the site and personal dictionaries are ASCII text files and can be edited by hand. However, it usually makes more sense to edit dictionaries with FrameMaker's dictionary management tools (described later in this section).

WINDOWS NOTE If you get an error message that says you cannot write to your user dictionary, use the File Manager to see if the file USER.DCT is marked read-only or hidden. If it is, remove the read-only or hidden attribute.

FrameMaker automatically creates a dictionary for the current document when you click Allow in Document in the Spelling Checker window (see Figure 11.13). The document dictionary is stored as part of the document.

Changing FrameMaker Dictionaries

You can modify your personal dictionary and the document dictionary by using the Dictionary Functions window shown in Figure 11.15. To get there, click on the Dictionaries button in the Spelling Checker window (see Figure 11.13).

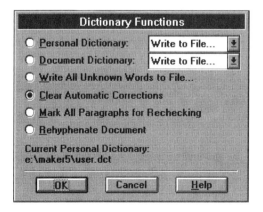

Figure 11.15 **The Dictionary Functions window**

The Dictionary Functions dialog box contains file management options and document options. The file management options allow you to do a number of things.

From the Personal Dictionary pull-down list, you can:

▶ Write your personal dictionary to another file (in other words, make a copy of the file).

▶ Merge a file into your personal dictionary.

▶ Change your personal dictionary (by using a different file).

▶ Turn off the use of any personal dictionary.

From the Document Dictionary pull-down list, you can:

▶ Write the document dictionary to a file (recall that the document dictionary is kept inside the document).

▶ Merge a file into the document dictionary (in other words, add words to the dictionary kept inside the document).

▶ Clear (delete) the document dictionary from the document.

 MAC NOTE In the Mac version, the Dictionary Functions dialog box also contains a Site Dictionary pull-down list that lets you change the site dictionary or turn off its use.

Access these functions by selecting an option from one of the pull-down lists and then pressing OK. You will then see a dialog box appropriate to your platform. From there, you can specify which file to read, write, or merge from.

In the Mac version, the site dictionary is managed in the same way. There is a Site Dictionary pull-down list in the Dictionary Functions dialog box that lets you change the site dictionary or turn off its use. In the Windows and UNIX versions, the name and location of the site dictionary is listed in the MAKER.INI file or Maker file, respectively. Edit these files to change the site dictionary. (In UNIX, you can also make $FMHOME/fminit/site.dict a link to another file or a null file.)

More Functions from the Dictionary Functions Box

Other choices in the Dictionary Functions dialog box allow you to:

▶ Run the Spelling Checker on a document without stopping, and then write all the unknown words in the document to a file (in other words, create a file of unknown words in FrameMaker dictionary format).

▶ Clear the stored list of automatic corrections (see the discussion of the Automatic Corrections check box in Spelling Checker, above).

▶ Mark paragraphs for rechecking when the Spelling Checker is next run. FrameMaker speeds spell-checking by marking paragraphs with no errors and no recent edits, then skipping those paragraphs until they are edited again. Marking paragraphs for rechecking is useful when you change dictionaries or spell-checking options.

▶ Force rehyphenation of the document. Do this after changing the hyphenation of a word or words. FrameMaker will not execute the changes unless you tell it to do so.

Editing FrameMaker's Dictionary Files

FrameMaker's ASCII dictionaries—the site dictionary, your personal dictionary, and any dictionary list FrameMaker writes to an external file—have a simple structure for listing words. You might find it easier to open these files in a text editor and work with them by hand than to use FrameMaker to modify them for you. If you do, keep the following in mind.

The first line of the dictionary must contain only the following text:

```
<MakerDictionary 2.0>
```

Each line after that has a correctly spelled and hyphenated word, with the hyphens shown, like so:

```
Green-street
```

To force FrameMaker to leave a word unhyphenated, precede the word with a hyphen character:

```
-Lorre
```

Everything You Need to Know about Hyphenation

To see the hyphenation of a word:

1. Type the word in the Word text box of the Spelling Checker window.
2. Click Show Hyphenation.

To change the hyphenation of a word:

1. Type the word in the Word text box.
2. Click Show Hyphenation.
3. Correct the hyphenation in the Word text box.
4. Click Learn.

To rehyphenate a document:

1. Click Dictionaries in the Spelling Checker window.
2. Click Rehyphenate Document.
3. Click OK.

To find all automatically inserted hyphens in a document:

1. Open the Find/Change palette by choosing Edit ➤ Find.
2. Select Automatic Hyphen from the Find pull-down list.
3. Click Find.

To force FrameMaker to use a hyphen when spelling a word, precede the hyphen with a backslash (\):

```
cross\-reference
```

If FrameMaker doesn't see hyphens in a dictionary word, it tries to hyphenate the word according to its hyphenating algorithm. That's why the preceding hyphen is needed—to force FrameMaker not to try to hyphenate.

Keyboard Shortcuts for Spell-Checking

Table 11.6 lists keyboard shortcuts for spell-checking. All are Escape key combinations. They include the letter *l* (as in *spell*), not the number *1*.

To Action	Press
Check the current selection	*Esc l s*
Check word at insertion point	*Esc l s*
Check entire document	*Esc l e*
Check current page	*Esc l p*
Correct a word	*Esc l c w*
Add word to personal dictionary	*Esc l a p*
Add word to document dictionary	*Esc l a d*
Add word to internal list of automatic corrections	*Esc l a c*
Delete word from personal dictionary	*Esc l x p*
Delete word from document dictionary	*Esc l x d*
Clear internal list of automatic corrections	*Esc l c a*
Display Spelling Check Options dialog box	*Esc l o*
Display Dictionary Functions dialog box	*Esc l c d*
Create file of unknown words in current document	*Esc l b*
Mark all paragraphs for rechecking	*Esc l r*
Show hyphenation of current word	*Esc l –*
Rehyphenate a document	*Esc l R*

Table 11.6   Keyboard Shortcuts for Spell-Checking

Using the Thesaurus to Find the Right Word

FrameMaker's thesaurus contains synonyms, *antonyms* (words that are opposite in meaning), and words related to the word you are looking up. It even has word definitions.

To look up words in FrameMaker's thesaurus, choose Edit ➤ Thesaurus. One of two things will happen:

▶ If no words are currently selected (highlighted) in the document, you see the Thesaurus Look Up dialog box shown below. Here you can enter a word to look up:

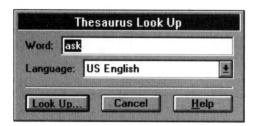

▶ If a word is currently selected, you see either the main Thesaurus window (a palette that stays open as you work), as in Figure 11.16, or a message that tells you that the selected word was not found.

From the Thesaurus window, you can continue to look up related words, call the Thesaurus Look Up window, and move words from the Thesaurus into the document, either as insertions or replacements. The Frame-Maker Thesaurus also allows you to look up words in any language for which a Thesaurus is installed.

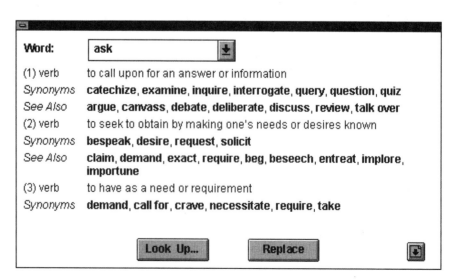

Figure 11.16 **The Thesaurus window**

The Thesaurus Window

The Thesaurus window contains a few obvious features. The Word box displays the current word you have looked up. From the pull-down list, you can see the last ten words you looked up. Choose a word from the pull-down list if you want FrameMaker to look it up again.

The main part of the window shows definitions, synonyms, and antonyms for the word, as well as related words that you can also look up. Click on any boldfaced word to look it up.

The button labeled Look Up opens the Thesaurus Look Up window. Click this button if you want to manually enter a new word to look up.

The button labeled Replace replaces the word selected in the document with the word shown in the Word box. If no word is selected, the word is inserted at the insertion point.

The Thesaurus Look Up Window

The Word text box in the Thesaurus Look Up window allows you to type the word you want to look up.

The Language pull-down menu lists the languages available for selection, from among the thesauruses that are installed. The complete list can include US English, UK English, German, Swiss German, French, Canadian French, Spanish, Italian, Danish, Dutch, Norwegian, and Swedish.

Click the Look Up button to open the Thesaurus window. It displays information about the word in the Word text box.

Chapter 12

Controlling the Look of the Page

How text and graphics are presented in a document is as important as the information itself. An unattractive, hard-to-read layout distracts readers from the information or message you are trying to convey. On the other hand, an attractive, easy-to-read page enhances the information or message.

In addition, the first attempt by a reader to gain information usually comes by scanning the page layout. The layout is not just for beauty (though attractiveness is clearly important to us all). The layout tells readers—literally at a glance—what's important on the page. This is why, for example, the most important headings, sometimes called "Level 1 headings" or "A-headings," should stand out.

Creating a page layout that tells readers whether or not they need to read the page carefully is an important skill and art. And it is also the subject of this chapter.

Elements of a Page Layout

There are lots of elements in a page layout. When you first create a FrameMaker document, you are presented with an opportunity to create or confirm the layout of the pages. Afterwards, you can change the page layout at any time.

You can control the following page layout elements:

▶ Page size

▶ Whether the document is single-sided or doubled-sided

▶ Page margins

▶ The number and placement of columns

▶ The placement and contents of headers and footers

▶ Page numbering

▶ The way text flows through the text frames

In addition, in multicolumn pages, you can control:

▶ Whether text is balanced in pages that are partially full

▶ Whether text lines are padded vertically to fill text columns to the end

▶ Whether the baselines of the lines in different columns line up

Finally, you have many options for creating interesting headings. Headings can appear:

▶ Above text paragraphs

▶ Next to text in a special area called the "sidehead area"

▶ Above all columns (in multicolumn documents) or all columns and the sidehead area (in single- and multicolumn documents)

You can also make other elements straddle multicolumn layouts (tables and figures in anchored frames, for example) so that the page layout is varied and interesting.

NOTE   Before you begin this chapter, you may want to review Chapter 8. It offers information about important layout concepts, including text frames and text flows; body pages, master pages, and reference pages; anchored frames; text columns, sidehead areas, and "straddles."

Laying Out the Page

When you first create a document with the File ➤ New command, you either

▶ Create a document from an existing template (like the Portrait page template or one of the templates in a templates directory).

▶ Create a custom document and specify the layout for yourself.

Laying Out a New Document

When you create a new document, you can use the Custom Blank Paper dialog box shown in Figure 12.1 to control the following elements:

▶ Page size

▶ Margins for the text area

▶ Number of columns in the text frame

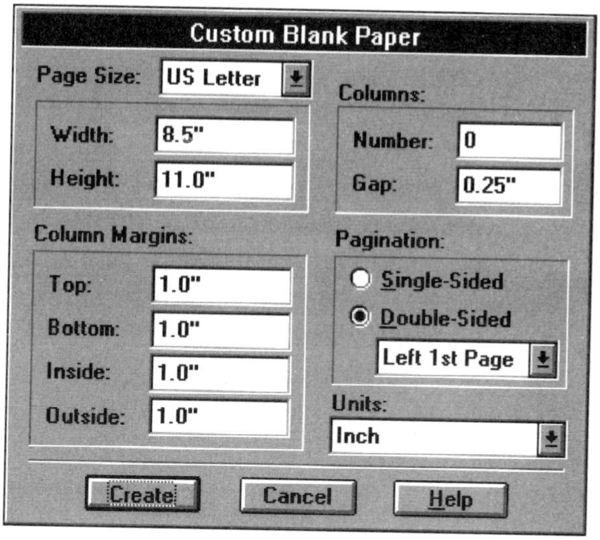

Figure 12.1 **The Custom Blank Paper dialog box**

▶ Whether the document is single- or double-sided (called "pagination" in this dialog box)

Set the page size to match the paper you will be printing on and the pagination according to whether the paper will be printed on one side only or on both sides.

The margins and columns settings should be set initially according to your best guess about what will look good, but most likely you will change these after you see the first drafts come out of the printer. In any case, don't spend too much time here adjusting these values. It's easy enough to change them later.

Changing the Layout of Existing Documents

After you've created a document, you can change its layout elements at any time.

Changing the Page Size

If you wish to change the page size and pagination (whether the document is single-sided or double-sided), as sometimes happens, select Format ➤ Page Layout ➤ Page Size and fill in the Page Size dialog box:

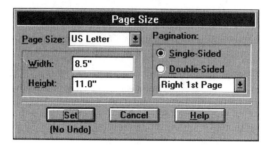

Working with Margins

It's not uncommon to change margins and columns sizes in a document, especially in a custom document. To change the margins or number of columns for an entire flow, including master pages, place the character cursor anywhere in the flow, select Format ➤ Page Layout ➤ Column Layout, and fill in the Column Layout dialog box shown in Figure 12.2. With this dialog box, you can also create a sidehead area, something that the Custom Blank paper dialog box does not allow.

Figure 12.2　The Column Layout dialog box

To change the margins and number of columns for a single text frame only, place the character cursor anywhere in the text frame, select Format ➤ Customize Layout ➤ Customize Text Frame, and use the Customize Text Frame dialog box shown in Figure 12.3. In this dialog box, margins are controlled with the Size and Offset text areas.

Customize Text Frame	
Type: Text Frame	
Unrotated Size:	**Color:** Black
Width: 5.25"	**Angle:** 0.0
Height: 7.792"	**Border Width:** 1.0 pt
Offset From:	**Flow Tag:** A
Top: 2.074"	X **Autoconnect**
Left: 1.625"	□ **PostScript Code**
	□ **Room for Side Heads:**
Columns:	
Number: 1	W**i**dth: 1.5"
Gap: 0.25"	G**ap**: 0.25"
□ **B**alance Columns	S**i**de: Left

| Set | Cancel | Help |

Figure 12.3   *The Customize Text Frame dialog box*

NOTE   You can also use the Customize Text Frame dialog box to change the sidehead area specification, but if you do, the change will be applied to the entire flow, not just to the current text frame.

Changing the Size and Position of Text Frames

You can also change the size or position of a body page text frame (in effect, its margins) by selecting it as an object (Ctrl+click in Windows and UNIX, Option+click on the Mac). Then, use the mouse to drag the text frame around or reshape it with its resizing handles. (Chapter 15 has more on manipulating text frames and other objects.)

Updating Changes from One Text Frame to an Entire Flow

If you use the Customize Text Frame dialog box to make any of the changes discussed above to just one text frame or body page, and later on you want to update the entire flow—including the master page—so it matches that frame or page, use the Format ➤ Page Layout ➤ Update Column Layout command. If the current body page contains overrides to the master page—for example, if the number of columns is different or the text frame has been moved or resized—you will see a confirming dialog box like this one:

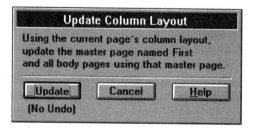

Click on Update to update everything in the flow to match the current page.

You can also change body pages globally by viewing master pages and changing the text frames and column layout there. When you view body pages again, FrameMaker will attempt to apply the changes on the master page to all body pages that use that master page.

▷ If all body pages using that master page matched that master page before you modified it, then those body pages are automatically updated.

▷ If some body pages using that master page contain individual layout overrides—that is, if their text frames were a different size from the one on the unmodified master page, for example—you see a warning dialog box. Here, you can choose to keep all overrides or remove all overrides while updating:

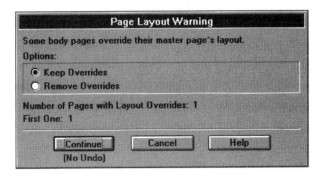

As Chapter 8 explains, you can create, delete, and rename master pages any time you like and reassign master page usage to any body pages you wish. Creating master pages is done with the Format ➤ Page Layout ➤ New Master Page command. Reassigning master page usage is done with Format ➤ Page Layout ➤ Master Page Usage.

Special master pages are typically used for the first page of a document or chapter and for special pages, like those with landscape (rotated) text frames that might be used for extra-wide tables or pictures.

Handling Headers and Footers

Among the most common page layout elements are headers and footers. A *header* is text and sometimes text and graphics (like a ruling line) that appears at the top of every page. Titles of documents or chapters, for example, as well as dates and page numbers, often appear in headers. A *footer* is text and sometimes graphics that appear at the bottom of every page. Page numbers, for example, are often placed in footers, along with ruling lines.

You can create and format text for headers and footers just as you would body text paragraphs. You can apply paragraph and character formats to the text, add and remove tabs, and add graphics elements like ruling lines. And headers and footers can include variable information, like the current page number and the current date.

Headers and footers can be sized and positioned. You can have more than one header or footer on a page. And you can have headers and footers for some pages that are different from the headers and footers on other pages.

Finally, a header or footer can get its text from the contents of a body page paragraph. For example, you can use the most recent Level 1 heading in a footer. Headers and footers that include headings are called *running headers* and *running footers* because they change throughout a document as the headings change.

Adding Headers and Footers to Master Pages

When you create a new document, each master page has a default text frame for a header and a footer. (One-sided documents have a master page named Right. Two-sided documents have master pages named Left and Right.) Header and footer text frames do not have flow tags, so they appear as background on each body page that uses that master page. They have the same side margins as the text frame that contains the named flow. They contain a single paragraph (tagged either Header or Footer) with a center tab in the center of the frame and a right tab at the right side of the frame. To begin with, header and footer text frames contain no text, of course.

You can modify these text frames in a number of ways. You can resize them, add a new header or footer text frame to a master page, and edit or reformat their text.

Resizing and Moving Headers and Footers

To resize or move a header or footer text frame:

1. Start from a body page whose header or footer you want to change and select View ➤ Master Pages.

2. To resize a header or footer text frame:

   - Select the text frame by Ctrl+clicking (Windows and UNIX) or Option+clicking (Macintosh) on it. Resizing handles appear around the border of the frame to show it is selected.

   - Drag the resizing handles into new positions until the frame is the right size. (You can also use Graphics ➤ Scale or Graphics ➤ Object Properties to resize a text frame.)

3. To move a header or footer text frame:

  - Select the text frame by Ctrl+clicking (Windows and UNIX) or Option+clicking (Macintosh) on it. Resizing handles appear around the border of the frame to show it is selected.

  - Drag the text frame border to move the frame to a new location. (You can also use the Graphics ➤ Align or Graphics ➤ Object Properties commands to reposition a text frame.)

4. Change headers and footers on other master pages as you wish.

5. When you are done, select View ➤ Body Pages. The body pages are updated with the new headers or footers. If you see the overrides warning message, you may keep or remove overrides as you wish without affecting the headers or footers you modified.

6. Save changes by selecting File ➤ Save.

Adding a Header or Footer to a Master Page

To add a new header or footer text frame to a master page:

1. Select View ➤ Master Pages.

2. Go to the master page to which you want to add the header or footer text frame.

3. Draw a text frame by using the Text Frame tool from the Tools palette. For information on how to draw a text frame, see Chapter 15. When you have finished, the Add New Text Frame dialog box shown in Figure 12.4 opens.

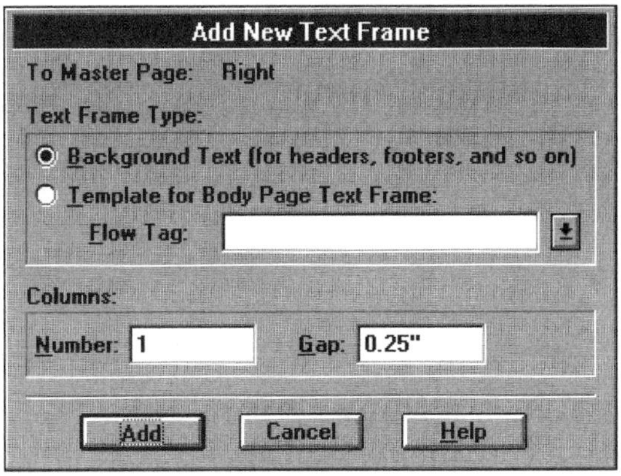

Figure 12.4 *The Add New Text Frame dialog box*

4. Select the Background Text radio button and click on Add.

5. Resize and/or move the text frame as you wish by using the instructions immediately above.

6. Add and format your header or footer text as you wish. (This is discussed in more detail throughout the rest of this section.)

7. Select View ➤ Body Pages to apply your changes. If you see the overrides warning message, you may keep or remove overrides as you wish without affecting the headers or footers you added.

8. Save your changes by selecting File ➤ Save.

Editing the Text in a Header or Footer

To edit or reformat text in a header or footer:

1. Select View ➤ Master Pages.

2. Go to the master page whose header or footer you want to modify.

3. Place the character cursor in the header or footer text frame and use normal text editing techniques to add, delete, or change the text.

4. Use paragraph and character formatting to format the text.

> **TIP** Remember that the default tags for headers and footers are called Header and Footer. It's a good idea to update these tags with all paragraph changes, so that all headers and footers look similar to each other.

5. When you are done, select View ➤ Body Pages. The body pages are updated with the new headers or footers. If you see the overrides warning message, you may keep or remove overrides as you wish without affecting the headers or footers you modified.

6. Save your changes by selecting File ➤ Save.

Including Page Numbers and Other Variables in Headers and Footers

FrameMaker provides a fast way to add the current date, the current page number, the total page count, and other variable information (like the current file name) to headers or footers:

1. Select View ➤ Master Pages.

2. Go to the master page that contains the header or footer you wish to modify.

3. Place the character cursor in the header or footer where you want the date, page number, or other variable to appear.

4. Insert a variable, as follows:

   - **Current page number**—Select Format ➤ Headers & Footers ➤ Insert Page # to insert the current page number at the character cursor.

   - **Last page of document**—Select Format ➤ Headers & Footers ➤ Insert Page Count to insert the number of the last page of the document at the character cursor. This variable is used to create header text like the following: "Page 1 of 12," in which case 12 is the last page of the document.

   - **Today's date**—Select Format ➤ Headers & Footers ➤ Insert Current Date to insert today's date (as your computer understands it) at the character cursor. The form of the date is *M/DD/YY*.

   - **Other variables**—Select Format ➤ Headers & Footers ➤ Insert Other to open the Variables dialog box and insert other variables. The Variables dialog box appears. Choose a variable from the list. If you have defined your own variables and added them to the list of system variables, they can be used in headers and footers also.

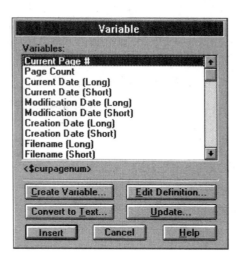

   NOTE   Variables and the Variable dialog box are discussed in detail in Chapter 19.

5.   Apply character formatting as you wish to the variables and other characters.

6.   When you are done, select View ➤ Body Pages. The body pages are updated with the new headers or footers. If you see the overrides warning message, you may keep or remove overrides as you wish without affecting the headers or footers you modified.

7.   Save your changes by selecting File ➤ Save.

You can use as many variables as you wish in a header or footer. For example, to create a header like "Page 1 of 12," type **Page**, enter a space, select Format ➤ Headers & Footers ➤ Insert Page #, enter another space, type the word **of**, enter yet another space, and then select Format ➤ Headers & Footers ➤ Insert Page Count.

Changing the Page Number Style

Page numbers can be shown in Arabic numbers (1, 2, and so on), Roman numerals (I, II, or i, ii, and so on), or letters (like a and b or A and B).

The page numbering style is part of a document's layout. By default, page numbering is done with Arabic numbers and starts on page 1, but you can choose a different page numbering style for your document and a different starting page number. Here's how:

1. Select Format ➤ Document ➤ Numbering. The Numbering Properties dialog box opens:

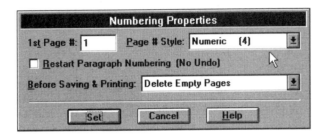

2. Type the number of the first page in the 1st Page # text box.

3. Select the page numbering style by using the Page # Style pull-down list. The choices are Arabic numbers (called "Numeric" in the pull-down list), upper- and lowercase Roman numerals (such as IV and iv), and upper- and lowercase letters.

4. Click the Set button.

5. Save your changes by selecting File ➤ Save.

NOTE When a document is part of a book, instead of using Format ➤ Document ➤ Numbering in the document window, use File ➤ Set Up File in the book window. This way, pages can be numbered correctly every time the book is updated. For more information on page numbers in books, see Chapter 16.

Creating Running Headers and Footers

Headers and footers that include information (other than the page number) that changes from page to page are called running headers and running footers. Many running headers, for example, include the most recent Level 1 heading. In the book you're holding in your hands, the running head on the right-hand page includes a running header with the most recent Level 1 heading in it.

FrameMaker creates running headers and footers with the four *Running H/F* system variables (*Running H/F 1*, *Running H/F 2*, and so on). These variables have initial definitions, which can be changed. Variables are made up of building blocks such as <*$lastpagenum*>, which represents the last page number in the document, and <*$fullfilename*>, which is a placeholder for the drive, path, and file name of the current file.

The initial definitions of the four Running H/F variables are as follows:

Variable	Definition	Meaning
Running H/F 1	<*$paratext[Title]*>	The text of the most recent paragraph tagged Title
Running H/F 2	<*$paratext[Heading]*>	The text of the most recent paragraph tagged Heading
Running H/F 3	<*$marker1*>	The text of the most recent marker of type *Header/Footer $1*
Running H/F 4	<*$marker2*>	The text of the most recent marker of type *Header/Footer $2*

These definitions are easy to change with the Variables dialog box, as shown below. At the very least, you want to replace the paragraph tags Title and Heading with tag names from your own document.

Modifying and Inserting Running Headers and Footers

To add a running header or footer to a document:

1. Select View ➤ Master Pages.

2. Go to the master page whose header or footer you wish to change.

3. Place the character cursor where you want the running header or footer inserted.

4. Select Special ➤ Variable. The Variable dialog box shown in Figure 12.5 opens.

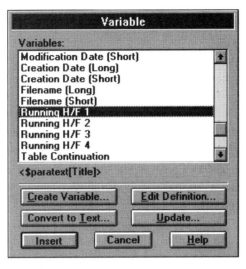

Figure 12.5 **The Variable dialog box**

5. Use the scroll list to find one of the Running H/F variables and select it. For example, *Running H/F 1*. The definition of the variable appears below the scroll list.

6. Change the variable definition, if you wish, by clicking on the Edit Definition button. The Edit System Variable dialog box opens:

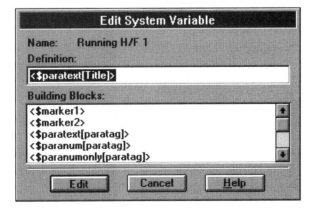

7. Edit the variable definition by typing directly into the Definition text box. You can insert building blocks into the definition by clicking on the building block in the Building Blocks scroll list.

Part 3

Formatting and Editing Text

8. Click the Edit button to change the definition. The Variable dialog box (see Figure 12.5) reopens.

9. Click the Insert button. The name of the variable is inserted into the header or footer. The name of the variable is a single unit, and double-clicking on it opens the Variables dialog box (another nice FrameMaker shortcut). (Note that the Insert button will be labeled Replace if you highlighted a selection in step 3.)

10. When you are done, select View ➤ Body Pages. The body pages are updated with the new headers or footers. If you see the overrides warning message, you may keep or remove overrides as you wish without affecting the headers or footers you modified.

11. Save your changes by selecting File ➤ Save.

Inserting Markers Used by Running Headers and Footers

If you used *<$marker1>* or *<$marker2>* in your Running H/F variable definition, the text of the variable is the text of the most recent marker of type *Header/Footer $1* or *Header/Footer $2*, respectively.

Markers are nonprinting characters inserted into the flow of a document. They contain text used for a variety of purposes. The marker type tells FrameMaker how to use the marker text. Some markers contain information entered by the user (for example, index markers, which are used to build document indexes); others contain text created by FrameMaker for its own uses (for example, cross-reference markers, which are used to store the information FrameMaker needs to display cross-references like "see page 12").

Header/Footer markers must be inserted and edited by hand. They are a handy way to place text into a header or a footer that does not appear as the text of a paragraph. (Note that all the other building blocks that take text from paragraphs take the *whole* paragraph, character for character. You cannot select a part of a paragraph and make it appear as text in a running header or footer.)

Header/Footer markers, when they are used with the *<$marker1>* and *<$marker2>* building blocks in Running H/F variables, allow you to decide for yourself which phrases appear in a running header or footer and when those phrases are superseded by other phrases.

To insert a Header/Footer marker into a document:

1. Go to the body page on which the marker should appear and place the character cursor in the text. The marker appears exactly where the character cursor is placed.

2. Select Special ➤ Marker. The Marker window (another palette) appears:

3. Select either Header/Footer $1 or Header/Footer $2 in the Marker Type pull-down list.

4. Type the text of the running header or footer exactly as you want it to appear in the Marker Text window.

5. Click on New Marker to insert the marker into the text.

6. Repeat this for each marker you wish to insert.

   If you wish to edit a marker, highlight the text containing the marker and select Special ➤ Marker. The Marker window shows the text of the current marker, and the button at the bottom says "Edit Marker" instead of "New Marker." You can change either the text or the marker type as you wish.

   If the text of a marker does not appear in the header or footer as you expect, check the marker type and, if necessary, change it to the appropriate Running Header/Footer marker type. Using the wrong marker type is a common mistake in working with FrameMaker markers.

Part
3

Formatting and
Editing Text

Doing More with FrameMaker

Chapter 13

Adding Graphics to Documents

Graphics are illustrations, diagrams, drawings, and pictures. A graphic can be worth a thousand words. A good one can be worth ten thousand. If it's a choice between writing ten thousand words or using a good graphic, a good graphic wins every time.

In this chapter you will learn about the graphic tools available in FrameMaker. You'll learn how to create line graphics in a document by using the graphic tools, and also how to import various types of graphics into a document.

Exploring the Tools Window

 Use the Tools window, another FrameMaker palette, to choose drawing tools and drawing properties. To open the Tools window, select Graphics ➤ Tools or press the Tools button on the side of the document window. The Tools window will appear. It will either be a large window, as in Figure 13.1, or a small window, as in Figure 13.2. To switch between the large and small window, click on the Zoom button.

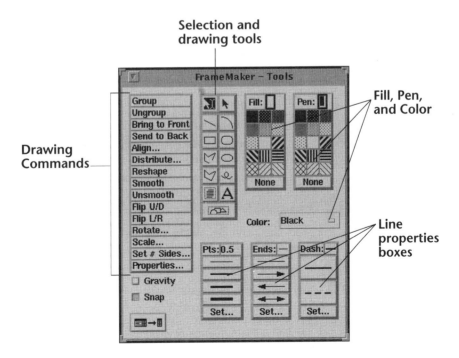

Figure 13.1 *The large Tools window*

Figure 13.2   **The small Tools window**

WINDOWS NOTE   On the Windows platform, only the small Tools window is available.

MAC AND UNIX NOTE   For UNIX installations, the small Tools window Zoom button is located at the bottom of the window, and the large Tools window Zoom button is located below the Drawing Properties area. The Mac Zoom button is the usual Zoom icon in the upper-right corner.

The large Tools window is divided into four main areas:

▶ **Selection and drawing tools**—The icons that allow you to select the Smart Selection tool, as well as the Line, Oval, Rectangle, and Text Frame tools.

▶ **Drawing commands**—The commands list, including items like Group, Scale, and Reshape.

▶ **Fill, Pen, and Color boxes**—The three boxes of patterns and colors for filling objects and borders.

▶ **Line properties boxes**—The boxes with sizes, ends, and dash patterns for lines.

Drawing commands are available only in the large Tools window, and in the small Tools window, the Fill, Pen, and Color buttons and the line properties buttons are located in the bottom half of the window.

The selection and drawing tools area of the Tools window offers two types of tools, as shown in Figure 13.3. The selection tools allow you to select the objects and text on which to perform operations, like grouping or aligning. The drawing tools let you draw objects such as lines and circles. The tools are labeled in Figure 13.3.

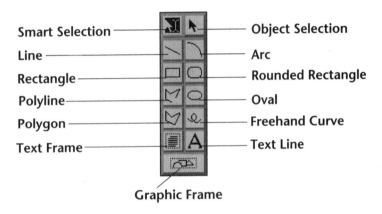

Smart Selection	Object Selection
Line	Arc
Rectangle	Rounded Rectangle
Polyline	Oval
Polygon	Freehand Curve
Text Frame	Text Line
	Graphic Frame

Figure 13.3   *The selection and drawing tools in the Tools window*

To select a tool, simply click on it. After you use the tool once, the tool is "deselected."

If you want to draw more than one of the same type object, like three rectangles, and you don't want to select the tool each time, Shift+click on the tool. The tool will stay selected and you can use it as needed until you click (or Shift+click) on another drawing or selection tool. (This does not work for the Text Frame tool, however.)

The Selection Tools

 With the *Smart Selection tool* you can select both text and objects. When you use this tool, the cursor changes shape, depending on what can be selected. If the cursor is over text, the cursor looks like a large thin letter *I*. If the cursor is over an object, it looks like an arrow.

When Smart Selection is on, you must use Ctrl+click to select text frames, text lines, and graphic frames as objects.

 MAC NOTE   On the Mac, Option+click selects text frames, text lines, and graphic frames as objects when Smart Selection is on.

 With the *Object Selection tool*, you can select only objects, not both text and objects. When you use this tool, the cursor looks like an arrow. By clicking on text in a text frame or a text line, you can select the text frame or text line without selecting any text contained in the frame.

Unless you Shift+click a new tool after you draw an object, you will return to the Smart Selection tool after each tool is used. To get the Object Selection tool after you draw an object, Shift+click the Object Selection button.

The Drawing Tools

Figure 13.3 shows what the drawing tools are in the Tools window. In this part of the chapter, we'll see what you can do with each of these tools. Let's look at them one at a time.

Line Tool

 The *Line tool* allows you to draw a line at any angle. To draw a line:

1. Click the Line tool button.

2. Move the cursor into the document. The cursor turns into a cross.

3. Place the cursor where you want to start the line.

4. Hold the mouse button and drag the cursor to where you want the line to end.

5. Release the mouse button.

TIP To draw a horizontal, vertical, or 45° straight line, hold the mouse button and Shift+drag the cursor to where you want the end of the line. Holding the Shift key constrains the line to the direction (horizontal, vertical, or a 45°) in which you drag the cursor.

Arc Tool

The *Arc tool* allows you to draw a 90° arc. The start and end points of the arc, both horizontally and vertically, cannot be on the same horizontal or vertical plane.

To draw an arc:

1. Click on the Arc tool button.

2. Move the cursor into the document. The cursor turns into a cross.

3. Place the cursor where you want to start the arc.

4. Hold the mouse button and drag the cursor to where you want the arc to end.

5. Release the mouse button.

Rectangle Tool

The *Rectangle tool* allows you to draw rectangles and squares. To draw a rectangle:

1. Click on the Rectangle tool.

2. Move the cursor into the document. The cursor turns into a cross.

3. Place the cursor where you want the corner of the rectangle to start.

4. Hold the mouse button and drag the cursor to where you want the opposite corner of the rectangle to be.

5. Release the mouse button.

To draw a square:

1. Click on the Rectangle tool button.

2. Move the cursor into the document. The cursor turns into a cross.

3. Place the cursor where you want the corner of the square to start.

Part
4

Doing More with
FrameMaker

4. Hold the mouse button and Shift+drag the cursor to where you want the opposite corner of the square to be.

5. Release the mouse button.

Rounded Rectangle Tool

 The *Rounded Rectangle tool* lets you draw rectangles or squares with rounded corners. Rounded rectangles look something like a TV screen, which also has rounded corners. To draw a rounded rectangle:

1. Click on the Rounded Rectangle tool button.

2. Move the cursor into the document. The cursor turns into a cross.

3. Place the cursor where you want the corner of the rounded rectangle to start.

4. Hold the mouse button and drag the cursor to where you want the opposite corner of the rounded rectangle to be.

5. Release the mouse button.

To draw a rounded square:

1. Click on the Rounded Rectangle tool button.

2. Move the cursor into the document. The cursor turns into a cross.

3. Place the cursor where you want the corner of the rounded square to start.

4. Hold the mouse button and Shift+drag the cursor to where you want the opposite corner of the rounded square to be.

5. Release the mouse button.

To change the radius of the corners on a rounded rectangle or square:

1. Select the rounded rectangle or square by clicking on it.

2. Select Graphics ➤ Object Properties. The Object Properties dialog box opens, as in Figure 13.4.

 NOTE For more information on the Object Properties dialog box, see "Changing the Size, Color, and Position of Objects" later in this chapter.

---

3. Click the Corner Radius text box and enter a new value in inches.

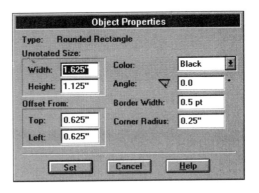

Figure 13.4   **The Object Properties dialog box showing rounded rectangle properties**

4.   Click the Set button.

Polyline Tool

 The *Polyline tool* allows you to draw a *polyline*, which is a line made of several segments that join end to end at different angles. A polyline looks like a jagged line. To draw a polyline:

1.   Click on the Polyline tool.

2.   Move the cursor into the document. The cursor turns into a cross.

3.   Place the cursor where you want to start the polyline.

4.   Click once and drag the cursor to where you want the first vertex to be.

5.   Click once and drag the cursor to where you want the second vertex to be.

6.   Continue clicking and dragging until the polyline is complete.

7.   At the end vertex, double-click. Reshape handles appear so you can reshape the polyline, if needed.

 TIP   To constrain a segment to horizontal, vertical, or 45°, Shift+click at a vertex.

Part
4

Doing More with
FrameMaker

Oval Tool

By clicking the *Oval tool*, you can draw an oval or a circle. To draw an oval:

1. Click on the Oval tool button.

2. Move the cursor into the document. The cursor turns into a cross.

3. Place the cursor where you want the oval to start. Hold the mouse button and drag the cursor diagonally to where you want the oval to end.

4. Release the mouse button.

To draw a circle:

1. Click on the Oval tool button.

2. Move the cursor into the document. The cursor turns into a cross.

3. Place the cursor where you want a corner of the circle to start.

4. Hold the mouse button and Shift+drag the cursor diagonally to where you want the circle to end.

5. Release the mouse button.

Polygon Tool

The *Polygon tool* lets you draw a *polygon*, which is a closed figure with three or more straight sides. To draw a polygon:

1. Click on the Polygon tool button.

2. Move the cursor into the document. The cursor turns into a cross.

3. Place the cursor where you want the polygon to start.

4. Click once to start and click once at each vertex of the polygon.

5. Double-click on the last vertex. Reshape handles appear so you can reshape the polygon, if needed.

TIP   To constrain a segment to horizontal, vertical, or 45° movement, Shift+click at a vertex.

To draw a polygon with all sides of equal length:

1. Draw a square or a circle.

2. Select the Set # Sides command from the left side of the Tools window (see Figure 13.1).

3. Enter the number of sides you want and the start angle.

4. Click the Set button.

Freehand Curve Tool

The *Freehand Curve tool* button is for drawing freehand lines. Using this tool is like using a pen to draw a curve on a piece of paper, which means it's possible to do it well or badly. Not all of us are cut out to use the Freehand Curve tool!

Freehand curves are made of something called Bezier curves. Bezier curves are easy to reshape. For more information, see "Working with Bezier Curves" later in this chapter.

To draw a freehand line:

1. Click the Freehand Curve button.

2. Move the cursor into the document. The cursor turns into a cross.

3. Place the cursor where you want the freehand line to start.

4. Hold the mouse button and drag the cursor. A line is drawn on the page as you drag the cursor.

5. Release the mouse button when you have finished drawing the line.

NOTE   If Snap is on, the invisible snap grid does not affect the drawing of the line, but the first point of the line will align with a grid point. The snap grid is discussed under "Aligning Objects with the Snap Grid" later in this chapter.

Part 4

Doing More with FrameMaker

Text Frame Tool

With the *Text Frame tool,* you can draw a text frame. You have seen text frames a number of times in these chapters. These are the frames that accept paragraphs of text. The Text Frame tool allows you to create them.

You can use text frames for multiline callouts, paragraphs of text, text you want to wrap, and a number of other things.

If a text frame is placed on a page in the middle of a text flow, the text will run around the text frame as long as text runaround is active. Text runaround is discussed later in this chapter in "Three More Drawing Commands: Join, Runaround, and Overprint."

To draw a Text Frame:

1. Click on the Text Frame tool button.

2. Move the cursor into the document. The cursor turns into a cross.

3. Place the cursor where you want the text frame to start.

4. Hold the mouse button and drag the cursor diagonally to where you want the text frame to end.

5. Release the mouse button.

6. Double-click in the text frame to place the insertion point in the text frame and type your text.

Text Line Tool

The *Text Line tool* lets you create a *text line,* a single line of text that is treated independently from other lines of text. A text line grows and shrinks as you edit it, add to it, or delete from it, but it doesn't wrap. A text line uses the format of the last character you typed or selected in the document. Characters in text lines can be selected and reformatted with either the Character Designer or the Format ► Font menu commands.

A text line does not move when you edit text around it. Text in a text flow is unaffected by a text line.

To draw a text line:

1. Click on the Text Line tool.

2. Move the cursor into the document. The cursor turns into a text cursor with a horizontal line through it.

3. Click where you want the text line.

4. Type the text you want the text line to contain.

    If you press ↵ at the end of a text line, you create a new text line below the first. This second text line is independent of the first text line.

Graphic Frame Tool

The *Graphic Frame tool* lets you draw a graphic frame. Graphic frames are frames that can contain graphic objects. They are like text frames, except that they do accept text paragraphs. A graphic frame is attached to the page on which it is drawn.

NOTE When a graphic frame is placed on a page in the middle of a text flow, the text in the flow runs around the frame if runaround is active for the frame. *Graphic frames* are used to hold and crop graphics and to hold reference graphics on a reference page. Text runaround is discussed in "Three More Drawing Commands: Join, Runaround, and Overprint" later in this chapter.

To draw a graphic frame:

1. Click on the Graphic Frame button.

2. Move the cursor into the document. The cursor turns into a cross.

3. Place the cursor where you want a corner of the graphic frame to start.

4. Hold the mouse button and drag the cursor diagonally to where you want the graphic frame to end.

5. Release the mouse button.

    If you draw a graphic frame on a reference page, the Frame Name dialog box appears. (It also appears if you select a graphic frame on a reference page and click the frame name in the status bar at the bottom of the document window.) The Frame Name dialog box allows you to name or rename a graphic frame on a reference page:

You must enter a name in the Name text box. If you do not enter a name, a graphic frame will not be created on the reference page. Click the Set button to apply the name.

Drawing Commands for Manipulating Graphics

The Drawing Commands area of the large Tools window is shown in Figure 13.5. In this area is a menu of drawing commands for manipulating graphics on the screen. Let's look at these commands one at a time.

To issue a command, select an object and then click on the command in the Tools window. Drawing commands are also available from the Graphics menu.

WINDOWS NOTE   Drawing commands are available only in the large Tools window. If you are using the Windows version of FrameMaker, issue drawing commands by using the Graphics menu.

Group: Combining Objects

The Group command combines independent objects (except frames) you've selected into a single object. To group objects, select the objects to be grouped, and then select the Group command. The combined object can then be manipulated as one object. You can use all of the drawing commands, except for Set # Sides, on grouped objects. You can also change the object properties of the combined objects as though all were a single object.

Using the Group command, you can group objects with other grouped or independent objects to form even larger groups.

Figure 13.5 **The drawing commands on the Tools window**

NOTE   You can also group objects by selecting Graphics ➤ Group.

Ungroup: "Uncombining" Grouped Objects

The Ungroup command separates grouped objects into independent objects.

To ungroup an object, select the grouped object, and then select Ungroup. If a large grouped object contains other, smaller grouped objects, ungrouping the larger object reveals the smaller groups of which the original object was composed but does not ungroup them. You can continue to ungroup combined objects until they are all separated into independent objects.

NOTE   You can also ungroup objects by selecting Graphics ➤ Ungroup.

MAC NOTE   You can use Ungroup to convert a PICT image into a Frame-Maker object. Just select the PICT image and click Ungroup.

Bring to Front: Moving Objects up Front

The Bring to Front command moves selected objects, including text frames and text lines, in front of other objects.

NOTE   You can also choose Bring to Front by selecting Graphics ➤ Bring to Front.

Send to Back: Moving Object Behind

The Send to Back command moves selected objects, including text frames and text lines, behind other objects. If an object disappears when you use Send to Back, simply select all of the objects in front and click on Send to Back again. This places the original hidden object in front of the other objects.

NOTE   You can also choose Send to Back by selecting Graphics ➤ Send to Back.

Align: Lining Up Objects

The Align command moves selected objects, excluding frames but including equations, so that a specific part of all the objects (for example, their left sides) lie along a straight line. You can also "align" a single object (including a grouped object) within a page or a frame with this command. Objects are aligned with a specific part of the *last* object you selected before the Align command was issued.

TIP   By using a "rubber band" selection border to select objects, you can align the objects with the frontmost object. See "Techniques for Selecting Objects" later in this chapter to learn about rubber band selection borders.

When you click on Align, the Align dialog box opens:

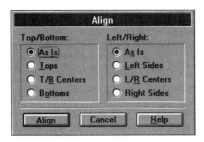

You can align objects both from top to bottom and from left to right. The top to bottom options are:

▶ **As Is**—Leaves Top/Bottom alignment unchanged.

▶ **Tops**—Aligns objects along their top edges.

▶ **T/B Centers**—Aligns objects along their top/bottom (vertical) center lines.

▶ **Bottoms**—Aligns objects along their bottom edges.

The left to right options are:

▶ **As Is**—Leaves Left/Right alignment unchanged.

▶ **Left Sides**—Aligns objects along their left sides.

▶ **L/R Centers**—Aligns objects along their left/right (horizontal) center lines.

▶ **Right Sides**—Aligns objects along their right sides.

Once you've clicked the options, press the Align button to perform the alignment. I recommend practicing with this one to see exactly how each option works. Try selecting objects in different orders before clicking the Align button.

NOTE   You can also align objects by selecting Graphics ➤ Align.

Distribute: Spreading Objects Out

The Distribute command moves objects, except for frames, horizontally or vertically until they are equally spaced. When you click on Distribute, the Distribute dialog box opens:

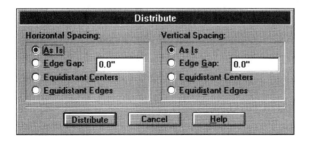

You can distribute objects both horizontally and vertically in the following ways:

▶ **As Is**—Leaves the spacing unchanged.

▶ **Edge Gap**—Moves all selected objects, except the leftmost object, to the left or right so that the gaps between the objects equal the value you entered in the text box. An edge gap of 0 makes the objects touch. A negative edge gap makes the objects overlap.

▶ **Equidistant Centers**—Moves all selected objects, except the leftmost and the rightmost, so that their centers are equally spaced.

▶ **Equidistant Edges**—Moves all selected objects, except the leftmost and the rightmost, so that their edges are equally spaced.

Click the Distribute button to perform the distribution.

NOTE   You can also distribute objects by selecting Graphics ➤ Distribute.

Reshape: Changing Objects' Shapes

The Reshape command allows you to change the shape of lines, polylines, polygons, arcs, and freehand curves.

When you select a line, polyline, or polygon and click Reshape, a reshape handle appears at each vertex. To reshape, simply drag a reshape handle. To add a vertex, Ctrl+click (⌘+Option+click on the Mac) on the point where you want a new vertex, then drag it into the new shape. To remove a vertex, Ctrl+click on it (⌘+Option+click on the Mac).

When you select a freehand line and click Reshape, reshape handles appear on the line and control points appear beside it. To change the shape of the line, drag a reshape handle. To change the curvature of the line, drag a control point.

To add a reshape handle to a curve, Ctrl+click (⌘+Option+click on the Mac) where you want the handle. To remove a reshape handle, Ctrl+click ⌘+Option+click on the Mac) on the handle you want removed.

When you select an arc and click reshape, a reshape handle appears at each end of the arc. To change the shape of the arc, drag one of the reshape handles.

NOTE   You can also reshape objects by selecting Graphics ➤ Reshape.

Smooth: Getting Softer Corners

The Smooth command does different things to different objects:

▶ For rectangles and squares, it rounds the corners.

▶ For rounded rectangles, it increases the corner radius.

▶ For polylines and polygons, it converts them into a series of Bezier curves. After the Smooth command is applied to a polyline or polygon, reshape handles and control points appear so you can reshape the curves. (For more information, see the "Working With Bezier Curves" later in this chapter.)

NOTE   You can also smooth objects by selecting Graphics ➤ Smooth.

Unsmooth: Getting Sharper Corners

The Unsmooth command does different things to different objects:

▶ For rounded rectangles and squares, it decreases the corner radius.

▶ For freehand curves, it converts them into polylines.

▶ For rectangles, squares, polylines, and polygons, it reverses the action of the Smooth command.

NOTE   You can also choose Unsmooth by selecting Graphics ➤ Unsmooth.

Flip U/D Turning Objects Upside Down

The Flip U/D (Up/Down) command flips an object along its horizontal axis so that the top of the object becomes the bottom. You can flip all objects except graphic frames, equations, and rotated text lines and text frames.

Part
4

Doing More with
FrameMaker

NOTE   You can also choose the Flip U/D command by selecting Graphics ➤ Flip Up/Down.

Flip L/R: Getting a Mirror Image of Objects

The Flip L/R (Left/Right) command flips an object along its vertical axis so that the left side of the object becomes the right side. In other words, it gives you a mirror image of an object.

You can flip all objects except for graphic frames, equations, and rotated text lines and text frames.

 NOTE   You can also issue this command by selecting Graphics ➤ Flip Left/Right.

Rotate: Spinning Objects

The Rotate command allows you to rotate objects. When you click on Rotate, depending on what object you have selected, one of several Rotate dialog boxes opens.

If you selected a graphics frame, equation, or table cell, a dialog box like this appears:

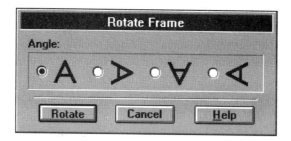

Here, you can rotate the object in 90° increments by clicking one of the radio buttons.

If you selected an object other than a graphics frame, equation, or table cell, the Rotate Selected Objects dialog box appears. Here is the Windows version of that dialog box:

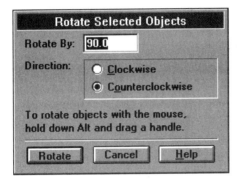

The Rotate By text box sets the rotation angle to any decimal value between 0 and 360 degrees, positive or negative. A negative angle rotates the object in a direction opposite to that set in the Direction area.

Select the direction to rotate the object in the Direction area of the dialog box. There are two choices, Clockwise and Counterclockwise. You can rotate several objects at the same time, whether or not they are grouped. Simply select the objects and click Rotate.

 TIP   On the Mac, you can rotate any object by selecting it, holding the ⌘ key, and dragging a reshape handle. In the Windows version, you can rotate objects in the same way with the Alt key. The UNIX version allows you to rotate objects with the Ctrl key and the right mouse button.

 NOTE   You can also rotate objects with the Graphics ➤ Rotate command.

Scale: Resizing an Object

The Scale command allows you to resize an object, except a text line or an equation, to either a percentage of its current size or to dimensions you specify. You can scale several objects at the same time, whether or not they are grouped.

Part 4

Doing More with FrameMaker

When you click on Scale, the Scale dialog box opens:

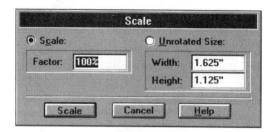

In the Scale area, enter a percentage to scale the object to a new size:

▶ 100% represents the object's current size.

▶ 50% represents half the object's size, both horizontally and vertically.

▶ 200% represents twice the object's size, both horizontally and vertically.

In the Unrotated Size area, you can enter numbers in the Width and Height text boxes to change those dimensions. The values you enter must be between 0.0125 and 3600 points. At first, the Width and Height text boxes contain the current dimensions of the object.

NOTE   You can also scale objects by selecting Graphics ➤ Scale.

Set # Sides: Changing Squares and Circles to Polygons

The Set # Sides command allows you to change a square or circle into a regular polygon with a number of equal sides. If you use Set # Sides with a rectangle, oval, or polygon, the new object will not have equal sides or equal angles. You might use this command when drawing flow charts, for example, to change triangles to rectangles.

When you click on Set # Sides, the Set Number of Sides dialog box opens:

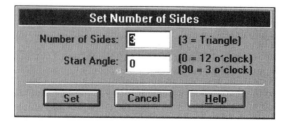

Fill in the dialog box like so:

▶ **Number of Sides**—Sets the number of sides for the polygon.

▶ **Start Angle**—Sets the clockwise rotation angle for the vertex of the polygon.

NOTE   You can also choose Set # Sides by selecting Graphics ➤ Set # Sides.

Object Properties: Changing Objects' Size, Color, Position

The Properties command, which you can also get by choosing Object Properties on the Graphics menu, allows you to view and change the properties of an object. These properties include size, color, position, border width, and angle of rotation.

For more information on this useful box, see "Changing the Size, Color, and Position of Objects" later in this chapter.

Picking Up Object Properties

By pressing the Shift key before you select Graphics, you can make the Object Properties command become the Pick Up Object Properties command. The Pick Up Object Properties command allows you to copy the properties of a selected object to the Tools Window. From there, you can change its properties both in the document you're working in and in other documents. For example, you can create your own customized arrowhead definitions.

Three More Drawing Commands: Join, Runaround, and Overprint

All of the drawing commands in Tools Window are also available in the Graphics menu. However, the Graphics menu gives you three commands that aren't in the Tools window—Join, Runaround Properties, and Overprint.

Join: Creating a Single Object from Many

The Graphics ➤ Join command connects objects, such as lines and arcs, to form a single object—for example, a single, longer line, or arc. You can then change the object's properties, including its line width, pen and fill patterns, and color. (Note that this is different from grouping the objects, which does not connect them to each other.)

You can join lines, polylines, smoothed polylines, arcs, and freehand curves to each other when their endpoints are touching. You cannot join objects that are part of grouped objects.

> **TIP**   If you join objects by mistake, use the Undo command (Edit ➤ Undo) immediately. There is no "unjoin" command!

Runaround Properties: Deciding How Text Flows around Objects

With the Graphics ➤ Runaround Properties command, you can specify how text flows around graphics. When you select Runaround Properties, you get the Runaround Properties dialog box shown in Figure 13.6.

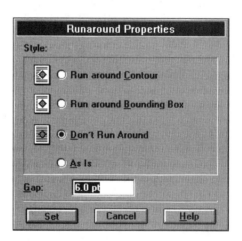

Figure 13.6   *The Runaround Properties dialog box*

Deciding how text runs around graphics is a complex issue, so I've devoted a whole section to it. See "Making Text Run Around Graphics" toward the end of this chapter.

The Overprint Command

When you choose Graphics ➤ Overprint command, the Overprint dialog box appears:

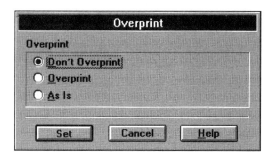

From here, you specify how overlapping objects are treated when color separations are printed.

NOTE See "Dealing with Color Separations" in Chapter 15 for the complete lowdown on color separations.

If you click the Overpint check box, all objects will be printed in their entirety, one over another, even if they are completely or partially hidden by other objects. Overprinting can cause the frontmost object to look murky on the printed page if there are other colored objects beneath it. (You can set Overprint for several objects at once by simply selecting the objects before choosing Overprint.)

If you click Don't Overprint, FrameMaker will print only the visible portions of objects. While this maintains the accuracy of the colors of the topmost objects, it may also cause a white border to appear at the overlap points when the color separations are registered (that is, laid on top of one another) for printing.

How to "Trap" in FrameMaker

If you decide not to overprint, you can make sure a white border doesn't appear by "trapping," a process familiar to graphic artists who work with four-color printing. Trapping creates a slight overlap between objects at their edges, so objects always at least touch where they should.

To trap objects in FrameMaker, create a duplicate of the top object, place it exactly on top of the object it duplicates, set fill to none (so its filled twin shows through from beneath it), define a thin border, and set the border color to match the other object's fill color. Then turn overprint on for the object with the border and leave overprint off for the filled object. The border will overprint, or "trap," the objects underneath.

Connecting Objects with the Gravity Feature

The Gravity feature helps connect objects to other objects. Turn it on by selecting Graphics ➤ Gravity or by clicking the check box next to the word *Gravity* under the drawing commands in the Tools window (see Figure 13.1).

When the Gravity setting is on, selected objects attract the pointer when you draw, resize, or reshape them. The corners and points of an object (where the handles are), and sometimes the center, exert a pull that attracts the pointer. In addition, as an object is dragged closer to a gravity point of another object, the first object automatically touches the gravity point of the second object.

Gravity extends the same distance on the screen regardless of the document zoom setting. So when gravity is on, you can zoom in to place an object close to a gravity point without the gravity point attracting the pointer or the other object.

Aligning Objects with the Snap Grid

The snap grid feature helps you align objects to an invisible grid. You turn it on by selecting Graphics ➤ Snap or by clicking on the check box next to the word *Snap* underneath the drawing commands in the Tools window.

When snap is on, selected objects are "attracted to" the invisible snap grid when you draw, resize, reshape, or move them. When you rotate objects, they snap to the snap rotation grid. As an object is dragged closer to a snap point, it automatically aligns itself to the invisible grid.

You can set the spacing of the invisible grid in the View Options dialog box.

1. Open the View Options dialog box, shown in Figure 13.7, by selecting View ➤ Options.

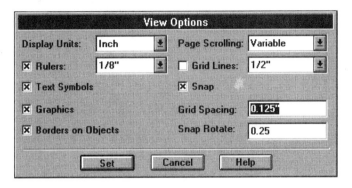

Figure 13.7 **The View Options dialog box**

2. Click the Snap check box.

3. Click in the Grid Spacing text box and change the value to what you want.

4. Click on the Set button.

 NOTE   See Chapter 3 for a more complete discussion of the invisible snap grid and the visible drawing grid.

Choosing Patterns and Colors for Objects

The Fill, Pen, and Color area of the Tools window are shown in Figure 13.8. (To bring up the Tools window, select Graphics ➤ Tools or press the Tools button.) You use these three tools to choose patterns and colors for objects and for their borders.

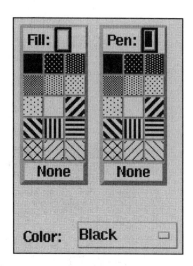

Figure 13.8   The Fill, Pen, and Color area of the large Tools window

Select a pattern that will fill an object from the Fill area. Select a pattern for the border of an object from the Pen area. To choose a color for the fill and pen pattern, use the Color pull-down menu.

NOTE   In the small Tools window, the Fill, Pen, and Color buttons are not together. The Fill and Pen buttons and indicators are immediately below the Graphics Frame Tool button. The Color button and indicator is the last of the group of buttons.

To choose a fill or pen pattern, select an object and click on the Fill and Pen pattern you want. To choose a color, select an object and then select a color from the Color pull-down menu.

In the large Tools window, the pattern that has been chosen is shown at the top of the Fill and Pen areas, respectively. The color that has been chosen is shown in the Color pull-down menu. In the small Tools window, the chosen fill and pen pattern and color are shown to the right of the boxes that call those pull-down menus.

Telling FrameMaker How to Draw Lines

The Line Properties area of the Tools window is where you tell Frame-Maker how to draw the lines in your graphics. You can select:

▶ The width of arcs, freehand curves, lines, polylines, and object borders

▶ The ends of arcs, lines, and polylines

▶ The style, solid or dashed, of lines and object borders

NOTE In the small Tools window, the Line Width, Line End, and Line Style buttons and indicators are located below the Fill and Pen buttons and above the Color button.

Choosing a Line Width

Use the Line Width menu to change the width of lines and objects properties, and also to set the line width for new objects.

In the large Tools window, the line width currently chosen is shown above the Line Width menu next to the Pts: label. In the small tools menu, it appears next to the button that calls the Line Width pull-down menu. Click on the current line width to apply it to a selected object.

The Line Width menu of both the large and small Tools window allows you to select one of four line widths as the new current line width. However, you can choose from more line widths by choosing Set from the Line Width menu. When you do, the Line Width Options dialog box appears:

Line Width Options			
0.5 pt	1.0 pt	3.0 pt	4.0 pt

(Use values between .015 and 360 points.)

Set	Get Defaults	Cancel	Help

Enter a width in any of the four text boxes. Each width must be between 0.015 and 360 points.

When you are done, click the Set button to apply the changes. Choose Get Defaults to reset the width to the default choices for lines to 0.5, 1.0, 3.0, and 4.0 points.

Choosing a Line End

The Ends menu, located below the label "Ends" in the large Tools window, is for changing the ends of arcs, lines, polylines, and freehand curves and for setting the end style of lines in new objects. Note that the arrows displayed on the Ends menu show only which direction the arrow will point when the object is drawn. They do not show the currently chosen arrow style.

In the large Tools window, the currently chosen line end is shown above the Ends menu next to the label "Ends." In the small Tools window, the currently chosen line is shown next to the button that calls the Line End pull-down menu. Click on the current line end to apply it to an object you've selected.

The menus on both the large and small Tools window allow you to select one of four line ends, but you can get other choices by clicking on Set from the Line Ends menu. When you choose Set, the Line End Options dialog box appears, as in Figure 13.9.

You can select from eight arrowhead styles in the Arrow Style area. The styles are listed with their base angles in degrees, their tip angles in degrees, and their lengths in points. There is also a graphic showing the arrow style. Click on the radio button next to a style to select it.

Designing Your Own Arrowhead   You can also design a custom style by clicking the radio button next to Custom and filling in the text boxes with the values you want.

▶ **Base Angle**—Can be any value between 5 and 175 degrees. The base angle must be at least 5 degrees greater than the tip angle.

▶ **Tip Angle**—Can be any value between 5 and 85 degrees.

▶ **Length**—Can be any value between 0 and 255 points. The length is specified for a 1.0 point line. The length will change as the line width changes.

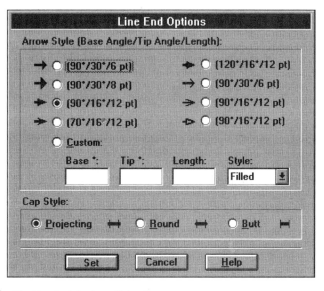

Figure 13.9   *The Line End Options dialog box*

▶ **Style**—You can choose Filled, Stick, and Hollow. If you choose Stick, the base angle setting is ignored (Stick arrows do not have a base).

Choosing a Cap Style   The Cap Style area is where you set the end style for lines that do not have arrowheads:

▶ **Projecting**—Lines ending with a square cap. This is the default.

▶ **Round**—Lines ending with a round cap.

▶ **Butt**—Lines ending with no cap.

When you are done choosing a style with which to end the line, click the Set button to apply your line end definitions to the object you selected.

Choosing a Line Style

The Line Style menu (in the Large Tools window, below the label "Dash") is for changing lines and object borders. You can make them solid or dashed. From this menu you also set the style to be used for new objects.

In the Large Tools window, the current line style is shown next to the label "Dash." In the small tools menu, the current line style appears next to the button that calls the Line style pull-down menu. Choices include Solid and Dashed.

Click on the current line style to apply it to a selected object. The type of dashed line available from the Line Style menu can be changed by clicking Set at the bottom of the menu. When you click Set, the Dashed Line Options dialog box appears, as in Figure 13.10.

This is where you can select a dashed pattern to use. There are eight patterns. To choose a dash pattern, click on one of the radio buttons. When you are done, click the Set button to apply the pattern to the object.

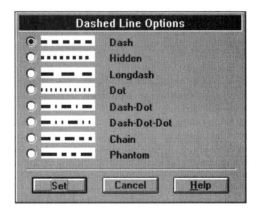

Figure 13.10   *The Dashed Line Options dialog box*

Creating a Drawing

Okay, let's put the drawing tools and drawing properties to work and make an original drawing. In this section, you will learn how to create a drawing. Hang on to the drawing you make here, because in subsequent sections you will learn how to manipulate it.

First, create a new document:

1. Select File ➤ New. The New file dialog box appears.

2. In the Use Blank Page area, click the Custom button. The Custom Blank Paper dialog box opens.

3. Click the Create button. A blank document opens.

Next, create an anchored frame in which to draw (anchored frames are discussed in Chapter 8):

1. Click in the text frame in the document to place the insertion point.

2. Select Special ➤ Anchored Frame. The Anchored Frame dialog box opens.

3. Under Size, change the Height to 4.0 inches.

4. Click the New Frame button. An anchored frame appears in the text frame.

Now, let's create a simple drawing:

1. Click the Tools button. The Tools window opens. (Mac and UNIX users: If the Small Tools window opens, click on Zoom to get the Large Tools window.) If necessary, turn the snap grid on by clicking the check box.

2. Shift+click the Rectangle Tool button, click the Fill pattern None and the Pen pattern solid black.

3. Move the cursor into the anchored frame. The cursor turns into a cross.

4. Move the cursor to the left side of the anchored frame. Hold the mouse button and drag the cursor diagonally to the right and down about two inches. Release the mouse button. Click to remove the selection handles.

5. Move the cursor so it is about half an inch to the right of the top of the rectangle you just created. Hold the mouse button and drag the cursor diagonally to the right and down about two inches. Release the mouse button. Click to remove the selection handles.

6. Click on the Line Tool button. Click on the Fill pattern solid black. Click on the Line End pattern of the right arrow.

7. Move the cursor into the anchored frame. The cursor turns into a cross.

8. Move the cursor so it's on top of the right side of the left rectangle about halfway between the top and the bottom. Hold the Shift key, hold the mouse button and drag the cursor to the right. (Holding the Shift key constrains the line to horizontal movement.) When the cursor is on top of the left side of the right rectangle, release the mouse button. An arrow appears pointing from the left rectangle to the right rectangle.

9. Click on the Text Line tool. Move the cursor into the anchored frame. The cursor turns into an insertion point with a small horizontal line through it. (The horizontal line shows where the bottom of the text line will be.)

10. Move the cursor into the left rectangle. Click near the center of the rectangle. A blinking cursor will appear.

11. Type **Start**.

12. Click on the Text Line tool. Move the cursor into the anchored frame. The cursor turns into an insertion point with a horizontal line. (The horizontal line shows where the bottom of the text line will be.)

13. Move the cursor into the right rectangle. Click near the center of the rectangle. A blinking cursor appears.

14. Type **End**.

15. Do not close the document.

That's it! You've just created a block diagram. The drawing should look something like this:

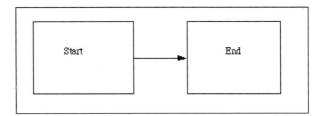

Don't worry if the drawing isn't perfect. Later in this chapter, you'll use drawing commands to correct inconsistencies.

Techniques for Selecting Objects

When you finish drawing an object, it is automatically selected. If an object is not selected, you can manually select it in either of two ways. You can

▶ Click on the object.

▶ Draw a "rubber band" selection box around the object. Do this by finding a point outside the object, holding the mouse button and dragging diagonally. A box appears. Continue dragging until the box encloses the object. Release the mouse button. The object is selected and handles appear.

You can also select more than one object at a time. You can do this in two ways. You can Draw a selection box around the objects. Do this by finding a point outside the objects, holding the mouse button and dragging diagonally. A box appears. Continue dragging until the box encloses all of the objects. When you release the mouse button, handles appear on the objects.

▶ Click on one object to select it. Add additional objects to the selection by holding the Ctrl key (Shift on the Mac) and clicking on an object.

Practice in Working with Graphic Objects

Once you've created a graphic object, you can manipulate it in several ways. For instance, you can use the drawing commands to change objects. You can also move objects or use Edit commands to copy, paste, or delete them.

In this section, you will learn how to manipulate graphic objects. You will use the block diagram drawing you created in the previous section as you do so.

Copying, Pasting, and Moving Objects

First, let's copy and paste the left rectangle:

1. Select the left rectangle by clicking on its border. Handles should appear.

2. Select Edit ➤ Copy.

3. Select Edit ➤ Paste. A new rectangle with handles appears slightly to the right and lower than the original rectangle. (Exactly nine points to the right and exactly nine points lower, in fact.)

Move the new rectangle:

1. Click and hold the mouse button anywhere on the border of the new rectangle except for a handle.

2. Drag the rectangle down and to the right until it is below the original rectangles and approximately centered in the gap between them. The drawing should look something like this:

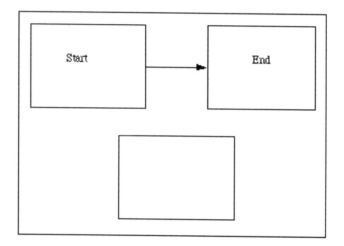

 TIP Another way to duplicate and move an object is to select the object, place the cursor anywhere on the object except on a handle, hold down the Alt key (Windows), the Control key (Mac), or the Ctrl key (UNIX), hold the mouse button (middle mouse button for UNIX users), and drag the object. A copy will appear.

Now we'll add an arrow, a fill pattern, and a caption:

1. Click on the Line Tool button. Click on the solid black Fill pattern and the solid black Pen pattern. Click on the Line End pattern of the right arrow.

2. Move the cursor into the anchored frame. The cursor turns into a cross.

3. Move the cursor so it's on top of the arrow halfway between the left and right rectangle. Hold the Shift key (to constrain the direction of the new arrow to vertical), hold the mouse button, and drag the cursor down to the bottom rectangle. When the cursor is on top of the top side of the

bottom rectangle, release the mouse button and Shift key. A vertical arrow appears.

4. Select the bottom rectangle by clicking on it.

5. Click on the shaded Fill pattern just to the left of the solid white pattern. The rectangle is filled with that pattern.

6. Click on the Text Line tool. Move the cursor into the anchored frame. The cursor turns into an insertion point with a small crosshatch. (The crosshatch shows where the bottom of the text line will be.)

7. Move the cursor into the bottom rectangle. Click near the center of the rectangle. A blinking cursor appears.

8. Type **End2.** The drawing should look something like this:

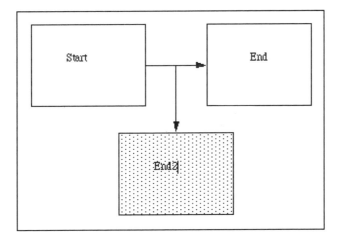

Now let's delete the new rectangle and arrow.

1. Select the bottom rectangle by clicking on it. Handles appear around the rectangle.

2. Select the text line *End2* by holding the Ctrl key and clicking on it.

 MAC NOTE   To do the above on a Mac, use Shift+Option+click.

3. Select the arrow that connects the bottom rectangle by holding the Ctrl key and clicking on it.

4. Press the Delete key. The rectangle, text line, and arrow are removed. The drawing should look something like the original.

5. Do not close the document. You will use it later in this chapter.

Moving Objects by Increments

As you just saw, one way to move objects is by clicking and dragging them to new locations. (You did this with the third rectangle you created for the simple drawing.) This method can be inexact, however.

When the snap grid is active and you move an object, the object aligns with the invisible snap grid. When the snap grid is inactive and you move an object, the object stays where you place it.

In either situation, you may not be able to place the object exactly where you need it to go, but you can get it close. At this point, you need a way to move the object in small increments. FrameMaker provides a way.

You can move an object in small, exact increments by holding the Alt key and pressing the ←, →, ↑, or ↓ key. This method moves an object a fixed distance on the screen.

 MAC AND UNIX NOTE   On a Mac, hold the Option key and press one of the arrow keys. In UNIX, hold the Ctrl key and press one of the arrow keys.

On a UNIX machine, this technique moves an object a fixed distance on the screen, but the actual distance the object moves depends on the Zoom setting of the display. If you are viewing a document at a Zoom setting of 100 percent, the object will move one point ($\frac{1}{72}$ inch) each time you press an arrow key. At a Zoom setting of 50 percent, pressing an arrow key moves the object 2 points. At a Zoom setting of 200 percent, pressing an arrow key moves an object half a point.

You can also move objects exactly 6 points at a time at a Zoom setting of 100 percent by holding the Alt+Shift keys and pressing an arrow key. (On a Mac, hold the Option+Shift keys and press an arrow key. On UNIX, hold the Control-Shift keys and press an arrow key.)

Pressing Alt+Shift+arrow at a Zoom setting of 50 percent, moves an object 12 points. Pressing Alt+Shift+arrow at a Zoom setting of 200 percent moves an object 3 points.

Working with Bezier Curves

A *Bezier curve* is a smooth, continuous curve. When you draw with the Freehand tool, FrameMaker uses a series of smooth, continuous Bezier curves to form the object. When you are finished drawing, handles appear on the object. There is a Bezier curve between each pair of handles along the curve. When you smooth a polyline or polygon, Bezier curves are used to form the converted object.

You can join two Bezier curves by moving them until their ends touch and selecting Graphics ➤ Join. Bezier curves and joined Bezier curves, like Freehand objects and smoothed polygons, can be manipulated like any other graphic object.

In addition, when you reshape a Bezier curve or joined Bezier curves, handles appear on the object. You can use these handles to change the curve's position. You can change the slope of the curve by using the control points that appear outside the object. Figure 13.11 shows handles and the control points on Bezier curves. The solid black squares are the handles. The squares with white centers are the control points.

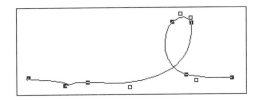

Figure 13.11   **Handles and control points on Bezier curves**

Aligning, Distributing, Rotating, and Scaling Objects

A drawing is ruined if some of its elements distract the viewer from the information that is being presented. For example, boxes of different sizes and uncentered text, as in the simple diagram drawing you created earlier in this chapter, are a distraction.

FrameMaker provides several drawing commands that can help you refine drawings. These include Align, Distribute, Rotate, and Scale. (For an explanation of these commands, see "Drawing Commands for Manipulating graphics" earlier in this chapter.)

In this section, you will use these commands to refine the simple block diagram you created earlier in this chapter. You will scale the rectangles, align them to each other vertically, distribute them horizontally, align the arrow to them, and rotate them.

First, let's resize the two rectangles so that they are the same size:

1. The Tools window (see Figure 13.1) should be open. If it isn't, open it now by clicking on the Tools button in the document window. (Mac and UNIX users: If the Small Tools window opens, click on Zoom to make it large.) If necessary, make the snap grid active by clicking on the Snap check box.

2. In the document, select the left rectangle by clicking on it. Handles appear around the border.

3. In the Tools window, click on Scale (or select Graphics ➤ Scale). The Scale dialog box opens.

4. In the Scale dialog box, set the Width to 2 inches (enter **2** in the text box) and the Height to 1 inch (enter **1** in the text box). Click the Scale button. The box is resized.

5. Repeat steps 2, 3, and 4 for the right rectangle.

Next, we'll vertically align the center of each rectangle to the others:

1. Select the right rectangle by clicking on it. Handles appear around the border.

2. Add the left rectangle to the selection by Ctrl-clicking on it. (Mac users should use Shift+Option+click.) Handles appear around the border.

3. In the Tools window, click on Align (or select Graphics ➤ Align). The Align dialog box opens.

4. Under Top/Bottom alignment, click the radio button next to T/B Centers. Under Left/Right alignment, click the radio button next to As Is. Click the Align button.

Now, let's distribute the rectangles horizontally:

1. Select the right rectangle by clicking on it. Handles appear around the border.

2. Add the left rectangle to the selection by Ctrl-clicking on it. (Again, Mac users use Shift+Option+click.) Handles appear around the border.

3. In the Tools window, click Distribute (or select Graphics ➤ Distribute). The Distribute dialog box opens.

4. Under Horizontal Spacing, select Edge Gap and enter **1** inch in the text box. Under Vertical Spacing, select As Is. Click the Distribute button.

Next, we'll align the text lines and arrow to the rectangles:

1. Select the text line *Start* by Ctrl+clicking on it. (On a Mac, Shift+Option+click on it.) Handles appear around the text line.

2. Add the left rectangle to the selection by Ctrl+clicking on it. (Mac users use Shift+Option+Click.) Handles appear around the border.

3. In the Tools window, click on Align (or use Graphics ➤ Align). The Align dialog box opens.

4. Under Top/Bottom alignment, click the radio button next to T/B Centers. Under Left/Right alignment, click the radio button next to L/R Centers. Click the Align button.

5. Repeat steps 1 through 4 to align the text line *End* and the right rectangle to each other.

6. Select the arrow by clicking on it. Handles appear at each end.

7. In the Tools window, click on Scale (or select Graphics ➤ Scale). The Scale dialog box opens.

8. In the Scale dialog box, set the Width to 1 inch (enter **1** in the text box). Notice that the Height is 0 because this is a horizontal arrow. Click the Scale button. The line is resized.

9. Click and hold the mouse button on the arrow and drag it until its left end is touching the right border of the left rectangle and its right end is touching the left border of the right rectangle. Release the mouse button.

10. Ctrl+click the left rectangle to add it to the selection. Handles appear around the border. (The arrow is already selected.)

11. In the Tools window, click on Align (or select Graphics ➤ Align). The Align dialog box opens.

12. Under Top/Bottom alignment, click the radio button next to T/B Centers. Under Left/Right alignment, click the radio button next to As Is. Click the Align button.

Your drawing should now look exactly like the following, except for the font used for the text line. Compare it to your original drawing.

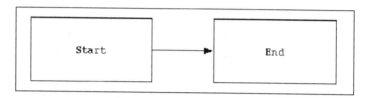

Finally, let's rotate the rectangles:

1. Select the right rectangle by clicking on it. Handles appear around the border.

2. Add the left rectangle to the selection by Ctrl+clicking on it (on the Mac, use Shift+Option+click). Handles appear around the border.

3. In the Tools window, click on Rotate (or select Graphics ➤ Rotate). The Rotate Selected Object dialog box opens.

4. In the Rotate Selected Object dialog box, select the defaults (Rotate By 90 degrees and Direction Counterclockwise). Click the Rotate button. The rectangle rotates.

5. Select the arrow by clicking on it. Handles appear at each end.

6. In the Tools window, click on Scale (or select Graphics ➤ Scale). The Scale dialog box opens.

7. In the Scale dialog box, change the Scale Factor to 200 percent by entering **200** in the text window. Click the Scale button.

Your drawing should now look like the following, except for the font used for the text line. Notice that once you align objects and manipulate them together, they maintain their alignment.

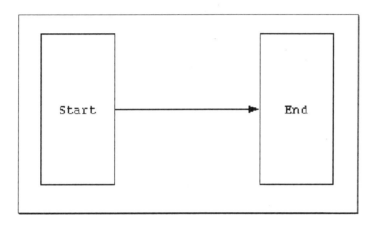

Importing Graphic Images

Using the Clipboard, you can import or paste graphics created in other applications, such as a paint program or a scanner, into a FrameMaker document. These can include bitmap graphics, vector graphic graphics, and Desktop Color Separation files.

 MAC NOTE   On a Mac with System 7 or above, you can also import Quick-Time movies. If QuickTime is installed on your system, you can even play QuickTime movies directly from a FrameMaker document.

Once an imported graphic is in a document, it is treated like a single graphic object, and you can manipulate it as you can other graphic objects. You can move it, scale it, anchor it to text, group it with other objects, cut it, copy it, and paste it.

You can also import PostScript files into a text frame. The PostScript appears on the screen as text (unless your system uses Display Post-Script), but when the document is printed on a PostScript printer, the image appears.

Importing Bitmap Images

In its truest sense, a bitmap image consists of a grid of black-and-white dots. Each dot is represented by one bit in the bitmap file. A zero (0) represents a white dot and a one (1) represents a black dot.

A gray scale or a color image also consists of dots, but each dot is assigned a shade of gray or a color. Therefore, each dot is represented by a group of bits, not just one. With 256 levels of gray scale or 256 colors, eight bits are required to represent each dot. Since bitmaps, gray scale images, and color images are all imported in the same way, the term *bitmap* will be used to apply to all of them.

Bitmaps can be created by a paint program, by a scanner, or by a screen-capture program. Also, a large number of clip art images are sold in bitmap format.

The bitmap formats in Table 13.1 are supported by FrameMaker.

Format	What It Is/How It's Used
BMP	Windows bitmap image. Windows only.
DCS	Desktop Color Separations. The images print correctly on all platforms, but display only if the preview image is supported by FrameMaker. All platforms.
DIB	Device Independent Bitmap. Windows only.
EMF	Enhanced Metafile. Windows NT only.
GEM	GEM Bitmap Image. All platforms.
GIF	Graphics Interchange Format. Windows and Mac only.
MacPaint	MacPaint format image. All platforms.
OLE	Object Linking and Embedding. Windows only.
PCX	PCX image. All platforms.

Table 13.1 **Bitmap Formats that FrameMaker Supports**

Format	What It Is/How It's Used
PICT	A raster and vector format. All platforms.
SGI-RGB	Silicon Graphics Red-Green-Blue image. UNIX only.
Sun raster	Sun Microsystems raster file. All platforms.
TIFF	Tagged Image File Format version 5 and 6 with CMYK extensions. All platforms.
WPG	WordPerfect Graphics. All platforms.
X11xwd	X Windows screen dump. All platforms.
Xbitmap	UNIX only.

Table 13.1 **Bitmap Formats that FrameMaker Supports (continued)**

To import a bitmap image:

1. Select where you want the image placed.

    - To place the image in a graphic frame, select the frame.

    - To place the image in a text frame, place the insertion point in the frame. The image will be imported into a newly created anchored frame.

    - To place the image directly on the page, click in the margin of the page. Do not have any other object or text selected.

    - To replace an image already in the document, select the image.

2. Select File ➤ Import ➤ File. The Import File dialog box opens, as in Figure 13.12.

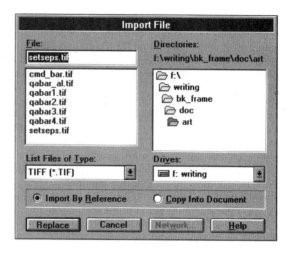

Figure 13.12   **The Import File dialog box**

3. Select the file you want to import. Use the scroll list and pull-down menu to locate the file, then click on it. If you need to choose the type of files that appear in the dialog box, use the List Files of Type pull-down menu.

 MAC NOTE   To choose the type of files that appear in the dialog box, use the Format pull-down menu or the Show All Files check box.

4. Select the Copy into Document or Import by Reference radio button.

   Copy into Document is the same as using the Copy and Paste commands. The image becomes part of the document. Importing by copy also increases the document's size by the size of the image. In addition, if you need to make changes to the image, you'll have to re-import the updated version.

   Import by Reference stores only the path to the image in the document. The image will be found and displayed each time the document is opened. If you make changes to the source file, the updated version will be displayed each time the page is redisplayed.

5. Click the Import button. The Imported Graphic Scaling dialog box opens, as in Figure 13.13.

6. Select a scaling factor (one of the radio buttons under Options).

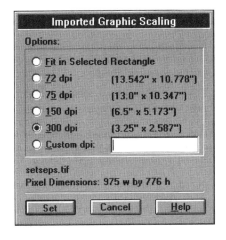

Figure 13.13 **The Imported Graphic Scaling dialog box**

For a better screen display, choose a value that divides evenly into your screen's resolution. For example, VGA screens are usually 96 dpi, while Macintosh screens have a resolution of 72 dpi.

For best printing results, choose a value that divides evenly into your printer's resolution. For example, for 300 and 600 dpi printers, choose 300, 150, 100, or 75 dpi. For other printers, you can specify a Custom dpi.

7. Click the Set button to import the image.

NOTE If you import an image directly on a page and it is placed over text, you can set the Text Runaround properties of the object. See "Making Text Run Around Graphics" later in this chapter.

Importing Vector Graphics

A *vector graphic* consists of a file that contains mathematical descriptions of the objects that appear in the graphic. Because of this, vector graphics retain their sharpness and clarity when they are resized.

An Encapsulated PostScript (EPS) file is a type of vector graphic. It uses the PostScript page description language to describe the objects in the graphic. An EPS file contains the information for printing. It may also contain a preview image that FrameMaker can display if the image is in

Part 4

Doing More with FrameMaker

a format that FrameMaker supports. If an EPS file does not have a preview image, or if the image is in an unsupported format, the image is displayed as a gray box on the screen.

Encapsulated PostScript Interchange (EPSI) files also use the PostScript page description language, but are designed specifically for cross-platform use. They contain a bitmap preview image that can be displayed on all platforms.

A vector graphic can be black and white, gray scale, or color. Table 13.2 lists the vector formats that are supported by FrameMaker.

Format	What It Is/How It's Used
CDR	CorelDraw version 3. All platforms.
CGM	Computer Graphics Metafile. All platforms.
DRW	Micrographx Draw. All platforms.
DFX	AutoCAD Drawing Interchange Format releases 10, 11, and 12. All platforms.
EPS	Encapsulated PostScript. The image is printed correctly on all platforms, but displays only if there is a preview image supported by FrameMaker. All platforms.
EPSI	Encapsulated PostScript Interchange. All platforms.
HPGL	Hewlett-Packard Graphics Language (used frequently for pen plotters). All platforms.
IGES	Initial Graphics Exchange Specification. All platforms.
PICT	A raster and vector format. All platforms.

Table 13.2 **Vector Formats that FrameMaker Supports**

Format	What It Is/How It's Used
PS	PostScript (PS). In a text frame defined as PostScript code, imported PS files appear on the screen as text, but print as the image they represent. All platforms.
WPG	WordPerfect Graphics. All platforms.
WMF	Windows Metafile. All platforms.

Table 13.2 **Vector Formats that FrameMaker Supports (continued)**

To import a vector graphic image:

1. Select where you want the image placed.

   - To place the image in a graphic frame, select the frame.

   - To place the image in a text frame, place the insertion point in the frame. The image will be imported into a newly created anchored frame.

   - To place the image directly on the page, click in the margin of the page. Do not have any other object or text selected.

   - To replace an image already in the document, select the image.

2. Select File ➤ Import ➤ File. The Import File dialog box (see Figure 13.12) opens.

3. Select the file you want to import. Use the scroll list and pull-down menu to locate the file, then click on it. To choose the type of files that appear in the dialog box, use the List Files of Type text box and pull-down menu.

 MAC NOTE To choose the type of files that appear in the dialog box, use the Format pull-down menu or the Show All Files check box.

4. Select Copy into Document or Import by Reference.

   Copy into Document is the same as using the Copy and Paste commands. The image becomes part of the document. This also increases the document's size by the size of the image. If you need to make changes to the image, you have to re-import the updated version.

   Import by Reference stores only the path to the image in the document. The image will be found and displayed each time the document opens.

If you make changes to the referenced image, the updated version is displayed each time the page is redisplayed.

5. Click the Import button.

> **NOTE** If you import an image directly on a page and it is placed over text, you can set Text Runaround properties for the object. See the "Making Text Run Around Graphics" later in this chapter.

Importing Desktop Color Separation Files

Desktop Color Separation (DCS) format is a standard used by many applications to allow the printing of process-color graphics in a Post-Script prepress system.

A DCS graphic consists of five files, all of which must be present for the graphic to be printed correctly. The five files include a main file that contains the preview image and a file for each of the four color separations (Cyan, Magenta, Yellow, and Black). The main file and the four color files must always be kept in the same directory.

You can import DCS graphics by reference or by copying them.

> **NOTE** If you import a DCS graphic by copying, all five files—the main and the four color files—are copied into the document. This greatly increases the size of the document.

To import a Desktop Color Separation (DCS) graphic:

1. Select where you want the graphic placed.

    -   To place the graphic in a graphic frame, select the frame.

    -   To place the graphic in a text frame, place the insertion point in the frame. The graphic will be imported into an anchored frame.

    -   To place the graphic directly on the page, click in the margin of the page. Do not have any other object or text selected.

    -   To replace a graphic already in the document, select the graphic.

2. Select File ➤ Import ➤ File. The Import File dialog box opens (see Figure 13.12).

3. Select the main file of the graphic you want to import. Use the scroll list and pull-down menu to locate the main file, then click on it. To choose the type of files that appear in the dialog box, use the List Files of Type text box and pull-down menu.

MAC NOTE To choose the type of files that appear in the dialog box, use the **Format** pull-down menu or the **Show All Files** check box.

4. Click the Copy into Document or Import by Reference radio button.

    Copy into Document is the same as using the Copy and Paste commands. The graphic becomes part of the document. This also increases the document's size by the size of the main file and color files. If you need to make changes to the graphic, you have to re-import the updated version.

    Import by Reference stores only the path to the main file in the document. The graphic will be found and displayed each time the document is opened. If you make changes to the referenced graphic, the updated version will be displayed each time the page is redisplayed.

5. Click the Import button.

NOTE If you import a graphic directly on a page and it is placed over text, you can set the Text Runaround properties for the object. See "Making Text Run Around Graphics" later in this chapter.

Importing QuickTime Movies (Mac Only)

On a Macintosh with System 7 or above, you can import QuickTime movies. They are imported the same way as other graphics. If QuickTime is installed on your system, you can also play the movies directly from the FrameMaker document.

You can cut, copy, paste, and resize a QuickTime movie, but if you resize a QuickTime movie, the playback quality is poorer.

When you import a QuickTime movie, it appears in the document with a control badge in the movie frame. Click on the control badge to make the movie control bar appear. If an anchored frame is created during

Part 4

Doing More with FrameMaker

import, the frame will be slightly taller than the movie frame to make room for the control bar.

When you print a document containing a QuickTime movie, the movie shows on paper as a rectangle with the movie title in it.

WARNING If you import the movie with the Copy command, only a small portion of the movie is copied into the document. So whether the movie is imported by copying or by reference, the original movie file should not be moved or deleted.

To import a QuickTime movie:

1. Select where you want the movie placed:

    - To place the movie in a graphic frame, select the frame.

    - To place the movie in a text frame, place the insertion point in the frame. The movie will be imported into an anchored frame.

    - To place the movie directly on the page, click in the margin of the page. Do not have any other object or text selected.

    - To replace a movie already in the document, select the movie.

2. Select File ➤ Import ➤ File. The Import File dialog box opens (see Figure 13.12).

3. Select the movie you want to import. Use the scroll list and pull-down menu to locate the movie, then click on it. To choose the type of files that appear in the dialog box, use the Format pull-down menu or the Show All Files check box.

4. Select the Copy into Document or Import by Reference radio button.

    Copy into Document is the same as using the Copy and Paste commands, except that only a small part of the movie is copied into the document.

    Import by Reference stores only the path to the movie in the document. The movie will be found and displayed each time the document opens. If you make changes to the referenced movie, the updated version is displayed each time the page is redisplayed.

5. Click the Import button.

> **NOTE** If you import a movie directly on a page and it is placed over text, you can set the Text Runaround properties for the object. See "Making Text Run Around Graphics" later in this chapter.

Importing PostScript Code

You can import PostScript code into a FrameMaker document. Unlike Encapsulated PostScript (EPS) files, which have a preview image, PostScript code does appear as an image on the screen (unless your system uses Display PostScript). When you print the file to a PostScript printer, the code is interpreted and printed as an image. You can also use PostScript code to create special effects, such as text on a radius.

To import PostScript code:

1. From the Tools window (see Figure 13.1), use the Text Frame tool to create a text frame.

2. Type in the PostScript code, paste in the code, or import the code.

3. Click the Import button.

4. Select the text frame by clicking on it.

5. Select Format ➤ Customize Layout ➤ Customize Text Frame. The Customize Text Frame dialog box opens.

6. Select PostScript Code.

7. Click the Set button. The text frame is now treated like an object and you cannot place the insertion point in the PostScript code.

> **NOTE** To edit the code in a PostScript Code frame, select Format ➤ Customize Layout ➤ Customize Text Frame. The Customize Text Frame dialog box opens. In the Customize Text Frame dialog box, deselect PostScript Code. You can edit the code. When you are done, open the Customize Text Frame dialog box and select PostScript Code.

Making Text Run around Graphics

There are three ways that text can interact with an anchored graphic object—that is, a graphic that doesn't move on the page:

▶ The text can ignore the graphic object and run right over the top of it.

▶ The text can follow the contours of the graphic object and not trespass on it.

▶ The text can follow the contours of the bounding box around the graphic object. The *bounding box* is the box that appears around the object when you select it.

To set how text runs around or doesn't run around an object, select the object and select Graphics ➤ Runaround Properties. The Runaround Properties dialog box appears. This dialog box is shown in Figure 13.14.

Figure 13.14   *The Runaround Properties dialog box*

Choose one of the radio buttons in this dialog box:

▶ **Run around Contour**—Makes the text follow the contours of the graphic object. How much space lies between the graphic object and the text is specified in the Gap text box. Here is what text looks like when it "runs around the contour":

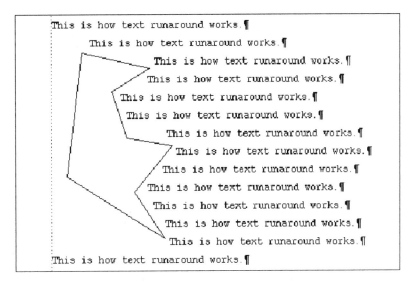

▶ **Run around Bounding Box**—Makes the text align vertically with the left or right side of the bounding box around the graphic object. Here's what text looks like when it keeps to the edge of the bounding box:

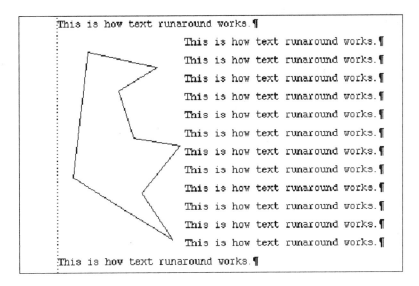

Part 4

Doing More with FrameMaker

▶ **Don't Run Around**—Makes the text run right over the graphic:

```
This is how text runaround works. ¶
This is how text runaround works. ¶
This is how text runaround works. ¶
This is how text runaround works. ¶
This is how text runaround works. ¶
This is how text runaround works. ¶
This is how text runaround works. ¶
This is how text runaround works. ¶
This is how text runaround works. ¶
This is how text runaround works. ¶
This is how text runaround works. ¶
```

▶ **As Is**—When several objects are selected, the As Is setting shows that the objects have different runaround properties. If you wish to change the runaround properties of all the selected objects, click on the radio button next to the setting you want and click Set.

Changing the Size, Color, and Position of Objects

The Object Properties command allows you to view and change the properties of an object. An object's size, color, position, and angle of rotation are called its "properties."

When you select an object and click on the Properties command in the Tools window or select Graphics ➤ Object Properties, the Object Properties dialog box opens and displays the properties of the selected object. This dialog box is shown in Figure 13.15.

The items in the Object Properties dialog box vary, depending on the type of object you selected. In this figure, the properties are those of a rectangle.

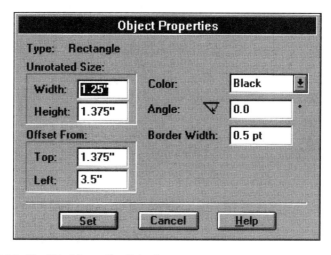

Figure 13.15 The Object Properties dialog box

NOTE If a text frame is selected when you bring up the Object Properties dialog box, a specialized version of the dialog box, called the Customize Text Frame dialog box, opens. For more information on text frames, see Chapter 8.

TIP The Object Properties and Customize Text Frame dialog boxes can be used both to see objects' properties and to change them. Editing properties with these boxes can be a useful way to control exactly how and where an object is displayed.

Depending on the object selected, the following items appear in the Properties dialog boxes. Change these items to change the properties of the object you selected. Once you've changed the properties, click the Set button to apply them to the object you selected.

Property	What It Shows
Type	The object type—for instance, a rectangle.
Unrotated Size	The height and width of the object before rotation was applied, if any. The height and width must be tetween 0.0125 and 3600 points.

Part 4

Doing More with FrameMaker

Property	What It Shows
Offset Position	The position of the object relative to the top or left side of the page or graphic frame.
Alignment Point Offset From	The position of the text line or equation baseline relative to the top or left side of the page or graphic frame. For text lines and equations only.
Alignment	The alignment of a text line (left, center, right) or an equation (left, center, right, manual). The alignment is maintained if you edit a text line or equation. For text lines and equations only.
Color	The object's color.
Angle	The object's clockwise rotation in degrees.
Border Width	The width of the border on the object. The width must be between 0.015 and 360 points.
Line Width	The width of a line or polyline, The width must be between 0.015 and 360 points. Lines and polylines only.
Corner Radius	The corner radius. The corner radius can be no more than half the size of the rectangle's shortest side. a rounded rectangle that is on inch by two inches can have a corner radius no larger than one half an inch. Rounded rectangles and squares only.
Start Angle	The start angle of an arc in degrees. The angle is measured clockwise from the 12 o'clock position on the page. Arcs only.
End Angle	The end angle of an arc in degrees. The angle is measured clockwise from the 12 o'clock position on the page. Arcs only.

Property	What It Shows
Facets	The facets that are present for an imported graphic. A *facet* is a representation of an inset. Some facets (such as PICT, FrameImage, and PostScript) are used to display and print graphics. Imported graphics only.
Language	The language used when spell-checking the text line. Text lines only.
Size	The size (small, medium, large) of the equation. Equations only.
Automatic Line Break After	Where the equation breaks automatically across lines.
Flow Tag	The tag of the text flow in the frame. Text frames only.
Autoconnect	Whether a page will be added automatically after the last text frame in the flow is filled. Text frames drawn with the text Frame tool have Autoconnect turned off. Text frames only.
PostScript Code	Interprets PostScript code in a text frame as an image and displays it when you print the document. The PostScript code will display as an image if your system uses Display PostScript. If PostScript code is not selected, the contents of the text frame is treated as normal text. Text frames only.
Room for Side Heads	Whether or not room will be left in the text frame for sideheads, and if so, how much (Width), the gap between the sidehead area and the next column, and the side (Left, Right, Side Closer to Binding, or Side Farther from Binding). Text frames only.

Part
4

Doing More with
FrameMaker

Property	What It Shows
Columns	The number of columns in the text frame, the gap between them, and whether or not they are balanced in the frame. Text frames only.
Room for Side Heads	Whether or not room will be left in the text frame for sideheads, and if so, how much (Width), the gap between the sidehead area and the next column, and the side (Left, Right, Side Closer to Binding, or Side Farther from Binding.) Text frames only.

If you hold the Shift key while you choose Properties in the Tools window, the Object Properties command changes to Pick Up Object Properties. This command changes the setting in the Tools window to match those of the selected object.

You can also choose Properties by selecting Graphics ➤ Object Properties. Object Properties becomes Pick Up Object Properties if you hold down the Shift key before selecting the Graphics command.

Chapter 14
Working with Tables

Tables are a versatile feature of FrameMaker 5. You can create and modify tables of any size, and use FrameMaker's powerful table-formatting capabilities to make tables look as interesting and professional as any you'll find in a printed publication.

Tables have properties, just like characters and paragraphs do. Frame-Maker lets you change the properties of tables with a designer window, called (you guessed it) the Table Designer. You can also save named sets of table properties for later use in a table catalog, so they'll be handy whenever you need them.

This chapter shows you how to create tables, add and change table cells, and use the Table Designer and the Custom Ruling and Shading windows to control the look of tables. You'll also see how to change plain text into tables, and how to copy table formats from one document to another. Finally, you'll learn another use for tables—as a place to put figures and figure captions. Once you learn the principles, you'll find working with tables fast and easy.

 NOTE Even though there is a table catalog (that is, a place in each document where the program stores table formats), there is no Table Catalog window you can use to apply these formats. Instead, formats from the table catalog must be applied using the Table Designer.

How Tables Work in FrameMaker

Tables are like anchored frames, except that you can control the space above and below them. A table is anchored to the text and moves when the text (and anchor symbol) moves. You can change the position of a table at any time with the Table.

Tables can straddle either all columns or all columns and the sidehead area, if it exists. Tables that are wider than one column in a multicolumn document will straddle all columns. Tables that are wider than all columns in the text area (in both single- and multicolumn documents) straddle all columns in the text area *and* the sidehead area, if there is one. Tables can also be positioned to "float" in the same way as anchored frames.

Heading and footing rows are repeated automatically at the top and bottom of each page whenever a table breaks across pages. You have probably seen tables with heading rows, also known as column heads.

Footing rows, which is where footnotes go, often contain explanations of the special symbols or abbreviations used in the table.

TIP   To get all of the placement options of anchored frames for tables, draw an anchored frame, put a text frame inside it, and then put the table in the text frame. A table can go anywhere an anchored frame can go, including the margins of the page. A table can also appear inside a paragraph with text wrapped around it.

Creating and Editing New Tables

Tables can be created from scratch, or you can convert existing text into a table. If you are importing information from a spreadsheet or database program, you will probably use the latter technique (it's covered later in this chapter). But most of the time, you'll create tables and then fill them in.

Creating an Empty Table in a Document

To create an empty table:

1. Place the character cursor in the line of text below which you want the table to be inserted. An anchor symbol appears at the character cursor. The table itself will be displayed below the line containing the anchor symbol.

2. Select Table ➤ Insert Table. The Insert Table dialog box appears, as in Figure 14.1.

3. Select a format from the Table Format list. (See below for an explanation of these formats.)

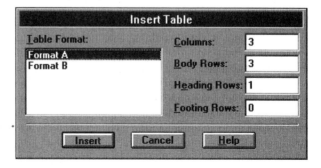

Figure 14.1   **The Insert Table dialog box**

4. Select the number of Columns, Body Rows, Heading Rows, and Footing Rows.

5. Click Insert at the bottom of the dialog box.

Default A and B Table Formats in New Documents

Most new documents in FrameMaker have two built-in formats, called Format A and Format B. These are simple table formats with column and row ruling lines, and distinctive heading and footing ruling lines. Figure 14.2 shows tables that use Format A and Format B. Note that these formats differ in their use of ruling lines.

Table 1:	Ribebis	
Ego ille	Quem nosti	Apros et quidem
Pulcherrimos	1980	Cepi.
Inquis	1984	Ipse; non tamen ut omnino ab inertia mea et quete discederem.
Ad retia	1983	Erat in proximo no venabulum aut lancea.

Table 1:	Ribebis	
Ego ille	Quem nosti	Apros et quidem
Pulcherrimos	1980	Cepi.
Inquis	1984	Ipse; non tamen ut omnino ab inertia mea et quete discederem.
Ad retia	1983	Erat in proximo no venabulum aut lancea.

Figure 14.2 **Format A (left) and Format B table (right)**

They also differ in their alignment—Format A is left-aligned and Format B is center-aligned in the text frame.

Entering Text and Other Objects into Table Cells

If you turn text symbols on (with View ➤ Text Symbols), you'll see that the cells of a table contain end-of-flow symbols:

For the most part, these cells act like little text frames. Enter text into table cells just as you would into text frames.

> **NOTE**   A *cell* is a "box" in the table. Normally, a cell is one column wide and one row tall, though larger cells (cells that "straddle" more than one row and/or column) are not uncommon. In a table, each cell holds one piece of data.

Cells can contain one or more paragraphs, just as text frames can. You can also import text by reference and graphic images directly into table cells. Cells can also contain anchored frames. When you import graphics into a table cell, for example, an anchored frame is created to contain it. But there are other uses for anchored frames in table cells. By manually inserting an anchored frame into a cell and then placing a text frame into the anchored frame, you can put another table into the text frame, in effect putting one table inside another one!

To move between cells of a table, use the mouse to click in the cell you wish to edit. You can also use the Tab and Shift-Tab keys to move to the next or previous cells, respectively, in a table. All of the editing commands and keys (except the Tab key) that work in text frames also work in table cells. (Since the Tab key is used to move from cell to cell in a table, you must use Esc Tab to enter a tab character into a table cell.)

Cutting, Copying, and Pasting Table Cells

You can cut, copy, and paste whole cells or groups of cells in a table. Do this by selecting the cell or cells to cut or copy (by dragging through them until the right ones are highlighted), and then cutting or copying, just as you would with text. When you are copying or cutting, put the character cursor in the cell where you want to paste the cells and paste away.

Selecting Cells

You can use Ctrl+click (Option+click on the Mac) to select a cell or a group of cells quickly. To select a row, a column, or an entire table:

▶ **Row**—To select a row, drag through it.

▶ **Column**—To select a column, drag from a heading row downward or Ctrl+double-click in a heading row (Option+double-click on the Mac).

▶ **Table**—To select a whole table, select a cell and then select Edit ➤ Select All of Table. You can also Ctrl+triple-click anywhere in the table (Option+triple-click on the Mac).

Pasting Cells

To paste a row or column into a table, place the character cursor anywhere in a row or column of the same or another table. When you select Edit ➤ Paste, you see a dialog box that allows you to replace the current row or column, or paste the new row or column next to it:

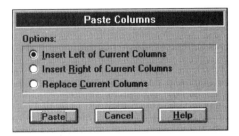

If you are pasting one cell, the new cell and its contents replace the old one. If you are pasting groups of cells, the new top-left cell of the new group is pasted into the cell with the character cursor, and the rest of the cells are pasted into neighboring cells.

To paste any group of table cells—either a whole table or part of a table—into the main flow of text, just place the character cursor at an insertion point in the text and then paste as you normally would. In effect, you are creating a new table. Tables and parts of tables can be copied and moved in this way.

WARNING Be careful when cutting, copying, and pasting from and to tables. Selecting a group of characters *in* a table cell is different than selecting the whole cell itself. When you select characters in a cell (even whole paragraphs), only those characters are highlighted. When you select an entire cell, the *whole* cell is highlighted (not just its contents) and there is a control handle on the side for dragging the column border. Before you cut, copy, or paste, make sure you've selected what you want—some of the contents of a cell, or the cell itself.

Part
4

Doing More with
FrameMaker

Adding New Rows and Columns to Tables

To add rows or columns to a table, select Table ➤ Add Rows or Columns. The Add Rows or Columns dialog box appears. Simply make a choice from the dialog box and click Add.

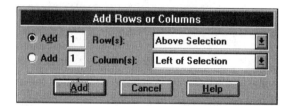

Changing the Shape and Look of a Table

Once your table is inserted and the data has been put into it, you may find that the columns and rows are not right. One column may be too narrow, for example, and another one too wide. You can change the size of columns and rows easily, and even rotate cells so that the text in them appears on its side.

Changing the Size of Columns and Rows

To change the width of a column, select any cell in the column and drag the resizing handle on the right side of the cell:

The whole table will become wider or narrower. To change the width of a column without changing the width of the table, hold down the Shift key as you drag the boundary of the cell. (If snap is turned on, the column margins will snap to the snap grid.)

To be more precise about changing the width of columns, you can select a column or a group of columns, then choose Table ➤ Resize Columns and use the Resize Selected Columns dialog box to resize columns more exactly. This dialog box is shown in Figure 14.3.

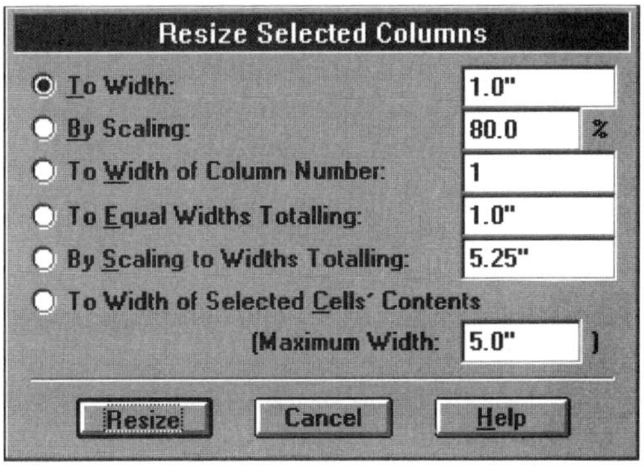

Figure 14.3   **The Resize Selected Columns dialog box**

There are a number of options here. You can use the To Width radio button to resize columns to exact dimensions, for example, or the To Width of Selected Cells' Contents button to "shrink-wrap" the column to the width of the cell containing the most contents (among the cells selected).

You can also scale each of the columns selected by some percentage, or scale them all proportionately so that their total width equals a number you select. (This last option is useful for scaling an entire table to fit some specified width without changing the relative widths of the columns it contains.)

To change the size of rows, select Table ➤ Row Format. The Row Format dialog box shown in Figure 14.4 appears. It allows you to set not only the height of a row, but other formatting options as well.

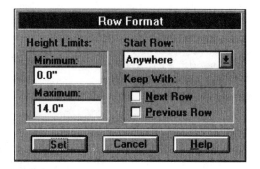

Figure 14.4   **The Row Format dialog box**

Making Cells Straddle Columns and Rows

You can join cells so that they straddle across rows or columns in a table. To do this, select the cells and choose Table ➤ Straddle. The result will look something like this:

Table 1: Ribebis		
Ego ille	Quem nosti	Apros et quidem
Pulcherrimos	1989	Cepi.
Inquis		Ipse; non tamen ut omnino ab iner- tia mea et quete discederem.
Ad retia	1983	Erat in proximo no venabulum aut lancea.

To reverse the process, select the straddling cell and select Table ➤ Unstraddle.

Rotating Cells

You've already learned that cells can be rotated in a table. Rotating a cell doesn't change its dimensions—you must do that by hand. But it does change the direction of the text within the cell and turn the letters on their sides or even upside-down.

To rotate a cell or a group of cells, first select the cells, and then select Graphics ➤ Rotate. The Rotate Table Cells dialog box appears, as in Figure 14.5. Use it to rotate cells in 90° increments.

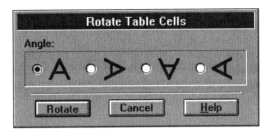

Figure 14.5 **The Rotate Table Cells dialog box**

Controlling How Tables Look

Controlling how tables look, also called "formatting tables," is done with the Table Designer. The Table Designer allows you to create table tags and assign tags to tables, and thus change the way tables look. You can also directly change the look of a table with the Table Designer, without using table tags to do so. To open the Table Designer window, select Table ➤ Table Designer. The Table Designer window appears, as in Figure 14.6.

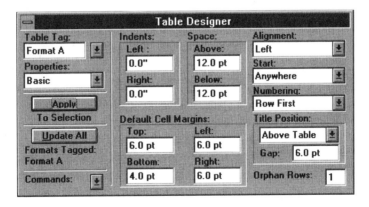

Figure 14.6 **The Table Designer window**

On the right side of the Table Designer are groups of table properties. The properties determine what the table looks like. On the left side of the window are the controls. Notice the pull-down list labeled Properties on the control side of the dialog box. This list determines which set (or "page") of properties is displayed in the right side of the window. These properties include Basic, Ruling, and Shading properties. When the window is first opened, the Basic set of properties is displayed. To see another set of properties, make another selection from the Properties pull-down list.

In this section, we'll examine the pages of properties one at a time, starting with the Basic properties. Then we'll look at the controls. The types of properties are:

Property	What It Does
Basic	Offers ways of controlling how far the table is indented from the text frame, how much space goes between the table and the preceding and following paragraph, how much space goes between the text and the walls of the table cells, how the table is aligned in the text frame or column, where tables appear on the page, and where the title goes.
Ruling	Lets you include ruling lines in tables between columns, between body rows, between the body of the table and heading/footing rows, and around the table itself. *Ruling lines* are dark lines that help direct the reader to important parts of a table.
Shading	Lets you shade certain rows and columns of a table to direct the reader's attention there; also lets you apply regular shading (to every other row, for example) to break up the landscape in large, hard-to-read tables.

NOTE All table properties in the Table Designer can be set to the As Is setting. This important setting is explained in Chapter 9. See that chapter for more information on what As Is means and how it is used.

Basic Table Properties

When you select Basic from the Properties pull-down list, you see the Basic set of properties. This set is shown in Figure 14.6. Let's look at these properties one at a time.

Indentation Settings   In the Indent area you can specify the left and right indentation for the table as a whole. The Left setting is used for left-aligned tables, and the Right setting is used for right-aligned tables. Centered tables use neither setting. Both indentations are measured from the edge of the text frame, not the edge of the page.

Space Above and Below the Table   The Space Above setting tells how much white space appears above the table. The Space Below tells how much white space appears below the table. Both measurements are presented in points.

When a table appears below a paragraph, the larger of the applicable space settings—space above the table and space below the paragraph—is used to determine the spacing. A similar rule applies when a table appears above a paragraph.

Default Cell Margins   The Default Cell Margins area offers settings for how much space lies between the text and the top, bottom, left, and right margins of the cells in the table. Text may come no nearer the cell boundaries than these margins allow.

TIP   You can override the cell margin settings for individual cells with the Table Cell properties of the Paragraph Designer.

Alignment   Alignment is a pull-down list with the following options: Left, Center, and Right alignment, and for double-sided documents, Side Closer to Binding and Side Farther from Binding. These alignment settings are relative to the borders of the text frame or column, not to the edge of the page.

Start   The Start pull-down lets you determine where a table starts. Choices include Anywhere, Top of Column, Top of Page, Top of Left Page, Top of Right Page, and Float. Anywhere places the table wherever it will fit, usually immediately below the line that contains the table anchor. The Top of Column and Top of Page settings place the table at the top of the next column or page that will hold it.

Float allows the table to "float" away from its anchor if there isn't enough room below the anchor for the table to fit. With Float on, many lines of text can appear between the anchor and the table. With Float off, the table and the anchor are kept together, even if the anchor must be moved out of a text frame or column that is not completely full and into the next one. (Floating tables are similar to floating anchored frames.)

Cell Numbering   With the options on the Number pull-down list, you can determine the direction in which cell paragraphs are numbered when cell paragraphs contain autonumbering and footnotes. Choices are Row First and Column First.

Title Position   Title Position specifies a place for a title (Above Table or Below Table). There is also a No Title option. The Gap text box lets you place white space (measured in points) between the title and the table.

> **NOTE**   Table titles are formatted with the Paragraph Designer and, optionally, paragraph tags. Using paragraph tags is recommended, since tables are often numbered, and autonumbering is the most efficient way to do this. See Chapter 10 for information about paragraph formatting and the Paragraph Designer.

You can also add two special variables to table titles, Table Continuation and Table Sheet. These variables are used with multipage tables. Table Continuation places a word like "Continued" in the table title. Table Sheet shows the current table page (called a "sheet") in a form like "Sheet 2 of 3." These variables can be also added to heading and footing rows. See Chapter 19 to learn more.

Orphan Row Control   The Orphan Rows setting determines the minimum number of table rows that may be isolated from the rest of the table by a page break.

Ruling Lines Properties

The Ruling properties page of the Table Designer, shown in Figure 14.7, is for specifying how ruling lines appear in the table. Ruling lines are dark lines that "dress up" the look of a table.

You can also customize ruling lines for any cell or group of cells (to make a group of cells stand out, for example) by using the Custom Ruling and Shading dialog box, which is covered later in this chapter.

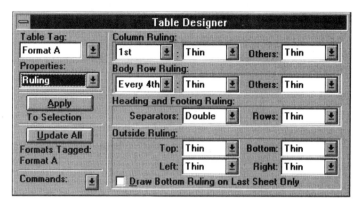

Figure 14.7   The Ruling Properties page of the Table Designer

Column Ruling   The Column Ruling area lets you set a ruling style for the right edge of one column separately from the ruling style of the right edges of all other columns. Ruling styles initially include None, Double, Medium, Thick, Thin, and Very Thin. In effect, this setting lets you place a darker line on one column, most likely the leftmost one where the column labels are.

NOTE   Ruling styles can be edited with the Custom Ruling and Shading dialog box. See later in this chapter for more information.

To use this setting, specify a column (1st, 2nd, and so on) in the first pull-down list, then a ruling style for the right edge of that column from the second pull-down list, and finally a ruling style for all other columns from the third pull-down list. Then apply your changes. (To see how to apply changes, see the section on Table Designer Controls later in this chapter.)

To make all column rulings look the same, make the settings in the second and third lists identical and apply your changes. (In this case, it doesn't matter what appears in the first list.)

Body Row Ruling   The Body Row Ruling area is similar to the Column Ruling area. It allows you to set a ruling style for the bottom edges of every second, third, fourth (etc.) row separately from the ruling style of the rows in between. (Again, ruling styles initially include None, Double, Medium, Thick, Thin, and Very Thin, but they can be edited.) You could, for example, make every second row end in a thick line. Or every third row could end in a double line, while the others had very thin lines in between.

To use this setting, specify a group of rows (Every 2nd, Every 3rd, and so on) in the first pull-down list, then a ruling style for the bottom edges of those rows from the second pull-down list, and finally a ruling style for all other rows from the third pull-down list. Then apply your changes.

To make all row rulings look the same, ignore the setting in the first box, make the settings in the second and third lists identical, and apply your changes.

Heading and Footing Ruling   The Heading and Footing Ruling area contains two boxes—one called Separators that sets a ruling style for the border between all heading or footing rows and the body of the table, and another called Rows that sets a ruling style between multiple heading and/or footing rows, if there are more than one. The Ruling styles here are the same ones that are available elsewhere in the Table Designer.

Outside Ruling   The Outside Ruling area offers four settings—Top, Bottom, Left, and Right. With these settings, you can set ruling styles separately for these borders of the table. In addition, there is a Draw Bottom Ruling on Last Sheet Only check box at the bottom of the page that allows you to decide whether the Bottom setting is applied to all bottom lines of a multipage table. (Keep in mind that pages of a table are called "sheets".)

Shading Properties

The Shading properties page of the Table Designer is shown in Figure 14.8. This is where you tell FrameMaker to shade the rows and columns of the table. "Shading" is really a fill pattern of dots and a color for those dots. The cell can be filled with no dots, a few dots, or many dots. You can choose from a number of dot densities. You can also fill columns or rows entirely with the color.

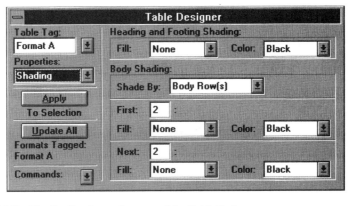

Figure 14.8   The Shading Properties page of the Table Designer

 NOTE   You can also shade a cell or group of cells with the Custom Ruling and Shading dialog box, which is discussed later in this chapter.

Heading and Footing Shading   From the Heading and Footing Shading area, you can specify a fill pattern and a color for all heading and footing rows. The Fill setting fills the cell with white or with dots of the specified color, expressed as a percentage ranging from None to 100%. The higher the percent, the more colored dots fill the cell. A setting of 100% fills the cell completely and, in effect, blackens (or colors) it out.

 NOTE   The Color list offers all colors that have been defined for the document, including user-defined colors. See Chapter 15 for information on defining or importing custom color definitions.

Body Shading   From the Body Shading area you can specify alternating bands of shading for either sets of body rows or body columns. Fill and Color choices for these bands are the same as elsewhere in the Table Designer.

To shade either rows or columns in alternating bands, choose either Body Row(s) or Column(s) in the Shade By pull-down list. Then type the number of rows or columns in the first band in the box labeled First and choose a Fill and Color for that band. Finally, type the number of rows or columns in the second band in the box labeled Next, choose a Fill and Color for that band, and apply your changes.

To shade all body cells alike, set both the Fill and Color boxes to the same setting and apply your changes.

Table Designer Controls

The control area of the Table Designer is identical to the control area of the Paragraph Designer. It has a Table Tag pull-down menu, a Properties pull-down list, an Apply button, an Update All button, and a Commands pull-down menu. If you're familiar with the Paragaraph Designer, you're all set. Otherwise, read on.

You already know about the Properties pull-down list. It allows you to "page" through the groups of table properties, from Basic through Shading. You can also page though these properties by pressing PgUp and PgDn.

What Are Table Tags?

The Table Tag field lists all the table tags that have been defined for the current document. As you have already seen, a "table tag" is a predefined set of table properties. To see the definition of a table tag, select the tag from the Table Tag pull-down list. The Table Designer property settings display the tag's definition. If the Table Tag field is blank, it means that no table tag has been defined for the tables selected in the document, or multiple tags are present. Blank is the field's usual condition.

To create new table tags or modify existing ones, see Chapter 9, "Characters and Character Formats." The procedures for working with table formats and tags are nearly identical to those for working with character formats and tags (and also paragraph formats and tags).

Applying a Table Tag

To apply a table tag to selected text, select the tag you wish to apply from the Table Tag pull-down list. Then click Apply, Update All, or select Global Update Options. All are described below.

Apply Button   The Apply button applies the properties in the current page of the Table Designer, including the tag, if any, to the tables that have been selected (highlighted) in the current document. The Apply button does *not* update the definition of a tag in the table catalog.

Update All Button The Update All button is actually several buttons in one. If the text below the button says "Tables" (meaning "Update All Tables"), then Update All brings up the Global Update Options dialog box shown in Figure 14.9. From here, you can choose several options. First, decide which properties to update, All Properties in the Table Designer (i.e., all pages of properties) or the properties of the current page only.

Figure 14.9 **The Global Update Options dialog box**

Then decide where to apply those properties:

▶ **All Tables and Catalog Entries**—Changes all tables in the document and all table tag definitions.

▶ **All Matching Tags in Selection**—Changes only those tags in the tables selected in the document, if tables of more than one tag were selected.

▶ **All Tagged**—Allows you to make changes to only one tag, the one selected from the pull-down list.

The changes are applied both to tables of a particular tag and to the tags themselves.

If the text below the Update All button says "Formats Tagged" (meaning "Update All Formats Tagged *XXX*", where *XXX* is a table tag), then Update All makes changes to only one tag (the one called *XXX*) and to the tables that have that tag.

You see "Update All Tables" when the selected text either has no tag or contains tables with more than one tag. You see "Update All Formats Tagged" when the selected text contains tables that all have the same format tag, or when you select a table tag from the Table Tag pull-down list.

The Commands Menu

The Commands pull-down menu gives you access to several useful commands, all of which you have seen in the other designer windows:

▶ **New Format command**—Creates a new table format using the properties in the Table Designer. The New Format command brings up the New Format dialog box. Enter the name of the new tag and choose whether to store the tag in the catalog and/or apply it to the selected text.

▶ **Global Update Options**—Brings up the Global Update Options window, the same box that appears when you select the Update All button. The only thing to remember about using this command is that if a table tag appears in the Table Tag field, the update will retag selected tables in the document. If no tag name appears in the Table Tag field, only properties of selected tables will be updated.

▶ **Delete Formats**—Displays the Delete Formats from Catalog dialog box so you can delete a format. To delete a format from the catalog, select a format and click Delete. When you are done, select Done.

(Formats are not actually removed from the document until you select Done.)

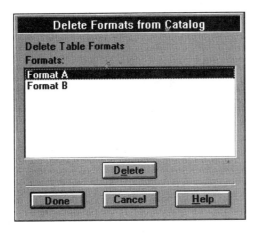

▶ **Set Window To As Is**—Sets all properties in the current page of the Table Designer to As Is.

▶ **Reset Window from Selection**—Resets the current Table Designer properties to the properties of the table(s) selected in the document.

Customized Ruling Lines and Shading

You can change ruling lines for selected cells individually. You can also shade them this way. Moreover, you can customize the way that ruling styles appear. Do all of this with the Custom Ruling and Shading dialog box shown in Figure 14.10. To see this box, select Table ➤ Custom Ruling & Shading.

As you can see, this box has two areas—Custom Cell Ruling and Custom Cell Shading. They operate independently of one another. Each has a check box that determines whether its settings are applied when you click the Apply button. The Show Current Settings button on the bottom of the dialog box (next to Apply) simply displays the current settings of the table cells.

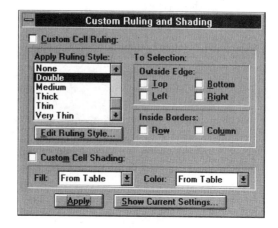

Figure 14.10   *The Custom Ruling and Shading dialog box*

Playing with the Ruling Lines

The Custom Cell Ruling area lists all the ruling styles defined for the document. It also specifies where to apply changes to the ruling lines in the cells. The various Outside Edge and Inside Borders check boxes allow you to specify any combination of outside and inside edges whose ruling lines you wish to change.

What's that Edit Ruling Style button for? It allows you to edit the list of ruling styles. You can delete an existing style, change its definition, or add a style or styles of your own. (Ruling styles are saved with the document and imported when table formats are imported.) When you press the Edit Ruling Style button, you see the Edit Ruling Style dialog box:

Initially, the Name field contains the name of the style highlighted in the Custom Ruling and Shading dialog box. If you change the Color, Pen Pattern, Width, or Number of Lines of the named style and then press Set, the definition of that style will be changed.

 WARNING There is no Undo command in the Edit Ruling Style dialog box, nor is there a "get defaults" button. When you press Set, the box closes and the changes take place whether you like it or not!

Be careful with this box. If you type the name of an existing style in the Name field, the other fields aren't updated with the settings of that style. It's therefore possible to change a style and not be aware of it. The best way to edit a style is to select that style first from the scroll list and then click the Edit Ruling Style button. This way, the box will always display the current definition of the style.

Your Own Customized Shading

The Custom Cell Shading area of the Custom Ruling and Shading dialog box (see Figure 14.10) offers the same Fill and Color options as the Shading Properties page of the Table Designer. And it offers one more setting besides, the From Table option. Use this option to reset the fill and color to the settings already specified for the cells by the Table Designer.

From Text to Tables and Back Again

Paragraphs of text can be converted into tables, and tables can be converted into paragraphs of text. This section explains how to do that.

Converting Text into Tables

Data that has been exported from a spreadsheet or database program started life as a table. Therefore, it can be reconverted by FrameMaker and made into a table again. You can also convert paragraphs into tables as long as the data was entered originally in a document so it could be converted into a table.

Most spreadsheet and database programs export their data as text. They write the information out row by row or record by record, with a tab, comma, or other delimiter to separate the cells in each row (or the fields in each record) from one another. After you import this kind of text into FrameMaker, one look will tell you how it is structured and what the delimiter is, if any. With this information, you are ready to proceed.

Convert text paragraphs into a table by highlighting the paragraphs to be converted and selecting Table ➤ Convert to Table. The Convert to Table dialog box appears, as in Figure 14.11. When paragraphs are converted into a table, each paragraph can be treated as either a row of cells, with the cells separated by whatever delimiter you specify, or as a single cell.

Use the first set of options under Treat Each Paragraph As for data derived from spreadsheets and database programs. With these options, the paragraph is treated as a row of cells. Just identify and specify the delimiting character with one of the three radio buttons.

The second option, is for specifying a number of columns for the table. With this option the paragraphs are written into the table one row at a time.

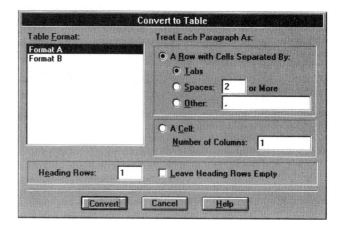

Figure 14.11   **Convert to Table dialog box**

Converting Tables into Text

Converting tables into text is useful if you want to send information in table form and the only way to transmit it is via a carrier that accepts only plain text. For example, you have to convert tables to text before you can send them in e-mail messages. The table could be converted into text paragraphs at your end, mailed to your recipient, and reconverted into a table there.

To convert a table into text, place the character cursor anywhere in a table and select Table ➤ Convert to Paragraphs. The Convert to Paragraphs dialog box appears:

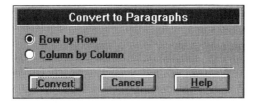

When a table is converted to text, each cell is written out as one or more paragraphs into the text frame or column at the current location. Cells are written so they can be read across, row by row, if you select the Row by Row radio button, or written so they can be read down, column-by-column, if you select the Column by Column radio button.

Copying Table Formats from One Document to Another

Just as you can copy character formats from one document to another, you can copy table formats and rulings styles also. To do so:

1. Open both the document you want to copy the formats from and the new document.

Part 4

Doing More with FrameMaker

2. With the new document active, select File ➤ Import ➤ Formats. The Import Formats dialog box appears as in Figure 14.12.

3. Select the document to copy from by using the Import from Document pull-down list. (With only two documents open, there are only two selections.)

4. In the Import and Update section of the window, click the Table Formats check box. You can also select any or all of the other choices.

5. Click the Import button. The table catalog in the new document is updated with all the formats and ruling styles from the original document.

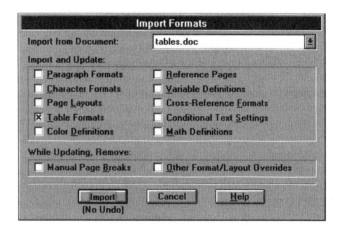

Figure 14.12   *The Import Formats dialog box*

Advanced Features

5

Chapter 15
Working with Color

FrameMaker comes with a variety of color options. In a Frame-Maker document, you can apply color to text and to objects. You can define custom colors—that is, colors other than those that come with the program—and set up different document views to see colors. You can also use FrameMaker to create color separations, the special printed pages that commercial printers use to print color documents. This chapter covers all of these options.

FrameMaker also comes with all the color definitions of the Pantone Matching System (PMS). This is the system printers use to specify ink colors exactly. It is especially handy if you are sending your work to a print shop. You can use the Pantone color model to see what your work will look like after it has been printed professionally, either by viewing your work onscreen or by printing it on your own color printer.

Of course, to view colors in a FrameMaker document, you must have a color monitor; and to print colors from FrameMaker, you must have a compatible color printer.

Adding Color to Text and Graphics

You can add color to a document in a number of ways, all of which are discussed in this section.

▶ With the Paragraph Designer or Character Designer, you can change the color of text to something other than black.

▶ With the Tools window, you can change the color of text, backgrounds and borders on text frames, anchored frames, and drawn objects.

▶ You can import graphics (pictures, drawings, and scanned images) that have color in them.

You can also display conditional text in colors, and control the colors used by the document comparison feature.

Adding Color to Text

There are several ways to add color to text. You can use the Character Designer or the Paragraph Designer.

With the Character Designer, you can Change the color of selected letters or words. You can also define character tags that apply colors to selected characters. With the Paragraph Designer, you can change the color of text in selected paragraphs. You can also define paragraph tags so that the text of certain paragraphs is always displayed in a certain color.

Let's look at the Character Designer first.

Adding Color with the Character Designer

You can use the Character Designer and character tags to add color to characters, words, and text lines created with the Tools window, and to the entire contents of paragraphs. For more information about the Character Designer, see Chapter 9.

 NOTE Changing the properties of characters in a paragraph does not change the properties of either the paragraph itself or the paragraph tag that applies to it.

To change the color of selected text characters (without using a character tag):

1. Open the document. (If you wish to practice, use a fresh copy of TRUDY.DOC, the document created in the first five chapters of this book.)

2. Open the Character Designer by selecting Format ➤ Characters ➤ Designer or by pressing Ctrl+D (⌘+D on the Mac). You'll see the dialog box shown in Figure 15.1.

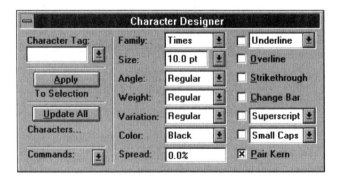

Figure 15.1   The Character Designer

3. Select the text you want to color. (For example, in TRUDY.DOC you might want to color the words *past due*.)

4. In the Character Designer, select a color (red is a nice "past due" color) from the Color pull-down menu.

5. Click on the Apply button. The selected text, in this case *past due*, is displayed in color.

   If you are working with TRUDY.DOC, don't close the document. We can use it in the next procedure.

To define a character tag that applies color to selected text:

1. Open the Character Designer by selecting Format ➤ Characters ➤ Designer or by pressing Ctrl+D (⌘+D on the Mac).

2. Select Set Window to As Is from the Commands list.

3. Select a color from the Color pull-down menu.

4. Make other changes to character properties, if you wish.

5. Type a name for the new tag in the Character Tag text box.

TIP   You can name a character tag by its color or by its purpose. For example, if the reason for the tag is to make something red, then "Red" is a good tag name. But if the reason for the tag is to highlight special terms—for example, words that are defined in a glossary at the end of an article, or words that are also hypertext links—then "Glossary" or "HT Link" would make better tag names than "Red" would. Naming tags by purpose instead of by color allows you to change colors in character tags without having to rename them.

---

6. Click Apply. The New Format dialog box appears, as in Figure 15.2.

Figure 15.2 *The New Format dialog box*

Part
5

Advanced Features

7. Click on the Store in Catalog check box to make this character tag available for other text.

8. Click the Apply to Selection check box to turn it off (unless, of course, you have already selected text to which to apply the tag).

9. Click the Create button.

10. If you wish, bring up the Character Catalog to see your new tag in the list.

    If you are using TRUDY.DOC, don't close the document. We can use it in the next procedure.

    Apply this tag as you would any other character tag, by highlighting text and clicking on the tag name in the Character Catalog.

Adding Color with the Tools Window

You can use the Tools window instead of the Character Designer to add color to text:

1. Select the characters you want to make a different color.

2. Open the Tools window by selecting Graphics ➤ Tools.

3. Select a color from the Color pull-down menu and release the mouse button. The text changes color when the mouse button is released.

Adding Color with the Paragraph Designer

You can also add color to a document by using the Paragraph Designer window. Any paragraph in a document can be colored. For more information on the Paragraph Designer, see Chapter 10.

To change the color of characters in a paragraph (without using a paragraph tag):

1. Open the document. (If you used TRUDY.DOC in the last procedure, the words *past due* are already red.)

2. Open the Paragraph Designer by selecting Format ➤ Paragraphs ➤ Designer or by pressing Ctrl+M (⌘+M on the Mac).

3. From the Properties pull-down list, select Default Font. The Default Font page of the Paragraph Designer appears, as in Figure 15.3.

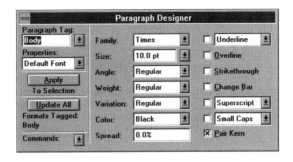

Figure 15.3   The Paragraph Designer with default font settings shown

4. Place the insertion point into the paragraph you want to change. (In TRUDY.DOC, let's place it anywhere in the paragraph that says "Sorry.")

5. In the Paragraph Designer, select a color from the Color pull-down menu. (For TRUDY.DOC, let's choose Blue for contrast.)

6. Click the Apply button. In TRUDY.DOC, notice that all of the text in the paragraph is now blue.

If you're using TRUDY.DOC, leave it open for now.

To define a paragraph tag that includes color as part of its definition, simply select a color other than black from the Color pull-down list in the Default Font page when you are creating or modifying paragraph formats.

Adding Color to Graphics

You can add color to graphics objects by using the Tools window. You can add color to lines and other drawn objects, to text lines, to text frames (both borders and backgrounds), to imported vector graphics, and even to text in a document. (For more information on the Tools window, see Chapter 13.)

To add color to a graphics object:

1. Open the document. If you have been using TRUDY.DOC, there is a paragraph that says *Sorry* in blue, and the words *past due* are in red.

2. Open the Tools window by selecting Graphics ➤ Tools or by clicking on the Tools button on the upper-right side of the document window.

Part 5

Advanced Features

3. Either select an object or draw one. In TRUDY.DOC, let's draw a small rectangle somewhere on the page. To do this:

    - Click on the picture of the rectangle in the Tools window.

    - Move the arrow into the document. Notice that the cursor changes into a cross.

    - Pick a spot on the page, click and hold the mouse button, and drag the mouse to the right and down. A small rectangle is formed.

    - Release the mouse button. Notice that the rectangle is selected (it has pull-handles around its edges).

4. In the Tools window, select a color using the Color button or menu (for TRUDY.DOC, let's use Red again). Note that when you release the mouse button, the color is applied to the selected object.

5. When you are done with the document, save it.

    For TRUDY.DOC, let's save under a new name by selecting File ➤ Save As, entering the file name TRUDY_C.DOC in the Save Document As text area, and clicking on the Save button.

Creating, Modifying, and Importing Colors

It is easy to create your own color definitions and add them to the list of colors available in the Paragraph Designer, Character Designer, Tools window, and other color lists. Not only can you change the definitions of existing colors, you can import color definitions from document to document.

What Is a Color Model?

Before we start creating colors, let's look at one of the basic concepts in color creation—the color model. A *color model* is simply a way of defining colors. There are many color models, and each works a little differently, as you will see below.

FrameMaker understands four common color models: CMYK, RGB, HLS, and the Pantone color matching system. Which color model you use in creating colors for a document depends on which system of

Two Rules for Using Color Effectively

There are a number of issues to consider when it comes to using color. Most of these issues, like which colors to use and where to use them, deserve (and get) books devoted just to them. But two issues, how much color to use and the cost of using color, are well worth considering here.

Just as you can use too much boldface text, you can also use too much color. Using color to highlight a word or phrase is effective, but using color for all the text in a document is not usually a good idea. Certain colors make text hard to read. For instance, yellow text on white paper strains the eye. And too many colors is downright confusing. Color, to be effective, should be used sparingly.

The cost of printing color should also be considered when applying color to documents that will be printed. A color page costs more to print than a black-and-white page, whether you print it at a print shop or with a color printer or copier. At a print shop, the more colors in the document, the more expensive it is to print, since each spot color requires a separate pass through the printing press. It is also costly to pay for all the labor involved in cleaning up the old ink and setting up each new ink. Four-color printing, for example, requires four passes through the press.

If you need only a few copies of a color document, color photocopying might be the answer. But if you need many copies, color photocopying will quickly become too expensive. In general, if you need lots of copies, limit the number of colors in the document, or if you can afford it, print the document using the four-color process.

defining color is easiest for you to use, and whether or not the document will be printed commercially.

In the following, keep in mind that a color model is simply a way for you to tell FrameMaker what a color should look like. Except for Pantone colors, all colors are stored by the system in all color models. Again, except for Pantone, you lose nothing by choosing one model over another.

CMYK Model   The CMYK (Cyan, Magenta, Yellow, Black) model is used by commercial printers with the "four-color printing process." Magazines and color newspapers use four-color printing. In the process, dots of the four colors listed above (Cyan, Magenta, Yellow, Black) are used in combinations to fool the eye into thinking it sees a variety of colors. CMYK is FrameMaker's default color model. (See "Four-Color Process Separations" near the end of this chapter for further explanation of four-color printing.)

Part
5

Advanced Features

RGB Model   The RGB (Red, Green, Blue) model defines colors in terms of their red, green, and blue components. It is sometimes useful to know the RGB components of a color because that's the way color television screens create colors, with dots of red, green, and blue. The dots are small and, used in combination, they fool the eye into thinking it sees all of the other colors.

HLS Model   The HLS (Hue, Lightness, Saturation) model was designed years ago by artists, and if you are an artist, you are probably very conformable defining colors in this way. Hue refers to the color itself, lightness (or luminosity) to how bright the chosen hue should appear, and saturation to how saturated (expressed as a percentage) you want the colored area to be with the hue you have chosen. If you've seen color wheels, you've had a glimpse of how the HLS model works.

Pantone Model   The Pantone model is a matching system. Pantone supplies sheets or cards printed with each of the Pantone-defined colors to artists and designers of brochures and documents, and it supplies pre-mixed ink in all of those colors to printers. When you ask a printer to use a Pantone color, you get what you ask for. (Pantone also supplies mixing instructions for printers who prefer to save money by mixing their own inks.)

In this sense, the Pantone way of defining colors differs from the other three. In those, you define a color by its components. Here, you define a color by finding its equivalent in a set of predefined colors.

Of course, Pantone also supplies ink to printers in the four process colors (Cyan, Magenta, Yellow, and Black) as well, so when you look at the Pantone charts, you will see the process colors listed.

Choosing a Color Model When You Define Colors

As you saw, the first three color models (CMYK, RGB, and HLS) define complex colors in terms of other, more basic colors or color characteristics. And once a color is defined in terms of one of these models, it can be redefined at any time in terms of another model.

So it makes no real difference whether you choose CMYK, RGB, or HLS—since you can see any color in terms of any of these models at any time. Just choose the way of defining colors with which you are most comfortable. (The program, in fact, supplies a "color picker" that allows you to choose a color by how it looks. It does the translation into CMYK, RGB, or HLS for you.)

The Pantone color model, however, is different. If you need the Pantone number for a color, you should define that color using FrameMaker's Pantone color selector. There is no other way to get the Pantone definition of a color.

A Word about the Term "Spot Color"

In a printed document—a document that is printed on a printing press—"spot color" refers to a color that is printed using an ink of that color. For example, when green ink is used to print a green line, the green is considered a spot color. In the CMYK model, on the other hand, which is used for four-color printing, no spot colors are used. Instead, the four standard process colors—cyan, magenta, yellow, and black—make up all the other colors. (See "Spot Color Separations" later in this chapter for all the details.)

In a document that is viewed—for example, a document you create on your screen or an online document—all colors are considered "spot colors", even if you use the CMYK model in FrameMaker to define them. They don't become process colors until they are actually separated into their CMYK components (with print separations) and printed using the four-color printing process. Color separations are discussed near the end of this chapter.

Creating New Colors

To create a new color for the current document:

1. Select View ➤ Color ➤ Definitions. The Color Definitions dialog box appears, as in Figure 15.4. Most likely, the default CMYK color model is selected, since that is FrameMaker's default color model.

2. Select New Color from the Name pull-down list.

3. Delete the name New Color and type your own color name.

    You can name colors with descriptions of their purpose or you can give them flat-out color names, like "Mauve." Often it is best to name colors by their purpose. For example, by using the name "Hypertext Color" for hypertext, you can change the color you use for hypertext without

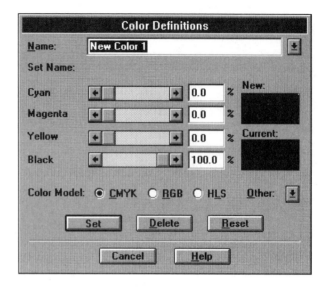

Figure 15.4   The Color Definitions dialog box

having to change the color assignment name. Of course, if your purpose is just to add dark blue to the list of colors, the name "Dark Blue" is just fine.

4. Select a color model to use when defining the new color. Your choices are CMYK, RGB, HLS, and from the Other pull-down menu, Common Color Picker or Pantone. (The Common Color Picker is a way of defining a color by "looks" and letting the program translate what you have chosen into its CMYK, RGB, or HLS components for you.) See "What Is a Color Model?" above if you're having trouble making a choice.

> **MAC AND UNIX NOTE**   In the Mac version, the choices on the Other menu are Apple Color Picker (a variation of the Common Color Picker) and Pantone. In the UNIX version, Pantone is the only choice.

5. What happens in step 5 depends on which choice you made in step 4. Read on.

If You Chose CMYK...   If you chose the CMYK color model, use either the slider bars or the % text boxes for the four colors (Cyan, Magenta,

Yellow, and Black) to specify how much of each should be present in the new color.

Unless you already know the CMYK definition of the color you want, you may have to experiment. The New color box, shown in Figure 15.5, shows you the results of your effort. Look in the New box to see what your color looks like. You can compare it with the color in the Current box, which is what you began with when you started experimenting.

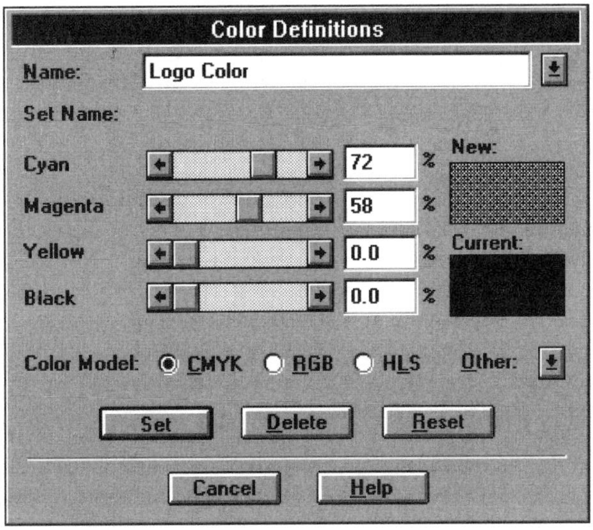

Figure 15.5   **The CMYK Color Definitions dialog box**

If You Chose RGB...   If you chose the RGB color model, use either the slider bars or the % text boxes for the three RGB colors (Red, Green, and Blue) to specify how much of each color should be present in the new color.

Here again, unless you already know the RGB definition of the color you want, you may have to experiment. As in Figure 15.6, the New color box shows you what your new color looks like.

If You Chose HLS...   If you chose the HLS color model in step 4, use either the slider bars or the % text boxes for the three qualities (Hue, Lightness or Luminosity, and Saturation) to specify the new color.

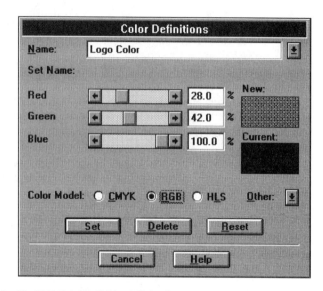

Figure 15.6   **The RGB Color Definitions dialog box**

When using HLS, it helps to remember that Hue walks you around a "color wheel" in degrees from one color to another. Lightness makes the color bright or dark, and saturation makes it paler or richer. It therefore makes sense that 0% Lightness is always black, no matter what the other settings are, and 100% Lightness is always white. In the same way, 0% Saturation is always a shade of gray, no matter what the other settings happen to be.

Check out the New box on the right side of the dialog box shown in Figure 15.7 to see what your new color looks like.

If You Chose Common Color Picker...   If you chose Common Color Picker from the Other pull-down menu in step 4, you see the Color Picker dialog box. It is shown in Figure 15.8. Here's how to create a new color with the Color Picker:

▶ The large box with all the colors in it shows Hues across the horizontal axis (from 0% on the color wheel to 360%), and Saturation along the vertical axis (from 0% or 100%). Select a Hue/Saturation combination by clicking anywhere in this box with the mouse.

▶ A separate vertical bar on the right side of the dialog box lets you specify a Luminosity (brightness) for the Hue/Saturation combination in the

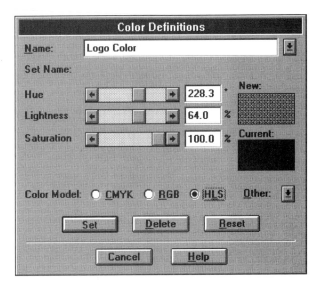

Figure 15.7 The HLS Color Definitions dialog box

large box. Select a Luminosity in the same way, by clicking with the mouse or using the slider triangle to the right of the vertical bar.

▶ The HLS and RGB definitions of the color you selected are shown in the text boxes. You can also type your own values into these boxes.

 MAC NOTE   In the Mac version, the Apple Color Picker appears instead of the Color Picker in Figure 15.8. This screen has two flavors, called Apple HLS and Apple RGB, which together provide the functions of the Common Color Picker, discussed above.

If You Chose Pantone...   If you chose Pantone from the other pull-down menu, you see the Pantone Colors dialog box shown in Figure 15.9. Here's how to select a color from this box:

▶ In the middle of the box are two columns of Pantone colors, starting with the Process colors and their substitutes and moving through the numbered colors. Select any of these colors by clicking on it with the mouse.

▶ Below the colors display is a slider bar for moving different colors into the display columns. By moving the slider to the right, you see the higher

Part 5

Advanced Features

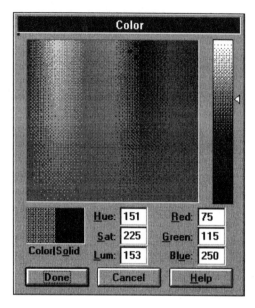

Figure 15.8 *The Color Picker dialog box (Windows)*

numbered Pantone colors, in the order in which those colors appear in the Pantone Color Formula Guide.

▶ Above the color display is a Find Pantone text box. Type a number or a Pantone name into this box to put that color somewhere in the color display and select it (just as though you had chosen that color with the mouse).

NOTE The Pantone Colors display generally shows Pantone colors in columns of seven colors, just as they appear in the Pantone color guide. That is, the top color in the column is the top color in the Pantone color strip—*except* for the colors above Pantone 448. Between 447 and 448, the numbered colors are interrupted by the named gray colors (warm grays and cool grays). Since there are 22 grays, the alignment of colors in the columns gets out of sync (by one) with the display of colors in the Pantone books.

6. When you have selected the color you want in the CMYK, RGB, HLS, Color Picker, or Pantone Color Definitions dialog box, click on the Done button. You will see the Color Definitions dialog box again, and the New color box will show the results of your effort.

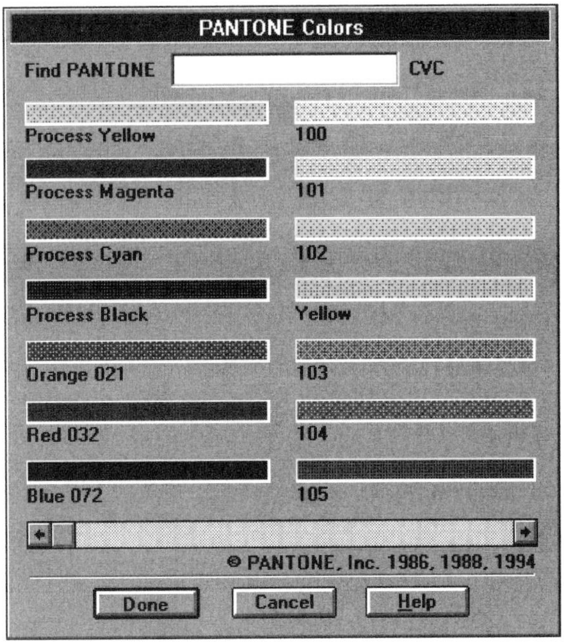

Figure 15.9 **The Pantone Colors dialog box**

If you used the Color Picker to select a color, it will be converted to whatever color model was last in use. Feel free to choose another color model if you wish.

If you used the Pantone Color Definition dialog box, the Set Name line near the top will show the Pantone name of the color, even if you typed in a new name for your color prior to selecting it. You can return to your old name now, if you like, by typing it (again) into the text box. Of course, having the Pantone name be the color name is awfully convenient.

7. Select the Set button to add your new color name and definition to the list of colors defined in the current document.

8. Repeat the process for each new color you want to create.

9. Select Done when you are finished defining colors.

> **NOTE** Colors you have created can be deleted with the Delete button. Predefined colors can't be deleted.

Changing the Definition of a Color

You can change the definition of any color you have defined. (Only the color definitions that come predefined for every document—Black, Red, and so on—cannot be changed.)

To modify an existing user-defined color definition for the current document:

1. Select View ➤ Color ➤ Definitions. The Color Definitions dialog box appears (see Figure 15.4).

2. Select the color to be redefined from the Name pull-down list.

3. Select the Color Model to use when redefining the color. Your choices are CMYK, RGB, HLS, and from the Other pull-down menu, Common Color Picker and Pantone.

4. Use the controls appropriate to the color model to modify the color. (See the previous sections for more information on how to get what you want from these color model controls.) The New color box will show you the effect of your changes.

5. When you are satisfied with your efforts, click on the Set button. (You can always cancel your work by pressing Cancel, or return the color to its original definition and start over by pressing the Reset button.)

Importing Color Definitions from Other Documents

You don't have to keep redefining color definitions whenever you need a new color. You can copy, or import, color definitions from other documents into the document you want to use the new color in. In addition, you can make documents with particularly useful color definitions into templates (see Chapter 6 for more on templates).

To import color definitions from another document:

1. Open both documents.

2. In the document that will *receive* the color definitions, select File ➤ Import ➤ Formats. The Import Formats dialog box appears, as in Figure 15.10.

3. From the Import from Document pull-down list, select the document that contains the color definitions to be imported.

4. In the Import and Update area, deselect (uncheck) all formats except Color Definitions, as shown in Figure 15.10.

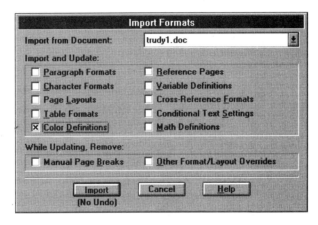

Figure 15.10   Importing color definitions with the Import Formats dialog box

5. Click on the Import button. The new color definitions are added to the current document.

Changing How
Colors Are Shown on the Screen

You can choose how colors are displayed on the screen. You can decide which colors are visible, which colors are cut out, and which colors are invisible. A definition of which colors are visible and which are not is called a *color view*.

You can use different color views for a number of purposes. When you edit a document, for example, you can put one reviewer's comments and changes in red, and another's in blue. Then, by changing the view, you can see one reviewer's comments, the other reviewer's comments, both reviewer's comments, or no comments whatsoever.

Part
5

Advanced Features

You can have up to six color views in a document. To create and edit color views:

1. Select View ➤ Color ➤ Views. The Define Color Views dialog box appears, as in Figure 15.11.

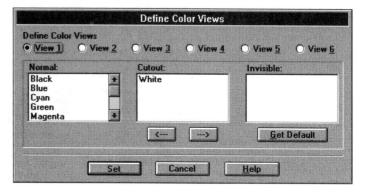

Figure 15.11   **The Define Color Views dialog box**

Note that six color views (View 1 through View 6) have already been defined. To find out how a view is defined, click on the radio button and look in the Normal, Cutout, and Invisible scroll lists.

2. To change any of the six views, click on the radio button next to its name.

3. Highlight the color you wish to use.

4. Press the left and right arrow buttons to move selected (highlighted) color names among the three scroll lists:

    • In the Normal scroll list, list the colors that you want to display or set up in the view.

    • In the Cutout scroll list, list the colors that should be cut out in the view. These colors are shown as white ("cut out") when they overlap other, nonwhite objects.

    • In the Invisible scroll list, list the colors that should be hidden in the view. Text and objects with those colors are not visible.

5. When you are finished defining that view, you can click on the name of another view and define it.

6. When you are finished defining all views, select the view you want to appear in the document and click the Set button.

Dealing with Color Separations

If you plan to send a color document to a print shop (as opposed to a copy shop, which photocopies documents), you need to print color separations.

A *color separation* is simply one color component of a document. To create color separations, you divide, or "separate," all the colors used in the document into color components and print one page for each component. You end up with several pages, printed in black, each of which shows where one color component goes.

A commercial printer uses these pages to make plates, one for each color, with which to print the various colors, using colored ink. (Plates are used to transfer ink from the press to the paper as it moves through the rollers.) When all of the colors have been printed using all of the plates, you have a finished document.

There are two kinds of color separations:

▶ Four-color process color separations

▶ Spot color separations

FrameMaker can create both of these kinds of color separations for you. Let's look at spot color separation first, since it is a simpler concept.

Spot Color Separations

Let's say you have a one-page document with three colors—black for the text, red for the border around the page, and green for a table on the page.

One way to print this page commercially is to give the print shop three sheets of paper, all printed in black:

▶ The first sheet shows where the black text should be printed. Where the other colors (red and green) appear, the sheet is blank.

▶ The second sheet shows only where the border will be printed.

▶ The third sheet shows only where the green table will be printed.

The print shop uses the three sheets to make plates:

▶ The first plate is used with black ink to print the black text.

▶ The second plate is used with red ink to print the red border.

▶ The third plate is used with green ink to print the green table.

Finally, the printed document is run through the press three times, once for each of the three colors. When that is done, you have a finished, printed, three-color document.

The procedure works fine for documents with one or two colors other than black. But what about a document with many colors? In that case, you need four-color separations.

Four-Color Process Separations

To print a document commercially that has many colors, another process is used. Instead of printing each color separately, all colors are first separated into their CMYK (cyan, magenta, yellow, and black) components.

By now the idea of dividing a color into its CMYK components should be familiar to you—you've seen it above when color models were discussed. Every color imaginable can be divided into some combination of these four colors. The color blue, as defined in FrameMaker's default color list, is 100% cyan + 100% magenta + 0% yellow + 0% black. Change the percentages of these components and you change the color.

To print a document commercially with four-color process color printing, you must divide each color—including black—into its CMYK components, then print four black sheets that show where each CMYK component goes. One sheet shows where cyan ink goes, another where magenta ink goes, another where yellow ink goes, and the last where black ink goes.

The whole process, from FrameMaker to printed page, works like this:

1. All of the colors on the page are separated into their cyan, magenta, yellow, and black components.

2. Four black pages are produced, one for each of the four process colors. Each page shows where each color goes.

3. Four plates are produced from these pages, one for each of the four process colors.

4. The plate that shows where yellow should go is placed onto the press, yellow ink is loaded, and the document is sent through the press once, where it receives the yellow ink in the right places.

5. The press is cleaned and the plate that shows where cyan should go is placed onto the press. Cyan ink is loaded and the document passes through the press a second time, where it receives the cyan ink in the right places.

6. The above process is repeated for magenta ink, and then for black ink.

After four passes through the press, the document is printed.

> **WARNING** Keep in mind that the quality of the final printed product has a lot to do with the resolution of your output device (printer). If you print your separations on a 300dpi (dots-per-inch) laser printer, your final document will have a 300dpi resolution. If you print on a 600dpi printer, your document will look twice as sharp. But if you print to a PostScript file, take the file to a "service bureau" and get it printed on a 1200 or 2400dpi typesetter, your final document will look quite professional.

Printing Spot Color Separations

This section explains how to print color separations for a document that uses spot color (one or two discrete colors in addition to black). As a sample, we will use TRUDY_C.DOC, the letter from Trudy Dutweiler that now has three colors in it—black text, a red rectangle, the words *past due* in red, and a paragraph ("Sorry") in blue. This oddly colored letter was created in exercises earlier in this chapter. If you didn't create it, use a document of your own.

> **MAC NOTE** To print color separations, you need to use either the Apple LaserWriter 8 or Adobe PS Printer driver 8. In addition, you must also have selected a nongeneric PostScript Printer Description (PPD) file for a printer that supports color separations.

Here's how to print color separations:

1. Open the document (in this case, TRUDY_C.DOC).

2. Select File ➤ Print. The Print Document dialog box opens, as in Figure 15.12.

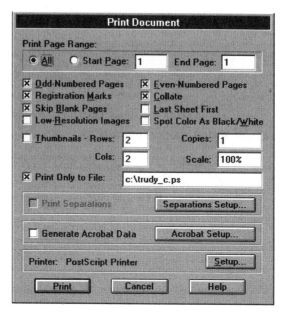

Figure 15.12   The Print Document dialog box

3. Turn *on* the following:

- Odd-Numbered Pages

- Even-Numbered Pages

- Registration Marks

- Collate

- Skip Blank Pages

NOTE   Registration marks won't be printed if the document is the same size as the paper in your printer (and you'll get a warning to that effect), but it's a good idea to turn them on every time you do work that will go to a print shop.

UNIX NOTE   In the UNIX version, Skip Blank Separation Pages is located in the Set Print Separations dialog box, which you will encounter later in this procedure.

4. Turn *off* the following:
   - Last Sheet First
   - Low-Resolution Images
   - Spot Color as Black/White

 MAC NOTE In the Mac version, to see the Spot Color as a Black/White setting, select Options. Black and White should be turned off.

5. Make sure the Print Range is All and Copies is set to 1.

6. If you are going to get your separations printed at a service bureau, select Print Only to File and enter a file name for your file. Otherwise, the separations will be sent to your printer.

 MAC NOTE To print to a file, select File from the Destination list.

7. Select a PostScript printer or print driver that is capable of printing separations (Mac and Windows only).

 WINDOWS NOTE If you change printer drivers now, you may get a message saying that the font information for your document has changed. This message is a function of your system configuration—which fonts are loaded, and so on. To avoid this message, create your document with a PostScript printer already selected.

8. Click Set Up Separations. The Set Print Separations dialog box appears, as in Figure 15.13 or 15.14. (Figure 15.13 shows the Windows version of this box, and Figure 15.14 shows the UNIX version. The Mac version of Set Print Separations is similar to the Windows version.)

9. Select the color you wish to use, then click the left and right arrow buttons and move each of the colors for which you want a spot color separation into the Print As Spot scroll list. (Depending on your system, you may see all the colors listed in this box already.)

Part
5

Advanced Features

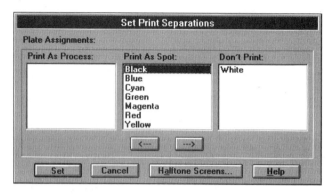

Figure 15.13   *The Set Print Separations dialog box (Windows version)*

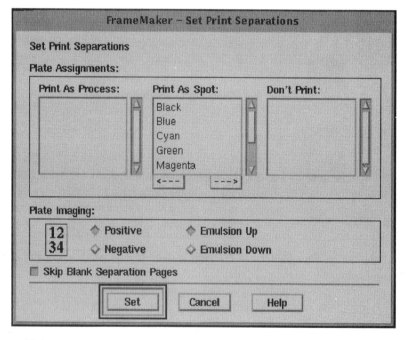

Figure 15.14   *Set Print Separations dialog box (UNIX version)*

A page will be printed for each name in the list (unless the page would be blank), so there should be one entry for each color in the document, including black. (For TRUDY_C.DOC, you should have three colors in the list—Black, Red, and Blue.)

10. Click the left and right arrow buttons, move all of the other color names into the Don't Print column. (The document should contain none of these colors anyway.)

11. Click the Set button. The Set Print Separations box closes.

12. Click the Print button in the Print Document dialog box (see Figure 15.12). The separations will be printed, either to the printer or to a file, whichever you selected.

When you are done, you will have as many printed pages as there were spot colors in the Print As Spot list (unless you tried to print a spot color that didn't appear in the document). Either that, or you will have a PostScript file that contains those pages in PostScript code. For TRUDY_C.DOC, note that you have three pages. One contains all of the black text, one only the red parts (the words "past due" plus a rectangle), and one only the text of the blue paragraph.

Printing Four-Color Separations

The procedure for creating four-color separations is similar to the procedure for printing spot color separations. To print four-color process separations:

1. Open the document (as an example, let's use TRUDY_C.DOC again).

2. Select File ➤ Print. The Print Document dialog box opens (see Figure 15.12).

3. Turn *on* the following:

   • Odd-Numbered Pages

   • Even-Numbered Pages

   • Registration Marks

   • Collate

   • Skip Blank Pages

NOTE   Registration marks won't be printed if the document is the same size as the paper in your printer (and you'll get a warning to that effect), but it's a good idea to turn them on every time you do work that will go to a print shop.

UNIX NOTE   In the UNIX version, Skip Blank Separation Pages is located in the Set Print Separations dialog box, which you will encounter later in this procedure.

4. Turn *off* the following:

    • Last Sheet First

    • Low-Resolution Images

    • Spot Color as Black/White

MAC NOTE   In the Mac version, to see the Spot Color as a Black/White setting, select Options. Black and White should be turned off.

5. Make sure the Print Range is All and Copies is set to 1.

6. If you are going to get your separations printed at a service bureau, select Print Only to File and enter a file name for your file. Otherwise, the separations will be sent to your printer.

MAC NOTE   To print to a file, select File from the Destination list.

7. Select a PostScript printer or print driver that is capable of printing separations (Mac and Windows only).

WINDOWS NOTE   If you change printer drivers now, you may get a message saying that the font information for your document has changed. This message is a function of your system configuration—which fonts are loaded, and so on. To avoid this message, create your document with a PostScript printer already selected.

8. Click on Set Up Separations. The Set Print Separations dialog box appears (see Figure 15.13).

9. Clicking the left and right arrow buttons, move each of the colors that you want separated into the Print As Process scroll list. There should be one entry for *each color* in the document except white. (For TRUDY_C.DOC, list all colors except white.) Do *not* select just cyan, magenta, yellow, and black. If you do, any color not in that group—red, for example—will not get separated.

10. Move white into the Don't Print column.

11. Select the Halftone Screens button. The Halftone Screens dialog box appears, as in Figure 15.15.

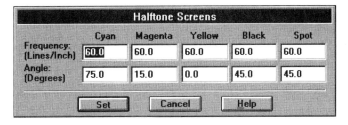

Figure 15.15 *The Halftone Screens dialog box*

12. Modify the settings for the halftone dots frequency and angle as you or your commercial printer wishes, and then click the Set button. To accept the settings you see (which you do most of the time), just click Set without making changes. The Halftone Screens dialog box closes.

 UNIX NOTE To change halftone screen settings in the UNIX version of FrameMaker, you must edit one of the ps_prolog files. If you edit your personal ps_prolog file (the one found or placed in $USER/fminit), your changes affect only your account. If you edit the system ps_prolog file (found in $FMHOME/fminit), your changes may affect other users.

13. In the Set Print Separations dialog box, click the Set button. The Set Print Separations box closes.

14. Select Print in the Print Document box. The separations will be printed, either to the printer or to a file, whichever you selected.

Part
5

Advanced Features

When you are done, you will have four printed pages, one each for the cyan, magenta, yellow, and black components of the colors in your document. Either that, or you will have a PostScript file that contains those pages in PostScript code.

For TRUDY_C.DOC, for example, you have four pages. If you look at those pages, you will see the following:

▶ A page for black ink that contains all of the black text.

▶ A page for magenta that contains the paragraph that was originally in blue, plus the words *past due* and the rectangle, both of which were originally red. (Recall that FrameMaker blue is magenta + cyan, and FrameMaker red is magenta + yellow.)

▶ A page for cyan that contains only the paragraph that was originally blue (FrameMaker blue is magenta + cyan).

▶ A page for yellow that contains the words *past due* and the rectangle, both of which were red (FrameMaker red is magenta + yellow).

Plate Imaging in UNIX

The UNIX version of the Set Print Separations dialog box contains an additional area for plate imaging. *Plate imaging* specifies how the color separation plates are printed:

▶ Positive prints a positive image of the page—white appears as white, and black appears as black.

▶ Negative prints a reverse image of the page—white appears black, and black appears white.

▶ Emulsion Up specifies that the photosensitive side of the paper or film be up, or facing toward you—a selection usually used for printing on paper.

▶ Emulsion Down specifies that the photosensitive side of the paper or film be down, or facing away from you—a selection that prints a mirror image of the page and is usually used for printing on film.

In the UNIX version, these settings are specified here. In the Mac and PC versions of the product, these capabilities, if they exist, are handled by the print drivers installed with your system, under the Advanced group of options.

Chapter 16

Creating and Working with Book Files

With FrameMaker, you can group separate but related documents together into a single unit, called a *book*. A book is simply a group of documents that can be manipulated either separately or together. You can open individual files in a book and work on them, for example, or you can print an entire book.

"Creating a book" means creating a book file that lists the files in the book. The book file has a Book File window. You can open, edit, format, and save documents directly from the Book File window. You can also control the formatting, page and paragraph numbering, cross-referencing, and printing of the documents in the book from a Book File window. You can even compare two versions of a book to see exactly how they differ.

This chapter shows you how to:

Create a new book file

Add and set up the documents in a book

Specify page and paragraph numbering for the document files in a book

Manipulate documents from the Book File window

Compare two versions of a book

NOTE   You can generate a table of contents, index, or other lists (like a list of tables) for the documents in a book. How to do that is the subject of the next chapter.

Creating a Book

Creating a book is easy and involves only a few simple steps:

▶ Gathering and preparing the files that will be part of the book

▶ Generating a book file

▶ Naming and saving a book

▶ Adding more documents to a book file

▶ Making the different files in the book consistent with one another

How to perform these simple steps is discussed in the following sections.

Gathering and Preparing Files for a Book

The first step is to gather and arrange the files that will be assembled into the book. Here are some hints to help organize your work and make the job easier.

Separate the Book into Chapters   Make each chapter or section of the book a separate document. If you have long documents over 50 pages, divide them into separate, shorter documents. Though FrameMaker is an excellent long document program (perhaps the best on the market), it works faster with shorter documents than with longer ones.

When you divide the document, be sure that each new document begins at the top of a page. This ensures continuity across the new documents. Also, don't split sentences, paragraphs, or tables between documents. Instead, divide a document where a natural break occurs, at the end of a section or before a major heading.

Name Document Files Similarly   It's easier to work with book file documents if your document files have similar names. You can use a system as simple as CH1.DOC, CH2.DOC, and so on (to use the Windows naming conventions), or something as elaborate as FMBK_CH1.DOC, FMBK_CH2.DOC, and so on, if you want to include the name of the book in the file name (in this case, FMBK stands for "FrameMaker Book").

If you want your chapters to appear in the right order in an alphabetical list of files, remember to use 01, 02, etc., in file names. Naming a file CH3.DOC instead of CH03.DOC puts the third chapter after the twenty ninth, since CH3 comes after CH29 in alphabetical order.

You can even include the title of the chapter in the file name by abbreviating it. And if you are a UNIX or Mac user, you can give files lengthy file names, so your naming system can get quite elaborate.

The benefits of consistent file names are many:

▶ You can see at a glance which files contain what contents, and even which files belong to what book.

▶ The file names are listed in the right order in any alphabetical list of file names.

▶ If you are a Windows or UNIX user, you can use wildcards to narrow the list of files in a directory listing, so that you see only the files you are interested in.

TIP It's a *lot* less work to change the name of a document file before it has been added to a book file than afterward. Try to make final decisions about the names of document files before creating book files. You'll save yourself a lot of trouble if you do.

Create a Directory for the Files in the Book When you are ready to create a book file, create a new directory (or folder) to hold the parts of the book, and place all the documents that will go into the book into this directory. Use this directory to hold the book file and all generated files for the book. Your new book directory is also a good place to store graphics that are included by reference in the book.

Generating a Book File

You can generate a book file from any document. When the book file is created, it will have a single entry—the document you used to generate the book file. Later, you can add other files to the book.

To create a book file:

1. Open any one of the documents to be included in the book. Select File ➤ Open and use the scroll list to select the document. (For this procedure, I used a file named COVER.DOC. If you are doing this for practice, you can use any document file you wish.)

2. Select File ➤ Generate/Book. The Generate/Book dialog box opens, as in Figure 16.1.

3. Click on the New Multifile Book radio button.

4. Click the Generate button. The Book File window opens, as in Figure 16.2. Notice that it contains just one document—the document used to generate the book file. The Book File window is temporarily named after the document that was open when you generated it.

You have just created a book. Now let's rename and save the book file.

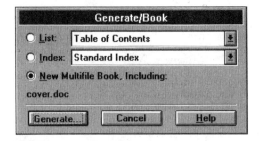

Figure 16.1　*The Generate/Book dialog box*

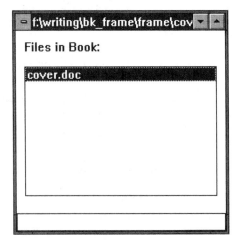

Figure 16.2　*The Book file window*

Renaming and Saving a Newly Created Book File

A newly created book file adopts the name of the document that was used to generated it. In the example above, I used a file called COVER.DOC to generate the book file, so my new book file is named COVER.BK. However, you will probably want to save your book file with a name more suited to your book.

To rename and save a new book file:

1. Make the Book File window active and select File ➤ Save As.

NOTE In the UNIX and Mac versions of the program, the main menu is at the top of each document window. In the Windows version, it is at the top of the FrameMaker application window. In all three versions, the File and Edit menus for book files differ significantly from the File and Edit menus for document files. Book file menus are discussed below.

2. In the Save Book dialog box, change to the directory or folder where you have assembled the files for the book.

3. Enter the new name of the book in the text box.

4. Click the Save button.

Adding Document Files to a Book

Once you have created a book file, you can add files to the book file list and make those files part of your new book. You can add two kinds of files, document files (chapters and cover pages) and "generated" files (a table of contents or an index). This section covers adding documents to books. For information on adding generated files, see Chapter 17.

When you add a file to a book, you are not adding the file itself. FrameMaker does not generate a huge file that contains all of the files in the book. A book file is simply a list of other files with information about where those files are located and how they are to be treated.

WARNING You can add files to a book only if they are saved in Normal FrameMaker format. Maker Interchange Format (MIF) and text files cannot be added to a book file.

To add a document file to a book:

1. Make the Book File window active (see Figure 16.2) and select File ➤ Add File. The Add File to Book dialog box opens, as in Figure 16.3.

2. Click the Document File radio button and use the scroll list on the left to locate the file or files you want to add to the book:

   • To add a single file to the book, select the name of the file in the scroll list by clicking on it. Remember, the file must be in Normal FrameMaker format.

Part
5

Advanced Features

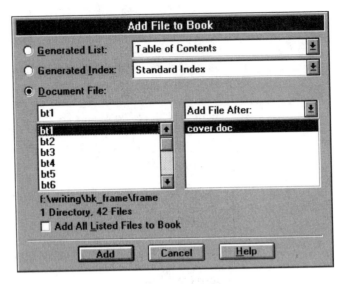

Figure 16.3   The Add File to Book dialog box

- To add all the files in the scroll list, click the Add All Listed Files to Book check box near the bottom of the dialog box.

3. Use the Add File pull-down menu and scroll list to select where in the book you want to add the files:

- From the pull-down menu, choose Add File After or Add File Before.

- From the scroll list, select a file after or before which to add the new files.

4. Click the Add button. The file name or file names appear in the right-hand scroll list where you specified. Note that the Cancel button will say "Done."

5. Repeat steps 2 through 6 for each file you want to add to the book.

6. When you are finished adding files, click Done. The dialog box closes and the file name or file names appear in the Book File window where you specified.

7. Save the book file by selecting File ► Save.

WINDOWS AND UNIX NOTE   You can use wildcards to limit the number of file names in the Document File scroll list of the Add File to Book dialog box. To do this, click Document File, type a wildcard in the text box above the list, and press Enter. This technique is useful for adding files with similar names to a book. For example, to display only files that have names ending with *.DOC*, type *.DOC in the text box and press Enter. To display only document files starting with *CH*, type CH*.DOC in the text box and press Enter. To see the entire contents of a directory after using a wildcard, type *.* and press Enter. You can also use the ? wildcard.

If you make a mistake in adding files, you can always delete or rearrange files you have added. See "Deleting and Rearranging Document Files" later in this chapter.

Setting Up Document Files

The final step in creating a book file is to specify the document file properties that affect the entire book. For example, you could number the pages in the book file consecutively from one chapter to the next, or you could start numbering all over again at page 1 in certain chapters. You can do the same for the figure numbers or table headings.

These properties are set in the book file separately for each chapter in the book. FrameMaker calls this process "setting up the file." To set up a document file in a book file:

1. Make the Book File window active (see Figure 16.2) and select the file whose properties you want to set up by clicking once on it. (If you double-click on the file, it will be opened.)

2. Select File ➤ Set Up File. The Set Up File dialog box appears, as in Figure 16.4.

3. Select a starting page side from the Starting Page pull-down menu:

   • **Read from File**—Use the current first page side setting from the document file.

   • **Next Available Side**—Use the page side that would naturally follow, based on where the previous document ended. This setting is helpful when a chapter has been split into two files in a two-sided book, or

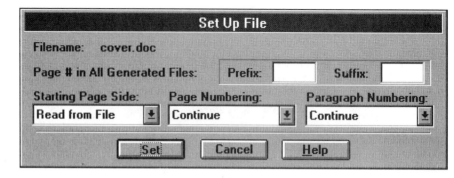

Figure 16.4   **The Set Up File dialog box**

when a chapter can start on either side of the page in a two-sided book.

- **Left or Right**—Always use either the left- or right-hand page.

4. Select a page numbering scheme from the Page Numbering pull-down menu:

   - **Continue**—Continue numbering pages from the previous file in the book. Thus, if the last chapter or document ended on page 12, this document starts on page 13.

   - **Restart at 1**—Restart page numbering at 1 for this document.

   - **Read from File**—Use the page number setting from the document file. In other words, let the file keep its original numbering scheme.

5. If necessary, select a paragraph numbering scheme for the document by selecting a setting from the Paragraph Numbering pull-down menu. Paragraph numbering affects the numbering of headings in chapters with outline-style headings (1.0, 1.1, etc.) and other autonumbered paragraphs, such as table and figure titles. The choices are similar to the paragraph numbering choices:

   - **Continue**—Continue paragraph numbering from the previous chapter or document in the book.

   - **Restart**—Restart paragraph numbering with this document.

6. If you want text to be added to the page numbers of the document when page numbers appear in generated files (like indexes or tables of contents), fill in the Page # in All Generated Files text boxes.

Text you enter in the Prefix box will appear before each page number. For example, if you enter **3-** for a Chapter 3 page number, your Chapter 3 pages will be numbered 3-1, 3-2, etc. The text you enter in the Suffix box will appear after each page number.

TIP If the prefix or suffix contains a hyphen, use a nonbreaking hyphen; otherwise, lines in generated files may break at the hyphen. To type a nonbreaking hyphen, type \+ (a backslash followed by a plus sign) in Windows, press 2 +grave accent on the Mac, or press Meta+hyphen on UNIX machines.

7. When you are finished, click the Set button. The changes will appear the next time you generate and update the book.

8. Save the changes to the book file by selecting File ➤ Save.

Working with Book Files

You can do a lot of things with book files. Like other files, book files can be opened, saved, and closed. You can also open, save, and close one or all of the document files in a book by using the Book File window.

Having organized several documents in a book, you can communicate changes, like updated formats, from any open document to some or all of the book file documents with a single command. Not only can documents be added to books, they can be rearranged and deleted as well.

This section deals with all of these capabilities. But let's first look more closely at the book File menu. As you've no doubt noticed, it's different from the File menu for documents.

NOTE In the UNIX and Mac versions of the program, the main menu appears at the top of each document or Book File window. In the Windows version, the main menu appears in one place—at the top of the FrameMaker application window. In both cases, the document menu and the book menu are different. The Windows main menu shows this difference by changing from the document version to the book version, depending on whether a document window or a Book File window is active. The menu references in this chapter assume that you are aware of these variations in the main menu.

Part 5

Advanced Features

When the Book File window is active, the number of menu choices is reduced to five: File, Edit, View, Window, and Help.

MAC AND UNIX NOTE   The Macintosh version of the book menu also contains another item, Scripts, containing a single selection, Add Temporary, which provides access to the system scripting function. Of course, in the UNIX version there is no Window menu.

The File pull-down menu contains the following items:

▶ **New**—Creates a new document from blank paper or a template.

▶ **Open**—Opens a file.

▶ **Close Book**—Closes the book file.

▶ **Save**—Saves the book file.

▶ **Save As**—Saves the book file under a new name.

▶ **Revert To Save**—Closes the book without saving it and opens the most recently saved version of the book.

▶ **Import ▶ Formats**—Merges formats from another document with the formats from one or all of the documents in a book.

▶ **Page Set Up**—Sets up the current printer *(Macintosh only)*.

▶ **Print**—Prints the book. See the section on printing later in this chapter for more information.

▶ **Print Setup**—Sets up the printer and allows printers to be changed *(Windows only)*.

▶ **Add File**—Adds a file or files to the book. See "Adding Files to a Book" later in this chapter.

▶ **Set Up File**—Sets up page and paragraph numbering schemes for the files in the book.

▶ **Rearrange File**—Rearranges and deletes files in a book.

▶ **Generate/Update**—Generates "auto-generated" files, like Tables of Contents and Indexes, and updates page numbering, paragraph numbering, and cross-references in the files of the book.

▶ **Utilities ▶ Compare Books**—Compares two versions of a book and shows their differences.

▶ **Preferences**—Sets FrameMaker preferences.

▶ **Recently Opened Files**—Lists the five most recently opened files.

▶ **Quit *or* Exit**—Quits FrameMaker.

If you hold the Shift key while you select the File pull-down menu, the New, Open, Close, and Save menu items change into these useful choices:

▶ **Repeat Last New**—Creates a new document with the same set up as the last new document created *(Macintosh only)*.

▶ **Open All Files In Book**—Opens all the files in the book.

▶ **Close All Files In Book**—Closes all open files in the book, including the book file.

▶ **Save All Files In Book**—Saves all the open files in the book, including the book file.

The Edit pull-down menu contains only one item:

▶ **Suppress Automatic Reference Updating**—Stops or resumes automatic updating of cross-references and text inserts when book files or documents are opened.

Opening, Saving, and Closing Book Files

Book files can be opened, saved, and closed in the same way as other FrameMaker documents:

▶ To open a book file, select File ➤ Open, choose the book file from the list of files and directories, and click Open.

▶ To save a book file, select File ➤ Save. The book file will be saved under its current name, whatever that happens to be.

▶ To save a book file under a new name or to a new location, select File ➤ Save As and use the Save Book dialog box. There are only two format choices for book files, Normal FrameMaker Book format and MIF. (For information on MIF, or Maker Interchange Format, see Chapters 6 and 7.) As always when you use the Save As command to save a file, you get two files, one book file with the old name and one with the new name.

NOTE   When you save a book file to a new location, only the book file goes to the new directory. The document files stay where they are.

Part
5

Advanced Features

▶ To close a book file, select File ➤ Close Book. If changes were made to the book file since it was last saved, a dialog box will appear and ask if you want to save those changes.

Operating on Document Files

The Book File window and its menu commands allow you to perform many document file operations quick and easy. These include opening, saving, and closing files. You can also import formats from one document file to all the files in a book at once. The section that follows this one will show you how.

Opening Document Files in a Book

From the Book File window, you can open one or all of the document files in the list.

▶ To open a single file, double-click on the file name in the Book File window or click on the file name and press Enter. The document will open.

▶ To open all the files in a book, make the Book File window active, hold the Shift key, and select File ➤ Open All Files in Book. All the documents in the book will open.

TIP To open all files in a book quickly, suspend the automatic updating of references (cross-references and text insets). To do this, make the Book File window active and select Edit ➤ Suppress Automatic Reference Update. In the Suppress Automatic Reference Update dialog box, select Suppress Automatic Update and click Set. Note that this option suppresses automatic reference updating only when the Open All Files in Book command is used—it does not affect automatic updating when you open an individual file in the book.

Saving and Closing Document Files in a Book

From the book window, you can save or close all open files in a book at the same time.

▶ To save all the open files in a book, make the Book File window active, hold down the Shift key, and select File ➤ Save All Files in Book. All open files that have changed, as well as the book file itself, will be saved.

▶ To close all open files in a book, make the Book File window active, hold down the Shift key, and select File ➤ Close All Files in Book. All open files and the book file itself will be closed.

Changing and Updating the Format of Document Files

Occasionally, you may want to change the page layout or paragraph formatting or book files, or make other format changes to all or some of them. You may, for example, want to increase the margins, or change the fonts of the paragraph tags. FrameMaker allows you to make these changes to one document (which may or may not be in the book already) and then update those changes to a selected list of documents in the book automatically.

You can update any of the following in this way:

▶ Paragraph formats

▶ Character formats

▶ Page layouts (i.e., master pages)

▶ Table formats (including line ruling styles)

▶ Color definitions

▶ Reference pages

▶ Variable definitions

▶ Cross-reference formats

▶ Conditional text settings

▶ Math definitions

To change and update the format of document files in a book:

1. Open the file you wish to change and make whatever changes you wish to the items listed above. This file may or may not be a file already in the book.

2. Save the file after making all the changes, but leave the file open.

3. Open the book file or make it active, and then select File ➤ Import ➤ Formats. The Import Formats dialog box opens, as shown in Figure 16.5.

Part 5

Advanced Features

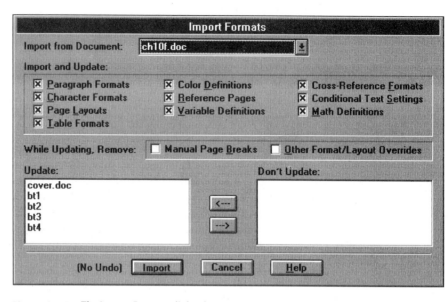

Figure 16.5   *The Import Formats dialog box*

4. Use the Import from Document pull-down list to select the source file—the file whose formats you want to use. Since this is a list of open documents, the source document must be open. The document you modified in step 1 above is your source document.

5. In the Import and Update section, select the settings you want to import by clicking on them.

6. Move the documents you do *not* want to update from the Update scroll list to the Don't Update scroll list by selecting the file name and clicking on the right arrow button. (Note that files that receive these changes do *not* have to be open.)

7. To remove format overrides, click the While Updating, Remove settings. Overrides are any properties manually applied to characters, paragraphs, tables, and pages that are not included in the various format tags or master page layouts.

   - If you select Manual Page Breaks, page breaks that are not part of a paragraph's format definition are removed.

   - If you select Other Format/Layout Overrides, character formatting, paragraph formatting, table formatting, and page layout overrides are removed.

8. Click the Import button.

> **TIP** To update file formats faster, open as many files as you can before using the Import ➤ Formats command. This speeds the process by updating files in computer memory, a much faster operation than updating them on the disk.

9. Save all open files in the book by holding down the Shift key and selecting File ➤ Save All Files in Book. If a file that will receive changes is open, it is updated in computer memory only and not on disk. The file must be saved to retain the changes you've made to it.

Deleting and Rearranging Document Files

Files can not only be added, they can be deleted from a book file list. They can also be rearranged within a list.

> **NOTE** Deleting a file from a book does not delete the file from the disk. It simply deletes the file from the list of files in the book.

You can delete files easily from a book:

1. Make the Book File window active (see Figure 16.2) and select File ➤ Rearrange Files. The Rearrange Files dialog box opens, as in Figure 16.6.

2. Select a file by clicking on its name.

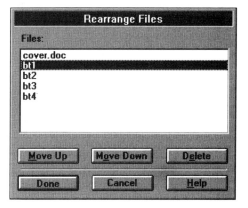

Figure 16.6 **The Rearrange Files dialog box**

3. Click the Delete button. The file name will be removed from the scroll list.

Part
5

Advanced Features

4. Repeat steps 2 and 3 for each file you want to delete. (Files are not actually deleted from the list until you press Done.)

5. When you are finished, click the Done button. The Rearrange Files dialog box closes and the deleted files are removed from the book.

6. If you are certain that you want to delete the file, save the book file by selecting File ➤ Save.

To change the order of files in a book:

1. Make the Book File window active and select File ➤ Rearrange Files. The Rearrange Files dialog box opens (see Figure 16.6).

2. Select a file by clicking on its name.

3. Click the Move Up or Move Down button until the file is where you want it.

4. Repeat steps 2 and 3 for each file you want to move. (Files are not actually moved until you press Done.)

5. When you have finished moving files, click the Done button. The files will be rearranged in the book file.

When Document Files Are Renamed...

When you use the File ➤ Save As command to change the name or location of a document file (or when the operating system does it through a copy or move command), the book file in which the document file is listed is *not* automatically updated. In other words, a book file doesn't know when one of its documents has been renamed. You have to tell the book file about the document name change yourself.

To do this, delete the old file name from the book file, and then add the new file name to the book file list:

1. Open the book file by selecting File ➤ Open.

2. With the Book File window active, select File ➤ Rearrange Files. The Rearrange Files dialog box opens (see Figure 16.6).

3. Select the old file name by clicking on it.

4. Click the Delete button.

5. Click the Done button. The old file is removed from the book.

Now you have to put the new file in the book file:

6. Make the Book File window active and select File ➤ Add File. The Add File to Book dialog box opens (see Figure 16.3).

7. Click Document File and, using the scroll list, select the new file you want to add to the book by clicking on it. Remember, the file must be in Normal FrameMaker format.

8. Use the Add File pull-down menu and scroll list to select where you want to add the file in the book—i.e., above or below which file in the book.

9. Click the Add button. The file name appears in the Add File scroll list where you specified.

10. Click Done. The Add File to Book dialog box closes and the book file shows the new file name.

11. Save the book by selecting File ➤ Save.

Printing a Book

Once you've put your book together and formatted it, it is ready to be printed. You can print one or more document files from the Book File window (see Figure 16.2). All the normal printing options are available except for the Print Range option, so you can print entire files but not page ranges.

To print one or more files from a book:

1. Make the Book File window active and select File ➤ Print. The Print Files in Book dialog box opens, as in Figure 16.7.

2. Move the files you do not want to print from the Print scroll list to the Don't Print scroll list by either clicking on the file name and then clicking on the right arrow button or double-clicking on the file name.

3. When you've moved all the files, click the Print button. The Print dialog box opens.

4. Set the printing options you want. (For more information on printing options, see Chapter 7.)

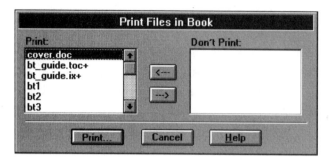

Figure 16.7 **The Print Files in Book dialog box**

5. If you're using a PostScript printer driver, you can print to a PostScript file by selecting Print Only to File (Windows and UNIX) or File (Macintosh) and specifying the path and name of the file.

6. Click the Print button.

    You can print specific pages or a range of pages from a file in a book by opening the file, selecting File ➤ Print, specifying the start and end pages in the Print dialog box, and clicking Print.

Comparing Books

As you work on a book, you may want to keep different versions of it so you can compare the different versions to see what has changed and whether you like the changes. A comparison of books examines text, footnotes, markers, anchored frames, text insets, variables, and cross-references and records where and how changes to these things were made.

Though the book files to be compared can have different file names, document files within books must have the same file names to be compared. (Of course, this assumes that the files to be compared are in separate directories.)

When versions of a book are compared, FrameMaker creates two documents to show where the changes were made. The first document is a general summary of differences between the "older" document and the "newer" one. (You get to say which book is older and which is newer.) The second is a composite document file that "adds together" the contents of each document file being compared.

The *summary document,* shown in Figure 16.8, is a list of differences between versions. When the comparison is finished, the summary document is opened and made active. The summary document lists differences made when you inserted, deleted, and otherwise changed the contents of the files in the books. If you created the summary document with the Create Hypertext Links option turned on, you can click on the change in the summary document and "jump" to the place where that change occurs in either document or in the composite document. (Using hypertext links in files that FrameMaker generates is discussed more fully in Chapter 17.) The summary document has the name SUMMARY (Windows), *newerbook*Summary (Macintosh), or *newerbook*Summary (UNIX), where *newerbook* is the name of the book file called "Newer Book" in the Compare Books dialog box. It is a view-only document created in memory only. When you quit the summary document, you will be prompted to save it.

The *composite document* shows the differences between the documents being compared. The composite document contains all text and other

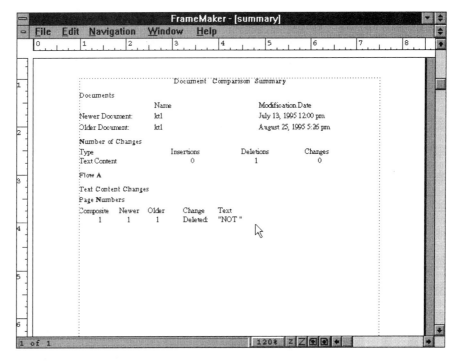

Figure 16.8 **A summary document**

items found in either document. Any item found only in the "newer" document is marked as an "insertion." Any item that appears only in the "older" document is marked as a "deletion." Any item that has moved is marked as both a deletion and an insertion.

Figure 16.9 shows a composite document. Note the use of change bars to show where insertions and/or deletions have occurred. As soon as it is created, the composite document is saved in the directory or folder that contains the newer book. It is named *FILENAME*.CMP (Windows), *filename*CMP (Macintosh), or *filename*CMP (UNIX).

The composite document uses FrameMaker's conditional text feature to identify insertions and deletions. If you select the default options when comparing documents in a book, FrameMaker creates a composite document that uses the conditional tag Inserted for inserted text (which is then marked with an underline and colored green), and the conditional tag Deleted for deleted text (which is then marked with a strikethrough and colored red). You can change these settings if you wish. Conditional

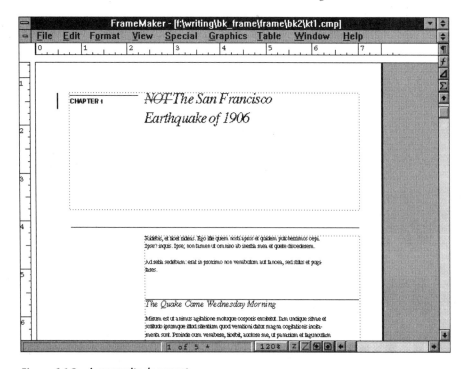

Figure 16.9 **A composite document**

text is covered in Chapter 19. Look ahead to that chapter for more information on using and modifying conditional tags in documents.

To compare two versions of a book:

1. Open both versions of the book by selecting File ➤ Open. Use the scroll list to locate the book files.

2. Make the *newer* version of the book active, and select File ➤ Utilities ➤ Compare Books. The Compare Books dialog box opens, as in Figure 16.10.

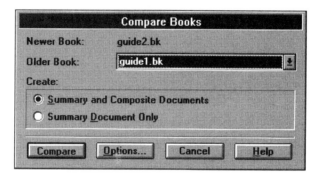

Figure 16.10 **The Compare Books dialog box**

3. Select the older version of the book from the Older Book pull-down menu. The Older Book pull-down menu lists all open, named books.

4. Select which comparison documents you want to create, both the Summary and Composite Documents or the Summary Document Only.

5. To set up the comparison options, click the Options button. The Comparison Options dialog box, shown in Figure 16.11, opens.

6. Select the condition tags you want to apply to inserted and deleted text in the Mark Insertions With and Mark Deletions With boxes. Click on the button next to your choice.

7. If you want change bars, select Mark Changes with Change Bars by clicking on the check box next to it. A change bar is a line along the right margin that shows where changes have been made.

8. If you want entries to be linked by hypertext from the summary document to all other documents—the composite and both the source documents—click on the Create Hypertext Links in Summary check box.

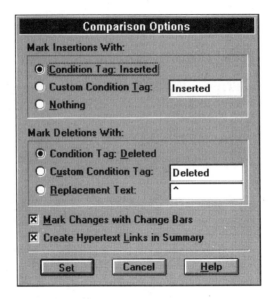

Figure 16.11 **The Comparison Options dialog box**

9. Click the Set button to go back to the Compare Books dialog box.

10. Click the Compare button.

    If there are differences between the books, a summary document is
    displayed when the comparison is finished. If a composite document
    is selected, it is saved in the directory or folder that contains the newer
    book file. If there are no differences between any of the chapters in the
    two books, an alert message is displayed and neither the summary nor
    the composite document is created.

    The summary document, which is opened when the comparison is
    finished, can be saved for future use. The various composite documents
    can be opened and examined for changes.

Chapter 17

Tables of Contents, Indexes, and Other Book Features

The last chapter explained how to create and print books with FrameMaker. In this chapter, you'll learn how to generate tables of contents (TOCs), indexes, lists of figures and tables, and other lists to make your books more useful.

TOCs and indexes are "generated lists," and each is usually placed in a separate file, called a "generated file." Let's look first at generated files more closely. Then we'll see how to create the two types of generated files—a file containing a list of paragraphs (like a table of contents, which is really a list of heading paragraphs) and a file containing a list of "markers" (like an index).

Generated Files

You can create a generated file from a book or from a single document. There are two types of generated files:

▶ A list of selected paragraphs in the source document(s). Items are listed in the order in which they appear, usually with page numbers. This type of generated file includes the table of contents, a list of figures (which lists paragraphs marked as figure titles), a list of tables (which contains paragraphs marked as table titles), and so on.

▶ A list of the contents of markers that have been placed in the text of the source document(s). Items are usually listed alphabetically, and again, usually with page numbers. This type of generated file includes the standard index and others, like an index of references.

Keep these differences in mind—lists of paragraphs in the order of appearance, and lists of markers in alphabetical order. It will help you in the discussion that follows.

 NOTE   The procedures in this chapter assume that lists are being generated with book file commands, but these procedures are applicable to lists generated from single documents as well.

Creating a Table of Contents

A table of contents (TOC) lists heading paragraphs that appear in the chapters of a book. Usually, a page number is printed next to the headings so readers know which page to turn to. You select which headings appear in a table of contents by selecting paragraph tags. All tagged headings will appear in the TOC.

Making Sure Source Documents Are Tagged Correctly

Before you generate a table of contents, go through the source document(s) and make sure they are prepared properly. Make sure you use consistent tag names in heading paragraphs that will be included in the TOC. For example, if you use the tag *Heading1* for first-level headings and *Heading2* for second-level headings, do so throughout all your source documents. Don't use *Heading 1* (with a space) or *FirstLevelHeading*, for example.

Make sure that each tagged heading is a single paragraph. A heading that covers two paragraphs creates two separate entries in the generated list. Similarly, don't use new-line characters (forced returns) in headings.

Generating a Table of Contents

Once you've prepared the heading paragraphs in the document or book, you can create the table of contents. Creating the TOC for a book involves two main steps:

1. Adding a table of contents document to the book file.

2. Generating the table itself.

To generate a TOC for a single document, you can skip step 1. The procedures for generating a TOC from a single document and for a book are a little different. Following are instructions for doing both. Where the procedures for generating the book TOC and document TOC are different, I will note them.

To create and generate a table of contents for a book or single document:

1. Make the Book File window active and select File ➤ Add File. Either the Add File to Book dialog box (for a Book) or the Generate/Book dialog box (for a single document) opens, as in Figure 17.1.

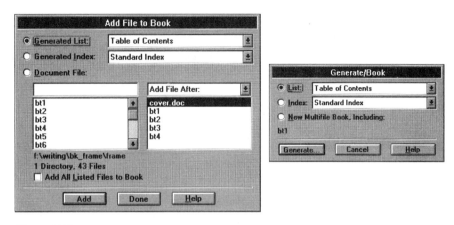

Figure 17.1 **The Add File to Book dialog box (left) and the Generate/Book dialog box (right)**

2. Select Table of Contents from the Generated List or List pull-down menu. If you're creating a TOC for a single document, skip to step 5.

3. Click on the file in the scroll list that is above or below where you want the TOC file to go.

4. Use the Add File pull-down list to select whether to add the file before or after the selected file.

5. Click the Add button if you're working on a book, or the Generate button if you're working on a single document. The Set Up Table of Contents dialog box appears, as in Figure 17.2.

6. In general, leave the text in the Filename Suffix box alone. In the Windows version, the table of contents document is given the file name extension *file name*.TOC. In the Mac and UNIX versions, the table of contents document is given the file name suffix *file name*TOC. In both cases, *file name* is the name of the source book or document file.

7. Move the paragraph tags you want to include in the TOC from the Don't Include scroll list to the Include Paragraph Tagged scroll list by clicking on the paragraph tag and then clicking on the left arrow button.

Part
5

Advanced Features

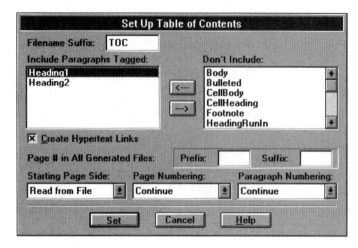

Figure 17.2 *The Set Up Table of Contents dialog box. This dialog box is for TOCs based on book files.*

8. If you want hypertext links to be created from the TOC to the various source documents, click on Create Hypertext Links. Hypertext is explained at the end of this chapter. Skip to step 10 if you're working on a single document.

9. Set the page and paragraph number properties—Page # in All Generated Files, Starting Page Side, Page Numbering, and Paragraph Numbering. For a full explanation of these settings, see "Changing and Updating the Format of Document Files" in Chapter 16.

10. Click the Set button if you're working on a TOC, or the Generate button if you're working on a single document.

   If you're working on a TOC for a single file, a file based on the name of the source document—*filename*.TOC (Windows) or *filename*TOC (Mac and UNIX)—is generated and opened. You're done!

   If you're working on a TOC for a book file, a file based on the name of the source book—*bookname*.TOC (Windows) or *bookname*TOC (Mac and UNIX)—is added to the book file. The plus sign (+) behind the file name in the Book File window means that the file is a generated file.

If you're working on a book TOC:

11. Click the Done button to close the Add File to Book dialog box.

12. Select the table of contents in the book file by clicking on the file name with the *TOC* suffix or extension.

13. Select File ➤ Generate/Update. The Generate/Update Book dialog box shown in Figure 17.3 opens. The TOC file name appears in the Generate scroll list.

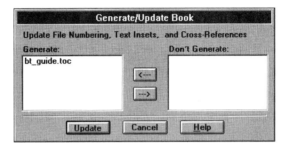

Figure 17.3 **The Generate/Update Book dialog box for creating generated files for books**

14. Click the Update button. FrameMaker opens and scans the documents in the book for the paragraph tags included in the table of contents. When the process is complete, the new TOC is opened and becomes active.

15. Save the TOC document by selecting File ➤ Save.

Regenerating a Table of Contents

When you make changes to a source document that affect the TOC, the TOC needs to be regenerated. To do this for a book file TOC:

1. Make the Book File window active and select File ➤ Generate/Update. The Generate/Update Book dialog box (see Figure 17.3) opens.

2. Move the file name of the table of contents to the Generate scroll list.

3. Click the Update button.

If the TOC was closed, it will be updated, but not opened. If the table of contents was open, it will be updated in computer memory only and must be saved to disk.

Part
5

Advanced Features

To regenerate a table of contents created from a single document, follow the procedure used to generate it originally:

1. Select File ➤ Generate/Book.

2. In the Generate/Book dialog box, make sure Table of Contents is selected and click Generate. The Set Up Table of Contents dialog box opens, as in Figure 17.4.

3. Check the paragraph tags list and click Generate again.

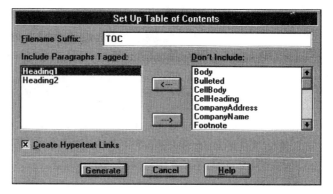

Figure 17.4   **The Set Up Table of Contents dialog box**

Formatting a Table of Contents

When you create a table of contents, the page layout and formatting are taken either from the source document or from a template (if you used one). If the formatting came from a source document, all TOC entries have the same nondescript paragraph format. After you generate a table of contents, however, you can change the page layout and other formats. Your changes are retained whenever you regenerate the TOC.

Much of a TOC's formatting and structure is determined by a special text flow on a reference page (often not the first reference page) of the document. This text flow has the default tag *TOC*.

Each document paragraph tag (for example, *Heading1*) in a table of contents list has a corresponding paragraph tag in the Paragraph Catalog of the TOC document (in our example, *Heading1TOC*). So if three document paragraph tags were used to generate the TOC, there would be three corresponding paragraph tags in the TOC Paragraph Catalog.

NOTE The formatting and structure of lists like a TOC—such as a list of figures or a list of tables—are determined by their own text flows. The list of figures text flow, for example, is called *LOF*; the list of tables flow is called *LOT*.

In addition, each of the paragraph tags is applied to a special paragraph in the *TOC* flow on the reference page. These paragraphs are special because they are made up of *building blocks* that insert information like page numbers in specific places in paragraphs.

FrameMaker's Building Blocks

Building blocks represent variable information that FrameMaker gathers and inserts in a document at a specified location. Examples of building blocks include *<$pagenum>*, which is replaced by a referenced page number, and *<$paratext>*, which is replaced by the text of a referenced paragraph.

Building blocks are always made up of a string of characters that starts and ends with angle braces (< and >). FrameMaker treats each building block as single unit.

As this chapter will show, building blocks are essential in creating entries in generated files. FrameMaker uses building blocks in other ways as well—for example, in headers and footers, in paragraph autonumbers, in text as variables, and to format cross-references.

The following types of building blocks are available (for a complete list of building blocks, see the online help provided with the program):

Autonumbering—These building blocks represent information used in paragraph autonumbering—for example, numeric (*<n>*, *<N>*), alphabetic (*<a>*, *<A>*), and Roman numeral (*<r >*, *<R>*) counters. See Chapter 10 for more information.

Cross-Reference—These building blocks insert information into cross-references. Examples include *<$pagenum>*, *<$paratext>*, and *<$fullfile name>*.

Variable—These insert page numbers, dates, file names, and other variable information into the text of documents. Examples include *<$lastpagenum>* for the last page number of a document (used to create text like "page 3 of 12"), *<$dayname>* for the name of the day, and *<$file name>*.

Header and Footer—These building blocks insert page numbers and other information into headers and footers, and can be used to create running heads that automatically contain the most recent heading of a certain type.

List and Index—These building blocks insert information into generated lists and indexes. This is the type of building block discussed in this chapter.

Figure 17.5 shows some reference page entries. These entries were taken from the second reference page of the Book TOC template included with FrameMaker 5. The first paragraph, tagged *ChapterTitleTOC*, is used to format all TOC entries that come from paragraphs tagged *ChapterTitle* in source documents. It includes several building blocks:

▶ *<ChapterNumber>*, *<Default Para Font>*, and *<PageNumber>* are the names of character tags in the TOC document. They will be applied at the specified locations.

▶ *<$paranum>* inserts each chapter's "paragraph" number, in this case the autonumbered chapter title, including text that appears with the number, like the word "Chapter."

▶ *<$paratext>* inserts the text of each paragraph entry.

▶ *<$pagenum>* inserts the page number on which each entry is found.

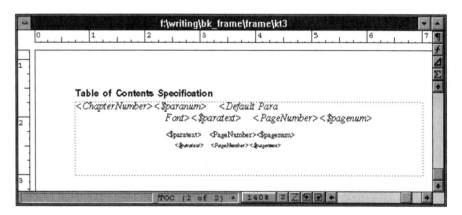

Figure 17.5   Example TOC flow on the TOC reference page

ChapterTitle entries have the font of the *ChapterTitleTOC* paragraph, with the same margins and tabs. The building blocks and other text specifies what the entries contain and how they appear in the generated list.

TIP This might be a good time to look at the sample book template files provided with FrameMaker. Check out the chapter file first, look at its Paragraph Catalog, and then open the TOC and look at it. Examine especially the relationship between the paragraphs in the reference page flow named *TOC* and the corresponding paragraphs in the generated body pages. (You can ignore the other flows on the reference page. They do not affect the TOC body pages.)

Simple Formatting for TOCs from Single Documents

If you are creating a table of contents from a single document without going though a book file, store all the formatting information, including the *TOC* text flow, in the source document. Then generate the TOC. The generated file will take all of its formatting from the source document, including the formatting of the *TOC* flow on the reference page.

Rearranging Information in a TOC Entry

If you don't like the arrangement of information in an entry, you can rearrange it. For example, you can make the page number come before the paragraph text instead of after it. To rearrange items in a TOC entry:

1. Make the table of contents active and display reference pages by selecting View ➤ Reference Pages.

2. Move to the reference page that contains the *TOC* text flow.

3. Rearrange the building blocks in the paragraph that correspond to the entry paragraph you want to change.

   Remember to treat the building blocks (including the left and right angle bracket) as single units. For example, instead of having paragraph text followed by a page number:

   ```
   <$paratext> <$pagenum>
   ```

   you can place the page number in front of the paragraph text:

   ```
   <$pagenum> <$paratext>
   ```

4. Display body pages by selecting View ➤ Body Pages.

5. Open the book file (or source document) and regenerate it. The change you made will appear in the appropriate entries.

6. Save the changes by selecting File ➤ Save.

Changing the Character Format of TOC Entries

You can change the character format of any entry in a TOC. For example, you can make the text bold and the page number italic. This can be done in two ways, by using building blocks based on the character tags in the TOC Character Catalog or by applying a character format directly to the building block itself. Let's look at the first way:

1. Make the TOC active, create a new character format with a descriptive name, and store it in the Character Catalog.

2. Display reference pages by selecting View ➤ Reference Pages.

3. Move to the reference page that contains the *TOC* text flow.

4. In the paragraph that corresponds to the entry paragraph, type in the name of the character format (enclosed between a left and right angle bracket, but with no $ sign). Type it immediately to the left of the building block to which you want to apply the new character format. For example, apply the format *BOLD* to the paragraph text building block as follows:

    ```
    <BOLD><$paratext> <$pagenum>
    ```

5. Type **<Default Para Font>** where you want to change back to the paragraph's default font—for example, before the page number:

    ```
    <BOLD><$paratext><Default Para Font> <$pagenum>
    ```

6. Display body pages by selecting View ➤ Body Pages.

7. Open the book file (or source document) and regenerate the TOC. The change you made will appear in the appropriate entries.

8. Save changes to the index by selecting File ➤ Save.

   Change the character format of text in the TOC by applying a character format directly to the building block itself—for example, the *<$pagenum>* building block:

1. Make the table of contents active, create a new character format with a descriptive name, and store it in the Character Catalog.

2. Display reference pages by selecting View ➤ Reference Pages.

3. Move to the reference page that contains the *TOC* text flow.

4. Select the text of the building block to which you want to apply the new character format—for example, *<$paratext>*. Select the entire building block including the left and right angle brackets.

5. Open the Character Catalog by selecting Format ➤ Characters ➤ Catalog.

6. Click on the character format tag you want to apply—for example, *BOLD*.

7. Display body pages by selecting View ➤ Body Pages.

8. Open the book file (or source document) for the TOC and regenerate it. The change you made will appear in the appropriate entries.

9. Save the changes by selecting File ➤ Save.

Inserting Text into a TOC Entry

You can insert any text you want in a TOC entry. You might, for example, want to enclose the page number in parenthesis. To insert text in an entry:

1. Make the TOC active and display reference pages by selecting View ➤ Reference Pages.

2. Move to the reference page that contains the *TOC* text flow.

3. Type the text you want to add into the entry you want to change. For example, the following places parentheses around the page number building block:

```
<$paratext> (<$pagenum>)
```

4. Display body pages by selecting View ➤ Body Pages.

5. Open the book file (or source document) for the TOC and regenerate it. The change you made will appear in the appropriate entries.

6. Save the changes by selecting File ➤ Save.

Including Autonumbers in TOC Entries

You can use autonumbers from source paragraphs in a TOC and other generated lists. Autonumbers are the numbers, as well as text, that are automatically inserted at the beginning of a paragraph. For example, your first-level headings might be autonumbered 1.0, 2.0, and so on, while second-level entries are numbered 1.1, 1.2, 2.1. You probably will want these numbers to be retained in the TOC entries.

To apply autonumbering to TOC entries, add a *<$paranum>* and *<$paranumonly>* building block to the paragraphs on the reference page that correspond to the entry paragraphs:

Building Block	What It Does
<$paranum>	Specifies that the entire auto-numbering specification of the source paragraph, including the text and the autonumber itself, be printed with the entry (for example, "Figure 3. ").
<$paranumonly>	Prints just the number itself with the entry (in the example above, just "3").

The following shows how this works:

1. Make the table of contents window active and display reference pages by selecting View ➤ Reference Pages.

2. Move to the reference page that contains the *TOC* text flow.

3. Type the autonumbering building block where you want it to appear. For example, to add only the number itself from the source entry, use:

```
<$paranumonly> <$paratext> <$pagenum>
```

4. Display body pages by selecting View ➤ Body Pages.

5. Open the book file (or source document) for the table of contents and regenerate it. The change you made will appear in the appropriate entry.

6. Save the changes by selecting File ➤ Save.

Keeping the Page Number with the Entry Text

Sometimes an entry fills a line completely or spans several lines. In these cases, the page number for the entry may appear alone on a line below the entry text. This can look pretty bad, but it can be prevented:

1. Make the table of contents window active and display reference pages by selecting View ➤ Reference Pages.

2. Move to the reference page that contains the *TOC* text flow.

3. Place a nonbreaking space, an en space, or an em space between the building blocks *<$paratext>* and *<$pagenum>* in the entry you want to change.

4. Display body pages by selecting View ➤ Body Pages.

5. Open the book file (or source document) for the TOC and regenerate the TOC. The change you made will appear in the appropriate entry.

6. Save the changes by selecting File ➤ Save.

Adding Tabs and Leader Dots to TOC Entries

Instead of spaces between the entry text and page number, or in addition to them, you can use tabs and leader dots:

1. Make the TOC window active and display reference pages by selecting View ➤ Reference Pages.

2. Move to the reference page that contains the *TOC* text flow.

3. Select the space between the building blocks *<$paratext>* and *<$pagenum>* in the paragraph for the entry you want to change.

4. Press the Tab key.

5. Use the Paragraph Designer to add a tab stop to the appropriate paragraph tag (for example, *Heading1TOC*) in the place you want. Choose the tab alignment (Left, Right, or Center) and leader dot pattern you want.

6. Apply the change to all paragraphs with the same tag by clicking the Update All Formats Tagged button in the Paragraph Designer. This stores the new format in the Paragraph Catalog so it can be used when the TOC is regenerated.

7. Display body pages by selecting View ➤ Body Pages.

8. Open the book file (or source document) for the TOC and regenerate the TOC. The change you made will appear in the appropriate entry.

9. Save the changes by selecting File ➤ Save.

Part 5

Advanced Features

Adding a Title to a Table of Contents

You can also add a title to the body page that starts the list of TOC entries:

1. After you have generated the TOC for the first time, create a new paragraph *before* the first entry in the list on the first body page.

2. Place the insertion point in the new paragraph and type the title.

3. Bring up the Paragraph Designer by selecting Format ➤ Paragraph ➤ Designer.

4. Create a new paragraph tag for the title paragraph that does *not* end in the *TOC* suffix by typing the name in the Paragraph Tag text box of the Paragraph Designer.

NOTE **Step 4 is important. Paragraphs with the *TOC* suffix get updated when the table of contents is regenerated, and you want your title to go untouched during updates.**

5. Select New Format from the Commands pull-down menu in the Paragraph Designer and check both Store in Catalog and Apply to Selection in the New Format dialog box.

6. Press Create to create the new format.

7. Using the Paragraph Designer, modify the paragraph to look the way you want it and click Update All after each group of changes. You want to modify both the paragraph itself and the format definition stored in the catalog.

8. When you are done creating and modifying the paragraph and its tag, save changes to the TOC by selecting File ➤ Save.

Using a Template to Format a Table of Contents

If you don't want to spend time formatting your TOC, you can use either an existing TOC or a template TOC to do the formatting for you. (The existing TOC or the template should have the formatting you want, or a format close to it.) This can be done in one of two ways—by using the formatted TOC directly, as though it were your own, or by importing formats from the formatted document into yours.

If TOC Formatting Is Not Retained after an Update...

When you regenerate a table of contents, all formatting should be carried over to the updated version. If some or all of the formatting is not retained, check to make sure that:

▶ The table of contents file name and location haven't changed. The TOC document must be in the same directory as the source book file (or document) and must use the file name FrameMaker assigns it.

▶ The title added to the first page does not have a paragraph tag that ends in the suffix *TOC*.

▶ All paragraph format changes were stored in the Paragraph Catalog *and* applied to paragraphs in the document.

▶ You stored any new character formats in the Character Catalog.

▶ All format changes that affect the *TOC* text flow were made in that flow and not somewhere else. Also make sure that these changes made it to the Paragraph Catalog.

Using a Copy of a Template to Format Your TOC   If you place a properly named template TOC—one that already contains the formatting you want—into the directory where FrameMaker expects to find your own TOC, then you simply generate or regenerate your own TOC, the formatted template will be updated with the new TOC information.

Here's the process step by step:

1. In the procedure for creating a TOC provided earlier in this chapter (see "Generating a Table of Contents"), perform steps 1 through 10. That will take you to the Add File to Book dialog box.

2. Copy the template document into the directory or folder that contains the book file or source document. The template document can be an existing TOC from another book, a template from FrameMaker's templates directory, or a template you or someone else has created.

3. Give the template the name that FrameMaker assigned to the your own TOC.

   For example, if you are using a book file named MYBOOK.BK (Windows-style), the generated TOC will be named MYBOOK.TOC (without the plus sign that appears in the book file list), and your template should also be named MYBOOK.TOC.

Part 5

Advanced Features

4. Finish the procedure for generating a table of contents. When you generate or regenerate the TOC, FrameMaker will update the template with the new TOC listings, just as though it were your own. The new TOC will have both correct table of contents information and the template's formatting.

Importing Formats from a Template TOC   You can also change the formats of your own TOC by importing formats from either another TOC or from a TOC template:

1. Open both your own table of contents document and the template document.

2. Make your own TOC active and select File ➤ Import ➤ Formats.

3. In the Import Format dialog box, select the name of the open template document from the Import from Document pull-down list.

4. Select all check boxes in the Import and Update section.

5. Click the Import button.

6. Save the changes to your modified table of contents by selecting File ➤ Save.

Troubleshooting a Table of Contents

Generally, problems with generated TOCs are caused by problems in the source document. For example, an incorrectly tagged heading may not show up in the table of contents, or a body paragraph that has a heading tag may be included erroneously. These problems must be fixed in the source document. If they are fixed in the table of contents, the corrections will disappear when the table of contents is regenerated. Following are some hints to help you fix the more common TOC problems.

Heading Missing   If a heading is missing from the table of contents, check the tag of the missing heading in the source document. You probably need to change it to a tag that is included in the TOC. Then regenerate the TOC.

Using Hypertext Links during Debugging

To trace a TOC entry back to its source easily, select Create Hypertext Links in the Set Up dialog box when you generate the table of contents. You can now use these links, which are described near the end of this chapter, to move from the TOC to the source document, even when the source documents are not in view-only mode. To move from a hypertext link in the TOC to its source heading in an editable (non-view-only) document, use one of the following mouse/keyboard shortcuts on the TOC entry:

In Windows, use Alt+Ctrl+click.

On the Macintosh, use 2 +Option+click

In UNIX, use Ctrl+click

When a hypertext link is selected in this way, the source document opens to the page that contains the TOC heading and the heading is selected.

All Headings of One Kind Missing If all headings with a particular paragraph tag are missing, make sure that the Include Paragraph Tagged scroll list in the Set Up Table of Contents dialog box (see Figure 17.2) contains that tag. If the tag is missing, move it to the scroll list and regenerate the table of contents.

Wrong TOC Entry If an entry doesn't belong in the table of contents, change the tag of the source paragraph to a tag not included in the TOC. Then regenerate it.

Blank Line with Page Number If a blank line with a page number appears, either delete the corresponding blank paragraph in the source document or change its tag and regenerate the table of contents.

Entry on Two Lines If an entry is broken and appears on two lines, each with a page number, make the corresponding paragraphs in the source document one paragraph. If you want the paragraph to appear on two lines in the source document, change the right indent of the paragraph until you get the desired result. If the paragraph is centered, change the right and left paragraph indents. Then regenerate the TOC.

Part
5

Advanced Features

Line Breaks in the Wrong Place   If line breaks appear in the wrong place in the TOC (for example, if page numbers appear on separate lines or lines break at hyphens in page numbers), there are several things you can do:

▶ Change the Allow Line Breaks After list for the TOC document. With the table of contents window active, select Format ➤ Document ➤ Text Options and change the list of Allow Line Breaks After characters. For example, remove the en dash from the list. Then regenerate the TOC.

▶ Put nonbreaking spaces between the TOC heading text and the page number. Do this for each heading level in the *TOC* text flow. Then regenerate the TOC.

▶ Remove all new-line characters from the source heading paragraph.

▶ Use a nonbreaking hyphen in the Page # in Generated Files specification of each source document file. For each source document file, click on the document file name in the book file list, select File ➤ Set Up File, and insert a nonbreaking hyphen in the Prefix and Suffix text boxes in place of regular hyphens, and regenerate the TOC. (For more information, see the section Setting Up Files earlier in this chapter.) To enter a nonbreaking hyphen into a dialog box, type \+ (backslash+plus) in Windows, press %+grave accent on the Mac, or press Meta+hyphen in UNIX.

Creating an Index

Indexes are invaluable in books that provide a lot of information. If you're producing a book or manual that your readers will refer to often, consider including an index. This part of the chapter tells you everything you need to know to generate and format an index.

In FrameMaker, indexes are generated using markers. A *marker* is a nontext item inserted into the flow of the characters. Each marker has text contents of its own, inserted either by you or by FrameMaker, and is used for a special purpose, depending on the kind of marker it is.

When text symbols are turned on, you can see markers in the text along with other symbols like the paragraph symbol. A marker looks like this:

The Quake Came Wednesday Mo

Mirum est uṫ animus agitatione motuque corporis
solitudo ipsumque illud silentium quod venationi

There are many kinds of markers, each with a special purpose. Some markers contain text used for running headers and footers, some contain information used to create cross-references, some contain hypertext commands, and others are used as anchors for tables and anchored frames.

An *index marker* contains index text. Index markers generally sit in the source document in the paragraph or next to the word they refer to (though this is not necessary, since index markers can be placed anywhere). The location of the index marker determines the page number of the index entry or entries generated by that marker.

When you generate a FrameMaker index, the following occurs:

▶ All markers in the source document are scanned.

▶ The text in the markers is stored in a list, along with the page number on which the marker appears.

▶ The list is sorted alphabetically and grouped by letter.

To create an index, you must complete four steps:

1. Prepare the source document or documents by adding the index markers, including markers for subentries (indented second-level entries) and index cross-references ("see also" comments in index entries).

2. Generate the index.

3. Format the index. (If you use a template when you generate the index, the template handles formatting.)

4. Fix problems, if any, with the index.

In this part of the chapter, we'll look closely at these four steps. This chapter explains how to mark documents for an index. It also describes how to refine index entries, all of which use characters with special punctuation (like the colon and the semicolon), and the set of building blocks used with indexes.

NOTE   The procedures for creating indexes can also be applied to other lists generated from markers, such as lists of cross-references.

Part 5

Advanced Features

Marking Documents for an Index

Before you create an index, the source documents need to be prepared. This means marking all the index entries by inserting index markers into the text. A marker appears in text only as a symbol, but FrameMaker uses the symbol to store the text of the index entry.

To see the contents of a marker, select Special ➤ Markers.

TIP   To see marker symbols where they appear in text, select View ➤ Text Symbols.

Marker text is viewed and edited with the Marker window. To bring up the Marker window, shown in Figure 17.6, select Special ➤ Marker. If a marker (or text containing a marker) is selected in your document, the button says "Edit Marker" and the window shows the type and text contents of the selected marker. To edit the marker, make whatever changes you wish and click on the Edit Marker button. (Markers can be selected in several ways—by selecting text that includes the marker or by using the Find/Change window to find markers themselves. Markers at the beginning of a word can be selected by selecting the word.)

Figure 17.6   **The Marker window**

If a marker, or text containing a marker, is not already selected in your document, the button in the marker window says "New Marker." Entering text in the marker window and pressing New Marker places a marker of the type listed in the text at the insertion point (the place where the character cursor is sitting).

You will use these two techniques in the procedures that follow. (Note, by the way, that the Marker window is a palette that stays open until you close it. When you are building an index, this window will stay open a lot.)

Besides the text of index entries, index markers can contain special characters and index building blocks that change the format of the entry. (For more information, see "FrameMaker's Building Blocks" earlier in this chapter.) You can use special characters and index building blocks to create subentries and index cross-references, and to identify page ranges for index entries that span more than one page. You can also use them to change the character format of parts of an entry or to change how an entry is alphabetized in the index.

Creating a Simple Index Entry

To use the Marker window to create a simple index entry:

1. Open the Marker window (see Figure 17.6) by selecting Special ➤ Markers.

2. Place the insertion point in the document where you want the marker to appear. Index markers can only be placed in text frames; they cannot appear in a text line created with the Text Line graphics tool.

TIP　It is good practice to place an index marker at the beginning or end of a paragraph, or at the beginning of a word in a paragraph. This will allow you to edit the paragraph without having the marker interfere with your work. Once index markers are added to a document, always edit with View ➤ Text Symbols on to keep from deleting index markers accidentally.

---

3. In the Marker window, select Index from the Marker Type pull-down list.

4. In the Marker Text area, type the text of the index entry. Marker text can be up to 255 characters long.

For example, to create an index marker with the text "Picard, Jean-Luc," simply type that text into the Marker window text box. When the index is generated, an entry will be created for "Picard, Jean-Luc," alphabetized on the first word ("Picard"). The entry will include the page number on which the marker appears. If there are three markers with identical

Special Characters in Index Markers

Several characters have special meanings when used in index markers. When they appear, they are interpreted and not printed. These special characters include the colon (:), semicolon (;), square brackets ([ ]), angle braces (< >), and the backslash (\).

If you wish to print one of these symbols with the rest of the marker text, precede it with a backslash (\). For example, to print a colon in an index, type backslash+colon (\:). To cause a backslash to be printed, type backslash-backslash (\\).

text ("Picard, Jean-Luc") on three different pages, there will be one index entry (again, "Picard, Jean-Luc"), followed by the three page numbers. In its basic form, indexing is really that simple.

Note, however, that the text of all three markers must be identical, character for character, in order for the entry to reference three different page references; if the entry is not identical, separate and slightly different index entries will be created, one for each variation in the marker text. In our example, you could end up with separate entries for "Picard, Jean-Luc" and "Picard, Jean Luc" (note the hyphen in the first entry. Similar but unidentical index entries are one of the more common index errors.

5. Click the New Marker button. A marker is inserted in the document.

6. Repeat steps 2 through 5 for each index marker you want to insert.

7. When you have finished inserting index markers, select File ➤ Save.

Quick Ways to Insert Index Markers

Marker text can be created quickly in two ways.

To index a single word, place an index marker without text at the beginning of a word. The word to the right of the marker becomes the text of the marker after the index is generated.

To index a word or phrase, select the word or phrase (and make sure it doesn't already contain a marker). The selected word or phrase will appear automatically in the text box of the Marker window, and you can insert the marker by just clicking the New Marker button.

Editing Index Entries

From time to time, you will want to go back and modify index entries. To edit the text of an index entry, edit the marker like so:

1. Open the Marker window by selecting Special ➤ Marker.

2. Select the index marker by selecting any text in the document that contains the marker. The text of the selected marker will appear in the Marker window, and the button will say "Edit Marker." If the marker is at the beginning of a word (as most will be), selecting the word automatically selects the marker. If you select text containing more than one marker, only the first marker will be displayed in the Marker window.

3. As a general rule, first make sure the Marker Type pull-down list says "Index."

4. Edit the text in the Marker Text area as you wish.

5. Click the Edit Marker button.

6. Repeat steps 2 through 5 for each index marker you want to edit.

7. When you are done editing markers, select File ➤ Save.

Using Special Characters and Building Blocks in Indexes

The special characters and building blocks in Table 17.1 can be used in index markers to control the formatting and sort order of an entry and to create subentries.

Creating Subentries in an Index

You can create second-level index entries, called *subentries*, under a main entry. For example, instead of listing "Picard, Jean-Luc, birth" and "Picard, Jean-Luc, accomplishments" as separate entries, you can list them both in a two-level entry that looks like this:

Picard, Jean-Luc
    accomplishments, 5
    birth, 3

Special Character(s)	What It Does
colon (:)	Separates entries from their subentries.
semicolon (;)	Separates first-level index entries in the same marker.
square brackets ([*word*])	Specifies that an entry be alphabetized as though it started with *word*.
angle braces (<*text*>)	Specifies that *text* is a FrameMaker building block.
backslash (\)	Produces special characters in index entries.

Index Building Block	What It Does
<*$startrange*>	Specifies that this entry and each entry following in the same marker is the start of a page range. Used with <*$endrange*>, where <*$startrange*> and <*$endrange*> markers have identical marker text.
<*$endrange*>	Specifies that this entry and each entry following in the same marker is the end of a page range. Used with <*$startrange*>, where <*$startrange*> and <*$endrange*> markers have identical marker text.
<*$nopage*>	Specifies that this entry and each entry following in the same marker be listed without a page number. Used with numberless entries like "Dracula *See* Lugosi, Bela."
<*$singlepage*>	In a marker that contains several entries, restores single page numbering after the appearance of a <*$startrange*>, <*$endrange*>, or <*$nopage*> building block.

Table 17.1   **Special Characters and Building Blocks in Indexes**

Special Character(s)	What It Does
<tag>	Changes the character format to *tag* for all text that follows in the same entry, where *<tag>* is a character tag between angle braces. If placed at the end of an entry, changes the format of the page number only. Note that character tag building blocks do *not* contain a dollar sign (*$*).
<Default Para Font>	Restores the paragraph's default font for all text that follows in the same entry. If placed at the end of an entry, restores the format of the page number only. Note that character tag building blocks do *not* contain a dollar sign(*$*).

Table 17.1 **Special Characters and Building Blocks in Indexes (continued)**

Subentries can be created down to many levels, but most indexes usually have one, or at most two, subentry levels.

To create an index subentry in a marker:

1. Open the Marker window (see Figure 17.6) by selecting Special ➤ Markers.

2. Place the insertion point in the document where you want the marker to appear.

3. In the Marker window, select Index from the Marker Type pull-down list.

4. In the Marker Text area, type the main entry, a colon (:), and then the subentry. For example:

   ```
   Picard, Jean-Luc:birth
   ```

   In marker text, the main entry always comes first. Be sure to type the main entry in the same way, character for character, each time you use it. Space characters count as characters (i.e., "Picard " is not the same entry as "Picard").

5. Click the New Marker button.

6. Repeat steps 2 through 5 for each subentry you want to create.

7. When you have finished inserting index markers, save changes to the document by selecting File ➤ Save.

Creating Page Ranges in an Index Entry

If an index reference spans several pages, you can create markers that identify the start and end of the range. When the index is generated, the combined entry looks like this:

Picard, Jean-Luc, 3-12

To mark a range of pages for an index entry:

1. Open the Marker window (see Figure 17.6) by selecting Special ➤ Markers.

2. In the document, place the insertion point at the start of the index entry.

3. In the Marker window, select Index as the Marker Type.

4. In the Market Text area, type **<$startrange>** and then the text of the entry. For example:

    ```
    <$startrange>Picard, Jean-Luc
    ```

5. Click the New Marker button.

6. In the document, place the insertion point at the end of the index entry.

7. In the Marker window, select Index as the Marker Type.

8. In the Market Text area, type **<$endrange>** and then the text of the entry. Make sure the text of the two markers is identical.

9. Click the New Marker button.

10. Repeat these steps for each set of page range markers you wish to insert.

11. When you are done, select File ➤ Save.

Adding Cross-References to Index Entries

An index cross-reference is an entry that directs the reader to another entry in the same index, like both of these:

Babe Ruth *See* Ruth, George Herman (Babe)

Sultan of Swat *See* Ruth, George Herman (Babe)

Cross-references are used in indexes to keep entries, subentries, and page numbers from being duplicated. In the example above, the "Ruth, George Herman (Babe)" entry would list all the page numbers and subentries, on the assumption that most people would look up references to a person under his or her last name, not a nickname or a title.

WARNING Readers do not take kindly to cross-references that point to other cross-references. Make sure all cross-references refer to index entries with real page numbers.

To create an index entry containing a cross-reference:

1. Open the Marker window (see Figure 17.6) by selecting Special ➤ Markers.

2. Place the insertion point in the document where you want the marker to appear.

3. In the Marker window, select Index from the Marker Type pull-down list.

4. In the Marker Text area, type **<$nopage>** and the text of the cross-reference. For example:

   ```
   <$nopage>Sultan of Swat See Ruth, George Herman (Babe)
   ```

The *<$nopage>* building block stops the page number from appearing with the cross-reference entry in the index.

5. Click the New Marker button.

6. Repeat steps 2 through 5 for each cross-reference marker you want to insert.

7. When you are done, select File ➤ Save.

Generating and Regenerating an Index

After you have inserted and saved index markers in the documents of a book (or in a single document, if you are not working with a book file), you're ready to create and generate the index.

TIP   If you are generating an index from a single document, simply select File ➤ Generate/Book from the document's main menu.

The procedures for creating and generating an index for a book and for a single document are a little different. Following are instructions for doing both. Where the procedures are different, I will note them.

To create and generate an index for a book or a single document:

1. Make the Book File window active and select File ➤ Add File. Either the Add File to Book dialog box (for a book) or the Generate/Book dialog box (for a single document) opens, as shown in Figure 17.7.

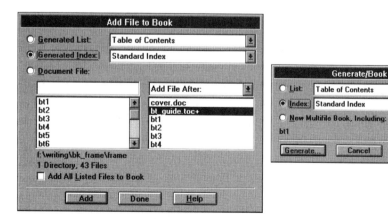

Figure 17.7   *The Add File to Book dialog box (left) and the Generate/Book dialog box (right)*

2. Select Standard Index from the Generated Index or Index pull-down menu. If you're working on a single document, the Set Up Standard Index dialog box appears and you can go to step 6. If you're working on a book, read on.

3. Click on the file in the scroll list that is above or below where you want the index file to go.

4. Use the Add File pull-down list to select whether to add the file before or after the selected file.

5. Click the Add button. The Set Up Standard Index dialog box opens, as shown in Figure 17.8.

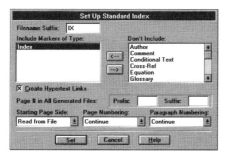

Figure 17.8 The Set Up Standard Index dialog box. The one on the left is for indexes based on book files; the one on the right is for single documents.

6. In general, leave the text in the File name Suffix box alone.

In the Windows version, the index document is given this file name extension (*file name*.IX). In the Mac and UNIX versions, the index is given this file name suffix (*file name*IX). In both cases, *file name* is the name of the source book or document file.

7. Move all of the marker types except Index from the Include Marker of Type scroll list to the Don't Include scroll list by clicking on the marker and then clicking on the right arrow button. When you are done, only the Index marker should be in the Include Marker scroll list.

Part
5

Advanced Features

8.　If you want hypertext links to be created from the index to the various source documents, click on Create Hypertext Links. If you're working on a single document, skip to step 10.

9.　Set the page and paragraph number properties—Page # in All Generated Files, Starting Page Side, Page Numbering, and Paragraph Numbering. For a full explanation of these settings, see "Changing and Updating the Format of Document Files" in Chapter 16.

10.　Click the Set button (for books) or the Generate button (for single documents).

If you're working on an index for a single file, a file based on the name of the source document—*filename*.IX (Windows) or *filename*IX (Mac and UNIX)—is generated and opened. That's all you need to do.

If you're working on an index for a book file, a file based on the name of the source book—*bookname*.IX (Windows) or *bookname*IX (Mac and UNIX)—will be added to the book file. The plus sign (+) behind the file name indicates that the file is a generated file. The Add File to Book dialog box will reappear.

If you're working on a book, complete these remaining steps:

11.　Click the Done button. The Add File to Book dialog box closes.

12.　Select the index in the book file by clicking on the file name ending with the *IX* suffix or extension.

13.　Select File ➤ Generate/Update. The Generate/Update Book dialog box shown in Figure 17.9 opens. The index file name appears in the Generate scroll list.

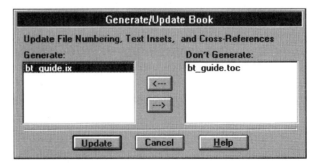

*Figure 17.9　**The Generate/Update Book dialog box, used to create generated files for books***

14. Click the Update button. The documents in the book will be opened and scanned for index markers. When the process is completed, the index document will open and become active.

15. Save the index document by selecting File ➤ Save.

Simple Formatting for Indexes from Single Documents

If you are creating an index from a single document without going though a book file, store all the formatting information, including the *IX* text flow, in the source document. Then generate the index.

The generated file will take all of its formatting from the source document, including the formatting of the *IX* flow on the reference page.

Regenerating an Index

When you make changes to a source document that affect the index, the index needs to be regenerated. To do this for a book file index:

1. Make the Book File window active and select File ➤ Generate/Update. The Generate/Update Book dialog box (see Figure 17.9) opens.

2. Move the file name of the index to the Generate scroll list.

3. Click the Generate button. If the index was closed, it will be updated but not opened. If the index was open, it will be updated in computer memory only and must be saved to disk.

To regenerate an index created from a single document, follow the procedure used to generate it originally:

1. Select File ➤ Generate/Book.

2. In the Generate/Book dialog box, make sure Standard Index is selected and click Generate.

3. In the Set Up Standard Index dialog box (see Figure 17.8), check the Include Marker Types list and click Generate again.

Formatting an Index

When you create an index, the page layout and formatting are taken either from the source document or a template (if you used one). If the formatting came from a source document, all entries have the same nondescript paragraph format. After you generate an index, however, you can change the page layout and other formats. Your changes will be retained when the index is regenerated.

Much of the index formatting and structure is determined by a special text flow on a reference page (often not the first reference page) of the index document. This text flow has the default tag *IX*, for "index." It might look like Figure 17.10. This example was taken from the second reference page of the Book Index template included with FrameMaker 5.

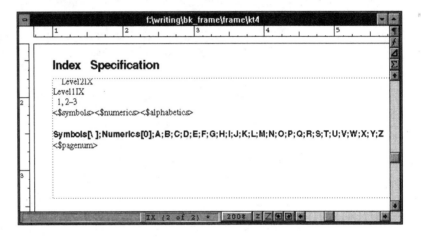

Figure 17.10 **Example Index flow on the IX reference page**

Each marker type in an index has a corresponding paragraph, tagged for that marker, on the reference page that adds and formats the page number. For a standard index, there is one marker (Index) and one paragraph on the reference page tagged *IndexIX*—it's the one with the *<$pagenum>* building block. If three different marker types were included in the index, there are three paragraphs on the reference page with *<$pagenum>* building blocks, each with its own paragraph tags ending in *IX*. As you can see from Figure 17.10, there are other paragraphs on the reference page as well. These will be discussed later in this section.

If the index is generated with hypertext links turned on, there is also a paragraph on the reference page that specifies the form of the hypertext commands. The paragraph will have a tag that starts with the word *Active*.

The rest of this section offers instructions for performing basic index formatting. Similar instructions apply to formatting other generated indexes.

Changing the Character Format of Index Entries

You can change the character format of any part of the text in an index entry. For example, you can italicize the word *See* in cross-references without changing the format of the rest of the entry. To do this:

1. Make the source document (the one with the markers) active and turn text symbols on.

2. Create a new character format with a descriptive tag and store it in the Character Catalog. (For information on creating character formats, see Chapter 9.) For example, you might create an italics character format named *ITALIC*.

3. Select an existing index marker in the source document by highlighting it.

4. Bring up the Marker window by selecting Special ➤ Marker. The text of the selected marker appears in the Marker Text area of the Marker window.

5. In the Marker Text area, type the name of the character format (enclosed between a left and right angle bracket, but with no $ sign) before the part of the marker you want changed. Then type **<Default Para Font>**. For example:

```
Sultan of Swat <ITALIC>See<Default Para Font> Ruth, George
Herman (Babe)
```

6. When you are finished, click the Edit Marker button.

7. Repeat these steps for each marker you want changed.

8. When you are finished, save the document and regenerate the index.

Changing the Character Format of Page Numbers

To change the page number character format of selected entries or all entries of a certain marker type in the generated index:

1. Make the source document (the one with the markers) active and turn text symbols on.

Part
5

Advanced Features

2. Create a new character format with a descriptive tag and store it in the Character Catalog. (For information on creating character formats, see Chapter 9.) Let's say you created a character format named *BOLD*.

3. Select an existing index marker in the source document by highlighting it.

4. Bring up the Marker window by selecting Special ➤ Marker. The text of the selected marker appears in the Market Text area of the Marker window.

5. In the Marker Text area, type the name of the character format (enclosed between a left and right angle bracket, but with no $ sign) at the end of the index entry. For example:

   ```
   Picard, Jean-Luc<BOLD>
   ```

6. When you are finished, click the Edit Marker button.

7. Repeat these steps for each marker you want changed.

8. When you are finished, save the document and regenerate the index.

   To change the page numbers character format of all entries of a certain marker type:

1. Make the index window active, create a new character format with a descriptive tag, and store it in the Character Catalog. For example, you might create a bold character format named *BOLD*.

2. Display reference pages by selecting View ➤ Reference Pages.

3. Move to the reference page that contains the *IX* text flow.

4. Find the paragraph tagged for the marker type whose page number you wish to reformat. (For standard index markers, look for the paragraph tagged *IndexIX*.) This paragraph probably contains the building block *<$pagenum>*.

5. Type the name of the character format (enclosed between a left and right angle bracket, but with no $ sign) before the building block. For example, apply the format BOLD to page numbers as follows:

   ```
   <BOLD><$pagenum>
   ```

   You can accomplish the same thing by selecting the entire IndexIX paragraph and applying the character format BOLD with the Character Catalog.

6. Display body pages by selecting View ➤ Body Pages.

7. Open the book file (or source document) for the index and regenerate it. The changes you made will appear in the appropriate entries.

8. Save changes to the index by selecting File ➤ Save.

Removing Page Numbers from an Index

You can use the procedure in the previous section to remove page numbers completely from index entries. Just substitute the *<$nopage>* building block for the *<$pagenum>* building block in the *IX* flow paragraph for that marker type (for example, in the *IndexIX* paragraph).

Unnumbered indexes can be useful if you just want to produce a sorted list. A list of 150 words, for example, can be sorted alphabetically in almost no time if each word is put in an index marker and then a numberless index is generated from those markers. Recall that empty index markers can be used at the start of a word to index that word. Adding empty index markers can be done very quickly.

Joining Consecutive Page Entries into a Page Range

You can automatically join entries that refer to consecutive pages and make the entry show a single page range instead. For example, the second "Enterprise" entry shown here is far superior to the first:

Enterprise, 6, 7, 8, 9, 10, 11

Enterprise, 6-11

You can compress entries for any given marker type by adding the building block *<$autorange>* to the beginning of the reference page paragraph named for that marker type—for example, to the beginning of the paragraph tagged *IndexIX*. The procedure is pretty simple:

1. Make the index active and display reference pages by selecting View ➤ Reference Pages.

2. Move to the reference page that contains the *IX* text flow.

3. Find the paragraph tagged for the marker type whose page number you wish to autorange. (For standard index markers, look for the paragraph

tagged *IndexIX*.) This paragraph probably contains the building block <*$pagenum*>.

4. Type the <*$autorange*> building block at the beginning of the paragraph:

   <$autorange><$pagenum>

5. Display body pages by selecting View ➤ Body Pages.

6. Open the book file (or source document) and regenerate the index. The index entry page numbers will be automatically compressed into a page range where applicable.

7. Save changes to the index by selecting File ➤ Save.

Changing Separator Characters in an Index

The text of a typical index entry usually contains the following separators: a space character (usually an em space or an en space) between the text of the entry and the page number list, a comma and a regular space between page numbers, an en dash between page numbers to show a page range, and nothing after the last number, like so:

Enterprise, 6, 12-23

You can change each of these separators by editing the Separator paragraph tagged *SeparatorsIX* in the *IX* text flow on one of the reference pages of the index. The separator paragraph is often at the top of the *IX* flow and must have the following form (note the space character before the number *1*):

   , 1, 2–3.

 NOTE While the separators (the initial space character, the comma+space, and the dash) can be changed to anything you like, the numbers *1*, *2*, and *3* are mandatory in this paragraph.

To change page number separators:

1. Make the index window active and display reference pages by selecting View ➤ Reference Pages.

2. Move to the reference page that contains the *IX* text flow.

3. Find the paragraph tagged *SeparatorsIX*. It should look like this:

   ```
   1, 2–3
   ```

4. Edit the separators in any way you want. (Just don't change the numbers themselves.)

   For example, to change the separator between the last word in the entry and the first page number from one space to four, make the paragraph look like this:

   ```
   1, 2–3.
   ```

   You can also change the en dash between page ranges to the word *to,* like this:

   ```
   1, 2 to 3
   ```

   And, of course, you could italicize the word *to* with the character tag *ITALIC* (if the tag exists in the Character Catalog of the index), as follows:

   ```
   1, 2 <ITALIC>to<Default Para Font> 3
   ```

5. When you are finished, display body pages by selecting View ➤ Body Pages.

6. Open the book file (or source document) and regenerate the index. The changes you made will appear in the index entries.

7. Save changes to the index by selecting File ➤ Save.

Aligning Page Numbers in an Index

The page numbers in an index entry are usually separated from the last part of the entry text by an en space (a space about as wide as the character *n* in the current font). These page numbers are not aligned with each other:

Picadilly (starship), 37
Picard, Jean Luc
   accomplishments, 5
   birth, 3

Aligned page numbers look something like this:

Picadilly (starship)..............37
Picard, Jean Luc
    accomplishments.............5
    birth................................3

To align the page numbers with each other, use a tab character (usually a right tab), with or without leader dots, instead of a space in the paragraph tagged *SeparatorIX* in the *IX* text flow:

1. Make the index window active and display reference pages by selecting View ➤ Reference Pages.

2. Move to the reference page that contains the *IX* text flow.

3. Find the paragraph tagged *SeparatorsIX*. It should look something like this:

   1, 2–3

4. Select the space before the number *1* in the Separators paragraph and insert a tab character by pressing the Tab key.

5. Use the Paragraph Designer to add a tab stop to the first paragraph tag you wish to modify. Place the tab where you want the numbers to appear. You can do this for index entries of any level, and you can choose any dot leader pattern you wish.

   For example, to right-align the page numbers of first-level index entries, add a right tab stop near the right margin of the paragraph tagged *Level1IX*.

6. After changing the tag for the paragraph, apply changes by clicking the Update All Formats Tagged button in the Paragraph Designer. This changes the paragraphs in the *IX* text flow, as well as the paragraph tags themselves stored in the Paragraph Catalog.

7. Repeat the last two steps for each paragraph tag you wish to modify.

8. Display body pages by selecting View ➤ Body Pages.

9. Open the book file (or source document) and regenerate the index. The changes you made will appear in all entries.

10. Save changes to the index by selecting File ➤ Save.

Changing Which Characters Are Ignored during Alphabetization

When index entries are sorted alphabetically, some characters that appear either between words or within words—hyphens, nonbreaking hyphens, en and em dashes—are ignored by default. These characters are specified in the *IgnoreChars* paragraph (the paragraph tagged *IgnoreCharsIX*) in the *IX* text flow on the reference pages of the index. You can modify this list by deleting or adding characters to the paragraph.

To change which characters are ignored when index entries are alphabetized:

1. Make the index window active and display reference pages by selecting View ➤ Reference Pages.

2. Move to the reference page that contains the *IX* text flow.

3. Find the paragraph tagged *IgnoreCharsIX*. It should look like this:

    ---—

    The default list includes a regular hyphen, a nonbreaking hyphen, an en dash, and an em dash. (If the paragraph does not exist, you can create it. If you do, be sure to create the *IgnoreCharsIX* tag also.)

4. Edit the paragraph by adding characters you want to be ignored or deleting the characters you want to be "unignored" (that is, considered during alphabetization). To cause spaces between words to be ignored when entries are alphabetized, place a space character *at the beginning* of the *IgnoreChars* paragraph.

5. Display body pages by selecting View ➤ Body Pages.

6. Open the book file (or source document) and regenerate the index. The changes you made will appear in all entries.

7. Save changes by selecting File ➤ Save.

Changing the Sort Order of an Index Entry

Index items are generally sorted alphabetically word by word, starting with the first word. For some entries, however, this produces unusual results. An entry for a year, say, *1995*, would normally appear with the other numbers in the index, but you might want it to appear under *N* (for nineteen ninety five). In the same way, you might want an entry for a book called *The Carnival Barker* to be alphabetized with the *C*s and not the *T*s.

You can specify what word will be used to sort an index entry, even if that word doesn't appear in the entry, by adding that word (or group of words) in square brackets ([ ]) at the end of the of the index entry text in the Marker window.

To change how an index entry is sorted:

1. Make the source document active and select the marker whose sort order you want to change.

2. Open the Marker window (see Figure 17.6) by selecting Special ➤ Marker. The text of the marker appears in the Marker Text text box.

3. At the end of the entry, type the word or phrase by which you want the entry sorted, enclosed in square brackets ([ ]).

For example, to sort an entry like *1995* under the letter *N* instead of with the rest of the numeric entries, like so:

neighbor, 32
1995, 80
numbering, 57

you would make the entry in the Marker Text area like this:

```
1995[nineteen ninety five]
```

To sort a subentry like "in movies" on the word *movies* instead of on the word *in*, like so:

animation
  kinescope, 6
  in movies, 24

you would make the entry in the Marker Text area look like this:

```
animation:in movies[animation:movies]
```

To make a cross-reference like "*See also* cartoons" the last subentry under a main entry, like so:

animation
    kinescope, 6
    in movies, 24
    See also **cartoons**

you would use *zzz* as the subentry sort word in square brackets, like this:

```
<$nopage>animation:See also cartoons[animation:zzz]
```

After you've decided how you want the entry sorted:

4. Press Edit Marker to insert the new marker into the document.

5. When you are finished editing markers, save changes to the document by selecting File ➤ Save.

6. Regenerate the index.

Changing the Sort Order of the Index

You can also change the sort order of the index itself. You can do this in two ways, by changing the order in which groups of entries appear (the group being entries starting with symbols like *$* and *&*, entries starting with numbers, and entries starting with alphabetic characters), or by changing the order of entries within any of those groups.

Changing the Order of Groups of Entries   Normally, indexes are sorted so that entries starting with symbol characters are followed by entries starting with numbers, which are followed by entries starting with alphabetic characters. But you can change the order in which any of these groups appear. For example, you may want entries that start with numbers to appear last, after entries that start with alphabetic characters. You can even change the sort order within the groups themselves.

The sort order is specified in the *SortOrder* paragraph (the paragraph tagged *SortOrderIX*) in the *IX* text flow on the reference pages of the index. The sort order is specified by these building blocks:

```
<$symbols><$numerics><$alphabetics>
```

First, let's change the sort order of the groups themselves by changing the order of the *SortOrder* building blocks. The procedure is pretty simple:

1. Make the index active and display reference pages by selecting View ➤ Reference Pages.

2. Move to the reference page that contains the *IX* text flow.

3. Edit the paragraph tagged *SortOrderIX* by rearranging the building blocks. Be sure to treat each building block (including the angle brackets) as a single unit. For example, to make entries beginning with numbers appear at the end of the index, arrange the building blocks like this:

   <$symbols><$alphabetics><$numerics>

4. Display body pages by selecting View ➤ Body Pages.

5. Open the book file (or source document) and regenerate the index. The changes you made will appear in all entries.

6. Save changes to the index by selecting File ➤ Save.

Changing the Order of Entries within Groups   You can also change the sort order within groups. You can specify your own sort order for symbols, numbers, or alphabetic characters by editing the *SortOrder* paragraph to replace the building block for that group with the corresponding characters in the order you want them arranged.

The procedure for editing the SortOrder paragraph is given above. Let's look at the three groups one at a time, first at numerics, then at alphabetics, and then at symbolics.

The numerics group comprises the group of entries that starts with numbers and is represented by the *<$numerics>* building block. Numbers have the following default sort order: 0 1 2 3 4 5 6 7 8 9. If you replace the *<$numerics>* building block with that list, the index sort order will not be changed. By replacing the *<$numerics>* building block with a variation of that list, you can change the sort order of entries within the numerics group.

For example, the following change to the SortOrder paragraph sorts entries starting with symbols in their default order, followed by entries starting with numbers in the order 8 5 4 9 1 7 6 3 2 0, followed by the alphabetic entries in their default order:

```
<$symbols>8 5 4 9 1 7 6 3 2 0<$alphabetics>
```

Sorting entries starting with numbers in this way wouldn't make sense, of course, but the example shows how to make these kinds of changes.

The alphabetics group comprises entries that start with letters of the alphabet, represented by the building block *<$alphabetics>*. By replacing the *<$alphabetics>* building block with a list of your own, you can change the sort order of entries that start with letters.

The symbolics group comprises entries that start with symbol characters and is represented by the building block *<$symbolics>*. It contains all of the nonalphabetic and non-numeric symbols (such as / and $) and is sorted by default in ASCII order. You can sort the characters in another way by replacing the *<$symbolics>* building block with a space-separated list of your own choosing.

NOTE Because angle braces indicate the start and end of a building block, you must use a backslash before angle braces in the symbolics list (i.e., \< and \>).

Modifying Index Group Titles

In the index itself, entries are grouped by default one letter at a time, with each group separated by spaces from under the title of that group. All the entries beginning with *A* are grouped first under the title A, then all the entries beginning with *B* are grouped, and so forth. Entries starting with symbols are grouped under the title Symbols, and entries starting with numbers are grouped under the title Numerics.

If you have a small index, however, or if there are consecutive groups with few entries, you may want to combine the groups and group titles. For example, if only a couple of entries are under *X*, *Y*, and *Z*, you may want to have only one group, *X–Z*. Or you might want to eliminate some titles (Symbols, for example) or eliminate all titles altogether. It's even possible to change the default font and spacing of all group titles.

Groupings and group titles are controlled by the paragraph tagged *GroupTitlesIX* in the *IX* flow of the index reference pages. The default GroupTitles paragraph looks like this:

```
Symbols[\ ];Numerics[0]
;A;B;C;D;E;F;G;H;I;J;K;L;M;N;O;P;Q;R;S;T;U;V;W;X;Y;Z
```

The words and letters outside the square brackets are the titles themselves, separated by semicolons. The square brackets provide sort information for the title—they tell where in the index list the titles are to be inserted.

In this section you'll see how to change the groupings and the titles themselves, and how to modify the paragraph format of all group titles in the index.

A Word about Sort Information

As you know, the *SortOrder* paragraph specifies the sort order of entries in the index. By default, FrameMaker inserts group titles exactly where they would go if they were index entries (in case of a tie, the title comes first). Thus, the title "A" is automatically inserted before the first entry starting with *A*. And that's why the "Symbols" and "Numerics" titles need sort information—to keep them from being inserted among the *S* and *N* entries, respectively.

The sort information in square brackets acts exactly like sort information does in an index entry: It "re-alphabetizes" the entry (in this case, the title) according to the word in the brackets.

In this case, sort information is used to place the title "Symbols" ahead of the entries beginning with symbols, and the title "Numerics" at the start of the entries beginning with numbers. The *[\ ]* (backslash-space) after the title "Symbols" says, "Place this title before the first entry that starts with a space character," and that entry happens to be the first symbol in the default *<$symbolics> SortOrder* list. The *[0]* after the title "Numerics" says, "Place this title before the first entry starting with a *0*," which, logically enough, is the first number in the default *<$numerics> SortOrder* list. (Recall that in case a title and an entry contain identical text, the title comes first.)

Changing Groupings and Title Listings   To change the groupings and title listings of index entries:

1.   Make the index active and display reference pages by selecting View ➤ Reference Pages.

2. Move to the reference page that contains the *IX* text flow.

3. Edit the paragraph tagged *GroupTitlesIX*. Replace group titles (the characters between the semicolons) with new group titles, or delete the titles you don't want. To specify where group titles should appear in the index, enclose sort information between square brackets.

Following are some examples.

To group the X, Y, and Z entries under one title, change the *GroupTitles* paragraph to look like the following. Note that in the title *X–Z[X]*, the sort information *[X]-* places the title ahead of every entry starting with *X*:

```
Symbols[\ ];Numerics[0]
;A;B;C;D;E;F;G;H;I;J;K;L;M;N;O;P;Q;R;S;T;U;V;W;X–Z[X]
```

To change the title "Numerics" to "Numbers," make the GroupTitles paragraph look like this:

```
Symbols[\ ];Numbers[0]
;A;B;C;D;E;F;G;H;I;J;K;L;M;N;O;P;Q;R;S;T;U;V;W;X;Y;Z
```

To eliminate the titles "Symbols" and "Numerics" but keep the spacing by placing empty paragraphs above these two groups, make the Group-Titles paragraph look like this:

```
[\ ];[0]
;A;B;C;D;E;F;G;H;I;J;K;L;M;N;O;P;Q;R;S;T;U;V;W;X;Y;Z
```

To use empty paragraphs as separators above all groups, make the *GroupTitles* paragraph look like this:

```
[\ ];[0];[A];[B];[C];[D];[E];[F];[G];[H];[I];[J];[K];[L];
[M];[N];[O];[P];[Q];[R];[S];[T];[U];[V];[W];[X];[Y];[Z]
```

Finally, to create an index with no titles or space separation at all between groups of entries, delete everything in the GroupTitles paragraph, but keep the paragraph symbol.

Once you've edited the paragraph tagged *GroupTitlesIX:*

4. Display the body page by selecting View ➤ Body Pages.

5. Open the book file (or source document) and regenerate the index. The change you made will appear in all entries.

6. Save changes to the index by selecting File ➤ Save.

Part 5

Advanced Features

Changing the Paragraph Format of Group Titles You can use the Paragraph Designer to change the paragraph format of the *GroupTitles* paragraphs and the *GroupTitlesIX* tag in order to change the way group titles appear in the generated index. In this way, you can alter the font of the titles, increase space above and below, and make any other changes the Paragraph Designer allows. To do this:

1. Make the index active and display reference pages by selecting View ▶ Reference Pages.

2. Move to the reference page that contains the *IX* text flow.

3. Bring up the Paragraph Designer by entering Format ▶ Paragraph ▶ Designer or by using one of the keyboard shortcuts.

4. Modify any aspect of the paragraph you wish. Likely candidates are the space above and below the paragraph (on the Basic properties page) and the look of the font (on the Default Font properties page).

5. When you are done, click Update All to change both the *GroupTitles* paragraph and the *GroupTitlesIX* tag.

6. Display the body page by selecting View ▶ Body Pages.

7. Open the book file (or source document) and regenerate the index. The change you made will appear in all entries.

8. Save changes to the index by selecting File ▶ Save.

Adding a Title to an Index

You can also add a title to the body page that starts an index:

1. After you have generated the index for the first time, create a new paragraph *before* the first entry on the first body page.

2. Place the insertion point in the new paragraph and type the title.

3. Bring up the Paragraph Designer with the Format ▶ Paragraph ▶ Designer command.

4. Create a new paragraph tag for the title paragraph that does *not* end in the *IX* suffix by typing the name in the Paragraph Tag text box of the Paragraph Designer. This step is important. Paragraphs with the *IX* suffix get updated when the index is regenerated, and you want your title to go untouched during updates.

5. Select New Format from the Commands pull-down menu in the Paragraph Designer and check both Store in Catalog and Apply to Selection in the New Format dialog box.

6. Press Create to create the new format.

7. Using the Paragraph Designer, modify the paragraph to look the way you want it and click Update All after each group of changes. You want to modify both the paragraph itself and the format definition stored in the catalog.

8. When you are done creating and modifying the paragraph and its tag, save changes to the index by selecting File ➤ Save.

If Index Formatting Is not Retained after an Update...

Formatting changes made to an index should be retained when the index is regenerated. If some or all of them are not retained, check to make sure that:

▶ The index file name and location haven't changed. The index must be in the same directory as the source book file (or document) and must use the file name FrameMaker assigns it.

▶ The title added to the first page does not have a paragraph tag that ends in the suffix *IX*.

▶ All paragraph format changes were stored in the Paragraph Catalog *and* applied to paragraphs in the document.

▶ You stored any new character formats in the Character Catalog.

▶ All format changes that affect the *IX* text flow were made in that flow and not somewhere else. Also make sure that these changes made it to the Paragraph Catalog.

Using a Template to Format an Index

If you don't want to spend time formatting your index, you can use either an existing index or a template index to do the formatting for you. (The existing index or the template should have the formatting you want, or one close to it.) You can use a template in either of two ways, by using the formatted index directly as though it were your own, or by importing formats from the formatted document into your document.

Part
5

Advanced Features

Using a Copy of a Template to Format Your Index   If you place a properly named template index that already contains the formatting you want into the directory where FrameMaker expects to find your own index, then simply generate or regenerate your own index, the formatted template will be updated with the new index information.

Here's the process step by step:

1. Perform steps 1 through 10 under "Generating and Regenerating an Index" earlier in this chapter. That will take you to the Add File to Book dialog box.

2. Copy the template document into the directory or folder that contains the book file or source document. The template document can be an existing index from another book, a template from FrameMaker's templates directory, or a template you or someone else has created.

3. Give the template the name that FrameMaker has assigned to your index. For example, if you are using a book file named MYBOOK.BK (Windows-style), the generated index will be named MYBOOK.IX (without the plus sign that appears in the book file list), and your template should also be named MYBOOK.IX.

4. Finish the procedure by following the instructions for creating an index given earlier in this chapter.

When you generate or regenerate the index, FrameMaker will update the template with the new index entries, just as though it were your own. The new index will have both correct index information and the template's formatting.

Importing Formats from a Template Index   You can also change the formats of your own index by importing formats from either another index or from a template index:

1. Open both your own index and the template index.

2. Make your own index active and select File ➤ Import ➤ Formats.

3. In the Import Format dialog box, select the name of the open template index from the Import from Document pull-down list.

4. Select all check boxes in the Import and Update section.

5. Click the Import button.

6. Save the changes to your modified index by selecting File ➤ Save.

Troubleshooting an Index

Problems in source documents cause problems in indexes. For example, a marker with incorrect text is not sorted correctly in an index. Entries that belong together may be separate entries. These problems must be fixed in the source document. If they are fixed in the index, the fixes will disappear when you regenerate the index.

Using Hypertext Links during Debugging

To trace an index entry back to its source easily, select Create Hypertext Links in the Set Up dialog box when you generate the index.

You can now use hypertext links to move from the index to the source documents, even when the source documents are not in view-only mode. To move from a hypertext link in the index to its source heading in an editable (non-view-only) document, use one of the following mouse/keyboard shortcuts:

▶ In Windows, Alt+Ctrl+click on the index entry

▶ On the Macintosh, use 2 +Option click

▶ In UNIX, Ctrl+click on the index entry

When a hypertext link is selected in this way, the source document opens to the page that contains the index marker and the marker is selected.

The basic procedure for changing an index entry is to:

1. Select the marker in the source document.

2. Change the text in the Marker window.

3. Click the Edit Marker button.

4. Save the source document.

5. Regenerate the index.

Some index markers may have to be deleted. To delete an index marker, go to the source document and select *only* the index marker you want to delete. Do this with the Find/Change window:

1. In the source document, place the character cursor ahead of the marker to be deleted.

2. Open the Find/Change window (with Edit ➤ Find/Change).

3. Select Marker of Type in the Find pull-down list.

4. Type Index in the Find text box.

5. Click the Find button. FrameMaker will locate the next marker of type Index.

6. Make sure the marker you want deleted is selected by looking in the Marker window. If the marker is selected, you will see the text of the index entry, and the button will change from New Marker to Edit Marker.

   Once you've selected the index marker:

7. Press the Del key to delete it. The Marker window will show no marker text, and the button will change to New Marker.

8. Repeat the above steps for as many markers as you want to delete.

9. Save the source document by selecting File ➤ Save.

10. Regenerate the index.

   Following are some hints for fixing common index problems.

   Entry Missing   If an entry is missing from an index, the reason could be one of several:

   ▶ The marker may be of an incorrect marker type (for example, *Header/Footer* instead of *Index*). Check this by selecting the marker and looking at its type in the Marker window. To correct this problem, change the marker type to *Index*.

   ▶ The marker could be sitting in hidden conditional text. Fix this by using the command Special ➤ Conditional Text to show all conditional text.

   ▶ The marker may have been deleted inadvertently during text editing. Fix this by adding a new marker for the entry.

   Double Question Marks in the Index   If an index entry contains double question marks (??), it means that one of the page range markers is missing, or that the text of the *<startrange>* marker is different from the text of the *<endrange>* marker. When you have corrected the problem, regenerate the index.

Entry Incorrectly Sorted or Grouped If an entry is incorrectly sorted or grouped, check that the sorting information in the *IX* text flow on the reference page is correct. Also check that the text in the marker itself does not contain extra spaces, that all punctuation is correct, that any sorting information between square brackets ([ ]) appears at the end of the entry, and that the sorting information is correct.

Cross-Reference with Page Number If a cross-reference has a page number, check that the cross-reference marker text contains the *<$nopage>* building block at the beginning of the entry.

Line Breaks in Wrong Place If line breaks appear in the wrong place in a generated index (for example, if they appear between the numbers in a page range or between the end of the entry and the page number), there are several things you can do:

▶ Change the Allow Line Breaks After list for the index document. With the index active, select Format ➤ Document ➤ Text Options and change the list of Allow Line Breaks After characters. For example, remove the en dash from the list.

▶ Put nonbreaking spaces between the entry and the page number. Do this by changing the first space character in the Separators paragraph in the *IX* text flow into a nonbreaking space.

▶ Use a nonbreaking hyphen in the Page # in Generated Files specification of each source document file. For each source document file, click on the document file name in the book file list, select File ➤ Set Up File, and insert a nonbreaking hyphen in the Prefix and Suffix text boxes in place of regular hyphens.

Creating Master Indexes and TOC That Cover Several Books

If you are writing a series of related books, you may want to create an index or table of contents that covers all of them. To create a master index or table of contents:

1. Create a new book file that contains all the files from all the other books.

Follow the procedure for creating a book given in Chapter 16. If you add generated files from the original books to the new book, add them like regular document files. Do *not* add them as generated files.

2.   Create a generated index or table of contents for the new book file.

3.   Make the Book File window active and set up page and paragraph numbering for each file in the book by selecting File ➤ Set Up File for each one. Follow the procedure for setting up files. It can be useful to use the prefix or suffix specification to identify the source book from which the document came.

4.   Generate the index or table of contents by selecting File ➤ Generate/Update.

Table, Figure, Paragraph, and Other Generated Lists

The two types of files that can be generated from a book or single document are lists of paragraph tags (such as a table of contents) and lists of markers (such as a standard index).

Besides a table of contents, you can generate other lists of paragraph tags, including:

▶   A list of tables (using table title paragraphs)

▶   A list of figures (using figure caption paragraphs)

▶   A list of paragraphs

▶   A list of markers (you can specify which marker types are included)

▶   An alphabetical list of markers

▶   An alphabetical list of paragraphs

▶   A list of references (fonts, resolved or unresolved cross-references, imported graphics, resolved or unresolved text insets, and/or conditional text tags)

In all but the alphabetical lists, items are listed with page numbers by their appearance in the source documents.

To add, create, or generate a list of paragraph tags, follow the procedures given above under "Creating a Table of Contents," but substitute the paragraph tags you want to generate for the paragraph tags used to create a table of contents.

Besides an index, you can generate other lists of markers, including:

▶ An author index (using the Author marker type)

▶ A subject index (using the Subject marker type)

▶ An index of markers (you can specify which marker types are included)

▶ An index of references (fonts, resolved or unresolved cross-references, imported graphics, resolved or unresolved text insets, and/or conditional text tags)

Items in indexes are sorted alphabetically.

To add, create, and generate any list of markers, follow the procedures under "Creating an Index" and substitute the appropriate marker type for the index marker.

Using Hypertext in Generated Files

When you generate a file (like an index or table of contents), you can specify that hypertext links to the source document be inserted. Then, when you click on a generated item in the file (like an index entry or a heading listed in the TOC), the referenced document will be displayed and the corresponding marker (for indexes) or paragraph (for lists of paragraphs) will be selected.

Hypertext can be used with both editable and view-only documents.

Hypertext in Editable Documents

In editable documents, as you have already seen, hypertext can be used to move quickly from a generated item that contains an error (such as a bad line break in a TOC or a misspelled index item) to the source of that item. In addition, some generated lists and indexes, like the list of unresolved cross-references, are designed to help correct errors in documents.

You can also "hypertext-click" on cross-references in editable documents, or on any hypertext buttons or menus built into the files.

In an editable document, simply clicking on the hypertext area is not enough. To use a hypertext link in an editable document, select the item as follows:

▸ In Windows, Alt+Ctrl+click on the active item

▸ On the Macintosh, ⌘+Option-click on the active item

▸ In UNIX, Ctrl+click on the active item

Hypertext in View-Only Documents

When files, especially books, are saved as view-only documents, all hypertext links become active and can be selected just by clicking on them.

With no further work on your part, view-only book files already have hypertext links between all generated lists and the source documents, and from all cross-references to the paragraphs referenced. In addition, using the broad range of hypertext capabilities FrameMaker provides, sophisticated hypertext buttons and menus can be built into any document.

Chapter 18

Using Hypertext in View-Only Files

Most documents created using FrameMaker are printed. But FrameMaker can also be used to make view-only hypertext documents for use on a computer monitor. View-only documents are an excellent way to disseminate (i.e., publish) information—everything from online documentation of computer programs and hardware, to professional training manuals and business presentations, to stories, letters, essays, and poetry.

In a hypertext document, certain areas are *active*—when they are clicked with the mouse, they take you to other places in the document, bring up a menu, or execute commands. An active area is an area of text or graphics that contains an embedded hypertext command that performs particular functions when clicked. These active areas can link to next or previous pages, jump to references in the same or different documents, display pull-down menus that can have submenus, display alert messages, close documents, and exit FrameMaker.

FrameMaker has two ways of inserting hypertext links and commands into documents—automatically and manually. Hypertext links can be inserted by FrameMaker automatically into generated files, like tables of contents and indexes, so that users can click on the entries in these files and jump to the paragraphs or words they refer to. Hypertext links can also be created automatically from cross-references such as "See page 12 for more information" that FrameMaker can create and manage for you. (Chapter 17 offers information about using hypertext in generated files. See the next chapter for coverage of the cross-references feature.)

A number of hypertext commands, however, must be inserted manually into documents. This chapter covers these commands and the techniques for using them.

View-Only Documents

A *view-only document* is a FrameMaker document that can be viewed and printed, but not edited and saved. You create view-only documents from editable documents when you save the editable document in view-only format. (See Chapter 6 for more on how to save documents in different formats.) View-only documents are useful because they allow you to distribute and update files and information without allowing anyone else to tamper with them.

You can also change a document from editable to view-only and back again while you are working on it by pressing *Esc F l k*. This combination works like a toggle—it both "locks" (i.e., changes to view-only) and unlocks a document.

Though hypertext commands can be executed from within editable documents by using special mouse-keyboard combinations, their greatest usefulness is in noneditable, view-only documents. When a Frame-Maker document is converted to view-only format (by saving it as view-only or by locking it with *Esc F l k*), all hypertext commands in active areas (whether they were automatically created by FrameMaker or manually inserted by you, the user) can be executed simply by clicking on them.

View-Only Documents vs. Editable Documents

A view-only document has fewer menu items than an editable one. Its primary menu items are File, Edit, and Navigation. (Of course, depending on the FrameMaker version you are using, there may be other menu items as well, such as the Window item for the Windows version.)

All versions of the File menu contain at least these items: New, Open, Close, Print, and Preferences. The Edit menu contains the following: Copy, Copy Special, Select All on Page, Find, and Find Next. The Navigation menu contains the commands Go To Page, Next Page, Previous Page, First Page, Last Page, Go Back. (The Mac Navigation menu also allows you to click on a list of the currently open document windows.)

Setting Up Hypertext Areas

A reader navigates through hypertext links and commands by clicking on active areas and executing commands contained in hypertext markers—markers of type "Hypertext"—found within those areas. You've already seen several other kinds of markers in previous chapters. For a hypertext marker, the text of the marker is the hypertext command itself. (Hypertext commands will be covered later in this chapter.)

As noted before, active areas can be words or groups of words in the text, or areas of the page that contain artwork, drawings of buttons, or other visual indicators that can be clicked to perform some function. You can set up active hypertext areas on a body page, or you can place them as background elements on master pages so they appear on all body pages that use that master page.

Making Text Active

You can make any text active—from a single character to a word, phrase, or entire paragraph. To do this, just insert a hypertext marker containing a hypertext command in the text itself, and you're done. The text is active as soon as the marker is inserted. (Inserting, deleting, and editing hypertext markers is discussed later in this chapter, and hypertext commands themselves are covered in the section following that.)

Boundaries of a Hypertext Text Area

Before you start setting up your own markers, you need background on how they work. When you place a hypertext marker in a paragraph of text, an area surrounding the marker becomes active. That active area has the following boundaries:

▶ If the paragraph contains character format changes, the area surrounding the marker *and bounded by the previous and/or next format change* is active. (In other words, if you place a marker in the middle of bold text, the bold text is active.)

▶ If the paragraph contains hypertext markers and no character format changes, the area surrounding the marker and *bounded by the previous and/or next hypertext marker* is active. (In other words, if you place a marker in plain text surrounded by hypertext markers, the text between the previous and following hypertext markers is active for the marker you just inserted.)

▶ If the paragraph contains no character format changes and no hypertext markers, *the entire paragraph is active*, no matter where in the paragraph the marker is placed.

You can use any of these methods to delineate active text areas, though the first method—using character format changes—is the easiest for users to deal with.

Part
5

Advanced Features

Using Format Changes to Mark Hypertext Text

Most of the time, hypertext markers in text are associated with words or phrases that have a character format change—either they are displayed in a different color, or they are boldfaced, underlined, italicized, or the like. Otherwise, users will not know which areas of a page are active and which are not.

You can apply this format change directly to the text—by using the Character Designer, for example, or one of the QuickAccess Bar buttons—or you can apply it using a character tag created for marking hypertext phrases.

You will probably find the character tag method to be the most useful. It allows you to define the look of all hypertext areas at one time and to change that look if you want to, simply by redefining the tag. For example, if you decide you want your hypertext areas to be blue and not green, editing a tag called *HT Links* can make that change for all active text areas at once. Chapter 9 has lots of information on how to create and apply character tags.

> **NOTE** If a hypertext marker itself contains no text, clicking on an active area will produce no result, even if all the other rules are followed. To correct this problem, make sure there is text in the marker. (See below for information on how to edit hypertext markers.)

Making Graphics Active

Any rectangular area of the document, typically an area containing a graphic or part of a graphic, can be made active by placing an invisible text frame on the page (on *top* of the graphic, not under it) and then inserting a single hypertext marker—and nothing else—into the text frame. We'll cover this in detail below. Note that it's not the graphic that becomes active, but the invisible text frame. The graphic only *appears* to be active to the user.

The graphic under the text frame can be any picture—a drawing of a button with a label or icon, an imported piece of art, a drawing of a bookshelf with book spines and titles, or any other visual element. The active area (that area covered by the invisible text frame containing the marker) can overlay the entire drawing or any part of it.

NOTE If the text frame contains only the marker and the end-of-flow symbol (§), the entire frame is active, and you can click anywhere in its boundaries to execute the hypertext command. If the text frame contains a paragraph symbol (¶), only the paragraph is active, and you have to click on the paragraph symbol itself to execute the command. This is why the text frame must be completely empty to be used in this way. If there's even so much as an empty paragraph symbol, the clickable area is greatly reduced.

When an entire text frame is active, any part of the text frame can be selected to activate the hypertext command in the marker. The user, of course, thinks the graphic is being selected, since the text frame on top of the graphic is invisible, but in fact the text frame with the hypertext marker is being selected, and not the graphic. (Of course, you could also set up a hypertext area in a part of a page that has no graphic under it, but the user would not then know what to do with it, or even know it's there!)

Setting Up Active Areas on Body Pages

This section contains procedures for making areas containing graphics active. As you saw in previous chapters, graphic images can be placed in FrameMaker documents in either of two ways—they can be pasted directly to pages (with or without a graphic frame around them), or they can be imported into anchored frames that move when the text in the flow is edited.

▶ If your graphic is pasted to the page, the text frame that will be made active must also be pasted to the page—right over the graphic.

▶ If the graphic is in a frame that is pasted to the page, the text frame should be placed within the graphic frame with the graphic.

▶ If the graphic is in an anchored frame, the text frame must also be placed within the anchored frame. Otherwise, the anchored frame will move when the text moves, but the active text frame will not.

Creating Active Body Page Areas To set up an active area over all or part of a graphic image:

1. If the graphic is in a frame, either an anchored frame or a frame pasted to the page, select the frame.

2. Open the Tools window by selecting Graphics ▶ Tools.

Part 5

Advanced Features

3. Draw a text frame around either the entire graphic or the part of the graphic you wish to make "clickable." To do that:

    - Click on the Text Frame tool.

    - Click and hold on the upper-left corner of the graphic or the area of the graphic to be made active.

    - Drag to the lower-right corner of the graphic or the area of the graphic to be made active.

    - Release the mouse button.

    - When the Create New Text Frame dialog box appears, click on the Set button.

    A text frame will appear *over* the graphic (it's important that the text frame be on top of the graphic, not underneath it), and the text frame will be selected.

4. Use the Tools palette to set the text frame Fill to *None* and Pen to *None*. This makes the text frame both transparent and invisible, so that only the graphic will appear on the body page.

5. Insert a marker of type Hypertext into the text frame, and place a hypertext command in the marker. (Inserting, deleting, and editing hypertext markers is discussed later in this chapter; hypertext commands themselves are covered in the section following that.)

6. Repeat the above steps for each area of the picture or drawing to be made active.

Setting Up Active Areas on Master Pages

It is easy to activate the same area on several pages. For example, a Next Page and a Previous Page button can appear on every body page in the document. You can do this by setting up active areas on one or more master pages, and then using those master pages as background for one or more body pages.

To create an active area on a master page, open or create a master page, and then follow the procedure given above for creating an active area on a body page.

Overriding Active Master Page Areas A master page active area can be overridden on a body page by laying something over it. For example, on the last body page of a document, you might want the Next Page button to disappear. You could do this by pasting a white rectangle over it, so that the user no longer sees the button and its hypertext link does not work.

But perhaps instead of hiding the Next Page button on the last page of the document, you'd like to make it jump to the first page of another document. For any individual body page, you can change the action performed by a master page hypertext area by pasting a new hypertext area (and even a new graphic) in the same location on the body page. If the body page hypertext area covers the master page hypertext area, the body page command will be executed when the area is clicked. In this way, the Next Page button on the last page of a document could be made to execute a different command than the Next Page buttons on the other pages.

If the "Active" Area Isn't Active

If you click on an active area and nothing happens, there are a few things you should check. If for some reason the text frame containing the hypertext marker gets placed behind (underneath) the graphic, clicking on the graphic will not activate the hypertext command. To correct this problem, use the Graphics ➤ Bring To Front command to place the text frame in front of (on top of) the graphic.

If the hypertext marker contains no text, clicking on the active area will produce no result. To correct this problem, make sure there is text in the marker. (See below for information on how to edit hypertext markers.)

Preventing Hypertext Graphics from Being Printed

You may want the graphics associated with hypertext areas to appear when the document is viewed, but not when the document is printed. To do this:

1. Create a new, uniquely named color for hypertext graphics by selecting View ➤ Color ➤ Definitions and using the Color Definitions dialog box.

2. Assign that color to all hypertext graphics and text areas using the Tools window.

3. Select File ➤ Print, open the Set Print Separations dialog box, and set up print separations so that the hypertext color you've created appears in the Don't Print scroll list.

4. Make sure that Print Separations is selected, and save the document.

   When the document is converted to view-only and distributed, selecting File ➤ Print will bring up your preset Print Document dialog box, and unless the user overrides your settings, the hypertext color will not be printed.

> **NOTE**   This will work only if one other color (presumably black) is used in the document. Otherwise, the Print Separations setting will cause one set of pages to be printed for each additional color in the document.

For more information on defining and using colors and on the Set Print Separations dialog box, see Chapter 15.

Working with Hypertext Markers

Hypertext areas are active because they contain markers of type Hypertext with valid hypertext commands in them. After the hypertext commands are inserted, you can edit or delete them.

This section contains instructions for inserting, editing, and deleting hypertext markers. For a list of hypertext commands and what they are used for, see "Hypertext Commands: A Quick Reference" later in this chapter.

Inserting Hypertext Markers and Commands

To insert a hypertext marker and command in either text or a text frame you wish to make active:

1. Make sure the document is editable (not in locked, view-only mode).

2. Turn on text symbols, if necessary, by selecting View ➤ Text Symbols.

3. Click to place the insertion point in the text flow or in the empty text frame.

4. Open the Marker window shown in Figure 18.1 by selecting Special ➤ Marker.

5. From the Marker Type pull-down list, select Hypertext.

6. Type the hypertext command in the Marker Text area. For more information on hypertext commands, see the next section.

Figure 18.1   **The Marker window**

7. Click the New Marker button. A hypertext marker is inserted into the active area at the insertion point.

8. When you are done, save changes to the document by selecting File ➤ Save.

Editing Hypertext Commands

Once a hypertext command has been inserted into a marker, you may need to edit it. For example, you may have mistyped the name of a link, or executing a command may not have had the effect you wished.

To edit a hypertext marker and command:

1. Make sure the document is editable (not in locked, view-only mode).

2. Turn on text symbols if necessary by selecting View ➤ Text Symbols.

3. Select Special ➤ Marker to open the Marker window (see Figure 18.1).

4. Select the hypertext marker you want to edit by selecting the area of text containing that marker.

NOTE   An alternate way to select a hypertext marker is to place the character cursor somewhere ahead of the marker you wish to edit, bring up the Find/Change window using Edit ➤ Find/Change, select Marker of Type from the Find pull-down list. Type Hypertext into the Find text box, and click on the Find button.

Part
5

Advanced Features

5. Edit the hypertext command in the Marker Text text box of the Marker window. For more information on hypertext commands, see the next section.

6. Click the Edit Marker button to change the marker in the document.

7. When you are done, save changes to the document by selecting File ➤ Save.

Deleting Hypertext Markers

Once a hypertext marker has been inserted, you may need to delete it—for example, because the part of the document used in a link might no longer exist. To delete a hypertext command:

1. Make sure the document is editable (not in locked, view-only mode).

2. Turn on text symbols if necessary by selecting View ➤ Text Symbols.

3. Select Special ➤ Marker to open the Marker window (see Figure 18.1).

4. Select only the hypertext marker you want to delete, not the text surrounding it. Do this with the Find/Change window:

   - Place the character cursor somewhere in front of the hypertext marker you wish to delete.

   - Select Edit ➤ Find/Change.

   - Select Marker of Type from the Find pull-down list.

   - Type Hypertext into the Find text box.

   - Click on Find.

   When the hypertext marker has been found, you will see its contents in the Marker window.

5. Press the Delete or Backspace key to delete the marker.

6. If the hypertext command was in a text frame over a graphic, delete the marker by deleting the text frame (and the graphic behind it!) by selecting them and pressing the Delete or Backspace key.

7. When you are done, save changes to the document by selecting File ➤ Save.

Hypertext Commands: A Quick Reference

This section contains reference information for the hypertext commands available with FrameMaker. But first, a few notes about these commands:

▶ A full hypertext command can contain up to 255 characters.

▶ Hypertext commands are case-sensitive. The command names themselves must be entered as lowercase. Optional parameters, such as file names or link names, can be entered as either upper- or lowercase, as long as file names are typed as they appear to the appropriate operating system (DOS, Mac, or UNIX) and link names are identical everywhere they appear.

▶ A file name can include a path name.

▶ In path names, directories or folders are separated by a slash (/) character, regardless of platform. (Windows-users take note!) Do not use DOS-style path names which use a backslash (\). They will not be recognized when the hypertext command is interpreted.

▶ Absolute path names begin at the top of the system. In Windows, an absolute path name begins with a drive specifier (entered as *c:/*, for example) and continues with the directory structure. An absolute path name in Windows cannot be used on other platforms. On the Mac, the absolute path name begins with a slash (/) and includes the drive name (for example, */MacHD*). On a UNIX system, the absolute path name begins with a slash (/).

▶ You can use relative path names beginning in the current directory or folder. A double period (..) indicates the directory or folder above the current directory or folder. A file in a directory or folder at the same level as the current directory or folder can be referred to as *../newdir/filename*. A file, directory, or folder in the current directory or folder can be referred to as *newdir/filename*.

▶ Hypertext jumps are stored using *stacks*, places to store a user's hypertext jumps as they are executed. There is one stack for each open document window, each having the user's most recently executed jump on top. The program uses these stacks to allow the user to retrace his or her hops through a document. Each stack can store up to 69 jumps. Some hypertext commands affect the current stack, and some do not. Commands that affect the stack are noted below.

alert The *alert* command displays an alert box with a message. *alert* does not affect the stack.

The syntax is:

```
alert MESSAGE
```

where *MESSAGE* is the text you want displayed in the alert box. The message can be up to 249 characters long.

alerttitle The *alerttitle* command displays an alert box with a message and a title other than "FrameMaker—Alert". (On the Mac, alert boxes do not have titles, and the *alerttitle* command works like the *alert* command. *alerttitle* does not affect the stack.

The syntax is:

```
alerttitle TITLE:MESSAGE
```

where *TITLE* is the alert box title, and *MESSAGE* is the text in the alert box. The message and title combined can be up to 243 characters long.

exit The *exit* command exits FrameMaker. It works the same as the File ➤ Exit command in Windows, the File ➤ Quit command on Macintosh, and the Exit command on the Main command window on UNIX.

The syntax is:

```
exit
```

gotolink The *gotolink* command jumps to a page containing a *newlink* marker with an identically spelled link name as the current marker. The *newlink* marker may be in the current document or a different document.

When *gotolink* is executed, the page with the *newlink* marker is displayed in the same document window. (Compare *openlink*, which displays the new page in a new document window.)

gotolink stores the current location on the stack for the current window.

The syntax is:

```
gotolink FILENAME:LINKNAME
```

where *FILENAME* is the file name of the document and *LINKNAME* is the name of the link in the corresponding *newlink* command. If

FILENAME is absent, the current file is assumed. *FILENAME* may include an absolute or relative path name.

gotolinkfitwin The *gotolinkfitwin* jumps to a page containing a *newlink* marker with an identically spelled link name as the current marker. The *newlink* marker may be in the current document or a different document.

When *gotolinkfitwin* is executed, the page with the *newlink* marker is displayed in the same document window, and the window is resized as necessary—from portrait to landscape, for example. (Compare *openlinkfitwin*, which displays the new page in a new document window.)

gotolinkfitwin stores the current location on the stack for the current window.

The syntax is:

```
gotolinkfitwin FILENAME:LINKNAME
```

where *FILENAME* is the file name of the document and *LINKNAME* is the name of the link in the corresponding *newlink* command. If *FILENAME* is absent, the current file is assumed. *FILENAME* may include an absolute or relative path name.

gotopage The *gotopage* command jumps to a specified page in the same or a different document.

When *gotopage* is executed, the new page is displayed in the same document window. (Compare *openpage*, which displays the new page in a new document window.)

gotopage stores the current location on the stack for the current window.

The syntax is:

```
gotopage FILENAME:PAGENUMBER
gotopage FILENAME:firstpage
gotopage FILENAME:lastpage
```

where *FILENAME* is the file name of the document and *PAGENUMBER* is the number of the page to which to jump. If *FILENAME* is absent, the current file is assumed. *FILENAME* may include an absolute or relative path name.

Part 5

Advanced Features

matrix   The *matrix* command creates a matrix of equal-sized cells in text frame, typically drawn over a graphic of equally sized buttons. The hypertext commands that are activated when the cells are clicked are listed in a named text flow on a reference page of the document.

The syntax is:

```
matrix ROWS COLUMNS FLOWNAME
```

where *ROWS* and *COLUMNS* specify the number of rows and columns in the matrix and *FLOWNAME* is the name of the reference page flow that lists the hypertext commands to be executed. In *FLOWNAME*, each command is listed in a separate paragraph, with row 1 commands listed first, then row 2 commands, and so on.

message openfile (Macintosh Only)   The *message openfile* command starts a Macintosh application or opens a file in an application. If AppleScript software is installed, *message openfile* can start an AppleScript script. *message openfile* does not affect the stack for the current window.

The syntax is:

```
message openfile PATHNAME
```

where *PATHNAME* is the path to the application, file, or script to be started or opened.

message system and message winexec (Windows Only)   The *message system* and *message winexec* commands start another Windows application. *message system* and *message winexec* do not affect the stack for the current window.

The syntax is:

```
message system APPLICATION PATHNAME,WINDOWSTATE
message winexec APPLICATION PATHNAME,WINDOWSTATE
```

where *APPLICATION* is the file name (with path name if necessary) of the application's executable file, *PATHNAME* is an optional command-line parameter, typically the path and file name of a file for the application to open, and *WINDOWSTATE* specifies the state of the opened window.

WINDOWSTATE can be any of the following:

SW_HIDE

SW_MINIMIZE

SW_RESTORE

SW_SHOW

SW_SHOWMAXIMIZED

SW_SHOWMINIMIZED

SW_SHOWMINNOACTIVE

SW_SHOWNA

SW_SHOWNOACTIVATE

SW_SHOWNORMAL

If *WINDOWSTATE* is not specified, the default value is SW_SHOWNORMAL.

For more information on window states, refer to the documentation in the Microsoft software development kit.

newlink The *newlink* command names a link that marks the destination of a *gotolink, openlink, gotolinkfitwin,* and *openlinkfitwin* command. The *newlink* command does not affect the stack for the current window.

The syntax is:

```
newlink LINKNAME
```

where *LINKNAME* is the same as the link name used in the *gotolink, gotolinkfitwin, openlink,* or *openlinkfitwin* command. The link names must match exactly, character for character.

nextpage The *nextpage* command displays the next page of the current document. If the last page is already displayed, *nextpage* has no effect.

nextpage stores the current location on the stack for the current window before jumping to the next page.

The syntax is:

```
nextpage
```

Part
5

Advanced Features

openlink   The *openlink* command jumps to a page containing a *newlink* marker with an identically spelled link name as the current marker. The *newlink* marker may be in the current document or a different document.

When *openlink* is executed, the page with the *newlink* marker is displayed in a new document window. (Compare *gotolink*, which displays the new page in the same document window.)

openlink creates a separate stack for the new window and leaves the stack for the current window unchanged.

The syntax is:

```
openlink FILENAME:LINKNAME
```

where *FILENAME* is the file name of the document and *LINKNAME* is the name of the link in the corresponding *newlink* command. If *FILENAME* is absent, the current file is assumed. *FILENAME* may include an absolute or relative path name.

openlinkfitwin   The *openlinkfitwin* jumps to a page containing a *newlink* marker with an identically spelled link name as the current marker. The *newlink* marker may be in the current document or a different document.

When *openlinkfitwin* is executed, the page with the *newlink* marker is displayed in a new document window, and the window is resized as necessary—from portrait to landscape, for example. (Compare *gotolinkfitwin*, which displays the new page in the same document window.)

openlinkfitwin creates a separate stack for the new window and leaves the stack for the current window unchanged.

The syntax is:

```
openlinkfitwin FILENAME:LINKNAME
```

where *FILENAME* is the file name of the document and *LINKNAME* is the name of the link in the corresponding *newlink* command. If *FILENAME* is absent, the current file is assumed. *FILENAME* may include an absolute or relative path name.

opennew   The *opennew* command opens another document (for example, a document template) in a new window as a new, unnamed document. *opennew* does not affect the stack for the current window.

The syntax is:

```
opennew FILENAME
```

where *FILENAME* is the path and file name of the document to be opened.

openpage   The *openpage* command jumps to a specified page in the same or a different document.

When *openpage* is executed, the new page is displayed in a new document window. (Compare *gotopage*, which displays the new page in the same document window.)

openpage creates a separate stack for the new window and leaves the stack for the current window unchanged.

The syntax is:

```
openpage FILENAME:PAGENUMBER
```

where *FILENAME* is the file name of the document and *PAGENUM-BER* is the number of the page to which to jump. If *FILENAME* is absent, the current file is assumed. *FILENAME* may include an absolute or relative path name.

popup   The *popup* command displays a pop-up menu from which items can be selected. The menu selections are contained in a named text flow on a reference page. *popup* does not affect the stack for the current window, though the commands in the menu items may.

The syntax is:

```
popup FLOWNAME
```

where *FLOWNAME* is the name of the text flow on a reference page that lists the pop-up menu items, one per paragraph. The hypertext commands for each menu item appear in a hypertext marker in the paragraph that contains that menu item.

To create a submenu, include the *popup* command in a marker of popup menu items on the reference page and refer to another named flow.

previouslink   The *previouslink* command executes the most recent hypertext command on the current stack.

The syntax is:

```
previouslink FILENAME:LINKNAME
```

where *FILENAME* and *LINKNAME* identify a file and link name to which to jump if the current stack is empty. If the stack is empty and *FILENAME:LINKNAME* are unspecified, nothing happens when the command is executed.

previouslinkfitwin   The *previouslinkfitwin* command executes the most recent hypertext command on the stack, and resizes the window if necessary—from portrait to a landscape, for example.

The syntax is:

```
previouslinkfitwin FILENAME:LINKNAME
```

where *FILENAME* and *LINKNAME* identify a file and link name to which to jump if the current stack is empty. If the stack is empty and *FILENAME:LINKNAME* are unspecified, nothing happens when the command is executed.

previouspage   The *previouspage* command displays the previous page of the current document. If the first page is already displayed, *previouspage* has no effect. *previouspage* stores the current location on the stack before jumping to the previous page.

The syntax is:

```
previouspage
```

quit   The *quit* command closes the current document. It works like the File ➤ Close command.

The syntax is:

```
quit
```

quitall   The *quitall* command closes all open view-only documents. It works like the File ➤ Close All Open Files command. In Windows, the *quitall* command also closes all view-only documents which are displayed as icons.

The syntax is:

```
quitall
```

Testing a Hypertext Document for Incorrect Links

When adding hypertext links to editable documents, you'll most likely do a lot of testing to make sure your links are set up correctly. One way to test these links is to lock the document (with *Esc F l k*), then select the link by clicking to make sure the correct area is active and see what the command does.

Another, faster way to test hypertext links is to keep the document unlocked and select the link by clicking, this time using the keyboard modifier for your version. In Windows, Ctrl+Alt+click selects an active hypertext link in an unlocked document. On UNIX systems, do this with Ctrl+Right click. On the Mac, use Control+Option+click.

To test whether an active area is indeed active without actually executing the command embedded in the marker, use the keyboard modifier for your system, hold down the correct mouse button, then pass the mouse cursor over the area, but *don't release the mouse button*. The active area will be highlighted when you pass over it, but not selected.

You can also quickly check all hypertext commands by generating a list of hypertext markers. To do this:

1. Select File ➤ Generate/Book.

2. In the Generate/Book dialog box, select List of Markers from the List pull-down menu and click the Generate button.

3. In the Set Up List of Markers dialog box, move Hypertext to the Include Markers of Type scroll list, and click the Generate button.

    The generated file will list all hypertext commands in the document and the page numbers they are on.

Part
5

Advanced Features

Linking Back to Generated Files

Generated files—for example, tables of contents or indexes—contain hypertext links to their source documents (if creation of hypertext links was turned on when the file was generated).

To complete an online document viewing system, you should also create links from the source document back to the generated file, so that a user who goes to the source document can get back to the document he or she started from. These links must be added by hand. They can be buttons on the master page (and thus on every body page) that take the user back to the TOC or index document, or they can be built into a hypertext menu of "go to" options that appears on the master page.

Chapter 19

Other FrameMaker Features

FrameMaker provides many features that help automate document creation, editing, and use. This chapter discusses cross-references, footnotes, variables, conditional text, change bars, document comparison, equations, and converting FrameMaker documents into HTML documents.

Placing Cross References in Documents

A *cross-reference* is a pointer to a source location in the current document or a different document. The source location is identified with a marker placed there by FrameMaker. The cross-reference pointer gets its information from the marker.

With FrameMaker, cross-references do not have to be typed manually. Several standard cross-reference formats (that is, standard phrases that can contain cross-reference information) are provided, and you can create your own cross-reference formats as well.

Here is an example of a cross reference format. Note that part of the format is "canned" (it contains phrases that never change) and part of it contains words provided by FrameMaker:

For more information, see "Astronavigation Basics" on page 12.

FrameMaker provided the phrase *Astronavigation Basics* (that was the text of the heading paragraph being referenced) and the number *12* (the page on which that heading appears). The format provided the rest of the words and the punctuation.

Cross-references can be updated with a simple command when page numbers or referenced text changes.

Two types of cross-references can be used in FrameMaker—a paragraph cross-reference (as in the example above) and a spot cross-reference.

Paragraph Cross-References A *paragraph cross-reference* points to an entire paragraph—for example, a heading paragraph or a paragraph that contains information about a subject. When the cross-reference is created, FrameMaker places a cross-reference marker at the beginning of the referenced paragraph, and then, in another place in the document, refers the reader to that location by reprinting the text of the paragraph and/or the page number where the marker is located. When the paragraph breaks across two pages, the location of the marker (in this case, at the start of the paragraph) provides the page number in the cross-reference.

Spot Cross-References A *spot cross-reference* is like a paragraph cross-reference, except that it points to a particular spot or location within a paragraph (identified by a marker *you* create) and not to the beginning of the paragraph (identified by a marker FrameMaker creates). For example, a sentence in the middle of a paragraph on an earlier page may contain the definition of a term used in the current paragraph. In this case, you can place a cross-reference marker at the start of that sentence yourself, and then refer to that marker by page number in the current paragraph. This allows you to point to the exact page number on which that sentence starts, even when that sentence is on a different page as the beginning of the paragraph that contains it. Note, however, that the format options are the same with both types of cross-reference. In general, you can include the whole text of a paragraph (not parts of a paragraph) and page numbers in which the cross-reference markers reside.

Inserting Cross-References

Each type of cross-reference, paragraph and spot, is inserted in a different way. When you insert a paragraph cross-reference, Frame-Maker automatically inserts a cross-reference marker at the beginning of the source paragraph. When you insert a spot cross-reference, you must manually place the source marker before inserting the cross-reference.

With both paragraph and spot cross-references, you must select a format to determine how the cross-reference reads and how it is punctuated. (To place a cross-reference in a text inset, you must insert the cross-reference into the source document of the text inset, since text insets cannot be directly edited.)

To insert a paragraph cross-reference:

1. If you are cross-referencing a source paragraph in another document, open that document. It must be a named, saved document.

2. Click to place the insertion point where you want the cross-reference to appear. You can insert a cross-reference only in a text frame, not in a text line.

3. Select Special ➤ Cross-Reference. The Cross-Reference dialog box opens, as in Figure 19.1.

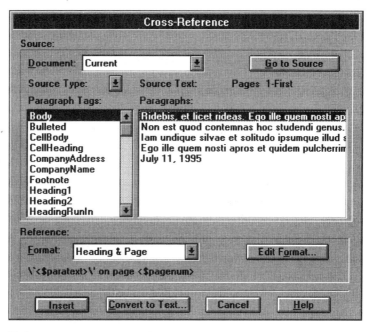

Figure 19.1   **The Cross-Reference dialog box for paragraphs**

4.   If the source paragraph is in a different document, select that document from the Document pull-down list.

5.   From the Source Type pull-down list, select Paragraphs.

6.   In the Paragraph Tags scroll list, click on the tag of the paragraph you are cross-referencing.

7.   In the Paragraphs scroll list, find and click on the specific paragraph you are cross-referencing. The Paragraph scroll list displays the text of all paragraphs with the tag you selected in the Paragraph Tags scroll list.

8.   From the Format pull-down list, select the format you want to use. The Format pull-down list displays the cross-reference formats available in the current document. For more information on cross-reference formats, see "Creating Cross-Reference Formats" later in this chapter.

9.   Click the Insert button. The cross-reference is inserted at the insertion point and a marker is placed at the beginning of the source paragraph.

Part 5

Advanced Freatures

> **WARNING** Do not edit the text of a cross-reference marker created by FrameMaker, even if, after the marker is moved, the text looks wrong to you. If you edit this marker in any way, FrameMaker will not be able to find it again when cross-references are updated, and you will have an unresolved cross-reference that must be reinserted. (See below for more information on updating and resolving unresolved cross-references.)

To insert a spot cross-reference:

1. Place the insertion point by clicking where you want to insert the marker. The marker may be inserted anywhere in a column of text. The location of the marker will determine the page number contained in any cross-reference that points to it.

2. Select Special ➤ Marker. The Marker dialog box opens, as in Figure 19.2.

Figure 19.2 **The Marker dialog box**

3. From the Marker Type pull-down list, select Cross-Ref.

4. In the text box called Marker Text, type a description of the marker. Marker text can be up to 255 characters long. This text does not appear in the cross-reference. It is only a label that allows you to know which Cross-Ref marker is which.

5. Click the New Marker button.

6. Now follow the procedure for inserting a paragraph cross-reference provided earlier in this chapter, but do it slightly differently this time.

   • In step 5, select Cross-Reference Marker (instead of Paragraph) from the Source pull-down list. The Cross-Reference dialog box will now display a list of marker types instead of paragraph tags, as shown in Figure 19.3.

- Ignore step 6, since the Marker Type scroll list contains only one item, Cross-Ref, which is already selected.

- In step 7, select the text of the marker you want to refer to in the cross-reference. (Again, this marker text will not appear in the cross-reference—its only purpose is to label the marker for you.)

7. Perform the rest of the procedure as you normally would, by selecting a format and clicking Insert. (Note again that your format options are the same for both types of cross-references.)

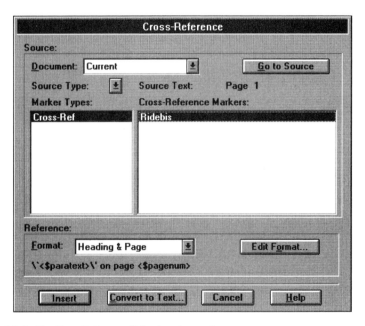

Figure 19.3   **The Cross-Reference dialog box for markers**

Part
5

You can edit a cross-reference at any time to change its source or format, and to cut, copy, paste, or delete it. Cut, copy, and paste cross-references just like you do text. Simply select the cross-reference and cut or copy and paste it in a new location.

TIP Double-clicking on a cross-reference brings up the Cross-Reference dialog box. This is an extremely handy shortcut, but it can be troublesome when you are selecting phrases or paragraphs that include cross-references. Remember that to select a cross-reference for cutting, copying, or pasting, single-click on the cross-reference, or double-click on words around the cross-reference and drag to include the cross-reference in the selection.

To delete a cross-reference, select it and press the Backspace or Delete key.

To change the source or format of a cross-reference, double-click on the cross-reference. This opens the Cross-Reference dialog box (see Figure 19.1). Select a new format from the Format pull-down list or change the source paragraph or marker as you wish, and then click the Replace button. The new cross-reference will replace the old one.

Updating Cross-References

A cross-reference gets its information (for example, a page number and paragraph text) from the location of the source marker and the text of the source paragraph that contains it. If the source marker moved, or the text of the paragraph that contains it is modified, the cross-reference that points to that paragraph may not be accurate—it will either name the wrong page (the old page number) or it will print the text of the source paragraph incorrectly. In cases like this, the cross-references need to be updated so their information reflects recent edits to the document.

FrameMaker automatically updates all cross-references when you open or print a document, unless you have suppressed automatic updating, but this may not be often enough. You can manually update cross-references whenever you wish, for example, after editing a number of source paragraphs. (Keep in mind that FrameMaker cannot update cross-references with markers in hidden conditional text. If you wish to update these cross-references, show all conditional text before updating.)

 WARNING When cross-references are updated for printing, the version of the document on disk is updated, not the version of the document in memory. To ensure that all changes you've made are reflected in the update, save the document before printing.

Manually Updating Cross-References

To manually update cross-references:

1. Select Edit ➤ Update References. The Update References dialog box opens, as in Figure 19.4.

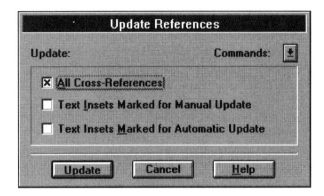

Figure 19.4 **The Update References dialog box**

2. Select All Cross-References.

3. Click the Update button.

When cross-references are updated and FrameMaker can't resolve a cross-reference (that is, it can't find the source marker), you will see the Unresolved Cross-References dialog box, and you will have to resolve any unresolved cross-references. To do this, use the procedure in the next section, starting with step 3.

Resolving Unresolved Cross-References

Unresolved cross-references occur for a number of reasons. The most common one is that the source marker was inadvertently deleted when a paragraph was modified. For this reason, it's a good idea to edit documents containing markers with Text Symbols turned on.

Also, if you edit the text of a cross-reference marker in any way, a cross-reference that points to that marker will not be able to find it. Cross-reference markers can be moved, but they should not be edited.

Part
5

Advanced Freatures

To resolve unresolved cross-references:

1. Select Edit ➤ Update References. The Update References dialog box opens (see Figure 19.4).

2. From the Commands pull-down list, select Update Unresolved Cross-References. The Update Unresolved Cross-References dialog box opens, as in Figure 19.5.

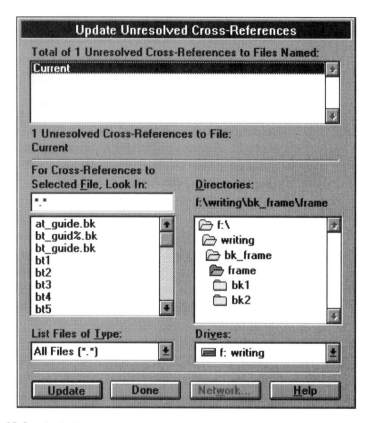

Figure 19.5   **The Update Unresolved Cross-References dialog box**

3. In the Files Named scroll list, select the file that used to contain the cross-reference. If it's the current document, select Current.

4. In the Look In scroll list, select the file that may now contain the source of the cross-reference.

5. Click the Update button. If the marker cannot be found in the selected document, select a different file in the Look In scroll list.

6. If a marker or group of markers still cannot be found, they were probably deleted. If that is the case:

   - Close the Update Unresolved Cross-References dialog box by clicking Done.

   - Find the first unresolved cross-reference (you can use the Find/Change dialog box to do this).

   - Double-click on the cross-reference to open the Cross-Reference dialog box.

   - Re-create the cross-reference.

Getting a List of Unresolved Cross-References

You can use the autogenerated file feature you saw in Chapter 17 to generate a list of unresolved cross-references for a given file. The list will show if the source is internal (in the current document) or external (in a different document), as well as the paragraph tag, text, and page number of each unresolved cross-reference. To do so:

1. Save the file containing the unresolved cross-references (this step is required).

2. Select File ➤ Generate/Book. The Generate/Book dialog box opens.

3. From the List pull-down menu, select List of References.

4. Click the Generate button. The Setup List of References dialog box opens.

5. Move Unresolved Cross-Refs to the Include References scroll list.

6. Click the Generate button. The document will be searched for unresolved cross-references, and a document containing the list will be created and opened. If there are no unresolved cross-references, the document will be empty.

Creating Your Own Cross-Reference Formats

A *cross-reference format* determines the wording, punctuation, and appearance of a cross-reference. Cross-reference formats allow you to be consistent in the way you use cross-references. Cross-reference formats are created using text and building blocks (for example, <*$pagenum>*). The building blocks allow FrameMaker to automatically insert and update variable parts of the cross-reference, for example, the page number of the source marker, or the text of the source paragraph.

When you create a new document (with File ➤ New), FrameMaker provides several cross-reference formats already, or you can create your own. Formats already available with new documents are:

Name	Definition	Example
Heading & Page	"<$paratext>" on page <$pagenum>	"Astronavigation" on page 12
Page	page <$pagenum>	page 12
See Heading & Page	See "<$paratext>" on page <$pagenum>.	See "Astronavigation" on page 12.
Table All	Table <$paranumonly>, "<$paratext>," on page <$pagenum>	Table 6, "Basic Astronavigation Terms," on page 12
Table Number & Page	Table <$paranumonly> on page <$pagenum>	Table 6 on page 12

To create or edit a cross-reference format:

1. Select Special ➤ Cross-Reference. The Cross-Reference dialog box opens (see Figure 19.1).

2. Click the Edit Format button. The Edit Cross-Reference Format dialog box opens, as in Figure 19.6.

What you do next depends on whether you are creating a new format or editing an existing one. To create a new format, do these three steps next:

3. Type in a name in the Name text box.

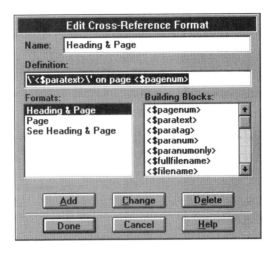

Figure 19.6   The Edit Cross-Reference Format dialog box

4. In the Definition text box, type in text and insert building blocks from the Building Blocks scroll list by clicking on them. To change the character format of a cross-reference, add a character format building block (for example, <Emphasis>) to the format definition.

5. Click the Add button.

    If you are editing an existing format, after following steps 1 and 2 above, do these four steps next:

1. Click on the name of the format in the Formats scroll list. The name and definition of the format will be displayed.

2. Edit the definition in the Definition text box. To change the character format of a cross-reference, add a character format building block (for example, <Emphasis>) to the format definition.

3. Click the Change button.

4. When you are done making all changes to cross-reference formats, click the Done button.

Deleting a Cross-Reference Format

To delete a cross-reference format, open the Edit Cross-Reference Format dialog box (see Figure 19.6), click on the format you want to delete in the Formats scroll list, click the Delete button, and click the

Part 5

Advanced Freatures

Done button. If you delete a format that is used in the document, you will be asked if you want to convert the cross-reference into text.

Converting Cross-References to Text

You can convert cross-references to text. You can convert all cross-references, cross-references with a specific format, or an individual cross-reference. To convert a cross-reference to text:

1. Click to place the insertion point anywhere in the document.

2. Select Special ➤ Cross-Reference. The Cross-Reference dialog box (see Figure 19.1) opens.

3. If you wish to convert a selected cross-reference (as opposed to all cross-references or all cross-references with a particular format), highlight it now.

4. Click the Convert to Text button. The Convert Cross-References to text dialog box opens, as in Figure 19.7.

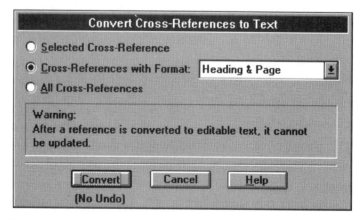

Figure 19.7 **The Convert Cross-References to Text dialog box**

5. Select which cross-references you want to convert. Your choices are the currently selected cross-reference, all cross-references of a particular format, or all cross-references.

6. Click the Convert button. The Cross-Reference dialog box (see Figure 19.1) returns.

7. If you wish to convert another selected cross-reference, repeat these steps.

8. When you are finished converting cross-references to text, click the Done button.

    Once a cross-reference is converted to text, you cannot update it, but you can edit the text.

Importing Cross-Reference Formats

Suppose a different document contains cross-reference formats that you want to use in the current document. You can import them. To import cross-reference formats:

1. Open the source document—the document containing the cross-reference formats you wish to import.

2. In the current document, select File ➤ Import ➤ Formats. The Import Formats dialog box opens, as in Figure 19.8.

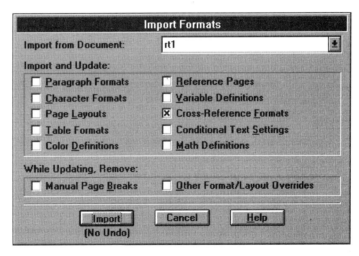

Figure 19.8 *The Import Formats dialog box*

3. Select the source document (the one to import from) in the Import from Document pull-down list.

4. In the Import and Update area, select Cross-Reference Formats.

5. Click the Import button.

Part
5

Advanced Freatures

Including Footnotes and Endnotes in Documents

A *footnote* is an explanatory note, comment, or reference about the text. Usually, footnotes are placed at the bottom of a page. An *endnote* is an explanatory note, comment, or reference about the text usually placed at the end of a document.

FrameMaker makes adding footnotes easy for you. All you need to do is identify the text you want to footnote and type in the footnote text. FrameMaker does the rest. It creates, numbers, and positions the footnote and adds a separator if the footnote is the first one in the column. You can use the default footnote format or create a custom format.

FrameMaker automatically manages footnotes for you. For example, if you insert a footnote before another footnote, FrameMaker adjusts the numbering of all succeeding footnotes in the document.

You can also create a footnote for individual table cells, refer to the same footnote from several points in the text or several table cells, and create endnotes.

How FrameMaker Handles Footnotes

In text, a footnote and the footnote reference always appear in the same text column. If the footnote reference moves to another column or page, the footnote moves along with it.

A table cell footnote always appears at the end of the table. If the table breaks across a page, the footnote will still be at the end of the table, regardless of which page the footnote reference is on.

In a multicolumn document with a paragraph that straddles columns, a footnote's position depends upon its Across All Columns setting on the Pagination properties page of the Paragraph Designer. If Across All Columns is selected, a footnote with a reference above the straddle paragraph appears below the straddle paragraph, at the bottom of the column (usually the bottom of the page). If Across All Columns is not selected, a footnote with a reference above the straddle paragraph appears just above the straddle paragraph, at the bottom of the column that contains the reference.

Inserting Footnotes

To insert a footnote:

1. Place the insertion point by clicking where you want to add the footnote. You can add a footnote to a text column or a table cell.

2. Select Special ➤ Footnote. The footnote reference is inserted, the footnote is created, and the insertion point is placed in the footnote. Any footnote that follows this one is renumbered.

3. Type the footnote text.

4. Return to the main text by clicking in it.

    After the footnote is created, you can edit footnote text just like you edit other text, but you cannot change the footnote number which is automatically maintained by FrameMaker.

Deleting a Footnote

To delete a footnote:

1. Select the footnote reference, not the footnote.

2. Press the Delete key.

    The footnote reference, the footnote, and the separator (if this footnote is the only one in the column) are deleted and any succeeding footnotes are renumbered.

    Two footnote references can be placed together, if you separate them with a space or a comma in the text. However, if you try to insert another footnote without a space or a comma, a second footnote will not be created. If the footnote references are superscripted, the space and the comma should also be superscripted.

Referencing a Footnote from Several Places

You can reference the same footnote from several places in text or from several table cells. The first footnote is created in the standard way and subsequent footnotes use cross-references. To create several references to a single footnote:

1. Insert the first footnote.

2. Create a cross-reference format for the additional footnote references.

   Make the cross-reference format the same as the footnote reference format. For example, create a cross-reference format for a superscripted reference, such as *<Superscript><$paranumonly>*. To do this, first create a character format with superscript called "Superscript." Since the footnote is an autonumbered paragraph, the cross-reference format should display the autonumber.

3. Place the insertion point by clicking where you want to add another reference to the first footnote.

4. Insert a cross-reference to the footnote. Use the cross-reference format you created in step 2 above. Make sure you select the paragraph tag of the footnote in the Paragraph Tags scroll list of the Cross-Reference dialog box.

5. Repeat steps 3 and 4 for each additional reference to the first footnote.

   After editing a document, the cross-reference to a footnote may not be accurate. For example, the footnote number may be wrong because you added new footnotes before the cross-referenced footnote. To ensure these cross-references are accurate, update all the cross-references in the document.

Separators for Dividing the Text from Footnotes

A *separator* is the graphic frame that is automatically inserted between the text in a column or a table and the first footnote in that column. The footnote graphic frame usually contains a line or other graphic object that acts like a visual break between the text in the column or a table and the footnote. The height of the graphic frame sets the gap between the text in the column or a table and the first footnote below it.

For a new FrameMaker document, the footnote graphic frame and the table footnote graphic frame are located on the first reference page of the document. The names of these graphic frames are the same as the names of the paragraph format tags used for these footnote types— *Footnote* and *TableFootnote*. You can change the separator by changing the graphic object or changing the graphic frame on the reference page.

To change a separator:

1. Select View ➤ Reference Pages.

2. Move to the page that contains the graphic frame for the separator.

3. Edit the graphic object or the graphic frame as you wish. For more information on working with graphics, see Chapter 13.

4. Select View ➤ Body Pages.

Formatting Footnotes

You may want to change the default footnote format to match more closely the style of your document. You can change the style of the numbers, the numbering format, and the paragraph format. There are separate formats for text and table footnotes. If your document contains both types of footnotes, you need to set the footnote properties for both types.

To change the footnote format:

1. Click to place the insertion point—in text to change the text footnote format, or in a table cell to change the table footnote format.

2. Select Format ➤ Document ➤ Footnote Properties. Depending on where you placed the insertion point, FrameMaker opens either the text Footnote Properties dialog box, shown in Figure 19.9, or the Table Footnote Properties dialog box, shown in Figure 19.10.

3. Set the properties (the format) of the footnote. See below for information on each of the properties.

4. Click the Set button.

For a text footnote, you can set the maximum height that the footnotes and the separator occupy in a text column. If the maximum height is exceeded, FrameMaker moves the last footnote into the next column.

The format of the footnote is taken from the format listed in the Paragraph Format text box. All newly created FrameMaker documents use the built-in paragraph formats *Footnote* and *TableFootnote* for footnotes. You can change the format of your footnotes by editing these built-in paragraph formats (with the Paragraph Designer) or by entering the name of another paragraph format in the Paragraph Format text box.

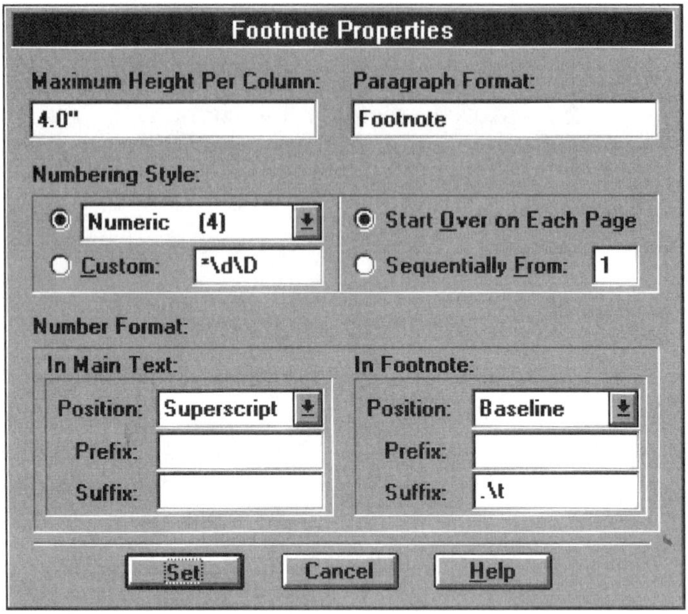

Figure 19.9   The Footnote Properties dialog box

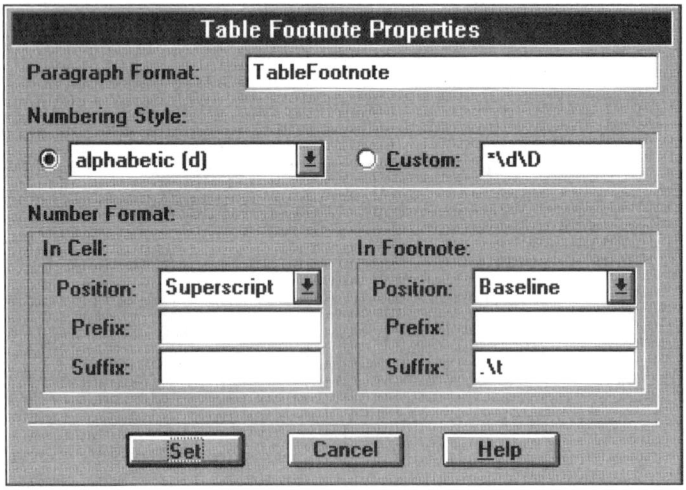

Figure 19.10   The Table Footnote Properties dialog box

The new format may be one that comes with the document or one that you create yourself.

In the Numbering Style area of the Footnote Properties dialog boxes (Figures 19.9 and 19.10), you can select a numbering style from the pull-down list. The choices are:

▶ Numeric (1, 2, 3, 4)

▶ roman (i, ii, iii, iv)

▶ ROMAN (I, II, III, IV)

▶ alphabetic (a, b, c, d)

▶ ALPHABETIC (A, B, C, D)

You can also create a custom style. The custom style can use numbers, letters, and symbols. Many people, for example, use asterisks (*), daggers, and double-daggers for footnote symbols. Just type in the characters you want to use, in the order you want to use them, in the Custom text box. Footnotes will be "numbered" sequentially using these symbols. When the list is used once, it will be repeated, only this time two symbols will be used instead of one. (Custom styles are best used with footnotes whose numbering starts over on each page. Otherwise, you might get a footnote whose "number" is eight daggers!)

For text footnotes, you can number footnotes sequentially from the start of the document or you can start numbering on each page. For sequential numbering, you can specify the starting number by typing the number in the Sequentially From text box. For table footnotes, the numbering is consecutive through the table and starts over for each table.

In the Number Format area of the Footnote Properties dialog boxes, you can select the format of the footnote reference. Select a position for the footnote number from the Position pull-down list. The choices are Superscript, Baseline, and Subscript. The default is Superscript. You can specify a prefix or a suffix by typing it into the Prefix or Suffix text boxes.

You can also select the format of the footnote number in the footnote. Select a position for the footnote number from the Position pull-down list. The choices are Superscript, Baseline, and Subscript. The default is Baseline. You can specify a prefix or a suffix by typing it into the Prefix or Suffix text boxes. The default Suffix is a tab.

Part
5

Advanced Freatures

Creating Endnotes

An *endnote* is an explanatory note, comment, or reference about the text. Usually, endnotes are placed at the end of documents. Endnotes are typed in as regular text and then cross-references are used in text to refer to the appropriate endnote. Since you use cross-references to refer to endnotes, you can combine text and table footnotes in one location.

To create endnotes:

1. Create an autonumber paragraph format for endnotes. For more information on paragraph formats, see Chapter 10.

2. Create a cross-reference format for endnote references. For more information on cross-reference formats, see the section on cross-references earlier in this chapter.

3. Go to the end of the document, type the endnote, and apply the endnote autonumber paragraph format to it.

4. Place the insertion point by clicking where you want to place the endnote reference.

5. Insert a cross-reference to the endnote. Make sure that you select the paragraph tag of the endnote in the Paragraph Tags scroll list and the cross-reference format you created in the Format pull-down list.

6. Repeat steps 3, 4, and 5 for each additional endnote.

Variables

Variables represent text, usually text that will change, such as the revision date of the document. But variables can also be any phrase that is repeatedly used throughout a document, such as the document's name. Using a variable saves you the trouble of changing this phrase by searching through the document to find every instance where it is used. You can change the phrase by changing the definition of the variable in one location, and all instances of that variable in the document will be updated automatically.

System Variables and User Variables

There are two types of variables—system and user. *System variables,* such as today's date, get their information from FrameMaker and your computer system. *User variables,* such as your name, are defined by you, the user.

System Variables

Each newly created FrameMaker document comes with a default set of system variables. System variables on master pages are updated whenever the value of the variable changes, and these updated variables automatically appear on body pages that use these master pages as background. System variables on body or reference pages are updated whenever the document is opened or printed. You can also manually update all system variables whenever the document is open.

Each FrameMaker variable has a name and a definition. You cannot add, delete, or rename a system variable, but you can change its definition. The set of system variables and their default definitions included in each FrameMaker document are shown in Table 19.1. System variables are listed in the Variable dialog box, which is shown in Figure 19.11.

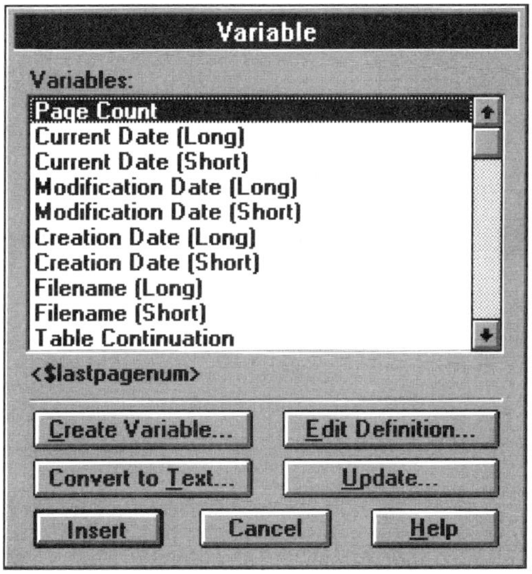

Figure 19.11   The Variable dialog box

Part
5

Advanced Freatures

Most of these variables are obvious. The variables labeled Running H/F are used in headers and footers. The variables labeled Table Continuation and Table Sheet are used in the titles of tables. (Pages of a multipage table are often called "sheets.")

You can redefine the six date and time variables—Current Date (Long), Current Date (Short), Modification Date (Long), Modification Date (Short), Creation Date (Long), and Creation Date (Short)—by using the date and time building blocks (for example, *<$seconds>*, *<$dayname>*, and *<$ampm>*).

System Variable	Default Definition
Current Page #	*<$curpagnum>*
Page Count	*<$lastpagenum>*
Current Date (Long)	*<$monthname> <$daynum>, <$year>*
Current Date (Short)	*<$monthnum>/<$daynum>/<$shortyear>*
Modification Date (Long)	*<$monthname> <$daynum>, <$year>,* *<$hour>:<$minute00> <$ampm>*
Modification Date (Short)	*<$monthnum>/<$daynum>/<$shortyear>*
Creation Date (Long)	*<$monthname> <$daynum>, <$year>*
Creation Date (Short)	*<$monthnum>/<$daynum>/<$shortyear>*
Filename (Long)	*<$fullfilename>*
Filename (Short)	*<$filename>*
Running H/F 1	*<$paratext[Title]>*
Running H/F 2	*<$paratext[Heading1]>*
Running H/F 3	*<$marker1>*
Running H/F 4	*<$marker2>*
Table Continuation	*(Continued)*
Table Sheet	*(Sheet <$tblsheetnum> of <$tblsheetcount>)*

Table 19.1   **System Variables**

You can also change the text of the table variables, and convert all system variables to text.

TIP The Variables dialog box appears when you select Special ➤ Variable, but you can access it quickly by double-clicking on any variable in the document.

User Variables

User variables are created by you, the user. When you create a user variable, you name it, define it, and define its character format as well. You can use any combination of text, symbols, and character formats. (You cannot, however, use building blocks like *<$pagenum>* in a user variable. If you enter one of these building blocks, it will be treated as text.)

You can change the definition of a user variable at any time. When you change the definition, all occurrences of the variable in the document are updated. You can also convert user variables to text.

Creating User Variables

To create a user variable, select a name, a definition, and a character format:

1. Click to place the insertion point in the document.
2. Select Special ➤ Variable. The Variable dialog box opens.
3. Click the Create Variable button. The Edit User Variable dialog box opens, as in Figure 19.12.
4. Type a name for the variable in the Name text box. Pick a descriptive name.

NOTE Variable names are case-sensitive and will accept spaces. A nice way to indicate user variables in a shared document is to make user variables all uppercase—for example, SYSTEM NAME.

5. Type the definition of the variable in the Definition text box.
6. Click the Add button. The variable will be created and its name will appear in the User Variables scroll list.

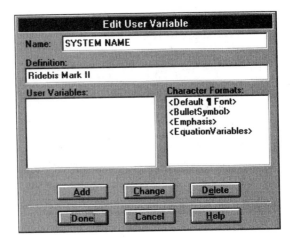

Figure 19.12   *The Edit User Variable dialog box*

7. Click the Done button. The Variable dialog box (see Figure 19.11) opens and the variable's name appears in the Variables scroll list after all the system variables.

8. Click the Done button to close the Variable dialog box.

Changing a Variable's Definition

You can change the definition of a system or user variable before or after you insert it into a document. You can use text, symbols, regular and nonbreaking spaces, and character formats. In system variables, you can also use building blocks. Whenever you change the definition of a variable, FrameMaker automatically updates the variable everywhere in the document.

To edit the definition of a variable:

1. Click to place the insertion point in the document.

2. Select Special ➤ Variable. The Variable dialog box (see Figure 19.11) opens.

3. Select a variable from the Variables scroll list by clicking on it.

4. Click the Edit Definition button. Depending on the type of variable you selected—system or user—the appropriate Edit Variable dialog box opens.

5. What you do next depends on whether you selected a system or user variable.

- If you selected a system variable, the Edit System Variable dialog box shown in Figure 19.13 opens. Redefine the variable by using text, symbols, or building blocks from the Building Blocks scroll list. When you are finished, click the Edit button. The Variable dialog box (see Figure 19.11) returns.

- If you selected a user variable, the Edit User Variable dialog box opens (see Figure 19.12). Redefine the variable by using text, symbols, or character formats. You can also change the name. When you are finished, click the Change button. The Variable dialog box (see Figure 19.11) returns.

6. In the Variable dialog box, click the Done button.

You can delete a variable from text by selecting it and pressing the Backspace or Delete key. (Single-click to select a variable. If you double-click on it, the Variables dialog box will open.)

You can delete a user variable from the document by selecting the variable name in Variables scroll list in the Variable dialog box and clicking the Edit Definition button. In the Edit User Variable dialog box, click the Delete button, and then click the Done button.

You cannot delete a system variable from the document.

Part 5

Advanced Freatures

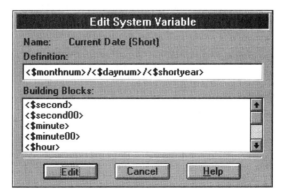

Figure 19.13 **The Edit System Variable dialog box**

Inserting Variables in a Document

You can insert variables into text on body pages, into reference pages, and into master pages. To insert a variable into text:

1. Click to place the insertion point where you want the variable to appear.

2. Select Special ➤ Variable. The Variable dialog box opens.

3. Select a variable from the Variables scroll list. User variables are located after the system variables.

4. Click the Insert button.

You can also insert variables into headers and footers by following the procedure above.

In addition to the standard header and footer variables (page number, and so on), there are four special variables, Running H/F 1-4, that are used for running headers and footers. What a running header and footer variable does depends on the contents of the body pages. For example, you could use a running header variable to insert the name of the current first-level section in a header.

Conditional Text

Conditional text is text that can be turned "on" or "off," depending on the use of the document. For example, you might need two versions of your resume, one that lists your salaries along with your jobs, and one that does not. Your salaries could be formatted in FrameMaker as "conditional text," and then either hidden or made to appear, depending on which version of your resume you were printing.

Conditional text is tagged with a "conditional tag"—a name you can define yourself, and is identified by "conditional indicators" —changes in the way text is displayed, for example, in a different color. Each defined conditional tag in a document can have a different condition indicator.

A document that contains conditional text is a *conditional document.* Conditional documents usually appear in several versions, depending on which condition tags are hidden and which are not.

Condition Tags
for Setting the Document Version

Condition tags are used to identify text, graphics, tables, and other elements that will appear in given versions of the document.

In the resume example above, there is probably only one conditional tag, perhaps called Salary, that identifies the salaries associated with each job. This document has two versions, a "with salaries" version and a "without salaries" version. Other documents might use two or more conditional tags to permit many versions.

You can also use condition tags for text you don't ever want to be printed—for example, comments from people who have reviewed the document. In this case, you would use a different conditional tag for each reviewer, and you would probably hide all conditional text before final printing.

Each condition tag has condition indicators that determine how the conditional text will be displayed. You can change the condition indicators of a condition tag at any time. You can also create, edit, and delete condition tags.

Creating Condition Tags

Depending on which condition tags are shown and which are hidden, the displayed document will change. Condition tags have condition indicators which help distinguish different kinds of conditional text from one another. For example, one conditional tag may use the color blue and another orange.

> **TIP** When you create a condition tag, use a meaningful name that begins with a first letter that's not used by any other tag. This will speed up tagging from the keyboard.

To create a condition tag:

1. With the document active, select Special ➤ Conditional Text. The Conditional Text window opens, as in Figure 19.14.

2. Click the Edit Condition Tag button. The Edit Condition Tag dialog box opens, as in Figure 19.15.

3. Type the name of the condition tag in the Tag text box.

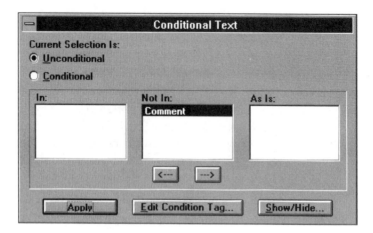

Figure 19.14   *The Conditional Text window*

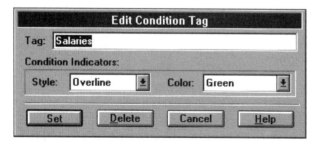

Figure 19.15   *The Edit Condition Tag dialog box*

4. From the Condition Indicators Style pull-down list, select a style
   The choices are As Is, Overline, Strikethrough. Underline, or Double
   Underline.

5. From the Condition Indicators Color pull-down list, select a color.

   The choices are As Is, Black, White, Red, Green, Blue, Cyan, Magenta
   and Yellow, but do not use the color magenta. Conditional text is
   displayed in magenta when it is assigned two or more condition tags
   each of which uses a different color as its condition indicators.

6. Click the Set button. The condition tag will appear in the Conditiona
   Text palette Not In scroll list.

7. Save the file. (The file must be saved before conditional tags can be edited.)

   Once a condition tag is created, you can change the condition indicators at any time. You can also delete the tag. When a tag is deleted, the conditional text that has that tag is not automatically deleted. Instead, FrameMaker gives you a choice of converting the conditional text to unconditional text or deleting the text.

   Changing Condition Indicators for a Tag   To change the condition indicators of a condition tag:

1. With the document active, select Special ➤ Conditional Text. The Conditional Text palette opens.

2. Select the tag in one of the scroll lists by clicking on it.

3. Click the Edit Condition Tag button. The Edit Condition Tag dialog box opens.

4. Select a style from the Condition Indicators Style pull-down list and a color from the Color pull-down list.

5. Click the Set button.

   Deleting a Condition Tag   To delete a condition tag:

1. With the document active, select Special ➤ Conditional Text. The Conditional Text palette opens.

2. Select the tag in one of the scroll lists by clicking on it.

3. Click the Edit Condition Tag button. The Edit Condition Tag dialog box opens.

4. Click the Delete button. If there is text in the document that only has this particular condition tag, the Delete Condition Tag dialog box shown in Figure 19.16 opens.

5. Select either Make the Text Unconditional or Delete the Text.

6. Click the OK button.

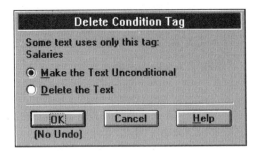

Figure 19.16   The Delete Condition Tag dialog box

Applying Condition Tags

You can apply a condition tag to text in a text frame, table cell, a footnote, an anchored frame and its contents, an entire table, a table row, a cross-reference, a marker, or a variable.

To apply a condition tag:

1. Select what you want to make conditional.

2. Select Special ➤ Conditional Text. The Conditional Text palette opens.

3. Select which condition tags you want to apply. You can apply more than one.

   - To apply a condition to the selected text, move the condition tag to the In scroll list.

   - To exclude a condition from the conditions to be applied, move the condition tag to the Not In scroll list.

4. Click the Apply button.

5. Close the Condition Text dialog box.

   The condition tag will be applied. If the condition tag is currently hidden, the selected item will disappear. If you did not select an item but only placed the insertion point into text, the condition tag will be applied to text you type until you move the insertion point or press Enter.

   If a condition tag is being used somewhere in the document, you can copy it and apply it to text elsewhere. To copy and apply a condition tag:

1. Click to place the insertion point in text that has the condition tag you want to copy.

2. Select Edit ➤ Copy Special ➤ Conditional Text Settings.

3. Select the item to which you want the tag applied.

4. Select Edit ➤ Paste.

Viewing Conditions

Unconditional text (text that has no conditional tags associated with it) is always displayed and printed. Conditional text is displayed or hidden depending on the Show/Hide setting. You can display all conditions (and the unconditional text, of course) or you can display only some conditions (or none).

To select which conditions to show or hide:

1. Select Special ➤ Conditional Text. The Conditional Text palette opens.

2. Click the Show/Hide button. The Show/Hide Conditional Text dialog box opens, as in Figure 19.17.

3. Select either Show All or Show. If you select Show, move the condition tags you want to show to the Show scroll list and move condition tags you want to hide to the Hide scroll list.

4. Click the Set button.

 TIP After you change the Show/Hide setting, you must update cross-references to ensure their accuracy.

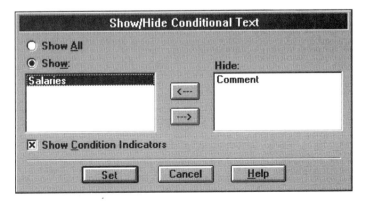

Figure 19.17 *The Show/Hide Conditional Text dialog box*

How Conditional Text Interacts with Other FrameMaker Features

Conditional text can be edited like unconditional (regular) text, but you can edit conditional text only if it's displayed. You can show all conditions (versions) to edit globally, or only selected conditions.

You can copy and paste conditional text by using the Copy and Paste commands. When you copy conditional text, you copy the text, the conditional text markers, and the condition tags. If you paste text into a different document and that document contains a condition tag not in the old document, FrameMaker automatically adds the condition tag to the new document.

You can delete conditional text by using the Cut command or the Delete key. You can apply paragraph and character format changes to hidden conditional text by selecting Update All in the appropriate designer palette.

The spelling checker only checks text that is displayed. To spell-check all conditional text in a document, select Show All in the Show/Hide Conditional Text dialog box.

If you want to compare the full text of two conditional documents, you must show all conditional text before the comparison. Select Show All in the Show/Hide Conditional Text dialog box.

You can search for the conditional text itself (conditional text that is displayed). To search for conditional text:

1. Select Edit ▶ Find/Change. The Find/Change window opens.

2. From the Find pull-down list, select Conditional Text. The Find Conditional Text dialog box shown in Figure 19.18 opens.

3. Move the conditions you want to find to the In scroll list. To find all conditions, place all condition tags in the As Is scroll list.

4. Click the Set button.

5. In the Find/Change window, click the Find button.

To print a version of the document, set the Show/Hide setting to show the condition tag or tags you want to be printed with the document. When you print, cross-references are automatically updated.

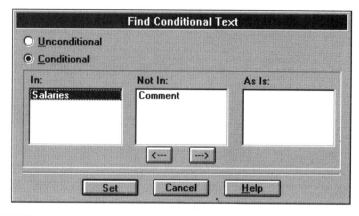

Figure 19.18 **The Find Conditional Text dialog box**

Things to Watch Out for with Conditional Text

When you change the Show/Hide setting to display a different condition tag, the pagination of the document may change. The newly displayed version of the document may have more or less text than the previously displayed version.

Whenever you change the view, display a different condition tag, but do not print the document. Instead, check the document visually to make sure page breaks fall properly, and then manually update all cross-references to check for those that might be unresolved as a result of hiding conditional text.

Change Bars for Marking Changes to Documents

When you edit or revise a document, you may want to visually mark the changes and additions that you've made. This will help you see what the changes and additions are. It can also indicate to a reader (whether it's someone who's reviewing the document or someone who is using the document) what material has changed or been added.

One way to mark all changes and additions is to use *change bars*. (Other ways of marking text changes and additions include changing the text color or using a different character format.) A change bar is a vertical line placed in the margin next to any text or graphic that has changed or been added. A change bar is usually placed in the margin of the page.

Change bars can be added automatically by FrameMaker whenever you make a change. With this technique, however, every change you make will be marked, and that may not be what you want. For example, you may change a word like "steal" to "steel" and not want that marked as a change that's important to notice.

You can also add change bars manually to selected changes and additions. For example, instead of marking every change, you may only want to mark changes that you want a reviewer to notice.

After change bars have been added to a document, you can remove all of them or only individual change bars. For example, when you finish a new document, you may want all the change bars you used in the review process removed.

When change bars are added to text, the paragraph format is changed so that it no longer matches the same format definition as stored in the Paragraph Catalog. If you then update the document by importing paragraph formats from another document and remove format overrides, the change bars will be removed. (You can get the same effect by "importing" formats from the current document and removing overrides.)

For change bars, the distance from the text column, the thickness, the position, and the color can be specified.

You can insert change bars into a newer version of a document by using the Compare Documents utility. For more information, see the section on document comparison later in this chapter.

Adding Change Bars Automatically

If you want every change or addition, no matter how small, to be marked with change bars, you can set FrameMaker to automatically add change bars. To select automatic change bars:

1. Select Format ➤ Document ➤ Change Bars. The Change Bar Properties dialog box opens, as in Figure 19.19.

2. Select Automatic Change Bars by clicking on the box next to the phrase.

3. Click the Set button.

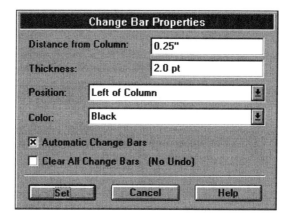

Figure 19.19 **The Change Bar Properties dialog box**

Adding Change Bars Manually

You can add change bars to selected text and to individual paragraphs in several ways. One way is to use the Character Designer, as follows:

1. Select the text you want to mark with change bars.

2. Select Format ➤ Characters ➤ Designer. The Character Designer window opens.

3. Select Change Bar by clicking on the box next to the words.

4. Click the Apply button. A change bar appears next to the selected text.

   Another way to add change bars to selected text is to select the text to be marked and use the keyboard combination *Esc c h*. This combination is a toggle—it can be used to either mark or unmark text.

   A third way to add change bars is to create a character format that adds change bars. If you are going to mark a lot of selected text, this is probably the easiest method. Simply select the text and apply the character format for change bars from the Character Catalog.

   A benefit of this method is that if you update paragraph formats by importing formats from a different document and remove format overrides, the change bars will remain. A drawback of this method, however, is that when you do remove all change bars from a document (per the procedure in the next section), the character tag persists, along with its definition. This can wreak havoc in autogenerated files, and therefore is not recommended.

Removing Change Bars

You can remove all of the change bars in a document or each change bar individually, regardless of how the change bars were added to the document.

▶ To remove all change bars in a document, select Format ➤ Document ➤ Change Bars. In the Change Bar Properties dialog box (Figure 19.19), select Clear All Change Bars and click the Set button.

▶ To remove a change bar from selected text, select the text marked with the change bar. Select Format ➤ Characters ➤ Designer, deselect Change Bars, and click the Apply button.

▶ A quicker way either to add or remove change bars is to select the appropriate text and press *Esc c h*. Text with change bars will lose them, and text without change bars will acquire them.

▶ To remove a change bar from an individual paragraph, place the insertion point by clicking in the paragraph. Select Format ➤ Paragraphs ➤ Designer. On the Default Font properties page, deselect Change Bar. Click the Apply to Selection button.

▶ To remove a change bar applied by a character format, select the text marked by the change bar. Select Format ➤ Characters ➤ Catalog. In the Character Catalog, click on Default ¶ Font. This removes the change bar and the character tag.

Formatting Change Bars

You can specify the characteristics of the change bars you add to documents. The format of change bars is set in the Change Bar Properties dialog box (see Figure 19.19). To open the Change Bar Properties dialog box, select Format ➤ Document ➤ Change Bars.

Set the Distance from Column of the change bar by typing a value into the text box. The distance from the column must be less than the distance of the edge of the paper or an adjacent column. The default distance is a quarter of an inch.

Set the Thickness of the change bar by typing a value in the text box. The thickness should be large enough to see easily, but not so large as to distract from the content of the document. The default thickness is two points.

Set the Position of the change bar by selecting one of the choices from the Position pull-down list. The choices are Left of Column, Right of Column, Side Closer to Page Edge, and Side Farther from Page Edge. On a multicolumn page, you do not want to use Side Farther from Page Edge. This places change bars for both columns in the gap between them and could confuse the reader.

Set the Color of the change bar by selecting a choice from the Color pull-down list. The choices are Black, White, Red, Green, Blue, Cyan, Magenta, and Yellow.

Document Comparison

As you work on a document, you may want to keep different versions of it. Different versions can be compared (two at a time) to see what has changed. Or perhaps you have received a revised document that does not contain change bars or anything else to mark the changed text. You can compare this revised version with the original to see what has changed.

The comparison between the documents looks at text flows with the same names on body and reference pages and checks text, footnotes, markers, anchored frames, tables, text insets, variables, graphics, and cross-references.

Items are compared as follows:

▶ Objects in anchored frames are checked to see if they are the same or in a different position.

▶ Text insets are checked for file name, modification date, relative path name, and how it was imported.

▶ Imported graphics are checked for contents and resolution (dpi).

▶ Equations are checked for size, position in the graphic frame, and the math expressions.

▶ Tables are checked for number of rows and columns, straddled cells, and rotated cells.

Part
5

Advanced Freatures

These items are not checked:

▶ Master page flows

▶ Graphic objects not in anchored frames

▶ Text lines not in anchored frames

▶ Anchored frame positions

▶ Footnote properties or numbers

▶ Character, paragraph, and table tags

▶ Text or table formatting

▶ Tags in the character, paragraph, or table catalogs

▶ Text in text insets

Comparing Documents

When documents are compared, FrameMaker creates two documents so you can see the results. The first document is a general summary and a list of revisions between the documents. When the comparison is finished, the summary document is opened and made active. The summary document considers differences to be either insertions, deletions, or changes. The summary document has the name *summary* (Windows, Macintosh, and UNIX). Hypertext links between the summary document and the source document can be created. These links can be used to quickly access the changes in the source document.

The second document is a composite document that shows the differences in the documents side by side. Each compared document that has differences creates a composite document. The composite document considers differences to be either insertions or deletions. The composite document is named the same as the newer version of the document: NEWERDOC.CMP (Windows), *newerdoc*CMP (Macintosh), or *newerdoc*CMP (UNIX).

The composite document is a conditional document. You can choose and change the condition tag you want to apply to the entries. When using the default condition tags (Inserted and Deleted), the changed text in the composite document is red to show deletions and green to show insertions.

To compare two versions of a document:

1. Open both versions of the document.

2. With the newer version of the document active, select File ➤ Utilities ➤ Compare Documents. The Compare Documents dialog box shown in Figure 19.20 opens.

3. Select the older version of the document by using the Older Document pull-down list. The Older Document pull-down list shows all open, named documents.

4. Select which documents you want created, both the Summary and Composite Documents or the Summary Document Only.

5. To set up the comparison options, click the Options button. The Comparison Options dialog box opens, as in Figure 19.21.

6. Select the options you want to use. For more information on options, see "Ways to Compare Documents" later in this section. Click the Set button when you're finished.

7. Click the Compare button.

    If there are differences between the documents, the summary document will be displayed when the comparison is finished. If the composite document is selected, it will also be displayed. If there are no differences between the documents, an alert will be displayed and no documents will be created. The summary and composite documents can be saved for future use.

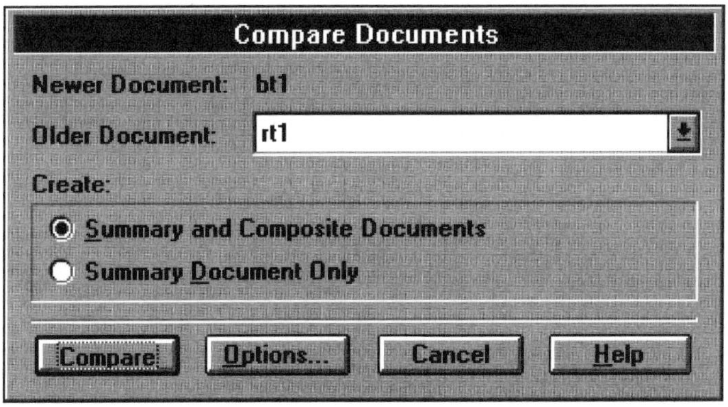

Part
5

Advanced Freatures

Figure 19.20   The Compare Documents dialog box

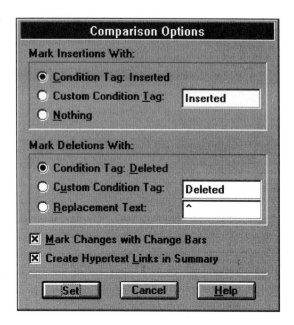

Figure 19.21   ***The Comparison Options dialog box***

Two documents with conditional text can have their full text compared by showing all conditions before beginning the comparison. Comparing some conditions from each document is a bit harder. Separate documents must be created showing the tags of the conditions you want compared. All other condition tags must be deleted.

In documents with multiple flows, FrameMaker compares only flows with the same names. Therefore, be sure that each flow you want compared has a tag that is different from the others in the document.

Ways to Compare Documents

You can select how to mark text in the composite document that has been inserted and deleted and you can create a hypertext linked summary document. Use the Comparison Options dialog box (see Figure 19.21) to set the comparison options.

Marking Insertions

You can select how to mark the inserted text in the composite document. Remember that in the composite document all changes are considered insertions and deletions. Note that in the composite document all conditional text is displayed and all condition indicators are on.

Inserted text can be marked with:

▶ The default Condition Tag *Inserted*. The condition indicators are green and text is underlined.

▶ A Custom Condition Tag you specify.

▶ Nothing.

Marking Deletions

You can select how to mark the deleted text in the composite document. Remember that in the composite document all changes are considered insertions and deletions. Note that in the composite document all conditional text is displayed and all condition indicators are on.

Deleted text can be marked with:

▶ The default Condition Tag *Deleted*. The condition indicators are red and text is "struck through."

▶ A Custom Condition Tag you specify.

▶ Replacement Text that can be anything. For example, you can replace the deleted text with the word *Deleted*. If you don't want the deleted text to show, select Replacement Text and leave the text box blank.

Marking Changes with Change Bars

You can mark all changes in the composite document with change bars. The change bars will be formatted using the settings in the Change Bar dialog box (Format ▶ Document ▶ Change Bars). For more information on change bars, see Change Bars earlier in this chapter. To mark all changes with change bars, select Mark Changes with Change Bars.

A quick way to add change bars to all changes in a newer version of a document without marking inserted text or showing deleted text is to compare documents. Select two versions of a document. Compare the documents with the following Comparison Options: Mark Insertions With Nothing; Mark Deletions With Replacement Text and leave the text

Part
5

Advanced Freatures

box blank; and Mark Changes with Change Bars selected. The composite document will be a copy of the newer version of the document with all changes marked with change bars. Save the composite document with a new name.

Hypertext Links in the Summary Document

Hypertext links between the summary document and the source document can be created. These links allow you to quickly access the newer version of the document, the older version of the document, and the composite document.

In a summary document with hypertext links, the page numbers are active areas. Simply click on the page number of a change, and the corresponding document (composite, newer version, older version) will be opened. To create hypertext links in the summary document, select Create Hypertext Links in Summary. For more information on hypertext and view-only documents, see Chapter 18.

Creating and Formatting Equations

You can create typeset equations by inserting an equation object into a document and then inserting math objects (numbers, symbols, operators, etc.) into the equation object. The equation is inserted into an anchored frame, where it can be formatted and edited. The equation's mathematical syntax is automatically adjusted.

FrameMaker understands the meaning of the math symbols it contains, and can evaluate equations according to the elements "definition." If a math element you need isn't available from the choices provided by FrameMaker, or if an element is not displayed in the form you want, you can create a new element (with its own custom definition) or edit the definition of an existing one. You can also "shrink-wrap" equations to fit in as small a space as possible.

Creating Equations

An equation is inserted into an anchored frame that is automatically created to hold it. An equation (and its anchored frame) can be placed within paragraph text so it will appear as an in-line equation, or in its own paragraph so it will appear as a "displayed" equation, separated from the text above and below it.

TIP If the characters in an equation are difficult to read on the monitor screen, zoom in until they are easy to read.

To create an equation:

1. Click in the document where you want to insert the equation (within the text of a paragraph, in a separate paragraph, or in a graphic frame). If you want to place an equation in a rotated text frame, you must unrotate the frame (to zero).

2. Select Special ➤ Equations or click on the Equations button in the document window.

The Equations window (another palette) opens.

3. Select a new equation command from the Equations pull-down menu. The commands available are New Small Equation, New Medium Equation, and New Large Equation. Small, Medium, and Large designate the font size used in the equation.

4. An anchored frame appears containing an "equation object," which is initially displayed as a question mark.

5. You are now ready to insert "math elements"—mathematical symbols and expressions—into the equation object. To do this, read on.

Math Elements

Once you have created an equation object, you can insert any math elements you wish into it. A math element can be an alphanumeric character, a symbol, an operator, or a string. When a math element is inserted into an equation, the mathematical syntax of the equation is automatically adjusted. For example, the math element in a fraction will be properly positioned depending on which part of the fraction is selected—the numerator, the denominator, or the whole fraction. You can edit math element definitions and create custom definitions.

Inserting Characters, Numbers, and Other Math Symbols

You can insert alphanumeric characters by simply typing them on the keyboard. You can insert any item in the Equations window by clicking on it. You can also use the keyboard to insert Equations window items (without opening the Equations window) by using backslash sequences. For information on backslash sequences, see FrameMaker's online help.

The Equations palette contains nine pages of math elements and commands. These are shown in Figure 19.22. You can select any page of elements by clicking on its name at the top of the palette.

The Equations window offers the following symbols:

Page	Symbols
Symbols	Greek characters, atomic symbols, diacritical marks, and strings. The Symbols page appears when you first open the Equations window.
Large	Sums, products, integrals, intersections, and unions.
Relations	Signs that show equals, less than, greater than, similar to, subset of, superset of, and proportional to.
Matrices	Matrices and matrix commands.
Operators	Roots, powers, signs, subscripts, superscripts, and logic symbols.
Delimiters	Parentheses, brackets, braces, and substitution symbols.
Calculus	Integrals, derivatives, partial derivatives, gradients, and limits.
Functions	Trigonometric, hyperbolic, and logarithmic function symbols. The Functions page also contains commands for evaluating equations and for creating and applying rules.
Positioning	Controls to adjust the position of an expression in an equation and the spacing around the expression.

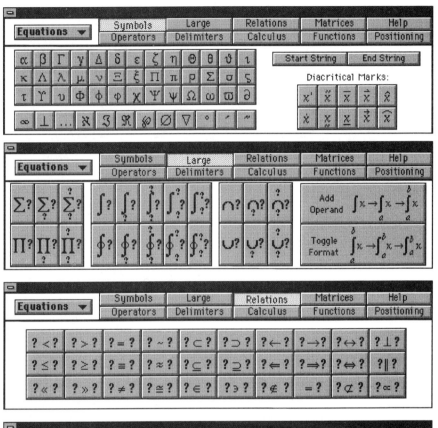

Figure 19.22   The Equations window

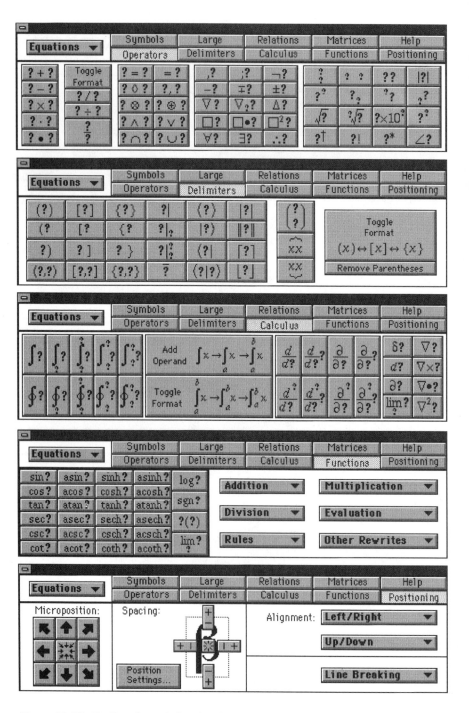

Figure 19.22   *The Equations window (continued)*

To insert a math element:

1. Select an insert point in the equation, or select an element or term of the equation.

2. If you're using the keyboard, type the math element. If you're using the Equations window, click on the page containing the math element you wish to insert and then click on the element symbol.

To insert a custom math element:

1. With the Equations window open, select an insert point in the equation, or select an element or term.

2. Select Insert Math Element from the Equations pull-down menu. The Insert Math Element dialog box opens.

3. Click on the custom math element you want to insert and click the Insert button. (See below for creating custom math elements.)

Creating and Redefining Math Elements

You can create and define a custom math element or redefine an existing math element. You can also update all math elements in the current document with definitions from another document.

Custom math element definitions are stored on special reference pages with names that begin with *FrameMath* (for example, FrameMath1). Each custom math element's definition is a text line in an unanchored graphic frame with the same name as the custom math element.

NOTE   The following types of math elements can be defined or redefined: atom, infix, prefix, postfix, delimiter, large, vertical list, function, and limit. The following types of math elements cannot be defined or redefined: script, derivative, diacritical mark, matrix, roots, substitution, vertical division bar, and horizontal list.

You can define or redefine a math element, but you cannot change its type. To create a custom math element or redefine a built-in math element:

1. From a Body page of a document, select View ➤ Reference Pages.

2. If a FrameMath reference page does not exist, create one named FrameMath1.

Part 5

Advanced Freatures

3. If there are FrameMath reference pages, display one.

4. Draw an unanchored graphic frame on the reference page. The Frame name dialog box opens.

5. Type the name of the custom math element. Or, if you're redefining a built-in math element, use the name of the existing math element. Click the Set button.

6. Add a text line to the graphic frame.

7. Insert a math element in the text line.

8. Select the graphic frame.

9. Open the Equations window by clicking the Equations button.

10. Choose Add Definition to Catalog from the Equations pull-down menu. The Add Math Element Definition dialog box opens.

11. Select the type of math element you are creating from the Type pull-down list.

12. Click the Add button.

To change a custom math element definition:

1. Display the special reference page (name FrameMath) that contains the custom math element definition. You can also select the custom math element in an equation and select Update Definitions from the Equations pull-down menu in the Equations palette.

2. Edit the text line containing the definition.

3. When you return to the body pages (View ➤ Body Pages), the custom math element will be modified.

To delete a custom math element definition, delete the graphic frame on the FrameMath reference page that contains the definition. If the math element appears in an equation, it will be surrounded by question marks.

Editing Equations

Once you have created an equation and inserted math elements, you can add, rearrange, or delete math elements (built-in and custom). You can select math elements by:

▶ Clicking and holding the mouse button next to a math element and dragging to select.

▶ Pressing the spacebar once to extend the selection to the next element.

▶ Pressing the spacebar twice to extend the selection to the next higher expression.

You can cut, copy, and paste math elements. You can also delete math elements, expressions, and entire equations, and you can delete the anchored frame containing an equation object. Simply select the math element, expression, equation, or anchored frame and press the Backspace or Delete key.

Formatting Equations

Math elements are automatically positioned according to their mathematical definition when inserted into an equation. However, once inserted, you can change the font, spacing, positioning, and alignment of the math elements in an equation.

Using the Positioning page of the Equations window, you can:

▶ Position the element or expression in small increments by using the arrow buttons in the Microposition area. The center square restores the element to its original position.

▶ Adjust the spacing around a math element or expression by using the Spacing area to add space above, below, to the left, or to the right.

▶ Set the alignment of an equation by selecting a setting from the Left/Right and Up/Down pull-down lists.

▶ Set manual line breaking characteristics of an equation by selecting either Manual (you add a manual line break) or Clear (removes a manual line break) from the Line Breaking pull-down list.

Evaluating Equations

Use the command groups on the Functions page of the Equations window to evaluate equations or parts of equations. These commands include operations associated with:

▶ Addition

▶ Multiplication

▶ Division

▶ Evaluation

▶ Creating and applying rules

See FrameMaker's online help for good descriptions of the exact operation of each of these commands.

HyperText Markup Language with FrameMaker

Hypertext Markup Language (HTML) is a descriptive language used on the World Wide Web. It is used to create hypermedia documents for Web browsers such as Mosaic and Netscape. HTML consists primarily of text, graphics, and tags that supply the Web browser with the information to display the text and graphics.

HTML tags provide the formatting (appearance) information used by Web browsers to display text and graphics. HTML tags are not displayed by the Web browser. The tags usually, but not always, come as pairs, an opening tag and a closing tag identified by a slash (/). The following are examples of HTML tags:

\<title\> \</title\>	Text between these tags appears in the Document Title area of a browser.
\<h1\> \</h1\>	Text between these tags appears as a large heading.
\<strong\> \</strong\>	Text between these tags appears in boldface.
\<em\> \</em\>	Text between these tags appears in italics.

An HTML document that can be accessed over the Web by a browser is referred to as a *Web page.* A Web page can contain text, graphics, and hypertext links to other parts of the document, different HTML documents, and even different HTML documents at other sites. You can create a Web page by using any text editor or word processor to insert HTML tags into the text of a document.

There are disadvantages to using the manual insertion method. Besides the work of inserting HTML into text (at the start and the end), revising a Web page that contains the HTML tags can be difficult and confusing.

FrameMaker comes bundled with WebWorks HTML Lite from Quadralay Corporation, a conversion program that converts FrameMaker documents to HTML documents. HTML Lite maps paragraph tags in a FrameMaker document to HTML tags and automatically inserts these tags into the correct locations in the document. The resulting text file can be opened by a Web browser and will be formatted correctly.

After installation of the Quadralay program, which should have occurred during FrameMaker installation, HTML Lite functions are made available from the File ➤ Utilities pull-down menu. Selections include HTML Mappings, HTML Convert, and HTML Info. To use these functions, you must have a FrameMaker document open.

For more information on HyperText Markup Language and WebWorks HTML Lite from Quadralay Corporation, refer to the HTML Lite manual and to the online help available from the HTML Lite notes file.

Part
5

Advanced Freatures

Appendices

Appendix A

Installing FrameMaker

This appendix presents installation information for all platforms (Windows, Macintosh, and UNIX). It also explains how to use FrameMaker's built-in introduction and tutorial.

Except for the UNIX version, installing FrameMaker is simple. When you install the UNIX version of the program, you have to make decisions about network and workgroup configuration, as well as decide on issues that deal with licensing daemons (yes, for you UNIX novices, "daemon" is a word). Few UNIX programs—FrameMaker included—are easy to install.

All about Your Serial Number

With each copy of the program (or, for UNIX users, with each purchased license), you receive a serial number in seven chunks in the form 00-0-01-01-5-999FF-123ABC. A serial number is actually several numbers. The first five chunks (00-0-01-01-5, for example) have a meaning for FrameMaker. They identify the product, the vendor, the version, and so on. The sixth chunk is a unique five-digit hexadecimal number for the copy of the product identified in the first five units. (A hexadecimal, or "hex," number is one that includes the counting numbers 1 through 9 as well as the letters A through F.)

These six chunks are displayed when you ask to see information about your program (by selecting Help ➤ Help About, for example, in Windows installations).

The seventh unit, the six-digit hexadecimal number, is critical. You will never see it displayed on the screen. (Windows users can find it in maker.ini, however, under RegNum.) FrameMaker has developed a coding (encryption) algorithm that takes the first six units of the serial number and translates them in a secret way into a six-digit hex number (in the example, 123ABC).

This is the number they gave you as part of your serial number. When you enter this seven-chunk serial number into FrameMaker during installation, the installer program checks the coding of the first six chunks against the seventh chunk. If that coding is incorrect, you're "hosed," as programmers say, and you cannot continue with the installation.

The bottom line is: Keep that number! It's the secret sauce that allows you to install FrameMaker.

Installing FrameMaker for Windows

To install FrameMaker for Windows, start by opening the package. You'll find:

▶ The installation disks

▶ The installation book (*Installing FrameMaker*)

▶ The small sheet of stick-on labels that contains your magic serial number

You may wish to read through *Installing FrameMaker* to familiarize yourself with the installation procedure, though installing the program is pretty straightforward.

Make sure you use the stick-on serial number labels appropriately. You are given several—one could go on one of the disks, one in the installation book, and one on the support information card. The serial number is important, since you cannot install FrameMaker without it.

The preliminaries over, you can start installing FrameMaker:

1. Insert Disk 1 into drive A (or B).

2. In the Program Manager, select File ➤ Run.

3. Type **a:\setup** (or **b:\setup**) in the Run dialog box and click the OK button.

4. Follow the instructions on the screen. (Be sure to type the serial number exactly, including the dashes. You don't want to have to type it twice!)

During installation, you are asked where to install FrameMaker and which of its many options you wish to put on your hard disk. It's all pretty self-explanatory. When the installation is complete, install the WebWorks HTML Lite product:

1. Insert the single HTML Lite disk into drive A or B.

2. Select File ➤ Run.

3. Enter **a:\setup** or **b:\setup** and click OK.

When the installation is complete, you will have a Program Manager group called Frame Products with two icons, one called FrameMaker and one called HTML Lite Notes, as in Figure A.1. Turn to Chapter 1 if you want to learn how to use FrameMaker.

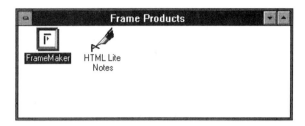

Figure A.1   **Frame Products icons (Windows)**

Installing FrameMaker for the Macintosh

Installing FrameMaker on the Mac is easy. First, open the package. You'll find:

▶ The installation disks

▶ The installation book (*Installing FrameMaker*)

▶ A small sheet of stick-on labels that contains your magic serial number

You may wish to read through *Installing FrameMaker* to familiarize yourself with the installation procedure, though it is pretty straightforward.

Make sure you use the stick-on serial number labels correctly. You are given several—for the disks, one for the installation book, and one for the support information card. The serial number is important, since you cannot install FrameMaker without it.

Now you're ready to get to the nitty-gritty:

1. Insert Disk 1 into a high-density disk drive. A window opens to show the contents of the disk, as in Figure A.2.

Figure A.2   **FrameMaker Installation Disk window (Mac)**

Appendices

2. Double-click on the ReadMeFirst icon and read the file to get the latest installation information.

3. Double-click on the FrameMaker Installer icon.

 NOTE On some machines, FrameMaker requires the presence of the Apple Shared Library Manager (ASLM). If ASLM is not installed, the FrameMaker Installer program will ask you to install it. ASLM software is provided on a separate disk.

During installation, you are asked where to install FrameMaker and, if you opted for a custom installation, which of its many options you wish to put on your hard disk.

When the installation is complete, install the WebWorks HTML Lite product:

1. Insert the single HTML Lite disk into a high-density drive.

2. Double-click on the floppy disk icon to open it.

3. Double-click on the README file and follow the installation instructions. Among other things, you will be asked to specify an HTML Lite installation folder.

When you are done, you will see a FrameMaker installation folder (named as you specified during installation) that looks like the one in Figure A.3. It contains these items:

▶ The FrameMaker5 program file

▶ A number of folders used by the program

▶ Three files—the overview document (see Figure A.3), a Frame Installer Log file, and a ReadMeFirst file

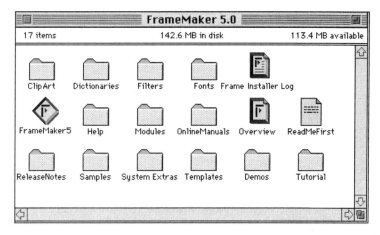

Figure A.3   **The FrameMaker folder after the installation is complete (Mac)**

You also have an HTML Lite installation folder that has, among other things, the HTML Lite README file icon, as shown in Figure A.4. Go to Chapter 1 if you need to know how to start the program.

Figure A.4   **The HTML Lite README file icon (Mac)**

Installing FrameMaker for UNIX

Installing the program on the UNIX platform can be done from either a tape drive or CD-ROM drive. Installing the program requires the use of FrameMaker's installation scripts. The following instructions assume you have read the installation manual, *Installing Frame Products*. The instructions here are provided only as a general guide, or overview, of installing FrameMaker for UNIX.

WARNING   Installing the UNIX version of FrameMaker involves making a number of important configuration decisions concerning the product (if you are a system manager for a workgroup) and the user's access to the product. You'll find information about installing FrameMaker for UNIX in the manual, *Installing Frame Products*. Read the manual carefully before you begin and refer to it often.

Installing FrameMaker for UNIX involves these general steps:

1. Create the directory into which FrameMaker will be installed. You must create a new, empty directory, even if you already have a version of FrameMaker on your system.

2. Load the CD-ROM or the tape into the appropriate drive. (On a network, the drive does not have to be local to your machine.)

3. Mount the CD-ROM or tape, if necessary. (*Installing Frame Products* offers excellent instructions for this step, if you need them.)

4. If you are root, exit and become yourself. (Only in the UNIX world does that sentence make sense!) It's best not to install FrameMaker as root.

5. If you are installing from a CD-ROM drive, change to the cdrom directory and run the installation script (**./read.cd**).

6. If you are installing from a tape drive, change to your installation directory, "tar" the script into that directory by typing:

   ```
   tar —xf
   ```

   and then run the script that installs the rest of the product from tape (**./readtape**).

7. Follow the instructions on the screen. You will be asked what options and languages you want to install. After you answer all the questions, get lunch. The process takes a while.

8. Check the installation by entering **bin/fmcheckinstall**. It's a good idea not to skip this step, even though you will probably find the installation went well. Go get lunch again.

9. Decide how to set up your user accounts.

   Frame provides a script for that (fmusersetup, in the install directory), but there are lots of options. Read Chapter 2 of *Installing Frame Products* and then think through how you want your users to use the product.

   The bare minimum is to define FMHOME for each user and to make sure they all have execute permission in their home directories. After that, I would add **$FMHOME/bin** to each user's path (if only one version of the program is installed at your site), or create an alias or script that sets FMHOME and calls maker for each version of FrameMaker the user has access to.

10. Deal with licensing. To do that, read Chapter 3 of *Installing Frame Products*, run the script fmsetupfls (this script sets up the license server, adds new licenses, creates other scripts needed by the license server, and sets up log files), set up user environments for workgroup operation if necessary, and set up personal licenses if necessary.

    Modify the startup scripts for the machine that will act as the network license server so that the Frame license server program will be restarted when that system is rebooted.

TIP If you are setting up a network installation for more users than yourself and you are using shared licenses, I recommend setting up FrameMaker as a workgroup installation, even though there may be only one (large) workgroup. A workgroup installation provides maximum flexibility in installation and customization, and is no more difficult to do than a standard installation. It may not be obvious right away why this advice is useful, but down the road you may be glad you followed it.

Using the FrameMaker Introduction and Tutorial

The first time you start FrameMaker after you install it, you see an introduction document called *Overview*. The first page is titled "Welcome to FrameMaker"! This is a good introduction to the product, and if you are a first-time user, I would take a few minutes to review it. (It's pretty short—it's not going to tie you up for long.)

After you close the document for the first time, it does not show up automatically again. To see it a second (or third) time, you have to open it. You can do that in one of two ways:

▶ Select File, and look at the list of recently opened files at the end of the File menu. A document named Overview may be listed there. If so, select it.

▶ Select Help ➤ FrameMaker Overview.

 NOTE On the last page of the overview document is an item you can click on to go straight to the tutorial.

The FrameMaker tutorial takes longer to work through, but it's pretty effective. To use the tutorial, select Help ➤ Tutorial. Then read the introduction, or click on the Lessons button to see a list of lessons to go to.

On the first page of the Tutorial, you can click on an item that takes you to the Overview document.

 NOTE Once you start the tutorial, FrameMaker closes any document you are currently working on. If there are unsaved edits, you will be prompted to save your changes.

Appendix B

FrameMaker Templates

A s you saw in Chapter 6, FrameMaker comes with some pretty useful templates. This appendix shows what the templates look like and provides descriptions of the tags in the Paragraph and Character Catalogs. Use this information when you work with these templates.

Business Templates

The business templates subdirectory contains templates for these kinds of documents:

▶ Letter

▶ Memo

▶ Fax cover page (with blank message page)

▶ Viewgraphs (tall and wide)

▶ Envelope

▶ Business cards (eight to a page)

Let's look at them one at a time. As you look at them, notice how well-coordinated they are—how Heading1, for example, has the same definition in each document. If you modify these templates or you design your own set, be sure to maintain this coordination.

Business Letter Template

The business letter template is shown in Figure B.1. The following list describes the paragraph formats, or tags, in the business letter template.

Paragraph Tag	Used For/Comments
Body	Used for body text paragraphs. Ten-point Times; 9 points space above.
Bulleted	Used for bulleted paragraphs. Uses character tag BulletSymbol to format the bullet; creates a hanging indent; 4 points space above.

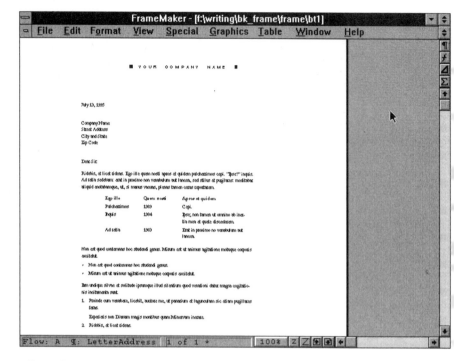

Figure B.1 *The business letter template*

Paragraph Tag	Used For/Comments
CellBody	Used for table cell paragraphs. Ten-point Times.
CellHeading	Used for table headings. Ten-point Times bold.
CompanyAddress	Used for the company address paragraph at the bottom of the letter. Eight-point Helvetica; 50-percent spread; the square bullets are rectangles inside anchored frames.

Paragraph Tag	Used For/Comments
CompanyName	Used for the company name paragraph at the top of the letter. Eight-point Helvetica; 50-percent spread; the square bullets are rectangles inside anchored frames.
Footnote	Used for footnotes. Ten-point Times.
Heading1	Used for first-level headings. Fourteen-point Times bold; 16 points space above.
Heading2	Used for second-level headings. Twelve-point Times bold; 12 points space above.
HeadingRunIn	Used for headings that run into the start of the next paragraph. Ten-point Times bold; 9 points space above; Next ¶ Tag = Body.
Indented	Used for indented paragraphs under paragraphs tagged Bulleted and Numbered. Four points space above.
LetterAddress	Used for the address lines (each of which is a paragraph) at the top of the letter. No space above or below.
LetterAuthor	Used for the "author name" paragraph and the "author title" paragraph. No space above or below.
LetterClose	Used for the "Sincerely" paragraph of the letter. Creates the space above and below the closing.

Paragraph Tag	Used For/Comments
LetterOpen	Used for the "Dear Joe" paragraph of the letter. Creates the space above and below the letter opening.
Numbered	Used for numbered paragraphs. Numbers start with the next available number from previous numbered paragraphs; creates a hanging indent for the number; 4 points space above.
Numbered1	Used for numbered paragraphs beginning with 1. Always restarts list numbering at 1; creates a hanging indent paragraph; 4 points space above; Next ¶ Tag = Numbered.
TableFootnote	Used for footnotes in tables. Ten-point Times.
TableTitle	Used for table titles. Ten-point Times bold.

The following list describes the character formats, or tags, in the business letter template.

Character Tag	Used For/Comments
Default ¶ Font	Used for default paragraph font. Resets characters to the paragraph-defined default.
BulletSymbol	Used to format the bullet symbol in paragraphs tagged Bulleted. Ten-point Courier bold.
Emphasis	Used to format emphasized text. Angle italic; everything else As Is.
EquationVariables	Used to format variables in equations. Angle italic; everything else As Is.

Business Memo Template

The business memo template is shown in Figure B.2. The following list describes the paragraph formats, or tags, in the business memo template.

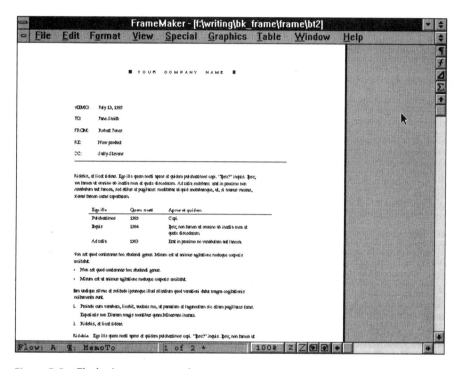

Figure B.2 **The business memo template**

Paragraph Tag	Used For/Comments
Body	Used for body text paragraphs. Ten-point Times; 9 points space above.
Bulleted	Used for bulleted paragraphs. Uses character tag BulletSymbol to format the bullet; creates a hanging indent; 4 points space above.

Paragraph Tag	Used For/Comments
CellBody	Used for table cell paragraphs. Ten-point Times.
CellHeading	Used for table headings. Ten-point Times bold.
CompanyAddress	Used for the company address paragraph at the bottom of the memo. Eight-point Helvetica; 50-percent spread; the square bullets are rectangles inside anchored frames.
CompanyName	Used for the company name paragraph at the top of the memo. Eight-point Helvetica; 50-percent spread; the square bullets are rectangles inside anchored frames.
Footnote	Used for footnotes. Ten-point Times.
Heading1	Used for first-level headings. Fourteen-point Times bold; 16 points space above.
Heading2	Used for second-level headings. Twelve-point Times bold; 12 points space above.
HeadingRunIn	Used for headings that run into the start of the next paragraph. Ten-point Times bold; 9 points space above; Next ¶ Tag = Body.
Indented	Used for indented paragraphs under paragraphs tagged Bulleted and Numbered. Four points space above.

Paragraph Tag	Used For/Comments
MemoCC	Used for the "CC" paragraph. Uses Labels character tag to format the label "CC:"; Next ¶ Tag = Body; 16 points space below; Frame Below creates ruling line.
MemoFrom	Used for the "FROM" paragraph. Uses Labels character tag to format the label "FROM:"; Next ¶ Tag = MemoSubject.
MemoSubject	Used for the "RE" paragraph. Uses Labels character tag to format the label "RE:"; Next ¶ Tag = MemoCC.
MemoTo	Used for the "TO" paragraph. Uses Labels character tag to format the label "TO:"; Next ¶ Tag = MemoFrom.
Numbered	Used for numbered paragraphs. Numbers start with the next available number from previous numbered paragraphs; creates a hanging indent for the number; 4 points space above.
Numbered1	Used for numbered paragraphs beginning with 1. Always restarts list numbering at 1; creates a hanging indent paragraph; 4 points space above; Next ¶ Tag = Numbered.
TableFootnote	Used for footnotes in tables. Ten-point Times.
TableTitle	Used for table titles. Ten-point Times bold.

The following list describes the character formats, or tags, in the business memo template.

Character Tag	Used For/Comments
Default ¶ Font	Used for default paragraph font. Resets characters to the paragraph-defined default.
BulletSymbol	Used to format the bullet symbol in paragraphs tagged Bulleted. Ten-point Courier bold.
Emphasis	Used to format emphasized text. Angle italic; everything else As Is.
EquationVariables	Used to format variables in equations. Angle italic; everything else As Is.
Labels	Used to format the autonumbered labels "TO," "FROM," etc. Nine-point Times.

Fax Cover Page Template

The fax cover page template is shown in Figure B.3. The following list describes the paragraph formats, or tags, in the fax cover page template.

Paragraph Tag	Used For/Comments
Body	Used for body text paragraphs. Ten-point Times; 9 points space above.
Bulleted	Used for bulleted paragraphs. Uses character tag BulletSymbol to format the bullet; creates a hanging indent; 4 points space above.
CellBody	Used for table cell paragraphs. Ten-point Times.
CellHeading	Used for table headings. Ten-point Times bold.

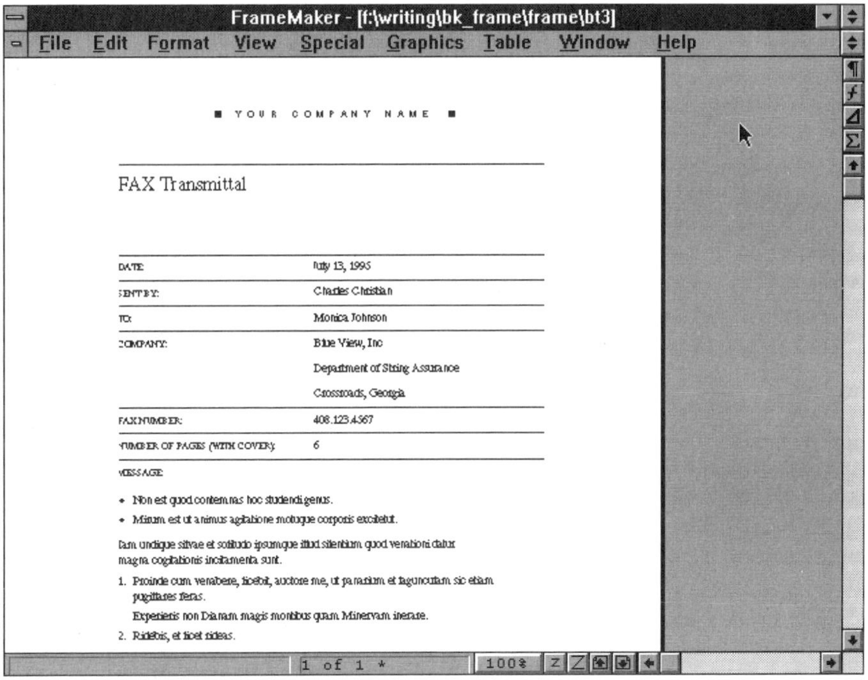

Figure B.3   *The fax cover page template*

Paragraph Tag	Used For/Comments
CompanyAddress	Used for the company address paragraph at the bottom of the fax form. Eight-point Helvetica; 50-percent spread; the square bullets are rectangles inside anchored frames.
CompanyName	Used for the company name paragraph at the top of the fax form. Eight-point Helvetica; 50-percent spread; the square bullets are rectangles inside anchored frames.
Footnote	Used for footnotes. Ten-point Times.

Paragraph Tag	Used For/Comments
Heading1	Used for first-level headings. Fourteen-point Times bold; 16 points space above.
Heading2	Used for second-level headings. Twelve-point Times bold; 12 points space above.
Indented	Used for indented paragraphs under paragraphs tagged Bulleted and Numbered. Four points space above.
Numbered	Used for numbered paragraphs. Numbers start with the next available number from previous numbered paragraphs; 4 points space above.
Numbered1	Used for numbered paragraphs beginning with 1. Always restarts list numbering at 1; creates a hanging indent paragraph; 4 points space above; Next ¶ Tag = Numbered.
TableFootnote	Used for footnotes in tables. Ten-point Times
TableTitle	Used for table titles. Ten-point Times bold.

The following list describes the character formats, or tags, in the fax cover page template.

Character Tag	Used For/Comments
Default ¶ Font	Used for default paragraph font. Resets characters to the paragraph-defined default.
BulletSymbol	Used to format the bullet symbol in paragraphs tagged Bulleted. Ten-point Courier bold.

Character Tag	Used For/Comments
Emphasis	Used to format emphasized text. Angle italic; everything else As Is.
EquationVariables	Used to format variables in equations. Angle italic; everything else As Is.

Viewgraph Templates

The tall viewgraph template is shown in Figure B.4. The wide viewgraph template is shown in Figure B.5.

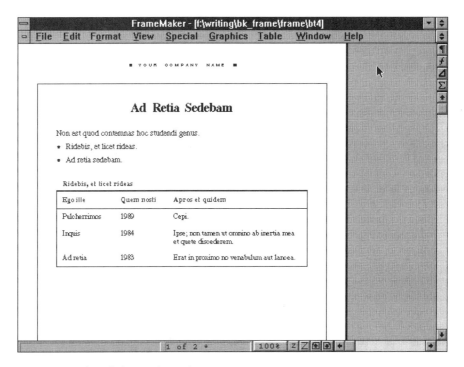

Figure B.4 **The tall viewgraph template**

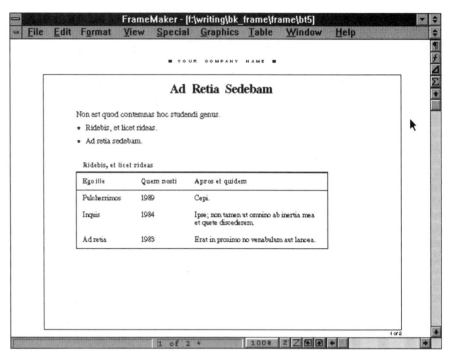

Figure B.5 **The wide viewgraph template**

The following list describes the paragraph formats, or tags, in the viewgraph templates.

Paragraph Tag	Used For/Comments
Body	Used for body text paragraphs. Sixteen-point Times; 12 points space above.
Bulleted	Used for bulleted paragraphs. Uses character tag BulletSymbol to format the bullet; creates a hanging indent; 6 points space above.
CellBody	Used for table cell paragraphs. Fourteen-point Times.
CellHeading	Used for table headings. Fourteen-point Times bold.

Paragraph Tag	Used For/Comments
Footnote	Used for footnotes. Twelve-point Times.
Heading1	Used for the centered title of the viewgraph. twenty-four-point Times bold; no space above; twenty-four-points space below.
Heading2	Used for headings in the viewgraph. Sixteen-point Times bold; 24 points space above; 9 points space below.
Indented	Used for indented paragraphs under paragraphs tagged Bulleted and Numbered. Six points space above.
Numbered	Used for numbered paragraphs. Numbers start with the next available number from previous numbered paragraphs; 6 points space above.
Numbered1	Used for numbered paragraphs beginning with 1. Always restarts list numbering at 1; creates a hanging indent paragraph; 6 points space above; Next ¶ Tag = Numbered.
TableFootnote	Used for footnotes in tables. Twelve-point Times.
TableTitle	Used for table titles. Fourteen-point Times bold.

The following list describes the character formats, or tags, in the viewgraph templates.

Character Tag	Used For/Comments
Default ¶ Font	Used for default paragraph font. Resets characters to the paragraph-defined default.

Appendices

Character Tag	Used For/Comments
BulletSymbol	Used to format the bullet symbol in paragraphs tagged Bulleted. Sixteen-point Courier bold.
Emphasis	Used to format emphasized text. Angle italic; everything else As Is.
EquationVariables	Used to format variables in equations. Angle italic; everything else As Is.

Business Envelope Template

The business envelope template is shown in Figure B.6. The following list describes the paragraph formats, or tags, in the business envelope template.

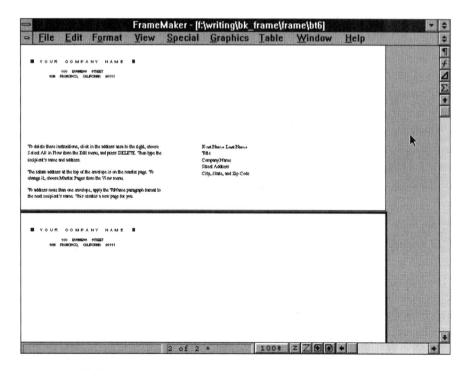

Figure B.6   *The business envelope template*

Paragraph Tag	Used For/Comments
CompanyAddress	Used for the company address paragraph in the return address of the envelope. Seven-point Helvetica; no spread.
CompanyName	Used for the company name paragraph in the return address of the envelope. Eight-point Helvetica; 50-percent spread; the square bullets are rectangles inside anchored frames.
ToAddress	Used for the address lines of the envelope (each of which is a separate paragraph). No space above or below.
ToName	Used for the name of the addressee. No space above or below.

The following list describes the character formats, or tags, in the business envelope template.

Character Tag	Used For/Comments
Default ¶ Font	Used for default paragraph font. Resets characters to the paragraph-defined default.
Emphasis	Used to format emphasized text. Angle italic; everything else As Is.
EquationVariables	Used to format variables in equations. Angle italic; everything else As Is.

Business Cards Template

The business cards template is shown in Figure B.7. The following list describes the paragraph formats, or tags, in the business cards template.

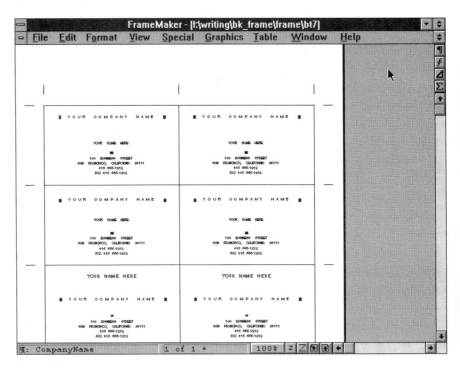

Figure B.7   The business cards template

Paragraph Tag	Used For/Comments
CompanyAddress	Used for the company address at the bottom of the letter. Seven-point Helvetica; no spread; the square bullets are rectangles inside anchored frames.

Paragraph Tag	Used For/Comments
CompanyName	Used for the company name at the top of the letter. Eight-point Helvetica; 50-percent spread; the square bullets are rectangles inside anchored frames.
YourNameLarge	Used for the name on the cards with large names. Ten-point Helvetica.
YourNameSmall	Used for the name on the cards with small names. Seven-point Helvetica.

The following list describes the character formats, or tags, in the business cards template.

Character Tag	Used For/Comments
Default ¶ Font	Used for default paragraph font. Resets characters to the paragraph-defined default.
Emphasis	Used to format emphasized text. Angle italic; everything else As Is.
EquationVariables	Used to format variables in equations. Angle italic; everything else As Is.

Reports Templates

The reports templates subdirectory offers three report styles:

▶ Plain (simple formatting, numbered headings)

▶ Numbered (fancy formatting, numbered headings)

▶ Sidehead (fancy formatting, unnumbered side-headings)

In addition to body page formatting, each of these templates has reference pages with specifications for a table of contents, list of figures, list of tables, and index. Thus, these templates can also be used as templates for generated files that contain these lists.

Appendices

Plain Report Template

The "plain" report template is shown in Figure B.8. The following list describes the paragraph formats, or tags, in the "plain" report template.

Paragraph Tag	Used For/Comments
Body	Used for body text paragraphs. Twelve-point Times; 12 points space above; 6 points space below.
Bulleted	Used for bulleted paragraphs. Uses character tag BulletSymbol to format the bullet; creates a hanging indent; 6 points space above.
BulletedCont	Used for indented paragraphs under paragraphs tagged Bulleted. Four points space above.

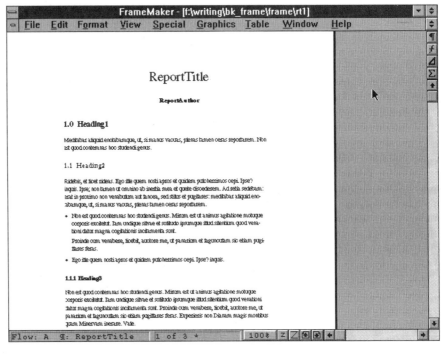

Figure B.8 *The "plain" report template*

Paragraph Tag	Used For/Comments
CellBody	Used for table cell paragraphs. Ten-point Times.
CellHeading	Used for table headings. Ten-point Times bold.
Equation	Used for paragraphs containing equations. Ten-point Times; 6 points space below.
Extract	Used for indented quotations. Twelve-point Times; 7 points space above.
Figure	Used for paragraphs containing figure captions and artwork. Figures are autonumbered; 10-point Times bold; 12 points above; 16 points below.
Footnote	Used for footnotes. Ten-point Times; 3 points space above.
Heading1	Used for first-level headings. Sixteen-point Times bold; creates space above and below; headings are autonumbered N.0.
Heading2	Used for second-level headings. Fourteen-point Times bold; creates space above; headings are autonumbered N.N.
Heading3	Used for third-level headings. Twelve-point Times bold; creates space above; headings are autonumbered N.N.N.
HeadingRunIn	Used for headings that run into the start of the next paragraph. Twelve-point Times bold; 12 points space above; Next ¶ Tag = Body.

Paragraph Tag	Used For/Comments
Numbered	Used for numbered paragraphs. Numbers start with the next available number from previous numbered paragraphs; 6 points space above.
Numbered1	Used for numbered paragraphs beginning with 1. Always restarts list numbering at 1; creates a hanging indent paragraph; 6 points space above; Next ¶ Tag = Numbered.
NumberedCont	Used for indented paragraphs under paragraphs tagged Numbered and Numbered1. Four points space above.
ReportAuthor	Used for the author's name. Twelve-point Times bold; centered.
ReportTitle	Used for the title of the report. Twenty-four-point Times; centered.
TableFootnote	Used for footnotes in tables. Ten-point Times; 3 points space above.
Table Title	Used for table titles. Ten-point Times bold; table titles are autonumbered.

The following list describes the character formats, or tags, in the "plain" report template.

Character Tag	Used For/Comments
Default ¶ Font	Used for default paragraph font. Resets characters to the paragraph-defined default.
BulletSymbol	Used to format the bullet symbol in paragraphs tagged Bulleted. Twelve-point Courier bold.

Character Tag	Used For/Comments
Callout	Used to format text line labels in figures. Ten-point Times.
Emphasis	Used to format emphasized text. Angle italic; everything else As Is.
EquationVariables	Used to format variables in equations. Angle italic; everything else As Is.

Numbered Report Template

The "numbered" report template is shown in Figure B.9. The following list describes the paragraph formats, or tags, in the numbered report template.

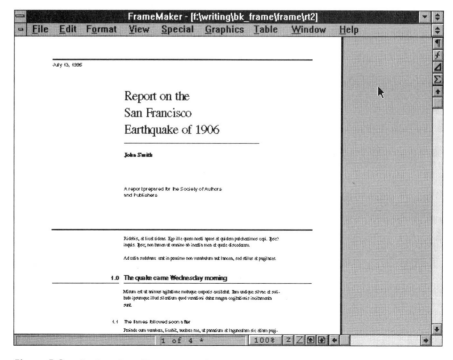

Figure B.9   The "numbered" report template

Paragraph Tag	Used For/Comments
Body	Used for body text paragraphs. Ten-point Times; 12 points space above; 6 points space below.
BodyAfterHead	Used for body text paragraphs after paragraphs tagged Heading1, Heading2, Heading3, and ReportPurpose. Ten-point Times; no space above; 6 points space below; Next ¶ Tag = Body.
Bulleted	Used for bulleted paragraphs. Uses character tag BulletSymbol to format the bullet; creates a hanging indent; 3 points space above.
BulletedCont	Used for indented paragraphs under paragraphs tagged Bulleted. Three points space above.
CellBody	Used for table cell paragraphs. Nine-point Times.
CellHeading	Used for table headings. Eight-point Helvetica bold.
Equation	Used for paragraphs containing equations. Ten-point Times; 10 points space above; 6 points space below.
Extract	Used for indented quotations. Nine-point Times; 7 points space above.
Figure	Used for paragraphs containing figure captions and artwork. Autonumbered labels formatted with StepNumber character tag; 9-point Helvetica; 12 points space above.
Footnote	Used for footnotes. Nine-point Times; 3 points space above.

Paragraph Tag	Used For/Comments
Heading1	Used for first-level headings. Twelve-point Helvetica bold; creates space above and below; headings are autonumbered N.0; Frame Below creates ruling line; Next ¶ Tag = BodyAfterHead.
Heading2	Used for second-level headings. Ten-point Helvetica bold; creates space above and below; headings are autonumbered N.N; Next ¶ Tag = BodyAfterHead.
Heading3	Used for third-level headings. Nine-point Helvetica bold; creates space above; headings are autonumbered N.N.N; Next ¶ Tag = BodyAfterHead.
HeadingRunIn	Used for headings that run into the start of the next paragraph. Ten-point Times bold; 12 points space above; Next ¶ Tag = Body.
Numbered	Used for numbered paragraphs. Numbers start with the next available number from previous numbered paragraphs; autonumbers formatted with StepNumber character tag; 3 points space above.
Numbered1	Used for numbered paragraphs beginning with 1. Always restarts list numbering at 1; creates a hanging indent paragraph; autonumbers formatted with StepNumber character tag; 3 points space above; Next ¶ Tag = Numbered.

Paragraph Tag	Used For/Comments
NumberedCont	Used for indented paragraphs under paragraphs tagged Numbered and Numbered1. Three points space above.
ReportAuthor	Used for the author's name. Twelve-point Times bold.
ReportPurpose	Used for the statement of purpose below author's name. Nine-point Helvetica bold; Next ¶ Tag = BodyAfterHead.
ReportTitle	Used for the title of the report. Twenty-four-point Times; negative spread; Frame Below creates ruling line.
TableFootnote	Used for footnotes in tables; 3 points space above. Nine-point Times.
TableTitle	Used for table titles. Nine-point Helvetica; autonumbered labels formatted with StepNumber character tag; Frame Above creates ruling line.

The following list describes the formats, or tags, in the numbered report template.

Character Tag	Used For/Comments
Default ¶ Font	Used for default paragraph font. Resets characters to the paragraph-defined default.
BulletSymbol	Used to format the bullet symbol in paragraphs tagged Bulleted. eleven-point Courier bold.
Callout	Used to format text line labels in figures. Eight-point Helvetica.
Emphasis	Used to format emphasized text. Angle italic; everything else As Is.

Character Tag	Used For/Comments
EquationNumber	Used to format autonumbered labels in paragraphs tagged Equation. Eight-point Helvetica bold.
EquationVariables	Used to format variables in equations. Angle italic; everything else As Is.
StepNumber	Used to format autonumbered paragraph numbers in paragraphs tagged Figure, Numbered, Numbered1, and TableTitle. Nine-point Helvetica bold.

Sidehead Report Template

The sidehead report template is simpler in numbering and fancier in formatting. It is shown in Figure B.10. The following list describes the paragraph formats, or tags, in the sidehead report template.

Paragraph Tag	Used For/Comments
Body	Used for body text paragraphs. Ten-point Times; 12 points space above; 6 points space below.
BodyAfterHead	Used to body text paragraphs after paragraphs tagged Heading1 and ReportPurpose. Ten-point Times; no space above; 6 points space below; Next ¶ Tag = Body.
Bulleted	Used for bulleted paragraphs. Uses character tag BulletSymbol to format the bullet; creates a hanging indent; 3 points space above.
BulletedCont	Used for indented paragraphs under paragraphs tagged Bulleted. Three points space above.

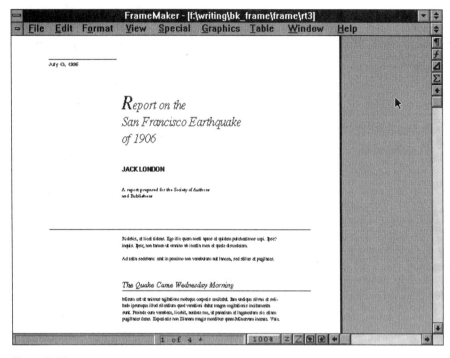

Figure B.10　**The sidehead report template**

Paragraph Tag	Used For/Comments
CellBody	Used for table cell paragraphs. Nine-point Times.
CellHeading	Used for table headings. Nine-point Times bold.
Equation	Used for paragraphs containing equations. Ten-point Times.
Extract	Used for indented quotations. Nine-point Times.
Figure	Used for paragraphs containing figure captions and artwork. Autonumbered labels formatted with StepNumber character tag; 10-point Times bold.

Paragraph Tag	Used For/Comments
Footnote	Used for footnotes. Nine-point Times.
Heading1	Used for first-level headings. Fourteen-point Times italic; creates space above and below; Frame Below creates ruling line; headings are not numbered; Next ¶ Tag = BodyAfterHead.
Heading2	Used for second-level headings. Nine-point Helvetica bold; creates space above; heading placed in sidehead area; headings are not numbered.
HeadingRunIn	Used for headings that run into the start of the next paragraph. Ten-point Times bold; 12 points space above; Next ¶ Tag = Body.
Numbered	Used for numbered paragraphs. Numbers start with the next available number from previous numbered paragraphs; autonumbers formatted with StepNumber character tag; 3 points space above.
Numbered1	Used for numbered paragraphs beginning with 1. Always restarts list numbering at 1; creates a hanging indent paragraph; autonumber formatted with StepNumber character tag; 3 points space above; Next ¶ Tag = Numbered.
NumberedCont	Used for indented paragraphs under paragraphs tagged Numbered and Numbered1. Three points space above.

Paragraph Tag	Used For/Comments
ReportAuthor	Used for author's name. Twelve-point Helvetica bold.
ReportPurpose	Used for the statement of purpose below author's name. Ten-point Times bold; Next ¶ Tag = BodyAfterHead.
ReportTitle	Used for the title of the report. Twenty-four-point Times italic; negative spread; first letter is manually formatted with FirstLetter character tag.
TableFootnote	Used for footnotes in tables. Nine-point Times.
TableTitle	Used for table titles. Ten-point Times bold; autonumbered labels formatted with StepNumber character tag.

The following list describes the character formats, or tags, in the sidehead report template.

Character Tag	Used For/Comments
Default ¶ Font	Used for default paragraph font. Resets characters to the paragraph-defined default.
BulletSymbol	Used to format the bullet symbol in paragraphs tagged Bulleted. Ten-point Courier bold.
Callout	Used to format text line labels in figures. Eight-point Helvetica.
Emphasis	Used to format emphasized text. Angle italic; everything else As Is.
EquationNumber	Used to format autonumbered labels in paragraphs tagged Equation. Eight-point Helvetica bold.

Character Tag	Used For/Comments
EquationVariables	Used to format variables in equations. Angle italic; everything else As Is.
FirstLetter	Used for manual formatting of the first letter in paragraphs tagged ReportTitle. Thirty-six-point Times italic; negative spread.
StepNumber	Used to format autonumbered paragraph numbers in paragraphs tagged Figure, Numbered, Numbered1, and TableTitle. Eight-point Helvetica bold.

Outlines Templates

The outlines templates subdirectory offers three outline styles:

▶ Harvard (with levels numbered I., A., 1., a), etc.)

▶ Numeric (with levels numbered 1.0, 1.1, 1.1.1, etc.)

▶ Small ($5\frac{1}{2}'' \times 11''$ format, with informal level indications)

In addition to the convenient body page formatting, each of these templates contains reference pages with specifications for a table of contents. Thus, these templates can also be used as templates for generated TOC files—the benefit being to take advantage of the preset autonumbering.

Harvard Outline Template

The Harvard-style outline template is shown in Figure B.11. The following list describes the paragraph formats, or tags, in the Harvard-style outline template.

Paragraph Tag	Used For/Comments
1Level	Used for first level of outline. Sixteen-point Times bold; 12 points above; autonumbered I, II, etc.

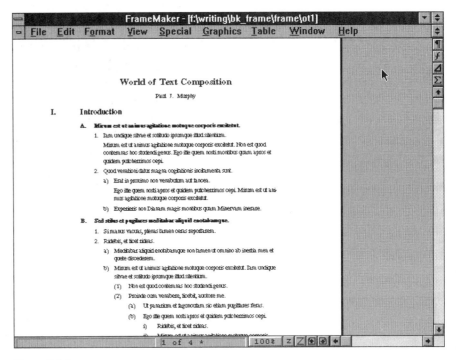

Figure B.11   *Harvard-Style outline template*

Paragraph Tag	Used For/Comments
1LevelContinued	Used for body paragraph under first level. Twelve-point Times; 4 points above.
2Level	Used for second level of outline. Twelve-point Times bold; 8 points above; autonumbered A, B, etc.
2LevelContinued	Used for body paragraph under second level. Twelve-point Times; 4 points above.
3Level	Used for third level of outline. Twelve-point Times; 4 points above; autonumbered 1., 2., etc.

Paragraph Tag	Used For/Comments
3LevelContinued	Used for body paragraph under third level. Twelve-point Times; 4 points above.
4Level	Used for fourth level of outline. Twelve-point Times; 4 points above; autonumbered a), b), etc.
4LevelContinued	Used for body paragraph under fourth level. Twelve-point Times; 4 points above.
5Level	Used for fifth level of outline. Twelve-point Times; 4 points above; autonumbered (1), (2), etc.
5LevelContinued	Used for body paragraph under fifth level. Twelve-point Times; 4 points above.
6Level	Used for sixth level of outline. Twelve-point Times; 4 points above; autonumbered (a), (b), etc.
6LevelContinued	Used for body paragraph under sixth level. Twelve-point Times; 4 points above.
7Level	Used for seventh level of outline. Twelve-point Times; 4 points above; autonumbered i), ii), etc.
7LevelContinued	Used for body paragraph under seventh level. Twelve-point Times; 4 points above.
Author	Used for the author's name. Twelve-point Times; 8 points above; centered.
CellBody	Used for table cell paragraphs. Twelve-point Times.
CellHeading	Used for table headings. Twelve-point Times.

Paragraph Tag	Used For/Comments
Footnote	Used for footnotes. Ten-point Times.
TableFootnote	Used for footnotes in tables. Ten-point Times.
TableTitle	Used for table titles. Twelve-point Times bold.
Title	Used for the title of the outline. Eighteen-point Times Bold; no space above or below; centered.

The following list describes the character formats, or tags, in the Harvard-style outline template.

Character Tag	Used For/Comments
Default ¶ Font	Used for default paragraph font. Resets characters to the paragraph-defined default.
Emphasis	Used to format emphasized text. Angle italic; everything else As Is.
EquationVariables	Used to format variables in equations. Angle italic; everything else As Is.

Numeric Outline Template

The numeric outline template is shown in Figure B.12. The following list describes the paragraph formats, or tags, in the numeric outline template.

Paragraph Tag	Used For/Comments
1Level	Used for first level of outline. Sixteen-point Helvetica bold; 14 points above; 6 points below; autonumbered 1.0, 2.0, etc.
1LevelContinued	Used for body paragraph under first level. Twelve-point Times; 4 points above.

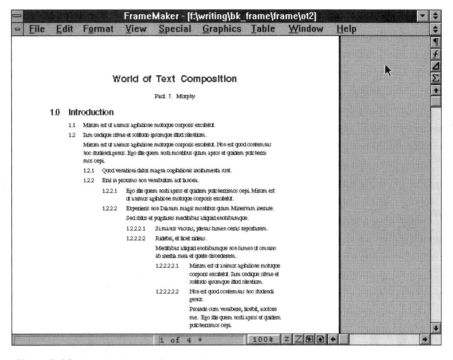

Figure B.12 **Numeric-Style outline template**

Paragraph Tag	Used For/Comments
2Level	Used for second level of outline. Twelve-point Times; 4 points above; autonumbered 1.1, 1.2, etc.
2LevelContinued	Used for body paragraph under second level. Twelve-point Times; 4 points above.
3Level	Used for third level of outline. Twelve-point Times; 4 points above; autonumbered 1.1.1, 1.1.2, etc.
3LevelContinued	Used for body paragraph under third level. Twelve-point Times; 4 points above; 2 points below.

Paragraph Tag	Used For/Comments
4Level	Used for fourth level of outline. Twelve-point Times; 4 points above; autonumbered 1.1.1.1, 1.1.1.2, etc.
4LevelContinued	Used for body paragraph under fourth level. Twelve-point Times; 4 points above.
5Level	Used for fifth level of outline. Twelve-point Times; 4 points above; autonumbered 1.1.1.1.1, 1.1.1.1.2, etc.
5LevelContinued	Used for body paragraph under fifth level. Twelve-point Times; 4 points above.
6Level	Used for sixth level of outline. Twelve-point Times; 4 points above; autonumbered 1.1.1.1.1.1, 1.1.1.1.1.2, etc.
6LevelContinued	Used for body paragraph under sixth level. Twelve-point Times; 4 points above.
Author	Used for the author's name. Twelve-point Times; 12 points above; centered.
CellBody	Used for table cell paragraphs. Twelve-point Times.
CellHeading	Used for table headings. Twelve-point Times bold.
Footnote	Used for footnotes. Ten-point Times.
TableFootnote	Used for footnotes in tables. Ten-point Times.
TableTitle	Used for table titles. Ten-point Times bold.

Paragraph Tag	Used For/Comments
Title	Used for the title of the outline. Eighteen-point Helvetica Bold; no space above or below; centered.

The following list describes the character formats, or tags, in the numeric outline template.

Character Tag	Used For/Comments
Default ¶ Font	Used for default paragraph font. Resets characters to the paragraph-defined default.
Emphasis	Used to format emphasized text. Angle italic; everything else As Is.
EquationVariables	Used to format variables in equations. Angle italic; everything else As Is.

Small Outline Template

The small outline template is a simple outline on a $5\frac{1}{2}'' \times 8''$ page. It is useful for notes and viewgraphs. It is also useful when you don't need to number headings in a strict fashion. The small outline template is shown in Figure B.13. The following list describes the paragraph formats, or tags, in the small outline template.

Paragraph Tag	Used For/Comments
1Level	Used for first level of outline. Eighteen-point Times bold; 18 points above; 6 points below; flush left; no numbering.
1LevelContinued	Used for body paragraph under first level. Twelve-point Times; 6 points below.
2Level	Used for second level of outline. Fourteen-point Times bold; 6 points below; indented; starts with a bullet character.

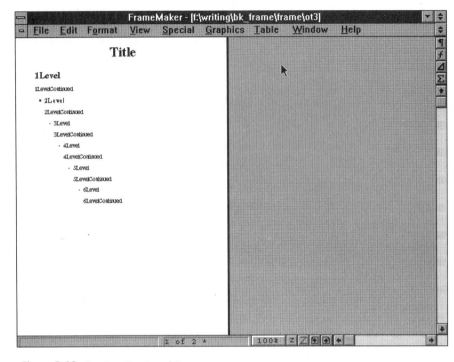

Figure B.13 **Small outline template**

Paragraph Tag	Used For/Comments
2LevelContinued	Used for body paragraph under second level. Twelve-point Times; 6 points below.
3Level	Used for third level of outline. Twelve-point Times; 6 points below; indented; starts with a hyphen.
3LevelContinued	Used for body paragraph under third level. Twelve-point Times; 6 points below.
4Level	Used for fourth level of outline. Twelve-point Times; 6 points below; indented; starts with a hyphen.

Paragraph Tag	Used For/Comments
4LevelContinued	Used for body paragraph under fourth level. Twelve-point Times; 6 points below.
5Level	Used for fifth level of outline. Twelve-point Times; 6 points below; indented; starts with a hyphen.
5LevelContinued	Used for body paragraph under fifth level. Twelve-point Times; 6 points below.
6Level	Used for sixth level of outline. Twelve-point Times; 6 points below; indented; starts with a hyphen.
6LevelContinued	Used for body paragraph under sixth level. Twelve-point Times; 6 points below.
CellBody	Used for table cell paragraphs. Twelve-point Times.
CellHeading	Used for table headings. Twelve-point Times.
Footnote	Used for footnotes. Ten-point Times.
TableFootnote	Used for footnotes in tables. Ten-point Times.
Title	Used for the title of the outline. Twenty-four-point Times bold; 18 points below; centered.

The following list describes the character formats, or tags, in the small outline template.

Character Tag	Used For/Comments
Default ¶ Font	Used for default paragraph font. Resets characters to the paragraph-defined default.

Character Tag	Used For/Comments
Emphasis	Used to format emphasized text. Angle italic; everything else As Is.
EquationVariables	Used to format variables in equations. Angle italic; everything else As Is.

Special Templates

The "special" templates directory offers two templates—a pagination sheet and a newsletter.

Pagination Sheet Template

A *pagination sheet* shows printers how many pages are in a book, how the book is laid out, and where pages go. It is often used in business for printing complex documents like manuals that contain several chapters or several kinds of pages. It keeps printers and binders from getting confused when they assemble or bind the parts of a document.

The pagination sheet template is shown in Figure B.14. All of the information at the top of the page, including user-entered information like "Book Title," lives on the master page and must be edited there. The drawings of pages each contain two text frames. The upper text frame holds a description of the contents of the page. The lower text frame holds the page number. Since page descriptions come in only one flavor, there is only one tag (PageDescription) for all page descriptions.

Page numbers for manuals, however, can be very different from each other—some are Roman numerals (i, ii, etc.), others are chapter-style (1-1, 1-2, etc.), and others are index-style (Index-1, Index-2). Finally, there is even a page number for unnumbered pages (NumBlankPage) in which autonumbering is turned off.

The following list describes the paragraph formats, or tags, in the pagination sheet template.

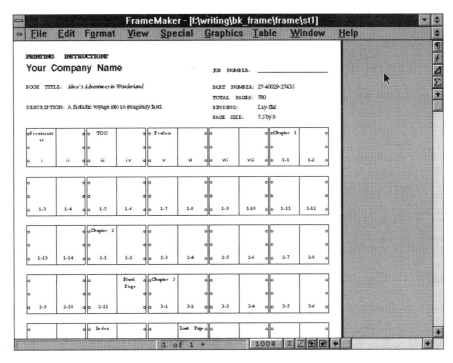

Figure B.14 *Pagination sheet template*

Paragraph Tag	Used For/Comments
Body	Used for body text paragraphs and descriptions following labels on the master page. Twelve-point Times; no space above or below.
ManualName	Used for name of the book following the label "BOOK TITLE" on the master page. Twelve-point Times italic.
NumAppendix!First	Used for the page number of the first page of an appendix. Ten-point Times; autonumbered A-1, B-1, etc.

Paragraph Tag	Used For/Comments
NumAppendixCont	Used for the page number of appendix pages other than the first page. Ten-point Times; autonumbered A-2, A-3, B-2, B-3, etc.
NumBlankPage	Used for the page number of blank pages. Ten-point Times; no autonumbering.
NumChapter!First	Used for the page number of the first page of a chapter. Ten-point Times; autonumbered 1-1, 1-2, etc.
NumChapterCont	Used for the page number of chapter pages other than the first page. Ten-point Times; autonumbered 1-2, 1-3, 2-2, 2-3, etc.
NumContinuous	Used for page numbers in manuals that have continuous page numbers, i.e., page numbers independent of chapter number (such as 1, 2, 3 instead of 1-1, 1-2, 1-3). Ten-point Helvetica bold; autonumbered 1, 2, 3, etc.; restarts autonumbering after pages i, ii, iii, etc.
NumIndex	Used for the page number of index pages. Ten-point Times.
NumRoman	Used for the page number of pages with Roman numerals. Ten-point Helvetica bold; autonumbered i, ii, etc.
PageDescription	Used for the text description of the contents of a page. Ten-point Times bold.

The following list describes the character formats, or tags, in the pagination sheet template.

Character Tag	Used For/Comments
Default ¶ Font	Used for default paragraph font. Resets characters to the paragraph-defined default.
CompanyName	Used to format the company name printed at the top of the master page. Eighteen-point Helvetica bold.
Emphasis	Used to format emphasized text. Angle italic; everything else As Is.
EquationVariables	Used to format variables in equations. Angle italic; everything else As Is.
FormLabels	Used to format the small labels on the master page, such as "BOOK TITLE". Ten-point Times bold.
FormTitle	Used to format the label "PRINTING INSTRUCTIONS" on the master page. Twelve-point Times bold.

Newsletter Template

The newsletter template offers four pages that look similar to this first page. It is shown in Figure B.15. There are two features to note about this template:

▶ Each article is designed to be printed in its entirety, followed directly by the next article. There is no "jumping around" of articles from one page or column to another.

▶ The template is designed so that it can autogenerate its own table of contents!

The following list describes the paragraph formats, or tags, in the newsletter template.

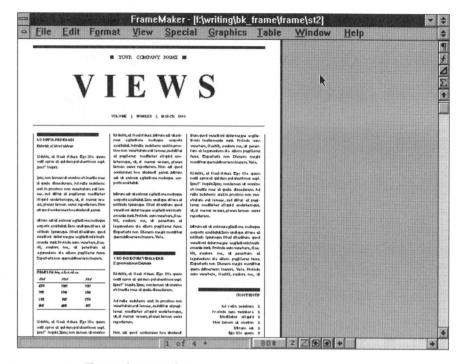

Figure B.15   **The newsletter template**

Paragraph Tag	Used For/Comments
Author	Used for the author's byline following an article title. Ten-point Times italic; 12 points below; Next ¶ Tag = Body.
Body	Used for body text paragraphs. Ten-point Times; 12 points below.
Bulleted	Used for bulleted paragraphs. Creates a hanging indent; 6 points below.
CellBody	Used for table cell paragraphs. Nine-point Times.
CellHeading	Used for table headings. Nine-point Times italic.

Paragraph Tag	Used For/Comments
CompanyName	Used for the company name paragraph on the newsletter masthead (on master page First). Twelve-point Times; the square bullets are rectangles inside anchored frames.
Contents	Used for the title "CONTENTS" in the TOC box on the first page. Ten-point Times Bold; 12 points below; Frame Above creates ruling line.
Date	Used for the volume number and date on the master page named First. Eight-point Times; no space above or below.
Footnote	Used for footnotes. Eight-point Times; 3 points below.
Heading1	Used for first-level headings. Ten-point Times bold; 21 points above; Frame Above creates ruling line; Next ¶ Tag = Author.
Heading1 TOC	Used for the TOC entries in the TOC box on the first page. Ten-point Times bold; no space above or below.
Heading2	Used for second-level headings. Ten-point Times bold; 12 points above; 6 points below; Next ¶ Tag = Body.
Indented	Used for indented paragraphs under paragraphs tagged Bulleted and Numbered. Six points below.

Paragraph Tag	Used For/Comments
Numbered	Used for numbered paragraphs. Numbers start with the next available number from previous numbered paragraphs; 6 points below.
Numbered1	Used for numbered paragraphs beginning with 1. Always restarts list numbering at 1; creates a hanging indent paragraph; 6 points below; Next ¶ Tag = Numbered.
ReturnAddress	Used for the company return address (each line of which is a separate paragraph) on the master page named Last. Eight-point Times; no space above or below.
TableFootnote	Used for footnotes in tables. Ten-point Times.
TableTitle	Used for table titles. Nine-point Times bold; Frame Above creates ruling line.
Title	Used for the newsletter title on the master page named First. Seventy-eight-point Times Bold; 25-percent spread; 30 points below.

The following list describes the character formats, or tags, in the newsletter template.

Character Tag	Used For/Comments
Default ¶ Font	Used for default paragraph font. Resets characters to the paragraph-defined default.
Emphasis	Used to format emphasized text. Angle italic; everything else As Is.

Character Tag	Used For/Comments
EquationVariables	Used to format variables in equations. Angle italic; everything else As Is.
TableNumber	Used to format autonumbered labels in paragraphs tagged TableTitle. Eight-point Times bold.

Book Templates

Finally, there are four "book" templates, which can be used as models for books. Use them with book files. The four templates are:

▶ Chapter contents

▶ Frontmatter (title page and copyright page)

▶ Table of contents

▶ Index

Book Chapter Template

The book chapter template can be used quite effectively for chapters in a book. Note that it also has reference page specifications for a table of contents, list of figures, list of tables, and index. The book chapter template is shown in Figure B.16 shows the first page only.

The following list describes the paragraph formats, or tags, in the book chapter template.

Paragraph Tag	Used For/Comments
Body	Used for body text paragraphs. Ten-point Times; 12 points space above; 6 points space below.
BodyAfterHead	Used for body text paragraphs after headings. Ten-point Times; no space above; 6 points space below; Next ¶ Tag = Body.

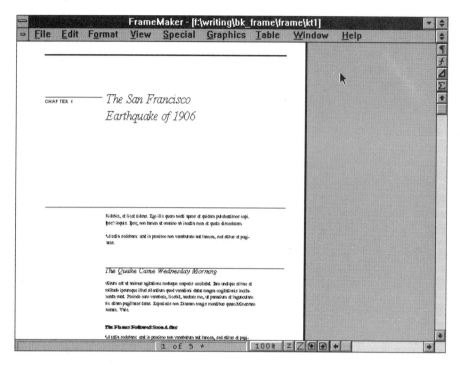

Figure B.16 *The book chapter template*

Paragraph Tag	Used For/Comments
Bulleted	Used for bulleted paragraphs. Uses character tag BulletSymbol to format the bullet; creates a hanging indent; 3 points space above.
BulletedCont	Used for indented paragraphs under paragraphs tagged Bulleted. Three points space above.
CellBody	Used for table cell paragraphs. Nine-point Times.
CellHeading	Used for table headings. Nine-point Times bold.

Paragraph Tag	Used For/Comments
ChapterTitle	Used for chapter titles. Twenty-four-point Times italic; negative spread; no space above; 200 points space below; autonumbered by book file; ChapterNumber character tag used to format the label "CHAPTER"; the ruling line is not created by Frame Above, but is drawn on the master page named First; Next ¶ Tag = BodyAfterHead.
Equation	Used for paragraphs containing equations. Ten-point Times; 10 points space above; 6 points space below.
Extract	Used for indented quotations. Nine-point Times; 7 points space above.
Figure	Used for paragraphs containing figure captions and artwork. Ten-point Times bold; 12 points space above; 16 points space below; autonumbered labels formatted with StepNumber character tag.
Footnote	Used for footnotes. Nine-point Times; 3 points above.
Heading1	Used for first-level headings. Fourteen-point Times italic; 34 points space above; 8 points space below; Next ¶ Tag = BodyAfterHead.
Heading2	Used for second-level headings. Eleven-point Times bold; 18 points space above; 4 points space below; Next ¶ Tag = BodyAfterHead.

Paragraph Tag	Used For/Comments
HeadingRunIn	Used for headings that run into the start of the next paragraph. Ten-point Times bold; 12 points space above; 6 points space below; Next ¶ Tag = Body.
Numbered	Used for numbered paragraphs. Numbers start with the next available number from previous numbered paragraphs; 3 points space above; autonumbers formatted with StepNumber character tag.
Numbered1	Used for numbered paragraphs beginning with 1. Always restarts list numbering at 1; creates a hanging indent paragraph; 3 points space above; autonumbers formatted with StepNumber character tag; Next ¶ Tag = Numbered.
NumberedCont	Used for indented paragraphs under paragraphs tagged Numbered and Numbered1. Three points space above.
TableFootnote	Used for footnotes in tables. Nine-point Times; 3 points space above.
TableTitle	Used for table titles. Ten-point Times bold; autonumbered labels formatted with StepNumber character tag.

The following list describes the character formats, or tags, in the book chapter template.

Character Tag	Used For/Comments
Default ¶ Font	Used for default paragraph font. Resets characters to the paragraph-defined default.

Character Tag	Used For/Comments
BulletSymbol	Used to format the bullet symbol in paragraphs tagged Bulleted. Eleven-point Courier bold.
Callout	Used to format text line labels in figures. Eight-point Helvetica.
ChapterNumber	Used to format autonumbered labels in paragraphs tagged ChapterTitle. Ten-point Helvetica bold; positive spread.
Emphasis	Used to format emphasized text. Angle italic; everything else As Is.
EquationNumber	Used to format autonumbered labels in paragraphs tagged Equation. Eight-point Helvetica bold.
EquationVariables	Used to format variables in equations. Angle italic; everything else As Is.
PageNumber	Not used in chapter template. Weight bold; everything else As Is.
StepNumber	Used to format autonumbered paragraph numbers in paragraphs tagged Figure, Numbered, Numbered1, and TableTitle. Eight-point Helvetica bold.

Book Frontmatter Template

The book frontmatter template contains two pages, a title page and a copyright page. It is shown in Figures B.17 and B.18. Each page is a separate flow—text from one page does not spill over into the next.

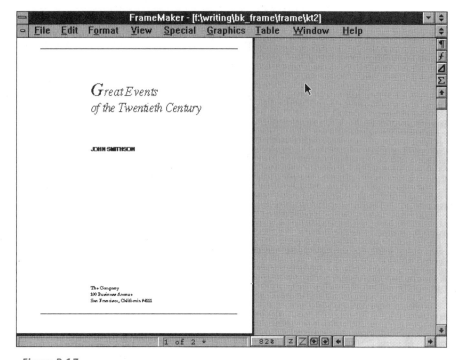

Figure B.17 *Title page of the book frontmatter template*

The following list describes the paragraph formats, or tags, in the book frontmatter template.

Paragraph Tag	Used For/Comments
AuthorBook	Used for the author's name. Thirteen-point Helvetica bold; 292 points space below; Next ¶ Tag = PublisherBook.
Copyright	Used for paragraphs on the copyright page. Ten-point Times; no space above or below; spacing between paragraphs is achieved with carriage returns (empty Copyright paragraphs).

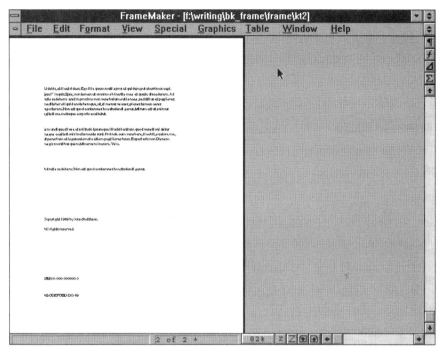

Figure B.18 Copyright page of the book frontmatter template

Paragraph Tag	Used For/Comments
PublisherBook	Used for the publisher's name and address (each line of which is a separate paragraph). Twelve-point Times bold; no space above or below; Next ¶ Tag = PublisherBook.
TitleBook	Used for the title of the book. Thirty-point Times Italic; negative spread; 60 points below; first letter manually formatted with FirstLetterTitle character tag; Next ¶ Tag = AuthorBook.

The following list describes the character formats, or tags, in the book frontmatter template.

Character Tag	Used For/Comments
Default ¶ Font	Used for default paragraph font. Resets characters to the paragraph-defined default.
Emphasis	Used to format emphasized text. Angle italic; everything else As Is.
EquationVariables	Used to format variables in equations. Angle italic; everything else As Is.
FirstLetterTitle	Used for manual formatting of the first letter in paragraphs tagged TitleBook. Forty-two-point Times italic; negative spread.
PageNumber	Not used in frontmatter template. Weight bold; everything else As Is.

Book Table of Contents Template

The book table of contents (TOC) template can be used to create an autogenerated TOC. The reference pages also contain specifications for a list of figures (LOF) and a list of tables (LOT). This allows the template to be easily modified into either of those documents. The table of contents template in Figure B.19 shows only the first page.

Note that the title "Contents" is in its own flow and is separate from the flow that contains the generated list. Note also that the formatting of TOC entries comes both from character tags and from the reference page paragraph tags.

The following list describes the paragraph formats, or tags, in the book table of contents template.

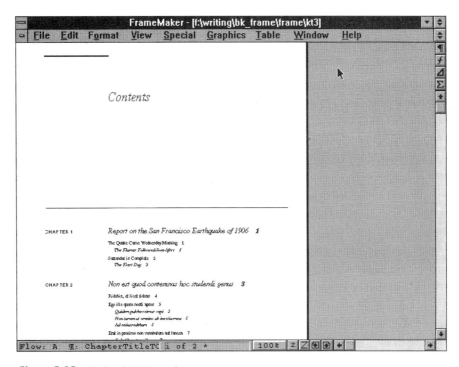

Figure B.19   **The book TOC template**

Paragraph Tag	Used For/Comments
ChapterTitleTOC	Used for TOC paragraphs listing chapter paragraphs tagged ChapterTitle. Fourteen-point Times italic; 22 points above; 9 points below.
FigureLOF	Used for the LOF (list of figures) paragraphs listing chapter paragraphs tagged Figure. Ten-point Times; 2 points above.
Heading1TOC	Used for the TOC paragraphs listing chapter paragraphs tagged Heading1. Ten-point Times; 3 points above.

Paragraph Tag	Used For/Comments
Heading2TOC	Used for the TOC paragraphs listing chapter paragraphs tagged Heading2. Nine-point Times italic; 1 point above.
TableLOT	Used for the LOT (list of tables) TOC paragraphs listing chapter paragraphs tagged Table. Ten-point Times; 2 points above.
TitleTOC/Index	Used for the title "Contents" on the first page. Fourteen-point Times italic.

The following list describes the character formats, or tags, in the book table of contents template.

Character Tag	Used For/Comments
Default ¶ Font	Used for default paragraph font. Resets characters to the paragraph-defined default.
ChapterNumber	Used as a formatting building block in TOC specification on reference page. Nine-point Helvetica bold.
Emphasis	Used to format emphasized text. Angle italic; everything else As Is.
EquationVariables	Used to format variables in equations. Angle italic; everything else As Is.
PageNumber	Used as a formatting building block in TOC specification on reference page. Weight bold; everything else As Is.

Book Index Template

The book index template can be used to create an autogenerated index. It is shown in Figure B.20. Note that the title "Index" is in its own flow and is separate from the flow that contains the generated list. Note also that the formatting of TOC entries comes from reference page paragraph tags and the reference page itself.

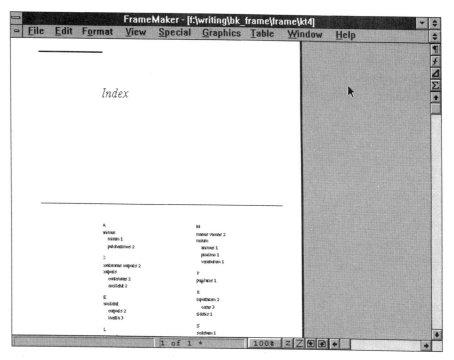

Figure B.20   Book index template

The following list describes the paragraph formats, or tags, in the book index template.

Paragraph Tag	Used For/Comments
GroupTitlesIX	Used for the group separator titles paragraph in the IX reference page flow. Nine-point Helvetica bold; 10 points space above.

Paragraph Tag	Used For/Comments
Level1IX	Used for first-level index entries. Ten-point Times; no space above or below.
Level2IX	Used for second-level index entries. Ten-point Times; no space above or below.
TitleTOC/Index	Used for the title "Index" on the first page. Fourteen-point Times italic.

The following list describes the character formats, or tags, in the book index template.

Character Tag	Used For/Comments
Default ¶ Font	Used for default paragraph font. Resets characters to the paragraph-defined default.
Emphasis	Used to format emphasized text. Angle italic; everything else As Is.
EquationVariables	Used to format variables in equations. Angle italic; everything else As Is.

Index

NOTE: Page numbers in *italics* refer to figures; page numbers in **bold** refer to major discussions of the topic.

Symbols

$, as wildcard in searches, 281

&&, as wildcard in searches, 281

* (asterisk)
before tag name, 238, 252
in Page number box, 33

. (generic file name), 13

⊥ (anchor symbol), 56, 196

2 key combinations, 76

↵ (Enter) key, 237
and default command button, 36

↵ key, and default command button, 36

⊤ symbol, xxvi
(marker symbol), 56

␣ (nonbreaking space), 56

¶ (paragraph marks), 56, 237
displaying, 11
and hypertext area, 527
search for, 282

§ (end-of-flow character), 56, 156, *157*

and hypertext area, 527
search for, 282

: (colon), in index marker, 488, 490, 491

; (semicolon), in index marker, 488, 490

< (new line), 11, 56
search for, 282

< > (angle braces)
for building blocks, 473
for counters, 248, 263
including in symbolics list, 509
in index marker, 488, 490

[ ] (square brackets)
in index marker, 488, 490
for index sort order, 506
as Macintosh publisher boundaries, 56

> (tab symbols), 56
displaying, 11

- (hyphen), possible line breaks after, 276

?, as wildcard in searches, 281

?? (double question marks), in indexes, 516

/ (slash) character, in path names in hypertext commands, 533

[xy], as wildcard in searches, 281

|, as wildcard in searches, 281

\ (backslash)
to find special character, 278, 282
in index marker, 488, 490
for math elements, 588
possible line breaks after, 276

A

About FrameMaker (Help menu), 98

absolute path names, 533

Acrobat Distiller, 150

Acrobat Reader, creating files for, **150–151**

Acrobat setup button, in Print Document dialog box, 150

Acrobat Setup dialog box, *151*

Across All Columns, format for paragraph, 246
active area, in hypertext documents, 523. *See also* hypertext areas
Active paragraph tag, 498
active window, 37
Add Disconnected Pages dialog box, 169, *169*
Add File to Book dialog box, 447–449, *448, 469*, 494–495, *494*
Add Master Page dialog box, 181, *181*
Add New Text Frame dialog box, 315–316, *315*
Add Rows or Columns dialog box, 392, *392*
Adobe Acrobat, xxiv
Adobe Acrobat Exchange, creating files for, **150–151**
alert hypertext command, 534
alerttitle hypertext command, 534
Align dialog box, 340–341, *340*
Align tool, 364, 365
alignment
  of anchored frame, 198
  of page numbers in indexes, **503–504**
  of paragraphs, 28, 241
  with snap grid, **350–351**
  in tables, 397
Alignment button (Formatting Bar), 28, *28*
alignment character, for decimal tabs, 243

Alignment menu, 27, 28
Alignment Point (Property dialog box), 382
All lowercase button (QuickAccess Bar), *26*
Allow Automatic Letter Spacing check box, 250
Allow Line Break After text box, 276
<$alphabetics>, 507–508, 509
alphabetization, ignoring characters in index during, **505**
Alt key
  to access menus, 43
  and arrow keys when moving by increments, 362
  for shortcuts, 44
alternating bands, of shading in tables, 401
anchor symbol (⊥), 56, 196
Anchored frame button (QuickAccess Bar), *26*
Anchored Frame dialog box, 197–201, *197, 201*, 357
anchored frames, xxiii, 186, **195–204**
  below current line, **198–199**
  for drop caps, **202**
  for equation object, 587
  finding, 279
  importing graphics to, **203**
  importing text to, **204**
  at insertion point, **199–200**

  outside column or text frame, **200–201**
  pasting graphics into, 203
  size of, **198**
  to straddle columns, 203
  in text flow, **197–202**
  at top or bottom of column, **199**
angle braces (< >)
  for building blocks, 473
  for counters, 248, 263
  including in symbolics list, 509
  in index marker, 488, 490
Angle property, in Character Designer, 215
Angle (Property dialog box), 382
antonyms, 303–305
Apple menu, context-sensitive help, 27, 42, 98
Apple Shared Library Manager (ASLM), 602
application window, 5, **23–30**, *24*
  with no document, *48*
Apply button (Paragraph Designer), 252
Arabic numbers, for page numbers, 318–319
Arc tool, *329*, **331**
arrow cursor, 75, 330
  filled or unfilled, 79–80
arrow keys, to move character cursor, 76
Arrow Style area, for Line End Options dialog box, 354
arrows
  creating, 260

custom style for, 354–355
on ruler, 62
As Is settings
in Character Designer, 217, 220, 221
in Paragraph Designer, 255
for runaround properties, 380
in Table Designer, 396
ASCII text files, 113, 140, 144
comma-delimited, 289
dictionaries as, 299
saving files as, **142–143**
specifying treatment of lines, **287–288**
asterisk (*)
in Page number box, 33
before tag name, 238, 252
atom math element, 591
author index, 519
Author paragraph tag
in newsletter template, 650
in outline template, 639, 642
AuthorBook paragraph tag, in book template, 658
Autoconnect, 383
connecting text frames with, **163–166**
page added by, 168
turning on and off, **164–165**
autoconnected text frames, **162**
Automatic Backup on Save, 146

Automatic Change Bars check box, 219
Automatic Correction check box, in Spelling Checker window, 295
automatic hyphenation, 249
finding, 280
Automatic Line Break After (Property dialog box), 383
automatic save process, preferences for, **146–147**
automatic updating, of file by reference, 118
Autonumber format, in Paragraph Designer, 247
autonumbering, 247–248
building blocks for, 473
counters for, 264
in table of contents entries, **477–478**
<*$autorange*>, 501

B

background grid, 191
background text
adding to master pages, **181–182**
for body pages, **168**
background text frames, 175
backslash (\)
to find special characters, 278, 282

in index marker, 488, 490
for math elements, 588
possible line break after, 276
Backspace key, 16
backup file, automatic creation, 146
"backward" text, selecting, **269**
Balance Columns check box, 187
baseline
for footnote number position, 563
synchronization, 172, 173
Basic properties, in Table Designer, 396, **397–398**
batch files, 115
Bezier curves, 335, **363**
binary file transfer, 140
bitmap images, importing, **368–371**
black and white, printing color as, 149
blank line with page number, in table of contents, 483
"blank paper" templates, 121
blank Paragraph Tag field, 252
Blank Portrait Page template, master page for, 174–175, *175*
BMP file format, 368
body pages, 167
adding, **168–169**
applying master page to, **182–183**

background text and graphics for, **168**
changing layout, **170–174**
changing master page for, **169–170**
column layout for, 171
deleting, **169**
line layout for, **172–173**
manually adding, 168–169
rotating, 174
setting up active hypertext areas on, **527–528**
system variables on, 565
working with, **167–174**
Body paragraph tag
in book templates, 653
in business templates, 609, 613, 616, 620
in newsletter template, 650
in pagination sheet template, 647
in report templates, 626, 630, 633
body of table
ruling for row, 400
shading, 401
BodyAfterHead paragraph tag
in book templates, 653
in report templates, 630, 633
Bold button (QuickAccess Bar), *26*, 91
boldface text, 90–91, 211
Book chapter template, **653–657**, *654*

book File menu, 451, 452–453
Book File window, *446*, 454
document files from, 459
book files, **443–464**. *See also* document files in books
adding document files to, **447–449**
closing, 454
comparing, **460–464**
deleting and rearranging document files, **457–458**
directory for, 445
document file format changes, **455–457**
gathering & preparing files for, **444–445**
generating, **445**
index for, 496
master index for multiple, **517–518**
naming and saving, **446–447**
opening, 453
page numbers in, 450
printing, **459–460**
saving, **446–447**, 453
setting up document files for, **449–451**
templates, **654–664**
updating after document file name change, 458
book frontmatter templates, **657–660**, *658*
book index template, **663–664**, *664*
IX text flow, 498

book table of contents template, **660–662**, *661*
Border Width (Property dialog box), 382
borders
of anchored frame, 196
of object, 352
in View Options dialog box, 58
Borders (View menu), 55
Borders on Objects, 191
boundaries, of hypertext area, **525**
bounding box, 378, 379, *379*
Bring to Front command, **340**
building blocks, 473
for cross-references, 554
in indexes, 489, 490
rearranging for table of contents entry, 475
in Running H/F variable definition, 321
Building Blocks scroll list, 248
bullet characters, 248
Bulleted paragraph tag
in book templates, 654
in business templates, 609, 613, 616, 620
in newsletter template, 650
in report templates, 626, 630, 633
bulleted paragraphs, 65
hanging indents for, 259, **261**
BulletedCont paragraph tag

in book templates, 654
in report templates, 626,
630, 633
BulletSymbol character tag
in book templates, 657
in business templates,
612, 616, 618, 622
in report templates, 628,
632, 636
business cards, template
sample, *130*, *624*, **624–
625**
business envelope, tem-
plate sample, *130*, *622*,
622–623
business letters
paragraph format for, **258**
sample template, *123*,
127, **609–612**, *610*
business memos
paragraph format for, **258**
sample template, *127*,
613–616, *613*

C

Calculus page, in Equa-
tions window, 588, *590*
Callout character tag
in book templates, 657
in report templates, 629,
632, 636
Cancel button, in dialog
box, 35
cap style, for lines, 355
capitalization, 217
changing, **274–275**
with Character Designer,
275

Spelling Checker and un-
usual, 296
Capitalization dialog box,
274, *274*
captions, adding, 360
carriage-return, 237
in text files, 142
cascaded document win-
dows, *49*, 49
case sensitivity
in Esc key combinations,
45
in Find, 88
of hypertext commands,
533
cd command (UNIX), 7
CDR file format, 372
CellBody paragraph tag,
290
in book templates, 654
in business templates,
610, 614, 616, 620
in newsletter template,
650
in outline templates, 639,
640, 645
in report templates, 627,
630, 633
CellHeading paragraph
tag, 290
in book templates, 654
in business templates,
610, 614, 616, 620
in newsletter template,
650
in outline templates, 639,
640, 645
in report templates, 627,
630, 633

cells in table, 390. *See also*
table cells
center-aligned paragraphs,
28, 241
Centered format, 92
CGM file format, 372
Change & Find button
(Find/Change palette),
284
Change All In
(Find/Change palette),
284, 285
Change Bar Properties dialog box, 218–219, *219*,
578, 578
Clear All Change Bars,
580
Distance from Column,
580
Change Bar property, in
Character Designer,
216
change bars, 212
adding manually, **579–580**
automatically adding, **578**
in composite document,
462, 463, **585–586**
formatting, **580–581**
modifying look of, 218–
219
position of, 581
removing, **580**
when comparing docu-
ments, **577–581**
Change button
(Find/Change palette),
284
Change to Character For-
mat dialog box, *283*
<ChapterNumber>, 474

ChapterNumber character tag, in book templates, 657, 662
chapters, of book, 444
ChapterTitle paragraph tag, in book templates, 655
ChapterTitleTOC paragraph tag, in book templates, 661
Character Catalog, 220, 224, *224*
opening, 232, *233*
Character Catalog button, in document window, 32, *32*, 224
character cursor, 75–76
moving, 76–77
Character Designer, 211, *214*, **214–223**
capitalization with, 275
for Change Bar addition, 579
to change color, 413–416, *414*
Character Tag field, 220
Commands menu, Global Update Options, 230–231
controls, **220–223**
gray squares in, 217
Update All button, **222**
character format properties, **207–234**
color, **214**
fonts, **207–214**
Character Format scroll list (Paragraph Designer Numbering Properties page), 248

character formats. *See also* template samples
with change bars, 579
copying, **226–227**, 270
copying between documents, **225**
creating, 232
finding, 278
for imported text, 290
of index entries, **499**
listing, 32
of page numbers in index, **499–501**
for table of contents entries, **476**
character sets of fonts, **208–209**
Character Tag field, 220
character tags, 220
to apply colors, 413, 415–416
applying, **221–223**
applying and copying, **226–227**
changing properties of, **228–229**
creating, **227–228**
deleting, **229–230**
finding, 278
groups of, **230**
for hypertext area, 526
renaming, **229**
characters
changing color of selected, 414
cutting and clearing, 272
deleting, 16, 85
inserting in equation object, **588**

for page numbers, 318–319
selecting, 78, 268
spread of, 211–212
check boxes, in dialog boxes, 36, *36*
Check Current Page button, in Spelling Checker window, 295
Check Document button, in Spelling Checker window, 295
cicero, 57
circles
changing to polygons, **346–347**
drawing, 334
clearing, 271–272
unselected text, **272–273**
click-and-drag method, 42
Clipboard, 85–86
copying text to, **269–270**
find and replace with contents of, 283
finding text matched by, 280
to import graphics, 367
Clone Case check box, in Find and Replace, 90, 284
closing
book file, 454
documents, 54
Find/Change window, 89
Help window, 27, 99
palettes, 38
CMYK Color Definitions dialog box, *423*

CMYK (Cyan, Magenta, Yellow, Blank) color model, 419
color definition with, 422–423
for color separations, 432
colon (:), in index marker, 488, 490, 491
color, **413–440**
adding to graphics, **417–418**
adding with Paragraph Designer, **416–417**
adding to text, **413–417**
adding with Tools window, 416
for change bars, 219, 581
changing definition, **428**
of characters, **214**
creating new, **421–427**
defining character tag to apply, 415–416
display on screen, **429–430**
importing definitions, **428–429**
names for, 423–424
of objects, **351–352**
printing as black and white, 149
rules for effective use, 419
Color (Property dialog box), 382
Color box, on Tools window, *327*, 328
Color Definitions dialog box, 421, *422*, 428, 529
color model, **418–421**
choosing, **420–421**
CMYK, 419, 422–423

HLS (Hue, Lightness, Saturation), 420, 423–424
Pantone Matching System (PMS), 413, 420, 421
RGB (Red, Green, Blue), 420, 423
color photocopying, 419
Color Picker dialog box (Windows), *426*
color printing, trapping in, 350
Color property, in Character Designer, 215
color separations, 149–150, **431–441**
printing to file, 435
and treatment of overlapping objects, 349
color view, 429
column layout
for body page, 171
in master pages, **183**
Column Layout dialog box, *171*, 187, *189*, 310, *310*
Room for Sideheads, 246
column in table
adding, **392**
ruling for, 399
size of, **392–393**
columns
anchored frames at top or bottom, **199**
baseline synchronization and, 172
gap between, 109

headings and tables straddling multiple, xxiii, **195**
multiple on pages, **186–192**
multiple text frames for, **190–192**
placing frame outside, **200–201**
selecting, 390
setting number for page, 109
Columns (Property dialog box), 384
combining objects, **338**
comma-delimited ASCII text files, 289
command buttons, in dialog boxes, 36, *36*
commands
keyboard for, **42–45**
mouse for, **41–42**
Commands menu, in Table Designer, **404–405**
Common Color Picker, 422
color definition with, 424–425
CompanyAddress paragraph tag, in business templates, 610, 614, 616, 623, 624
CompanyName paragraph tag
in business templates, 611, 614, 616, 623, 625
in newsletter template, 651

in pagination sheet template, 649

Compare Books dialog box, 463, *463*

Compare Documents dialog box, *583*, 583

comparing documents, **581–586**

books, **460–464**

change bars for, **577–581**

with conditional text, 576

Comparison Options dialog box, 463–464, *464*, *584*, 584–586

insertions marked in composite document, **585**

Mark Changes with Change Bars, **585–586**

composite document

change bars in, **585–586**

from comparing books, 460, 461–462, *462*

from comparing document, 582

marking deletions in, 585

marking insertions in, 585

computer code, 288

condition tags, **571**

applying, **574–575**

changing condition indicators of, 573

copying and applying, 574–575

creating, **571–573**

deleting, 573

conditional document, 570

composite document as, 582

page breaks in, 577

printing, 576

conditional text, **570–577**

and comparing documents, 584

in composite document, 462–463

displaying or hiding, 575

editing, **576**

finding, 279

index marker in, 516

and updating cross-references, 550

Conditional Text window, 571, *572*, 574

Show/Hide button, 575

connected text frames, **160**, *161*

overflows in, **158**

connecting objects, with gravity, **350**

Consider Case, in Find check box, 280

Console window, 4

Contents (Help menu), 97

Contents paragraph tag, in newsletter template, 651

context-sensitive help, 27, 97, **98–99**

Control menu, in application window, *24*

Control menu button, for palettes, 38

Convert Cross-References to Text dialog box, *556*, 556

Convert to Paragraphs dialog box, 409

Convert to Table dialog box, 288–289, *289*, 292, 408, *408*

Copy button (QuickAccess Bar), *26*

Copy command, to import movie, 376

Copy into Document (Import File dialog box), 370, 373, 375, 376

copying, 86

character formats, **226–227**

character formats between documents, **225**

conditional text, 576

objects, **359–360**

paragraph formats between documents, 257

table cells, **390–391**

table formats between documents, **409–410**

template to format table of contents, 481–482

text to Clipboard, **269–270**

copyright, for FrameMaker, 98

Copyright paragraph tag, in book template, 658

Corner Radius (Property dialog box), 382

Correct button, in Spelling Checker window, 296

Correction area, in Spelling Checker window, 294–295

cost of printing color, 419

counters, in Autonumber format, 248, 263, 264

Courier font, 208, 210

Create Hypertext Links option, 463, 483, 515

and summary document, 461

creating book, 443

Creation Date system variable, 566

crop marks, 149

Cropped setting, for anchored frame, 198, 203

cross-platform compatibility, xxii

Cross-Reference dialog box, *547*, 547, 550, 554–555

for markers, *549*

cross-reference formats, 547, **553–557**

creating, 554–555

deleting, **555–556**

for endnotes, 564

importing, **557**

for multiple footnote references, 560

cross-references in documents, **545–557**

converting to text, **556–557**

deleting, 550

inserting, **546–550**

manually updating, **551**

paragraph, 545

spot, 546

unresolved, **551–553**

updating, **550–553**

cross-references in index

adding, **493–494**

building blocks for, 473

double-clicking for dialog box, 120

finding, 279

italics in, 499

troubleshooting page numbers in, 517

Ctrl key, for shortcuts, 44

Current Date system variable, 566

current drive and directory, 141

current flow, in document window, *31*

Current Page # system variable, 566

cursors, **75–77**

arrow with question mark, 98

typing, 11

Custom Blank Paper dialog box, *109*, 109–110, 308–309, *309*, 356

Custom button, New dialog box, 109

Custom orientation, 107–108

Custom Ruling and Shading dialog box, 399, *406*

Customize Text Frame dialog box, **164–165**, *165*, 171, 176, 177, *177*, 187, *189*, *311*, 377, 381

Room for Sideheads, 192, *193*, 311

customizing

dictionaries, **298–301**

ruling in table, **405–407**

spelling checker options, **296–298**

Cut button (QuickAccess Bar), *26*

cutting, 86

to delete, 271

table cells, **390–391**

unselected text, **272–273**

vs. deleting, 86

D

dashed line, 355–356

Dashed Line Options dialog box, *356*

databases

converting imported text from, **288–289**, *289*

data exported from, 407–408

date, inserting in header or footer, 317

Date paragraph tag, in newsletter template, 651

<$dayname>, 473

DCS (Desktop Color Separation) format, 368

importing, **374–375**

decimal tabs, alignment character for, 243

Decrease Character button (QuickAccess Bar), *26*

Default ¶ Font character tag, 580

in book templates, 656, 660, 662, 664

in business templates, 612, 616, 618, 622, 623, 625

in newsletter template, 652

in outline template, 640, 643, 645

in pagination sheet template, 649
in report templates, 628, 632, 636
Default A table format, 389
Default B table format, 389
default button, in dialog box, 15, 36
default cell margins, 397
default master page, 168
<Default Para Font>, 474, 476, 491, 499
default text frame, for header and footer, 314
default unit of measurement, 109
Define Color Views dialog box, 430, *430*
definitions, adding to document from template, 125
Del (Delete) key, 16
Delete Condition Tag dialog box, *574*
Delete Empty Pages setting, 163, 165
Delete Formats from Catalog dialog box, 229, *230*, 255, 404–405, *405*
Deleted condition tag, 462, 582, 585
deleting, **271–272**
  body pages, **169**
  change bars, **580**
  character tags, **229–230**
  characters, 16, 85
  condition tag, 573
  conditional text, 576
  cross-reference format, **555–556**

cross-references, 550
custom math element definition, 592
document files in book, **457–458**
footnotes, **559**
format from Character Catalog, 224
hypertext markers, **532**
index marker, 515–516
master pages, 182
page numbers from indexes, **501**
paragraph format, **255**
preventing accidental for index markers, 487
reference pages, 185
selected text, 17
tab stops, 243
table formats, 404
text, **84–85**
text frame, 191
user variables, 569
vs. cutting, 86
delimiter math element, 591
Delimiters page, in Equations window, 588, *590*
delimiting character, 288–289
derivative math element, 591
deselecting
  objects, 84
  text frames, 84
Desktop Color Separation format, importing, **374–375**
desktop publisher, FrameMaker as, xxi–xxii

DFX file format, 372
diacritical mark math element, 591
dialog boxes, **35–37**, *36*
  default button in, 15
DIB file format, 368
dictionaries
  adding word to, 296
  changing, **299–300**
  customizing, **298–301**
  editing, **301**
  as read-only or hidden files, 299
  removing word from, 296
Dictionaries button, in Spelling Checker window, 295
Dictionary Functions window, 299, *299*, 300
didot, 57
directory
  for book files, 445
  changing references in MIF file, 114–115
  for file storage, 14, 141
  for opening document, 110–111
  for personal templates, 135
  for templates, 122
disconnected page, 166
discretionary hyphen, 56
  search for, 282
Display Units, in View Options dialog box, 57–58
Distance above Baseline, for anchored frames, 199–200
Distribute command, **341–342**, 365

Distribute dialog box, 341–342, *341*

.DOC file extension, 140

document dictionary, 298
adding word to, 296

document files in books
deleting and rearranging, **457–458**
format changes, **455–457**
opening, **454**
renaming, **458–459**
saving and closing, **454–455**
setting up, **449–451**

document icons, *30*

document templates, **120–136**. *See also* templates

document windows, *31*, **31–35**
cascaded, 49, *49*
maximizing, 50, *51*
Page Up and Page Down buttons on, 72
resizing, **34–35**
tiled, *50*, 50

documents. *See also* comparing documents; view-only documents
changing layout in existing, **309–313**
changing name or location, 141
conditional, 570. *See also* conditional document
creating, **107–110**
creating from templates, **8–12**, 121
defined, 150
formatting for table of contents, 475

importing, **111–120**
importing nonFrame-Maker, **112–116**
importing text from, **119–120**
marking for index, **486–494**
moving through by screen, 33
opening existing Frame-Maker, **110–111**
recently opened list on File menu, 48
ruler settings, 61
saving, **139–147**
size of, **34–35**
spell check of, **93–95**
templates to modify look of, **124–126**
viewing, **54–55**
view-only vs. editable, 524
zoom settings for, 66

Double Line reference frame, 183

double line spacing, 28

double underline, 212

double-sided document, 109, 149, 173

Double-space format, 92

dragging, 42
to select word, 17
windows, 53

Draw Bottom Ruling on Last Sheet Only check box, 400

drawing, creating, **356–358**

Drawing commands in Tools window, *327*, 328, **338–347**, *339*

Align command, **340**

Bring to Front command, **340**

Distribute command, **341–342**

Group command, **338**

Send to Back, **340**

Ungroup command, **339**

drawing tools, xxiii
on Tools window, *327*, 328, **330–338**

drive
for file storage, 14, 141
for opening document, 110

drop caps, anchored frames for, **202**

DRW file format, 372

E

Edge Gap, 342, 365

Edit button (Paragraph Designer Basic Properties page), 242

Edit Condition Tag dialog box, *572*, *572*, 573

Edit Cross-Reference Format dialog box, *555*

Edit menu
for book file, 453
➤ Clear, 84, 271
➤ Copy, 86
➤ Copy Special,
➤ Character Format, 270
➤ Conditional Text Settings, 270
➤ Paragraph Format, 270

➤ Table Column Width, 270

➤ Cut, 86, 272

➤ Find/Change, 276

for conditional text, 576

for hypertext markers, 531

➤ Find Next, 285

➤ Paste, 86, 270

for row or column, 391

➤ Spelling Checker, 93, 293

➤ Suppress Automatic Reference Update, 454

➤ Thesaurus, 304

➤ Undo, 87, 273

➤ Update References, 551, 552

in view-only document, 524

Edit Ruling Style dialog box, 406–407, *406*

Edit System Variable dialog box, *569*, 569

Edit Tab Stop dialog box, *243*

Edit User Variable dialog box, 567, *568*

editable documents

hypertext in, **519**

vs. view-only documents, 524

editing, **15–18, 75–95**

conditional text, **576**

cross-reference marker text, problems from, 551

dictionary files, **301**

equations, **593**

header or footer text, **316**

hypertext commands, **531–532**

index entries, **489**

index markers, 486

text inset properties, **292–293**

variable definition, 568

em dash, 212

ignoring in index alphabetization, 505

possible line breaks after, 276

search for, 282

em space, search for, 282

e-mail messages, 288

EMF file format, 368

Emphasis character tag, 220

in book templates, 657, 660, 662, 664

in business templates, 612, 616, 618, 622, 623, 625

in newsletter template, 652

in outline template, 640, 642, 646

in pagination sheet template, 649

in report templates, 629, 632, 636

empty pages, 163, **165–166**

en dash

ignoring in index alphabetization, 505

possible line breaks after, 276

search for, 282

en space, search for, 282

Encapsulated PostScript files, 371–372

Encapsulated PostScript Interchange (EPSI) files, 372

End Angle (Property dialog box), 382

End key, to move character cursor, 76

endnotes, 558, **564**

end-of-flow character (§), 56, 156, *157*

and hypertext area, 527

search for, 282

in table cells, 389, *389*

<*$endrange*>, 490, 492, 516

Enlarge Character button (QuickAccess Bar), *26*

Enter (↵) key, 237

and default command button, 36

envelope, template sample, *130*

EPS file format, 372

EPSI file format, 372

Equation paragraph tag

in book templates, 655

in report templates, 627, 630, 634, 636

Equation Variables character tag

in book templates, 657, 660, 662, 664

in business templates, 612, 616, 618, 622, 623, 625

in newsletter template, 653

in outline template, 640, 643, 645

in pagination sheet template, 649
in report templates, 629, 633, 637
EquationNumber character tag
in book templates, 657
in report templates, 633
equations, **586–594**
creating, **586–587**
editing, **593**
evaluating, **594**
formatting, **593**
inserting characters, numbers, and math symbols, **588**
math elements for, **587–588, 591–592**
Equations button, in document window, *32*, 32, 587
Equations Help window, *99*
Equations window, 587, 588, *589–590*
Equidistant Centers, for Distribute command, 342
Esc key, shortcuts using, 44–45. *See also* keyboard shortcuts
evaluating equations, **594**
even page count, 166
Even-Numbered Pages setting, in Print Document dialog box, 149
exit hypertext command, 534
Explore Standard Templates (New dialog box), 8, 122

extending selection, 79
Extra Spaces, Spelling Checker and, 297
Extract paragraph tag
in book templates, 655
in report templates, 627, 630, 634

F

Facets (Property dialog box), 383
Facing pages display, 59
Family property, in Character Designer, 215
fax cover page, template sample, *128*, **616–619**, *617*
feathering, 172, 173
Figure paragraph tag
in book templates, 655
in report templates, 627, 630, 634
FigureLOF paragraph tag, in book templates, 661
figures. *See also* graphics
list of, 518
file, of unknown words from Spelling Checker, 301
File menu
➤ Add File, 494
➤ Exit, 18, *19*
➤ Generate/Book, 445, 494, 553
➤ Generate/Update, 471, 496
➤ Import, 197

➤ File, 117, 203, 369, 373, 374, 376
➤ Formats, 124, 225, 257, 410, 429, 455, 482, 514, 557
➤ New, 8, 107, 121, 135, 308
Explore Standard Templates, 187
➤ Open, 48, 110
➤ Preferences, 67
➤ Print, 18, 147, 433
➤ Rearrange Files, 457
recently opened documents on, 48, 111
➤ Revert to Saved, 87, 145
➤ Save, 13, 14, 17, 123, 139
➤ Save As, 13, 14, 139, 144, 446
➤ Set Up File, 319, 449
➤ Text Symbols, 11
➤ Utilities, 595
➤ Compare Books, 463
➤ Compare Documents, 583
in view-only document, 524
File menu for book, 451, 452–453
➤ Close All Files in Book, 455
➤ Save All Files in Book, 454
<*$file name*>, 473
file names
generic (*.*), 13
in hypertext commands, 533

file transfer, binary, 140
Filename Suffix box, for
    Table of Contents files,
    469
Filename system variable,
    566
files
  for book, **444–445**
  printing color separations
    to, 435
  printing in Mac version,
    438
  saving all open, 139
Fill box, on Tools window,
    327, 328
fill pattern, 352, 361
  adding, 360
filter, 112
Find Backward option, 280
Find Character Format
    dialog box, *278*
Find Conditional Text dia-
    log box, 279–280, *280*,
    576, *577*
find and replace, **276–286**
  repeating from search,
    285
Find/change button
    (QuickAccess Bar), *26*
Find/Change palette, 88,
    276–286, *277*
  buttons on, 284–285
  Change area, **283–284**
  closing, 89
  Find area of, 277–279
finding text, **88**
First Baseline, for sidehead
    alignment, 194

FirstLetter character tag,
  in report templates,
  637
FirstLetterTitle character
  tag, in book templates,
  660
first-line margin, 240, 258
  changing, 63
First-Line Synchronization
  Limit, 173
Fixed check box (Para-
  graph Designer Basic
  Properties), 242
fixed spacing characters,
  209–210
Flip L/R (Left/Right) command, **344**
Flip U/D (Up/Down) com-
  mand, **343–344**
Float option, for table position, 398
Floating check box, for anchored frames, 198–
  199
Flow settings, in Custom-
  ize Text Frame dialog
  box, 165
flow tag, 176, 177
  master page text frame
  with, 182
Flow Tag (Property dialog
  box), 383
fmdictionary file (UNIX),
  298
FMHOME variable, 7
folder, 14. *See also* directory
font size
  greeking for small, 67

line spacing adjustment
  for, 242
fonts, **207–214**
  angle, **211**
  for business letters, 258
  font families, **209**
  for manuscripts and personal letters, 258
  style, **211–213**
  symbol set, **208–209**
  type size, **210**
  variation, **211**
footers. *See also* headers
  and footers
  on master page, 167
  on portrait orientation,
  108
footing in table
  repeating row across
  pages, 387–388
  ruling for, 400
  shading, 401
Footnote button (QuickAc-
  cess Bar), *26*
Footnote paragraph tag,
  560, 561
  in book templates, 655
  in business templates,
  611, 614, 616, 620
  in newsletter template,
  651
  in outline templates, 640,
  642, 645
  in report templates, 627,
  630, 635
Footnote Properties dialog
  box, 561, *562*
  Number Format area, 563

Numbering Style area, 563
Footnote reference frames, 183
footnotes, **558–563**
  deleting, **559**
  finding, 279
  formatting, **561–563**
  inserting, **559**
  management of, **558**
  referencing from multiple places, **559–560**
  separator for, **560–561**
  style for numbering, 563
Format area (Paragraph Designer Pagination Properties page), 246
Format menu
  ➤ Characters,
    ➤ Catalog, 224, 226, 477
    ➤ Designer, 214, 221, 226, 580
  ➤ Customize Layout, 174
  ➤ Connect Text Frames, 166, 192
  ➤ Customize Text Frame, 164, 171, 176, 177, 187, 311, 377
  ➤ Disconnect Both, 166
  ➤ Disconnect Next, 166
  ➤ Disconnect Previous, 166
  ➤ Rotate Page Clockwise, 174
  ➤ Rotate Page Counterclockwise, 174
  ➤ Split Text Frames, 166

  ➤ Unrotate Page, 174
  ➤ Document,
    ➤ Change Bar Properties, 218
    ➤ Change Bars, 578, 580
    ➤ Footnote Properties, 561
    ➤ Numbering, *165*, 165–166, 319
    ➤ Text Options, 217, 275
  ➤ Headers & Footers,
    ➤ Insert Current Date, 317
    ➤ Insert Page #, 317
    ➤ Insert Page Count, 317
  ➤ Page Layout,
    ➤ Column Layout, 171, 187, 310
    ➤ Line Layout, 172
    ➤ Master Page Usage, 169–170, 182, 313
    ➤ New Master Page, 181, 313
    ➤ Page Size, 173, 310
    ➤ Update Column Layout, 183, 312
  ➤ Paragraphs,
    ➤ Catalog, 256
    ➤ Designer, 39, 239, 416
  ➤ Style, 91
format overrides, 229
formatting. *See also* character format properties
  adding to document from template, 125
  change bars, **580–581**

  for cross-references in documents, **553–557**
  equations, **593**
  footnotes, **561–563**
  imported text, **286–293**
  indexes, **497–514**
  retaining in index after update, **513**
  table of contents, **472–482**
  of text, 90
Formatting Bar
  in application window, *24*, **27–29**, *28*
  asterisk (*) before name tag in, 238
  to change paragraph format, 92
  viewing, 29
FormLabels paragraph tag, in pagination sheet template, 649
FormTitle paragraph tag, in pagination sheet template, 649
four-color printing process, 419
four-color process separations, **432–433**
  printing, **437–440**
four-color slides, xxii
Frame Above/Below (Paragraph Designer Advanced Page), 250
Frame Name dialog box, 184, 337–338, *338*
Frame Products group, 3
FrameMaker
  introduction and tutorial, **606**
  quick tour, xx–xxii

quitting, 18, 20, 25
serial number, 98, **599**
starting, **3–7**
version 5 new features, xxii–xxiv
FrameMaker files, working with, xxii
FrameMaker icon, *4*
FrameMaker (Mac version)
Apple Color Picker, 422
application window, 23
character properties, 213
color separations, 433
Dictionary Functions dialog box, 300
editing actions, 77
file format conversion, 118
Formatting Bar, 29
Help facilities, 97
importing nonFrameMaker document, 112
importing QuickTime movies, 367
installation folder, *6*
installing, **601–603**
main menu for book file, 451
main screen, *6*
New file dialog box, 107
Preferences dialog box, 146
Print Document dialog box, 147, *148*
Publish-and-Subscribe, 116, 269
QuickAccess Bar display, 27
quitting, 20

Save dialog box, 13
site dictionary, 300
starting, **5**
Tools window, 328
Undo in, 273
FrameMaker Overview (Help menu), 98
FrameMaker (UNIX version)
document window, 31
editing actions, 77
formats for saving files, 144
Formatting Bar, 29
halftone screen settings, 439
Help facilities, 97
installing, **604–605**
main menu, 7, 24
main menu for book file, 451
New file dialog box, 107
plate imaging in, **440**
Preferences dialog box, 146
Print Document dialog box, 147
QuickAccess Bar display, 27
quitting, 20
Save Document dialog box, 13, 139
starting, **7**
Tools window, 328
Undo in, 273
FrameMaker view-only file mode, 144
FrameMaker (Windows version)
application window, *5*

closing Help screen, 99
installing, **600**
main menu for book file, 451
printer drivers, 435
starting, **3–4**
Tools window, 328
FrameMath reference page, 591
frames. *See* anchored frames; graphic frames; text frames
Freehand Curve tool, *329*, **335**
<$fullfilename>, 320
<$fullfilename>, 320
function math element, 591
Functions page, in Equations window, 588, *590*

G

gap between columns, 109
GEM file format, 368
Generate Acrobat Data, in Print Document dialog box, 150
Generate/Book dialog box, 445, *446*, *469*, 494–495, *494*
List of References, 553
Generate/Update Book dialog box, 471, *471*, 496, *496*, 497
generated files, 447, 450, **467**
hypertext in, **519–520**, **542**
generated lists, 467

of hypertext markers, 541
table of contents, **468–471**
generic file name (*.*), 13
GIF file format, 368
Global Update Options
in Paragraph Designer, 254
in Table Designer, 404
Global Update Options
dialog box, *222*, 222–223, 230, 252–253, *253*, *403*, 403
Go to Page dialog box, 34, 72–73, *73*
gotolink hypertext command, 534–535
gotolinkfitwin hypertext command, 535
gotopage hypertext command, 535
graphic frame, to separate footnotes, 560
Graphic Frame tool, *329*, **337**
graphic frames
adding to reference pages, **184–185**
importing bitmap to, 369
importing Desktop Color Separation graphic to, 374–375
importing QuickTime movie to, 376
importing vector graphic to, 373
sizing, 185
graphics, **327–384**. *See also* Tools window
as active hypertext area, **526–528**
adding color to, 417–418
background for body pages, 168, **181–182**
creating drawing, **356–358**
importing, **367–377**
importing bitmap, **368–371**
importing to table cell, 390
on master page, 176
preventing printing of hypertext, **529–530**
printing as gray boxes, 149
setting fixed distance for, 200
text following contours of, xxiii, 375–379, **378–380**, *379*
Graphics check box, in View Options dialog box, 59
Graphics menu, 338
➤ Align, 341, 364, 365
➤ Bring to Front, 340
➤ Distribute, 342, 365
➤ Flip Left/Right, 344
➤ Flip Up/Down, 34
➤ Gravity, 350
➤ Join, **347–348**, 363
➤ Object Properties, 164, 171, 294, 314, 332, 347, 380, 384
➤ Overprint, 349
➤ Reshape, 343
➤ Rotate, 345, 366
➤ Runaround Properties, **348**, 378
➤ Scale, 314, 346, 364
➤ Smooth, 343
➤ Tools, 327, 351, 416
➤ Ungroup, 339
➤ Unsmooth, 343
gravity, connecting objects with, **350**
gray items on menus, 35
gray scale, 368
gray squares, in Character Designer, 217
greeking, 66–67
Grid Lines (View menu), 55
grid lines, in View Options dialog box, 58
Grid Spacing check box, in View Options dialog box, 60
grids
background, 191
snap vs. visible, 60
Group command, **338**
Group read and write permissions for UNIX documents, 139
groups of character tags, **230**
groups of index entries
changing order, 507–508
changing order within, 508–509
empty paragraphs as separators between, 511
modifying titles, **509–512**
paragraph format of, 512
GroupTitlesIX paragraph tag, in book templates, 510, 663
gutter, 187

H

Halftone Screens dialog box, 439, *439*

handles, on Bezier curves, 363

hanging indent, 63–64
  paragraph formats for, **259–263**

Harvard outline style, 132, *133*, **637–640**, *638*

headers and footers, **313–323**
  adding to master pages, **314–316**
  building blocks for, 473
  editing text in, **316**
  inserting markers for use in, **322–323**
  on master page, 167
  on portrait orientation, 108
  resizing and moving, **314–315**
  running, 314, **319–323**
  variables in, **317–318**, 570

Heading1 paragraph tag
  in book templates, 655
  in business templates, 611, 614, 616, 620
  in newsletter template, 651
  in report templates, 627, 631, 635

Heading1TOC paragraph tag
  in book templates, 661
  in newsletter template, 651

Heading2 paragraph tag

in book templates, 655
in business templates, 611, 614, 616, 620
in newsletter template, 651
in report templates, 627, 631, 635

Heading2TOC paragraph tag, in book templates, 662

Heading3 paragraph tag, in report templates, 627, 631

Heading & Page cross-reference format, 554

heading in table
  repeating row across pages, 387–388
  ruling for, 400
  shading, 401

HeadingRunIn paragraph tag
  in book templates, 656
  in business templates, 611, 614
  in report templates, 627, 631, 635

headings
  capitalization of, 217
  missing from table of contents, 482
  straddling multiple columns, xxiii

Help, **97–104**
  context-sensitive, 27, 97, **98–99**
  index, *102*, **102–103**
  from QuickAccess Bar, 227

returning to previously viewed pages, 103
viewing online manuals, **101–102**

Help menu, *97*
  ➤ Contents, 100
  ➤ Context Sensitive, 27, 97
  ➤ FrameMaker Overview, 606
  ➤ Tutorial, 606

Help window
  closing, 27
  restoring with Windows task list, 103

Helvetica type, 209

hidden conditional text, 570. *See also* conditional text

highlight. *See* selected text

HLS Color Definitions dialog box, *425*

HLS (Hue, Lightness, Saturation) color model, 420
  color definition with, 423–424

Home key, to move character cursor, 76

horizontal list, 591

Horizontal page display, 59

horizontal straight line, 331

HPGL file format, 372

HTML output, xxiv

Hue, 420, 424

hypertext areas
  boundaries of, **525**
  format changes to mark, **526**
  graphics as, **526–528**

preventing printing of graphics, **529–530**
setting up on body pages, **527–528**
setting up on master pages, **528–529**
hypertext commands, 144, **533–540**
editing, **531–532**
inserting, **530–531**
hypertext documents
active area in, 523
testing for incorrect links, **541**
hypertext links
creating for table of contents, 470, 483
in generated files, **519–520**
from index, 496, 498
setting up, **524–529**
in summary document, **586**
in view-only documents, 150, **520**
when debugging index, **515**
hypertext markers, **530–532**
deleting, **532**
generating list, 541
inserting, **530–531**
selecting, 531
Hypertext Markup Language (HTML), **594–595**
hyphen
automatic, finding, 280
discretionary, 56, 282
forcing use of, 302

ignoring in index alphabetization, 505
nonbreaking, 451, 484, 517
possible line breaks after, 276
hyphenation, 295, **302**
automatic, 249
forcing changes, 301
Spelling Checker and unusual, 296

I

I-beam cursor, 75, 330
icons
document, *30*
FrameMaker, *4*
moving, 52
reducing windows to, 51
IGES file format, 372
IgnoreCharsIX paragraph tag, 505
Import by Reference button (Import File dialog box), 370, 372, 375, 376
Import File dialog box, 117, 369–370, *370*, 373, 374, 376
Import Formats dialog box, 124, *125*, 225, 225, *257*, 257, *410*, 410, *429*, 429, 455–456, *456*, 482, 514
Import Text File by Copy dialog box, 118, *287*
Import Text File by Reference dialog box, 118, 287–288, *287*, 292

Import Text Flow by Copy dialog box, 119, 290, *291*, 292
Import Text Flow by Reference dialog box, 119, *119*, 290, 292
Imported Graphic Scaling dialog box, 370–371, *371*
imported text
double-clicking for dialog box, 120
formatting, **286–293**
importing
color definitions, **428–429**
cross-reference formats, **557**
Desktop Color Separation format, **374–375**
documents, **111–120**
file by reference, xxiii, 111–112, 117, 279, 286
and formatting options, 290
formats from template index, 514
formats from template table of contents, 482
graphics into anchored frames, **203**
graphic images, **367–377**
graphics to table cell, 390
nonFrameMaker document, **112–116**
PostScript code, 377
QuickTime movies, 367, **375–376**
text, **116–120**

text into anchored frames, **204**

text from FrameMaker documents, **119–120**

text from nonFrame-Maker document, **118**

vector graphics, **371–374**

In Column format for paragraph, 246

incremental movement of objects, **362**

Indented paragraph tag

  in business templates, 611, 614, 616, 620

  in newsletter template, 651

indented paragraphs, format for, **259**

indents

  hanging, 63–64

  paragraph formats for, **259–263**

  Paragraph Designer settings for, 62, 240

  for tables, 397

Index button, on Help main menu screen, 100

index entries. *See also* groups of index entries

  adding cross-references, **493–494**

  changing, 515–516

  character format of, **499**

  creating simple, **487–488**

  editing, **489**

  missing, 516

  page range for, **492**

  sort order of, **505–507**

index markers, 485

  deleting, 515–516

inserting, 486

  preventing accidental deletion, 487

  quick ways to insert, 488

  special characters in, **488**

indexes, **484–517**

  adding title to, **512–513**

  building blocks in, 489, 490

  character format for page numbers, **499–501**

  double question marks (??) in, 516

  formatting, **497–514**

  generating and regenerating, 485, **494–497**

  hypertext links from, 496

  ignoring characters during alphabetization, **505**

  joining page numbers into page range, **501–502**

  marking document for, **486–494**

  master for multiple books, **517–518**

  page number alignment in, **503–504**

  removing page numbers from, **501**

  retaining formatting after update, **513**

  separator characters in, **502**

  special characters in, 489, 490

  steps to create, 485

  subentries in, 489, 491

  templates containing, 625

templates to format, **513–514**

troubleshooting, **515–517**

infix math element, 591

initial caps, changing text to, 274

Initial Page Layout, in Add Master Page dialog box, 181

in-line equations, 586

Insert Math Element dialog box, 591

Insert table button (QuickAccess Bar), *26*

Insert Table dialog box, 388–389, *388*

Inserted condition tag, 462, 582, 585

inserting

  cross-references in documents, **546–550**

  footnotes, **559**

  hypertext markers and commands, **530–531**

  index markers, 486

  text in table of contents entries, **477**

  variables, 570

  variables in headers and footers, 570

insertion point, anchored frames at, **199–200**

installing

  FrameMaker for Macintosh, **601–603**

  FrameMaker for UNIX, **604–605**

  FrameMaker for Windows, **600**

Internet publishing, xxiv

Italic button (QuickAccess Bar), *26*, 91
italic text, 90–91, 211
  in index cross-references, 499
.IX file extension, 495
IX text flow, 498
  character format for, 500–501
  GroupTitlesIX paragraph tag, 510, 511
  SeparatorsIX tag, 502, 503, 504, 517

J

jagged line, 333
Join command, **347–348**
joined Bezier curves, 363
Justified format, 92, 241
  word spacing in, 250

K

Keep With Next/Previous (Paragraph Designer Pagination Properties page), 245
kerning, 212
keyboard
  to change paragraph format, 92
  for commands, **42–45**
  repeating search from, 285
  for selecting text, 268

keyboard shortcuts, **18**, **43–45**
  for adding and removing change bars, 579, 580
  for capitalization, 274
  for Character Catalog, 224
  for Character Designer, 214
  Ctrl+M for Paragraph Designer, 40
  Ctrl+S for Save, 18
  for cut, copy and paste, 86
  for cutting and clearing text, 272–273
  for Find and Replace, 285, 286
  to lock document, 541
  for Paragraph Catalog, 256
  for selecting text, 268
  for spell checking, 302–303
  for Spelling Checker, **302–303**
  to switch between view-only and editable documents, 524
  to unlock view-only file, 145
Keyboard Shortcuts (Help menu), 97
keypad, 76–77

L

Labels character tag, in business templates, 616

Landscape button, 108
Landscape orientation, 107–108, 174
language
  selecting, 249
  for Thesaurus, 305
Language (Property dialog box), 383
large math element, 591
Large page, in Equations window, 588, *589*
Last Baseline, for sidehead alignment, 194
Last page of document, inserting in header or footer, 317
<*$lastpagenum*>, 320, 473
Launcher program (Mac), 5
leader characters
  in table of contents entries, **479**
  for tabs, 242
leading, 242
Learn button, in Spelling Checker window, 94, 296
Left-aligned paragraphs, 28, 92, 241
left-hand page, 173
Left master page, 168, 181
LetterAddress paragraph tag, in business templates, 611
LetterAuthor paragraph tag, in business templates, 611
LetterClose paragraph tag, in business templates, 611

LetterOpen paragraph tag, in business templates, 612

Level1IX paragraph tag, in book templates, 664

Level2IX paragraph tag, in book templates, 664

*n*Level paragraph tag, in outline template, 637–639, 640–642, 643–645

*n*LevelContinued paragraph tag, in outline template, 638–639, 640–642, 643–645

lightness of color, 420, 424

limit math element, 591

line breaks, 12, 275
  in index, 517
  in table of contents, 484

line end, **354**

Line End Options dialog box, 354–355, *355*

line layout, for body pages, **172–173**

Line Layout dialog box, 172–173, *172*

line properties boxes, on Tools window, *327*, 329

line spacing, 28, 242

line of text
  cursor movement by, 76
  cutting and clearing, 272–273
  deleting to end, 85
  preventing spelling check of, 294
  selecting, 268

Line tool, *329*, **330–331**, 357, 360

line width, **353–354**

Line Width (Property dialog box), 382

Line Width Options dialog box, 353–354, *354*

lines
  cap styles for, 355
  end style of, 354
  jagged, 333
  reshaping, 342
  style of, **355–356**

list of figures, templates containing, 625

list of figures text flow, 473

List Files of Type dropdown list (Save Document dialog box), 142

list of tables, templates containing, 625

list of tables flow, 473

location of documents, changing, 141

locking documents, 541

lowercase, 213
  changing text to, 274

Lowercase button (QuickAccess Bar), *26*

Low-Resolution Images check box, in Print Document dialog box, 149

luminosity, 420

M

Macintosh, xxii. *See also* FrameMaker (Mac version)

Macintosh publisher boundaries ([ ]), 56

MacPaint file format, 368

main dictionary, 298

main flow, 187

main menu
  in application window, *24*, **25**
  Help, 97
  Navigation, 102
  in Windows version, 43

Make Page Count Even, 166

Make Page Count Odd, 166

maker command (UNIX), 7

Maker file (UNIX), 300

MAKER.INI file, 300

Maker Interchange Format (MIF), **113–115**, 140, 144, 447

Maker Markup Language (MML) files, 113, **115–116**

ManualName paragraph tag, in pagination sheet template, 647

manuscripts, paragraph formats for, 258

margin graphics, 201

margins, 240, **310–311**
  changing first-line, 63
  for columns, 109
  for headers and footers, 314

marker symbol (⊤), 56

marker text, finding, 279

Marker of Type, finding, 279

Marker window, 323, *323*, 486, *486*
  Marker Text area, 499
markers, 484–485
  finding, 278
  generating list of contents, 467
  hypertext, **530–532**
  inserting for index, 486
  inserting for use in headers and footers, **322–323**
marking document for index, **486–494**
master indexes, for multiple books, **517–518**
Master Page Usage dialog box, 169–170, *170*
master pages, 79, 167, **174–183**
  adding, **180–181**
  adding background text and graphics, **181–182**
  adding to document from template, 125
  adding headers and footers to, **314–316**
  adding template text frames to, **182**
  applying to body page, **182–183**
  for Blank Portrait Page template, 174–175, *175*
  changes to, 312
  changing for body page, **169–170**
  column layout in, **183**
  deleting and renaming, 182

  headers and footers on, 167
  order of, 180
  rotating, **183**
  setting up active hypertext area on, **528–529**
  spelling checker for, 298
  system variables on, 565
math elements, **587–588, 591–592**
  creating and redefining, **591–592**
  deleting custom definition, 592
Matrices page, in Equations window, 588, *589*
matrix hypertext command, 536
matrix math element, 591
Maximize button
  in application window, *24*, 25
  in document window, 34
maximizing document window, 50, *51*
Maximum Inter-¶ Padding, 173
Maximum Interline Padding, 173
measurement unit, default, 109
MemoCC paragraph tag, in business templates, 615
MemoFrom paragraph tag, in business templates, 615

MemoSubject paragraph tag, in business templates, 615
MemoTo paragraph tag, in business templates, 615
menus
  gray items on, 35
  keyboard to access in Windows, 43
Merge Lines into Paragraph option, for ASCII text, 288
message openfile hypertext command, 536
message system hypertext command, 536–537
message winexec hypertext command, 536–537
messages, during startup, 4
Meta key (UNIX), for shortcuts, 44
Microsoft Word, 113
MIF (Maker Interchange Format), **113–115**, 140, 144, 447
Minimize button
  in application window, *24*, 25
  in document window, 34, 51
mirror image of objects, **344**
mistakes, undoing, **87**
MML (Maker Markup Language) files, 113, **115–116**
models, 135. *See also* templates
Modification Date system variable, 566

monospaced characters, 209–210

mouse
for commands, **41–42**
for selecting text, 268

moving
anchored frames, 198, 200
between cells in tables, 390
through documents by screen, 33
header or footer text frame, 315
icons, 52
objects, 81, 360
by increments, **362**
through pages, **71–73**
palettes, 39

multiple objects, selecting, 81

N

names
for book files, **446–447**, 453
changing for character tags, **229**
for character tags, **229**, 415
for colors, 423–424
for condition tag, 571
for document files in book, **458–459**
for files in book, 444–445
for master pages, 182
for reference pages, 185

saving documents under new, 14, 141
for text flows and import process, 119–120
for variables, 567

Navigation menu, 102
in view-only document, 524

Network button, in Save Document dialog box, 141

new documents, saving, **12–15**

New file button (QuickAccess Bar), *26*

New file dialog box, 8, *9*, 107, *108*, 121, *121*

New Format command
in Paragraph Designer, 254
in Table Designer, 404

New Format dialog box, 227–228, *228*, 254, *254*, 415–416, *415*

new line (<), 11, 56
search for, 282

New Marker button, in Marker window, 486

newlink hypertext command, 537

newlink marker, 534

newsletters
columns in, 190
template sample, *134*, 187, **649–653**, *650*

newspaper-style columns, 186

Next ¶ Tag setting (Paragraph Designer), 244

Next Page button, in document window, *31*

nextpage hypertext command, 537

"No Undo" comment, 87, 273

nonbreaking hyphen, 451, 484, 517
ignoring in index alphabetization, 505
search for, 282

nonbreaking space (␣), 56
in index entries, 517
search for, 282

nonFrameMaker document
importing, **112–116**
importing text from, 118

non-printing text symbols, displaying, 55

<$nopage>, 490, 493, 501, 517

"Normal FrameMaker Document Format," 140–141

"Note" paragraphs, **262–263**

notes, xxv

NumAppendixCont paragraph tag, in pagination sheet template, 648

NumAppendix!First paragraph tag, in pagination sheet template, 647

Numbered1 paragraph tag
in book templates, 656
in business templates, 612, 615, 616, 620

in newsletter template, 652

in report templates, 628, 631, 635

numbered paragraph, 65

Numbered paragraph tag
in book templates, 656
in business templates, 612, 615, 616, 620
in newsletter template, 652
in report templates, 628, 631, 635

numbered paragraphs, 65
format for complex, **263–264**
hanging indents for, 260
paragraph format for, 261–262

numbered report, template sample, *131*, *629*, **629–633**

NumberedCont paragraph tag
in book templates, 656
in report templates, 628, 632, 635

numbering footnotes, style for, 563

Numbering Properties dialog box, *319*, 319
Delete Empty Pages setting, 163, 165

numbers, inserting in equation object, **588**

NumBlankPage paragraph tag, in pagination sheet template, 648

NumChapterCont paragraph tag, in pagina-

tion sheet template, 648

NumChapter!First paragraph tag, in pagination sheet template, 648

NumContinuous paragraph tag, in pagination sheet template, 648

numeric outline, 132, *133*
template, **640–643**, *641*

numeric space, search for, 282

numeric underline, 212
<$numerics>, 507–509

NumIndex paragraph tag, in pagination sheet template, 648

NumRoman paragraph tag, in pagination sheet template, 648

O

object cursor, 75–76
converting text cursor to, 82
as filled or unfilled arrow, 79–80
to select objects, **79–84**

Object Properties command, **380**

Object Properties dialog box, 332–333, *333*, 380–384, *381*

Object Selection tool, *329*, 330

objects, 150
alignment of, **340**
alignment with snap grid, **350–351**
combining, **338**
connecting with gravity, **350**
copying and pasting, **359–360**
deselecting, 84
entering in table cells, **389–390**
equally spacing, 341–342
flipping, 343–344
mirror image of, **344**
moving, 81
patterns and colors of, **351–352**
resizing, **345–346**
selecting, **79–84**, **358–359**
selecting text frame as, 164, 178, 311, 330
selecting text lines and graphic frames as, 330
shapes of, **342**
snapping rotation to set angle, 60
ungrouping, 339

oblique characters, 211

Odd-Numbered Pages setting, in Print Document dialog box, 149

odd page count, 166

Offset Position (Property dialog box), 382

Offset, for superscripts and subscripts, 218

OLE file format, 368

online distribution, file format for, 144

online manuals
  for Help, **101–102**
  MIF Reference, 116
  MML Reference, 116
online tutorial, xxiv
Open dialog box, *110*
open documents, listing in
    Window menu, 52–53
Open file button
    (QuickAccess Bar), *26*
opening
  book file, 453
  Character Catalog, 232,
    233
  document files in book,
    454
  existing FrameMaker
    document, **110–111**
  folder, 14
  palettes, 38
openlink hypertext com-
    mand, 538
openlinkfitwin hypertext
    command, 538
opennew hypertext com-
    mand, 538–539
openpage hypertext com-
    mand, 539
Operators page, in Equa-
    tions window, 588, *590*
option buttons, in dialog
    boxes, *36*, 36–37
Orientation button
    (QuickAccess Bar), *26*
orphan lines, 246
  control for tables, 398
outline character property,
    213, 216
outlines templates, 132,
    133, 134, **637–646**

outside ruling, 400
Oval tool, *329,* **334**
overflows, **156, 158–159,**
    160–161
overline property, in Char-
    acter Designer, 212,
    216
Overprint command, **349**
overrides, 179–180, 229
  of active master page ar-
    eas, 528–529
  in book files, 456
  of paragraph tag proper-
    ties, 238
  updating, 313
Overview introduction
    document, 606

P

page breaks
  in conditional document,
    577
  preventing between para-
    graphs, 245
Page Count system vari-
    able, 566
Page cross-reference for-
    mat, 554
Page Down button, 72
Page Layout Warning dia-
    log box, *313*
page layouts, **307–323**
  changing in existing docu-
    ments, **309–313**
  creating special, **185–195**
  elements of, **307–308**
  headers and footers, **313–
    323**

multicolumn, **186–192**
for new documents, **308–
    309**
Page Number box, in
    document window, *31,*
    33
page numbers, 313
  alignment in indexes,
    503–504
  in book file, 450
  character format in in-
    dex, **499–501**
  in headers or footers, 317
  location in table of con-
    tents, **478–479**
  properties when generat-
    ing index, 496
  removing from index, **501**
  style of, **318–319**
  troubleshooting display
    in cross-references,
    517
page of properties, in Para-
    graph Designer, 239
page range
  for index entries, **492**
  joining index page num-
    bers into, **501–502**
Page Scrolling pull-down
    menu, in View Options
    dialog box, 59
page size, 309, **310**
  selecting, 109
Page Size dialog box, 173
Page Up button, 72
PageDescription para-
    graph tag, in pagina-
    tion sheet template,
    648

<$pagenum>, 473, 474, 498, 501
PageNumber character tag, in book templates, 657, 660, 662
pages, 155
 automatic addition, 162
 changing size, **173**
 empty, 163, **165–166**
 moving through, **71–73**
 in palettes, 40
 pagination, 309
 changing, **173**
pagination sheet template, **646–649**, *647*
Paging buttons (QuickAccess Bar), 26, *26*
Pair Kern property, in Character Designer, 216
pair kerning, 212
palettes, 23, 32, **37–41**
 Character Catalog as, 224, *224*
 closing, 38
 Marker window as, 487
 moving, 39
 opening, 38
 Spelling Checker as, 93
Pantone Color Formula Guide, 426
Pantone Colors dialog box, *427*
Pantone Matching System (PMS), 413, 420, 421
 color definition with, 425–427
Paragraph Catalog, 38, *38*, **238**, *256*
 applying tags with, **256**

deleting format from, 255
for portrait orientation document, 108
Paragraph Catalog button, in document window, 32, *32*, 256
paragraph cross-references, 545
 inserting, 546
Paragraph Designer, 39, 62, *63*, 238, *239*, **239–255**
 adding color with, 416–417
 Advanced Properties page, *249*, **249–250**
 Language, 294
 Basic Properties page, *240*, **240–244**
 Fixed Line Spacing off, 200
 Commands menu,
 Delete Formats, 255
 Global Update Options, 254
 New Format, 254, 480
 Reset Window from Selection, 255
 Set Window to As Is, 255
 control area, **251–252**
 creating new format with, **254**
 Default font page, *244*, **244–245**
 Default Font Properties page, 416, *417*
 Numbering Properties page, **246–249**, *247*, 261, *262*

Pagination Properties page, 194, 195, *245*, **245–246**, 265
Table Cell properties page, **250–251**, *251*
Update All button, **252–254**
Update All Formats Tagged button, 504
vs. ruler settings, 62
Paragraph Format menu, 28, 29, *29*
paragraph format samples, **258–265**. *See also* template samples
 for business memos and letters, **258**
 complex numbered paragraphs, **263–264**
 for hanging indents, **259–263**
 for indented paragraphs, **259**
 for manuscripts and personal letters, **258**
 "Note" paragraphs, **262–263**
 run-in paragraphs, **265**
paragraph formats, 237
 copying, 270
 copying between documents, 257
 creating, 39
 creating with Paragraph Designer, 254
 deleting, **255**
 for imported text, 290
 listing all, 32
paragraph marks (¶), 56, 237

displaying, 11
and hypertext area, 527
search for, 282
Paragraph Tag field, in
   Paragraph Designer,
   251–252
paragraph tags, 28, **238**
   applying with Paragraph
     Catalog, **256**
   defining to include color,
     417
   in document window, *31*
   finding, 278
   and imported text, 290
   including in table of con-
     tents, 469
   for index title, 512
   lists of, 518
   setting for next para-
     graph, 244
   in source documents, and
     table of contents, **468**,
     472, 483
   for table of contents title,
     480
   for tables, 398
   updating, 253
   viewing definition, 252
paragraphs, **237–265**
   as active hypertext area,
     525
   aligning, 28
   appearance after import-
     ing, **289–290**
   bulleted, 65
   changing look of, **91–93**
   cursor movement by, 76
   definition of, 237
   list of, 467, 518

marking for rechecking
   with Spelling
   Checker, 301
numbered, 65, 450
preventing page breaks
   between, 245
preventing spelling check
   of, 294
selecting, 78, 268
setting location of, 245
spacing of, 28, 241–242,
   258
<$paranum>, 474, 478
<$paranumonly>, 478
<$paratext>, 473, 474
Paste button (QuickAccess
   Bar), *26*
pasting, 86, **269–270**
   conditional text, 576
   graphics in anchored
     frames, 203
   objects, **359–360**
   table cells, **390–391**
   patterns of objects, **351–**
     352
PC computer, xxii
PCX file format, 368
PDF (Portable Document
   Format), 150
Pen box, on Tools window,
   327
percentages, customizing
   in Zoom menu, 71
personal dictionary, 298
   adding word to, 296
Personal Dictionary file
   (Macintosh), 298–299
personal letters, paragraph
   format for, **258**
PgDn key, 72

PgUp key, 72
photocopying, color, 419
picas, 57–58
Pick Up Object Properties
   command, 347, 384
PICT file format, 369, 372
pitch, 210
Plain button (QuickAccess
   Bar), *26*
plain report template, *131,*
   626, **626–629**
plain text, imported text
   flow as, 292
plate imaging in UNIX,
   440
plates, 431
playback quality, of Quick-
   Time movie, 375
PMS. *See* Pantone Match-
   ing System (PMS)
points, 57–58, 207, 210
Polygon tool, *329,* **334–335**
polygons
   changing circles or
     squares to, **346–347**
   reshaping, 342
   Smooth command and,
     343
polyline, reshaping, 342
Polyline tool, *329,* **333**
polylines, Smooth com-
   mand and, 343
popup hypertext com-
   mand, 539
Portable Document For-
   mat (PDF), 150
Portrait orientation, 107–
   108, 174
Positioning page, in Equations window, 588, *590*

postfix math element, 591
PostScript Code (Property dialog box), 383
PostScript files, 433, 437
Encapsulated, 371–372
importing, 367, **377**
posture, 67
power loss, and lost work, 15
preferences, for automatic save process, **146–147**
Preferences dialog box, *146*
Greek Screen Text, 67
prefix math element, 591
prepositions, ignoring in index sorting, 506
Previous Page button, in document window, *31*
previouslink hypertext command, 539–540
previouslinkfitwin hypertext command, 540
Previously View Page button, in Help, 103
previouspage hypertext command, 530
Print Document dialog box, 18, *19*, 37, 147–150, *148*, 433, *434*
Print file button (QuickAccess Bar), *26*
Print Files in Book dialog box, 459–460, *460*
print separations, 149–150
printer, changing, 149
printer drivers, in FrameMaker (Windows), 435, 438
printing, **18**, **147–151**
books, **459–460**

color as black and white, 149
conditional document, 576
cost of color, 419
document with Quick-Time movie, 376
four-color separations, **437–440**
preventing hypertext graphics in, **529–530**
spot color separations, **433–437**
thumbnails, 149
problem solving. *See* troubleshooting
process colors, 421
Properties command, **347**
Properties pull-down list
in Paragraph Designer, 239
in Table Designer, 395–396
proportionally spaced characters, 209–210
PS file format, 373
Public read and write permissions for UNIX documents, 139
Publish and Subscribe (FrameMaker Mac version), 269
publisher, finding, 279
PublisherBook paragraph tag, in book template, 659
pull-down menus, xxvi
in dialog boxes, 35, *36*

Q

Quadralay Corporation, 595
Question button (QuickAccess Bar), *26*, *27*
question marks, double (??), in indexes, 516
Quick Access Bar, Help button, *26*
QuickAccess Bar, xxiv, **26–27**, *26*
in application window, *24*
Bold button, 91
to cut, copy and paste, 86
Find/Change button, 277
horizontal or vertical, 27
Italic button, 91
Paste, 270
Underline button, 91
Undo button, 87
viewing, 27
quick-copying, **271**
QuickDraw PICT file format, 113
QuickTime movies
importing, 367, **375–376**
printing document with, 376
quit hypertext command, 530
quitall hypertext command, 530
quitting FrameMaker, 18, 20, 25
quotation marks, 275–276

R

radio buttons, in dialog
boxes, 36–37, *36*
read permissions for
UNIX documents, 139
Rearrange Files dialog
box, 457–458, *457*
recover file, 147
Rectangle tool, 177, *329*,
331–332, 357
rectangles, smoothing corners, 343
reference
automatic updating of file
by, 118
importing text by, xxiii,
111–112, 117, 204
reference frames, 250
reference pages, 167, **183–
185**
adding, 185
deleting, 185
graphic frame on, **184–
185**, 337–338
renaming, 185
system variables on, 565
TOC flow on, 473–474,
474
references
index of, 519
list of, 518
suspending automatic up-
dating, 454
registration marks, 434,
438
Registration Marks check
box, 149
Relations page, in Equa-
tions window, 588, *589*

relative path names, 533
repeated words, Spelling
Checker and, 296
ReportAuthor paragraph
tag, in report tem-
plates, 628, 632, 636
ReportPurpose paragraph
tag, in report tem-
plates, 632, 636
reports, templates for, *131*,
625–637
ReportTitle paragraph tag,
in report templates,
628, 632, 636
Reset Window from Selec-
tion command, in Para-
graph Designer, 255
Reshape command, **342**
reshape handle, 342
dragging to rotate object,
345
Resize Selected Columns
dialog box, *393*
resizing handles
for anchored frames, 197,
198
for header or footer text
frame, 314
resizing objects, **345–346**
resolution, of output de-
vice, 433
Return (⏎) key, 237
and default command
button, 36
ReturnAddress paragraph
tag, in newsletter tem-
plate, 652
reverse video, 77–78, 267
RGB Color Definitions
dialog box, *424*

RGB (Red, Green, Blue)
color model, 420
color definition with, 423
Rich Text Format (RTF),
113, 144
right-aligned paragraphs,
28, 92, 241
right-hand page, 173
Right master page, 168,
181
Roman-8 characters, 208
roman characters, 211
Roman numerals
as counters, 248
ignoring in Spelling
Checker, 298
for page numbers, 318–
319
Room for Side Heads
(Property dialog box),
383
Room for Sideheads (Col-
umn Layout dialog
box), 246
roots math element, 591
Rotate command, **344–345**
Rotate Selected Objects
dialog box, 345, *345*
Rotate Table Cells dialog
box, 394, *395*
Rotate tool, 366
rotating
body pages, 174
master pages, **183**
snapping objects to angle,
60
rounded rectangle, radius
of corners, 332
Rounded Rectangle tool,
329, **332**

Row Format dialog box, 393, *394*
row in table
  adding, **392**
  selecting, 390
  size of, **392–393**
RTF (Rich Text Format), 113, 144
"rubber band" selector box, 81, 359
  to select objects, 340
  to select text frame, 82–84
rulers, **60–65**
  to change paragraph format, 92
  objects snapping on, 59–60
  in View Options dialog box, 58
  vs. Paragraph Designer settings, 62
Rulers (View menu), 55
Ruling properties page, in Table Designer, 396, **398–400**, *399*
ruling in table, customizing, **405–407**
Run around Bounding Box, 379
Run into Paragraph Anchoring position, 202
runaround properties, As Is for, 380
Runaround Properties command, **348**
Runaround Properties dialog box, 348, *348*, 378–380, *378*

Run-In head, format for paragraph, 246
run-in paragraphs, format for, **265**
running footers, 314, **319–323**
Running H/F *n* system variables, 320, 321, 566, 570
running headers, 314, **319–323**

S

samples, of templates. *See* template samples
Samples & Clip Art (Help menu), 98
sans serifs font families, 209
saturation, 420, 424
Save As Text dialog box, 142–143, *143*
Save Document dialog box, 13, *13*, *15*, 123, *124*, 139, *140*
  Network button in, 141
Save file button (QuickAccess Bar), *26*
saved document, reverting to previous, 87
saving documents, **139–147**
  book files, **446–447**, 453
  document files in book, **454–455**
  new, **12–15**
  in "Normal FrameMaker Document Format," 140–141

  preferences for automatic process, **146–147**
  specialized formats for, 143–145
  as text file, **142–143**
  under new name, 14
Scale command, **345–346**
Scale tool, 364
screen, moving through document by, 72
screen display
  color on, **429–430**
  graphics on, 59
script math element, 591
Scroll bars, in document window, 30, *31*, **33**, 72
scroll box, 33
search and replace, **88–90**
See Heading & Page cross-reference format, 554
See references in indexes, **493–494**
selected text
  deleting, 17
  Esc key shortcuts for, 45
  extending, 79
  importing by reference and, 120
  replacing by typing, 14
  text cursor for, 77
selecting
  "backward" text, **269**
  characters in cell, 391
  hypertext marker, 531
  markers, 486
  multiple objects, 81
  objects, **79–84**, **358–359**
  table cells, **390–391**
  text, **267–268**
  text frames, 81–84

text frames as object, 164, 178, 311

tools, 329

selection tools, on Tools window, *327*, *328*, **330**

semicolon (;), in index marker, 488, 490

Send to Back command, **340**

sentences

cursor movement by, 76

cutting and clearing, 273

selecting, 268

separations, 149–150, **431–441**. *See also* color separations

Separations Setup button, 150

separator characters, in indexes, **502**

separators

for footnotes, **560–561**

between index entry groups, 511

for table headers and footers, 400

SeparatorsIX tag, 502, 503, 504

serial number, for FrameMaker, 98, **599**

series label, in Autonumber format, 247–248

serif font families, 209

service bureaus, files for, xxii, 433, 435

Set # Sides command, **346–347**

Set Find/Change Parameters dialog box, 285–286, *285*

Set Print Separations dialog box, 435, *436*, 439, 529

Set Up dialog box, Create Hypertext Links, 515

Set Up File dialog box, 449–451, *450*

Set Up Standard Index dialog box, 495, *495*

Set Up Table of Contents dialog box, 469, *470*

Create Hypertext Links, 483

Include Paragraph Tagged scroll list, 483

Set Window To As Is option, in Table Designer, 405

SGI-RGB file format, 369

shading, customizing in table, **405, 407**

Shading properties page, in Table Designer, 396, **400–402**, *401*

shadow character property, 213

Shift key

and menu commands, 139

for shortcuts, 44

shortcut buttons, in document window, *31*, **32**

shortcuts. *See* keyboard shortcuts

Show/Hide Conditional Text dialog box, *575*, 575

Show Hyphenation button, in Spelling Checker window, 295

sidehead report, template sample, *132*, **633–637**, *634*

sideheads, 186, **192–194**, *193*, 246, 310, 311

Single Line reference frame, 183

single line spacing, 28, 242

single-character words, ignoring in Spelling Checker, 297

<$singlepage>, 490

single-sided document, 109, 173

Single-space format, 92

SITE.DCT dictionary file (Windows), 298

site.dict dictionary file (UNIX), 298

site dictionary, 298

in FrameMaker (Mac version), 300

Site Dictionary file (Macintosh), 298

size

of anchored frame, **198**

of documents, **34–35**

of graphic frame, 185

Size property, 383

in Character Designer, 215

slanted characters, 211

slash (/) character, in path names in hypertext commands, 533

slide presentations, 160, *161*

small caps, 213

changing look of, **217–218**

changing text to, 274

Small Caps property, in Character Designer, 216

small outline template, 132, *134*, **643–646**, *644*

Small Tools window, 364

smart quotes, 275–276

Smart Selection tool, *329*, 330

smart spaces, 275

Smooth command, **343**

Snap feature, 191
  and Freehand Curve tool, 335
  on ruler, 63
  in View Options dialog box, 59–60

snap grid, **350–351**, 362, 364

Snap Rotate text box, in View Options dialog box, 60

sort information, **510**

sort order of index, **505–507**
  ignoring characters during, **505**
  ignoring prepositions when, 506
  problem solving, 517

sorted list, 501

SortOrder paragraph, editing, 508

SortOrderIX paragraph tag, 507

source document, links back to generated file, 542

spaces, smart, 275

spacing
  of font families, 209–210
  of paragraphs, 28

Spacing button (Formatting Bar), 28, *28*

Spacing menu, 27, 28

special characters
  backslash character (\) to find, 278, 282
  in index markers, **488**
  in indexes, 489, 490
  searching for, **282**

Special menu
  ➤ Add Disconnected Pages, 169, 192
  ➤ Add Master Page, 181
  ➤ Add Reference Page, 185
  ➤ Anchored Frame, 197, 202, 357
  ➤ Conditional Text, 571
  ➤ Cross-Reference, 546, 554
  ➤ Delete Page XXX, 185
  ➤ Delete Pages, 169
  ➤ Equations, 587
  ➤ Markers, 323, 486, 487, 499, 530
  ➤ Variable, 320

special templates, **646–653**

speed, graphics display and, 59

Spell-check button (QuickAccess Bar), *26*

Spelling Checker, **93–95**, **293–303**
  corrections by, **295–296**
  customizing dictionaries, **298–301**

customizing options, **296–298**

editing dictionary files, **301**

Ignore options for, **297–298**

keyboard shortcuts for, **302–303**

limitations of, 298

limits of, 95

preventing paragraph inclusion in, 249

Spelling Checker Options window, 296–298, *297*

Spelling Checker window, *94*, **293–295**, *294*
  Dictionaries button, 299

spot color, **421**

spot color separations, **431–432**
  printing, **433–437**

spot cross-references in documents, 546
  inserting, 548–549

spread of characters, 211–212

Spread property, in Character Designer, 216

spreadsheets, data exported from, 288, 407–408

square, rounded, 332

square brackets ([ ])
  in index marker, 488, 490
  for index sort order, 506

squares
  changing to polygons, **346–347**
  drawing, 331–332

smoothing corners, 343
stacks, for hypertext
   jumps, 533
Standard Space, 250
Standard Templates dialog
   box, 8, 9, 10, 122
Start Angle (Property dialog box), 382
Start Checking button, in
   Spelling Checker win-
   dow, 295
Start list (Paragraph De-
   signer Pagination Properties page), 245
Start setting, for table,
   397–398
starting FrameMaker, **3–7**
<*$startrange*>, 490, 492,
   516
status area
   asterisk (*) before name
      tag in, 238
   on document window, **33**
StepNumber character tag
   in book templates, 657
   in report templates, 633,
      637
straddle frames, anchored
   frames as, **203**
straddle paragraphs, **195**
   and anchored frame
      placement, 199
   and footnote position, 558
straddle tables, 387
straddling cells across columns and rows, **394**
Straight Quotes, Spelling
   Checker and, 297
strikethrough, 212, 216
subdirectory. *See* directory

subentries, in indexes, 489,
   491
subject index, 519
subscript, 213
   changing look of, **217–218**
   for footnote number posi-
      tion, 563
substitution math element,
   591
summary document
   from comparing book,
      461, 461
   from comparing docu-
      ment, 582
   hypertext links in, **586**
Sun raster file format, 369
superscript, 212–213
   changing look of, **217–218**
   for footnote number posi-
      tion, 563
Superscript property, in
   Character Designer,
   216
symbol set, **208–209**
<$symbols>, 507–508, 509
Symbols page, in Equa-
   tions window, 588, *589*
Synchronize ¶'s with Line
   Spacing Of, 173
synonyms, 303–305
system variables, **565–567**
   editing definition, 569

T

Tab character
   as delimiter, 288–289
   for index page numbers,
      504

in table cells, 390
tab leader, character for,
   243
tab stops
   adding, 64
   deleting, 243
Tab stops (Paragraph De-
   signer Basic Properties
   page), 242
tab symbols (>), 56
   displaying, 11
tab wells, 28
Table All cross-reference
   format, 554
table catalog, 387
table cells
   cutting, copying and past-
      ing, **390–391**
   footnote for, 558
   moving between, 390
   numbering, 398
   rotating, **394**
   selecting characters in,
      391
   straddling across col-
      umns and rows, **394**
table of contents, **467–484**
   formatting, **472–482**
   generating, **468–471**
   on Help screen, 99
   for multiple books, **517–
      518**
   page number position in,
      478–479
   paragraph tags in source
      documents, **468**
   regenerating, **471–472**
   template to format, **480–
      482**
   templates containing, 625

title for, **480**
troubleshooting, **482–484**
updating and format re-
tention, **481**
table of contents entries
autonumbering in, 477–
478
character formats for, **476**
inserting text, **477**
rearranging information,
475–476
tabs and leader dots in,
479
Table Continuation system
variable, 398, 566
Table Designer, 387, *395*,
395
Basic properties in, 396,
397–398
Commands menu, 404–
405
control area, **402–404**
Properties pull-down list
in, 395–396
Ruling properties page,
396, **398–400**, *399*
Shading properties page,
400–402, *401*
Table Footnote Properties
dialog box, 561, *562*
table formats
copying between docu-
ments, **409–410**
default, 389
Table menu
➤ Add Rows or Col-
umns, 392
➤ Convert to Para-
graphs, 409
➤ Convert to Table, 408

➤ Custom Ruling &
Shading, 405
➤ Insert Table, 388
➤ Resize Columns, 393
➤ Row Format, 393
➤ Straddle, 394
Table Number & Page
cross-reference format,
554
Table Sheet system vari-
able, 398, 566
table tags, **402**
applying, **402–404**
TableFootnote paragraph
tag, 560, 561
in book templates, 656
in business templates,
612, 615, 616, 620
in newsletter template,
652
in outline templates, 640,
642, 645
in report templates, 628,
632, 636
TableFootnote reference
frame, 183
TableLOT paragraph tag,
in book templates, 662
TableNumber Variables
character tag, in news-
letter template, 653
tables, **387–410**
appearance after import-
ing, **289–290**
converting text to, **407–
408**
converting to text, **409**
creating empty, **388–389**
entering text and objects
in cells, **389–390**

finding, 279
flexibility in placement,
388
formatting. *See* Table Designer
how they work, **387–388**
from imported text, 290
list of, 518
position on page, 397–
398
selecting, 391
shape and look of, **392–
393**
straddling multiple col-
umns, xxiii
tab character in, 390
white space above and be-
low, 397
writing to text file, 143
TableTitle paragraph tag
in book templates, 656
in business templates,
612, 615, 616, 620
in newsletter template,
652
in outline template, 640,
642
in report templates, 628,
632, 636
tabs
in counters, 248
for headers and footers,
314
search for, 282
in table of contents en-
tries, **479**
<*tag*>, 491
template samples, 122,
126–134, 609–664

Blank Portrait Page, 174–175, *175*

books, 475, **653–664**

business cards, *130, 624,* **624–625**

business envelope, *130, 622,* **622–623**

business letter, *123,* **127, 609–612,** *610*

business memo, *127, 613,* **613–616**

fax cover page, *128,* **616–619,** *617*

newsletter, *134,* 187, **649–653,** *650*

numbered report, *131, 629,* **629–633**

outlines, 132, *133, 134,* **637–646**

pagination sheet, **646–649,** *647*

plain report, *131, 626,* **626–629**

sidehead report, *132*

tall viewgraph, 129, *619,* **619–622**

wide viewgraph, 129, *619,* **619–622**

template text frames, adding to master pages, **182**

templates, **120–136**

  autoconnect for, 163

  creating, **135–136**

  creating documents from, **8–12, 121**

  directories for, 122, 135

  to format index, **513–514**

  to format table of contents, **480–482**

  to modify document look, **124–126**

  thumbnail view of, 10

text

  as active hypertext, **525–526**

  adding color, **413–417**

  capitalization of, 274

  changing look, **90**

  converting cross-references to, **556–557**

  converting to tables, **407–408**

  converting tables into, **409**

  cutting and clearing unselected, **272–273**

  deleting, **84–85**

  importing, **116–120**

  importing by reference, xxiii, 111–112, 117, 279, 286

  opening MIF file as, 114

  placement on page, 155–156

  replacing, **89–90**

  search for, 277

  selecting, **267–268**

text boxes, in dialog boxes, *36, 36*

text cursor, 75–76

  converting to object cursor, 82

  for selecting text, 77

text editor

  for dictionary files, 301

  for MML files, 115

text files, 113, 144. *See also* ASCII text files

text flow, 155, 156, *157*

  anchored frames in, **197–202**

  cursor movement to beginning or end, 77

  format for imported, 290, 292

  for index formatting, 498

  objects moving with. *See also* anchored frames

  for table of content formatting, 472

  updating text frame changes to, **312**

Text Frame tool, 315, *329,* **336**

text frames, 55, 62, 156, *157*

  anchored frames outside, **200–201**

  autoconnected, **162**

  changing margins and number of columns, 311

  changing size and position, **311–312**

  with columns, xxii

  connecting with Autoconnect, **163–166**

  connecting and disconnecting, **160,** *161,* **166**

  creating around graphic for hypertext, 528

  deleting, 191

  deselecting, 84

  for graphic as hypertext, 526–527

  importing bitmap to, 369

  importing Desktop Color Separation graphic to, 374–375

importing QuickTime movie to, 376
importing vector graphic to, 373
and indent setting, 240
multiple for multiple columns, **190–192**
multiple on newsletter front page, 191
overflows in, **158**, *159*
selecting, 81–84
selecting as object, 164, 178
and selecting text, 79
Text Inset Properties dialog box, 120, *120*, 292–293, *293*
text insets, 286
cross-references in, 546
editing properties of, **292–293**
Text Line tool, 202, *329*, **336–337**, 358, 361
Text Options dialog box, 217–218, *218*, *275*, 275–276
text overflows, **156, 158–159**, *160–161*
text runaround, 336, 337, **378–380**
text symbols, 56
in View Options dialog box, 58
Text Symbols (View menu), 55
Thesaurus, **303–305**, *304*
Thesaurus Look Up dialog box, 304, *304*, 305
thickness, of change bars, 219, 581

thin space, search for, 282
thumbnail view
printing, 149
of template, 10
TIFF file format, 369
tiling windows, 50, *50*
tips, xxv
title bar
for active window, 37
in application window, *24*, **25**
in document window, *31*
double-clicking to maximize window, 50
Title paragraph tag
in newsletter template, 652
in outline template, 640, 643, 645
TitleBook paragraph tag, in book template, 659
titles
adding to index, **512–513**
of index entry groups, **509–512**
position for tables, 398
for table of contents, **480**
TitleTOC/Index paragraph tag, in book templates, 662, 664
ToAddress paragraph tag, in business templates, 623
toggle command, 27
ToName paragraph tag, in business templates, 623
tools, selecting, 329
Tools button, in document window, 32, *32*, 357

Tools window, *327*, **327–356**, *328*
adding color with, 416
Color area, *352*
Drawing Commands, **338–347**, *339*
drawing tools on, *327*, 328, **330–338**
Ends, 354
Fill area, *352*
Line Properties area, **353–356**
Pen area, *352*
selection tools, **330**
Top Edge, for sidehead alignment, 194
trapping, 350
Treat Each Line as a Paragraph option, for ASCII text, 288
triangles, on ruler, 62
troubleshooting
indexes, **515–517**
marker text in header or footer, 323
retention of index formatting after update, **513**
table of contents, **482–484**
table of contents formatting after updating, **481**
testing hypertext document for incorrect links, **541**
unresolved cross-references, *551–553*
Tutorial, xxiv, 98, 606
Two in a Row, Spelling Checker and, 297

Type (Property dialog box), 381
type size, 210
typeface, 209
typeset-quality pages, xxii
typing cursor, 11

U

unanchored frames, 186
unconnected text frames, **160**, *161*
  overflows in, **158**
underline, 90–91, 212
Underline button (QuickAccess Bar), *26*, 91
Underline property, in Character Designer, 216
underlined letter, in menus, 43
Undo button (QuickAccess Bar), *26*
Undo changes, 271
  using save to, **145**
Undo command, after joining objects, 348
undoing mistakes, **87, 273–274**
Ungroup command, **339**
unit of measurement, default, 109
Units menu, in Custom Blank Paper dialog box, 109
UNIX, xxii. *See also* FrameMaker (UNIX version)

UNIX systems, Esc key combinations for, 44
Unknown File Type dialog box, 112, *112*, 118
Unlearn button, in Spelling Checker window, 296
unlocked documents, hypertext links in, 541
unlocking view-only file mode, 145
unresolved cross-references, *551–553*
  finding, 279
  list of, **553**
unresolved text inset, finding, 279
Unrotated Size (Property dialog box), 381
unsaved edits indicator, 33
unselected text, cutting and clearing, 272–273
Unsmooth command, **343**
unusual capitalization, Spelling Checker and, 296
unusual hyphenation, Spelling Checker and, 296
Update All button, in Paragraph Designer, **252–254**
Update References dialog box, 551, *551*, 552
Update Unresolved Cross-References dialog box, 552–553, *552*
uppercase, 213
  changing text to, 274

ignoring words in Spelling Checker, 298
Uppercase button (QuickAccess Bar), *26*
Use Blank Paper (New file dialog box), 107–108
USER.DCT dictionary file (Windows), 298
user variables, 565, **567–568**
  deleting, 569
  editing definition, 569

V

Variable dialog box, *565*
  Create Variable button, 567
  Edit Definition button, 568
Variable page display, 59
variables, **564–570**
  building blocks for, 473
  changing definition, **568–569**
  double-clicking for dialog box, 120
  finding, 279
  in headers and footers, **317–318**
  inserting, **570**
  system, **565–567**
  user, 565, **567–568**
Variables dialog box, 317–318, *318*, 320–321, *321*
Variation property, in Character Designer, 215

vector graphics, importing, **371–374**
Ventura Publisher files, 113
version, for FrameMaker, 98
vertex, removing, 342
vertical division bar, 591
vertical list math element, 591
Vertical page display, 59
vertical straight line, 331
View menu, 54–55
➤ Body Pages, 167, 175, 476
➤ Borders, 55
➤ Color,
  ➤ Definitions, 421, 428
  ➤ Views, 430
➤ Formatting Bar, 29
➤ Go to Page, 72
➤ Grid Lines, 55
➤ Master Pages, 167, 174, 176, 180, 314, 317
➤ Options, 56, 191
➤ QuickAccess Bar, 27
➤ Reference Pages, 167, 184, 475, 476, 500
➤ Rulers, 55
➤ Text Symbols, 11, 55, 486
View Options dialog box, 35, *36*, **56–59**, *57*
Borders on Objects, 191
Display Units, 57–58
Grid Lines, 191
Page Scrolling pull-down menu in, 59
Snap, 191

Snap feature in, 59–60, 62, *351*
spacing of invisible grid, 351
viewing
  documents, 10–11, **54–55**
  Formatting Bar, 29
  QuickAccess Bar, 27
view-only documents, 150, **523–542**
  hypertext in, **520**
  vs. editable documents, 524
view-only file mode, 101–102, 144
unlocking, 145

W

warnings, xxv
Web page, 595
WebWorks HTML Lite, 595
weight of font, 211
Weight property, in Character Designer, 215
white space
  above and below paragraphs, 241–242
  between paragraphs, 258
  above and below table, 397
  between title and table, 398
Whole Word option, for Find, 89, 280
widow lines, 246
width, of line, **353–354**
wildcards

in Add File to Book dialog box for file names, 449
in Find, 280, **281**
when saving file, 142
Window menu
➤ Arrange Icons, 52
➤ Cascade, 49, 68
list of open documents, 52–53
➤ Tile, 50
windows, **23–41**. *See also* application window; document windows
active, 37
arranging in working area, **49–54**
dialog boxes, **35–37**, *36*
dragging, 53
palettes, **37–41**
Windows Control menu button, 25
Windows task list, restoring Help screen with, 103
WMF file format, 373
word processor, FrameMaker as, xx–xxi
Word text box, in Spelling Checker window, 294
word-by-word sort, 505
WordPerfect files, 113
words
  adding to personal dictionary, 296
  capitalization of, 274
  cursor movement by, 76
  cutting and clearing, 272
  deleting, 85

forcing unhyphenated,
301
ignoring single-character
in Spelling Checker,
297
selecting, 17, 268
selecting with text cursor,
78
spacing in justified paragraphs, 250
Words containing text, ignoring in Spelling
Checker, 298
words with digits, ignoring
in Spelling Checker,
298
word-wrap, 143
working area
in application window,
24, **30**
arranging windows in, **49–
54**
World Wide Web, **594–595**
WPG file format, 369, 373
write permissions for
UNIX documents, 139

X

X11xwd file format, 369
Xbitmap file format, 369

Y

YourNameLarge para-
graph tag, in business
templates, 625
YourNameSmall para-
graph tag, in business
templates, 625

Z

Zoom Controls, in docu-
ment window, *31*
Zoom feature, **66–71**
and moving objects by in-
crements, 362
Zoom In button, 66, 67
Zoom menu, 34, *34*, 66
customizing percentages
in, 71
Fit Page to Window, 68,
70
Fit Window to Page, 68,
69, *70*
Zoom Menu Options dia-
log box, 71, *71*
Zoom Out button, 61, 66

FOR EVERY COMPUTER QUESTION, THERE IS A SYBEX BOOK THAT HAS THE ANSWER

Each computer user learns in a different way. Some need thorough, methodical explanations, while others are too busy for details. At Sybex we bring nearly 20 years of experience to developing the book that's right for you. Whatever your needs, we can help you get the most from your software and hardware, at a pace that's comfortable for you.

We start beginners out right. You will learn by seeing and doing with our Quick & Easy series: friendly, colorful guidebooks with screen-by-screen illustrations. For hardware novices, the Your First series offers valuable purchasing advice and installation support.

Often recognized for excellence in national book reviews, our Mastering titles are designed for the intermediate to advanced user, without leaving the beginner behind. A Mastering book provides the most detailed reference available. Add our pocket-sized Instant Reference titles for a complete guidance system. Programmers will find that the new Developer's Handbook series provides a more advanced perspective on developing innovative and original code.

With the breathtaking advances common in computing today comes an ever increasing demand to remain technologically up-to-date. In many of our books, we provide the added value of software, on disks or CDs. Sybex remains your source for information on software development, operating systems, networking, and every kind of desktop application. We even have books for kids. Sybex can help smooth your travels on the Internet and provide Strategies and Secrets to your favorite computer games.

As you read this book, take note of its quality. Sybex publishes books written by experts—authors chosen for their extensive topical knowledge. In fact, many are professionals working in the computer soft-ware field. In addition, each manuscript is thoroughly reviewed by our technical, editorial, and production personnel for accuracy and ease-of-use before you ever see it—our guarantee that you'll buy a quality Sybex book every time.

To manage your hardware headaches and optimize your software potential, ask for a Sybex book.

FOR MORE INFORMATION, PLEASE CONTACT:

Sybex Inc.
2021 Challenger Drive
Alameda, CA 94501
Tel: (510) 523-8233 • (800) 227-2346
Fax: (510) 523-2373

SYBEX

GET A FREE CATALOG JUST FOR EXPRESSING YOUR OPINION.

Help us improve our books and get a ***FREE*** full-color catalog in the bargain. Please complete this form, pull out this page and send it in today. The address is on the reverse side.

Name _____   Company _____

Address _____   City _____ State ___ Zip _____

Phone ( ) _____

1. How would you rate the overall quality of this book?

- ❑ Excellent
- ❑ Very Good
- ❑ Good
- ❑ Fair
- ❑ Below Average
- ❑ Poor

2. What were the things you liked most about the book? (Check all that apply)

- ❑ Pace
- ❑ Format
- ❑ Writing Style
- ❑ Examples
- ❑ Table of Contents
- ❑ Index
- ❑ Price
- ❑ Illustrations
- ❑ Type Style
- ❑ Cover
- ❑ Depth of Coverage
- ❑ Fast Track Notes

3. What were the things you liked *least* about the book? (Check all that apply)

- ❑ Pace
- ❑ Format
- ❑ Writing Style
- ❑ Examples
- ❑ Table of Contents
- ❑ Index
- ❑ Price
- ❑ Illustrations
- ❑ Type Style
- ❑ Cover
- ❑ Depth of Coverage
- ❑ Fast Track Notes

4. Where did you buy this book?

- ❑ Bookstore chain
- ❑ Small independent bookstore
- ❑ Computer store
- ❑ Wholesale club
- ❑ College bookstore
- ❑ Technical bookstore
- ❑ Other _____

5. How did you decide to buy this particular book?

- ❑ Recommended by friend
- ❑ Recommended by store personnel
- ❑ Author's reputation
- ❑ Sybex's reputation
- ❑ Read book review in _____
- ❑ Other _____

6. How did you pay for this book?

- ❑ Used own funds
- ❑ Reimbursed by company
- ❑ Received book as a gift

7. What is your level of experience with the subject covered in this book?

- ❑ Beginner
- ❑ Intermediate
- ❑ Advanced

8. How long have you been using a computer?

years _____
months _____

9. Where do you most often use your computer?

- ❑ Home
- ❑ Work

- ❑ Both
- ❑ Other _____

10. What kind of computer equipment do you have? (Check all that apply)

- ❑ PC Compatible Desktop Computer
- ❑ PC Compatible Laptop Computer
- ❑ Apple/Mac Computer
- ❑ Apple/Mac Laptop Computer
- ❑ CD ROM
- ❑ Fax Modem
- ❑ Data Modem
- ❑ Scanner
- ❑ Sound Card
- ❑ Other _____

11. What other kinds of software packages do you ordinarily use?

- ❑ Accounting
- ❑ Databases
- ❑ Networks
- ❑ Apple/Mac
- ❑ Desktop Publishing
- ❑ Spreadsheets
- ❑ CAD
- ❑ Games
- ❑ Word Processing
- ❑ Communications
- ❑ Money Management
- ❑ Other _____

12. What operating systems do you ordinarily use?

- ❑ DOS
- ❑ OS/2
- ❑ Windows
- ❑ Apple/Mac
- ❑ Windows NT
- ❑ Other _____

13. On what computer-related subject(s) would you like to see more books?

_____

_____

_____

_____

14. Do you have any other comments about this book? (Please feel free to use a separate piece of paper if you need more room)

_____

_____

_____

_____

- - - - - - - - - - - PLEASE FOLD, SEAL, AND MAIL TO SYBEX - - - - - - - - - - -

SYBEX INC.
Department M
2021 Challenger Drive
Alameda, CA
94501

SYBEX®

QuickAccess Bar 3—Graphics Editing

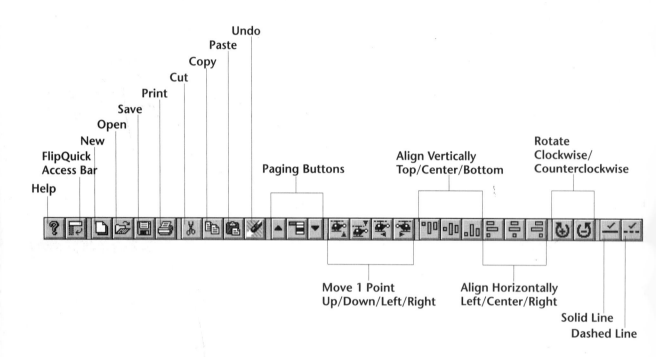

Help

FlipQuick
Access Bar

New

Open

Save

Print

Cut

Copy

Paste

Undo

Paging Buttons

Move 1 Point
Up/Down/Left/Right

Align Vertically
Top/Center/Bottom

Align Horizontally
Left/Center/Right

Rotate
Clockwise/
Counterclockwise

Solid Line

Dashed Line